VALUING A BUSINESS

The Analysis and Appraisal of Closely-Held Companies

VALUING A BUSINESS

The analysis and appraisal of closely-held companies

SHANNON P. PRATT, D.B.A., C.F.A., C.F.P., A.S.A.
President
Willamette Management Associates, Inc.

Dow Jones-Irwin
Homewood, Illinois 60430

ISBN 0-87094-205-0

Library of Congress Catalog Card No. 80–85475

Printed in the United States of America

11 12 13 14 15 K 0 9 8 7

To Millie

PREFACE

This book is a primer on the theory and practice of valuing a business or an interest in a business. It is intended for owners of businesses and business interests and for professional advisors to business owners, such as CPAs, attorneys, financial and estate planners, bankers, insurance agents, investment brokers, corporate finance specialists, and business consultants.

While there have been hundreds of articles and court cases dealing with various aspects of business valuation, little has been done to bring the essentials of this body of knowledge together in a single expository and reference manual. This book is an attempt to fill that need. It draws heavily on the relevant literature of the accounting, legal, and security analysis professions, as well as on court decisions and the personal experience of the author. For those who wish to go deeper into any aspect of business valuation, extensive bibliographical references are included.

It is expected that many of the readers of this book will have little or no background in business valuation. Each aspect of business valuation is described in basic, fundamental terms, with no prior knowledge on the part of the reader assumed. Each term or reference that might be esoteric in nature is defined or identified the first time it is used in the book. Extensive use is made of examples where appropriate.

This book presents both theoretical principles and generally accepted practices in business valuations. It explains why both the approaches used and the conclusions reached may vary depending on the purpose of the valuation.

With this background established, the book turns to the mechanics of doing a business valuation. It describes the internal and external data to be assembled, including a discussion of the most useful information sources. It covers the analysis of financial statements and the presentation of a valuation report, including a complete sample written case and a chapter on court testimony. Finally, it discusses valuations for specific purposes, such as gift and estate taxes, recapitalizations, employee stock ownership plans, buy-sell agreements, selling out the company, going public, other transactions, and valuation situations involving litigation or potential litigation.

This book treats both controlling interests and minority interests. It is applicable to all forms of business organization, such as regular corporations, Subchapter S corporations, professional corporations, general or limited partnerships, and sole proprietorships.

This book discusses the inextricable relationship between the public capital markets and the values of closely-held businesses. The markets for publicly-traded securities provide information on the cost of capital to businesses and statistics on the prices of alternative available investments. This book describes in detail what public market information is relevant, where to find it, and how to use it in the valuation of a closely-held business.

While basic principles remain intact over the years, the practice of business valuation is a dynamic discipline, constantly changing with economic and industry conditions, new laws, court decisions, and business practices. The author solicits reader comments and criticisms at 400 S.W. Sixth Avenue, Suite 1115, Portland, OR 97204.

Acknowledgments

This work has benefited from the assistance and cooperation of many people at every stage of the project, including conceptual discussions, research and compilation of information, critiques of the manuscript, and permission to use relevant material from other publications.

For permission to use material I wish to thank American Institute of Certified Public Accountants, American Society of Appraisers, Disclosure, Inc., Dow Jones-Irwin Co., Dun & Bradstreet, Georgia-Pacific, *The Journal of Taxation,* The McDermott Group, *Mergers & Acquisitions,* Robert E. Moroney, Robert Morris Associates, Mouldings, Inc., Oregon Portland Cement, Predicasts, Inc., Thomas A. Solberg, Standard & Poor's, Tax Corporation of America, and Warren Gorham & Lamont.

For critiques of all or portions of the manuscript I particularly thank Greg Gilbert, associate director of the valuation division of Willamette Management Associates, Inc. and the valuation analysts on the staff: Steve Brink, Marilyn Burr, John Curti, Richard Dole, Helen Ivaska, Andrew Labadie, Mark Pagano, and David Schue. I also thank Eric Haessler, Ed Hall, Richard Miller, and George Wagner, all attorneys, and Geoff Bruce, Joe Carey and Tom Dant, all CPAs. Particular thanks is extended to Dexter· D. MacBride, executive vice-president, American Society of Appraisers, and to C.E.O. Walker, a member of the A.S.A. Business Appraisal Committee, who also reviewed the manuscript.

Chapter 15, Pagano Supermarkets, Inc.—A Sample Case, was written by Mark Pagano and edited by Greg Gilbert and myself.

The entire bibliography, including the general bibliography at the end of the book, and the special subject sections of the bibliography found at the ends of certain chapters, was compiled by Marilyn Burr, who also assisted in the research and documentation of the material throughout the project.

The head typist for the manuscript was my wife, Millie, who also offered hundreds of editorial suggestions to help make the text more clearly and easily readable. Others assisting in typing included Dixie Sims, Susan Runckel, and my secretary, Kathie Martin.

Composition of the tabular data in the exhibits was done by Lenair Mulford, with the assistance of Charles Clifford.

To all of the above and to all the many others who extended a helping hand at one stage or another I extend my sincere thanks.

Shannon Pratt

CONTENTS

asset value. Stock value to asset value ratio adjusted to a debt-free basis. Combination approaches. Other factors to consider: *History of past transactions. Marketability. Extent of "elements of control" versus minority position. Other contractual rights or obligations.* Analyzing and balancing the valuation factors.

CODE OF ABBREVIATIONS

acq., acquiesced
aff'd sub nom., affirmed sub nomine
A.F.T.R., American Federal Tax Reports
A.L.R., American Law Reports
Am. Jur., American Jurisprudence
Am. Jur. P.O.F., American Jurisprudence Proof of Facts
app. dism'd, appeal dismissed
A. 2d Atlantic Reporter 2d
B.T.A., Board of Tax Appeals
cert. den., Certificate denied
C.L.U., Chartered Life Underwriter
C.F.R., Code of Federal Regulations
C.J.S., Corpus Juris Secundum
C.B., Cumulative Bulletin
ERISA, Employee Retirement Income Security Act
F. 2d, Federal Reporter 2d
F. Supp., Federal Supplement
I.R.C., Internal Revenue Code
P. 2d, Pacific Reporter 2d
reh. den., rehearing denied
rev'd, reversed
S.E.C., Securities and Exchange Commission
S. Ct., Supreme Court Reports
T.C., Tax Court
T.C.M., Tax Court Memorandum (Commerce Clearing House)
U.S.C.A., United States Code Annotated
U.S., United States Reports
U.S.T.C., United States Tax Cases
vac'd & rem'd, vacated and remanded

LIST OF EXHIBITS

I

PRINCIPLES OF BUSINESS VALUATION

1

THE GROWING NEED FOR BUSINESS APPRAISALS

GIFT, ESTATE, AND INHERITANCE TAXES AND ESTATE PLANNING
  Minimizing gift, estate, and inheritance taxes
  Planning a program of family gifts
  Recapitalization as a business and estate-planning tool
  Valuation considerations affecting income taxes
  Charitable contributions

FAIR AND ENFORCEABLE BUY-SELL AGREEMENTS

DETERMINING ADEQUACY OF LIFE INSURANCE
  Payment of taxes
  Liquidation of estate stock
  Continuity of business

BUYING OR SELLING SHARES IN THE COMPANY
  Estate and trust cases
  Transactions with employees
  Transactions with other stockholders

EMPLOYEE STOCK OWNERSHIP PLANS (ESOPs)

CORPORATE OR PARTNERSHIP DISSOLUTIONS

DIVORCES

GOING PUBLIC

GOING PRIVATE

STATUTORY MERGERS ("SQUEEZE-OUT" MERGERS) AND DISSENTERS' RIGHTS

SELLING OUT

SPINNING OFF PART OF COMPANY

MAKING AN ACQUISITION

COMPENSATORY DAMAGE CASES
  Breach of contract
  Antitrust
  Loss of business opportunity
  Condemnation

OBTAINING FINANCING

REORGANIZATION

ALLOCATION OF TOTAL VALUE
  Allocation among classes of securities
  Allocation among classes of assets

VALUING TRUST OR PORTFOLIO HOLDINGS

CONSIDERING ALTERNATIVES

More than ever, business owners, managers, and fiduciaries are recognizing the need for competent and frequent valuations of the enterprises with which they are associated. This heightened appreciation of competent business valuation is a natural outgrowth of the general trend toward increased sophistication among managers and owners of businesses of all sizes. Increased perception of the complexities of business valuation by all concerned parties is rendering obsolete the old seat-of-the-pants approaches to business valuation.

Catalysts encouraging more in-depth business valuations include more complex laws, more sophisticated legal cases and court interpretations of existing laws, where business valuation is an issue, and greater attention to fiduciary responsibilities by business people generally. It is increasingly important to have a competent and thoroughly documented valuation in the many situations where litigation or potential litigation may be involved.

Also, an appraisal of a company's value can be quite beneficial to management. The exercise of going through the business appraisal usually brings to light strengths and weaknesses that management may have partially or totally overlooked. The balance of this chapter discusses the role of the business valuation in facilitating the accomplishment of the many and diverse objectives of various business ownership situations.

GIFT, ESTATE, AND INHERITANCE TAXES AND ESTATE PLANNING

The typical owner of a closely-held business works a lifetime to build value and security for self and family, and then sacrifices far more than necessary of the hard-earned resources to federal and state governments in conjunction with the transfer of interests in the business enterprise to other people. All or a large part of his sacrifice can be avoided by a sound program of ongoing business valuation and estate planning.

Minimizing gift, estate, and inheritance taxes

As with income taxes, federal gift and estate taxes and most state inheritance taxes are established on a progressive basis, and the dollar increments at which each increase of tax rate becomes effective are not adjusted for inflation. Thus, the impact of gift, estate, and inheritance taxes, in real terms, increases automatically and on a disproportionately progressive basis with inflation. This is one of the critical reasons why careful business valuations for tax purposes become more important in terms of wealth remaining in the family's possession with every passing year.

The values of interests in closely-held businesses for gift and estate tax purposes are determined in accordance with Internal Revenue Service (IRS) Revenue Ruling 59-60, along with its various modifications and administrative and court interpretations. Gift taxes are levied on the donor, and estate taxes on the estate.

Most states also levy an inheritance tax, which is a tax on the receipt of property. Valuation criteria for state inheritance tax purposes tend to follow the criteria of Revenue Ruling 59-60, but there are many variations, resulting either from differences in wording of the state statutes or from changing state administrative or court interpretations.

While the established criteria for valuations of business interests for gift, estate, and inheritance taxes are spelled out in some detail in the law, many of the guidelines are very general, and the discrepancies found in their application and interpretation are immense. Working within the scope of discrepancies to obtain the most favorable tax treatment to which the business owner is entitled requires consultation with an expert who is experienced in dealing with the IRS and state departments of revenue, and who is familiar with court decisions on various points where the IRS and the taxpayer were unable to reach agreement. To be properly protected, the taxpayer must provide thorough documentation of the basis for the valuation used in each gift, estate, or inheritance tax incidence, in accordance with accepted valuation principles. This book provides an introduction to such principles, plus two chapters analyzing certain selected federal gift and estate tax cases which illustrate court decisions that involve several of the more important principles.

Under the current Federal Unified Gift and Estate Tax program, a person is entitled to transfer a certain amount of wealth free of federal tax regardless of whether it is during the person's life or through his estate. The combined gift and estate tax exclusion is now $325,000 per person, or $650,000 for a married couple. In addition, each person may gift up to $10,000 to each of as many people as he or she wishes each year with no federal gift tax.

Complete avoidance of federal gift and estate taxes would require a program of distributions that would keep the estate value down to $650,000 for a married couple, including any part of the lifetime unified gift and estate tax exemption already used up. Many, if not most, financially successful couples would be unwilling to maintain their estates at this low a level. However, by constantly monitoring the value of their business, along with other assets, they can consciously and objectively weigh the tax consequences of the many alternatives available to them in their estate planning.

Planning a program of family gifts

As noted in the previous section, the estate and gift tax bite can be reduced by using the maximum allowable tax-free gift of $10,000 per donor/donee combination each year ($20,000 per donee for a married couple). If the maximum is used, and gifts of stock or other business interests are included, it is important that the valuation of the stock or business interests transferred will be on a basis acceptable to the IRS, so that an audit will not result in a higher valuation, which would then have to be applied to the lifetime gift and estate tax exclusion.

If it appears that the business is rapidly increasing in value, it may be worthwhile to go ahead and use all or part of the lifetime exemption. In this way a larger percentage of the business could be transferred tax free than would be the case later on when the business became worth considerably more.

---

[1] *Will reach 600,000 and 1,200,000 respectively in 1987.*

If a business is growing rapidly in value, recapitalization is an acceptable technique to freeze the value of the estate of an older generation and allow all the future appreciation to accrue to the younger generation. The recapitalization can create two or more classes of stock, each with features designed to serve the needs of different stockholders or stockholder groups. In a recapitalization, it is essential both that the total business valuation be acceptable to the IRS and that the allocation of value among classes of stock be acceptable. The chapter on estate planning contains a section on recapitalization.

Recapitalization as a business and estate planning tool

There are a number of circumstances in which the transfer of a business interest potentially may be construed as an event subject to ordinary income tax on the value of the transfer. The most important aspect of valuation with respect to income taxes, in most cases, is to be sure that any transfer of a business interest, whether by gift or purchase, is so valued that the IRS will not come back and say it was worth much more than the gift value or purchase price placed on it—and thus construe the difference as taxable income to the recipient.

Valuation considerations affecting income taxes

It usually is to the taxpayer's advantage to have the highest possible value on stocks or other business interests to be donated as charitable contributions, because the value of such donations usually is deductible from taxable ordinary income. Since the values of business interests fluctuate in response to the company's own fortunes and to a variety of economic variables, the taxpayer's advantage lies in timing such charitable donations to when the value of the particular interest to be donated will most likely be at its highest level.

Charitable contributions

A good buy-sell agreement can be a powerful tool to assist a closely-held business in accomplishing a variety of objectives. Restrictive provisions can prevent the danger of ownership by unwanted outsiders. The agreement can facilitate transfers of shares under many circumstances. The agreement also can be instrumental in establishing values for gift, estate, and inheritance tax purposes.

The most critical and difficult aspect of most buy-sell agreements is the provision for valuation. A full chapter is devoted to buy-sell agreements, Chapter 21, including a special bibliography on the subject at the end of the chapter.

FAIR AND ENFORCEABLE BUY-SELL AGREEMENTS

Insurance is designed to provide adequate coverage of contingent needs. The contingency in life insurance related to a business is the death of a key person in the business. To program the insurance requirements, it is necessary

DETERMINING ADEQUACY OF LIFE INSURANCE

to determine the contingent needs that will arise from the death of the key person. Such contingent needs are payment of taxes, liquidation of the estate's business interest, and providing for continuity of the business.

Payment of taxes

Unless funds are available from some other source, life insurance commonly is used to provide for the payment of estate and inheritance taxes. It is necessary to have a reasonable approximation of the taxable value of the business interest to determine the amount of insurance necessary for this purpose. (In some cases, the insurance needs can be reduced by an extended estate tax payment schedule.)

Liquidation of estate stock

It frequently is desired by both the estate and the other stockholders to liquidate all or part of a business interest following the death of a stockholder or partner. There may be a buy-sell agreement in effect that would be difficult or even impossible to act on in the absence of the funding provided by life insurance. Obviously, to provide the proper funding to liquidate estate stock through life insurance proceeds, a good approximation of the value of the stock is required, and should be reviewed periodically.

From the viewpoint of persons remaining active in the business, it may be undesirable to have heirs who are not active in the business to continue as stockholders. From the point of view of the estate, an interest in a business in which the heirs are not active usually is not a very attractive investment holding. Even if it is considered desirable for the inactive heirs to retain some interest in the family business, a prudent business practice is to liquidate enough of the stock to provide diversification of the heirs' investments. My own rule of thumb would be to handle the estate planning so that no inactive heir would have over 10 to 20 percent of his assets in the family business.

Note that the insurance might be in favor of the corporation or an interested party or parties who would purchase the stock from the estate. These options are discussed in Chapter 21, Buy-Sell Agreements.

Continuity of business

Over and above the amount of insurance necessary to pay estate and inheritance taxes, it may be desirable to have additional proceeds available to the corporation to offset whatever discontinuities might result from the loss of a key man. It is common to have certain indebtedness subject to repayment from life insurance proceeds in the loss of a key man.

Enough life insurance should be provided to cover all the genuine needs of tax payment, estate stock liquidation, and business continuity.

BUYING OR SELLING SHARES IN THE COMPANY

Numerous instances arise when the company itself may want to buy or sell some of its shares, or when a stockholder may wish to buy or sell shares. A sound basis for determination of the value will help to safeguard fairness to all parties and to avoid any subsequent ill feelings or even litigation.

Whether or not there is a buy-sell agreement and whether or not there is funding through life insurance, the situation frequently arises when the company or a stockholder is in a position to purchase stock from the estate of a deceased stockholder or from a trust.

In the case of a corporate repurchase, the board of directors has a fiduciary responsibility to all shareholders and their beneficiaries to make the purchase on the basis of a price and a set of terms that is fair to the company and the stockholders. The board thus has the fiduciary responsibility to see that a proper valuation is made.

Similarly, the representative or trustee for the estate or trust has the fiduciary responsibility to make the transaction on a price and terms that are fair to the beneficiaries, which obviously requires a sound approach to valuation.

Anyone with a fiduciary responsibility should document the appropriateness of the price and terms of the transaction as thoroughly as is warranted by the size of the transaction. To the extent that any potential future animosity may be suspected of arising between any of the parties or their beneficiaries, the importance of such documentation assumes an even greater role.

Sometimes the board and the representative or trustee will prepare or have prepared separate valuation reports for such a transaction. In other cases, especially if the transaction is too small to warrant the expense of two valuation exercises and reports, the board and representative or trustee will agree on a qualified independent appraiser, who will be retained jointly to present an independent valuation report on which to base the transaction.

Any time that employees are involved in a stock transaction, it is necessary to have a fair valuation. One reason is that employee morale may be an important factor. It is desirable not only that the employee be treated fairly but also that the employee perceives without any reservations that he is being treated fairly, both for his own morale and also for the morale of others with whom the employee undoubtedly will communicate.

The typical situation is where the employee who owns some minority stock is quite sophisticated about doing his job but totally unsophisticated about understanding how to evaluate the stock of his company. In smaller companies this situation often prevails, even though the employee may be an officer or director of the company. The employee typically does not have the background to make an evaluation of the stock interest he is acquiring or disposing of, even though the person may have access to all the relevant material needed to make such an evaluation.

In these circumstances it is important for employee morale and also for the legal protection of controlling stockholders and other officers and directors to see that a fair valuation is made and documented and that the employee involved understands it as thoroughly as possible.

Transactions with other stockholders

Much the same caveats apply to transactions with other stockholders as to transactions with employees, except that other stockholders usually are at a further disadvantage by having less ready access to all the relevant information. A disgruntled outside stockholder may not create the same morale problem as a disgruntled employee stockholder, but he or she certainly can be a costly and aggravating nuisance.

EMPLOYEE STOCK OWNERSHIP PLANS (ESOPs)

The ESOP is a statutorily defined employee benefit plan providing for employees to own an interest in the company, with considerable income tax benefits to the company. To qualify for the tax benefits of an ESOP, the company's securities must be made available to employees on a basis that is nondiscriminatory, along the same basic guidelines for eligibility of participation as for pension or profit-sharing funds.

Employer securities may be contributed to the plan, and the value of such securities is a deductible expense for federal income tax purposes. Cash may be contributed, and used to purchase securities from existing stockholders.

An ESOP also can be used for tax advantages in connection with corporate borrowing. The net effect is that the principal of the loan as well as the interest can be paid in tax-deductible dollars.

The ESOP thus can be a useful tool in the closely-held business for both income tax advantages and for providing liquidity for existing stockholders. An adequate valuation, which must meet Employee Retirement Income Security Act (ERISA) and IRS standards, both initially and on an annual basis, is essential in an ESOP. The ESOP valuation guidelines are almost the same as for gift and estate taxes, although there are certain problems peculiar to the valuation of ESOP shares. This book contains a complete chapter on ESOPs, with a special ESOP bibliography at the end of the chapter.

CORPORATE OR PARTNERSHIP DISSOLUTIONS

It is common to find that one stockholder or partner "wants out," either for personal reasons or because of disagreements over management policy. The ability to arrive at a price and set of terms that are fair to all parties is crucial to resolving such situations amicably.

Sometimes elements of the business will be divided between the remaining and departing stockholders or partners. In such cases, the allocation of value between the different elements of the business takes on critical importance.

DIVORCES

To find either or both spouses involved in a business or professional practice at the time of a divorce is common. The business or professional practice needs to be valued for the property settlement. In my own business appraisal experience, these situations have been the most difficult types of business valuation to resolve amicably, because animosity and distrust between the parties tend to build as the divorce situation develops.

Occasionally, the two parties will retain a qualified independent appraiser to make a recommendation on the value of the business and will rely on the appraiser's report in the property settlement. The parties in such cases may or may not agree ahead of time to be bound by such a report. Sometimes the court will appoint an independent appraiser to make a recommendation to the court.

More commonly, each party hires his or her own independent appraiser to make a study of the value of the business. Sometimes the parties' attorneys succeed in reaching a settlement figure on the basis of the experts' opinions. More often it turns out that each appraiser presents expert testimony in court, and the final decision is made by the judge.

GOING PUBLIC

Obviously, if a company is going to offer securities to the public, a price must be determined. The process typically involves negotiation between the firm and its investment banker. The more knowledgeable the company's board of directors and negotiating representatives are about reasonable parameters for valuing the company's securities, the more successful such negotiations are likely to be in reaching an agreement that will best serve the stockholders' long-term interests. This book contains a section on going public in the last chapter.

GOING PRIVATE

Many companies have gone public and subsequently have been disenchanted with their role as a part of the public marketplace. The reasons for lack of satisfactory price and liquidity performance vary from company to company, some revolving around the company's own failure to achieve its earnings and growth objectives and others simply reflecting lack of satisfactory public market interest in the company's securities.

The rules adopted by the Securities and Exchange Commission (SEC) on August 2, 1979, require that a company going private retain an unaffiliated representative to act on behalf of the shareholders in negotiating and preparing an opinion on the fairness of the transaction.

A similar opinion may also be required in other transactions in the company's securities to insure fairness to unaffiliated shareholders.

STATUTORY MERGERS ("SQUEEZE-OUT" MERGERS) AND DISSENTERS' RIGHTS

Most states have statutes which allow a company (either private or public) to merge into another company, paying the stockholders of the merged company in cash or securities, or both, of the acquiring company. The percentage of stockholder vote that is required to authorize such a merger varies from state to state, but in most states is more than a simple majority and less than 100 percent.

The state statutes generally have a provision which allows stockholders who vote against the merger to dissent if they feel that the compensation offered the stockholders of the acquired company is inadequate. Stockholders who dissent cannot block the merger if the required percentage vote in favor is obtained, but they have the right to a court determination of the amount of compensation to which they are entitled.

A company that contemplates a statutory merger usually retains an expert business appraiser to advise it about the compensation to offer. Stockholders who are considering dissenting usually retain an appraiser to give them at least a preliminary report to help them make up their minds whether a dissent is warranted. Those who elect to dissent may seek an out-of-court settlement on compensation, or the appraisers for the respective parties may present their testimony in court and leave the final settlement to be determined by the judge. (In most states the parties have the right to have dissenters' stockholder suits tried by jury, but attorneys tend to waive the right to a jury in most such cases.)

Certain statutory mergers are referred to as "squeeze-out" mergers because in some cases they are undertaken specifically for the purpose of forcing out minority stockholders. Sometimes a special corporation is formed specifically for the purpose of acquiring the company that wishes to eliminate the minority stockholders.

SELLING OUT

One of the most important situations in which a valuation is necessary is when the company is faced with the prospect of selling out. For most closely-held companies it is the biggest financial decision that the company will ever make, and frequently the most important financial decision in the major owner's lifetime.

For most closely-held companies, the study of the selling company's value, the negotiations to sell, and the final decision do not get nearly the attention and resources that a decision of such magnitude deserves relative to other business decisions. An interest in selling may arise hastily in response to some event, such as the death of a key person. Or a potential buyer may express an interest when least expected. The company will be in a much better position to respond to such situations if it has made a point to keep some ongoing study or at least a rough idea of its own value, which it can then update and bring into sharper focus when the need arises.

If the company is contemplating selling out to another company for stock in the acquirer, then two valuations are really involved; that is, both the value of the selling company and the value of the stock in the acquiring company that will be received by the selling stockholders. When a public company acquires a private company for stock, it is commonly found that the stock to be issued is restricted from sale for some period, typically two years under usual circumstances. In this case, it is especially important that the seller have the benefit of a thorough valuation of the acquirer, since the seller will have at least two years before being able to liquidate the stock received as consideration in the sale. Back in the 1960s many good closely-held companies sold out for stock to public companies that had little substance and inflated stock prices, and which then tumbled to a fraction of the merger price before the selling stockholders were eligible to liquidate their holdings of the acquiring company's restricted stock issued in the acquisition.

SEC regulations now provide for the appointment of an independent appraiser to act as offeree representative on behalf of the stockholders of .companies selling out to publicly-traded companies. Even if the costs of the offeree representative are borne by the acquirer, as is frequently the case, the offeree representative has the fiduciary responsibility to act in the interests of the selling stockholders and to present them with an unbiased report on the fairness of the transaction. The offeree representative may or may not take a direct active part in the negotiations.

If the consideration to be received in selling out is part cash and part some type of bond or note receivable over a period of time, then the value of the consideration received also needs to be analyzed. One aspect to be analyzed is the risk of the receivable, that is, the buyer's apparent ability to meet the interest and principal payments when due. The other aspect is the adequacy of the interest rate for the type of receivable under the then-prevalent market conditions. An 8 percent nonmarketable note receivable from a middle-grade company certainly isn't worth face value if readily salable AAA bonds are yielding 12 percent. The appraiser must make a thorough analysis of the true value of whatever consideration other than cash may be received in a sale, not simply accepting it at face value.

SPINNING OFF PART OF COMPANY

Sometimes there is occasion to sell only a part of a company rather than the whole thing. The parts may operate better separately than together or the parts may be worth more separately than together. The portion of the company may be spun off to people managing it, to other buyers, or to the public.

The first task in such cases is to define what is to be spun off, in terms of operations, assets, and liabilities. If historical pro-forma statements can be constructed to aid in the valuation, that is desirable, but it is not always possible. If the people acquiring the spin-off are giving up stock in the rest of the company for it, then the situation requires valuation of both the spin-off and the remaining company in order to establish an exchange ratio for the stock.

MAKING AN ACQUISITION

Frequently the top officers of a company have a very good idea about whether another company would be a good acquisition as far as fitting into the acquirer's business plan, but do not have a very clear idea on how much they should consider paying. The result is that many overpriced acquisitions never fully justify themselves financially, or, conversely, good potential acquisitions never get made, because the acquirer's ideas of pricing are too low to be realistic. A sound, in-depth approach to the matter of valuation is an essential part of an effective acquisition program or of any single acquisition deliberation.

Besides serving its own interests, a company with a thorough approach to the valuation question frequently can present its case convincingly to a qualified acquisition candidate whose owners may be interested in merging but who may have unrealistically lofty notions about value. A well-documented valuation presentation may result in salvaging a sound merger that might otherwise go by the boards for lack of ability to reach agreement on price and terms.

COMPENSATORY DAMAGE CASES

Many situations give rise to lawsuits where the valuation of a business interest or business opportunity is the basis for measuring damages. These include cases involving breach of contract, antitrust violations, misrepresentations, condemnations, and a variety of other events. In such instances, it becomes the job of a credible independent business appraiser to provide expert testimony to assist the court in reaching a realistic value on which to base an award of damages.

Breach of contract

Time after time there are cases where a court finds that, as a result of some type of breach of contract, somebody has lost a business interest which needs to be valued to establish the amount of the damages.

The most common situation is where someone has been fired or somehow squeezed out of a business, where they either had been promised an interest, or where they actually had an interest but lost control of it for some reason. If the court feels that someone was denied a business interest to which he had a contractual right, the court may be inclined to make a very liberal interpretation of what the lost business interest might have been worth.

Antitrust

Some of the largest business valuation cases arise out of antitrust actions. If a court finds that someone was forced out of business, or forced out of some portion of his business, by activities that violated antitrust laws, the courts may be extremely liberal in awarding damages.

A great deal of conjecture is involved in such business valuation cases, because they have to deal not with an actual situation but with the hypothetical situation of what the business would have been worth if the activities that violated the antitrust laws had not occurred. The opposing parties usually are very far apart in their positions.

Loss of business opportunity

A valuation of a lost business opportunity is similar in some respects to a breach of contract or an antitrust case. If a court finds that someone usurped a business opportunity to which someone else legally should have been entitled, then damages generally are based on the value of the lost business opportunity.

A case involving condemnation of a business is similar in nature to a case involving condemnation of real estate. If there is business goodwill value attached to a location, or some other aspect of a business that is lost because of a condemnation proceeding, the business usually is entitled to compensation for the value of the loss.

Condemnation

Business valuations frequently are extremely helpful in obtaining financing. If it can be demonstrated convincingly that a business has significant value beyond what is readily apparent from its balance sheet and physical assets, both lenders and sources of equity capital tend to be more favorably disposed toward providing the financing.

OBTAINING FINANCING

Where potential equity value can be demonstrated, financing frequently can be worked out on a basis of debt with an equity "kicker," such as a debt instrument convertible into stock or debt with some stock purchase warrants included.

A business reorganization typically occurs from a cash flow inadequate to meet the company's current obligations, even though the business may have potential long-run viability. In other words, the business may be currently insolvent but not economically worthless.

REORGANIZATION

In such cases the typical approach is to attempt to value the business on a debt-free basis, and then to create a capital structure that, hopefully, will be viable. Sometimes such reorganizations are carried out by voluntary cooperation of the parties involved without court involvement, and in other cases reorganizations are carried out under court jurisdiction through utilization of the bankruptcy laws.

In many cases the valuation problem goes beyond just the total value of the business enterprise to include the matter of allocating the total value among two or more classes of securities. This sometimes is necessary under a company's existing capital structure, and almost always is necessary under conditions where a new capital structure is being created, such as in the recapitalization and reorganization situations discussed earlier.

ALLOCATION OF TOTAL VALUE

Allocation among classes of securities

The reasons for allocation of value may be because of the desire to sell or transfer some or all of one class of security, or it might be to establish a cost basis to be used in some future transfer. For example, if a company were to raise capital by selling "units" consisting of some debt and some stock, or some stock and some warrants, the price would have to be so allocated between the elements of the units that the capital gain or loss could be established when someone later disposed of one or the other element.

The most common reason to have to allocate total value among classes of assets is to determine allowable depreciation or amortization schedules. Most

Allocation among classes of assets

14

closely-held businesses want as much as possible of the total value allocated to those assets which can be depreciated or amortized most rapidly.

If one buys a professional sports team, how much of the purchase price is for the franchise (which the IRS would argue is a perpetual right and thus not amortizable for tax purposes) and how much is for player contracts (which should be amortizable for tax purposes over the life of the contracts)? How much of the price paid for a certain business is allocable to goodwill (not amortizable for tax purposes) versus patents and copyrights (amortizable over their remaining life)? It is common to find that a purchaser of a business liquidates the business by placing its assets into another corporate entity, and, in the process, allocating the total purchase price among the various classes of assets in such a manner that will generate the greatest depreciation and amortization write-offs that it deems will be acceptable to the IRS. The IRS has some complicated rules regarding the allocation of purchase price among asset categories.

VALUING TRUST OR PORTFOLIO HOLDINGS

There are many cases where a trustee or investment manager may have one or more closely-held business interests within a portfolio of assets that must be valued periodically for fiduciary or other reporting requirements. Even though a complete in-depth valuation generally is not warranted for each reporting period, at least some superficial valuation that is consistent with accepted valuation principles usually is better than just reporting a constant value from year to year without any recognition of improvement or deterioration in the value of the asset.

CONSIDERING ALTERNATIVES

A good idea of the value of a business or business interest is an essential background for the owner's deliberations about choices among the alternatives that he constantly faces. Sell out? Go public? Form an ESOP? Make stock gifts to family or charity or to both? Recapitalize the company? Make or change a buy-sell agreement? How much life insurance? Make an acquisition? Liquidate? Spin off part of the company? Go for debt or equity financing? Offer stock options to employees? Sell stock to employees or others? Buy in some of the outstanding stock?

This book is designed to help make the owner of a business or business interest consciously aware of the many alternatives available to him, as well as to assist in providing reasonable valuation guidelines that can be useful in making and implementing choices among available alternatives.

2

DEFINING THE APPRAISAL ASSIGNMENT

DEFINITION OF THE INTEREST TO BE APPRAISED
  Definition of entity appraised
  Definition of interest appraised relative to entity

DATE OR DATES OF VALUATION

PURPOSE OR PURPOSES OF THE APPRAISAL

FORM AND EXTENT OF WRITTEN OR VERBAL REPORT

DEFINITION OF WHO MADE AND WHO ACCEPTED THE ASSIGNMENT

RETAINING AN INDEPENDENT APPRAISER
  Scheduling
  Budget

I cannot overemphasize the importance of making a sharp definition of the elements of the appraisal assignment *at the onset of a business appraisal.*

It may seem obvious that the first step is to define the task. However, it is my own personal experience, undoubtedly shared by most other professional business appraisers, that most initial assignments are incomplete. This may be because the client does not have the experience to realize all the details that should be included in the appraisal assignment or has not thought through the implications of some aspects of the appraisal. The professional appraiser should give the client guidance in these details. Regardless of the reasons why the shortcomings tend to occur, failure to be thorough and explicit in the appraisal assignment is one of the greatest sources of errors, delays, excess costs, and misunderstandings between client and appraiser in business valuations.

The basic elements of the appraisal assignment are:

1. Definition of the interest or interests to be appraised.
2. Date or dates of valuation.
3. Purpose or purposes of the appraisal.
4. The form and extent of the required written or verbal report.

The definition of the assignment also should specify who made the assignment and who accepted the responsibility to carry out the assignment.

Two other critical matters to be addressed at this time are the schedule and the budget, including terms of payment for completing the assignment.

In many cases it is not possible at the outset to define all the relevant details of the foregoing appraisal assignment elements. In those cases the appraiser should make a list of the details remaining to be filled in, and such questions should be answered as soon as reasonably possible. Making the list focuses on the aspects that are unknown, and thus helps to prevent a material factor from being overlooked or misconstrued.

As the missing details are filled in, they should be added to the appraisal assignment file by appropriate written memoranda. If questions relevant to the assignment should be overlooked initially and uncovered later, such details should be added to the assignment file by memoranda. Similarly, if there are any subsequent changes in the assignment, appropriate memoranda should be filed.

DEFINITION OF THE INTEREST TO BE APPRAISED

Definition of entity appraised

If the entity in which the interest to be appraised is incorporated, it is necessary to indicate both the corporate name and the state where it was incorporated to adequately define the entity. The state of incorporation is necessary for an unambiguous definition of the entity, because there may be two or more corporations with identical names incorporated in different states. Furthermore, in some cases, the laws of the state of incorporation can have a bearing on the value of a particular business interest.

There may be instances in which the appraisal requires breakdowns on value attributable separately to a parent corporation and to interests in one or more subsidiaries, in which case such breakdowns need to be specified.

If the form of business organization is something other than a corporation, the form as well as the name must be specified. Some of the most common forms of business organization are sole proprietorships, general partnerships, limited partnerships, and cooperatives.

If the structure of the business organization could give rise to special tax or legal considerations in the valuation, such structure should be specified. Examples would be Subchapter S corporations (corporations taxed as partnerships), professional corporations, real estate investment trusts (REITs), investment companies registered under the Investment Company Act of 1940, and personal holding companies.

In some business organizations, especially sole proprietorships, there is a formal name of the entity and another name, called a *DBA* (''Doing Business As''), by which the public knows the entity, in which case it is desirable to identify the entity by both names in the appraisal assignment.

If the business to be appraised is some portion of a corporation or other business entity, such as a division or branch, then it is necessary to be explicit on exactly what aspects of the total company are included in the appraisal.

Definition of interest appraised relative to entity

One critical definition in the assignment is the question of whether the appraisal is of the assets constituting the entity, or of stock or some other interest, such as a partnership interest, in the entity. In selling a business, considerable tax implications rest on the question of whether it is assets or a stock, partnership, or other interest that is being transferred. In valuation of a business interest for gift or estate taxes, or for many other purposes, it can make a considerable difference whether one is valuing a direct interest in the assets comprising the business or whether a corporate, partnership, or some other entity intervenes between the investment assets and the owner of the business interest.[1]

If the business is incorporated, the appraisal assignment must indicate the number of shares to be valued and the number of shares outstanding. (Note, by the way, that treasury stock, which is stock once issued and subsequently reacquired by the corporation, is *not* outstanding, and must be subtracted from the shares issued in determining the number of shares outstanding.)

If there is more than one class of stock, such as voting and nonvoting, then the appraisal assignment should indicate what class of stock is being valued, and the proportionate interest of the number of shares being valued to the total equity capitalization, as well as to their own class of stock.

Any special restrictions attaching to the shares being valued should also be a part of the description of the interest being valued, since any restrictions normally would have a negative effect on value, all other things being equal.

---

[1]See, for example, *Edwin A. Gallun v. Comm.* 33 T.C.M. 284 (1974).

The most common category of such restrictions, which may or may not apply to all the securities of the class being valued, are restrictions on transferability. Public companies, for example, commonly issue restricted stock (also called "investment letter stock") in connection with acquisitions or raising capital through private placements. Closely-held companies may restrict transferability by having all or part of their shares subject to some form of buy-sell or repurchase agreement.

There also may be privileges which attach to the particular shares in question that may have a positive effect on value, such as the owner having a "put" option to sell the shares to the corporation under some circumstances. A *put* is an option to sell, exercisable at the discretion of the owner, under certain prescribed terms and conditions. Various forms of put options are found in employee stock ownership plans, for example, the result being that a share of stock owned by the ESOP, or by a beneficiary as a result of a distribution of stock from an ESOP, may be worth more than another share of the same company but not subject to the ESOP privileges.

If the interest is a partnership or joint venture interest, the percentage should be indicated. In a limited partnership, the respective percentage interests of the limited and general partners should be indicated.

Who owns the interest in question, or whether it is to be a newly created interest, also should be indicated. Sometimes the relationship of the owner of the interest to other members of the control group is thought to have a bearing on the value. In the case of an ESOP, the value per share will be less if it is to be newly issued stock than if the ESOP stock is to be acquired from an existing shareholder, since there will be dilution in the former case and not in the latter.

DATE OR DATES OF VALUATION

The specific valuation date or dates are critical variables to be determined at the outset. The value will vary from one date to another for various reasons. Sometimes the value can change fairly drastically within a short time as a result of certain events.

Sudden and substantial changes in the public's perception of the value of shares of a particular company's stock are demonstrated in the public marketplace every day. There are many court cases, especially involving tax litigation, where significantly different values have been justified within very brief time spans because of changes in relevant circumstances.[2]

Values of interests in business enterprises vary inversely with the cost of capital to businesses, a factor over which the individual business has no control. A sudden change in a company's earnings can have a substantial effect on the value of the company or an interest in it, especially if the sudden change might not have been anticipated. Key agreements, such as the signing or termination of a major customer contract, can have a significant impact on

[2]See, for example, *Morris M. Messing,* 48 T.C. 502 (1967), acq. 1968–1 C.B. 2. Even though the company made a public offering at over $36 shortly after a gift of stock, the court upheld a value of $13 for gift tax purposes as of the date of the gift.

value. A major event, such as selling out the company or making a public offering of the stock, can have a dramatic immediate impact on value. These are just a few examples of variables that can cause significant differences in value from one date to another, sometimes in a very short time.

In most business valuation cases, the value opinion will be based at least partly on other related transactions which have occurred. Such transactions commonly include prices at which stocks in the same industry are trading in the public marketplace relative to their earnings, assets, dividends, or other relevant variables. The valuation date for the business interest in question must be known so that the comparable transaction data can be compiled for the valuation date or as near to it as practically possible.

Sometimes there are multiple valuation dates, such as in a series of gifts of stock. Unless the dates are quite close together and relevant circumstances have not changed materially, a separate set of data needs to be gathered and taken into consideration for each date.

In many situations the relevant date is some undetermined time in the future when some as yet unscheduled event is expected to take place, such as a sale of a company, a public offering of stock, or a trial where the value of the business interest on the trial date will be at issue. This presents the appraiser with the challenge of the valuation date being a moving target, and the data to be used simply must be brought up as close to the current moment as possible.

Where the valuation must satisfy some aspect of Securities and Exhange Commission requirements, the usual rule is that the data must be current to within 90 days of the relevant event, such as an offering of stock. This stems from the fact that most public companies report earnings and other relevant data on a quarterly basis. The "current within 90 days" requirement of the SEC can be used as a rough guideline for other situations where no hard and fast rule exists.

In some valuation cases involving litigation, the valuation date itself is an issue to be resolved by the court. This increases the complexity of the valuation task, because the appraiser must be prepared to address the valuation at various times, sometimes not knowing until after the judgment is rendered what valuation date the court determined to be relevant. Since the choice of the valuation date in such cases will be a legal matter, the attorney for whom the expert appraiser will be testifying should take the responsibility, as a part of giving the appraiser his assignment, to consider all alternative valuation dates that the court might consider applicable, and to instruct the appraiser to be prepared to address the value as of each of the alternative dates.

PURPOSE OR PURPOSES OF THE APPRAISAL

Perhaps the most important point to establish in this chapter is that the purpose of the appraisal will have a substantial impact on the methodology used, and therefore possibly on the result, since different methodologies are acceptable for different purposes. If properly carried out in each respective case, there should be nothing incompatible between these different approaches and results.

The greatest differences among valuation methodologies for varied purposes arise from the relative degree of reliance on forward projections as compared with reliance on historical data. There is unanimous agreement among professional business appraisers that the present value of a business interest involves a prophesy about the future. However, in many cases it is difficult or impossible to agree on such a prophesy. Many of the differences in methodology or approach to different valuation problems, then, involve differences of degree between utilization of opinions about the future versus utilization of historical data and analysis of past and current circumstances.

The conclusion that the methods appropriate for a particular valuation depend at least partly on the purpose is well documented in literature relating to professional business appraisals. For example, as the *Harvard Law Review* pointed out:

Some appraisers and courts tend to assume that accounting valuations of corporations and of stock for other purposes can serve as models for appraisal valuation. Although this may sometimes be true, more often the method *should depend on the reason for the valuation.*[3] (Emphasis supplied.)

Victor I. Eber, a CPA and former chairman of the Business Management Institute, explains the critical importance of defining the purpose of the appraisal:

Appraisal techniques for income, estate, and gift tax purposes can substantially differ from methods used to appraise a business for purposes of acquisition, merger, liquidation, divestiture, split-up and spin-offs . . . the typical appraisal for commercial purposes will frequently deal with factors of concern to prospective purchasers, liquidators, or merger partners, as distinguished from a determination of an IRS-acceptable value of the business as a free-standing going concern.[4]

Eber elaborates with an example:

Many principals and their advisers in buy-sell situations consciously consider a limited number of variables in establishing a value. For example, a small loan holding company negotiating for the purchase of an additional office would concentrate almost entirely on the origin and condition of receivables, with minimum regard for the organization structure, the condition of the office, book values, or the past earnings of the business under existing management. Such truncated appraisal is based on the assumption that the acquiring company can supply those things. Thus, it appears that many essential factors are being ignored, on the recognized assumption that the principals expect to overcome the business deficiencies.

For estate and gift tax appraisals, such short cuts are not taken because the appraiser is typically valuing a business in a noncommercial, nonacquisition setting. Further it is a situation in which the appraiser must follow requirements.[5]

---

[3]"Valuation of Dissenters' Stock Under Appraisal Statutes," *Harvard Law Review* (May 1966), p. 1954.

[4]Victor I. Eber, "How to Establish Value for Close Corporation Stock That Will Withstand an IRS Audit," *Estate Planning* (Autumn 1976), pp. 28–29.

[5]Ibid., p. 28.

Chapter 4 presents the discounted future earnings (DFE) method of valuing a business. There is general agreement among students and practitioners of business appraisal that this method, or some variation of it, such as discounted future cash flow, is the theoretically most correct method for determining the value of a business investment. This approach is widely used for business decision making, such as the price to offer for a potential acquisition.

However theoretically correct some version of the discounted future benefits approach to valuation may be, the validity of the result is dependent on the accuracy of estimates of earnings, cash flow, or other variables for several years into the future. Courts tend to range from reluctant to totally unwilling to rely on such estimates in arriving at the value of a business. Therefore, in valuation situations involving litigation or potential litigation, much greater emphasis must be placed on valuation approaches that utilize historical and current data. Chapter 5 discusses such appraisals, and Chapter 17 provides further elaboration on guidelines for gift, estate, and inheritance tax appraisals.

To the extent that businesses tend to grow in value over time, one of the implications is that the forward-looking appraisal may tend to result in a higher value conclusion than the appraisal based primarily on past and current data. The seller of a business should try to get all he can for the speculative value of future opportunities in his business, and buyers are willing to pay for such opportunities if they believe that the opportunities offer good business risks. On the other hand, for gift and estate tax valuations, in the absence of unusual and extenuating circumstances, there is no requirement to base the valuation on earnings expectations beyond what the company's historical demonstrated earnings record would support as reasonable.

FORM AND EXTENT OF WRITTEN OR VERBAL REPORT

The purpose of the assignment will be a major determinant of the form of the report.

In cases involving taxes or tax implications, such as gift or estate tax valuations, ESOPs, or recapitalizations, the appraiser should prepare a formal written report that scrupulously satisfies the requirements of Revenue Ruling 59–60, which contains the guidelines for implementation of Treasury Regulation 20.2031. Such a report also will satisfy most state inheritance tax stipulations.

If a written report is to be prepared for presentation to prospective buyers for the purpose of selling the company, the report usually will focus heavily on projections, studies of markets for the company's existing and prospective products and services, and other factors to help convince a buyer that an attractive business opportunity is available. The language and documentation of the report normally will be much more informal than a report for tax purposes.

Where litigation is involved, the balance between written report and oral testimony will depend on the preferences of the court, the attorney involved, and the appraiser, who will have to present his findings as expert testimony. In some cases a judge might enter a pretrial order requiring each side's experts to prepare and exchange complete written reports prior to the trial, with copies to the court, and then limit verbal testimony to selected issues of significant disagreement.

In most cases, including most cases involving the SEC, such as making an offer to the stockholders to take a public company private, the only formal written output required is an opinion letter on the fairness of the transaction, which may be as brief as a page and may or may not reveal any significant details of the basis for the opinion.

In many cases only a verbal report to the client is required. This is common in estate planning, especially when the purpose of the exercise is to help the client to get a ballpark idea of the value of the business in order to decide what to do. When the client makes a decision to make stock gifts, form an ESOP, attempt to sell the business, or whatever, then a timely and complete report appropriate to the situation can be prepared.

It is common to give a very brief opinion letter report in the early stages of potential litigation regarding valuation disputes or potential disputes. The appraiser may take a cursory look at a situation and offer a preliminary range of potential values, usually qualified by the stipulation that he is not bound by such a preliminary conclusion if a more in-depth examination indicates otherwise. Such a preliminary opinion letter frequently provides the basis for a negotiated settlement between the parties. If the initial appraisal assignment is limited to such a preliminary opinion letter, it usually also is agreed that the appraiser will be willing to conduct a complete valuation study and testify about his findings in court if that becomes necessary.

In any case, the appraisal assignment should include as clear a specification as possible about the form and extent of written or verbal output product that is expected.

DEFINITION OF WHO MADE AND WHO ACCEPTED THE ASSIGNMENT

There are a number of reasons why the statement of the assignment should specify who the client is and who the appraiser is, besides the obvious reason of the need to know who is to bill whom and who is responsible for payment for the services. In most situations, the appraiser has a fiduciary responsibility to the client to release information about the appraisal only to the client or to others with the client's permission. In some circumstances involving litigation and potential litigation, the attorney involved may prefer to retain the appraiser rather than have the client retain the appraiser directly, on the theory that this relationship better protects the appraiser's working papers and files from subpoena by the opposing attorney.[6]

In cases where a business transaction is the probable ultimate outcome, it may be important to be specific about whom the appraiser represents, such as

---

[6]See, for example, Richard H. Dallas, "The Attorney-Client and the Corporation in Shareholder Litigation," *Southern California Law Review* (1977), pp. 303–36.

the board of directors of the buying or selling company, or one or more individual stockholders of the buying or selling company. In such cases, the relationship of the appraiser to the parties involved should be clear, since he may or may not be considered to be in a position of advocacy.

In specifying the appraiser, the distinction that usually needs to be made is whether the individual primarily responsible for the appraisal is being retained or whether it is the firm which employs the individual that is being retained. Among professional appraisers, as among certified public accountants who perform audits, the common practice is that the firm rather than the individual appraiser is retained. This protects the client, since the firm has the responsibility to complete the job without concern about anything that might impair the individual person's ability to perform the work. Also, it usually provides continuity for keeping and being able to refer to the working papers and related records if the occasion should arise to do so in later months or years, as is frequently the case.

RETAINING AN INDEPENDENT APPRAISER

For many appraisal situations, it is appropriate to retain an independent outside appraiser. This brings to the appraisal situation the benefits of professional training, experience, and third-party objectivity. When retaining an outside appraiser, all the foregoing elements of the appraisal assignment should be considered carefully, along with schedule and budget.

Scheduling

One of the most common practical problems in getting a business valuation done on a thorough and timely basis is the lack of proper scheduling, a problem which usually could be avoided with appropriate planning.

The scheduling problems usually arise from either procrastination in making the appraisal assignment and then winding up with a need or desire to have it completed on a crash basis, or from tardiness in providing the appraiser with some portions of the information needed. Another common source of scheduling problems is changing some aspect of the assignment midway through the project, which is another good reason for the client and the appraiser to think through and agree on the details of the appraisal assignment as thoroughly as possible at the outset.

Procrastination in getting the appraisal assignment made, and thus delay in getting the appraisal started, tends to arise partly from the client or his attorney or CPA failing to be decisive in defining the client's needs or objectives in making the appraisal, and partly from underestimating the lead time required to take all the steps required for a thorough business appraisal. Once the appraiser has been contacted, he should take the initiative to help the client avoid procrastination by spelling out clearly the steps to be taken and why adequate lead time is necessary. The reading of this book, I hope, will help to provide a better appreciation of the reasons why some lead time is important in getting the job done as well as possible. As far as indecision about the definition of the client's need for the appraisal, it frequently is helpful to call in the appraiser in the early stages of this decision process to help crystallize the appraisal requirements.

Hopefully, also, reading this book, and especially the checklist of documents and information to be used, covered in Chapters 6 and 7, will help those contemplating the need for an appraisal to gather the material needed on a timely basis so that last-minute scrambles for data and attendant delays in the appraisal work can be avoided.

The appraisal assignment should specify when the work is expected to be completed, but it should also make it clear that the appraiser's ability to meet the proposed schedule is dependent on getting the necessary material on a timely basis, and also that changes in the appraisal assignment during the project most probably will cause changes in the schedule if the schedule is already tight. One safety valve that is available in some tight scheduling situations, such as filing a gift or estate tax return by a specified date, is to specify that the appraiser will arrive at a figure by the required filing date, and that the formal written documented report will follow within a reasonable time.

Different business appraisal situations vary so much that it is very difficult to generalize broadly about reasonable overall scheduling. My firm has done an appraisal in a week, and we have been involved in appraisals that stretched over a year. If there is such a thing as a typical business valuation—let's say, an initial valuation of stock in conjunction with the formation of an ESOP for a relatively uncomplicated business with a few million dollars in sales—one might suggest that a roughly comfortable time schedule would be to allow for about 100 hours of applied effort by various staff levels of the appraisal firm, spread over a period of about 90 days.

Budget

The budget can be either a fixed price or a straight hourly basis, or some combination of the two. To the extent that the appraisal assignment is clearly and thoroughly defined, it is reasonable to expect the parties to agree to a fixed fee basis for the work. Like contracting for construction, changes in the specifications after the work is started usually result in increased costs. This is another good reason to be as complete as possible in specifying the appraisal assignment at the outset.

Where third-party independence of judgment is a requirement of the appraisal, as in any case where expert testimony in litigation or potential litigation may be involved, the appraiser's fees must be fixed, hourly, or set in some manner totally independent of the outcome of any litigation, or the appraiser's independent third-party status will be thrown into jeopardy.

In any case, the amount or basis for determination of the appraiser's fees should be considered at the time the appraisal assignment is made.

3

PRINCIPLES OF BUSINESS VALUATION—THEORY AND PRACTICE

Value, like beauty, is in the mind of the beholder. It is no wonder then, that there is so much controversy about the criteria by which to determine the value of a business or business interest. To quote a popular phrase of the younger generation, "It depends on where you're coming from."

DEFINITIONS OF VALUE

Before the valuation process can begin in any meaningful way, one must determine the definition of *value* that is applicable for the purpose of the valuation, since different definitions of value may be applicable for different purposes. Replacement cost or depreciated replacement cost value of the assets is the approach usually taken for insurance purposes. Liquidation value may be appropriate if liquidation is a prospect under consideration. However, most business valuation purposes are best served by arriving at a "going concern value," that is, the value of the business interest assuming that the business will continue to carry on without any significant interruption.

There are also different statutory definitions of value. Federal regulations are clear in stating that the value of a business interest for gift and estate tax purposes is "fair market value." The definition of fair market value is virtually universally accepted as "the price at which the interest would change hands between a willing buyer and a willing seller, both being adequately informed of the relevant facts, and neither being under any compulsion to buy or to sell."[1] Although not specifically written into the statutes, there is general agreement on the implication that the parties also must have the ability as well as the willingness to buy or to sell. Most state inheritance tax statutes adhere to the fair market value definition.

However, certain other statutes, notably state statutes defining dissenting stockholder rights, are much less clear, typically using the term *fair value* instead of *fair market value*. There is no universally accepted definition of fair value as there is for fair market value. The effect of this ambiguity is that the discrepancies between the value conclusions of opposing parties tends to be even wider where the statutory standard is fair value than in cases where the fair market value standard clearly applies.

In general, most of this book deals with arriving at fair market value on a going-concern basis. Where deviations from this standard of value are applicable, I think that they will be apparent.

GENERALLY ACCEPTED THEORY

There is a generally accepted theoretical structure underlying the process of valuing a business interest. In theory, the value of an interest in a business is dependent on the future benefits that will accrue to that interest, with the value of the future benefits discounted back to a present value at some appropriate discount (capitalization) rate. Thus, the theoretically correct approach is to

[1]For intensive historic and legal review, see "Power and Process, A Commentary on Market Value," ASA Monograph No. 1 (June 1969).

project the future benefits (usually earnings, cash flow, or dividends), and discount the projected stream back to a present value.

However, while there is general acceptance of a theoretical framework for business valuation, translating it into practice in an uncertain world poses one of the most complex challenges of economic and financial theory and practice.

Deviations from the theoretically correct approach to business valuation are, however, not necessarily, or even usually, inconsistent with the underlying theory.

Since the value of a business interest is dependent on its future benefits, direct implementation of the correct theoretical approach to valuation requires a quantified forecast of the benefits considered relevant in the case, be they earnings, cash flows, or dividends. The discounted future benefits approach is only applicable in practice to the extent that the projections and assumptions used are acceptable to the decision maker for whom the business valuation is being prepared.

Such projections may be difficult to make—and even more difficult to get two or more parties with different economic and business expectations to agree on. Therefore, practitioners of business valuation have developed various approaches that use historical rather than projected data to arrive at a valuation. In some cases, approaches using historical data may tend to be carried out in a manner that is a little more conservative than the discounted future benefits approach with respect to reflection of potential future growth. However, in general, approaches using historical data, properly carried out, should yield a result that is reasonably reconcilable with what would be arrived at by a well-carried-out discounted future benefits approach.

RELIANCE ON PROJECTED VERSUS HISTORICAL DATA

In the real world of business valuation practice, the situations that come closest to actually using a theoretical discounted future benefits model to arrive at a value are in the merger market, and, to a lesser extent, in the markets for publicly-traded securities.

In applying the discounted future benefit approach, someone has to make estimates of the future benefits with enough credibility that someone is willing to take action on them. Businessmen are trained and experienced in making and evaluating business and economic forecasts and using them as a basis for decision making on a daily basis. Thus, many merger and stock transaction decisions are made in this manner.

However, as a practical matter, because of lack of a set of projections and assumptions acceptable to all parties, most business valuations end up relying on historical data, which are evaluated to reflect reasonable expectations about foreseeable future changes.

It is not at all unreasonable, of course, in many cases to go through the valuation exercise based on projected data and also do a valuation based on historical data. The choice of which to rely on, or the relative weights to be assigned in reaching the final valuation conclusion, will depend on the circumstances of the particular case and the judgment of the appraiser.

In any business valuation involving litigation or potential litigation, the courts must rely on evidence. Historical facts usually make more credible evidence in the eyes of the court than forward projections of what somebody thinks will happen.

Therefore, the focus of attention in many business valuations for the purpose of transactions (mergers, sellouts, public markets, and the like) tends to be on future projections. Where legal evidence is required, the focus tends to be on the past record, tempered by any evidence that can be well supported about predictable future changes that might indicate the past record is inadequate to provide a basis for current valuation.

The extent to which a court will rely on projections as evidence in a valuation case probably is a function of the court's degree of confidence in the validity of those projections, or at least the general acceptability of the projections on the valuation date. It is not at all unreasonable that a prospective buyer in a merger situation, who may have an intimate knowledge of the industry involved, finds it easier to make judgments on the validity of the company's projections than does a judge in a courtroom.

A good example of a court's unwillingness to rely on future projections to arrive at a business valuation is provided in a recent Oregon Supreme Court opinion. Georgia-Pacific Corporation (GP) was defendant in a case involving an alleged breach of contract, and the issue at hand was the value on a particular date of an interest in a corporation called Montana Pacific International (MPI). The court's opinion included the following statement:

As evidence of the appropriate value plaintiffs point to a "pro forma" projection of MPI's anticipated profits over a ten-year period, prepared by GP in support of an application for bank financing. *We find these projected profits far too speculative to provide the basis for relief in this case.*[2] (Emphasis supplied.)

In this case, the court stated that it was unwilling to rely on the projections as a basis for determining the business value, for the purpose of assessing the amount of damages for which the defendant could be liable, even though the court stated that the projections were actually prepared by the defendant itself.

Discussing dissenter stockholder suits, Warren Banks stated that: ". . . it seems fair to say that the Delaware courts have been reluctant to base their valuations on a projection of future earnings. . . ."[3]

For example, in one case decided in the Supreme Court of Delaware, the opinion stated: "As between the valuation based on a forecast of the future and one based on actual figures, the latter method seems preferable."[4]

In another Delaware case, the court opinion's discussion of the matter of

---

[2]*Delaney v. Georgia-Pacific Corp.*, Or., 564 P.2d 277 (Or. 1977).

[3]Warren E. Banks, "A Selective Inquiry into Judicial Stock Valuation," *Indiana Law Review* (1972), p. 23.

[4]*Cottrell v. Pawcatuck Company*, 128 A.2d 224 (Del. S.C. 1956), p. 231.

estimated earnings included the following language: ". . . his estimate was based principally on long-range projections, a technique which has not met with approval in Delaware. . . ."[5]

There is one major category of exception in the historical versus forward-looking basis for judicial valuation decisions. Courts usually rely on capitalization of anticipated future earnings in business valuations in conjunction with reorganization proceedings under bankruptcy statutes.[6] It would seem almost essential to do so, since, unless there was a reasonable expectation that the future would be more economically rewarding than the past, the reorganization would appear to be a fruitless effort.

In summary, this difference in focus or emphasis between the historical record and future projections is dictated by what the respective decision makers are willing to rely on. There is a big difference in this respect between an investment decision in the market and a judicial decision in a court (other than bankruptcy cases). The businessman can and should, using his knowledge and experience in allocating resources entrusted to him for the purpose of taking business risks, accept calculated risks inherent in decision making based on forecasts of an uncertain future. The court typically perceives that it lacks such expertise and that its mandate should be to reduce the element of uncertainty or risk to the greatest possible extent in its decision-making process. To be practically useful, the business valuation procedure selected must be responsive to the criteria acceptable to those who ultimately decide what action will be taken as a result of the valuation process.

Chapter 4 addresses the procedure for valuing a business using the discounted future benefits approach, and Chapter 5 addresses general procedures for a business valuation relying on historical data.

BASIC VARIABLES AFFECTING VALUE

Whether one actually attempts to make future projections or whether one relies on historical data to derive some proxy for reasonable future expectations, there are certain key variables on which the business valuation will focus. The relative importance of the variables will be different in different types of situations. Theorists will continue to argue for longer than this book will be in print about what variables are the most appropriate ones on which to focus for various valuation situations.

The primary financial statement variables to be considered (not necessarily all in *every* case) are:

1. Earnings.
2. Cash flow.
3. Dividends or dividend-paying capacity.
4. Assets (broadly construed to include balance sheet analysis).
5. Gross revenues.

---

[5]*Levin v. Midland Ross Corp*, 194 A. 2d 50 (Del. Ch. 1963), p. 57.

[6]Banks, "A Selective Inquiry," pp. 33–37.

In many instances, a conclusion as to value may be tempered by other factors, such as:

1. Marketability.
2. Voting rights.
3. History of past sales in the company's securities.
4. Special ownership or management perquisites.

The key external variable is cost of capital.

Relative importance of financial statement variables

There is no clear-cut answer that is applicable in all situations about which variable among the future benefits deserves the greatest attention in the valuation. There is general consensus within the discipline of business valuation that earning power is the most important internal variable affecting the value of most operating companies, such as manufacturers, merchandisers, and service companies.

Earnings

One of the difficulties in trying to determine which is the most important variable or variables to focus on in any particular situation is the fact that, within the broad scope of generally accepted accounting principles (GAAP), the definition and measurement of "earnings" is elusive. Therefore, if anticipated future earnings is to play an important part in the valuation process, it is important that the parties involved in the analysis have a good understanding of how they are defining and measuring earnings. If earnings is defined in such a way that this variable offers some reasonable approximation of incremental value accruing to the business interest, before dividend payouts, then I am inclined to agree with the consensus that earnings is the best variable on which to focus for valuation purposes.

Cash flow

Focusing on discounted cash flow (DCF) has particular appeal in those situations where cash flow provides a better measurement of incremental value to the business than does earnings. This is generally applicable, for example, for companies whose main business is owning improved real estate that they lease or rent out. In these inflationary times, most well-maintained buildings hold their value or appreciate in terms of current dollars, and the depreciation charged against earnings for such companies does not really represent a decrement to the enterprise value. Thus, in valuing such companies as real estate investment trusts (REITs), analysts tend to focus more on cash earnings than net earnings.

Although considerably less ambiguous than earnings, cash flow also can be defined in a number of ways. The term *cash flow* is not necessarily synonymous with *cash earnings*. The term *cash earnings* usually means *net earnings plus book charges such as depreciation and amortization*. On the other hand, cash flow can be defined to include or exclude anything the analyst considers appropriate for the purpose. In some cases, even major capital expenditures may be deducted in measuring cash flow.

The basic arithmetic for valuing a company by the DCF method is exactly the same as for the discounted future earnings (DFE) method; it is just that different variables are used, including careful choice of a capitalization rate that is appropriate to the future benefit stream being measured.

Dividends

One of the earliest and most frequently cited works on the theory of valuation of a stock asserted the proposition that the value of a share was based entirely on its future stream of dividend payments, discounted back to a present value by an appropriate capitalization rate.[7] Despite John Burr Williams's classic pioneering work in this regard, contemporary business valuation theory and practice put considerably less weight on dividend paying capacity than on earning power in arriving at the value of the business. This is largely because dividend paying capacity stems primarily from earning capacity. Once the earning capacity is achieved, then it becomes a discretionary decision on the part of the directors whether available funds should be used for dividends or for retained earnings and further pursuit of the company's business opportunities.

The emphasis on capitalizing a dividend stream might be considered most appropriate in cases where the buyers of the stock attribute value to it primarily because of its dividends. Utility stocks are probably the industry group most commonly regarded in this manner. It also is generally recognized that dividends or lack of them should assume relatively greater importance in valuing a minority interest than in valuing a controlling interest, since the minority holder has no power to exercise discretion to pay dividends, even if adequate dividend paying capacity is available to the firm.

An alternative to valuing a stock by estimating its dividends in perpetuity and discounting them by an appropriate capitalization rate is to discount a stream of anticipated dividends for some finite number of years, plus some estimated terminal value, also discounted to a present value. Determining the terminal value (the price at which the interest presumably could be sold at some specified time in the future) is the obvious problem with this approach. Unless there is an expectation of some future event which would give rise to a terminal value with some degree of certainty, that would seem to me to be a formidable challenge.

Assets

It is important to dispel the popular misconception that ownership of a share of stock represents rights to a proportionate share of the underlying assets. That simply is not true. The importance of assets in the valuation process is dependent on the extent to which they can be utilized to generate the benefits

---

[7]John Burr Williams, *The Theory of Investment Value* (Cambridge, Mass.: Harvard University Press, 1938). Reprinted in Amsterdam by North Holland Publishing Co. in 1956.

already discussed, such as earnings, cash flows, or dividends, either through operations or through liquidation.[8] As George Lasry explains it:

A share of common stock does not represent a share in the ownership of the assets of a business. It represents a claim on the income derived from these assets by the people entrusted with their management.[9]

* * * * *

. . . a share of common stock is simply a share in the title to a claim on the income of the corporation. This title encompasses a claim on the residual income, the retained earnings and original capital, and the expected income produced by the assets of the corporation. Only the corporation itself holds title to all its assets and liabilities. A shareholder only owns a claim on income and not a share in the corporate title to its net property. A thirsty shareholder of a brewery cannot walk into "his" company and demand that a case of beer be charged to his equity account.[10]

If liquidation is contemplated, then, of course, asset values assume a major role in the valuation. In most operating companies, however, asset values are considered in a supportive role, providing the means to continue the earning power—and some defense against the magnitude of downside risk in the future value of the enterprise in case of periods of low earnings or losses.

The type of enterprise where assets typically would take on a relatively more important emphasis would be in a company that is primarily a holding company rather than an operating company. In a company whose primary business is holding a portfolio of real estate or securities, the underlying asset value usually takes on more weight than earnings, dividends, or cash flow.

Some companies are a hybrid, that is, a combination of operating and holding company. In such cases, it may be appropriate to value the company in two parts, with greater emphasis on earnings for the operating portion of the company and greater emphasis on asset values for the nonoperating portion of the company.

Sometimes, if an operating company owns certain nonoperating assets, especially if they are nonoperating assets not contributing to the present or foreseeable earnings stream in any way, the liquidating value of such assets, or some portion of it, may be added to the value otherwise determined on a capitalization of earnings basis.

Chapter 11 addresses analysis of the balance sheet to arrive at a total or per share asset value that will be useful to the extent that asset values are to be accorded weight in the particular valuation. The essential point to keep in mind in according weight to any asset value approach in valuing a business interest is that the corporate entity intervenes between the assets and the shareholder. Therefore, after an asset value per share has been determined

---

[8]An example of this point is found in the court's opinion on the *Gallun* case, discussed in a later chapter.

[9]George Lasry, *Valuing Common Stock* (New York: AMACOM, 1979), p. 1.

[10]Ibid., p. 15.

that is suitable to the valuation purpose at hand, another step remains before that figure can be used as part of the final valuation determination. Even when an asset value approach is used, a share of stock may be worth either more or less than the underlying asset value, remembering that the shareholder does not have a direct claim on the underlying assets. The techniques for translating underlying asset values into their implications for the value of a share of stock are discussed in later chapters.

Gross revenues

Gross revenues may be the primary focus of the valuation process in certain situations, usually service businesses, and especially in connection with a sellout or merger. Even if earnings are depressed or negligible, either from mismanagement or from management's expense and compensation policies, a buyer frequently is willing to pay some multiple of gross revenues for the established market share, with the buyer willing to accept the risk of making the operation satisfactorily profitable.

The valuation emphasis frequently tends to be on gross revenues when buying or selling various commission-type service agencies, such as advertising or insurance, or professional practices, such as medical or accounting. Sometimes emphasis on gross revenues is found in transactions in the publishing field.

It is unusual, however, even when heavy weight is accorded to gross revenues in the valuation, for this factor to be the sole value criterion. In comparing two similar service businesses with the same level of revenues, most people would pay more for the one with the better underlying earnings, cash flow, and asset base.

IMPACT OF OTHER VARIABLES

Marketability

The market pays a premium for liquidity, or, conversely, a discount for lack of it. For two given investments identical in all other valuation criteria, the market will accord a considerable premium to one which can be liquidated into cash instantly, especially without risk of loss of value, compared with one which cannot be so liquidated.

For this reason, a share in a privately-held company usually is worth less than an otherwise comparable share in a publicly-held company. Many factors affect the relative marketability of different business interests. Some are inherent in the nature of the business interest, and others are built in through specific contractual rights or restrictions. The size of the interest can have a bearing, too. In some cases a smaller block would be easier to market than a larger block, and in other cases the reverse could be true.

Voting rights

Voting rights constitute one of the most difficult variables to quantify in terms of impact on value. As a generality, the greater the extent to which the issue of control is involved, the greater the importance of voting rights in terms of value. For very small minority interests, the market accords very little value to voting rights. Where swing votes or control is involved, the value impact can be significant.

History of past sales

The greater the extent to which past sales truly can be considered arm's-length transactions among fully informed parties, the greater the extent to which such sales properly can be accorded weight as a factor in the valuation. Also, the more sales, the larger the sales, and the more recent the sales, the more weight they properly can be accorded.

If a stock enjoys an active public trading market, the public market price usually determines the value for gift, estate, and inheritance tax purposes. In a closely-held stock valuation, if there has been one or more carefully negotiated, recent, arm's-length transactions between fully informed and generally knowledgable parties, the price thus determined could be the most important factor in some valuation situations.

Other perquisites

Of course, in most closely-held businesses there are expense accounts, compensation, and other special arrangements accorded owners and others whom they may designate, not found in public companies. To some extent, these special arrangements can be taken into consideration in the valuation by appropriate adjustments to the earning power base. In other cases, the "psychic income" of certain satisfactions connected with ownership may defy valuation.

IMPACT OF RISK AND THE COST OF CAPITAL

The appraiser must be cognizant that the relevant variables need to be considered in two dimensions, magnitude and risk. For the purpose of discussion in this book, I will define *risk* as *the degree of certainty or lack of certainty as to the realization of future expectations*. For a given level of future expectations, the market will pay more to the extent that a realization of those expectations is more certain, or less to the extent that a realization of the expectations is less certain. In other words, for a given level of expected future earnings (or cash flow, dividends, and the like), the lower the risk, the higher the present value, or, conversely, the higher the risk, the lower the present value.

The element of risk can be handled in the valuation exercise in one of two ways. One is to make a downward adjustment to the expected future stream (earnings, cash flow, dividends, and so on) to reflect the uncertainty. The other is to reflect the risk by using an increased discount rate in valuing the expected stream. Sometimes (either consciously or unconsciously), a combination of these methods is used.

Bierman and Smidt make a convincing argument that the theoretically most correct way to handle the element of risk is to adjust the future expectations stream to what they call a "certainty adjusted equivalent." They adjust the expectations downward by some factor reflecting the probability that the expectations will be achieved. They then apply the same cost of capital to the valuation of all alternative investment choices. They do quite a good job, in my opinion, in explaining the rationale for this approach.[11]

Notwithstanding Bierman and Smidt's fine presentation, the more commonly used approach to taking risk into consideration in the valuation is to reflect it in the cost of capital. For the purpose of discussion in this book, we will adopt a commonly used definition of *cost of capital* as *the rate of return available in the marketplace on investments of comparable risk and other investment characteristics.* The definition could be paraphrased to say that the cost of capital is the expected rate of return an investor would require to induce him to purchase the business interest under consideration.

Thus, the cost of capital, one of the most important variables in the valuation of the business, is determined by the market, and is almost totally outside the control of the owners of the business enterprise. As the cost of capital goes up, the present value of a given stream of future expected dollars goes down, and vice versa.

One of the things the owners can do, of course, to lower their cost of capital, and thus to increase the value of their enterprise, is to lower the degree of risk associated with it. The lower the evaluators perceive the risk to be, the lower will be the cost of capital considered applicable in the valuation, and thus the higher the resulting value will be.

DIFFERENCES IN VALUE TO DIFFERENT PEOPLE

This final section of the chapter brings us full circle to the chapter's opening sentence: "Value, like beauty, is in the mind of the beholder." There are many valid reasons why any particular business interest may be perceived as having different values to different parties.

Among all the valuation factors discussed in this chapter, there may be considerable differences among different people on the appropriate weight to be assigned any given factor in any case. There also will be differences of opinion on the measurement of reasonable expectations regarding the various factors, such as earnings or values of assets, depending on different people's degree of knowledge and their optimism or pessimism regarding the outlook for the economy, the industry, and the company's ability to compete favorably.

As discussed earlier, one investor may apply a higher cost of capital, resulting in a lower valuation, because he perceives a high degree of risk; while another investor, with a higher degree of confidence in the company's future, evaluates it on the basis of a lower cost of capital. The cost of capital used by different people in the valuation analysis may vary for other reasons than the risk inherent in the enterprise itself. The business, standing alone,

---

[11]Harold Bierman, Jr., and Seymour Smidt, *The Capital Budgeting Decision* 4th ed. (New York: Macmillan Co., 1975). Chaps. 4 and 9 discuss this subject.

may be highly risky and require a high cost of capital when considered independently. On the other hand, a large company considering acquiring it may have a much lower cost of capital, and may use its own cost of capital in the valuation, assuming that the risk of the individual business unit will be reduced considerably as a result of viewing it as a division or integral part of the larger company.

A business may offer synergistic value to certain buyers, which it would not offer to other buyers. It may offer a company an important horizontal integration, such as entry into a key market area.

It should be noted, however, that most state statutes on the appraisal rights of minority stockholders dissenting to a statutory merger specify that the appraisal must be based on the company standing on its own. Any special economic value resulting from the combination with the acquiring company should not be taken into consideration to determine how much dissenting stockholders are entitled to be paid under dissenters' appraisal statutes.

Minority shares of a closely-held company probably would be perceived by members of the controlling family or company employees to have more value than an outsider among the general investing public would perceive such shares to have. In an inheritance tax case before the Oregon Supreme Court, the court decided that minority shares of a closely-held investment company should be valued at approximately a 66 percent discount from their underlying net asset value, using the fair market value standard, the same standard as is applicable for federal gift and estate tax valuations. The court concluded its opinion with this statement:

It may well be that the property subject to inheritance tax is worth more to the heirs than it would bring on the market between a willing buyer and a willing seller. It may also be true that these types of closely held family investment companies constitute a haven from inheritance and gift taxes. However, the legislature has determined that it is the market value of the inherited property which is to control and this court has consistently followed the statutory mandate. It is the province of the legislature, not the court, to change this standard if it is inequitable.[12]

---

[12]*Kingery* v. *Department of Revenue*, Or., 55 P. 2d 471 (Or., 1976) pp. 474–75.

4

THE "DISCOUNTED FUTURE EARNINGS" METHOD OF VALUATION*

*This chapter was partially adapted from Shannon P. Pratt and Craig S. Hugo, "Pricing a Company by the Discounted Future Earnings Method," *Mergers & Acquisitions* 7(Spring 1972):18–32.

The Valuation of an on-going business is the present worth of the future stream of net income.[1]

When someone buys a company, what is he really buying? Management? Markets? Technological skills? Products? Although each of these may be involved, what is actually being bought is a stream of future earnings. Thus the problem in valuing a business for acquisition purposes becomes a problem in predicting earnings and discounting them to a present worth. Bearing this out is the shifting emphasis in accounting from the balance sheet to the income statement, reflecting the increased recognition of earning power as the essential variable in a business.

A similar approach is to calculate future cash flows of a prospective firm to be acquired—a technique known as discounted cash flow (DCF). Either will work, but here we use earnings because both the stock market and the merger market tend to look at earnings rather than cash flow. The chapter focuses on the discounted future earnings (DFE) approach for mergers and acquisition, because that is the context in which it most often is used. However, the approach can be equally valid for other purposes.

DISCOUNTED FUTURE EARNINGS APPROACH

Remember Miss Grundy, the fourth grade teacher? "Invest $1 at 6 percent interest, and it will be $2 in 12.4 years." Thus she drilled the idea of compound interest into you and me and all of us.

Unfortunately, she forgot to teach the corollary: that $2 paid out 12.4 years from now is only worth $1 today. That's *discounting*, as opposed to compounding, and Jones's *Fourth Grade Arithmetic Reader* just never covered that subject.

Yet, for the merger maker, discounting is as important as compounding—perhaps even more so. For any acquisition, whether paid in stock or cash or debt, is an investment which represents payment *today* for a stream of future earnings. Thus, the same discounting model which has been used for many years in evaluating equipment purchases, plant additions, marketing programs, and other capital investment projects is equally applicable in buying a company.

This chapter demonstrates the technique of discounting expected future earnings to present value to evaluate a company. Proper understanding and application of this technique can be worth millions of dollars in a merger decision.

To turn the discounting process into concrete numbers, one must quantify two things: (1) The amounts of the expected future earnings stream, and (2) an appropriate discount rate.

The higher the expected future earnings stream, the higher the present

---

[1] Walter Jurek, *How to Determine the Value of a Business* (Stow, Ohio: Quality Services, Inc., 1977), p. 28.

value. On the other hand, the higher the discount rate (determined primarily by the cost of capital), the lower the present value.

The arithmetic of present value computations is shown in Exhibit 4–1. Tables that can be used to make present value calculations are included as Appendix Tables A–1 and A–2 at the back of the book. Many inexpensive pocket calculators are available today that work present value problems simply and virtually instantly. Exhibit 4–2 shows how to apply the arithmetic from Exhibit 4–1 to a hypothetical case problem.

Exhibit 4–1

ARITHMETIC OF PRESENT VALUE

Discounting future values back to present value is just the opposite of taking a present value and determining what its value will be at some time in the future at some given compound rate of return. The formula for determining the future amount of some present value growing at some compound rate is as follows:

$$FV_i = PV\,(1+r)^n$$

where;

FV_i = Amount at some future time (i)

PV = Present value

r = Rate of return (In varying contexts, this may appropriately be called the discount rate, the interest rate, the capitalization rate or the opportunity cost rate.)

n = Number of periods into the future for which the compounding is being computed (usually designated in years)

Problem: Assume that $1,000 is invested for three years at a 10% rate of return, what is the value of this investment at the end of the time period?

Using the formula: $FV_i = PV(1+r)^n$

Substituting: $FV_i = \$1000(1+.10)^3 = \$1331$

When we know or have a workable estimate of what some future amount "FV" (a projected earnings stream, for example) will be and we want to determine its present value, we work the above formula into a "present value" formula:

$$PV = \frac{FV_i}{(1+r)^n}$$

Problem: Assume that an investment has a value certain of $1,331 at the end of three years, and you want to know what you should pay for it today in order for the compound rate of return on to-day's investment to be equal to 10%:

Using the formula: $PV = \dfrac{FV_i}{(1+r)^n}$

Substituting: $PV = \dfrac{\$1331}{(1+.10)^3} = \underline{\underline{\$1000}}$

(Use Appendix A-1 to simplify this calculation.)

There is just one more wrinkle, and that is the fact that the return on most investments (certainly including acquired companies) is not just one lump sum at a single future time, but a series of sums over a number of future times. To account for this we need to introduce into our formula the standard mathematical notation "Σ," pronounced Sigma, which simply means to sum up all the numbers or expressions which directly follow it. Then the formula appears as:

$$PV = \Sigma\,\frac{FV_i}{(1+r)^n}$$

Problem: Assume that you are considering buying a $1,000 bond, issued several years ago and bearing an annual interest rate of 5½%, with three years remaining until maturity. Assume that, because of rising interest rates, comparable bonds now sell in the market to yield 10%. What would the present value of this bond be in the marketplace?

Using the formula: $PV = \Sigma\,\dfrac{FV_i}{(1+r)^i}$

Substituting: FV_1 = $55 (Interest at end of first year)

FV_2 = $55 (Interest at end of second year)

FV_3 = $1055 (Interest at end of third year plus repayment of face value at maturity)

$$PV = \frac{\$55}{(1+.10)^1} + \frac{\$55}{(1+.10)^2} + \frac{\$1055}{(1+.10)^3}$$

1st Yr. 2nd Yr. 3rd Yr.

(from Appendix A-1)

= $50 + $45.45 + $792.64

= $\underline{\underline{\$888.09}}$

The following case is slightly simplified by the fact that the amounts of the expected cash flows are the same for each of the future years.

Problem: Assume that you are considering the purchase of a $3000 equipment contract that pays $1000 at the end of each year for three years. What would you be willing to pay for this contract if you required a 10% rate of return on your investment?

Using the formula $PV = \Sigma\,\dfrac{FV_i}{(1+r)^i}$

Substituting:

$$PV = \frac{\$1000}{(1+.10)^1} + \frac{\$1000}{(1+.10)^2} + \frac{\$1000}{(1+.10)^3}$$

= $909.09 + $826.45 + $751.31

= $\underline{\underline{\$2486.85}}$

In each of the above cases, the present value of each of a series of future cash flows has been computed and then summed together to determine the present value of the total investment. This general approach can be applied to determine the present value of an acquisition, as well as most other investments.

Note that if a DFE return on a project is 20%, it is implicitly assumed that the earnings generated in each period will be reinvested at a rate of 20%. If periodically generated earnings don't earn 20% return, the DFE return on the original investment will not be 20%.

Exhibit 4–2

ANALYSIS OF PRESENT VALUE OF FIRM AS OF JAN. 1, 1981 BY THE DISCOUNTED FUTURE EARNINGS APPROACH

Assume that we have carefully projected a merger candidate's earnings for each of the first five years. In addition we have assumed an annual compound growth rate in earnings of 6% per year for the sixth through eleventh years, and no growth in future earnings thereafter. The projected earnings thus derived are as follows:

1981	$ 20,000	
1982	40,000	
1983	70,000	
1984	90,000	
1985	100,000	
1986	106,000	($100,000 \times 1.06^1$)
1987	112,000	($100,000 \times 1.06^2$)
1988	119,000	($100,000 \times 1.06^3$)
1989	126,000	($100,000 \times 1.06^4$)
1990	134,000	($100,000 \times 1.06^5$)
1991 and after	142,000	($100,000 \times 1.06^6$) per year

Beginning in the eleventh year, we have what is, in effect, a net level annuity in perpetuity. The value of such an annuity can be calculated simply by dividing the annual amount by the capitalization rate. Take, for example, a straight high-grade preferred stock with a $5 dividend. If the going market rate of return on such a security is 8%, the present value is found simply by dividing the amount, $5, by the rate, .08, giving a present value of $62.50. In the above problem, the same valuation procedure is applied to the assumed annuity in perpetuity starting with the eleventh year. Dividing the $142,000 by an assumed required rate of return of 20%, or 0.20, we value this annuity as of the beginning of the eleventh year at **$710,000 ($142,000 ÷ 0.20 = $710,000). But note that this is the value as of the end of the tenth year, and we still have to discount that value back for ten years in order to arrive at its present value.**

$$\text{Present Value} = \Sigma \frac{E_i}{(1+r)^i}$$

where:

- E_i = Earnings in the ith year in the future
- i = The year in the future in which the earnings are achieved
- r = The discount rate or required rate of return at which the future earnings are to be capitalized

Thus, **substituting** the assumed figures in our present value formula, the equation appears as follows:

$$PV = \overset{1981}{\frac{\$\ 20,000}{(1+.20)^1}} + \overset{1982}{\frac{\$\ 40,000}{(1+.20)^2}} + \overset{1983}{\frac{\$\ 70,000}{(1+.20)^3}} + \overset{1984}{\frac{\$\ 90,000}{(1+.20)^4}}$$

$$+ \overset{1985}{\frac{\$100,000}{(1+.20)^5}} + \overset{1986}{\frac{\$106,000}{(1+.20)^6}} + \overset{1987}{\frac{\$112,000}{(1+.20)^7}} + \overset{1988}{\frac{\$119,000}{(1+.20)^8}}$$

$$+ \overset{1989}{\frac{\$126,000}{(1+.20)^9}} + \overset{1990}{\frac{\$134,000}{(1+.20)^{10}}} + \overset{1991+}{\frac{\$142,000/.20}{(1+.20)^{10}}}$$

Using the present value tables (Appendix A), or any handy pocket financial calculator, this seemingly complex problem is easily solved:

$$PV = \$16,666.67 + \$27,777.78 + \$40,509.26$$
$$+ \$43,402.78 + \$40,187.76 + \$35,499.19$$
$$+ \$31,257.14 + \$27,675.60 + \$24,419.64$$
$$+ \$21,641.75 + \$114,668.96$$
$$= \$423,706.53$$

Note: As long as the year-to-year percentage increase in the assumed earnings is greater than the discount rate, the present value of each subsequent annual increment increases; but when the annual rate of growth is less than the discount rate, the present value of each additional year's increment decreases.

Using the same procedures and varying the discount rate applied from 14% to 26% in 2% increments, the range of present values for our merger candidate's projected future earnings would work out as follows:

Capitalization Rate	Present Value
14%	$684,049
16%	573,250
18%	489,050
20%	423,707
22%	371,432
24%	328,946
26%	293,872

Typically, an analyst could "pin down" an appropriate discount rate within a much narrower range than shown above, resulting in a much narrower range of relevant values. The wider range is shown above to illustrate the extent of the effect of varying the discount rate.

Source: Adapted from Mergers & Acquisitions (Spring 1972), © 1972 Information for Industry, Inc., 229 S. 18th Street, Philadelphia, Pennsylvania 19103.

FORECASTING FUTURE EARNINGS

The earnings forecast is the heart of the entire valuation process and requires a thorough knowledge of the complex factors influencing an investment venture. As a preliminary step, any company being considered for purchase should have at least a five-year operating plan, even if an outside consultant must be retained to prepare it. In merger analysis, the method of gaining reasonably reliable forecasts depends somewhat on the type of activity of the company being investigated. If its activity is closely related to that of the buying company, the buyer is obviously in a much better position either to make or to evaluate forecasts for the company being analyzed.

Even in the best of circumstances, forecasting a range of possible future returns for an investment is one of the most difficult aspects of the DFE model. However, the process is invaluable because it forces the buying company to take into account the many variables which will influence the acquired concern's earnings, thus facilitating a wiser investment decision.

Evaluation of the various elements involved—sales volume, wholesale and retail prices, costs of materials, operating expenses, the strength of the competition, to mention a few—must be undertaken by those executives best prepared to do so, which usually means that sales people estimate sales, production people provide production figures, and so on. The role of the financial analyst is primarily to initiate and coordinate the various segments of the analysis.

No matter how much care is taken in producing an earnings forecast, it can never be more than an estimate. As Edward G. Bennion stated in his article "Capital Budgeting and Game Theory":

It is impossible to make an economic forecast in which full confidence can be placed. No matter what refinements of techniques are employed, there still remain at least some exogenous variables. It is thus not even possible to say with certainty how likely our forecast is to be right. We must be brash enough to label a forecast as "most probable," but this implies an ability on our part to pin an approximate probability co-efficient on a forecast: 1.0 if it is virtual certainty, 0.0 if it is next to an impossibility, or some other co-efficient between these extremes. But, again, since we have no precise way of measuring the probability of our exogenous variables behaving as we assume them to do, there is no assurance that the estimated probability co-efficient for our forecast is anything like 100 percent correct.[2]

A decision maker armed with only a single "most probable" forecast is in no position to make a wise investment decision unless his forecast is 100 percent correct, an impossibility without an all-knowing crystal ball. To account for the fact that the forecasts for a given period may not materialize as anticipated, he should obtain a range of possible outcomes.

One rather simple approach for taking into consideration a range of earnings forecasts for any future year is borrowed from the PERT (Program Evaluation and Review Technique) approach to estimating times required for completion of jobs. Using this method, the forecaster gives his most optimistic estimate (in this case, the most he thinks the company could earn under the most favorable conditions), his most likely estimate (the amount of earnings he thinks has the highest probability of occurring), and his most pessimistic estimate (how much he thinks it would earn or lose under the worst circumstances he can envision).

---

[2]Edward G. Bennion, "Capital Budgeting and Game Theory," *Harvard Business Review* (November–December 1956), pp. 115–23.

With these estimates in hand, he can then calculate a weighted average expected return for each year using one of the following formulas. In the first equation, the possible outcomes are each assigned a numerical probability:

	Probability	×	Outcome	=	Expected value
Low	0.25		$ 800,000		$ 200,000
Probable	0.50		1,000,000		500,000
High	0.25		1,400,000		350,000
Weighted average	1.00				$1,050,000

An alternative for calculating a weighted estimated earnings figure is this:

$$E = \frac{a + 4m + b}{6}$$

where

E = estimated earnings (weighted)
a = most optimistic estimate
m = most likely estimate
b = most pessimistic estimate

Using the same example as above, the formula would work out as:

$$\frac{\$800,000 + 4(\$1,000,000) + 1,400,000}{6} = \$1,033,333$$

Either of these weightings is arbitrary, and may be too oversimplified for many situations. More exhaustive treatments of the subject of making and evaluating earnings forecasts can be found in the bibliography.

It is common to attempt specific forecasts for five years, an assumed percentage growth rate for five more years, and a flat stream of earnings in perpetuity after the tenth year. Some people feel it is only realistic to make specific earnings forecasts for three years, and then apply a percentage growth component. The percentage growth assumption need not be the same for all years. While it probably is more realistic to carry some growth projection out for 15 or 20 years instead of only 10, the effect of the difference is relatively small when using the high discount rates appropriate for equity analysis and projecting many years into the future.

TREATING THE ELEMENT OF RISK

In DFE analysis, *risk* may be defined as *the estimated degree of uncertainty with respect to the realization of expected future returns.* Risk, then, resides in the mind of the beholder. What seems very risky to one person may seem less risky to another, depending on his confidence in the predictions and his attitudes toward risk-aversion. This is perfectly appropriate in DFE analysis for merger and acquisition purposes, and will result in evaluators with less certainty placing a lower present value on a company than will someone who regards the same company's future with a higher degree of certainty.

Hopefully, this very desirable bias will lead acquirers to favor those companies whose business they know and understand best, and to lean away from those further outside their fields of expertise. Generally speaking, the wider the range of expected future returns around the "best estimate," the more risky the company.

There are two basic ways (each with many variants) to handle risk in the DFE analysis. One is to reduce the expected value of the future returns to a "confidence-adjusted equivalent," using a larger reduction factor to indicate greater risk. The other basic method is to vary the rate at which the expected future earnings stream is discounted, using a higher discount rate to reflect greater risk.

There are any number of ways to adjust the best estimates of future earnings to confidence-adjusted equivalents. One simple method is to multiply each best estimate by the probability of obtaining it. For example, if the best estimate of earnings for 1985 were $500,000, and it was felt there was an 80 percent chance (4 chances out of 5) of attaining it, we would multiply $500,000 by 0.8, giving us $400,000 as a confidence-adjusted equivalent expected earnings figure for 1985. If we had only 60 percent confidence in attaining our estimated earnings (3 chances out of 5), we would multiply the $500,000 best estimate by 0.6, giving us a $300,000 confidence-adjusted equivalent.

A more comprehensive discussion of arriving at a confidence adjusted equivalent is found in chapters 4 and 9 of the Bierman and Smidt book discussed in the preceding chapter.[3]

The other traditional way of taking account of risk, by varying the discount factor, is discussed in the next section.

Whatever the method, the main point in risk analysis is that a company with a given level of expected earnings which is highly uncertain has a lower present value than a company with the same expected earnings level which is more certain. The objective of risk analysis and evaluation is to quantify this difference.

SETTING THE DISCOUNT RATE

"Don't count your future returns before they are discounted" is a paraphrase of an old adage. The question is, At what rate should future returns be discounted? Volumes of material have been written on the subject, and it is still difficult to generalize.

Broadly speaking, the discount rate should be the expected rate of return available on alternative investment opportunities with comparable risk. In other words, the appropriate discount rate is in the nature of an "opportunity" cost, which is the rate of return available from other comparable investment media. This would be the rate that investors would expect to have their

---

[3]Harold Bierman, Jr., and Seymour Smidt, *The Capital Budgeting Decision* 4th ed. (New York: Macmillan Co., 1975), chaps. 4 and 9.

investment earn on equity to induce them to make the investment. If the capital markets are operating efficiently, this opportunity cost establishes the cost of capital.

For the discussion in this chapter, we will assume that what is being valued is the company's common equity, and that the cost of capital with which we are concerned is the cost of common equity capital. Minimizing the cost of common equity capital assumes that the company has an optimal capital structure. What is optimal is another debatable subject for any company, and will vary from industry to industry and from time to time as relationships among different segments of the capital markets change. A discussion of optimal capital structures is beyond the scope of this book.

Studies have shown that the long-term average rate of return earned by investors in NYSE-listed common stocks has been just under 10 percent. Since such companies tend to be the largest and most stable in the country, that figure might serve as a bottom limit when determining an appropriate discount rate or an expected rate of earnings on equity. The 10 percent figure, however, was arrived at by netting out large losses during the great Depression. In addition, interest rates and the cost of capital, in general, have risen sharply in recent years, along with inflation, so 14 percent might be a more realistic lower limit for earnings expectation on equity for the foreseeable future. This figure can then range upward, depending on the riskiness and other characteristics of the investment under consideration.

Another way to evaluate the lower boundary of cost of equity capital at any given time is to study utility stocks. Utilities generally have a captive market and are in a monopoly position to supply a needed service, so their cost of equity capital should be lower than for the average company. Utility commissioners in the 50 states allow utilities to charge rates that provide what is supposed to be a fair rate of return to the stockholders. In 1980, most of the allowed rates of return ranged from 13 to 16 percent, averaging about 14 percent. However, most utility stocks then were selling below book value, which indicates that the market did not consider the allowed rate of return to be adequate.

If the average utility stock were to sell at 85 percent of book value, and the average allowed rate of return on equity were 14 percent, the implied average market cost of equity capital to utilities would be .14/.85 = .1647, or about 16.5 percent.[4] This would be a reasonable bench mark to assess the minimum prevalent cost of equity capital given those relationships.

Another bench mark by which to gauge the cost of equity capital is by reference to yields available on long-term bonds and preferred stocks. Since common equity is junior to these, it is more risky, and thus requires a higher expected return. Various differences between return on long-term senior

---

[4]I believe that there would be a consensus among students of utility stocks that a rate of return on equity just high enough for the market to price such stocks at book value would not be adequate, since utility stocks should sell at some premium to book. However, that discussion is outside the scope of this book. The point of this illustration is merely to provide a bench mark on a lower boundary for the cost of equity capital.

securities and expected return to equity have been suggested, but there seems to be some consensus that the differential should be 300 to 600 basis points for high-grade companies and somewhat more for lower-grade companies. Thus, if the average return is 13 percent on long-term AAA bonds or AAA preferred stocks,[5] then this would imply a 16 to 17 percent minimum required return on cost of equity capital for AAA rated companies.

Exhibit 4–3 gives representative yields available as of early 1980 on various Standard & Poor's grades of preferred stocks. Considering the risks and other investment disadvantages of the typical closely-held corporation, compared to the publicly-traded companies shown as examples in Exhibit 4–3, it seems obvious that the cost of equity capital for most closely-held companies is over 20 percent as we enter the 1980s.

If risk has already been taken into account by reducing expected future earnings to a confidence-adjusted equivalent, as discussed in the previous section, the discount rate need not compensate for risk. It is more common, however, to use the best estimate of the future earnings stream without adjustment for risk, and to take risk into consideration by varying the discount rate used—the higher the risk, the higher the discount rate. It is not unreasonable to apply a discount rate of 30 percent or more to estimated future earnings streams that are extremely uncertain.

SAMPLE APPLICATION OF DFE ANALYSIS

Assume that the corporate planner of a large manufacturing concern is responsible for completing a DFE analysis in connection with the possible acquisition of a small manufacturing company that produces a limited line of specialty items.

As the coordinator of the analysis, his first step would be to instruct other executives in his company responsible for such areas as marketing, production, and finance to make forecasts for the candidate company.

The marketing man would supply forecasts on future expected unit sales, prices, advertising volume, and selling expenditures. The production executive would use these sales forecasts to estimate future plant requirements and additional costs of production. Someone from finance would incorporate the estimates from the various departments into projected earnings statements for future years. (If the candidate company already has pro forma statements prepared, the team doing the analysis for the acquirer probably would evaluate the available projections, rather than build their own from scratch.)

The analyst then must determine the discount rate that the company should use, taking into consideration the acquiring company's cost of capital, plus any

---

[5]Since preferred stocks are junior to bonds, one would expect some markedly higher return on preferred stocks than on bonds of the same rating. The reason that this is not so is because of the "intercorporate dividend exclusion," a tax advantage to the corporate holder of stock. Only 15 percent of the dividends received from another corporation are taxable to the recipient. Thus, for a corporation in the 46 percent tax bracket, the effective tax rate on dividends received is only 6.9 percent (.15 × .46). It is because of this feature that preferred stocks do not yield significantly more than bonds of comparable grade.

Exhibit 4–3
Preferred stocks, dividend yield summary

	CO's	ISSUES	RANGE LOW	HIGH	MEAN	MEDIAN
AAA	3	5	9.2% -	11.1%	10.26%	10.0%
AA	10	41	9.6% -	14.7%	11.78%	11.8%
AA−	6	17	11.2% -	13.9%	12.33%	12.5%
A+	5	25	10.7% -	15.0%	12.88%	13.0%
A	31	70	5.3% -	14.5%	11.91%	12.45%
A−	14	45	8.9% -	14.9%	12.68%	12.7%
BBB+	4	18	11.0% -	14.4%	13.53%	13.8%
BBB	36	108	5.2% -	14.7%	12.92%	13.05%
BBB−	2	4	11.4% -	13.5%	12.68%	12.9%
BB+	1	2	11.9% -	14.9%	12.95%	12.95%
BB	17	38	9.8% -	15.6%	13.27%	13.5%
BB−	4	10	10.5% -	15.7%	14.20%	14.9%
B	10	11	0.4% -	15.8%	11.65%	13.2%
CCC	3	4	10.5% -	14.4%	13.10%	13.75%
NR	11	12	0.0% -	12.7%	9.73%	11.05%
C	5	6	Non-Paying by Definition			

"AAA" This is the highest rating that may be assigned by Standard & Poor's to a preferred stock issue and indicates an extremely strong capacity to pay the preferred stock obligations.

"AA" A preferred stock issue rated "AA" also qualifies as a high-quality fixed income security. The capacity to pay preferred stock obligations is very strong, although not as overwhelming as for issues rated "AAA."

"A" An issue rated "A" is backed by a sound capacity to pay the preferred stock obligations, although it is somewhat more susceptible to the adverse effects of changes in circumstances and economic conditions.

"BBB" An issue rated "BBB" is regarded as backed by an adequate capacity to pay the preferred stock obligations. Whereas it normally exhibits adequate protection parameters, adverse economic conditions or changing circumstances are more likely to lead to a weakened capacity to make payments for a preferred stock in this category than for issues in the "A" category.

"BB," "B," "CCC" Preferred stock rated "BB," "B," and "CCC" are regarded, on balance, as predominately speculative with respect to the issuer's capacity to pay preferred stock obligations. "BB" indicates the lowest degree of speculation and "CCC" the highest degree of speculation. While such issues will likely have some quality and protective characteristics, these are outweighed by large uncertainties or major risk exposures to adverse conditions.

"CC" The rating "CC" is reserved for a preferred stock issue in arrears on dividends or sinking fund payments but that is currently paying.

"C" A preferred stock rated "C" is a non-paying issue.

"D" A preferred stock rated "D" is a non-paying issue with the issuer in default on debt instruments.

NR indicates that no rating has been requested, that there is insufficient information on which to base a rating, or that S&P does not rate a particular type of obligation as a matter of policy.

Plus (+) or Minus (−) To provide more detailed indications of preferred stock quality, the ratings from "AA" to "BB" may be modified by the addition of a plus or minus sign to show relative standing within the major rating caregories.

Source: All nonconvertible preferred shares listed in the March 1980 *Standard & Poor's Stock Guide.*

amount that should be added for special risks involved in the particular acquisition.

Since the entire discounted future earnings approach is based on valuing future events, which are uncertain at best, the analyst will want to come up with a range of reasonable values for each company being evaluated, rather than a single value. The greater the uncertainty regarding future expectations, the wider this range will be, and vice versa. More pessimistic estimates of future earnings will result in lower present values, as will application of a higher discount rate. Therefore, the lowest reasonable value to be paid for a company will be determined by applying a relatively high discount rate to a relatively conservative estimate of future earnings. Conversely, the highest price to be paid will be that calculated by applying the lowest reasonable discount rate to optimistic earnings projections.

The real value in a DFE analysis is that it lets any statement about a company's future earnings stream and the chances of attaining a predicted level of earnings be converted into a dollar price. "I think we have a damn good chance to make $1 million after tax in two years" can be converted into a reasonable price estimation when "damn good chance" is converted to "80 percent."

Exhibit 4–4 shows how the various values can be compared when using various discount rates and applying them to "pessimistic," "most likely," and "optimistic" earnings forecasts. Note that, in this case, earnings estimates are shown for ten years, and it simply is assumed that there will be a flat earnings stream in perpetuity from the end of the tenth year onward. The pessimistic projection shows the company at $75,000 earnings in the fifth year, and assumes about 7 percent annual growth for the next five years. The most likely projection brings the company to $90,000 earnings in the fifth year and assumes about 10 percent growth for the next five years. The optimistic forecast has the company at $95,000 in the fifth year and then assumes about 15 percent annual growth for the next five years.

Exhibit 4–4 suggests that a case can be made for pricing Ace Widget Company anywhere from $224,000 to $512,000, depending on future earnings expectations and choice of appropriate discount rate. While this may seem like a wide range, it places some upper and lower boundaries on what might be considered reasonable, along with the appropriate conclusion for each set of assumptions.

Note the phenomenon that each annual earnings increment increases in value to the extent that its growth rate over the previous year exceeds the discount rate, and decreases to the extent that it does not. Looking at the most likely forecast in the 20 percent discount rate column, the present value of each year's earnings increases through year four because the growth rate each year is greater than the 20 percent discount rate applied. The present value of the fifth year's earnings is exactly the same as the present value of the fourth year's earnings, because the year-to-year growth is exactly 20 percent (from $75,000 to $90,000), exactly the same as the discount rate. From year six onward, the present value of each year's earnings decreases, because the assumed growth of about 10 percent per year is less than the 20 percent discount rate. Moving over to the 28 percent discount rate column in the most likely forecast, we see that the present value of each year's earnings is less than the previous year, because there is no year in which the per-

Exhibit 4–4
Present value of Ace Widget Company
(by the discounted future earnings method)

Pessimistic Earnings Forecast

Year	Projected Earnings	Present Value Discounted at				
		20%	22%	24%	26%	28%
1	$ 36,000	$ 30,000	$ 29,508	$ 29,032	$ 28,571	$ 28,125
2	44,000	30,556	29,962	28,616	27,715	26,855
3	54,000	31,250	30,323	28,322	26,995	25,749
4	65,000	31,346	29,341	27,493	25,789	24,214
5	75,000	30,141	27,750	25,583	23,616	21,828
6	80,000	26,792	24,262	22,007	19,992	18,190
7	86,000	24,001	21,379	19,079	17,057	15,277
8	92,000	21,396	18,746	16,459	14,482	12,768
9	98,000	18,993	16,368	14,139	12,243	10,625
10	105,000	16,958	14,374	12,217	10,411	8,894
11	on 105,000	84,790	65,338	50,905	40,042	31,764
Total Value		$346,223	$307,621	$273,852	$246,913	$224,289

Most Likely Earnings Forecast

Year	Projected Earnings	Present Value Discounted at				
		20%	22%	24%	26%	28%
1	$ 40,000	$ 33,333	$ 32,787	$ 32,258	$ 31,746	$ 31,250
2	50,000	34,722	33,593	32,518	31,494	30,518
3	62,000	35,880	34,144	32,518	30,994	29,564
4	75,000	36,169	33,855	31,723	29,756	27,940
5	90,000	36,169	33,300	30,670	28,339	26,193
6	99,000	33,155	30,025	27,234	24,741	22,510
7	109,000	30,420	27,096	24,181	21,619	19,362
8	120,000	27,900	24,451	21,469	18,889	16,693
9	132,000	25,582	22,046	19,045	16,491	14,311
10	145,000	23,418	19,850	16,871	14,377	12,282
11	on 145,000	117,092	90,229	70,298	55,295	43,864
Total Value		$433,840	$381,376	$338,785	$306,741	$274,487

Optimistic Earnings Forecast

Year	Projected Earnings	Present Value Discounted at				
		20%	22%	24%	26%	28%
1	$ 44,000	$ 36,667	$ 36,066	$ 35,484	$ 34,921	$ 34,375
2	55,000	38,194	36,952	35,770	34,643	33,569
3	67,000	38,773	36,897	35,141	33,494	31,948
4	80,000	38,588	36,112	33,838	31,740	29,802
5	95,000	38,178	35,150	32,405	29,914	27,649
6	109,000	36,504	33,057	29,984	27,240	24,784
7	127,000	35,443	31,571	28,174	25,189	22,560
8	145,000	33,722	29,545	25,941	22,825	20,123
9	166,000	32,172	27,725	23,950	20,738	17,998
10	190,000	30,686	26,011	22,107	18,839	16,094
11	on 190,000	153,430	118,231	92,114	72,456	57,477
Total Value		$512,357	$447,317	$394,908	$351,999	$320,379

centage growth rate is assumed to be as high as the 28 percent discount rate applied.

Another phenomenon worth noting is the extent to which the choice of a discount rate magnifies the value conclusion, because the future earnings to be discounted are farther out in time. Again looking at the most likely forecast, the present value of the earnings in the sixth year is $33,155 discounted at 20 percent, or $22,510 discounted at 28 percent, a difference of a little less than a third. But the earnings for the 11th year on discounted at 20 percent have a present value of $117,092, compared with only $43,864 discounted at 28 percent, or 62 percent less for the higher discount rate. This demonstrates the critical difference that the choice of a discount rate can make in applying the discounted future earnings approach in valuation practice.

THE MYTH OF DILUTION

Almost anyone who has been involved in mergers has heard (or said), "We can't pay a price/earnings multiple for an acquisition higher than the P/E multiple our own stock sells at, because that will dilute our earnings per share." This myth has deadlocked many potentially sound merger negotiations.

An acquiring company *can* pay a higher multiple for an acquisition than its own stock commands and still come out ahead in the long run—provided the company being acquired has a higher expected future growth rate than the acquirer. While it is true that some dilution in earnings will occur in the short run, this can be more than overcome in a very short time if the differential in earnings growth between the two companies is substantial. The premium price paid in terms of a higher price/earnings multiple should be regarded as an investment that will be repaid over the years, and, like any other investment, a cost versus benefits comparison will determine whether it is justified.

One way to analyze how much of a premium is justifiable is to apply the DFE technique specifically to the *difference* in expected earnings growth between the two companies. This will provide a present value for only that part of the expected earnings which is over and above the earnings the acquired company would have were they to grow at the same rate as those of the acquirer.

Exhibit 4–5 shows the computation of the present value of the growth component of an acquired concern's expected future earnings and illustrates how quickly initial dilution can be overcome when the growth differential is substantial. Even though company A, which is selling at 10 times earnings, pays 13 times company B's earnings, the "dilution" is fully overcome in the third year. From that time on, the excess earnings are available for discretionary investments or dividend payout.

In the case shown in the exhibit, it is assumed that the price/earnings ratio for the acquirer remains constant. However, because of the increased rate of earnings growth resulting from the acquisition, one should reasonably assume that the acquirer stands a good chance of benefiting further by some increase in its own P/E ratio.

GARBAGE IN: GARBAGE OUT

Like all mathematical models, the discounted future earnings model is only as good as the inputs to it; it will produce a correct answer for any type of

Exhibit 4–5
The myth of dilution

THE MYTH OF DILUTION

Acquiring Company A		Acquired Company B	
Market Price	$ 10.00	Market Price	—
Total Earnings	400,000	Total Earnings	$100,000
Shares Outstanding	400,000	Shares Outstanding	100,000
Earnings Per Share	$ 1.00	Earnings Per Share	$ 1.00
Assumed Growth	None	Assumed Growth	12% per year

Company A stock is selling at 10 times earnings, but Company A pays 130,000 shares — or 13 times Company B's earnings — to acquire Company B. Company A now has 530,000 shares outstanding and $500,000 earnings, resulting in an immediate dilution in earnings per share from $1.00 to $.94/share. This dilution is soon recovered, however, as shown below:

	Company A Earnings	Company B Earnings	Earnings Per Share
Time of Merger	$400,000	$100,000	$500,000/530,000 = $ .94/share
End of Year 1	400,000	112,000	512,000/530,000 = $ .97/share
End of Year 2	400,000	125,440	525,440/530,000 = $ .99/share
End of Year 3	400,000	140,490	540,490/530,000 = $1.02/share

The "premium" paid can be regarded as 30,000 shares at $10.00 or $300,000. What Company A is buying is the extra earnings resulting from Company B's earnings growth (total earnings less $100,000). Discounted at 15%, this future growth is worth $660,268:

$$\frac{\$12,000}{(1.15)^1} + \frac{25,440}{(1.15)^2} + \frac{40,490}{(1.15)^3} + \frac{57,352}{(1.15)^4} + \ldots\ldots + \frac{121,068}{(1.15)^7} + \frac{147,596}{(1.15)^8} + \frac{177,307}{(1.15)^9} + \frac{210,584}{(1.15)^{10}} + \frac{210,584/.15}{(1.15)^{10}} = \$660,268$$

It is assumed that after 10 years, Company B's earnings will be constant and will experience no further growth. The extra earnings in year 10 are treated as an annuity in perpetuity having a value of $210,584/.15 or $1,403,893 at the end of the tenth year — resulting in a present value of $347,014.

Result: Company A has paid a "premium" of $300,000 for Company B over what it would pay for B's earnings if valued at A's price-earnings multiple. This was justified by Company B's projected future growth in earnings, the present value of which, discounted at 15%, is over twice the "premium" paid by Company A.

Source: Shannon P. Pratt and Craig S. Hugo, "Pricing a Company by the Discounted Future Earnings Method," Mergers & Acquisitions (Spring 1972), p. 26. Reprinted with permission from Mergers & Acquisition (Spring 1972). © 1972 Information for Industry, Inc., 229 S. 18th Street, Philadelphia, Pennsylvania 19103. All rights reserved.

input. The relevant question then is not how correct is the resulting answer, but how correct was the input data that produced the answer? For investment decisions involving large capital outlays, it is far better to be approximately right than precisely wrong. And if used improperly, the discounted future earnings model will produce just that: a precise answer that is completely wrong.

MAKING MONEY WITH THE DFE APPROACH

It costs money to do DFE analysis or to have it done. As a matter of fact, it's expensive. It's hard work. Outside consultants may be needed, because the know-how to do it properly is not found in every company. (Also, outside consultants may be more objective.) It also requires working with numbers and fitting these numbers into a formula or two, a process most businessmen find disconcerting. Some of the best executives suffer from symbol shock when faced with an algebraic formula.

But the discounted future earnings method is the most valid and accurate approach available for valuing a company in most merger situations. The exercise clearly establishes a reasonable price range within which negotiations can be confined. For the buyer, the discipline of working through the exercise may save money in situations where rampant enthusiasm and optimism about a proposed acquisition may otherwise overshadow sound judgment about its value.

For the seller, a good presentation using sound DFE analysis could easily make a difference of 20 percent in the price the company sells for. On a company that might otherwise go for $5 million, that's a cool $1 million!

There is no business decision bigger than that final one—the price at which a company is sold. The stakes are high. Few expenditures could be more worthwhile than that necessary to get it valued properly.

5

CONVENTIONAL APPROACHES TO VALUATION

CAPITALIZATION OF EARNING POWER
　　Arriving at the earning power base
　　Determining the appropriate price/earnings ratio
　　Price/earnings ratios adjusted to a debt-free basis

CAPITALIZATION OF CASH FLOW

CAPITALIZATION OF DIVIDENDS

CAPITALIZATION OF GROSS REVENUES

ASSET VALUE APPROACHES
　　Determining the appropriate asset value
　　Ratio of stock value to asset value
　　Stock value to asset value ratio adjusted to a debt-free basis

COMBINATION APPROACHES

OTHER FACTORS TO CONSIDER
　　History of past transactions
　　Marketability
　　Extent of "elements of control" versus minority position
　　Other contractual rights or obligations

ANALYZING AND BALANCING THE VALUATION FACTORS

Because of the difficulties in making future projections with enough reliability to apply a discounted future earnings or discounted cash flow approach and get a meaningful result, a number of approaches to valuation using historical data have found general acceptance in the discipline of business appraisal. It should be remembered, however, that historical data are used as a proxy for future expectations. Therefore, if the past history is not reasonably representative of current or foreseeable future conditions, appropriate modifications should be made. If the various approaches are applied properly, results of approaches using historical data should be reconcilable with results using discounted future projections.

Virtually all the conventional approaches to valuation using historical data can be grouped into four categories:

1. Capitalization of earning power or cash flow.
2. Capitalization of dividends.
3. Capitalization of gross revenues.
4. Asset value approaches.

In some cases, one of the above factors may be relied on solely or primarily in reaching a value conclusion. In other cases, two or more of the above factors may be combined in some manner in reaching a conclusion.

In addition to utilizing some measurement of one or more of the above factors, the valuation conclusion may be tempered or modified by any of the following factors:

1. History of past transactions in the securities.
2. Degree of marketability, or lack thereof.
3. Extent of control or minority position represented, including the effect of voting rights.
4. Other contractual rights or obligations connected to the securities.

CAPITALIZATION OF EARNING POWER

There is widespread consensus that capitalization of earning power is the most important single factor in the valuation of most operating companies, such as manufacturers, merchandisers, and companies providing various services. Conceptually, capitalization of earning power is a simple, two-variable approach, requiring a figure for the company's earning power and a figure for the appropriate price/earnings ratio. As one might suspect, however, the complexities in arriving at these two numbers offer intriguing challenges to the valuation analyst's knowledge and ingenuity.

Arriving at the earning power base

If one is to use historical reported earnings data to determine a company's earning capacity, one must analyze the data and adjust for any items which are not representative of the company's earning capacity. The types of items which most commonly require some adjustment are discussed in Chapter 11, Analyzing and Adjusting Financial Statements.

Besides making any appropriate adjustments to reported earnings, one must also decide what historical period should be used, and whether any weighting is appropriate. The analyst may consider using the statistical technique of computing an earnings trend line.

The key word in the choice of the historical period and weighting factors is "representative." In other words, what type of analysis of the historical record will produce a result that is representative of the company's ongoing earning capacity? The analyst cannot use a single formula in all situations, because the appropriate analysis will vary considerably from one set of circumstances to another.

Choice of time period. The most commonly selected historical period for evaluation of earning capacity is five years. The general idea is that, for many companies, analysis of five years' results goes back far enough to demonstrate some type of continuum, but not so far that the past results have no relevance to today's conditions or operations. The analyst, then, should vary from the conventional five-year historical period to the extent that this underlying assumption is not valid.

If, for example, the company changed its operations drastically three years ago, it might be more appropriate to consider data for only the three years that it operated in its current mode. On the other hand, if a company is in an industry that is subject to fairly lengthy business cycles, five years may be heavily weighted to a depressed or buoyant period for the company, and may not be long enough to be representative of the company's reasonable long-term fortunes. The analyst should consider the circumstances and exercise reasonable judgment in selecting the historical period on which to rely.

Unweighted, weighted, or trend line values. If there is no apparent pattern to the past earnings analyzed, or if what might appear to be a pattern may not reasonably be expected to continue, then a simple average of the historical earnings might serve adequately as being representative of earning capacity. If there appears to be a pattern set that may be extrapolated into the future, then it may be appropriate to accord more weight to the more recent earnings and less to the earlier years' earnings.

One technique for weighting the historical earnings that is commonly used, and that is appealing because of its simplicity, is the simple weighted average. It is computed in the same manner as the sum-of-the-years'-digits method of computing depreciation. If, for example, five years' earnings are being used, the most recent year is accorded 5/15ths the total weight, the next most recent year 4/15ths, and on back to the earliest year, which is weighted 1/15th.

If it can be assumed that the company has generated an earnings trend that may continue, then a trend line analysis may be appropriate. The trend line would be preferable to the weighted average in cases where the most recent year took an unusual upswing or downswing, and thus might not appropriately be accorded the most weight in the earning power evaluation. It should be noted, however, that a span of five years' data is a relatively short period over which to compute a statistical trend line, especially if the data are erratic. Trend lines have greater statistical validity to the extent that the number of points or "observations" are greater and to the extent that the data are "smooth," or reasonably consistent.

For a company with the seven-year earnings record shown in Exhibit 5–1, the earning power by the simple average, weighted average, and trend line methods would be computed as:

Simple average method

$$\frac{\$1.00 + \$1.15 + \$1.25 + \$1.50 + \$1.60 + \$2.00 + \$2.50}{7} = \$1.57$$

Weighted average method

$$
\begin{array}{rcl}
\$1.00 \times 1 & = & \$1.00 \\
1.15 \times 2 & = & 2.30 \\
1.25 \times 3 & = & 3.75 \\
1.50 \times 4 & = & 6.00 \\
1.60 \times 5 & = & 8.00 \\
2.00 \times 6 & = & 12.00 \\
2.50 \times 7 & = & 17.50 \\
\overline{28} & & \overline{\$50.55}
\end{array}
$$

$$\$50.55 \div 28 = \underline{\underline{\$\ 1.80}}$$

Trend line method

The formula to be solved is

$$Y = a + bX$$

Where:

$$b = \frac{N(\Sigma XY) - (\Sigma X)(\Sigma Y)}{N(\Sigma X^2) - (\Sigma X)^2}$$

$$a = \frac{\Sigma Y - b(\Sigma X)}{N}$$

X = Value for the years
Y = Value for earnings
N = Number of observations

In order to solve the formula the following format is suggested:

X	Y	X²	XY	N = 7 observations
1	1.00	1	1.00	
2	1.15	4	2.30	
3	1.25	9	3.75	
4	1.50	16	6.00	
5	1.60	25	8.00	
6	2.00	36	12.00	
7	2.50	49	17.50	
$\Sigma X = 28$	$\Sigma Y = 11.00$	$\Sigma X^2 = 140$	$\Sigma XY = 50.55$	

Exhibit 5–1
Seven years' earnings for Reliable Company, with trend line plotted

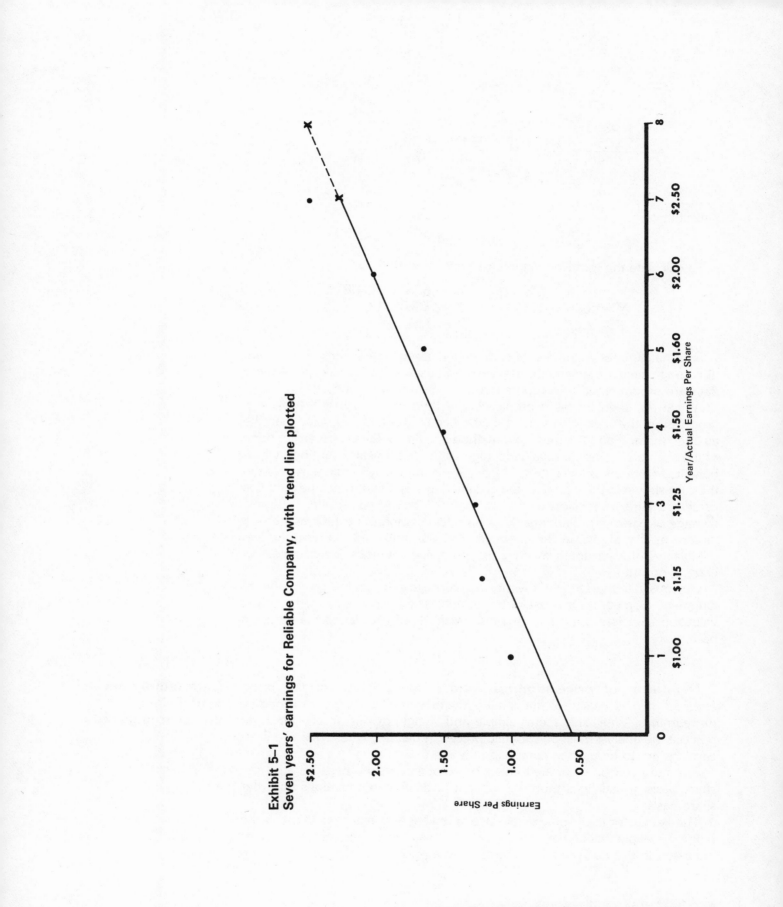

$Y = a + bx$

$b = \dfrac{7(50.55) - [(28)(11)]}{7(140) - (28)^2} = \dfrac{353.85 - 308}{980 - 784} = \dfrac{45.85}{196} = .234$

$a = \dfrac{11 - .234(28)}{7} = \dfrac{4.45}{7} = .636$

Substituting:

$$Y = .636 + .234(X)$$

To calculate the trendline value for years 7 and 8:

$Y = .636 + .234(7)$	$Y = .636 + .234(8)$
$Y = .636 + 1.64$	$Y = .636 + 1.87$
$Y = 2.28$	$Y = 2.51$

Fortunately, the arithmetic shown in the trend line example need not discourage the use of the method, since most business pocket calculators these days are programmed to compute trend line values in seconds.

As can be seen in this example, where there is a very stable earnings progression, the weighted average method computes a higher value than the average method and the trend line method a higher value yet. Even so, none of the methods compute a value as high as the latest year's earnings, which benefited from an unusual jump. Most people intuitively would agree that in the case shown in the example, the weighted average and trend line methods present a fairer estimation of the company's earning power than a simple average of past years' earnings. However, few companies exhibit as stable a pattern as that shown in the example. The less stable the pattern, the less reliable are the weighted average or trend line methods as estimators of earning power.

Obviously, the selection of the most appropriate earnings base is a matter of judgment. Sometimes it is useful for comparative purposes to work out the valuation exercises using two or more methods of calculating the earnings base.

Determining the appropriate price/earnings ratio

Definition of price/earnings ratio. The definition of the *price/earnings ratio,* is, exactly as the name of the ratio implies, *the price divided by the earnings.* While this seems simple and straightforward at first blush, in practice the analyst must be carefully precise in defining what price and what earnings are to be used in computing the ratio.

The ratio can be computed either on a total company basis or on a per share basis. It usually is more convenient to do the computations on a per share basis.

The key factor in defining what price and what earnings base to use in the ratio is comparability. For the purpose of valuing a business interest as discussed in this book, we are interested in a price on a particular valuation date, as defined in the description of the valuation assignment. Therefore, if we plan to use price/earnings ratios for shares of comparable companies as a guide to determining an appropriate price/earnings ratio for the subject company, the prices used for the comparable companies should be on our valuation date or as close to it as possible.

The figure to use for earnings usually will be derived in one of the manners described in the previous section. The key factor, again, is comparability. That is, if we define the price/earnings ratio a certain way for our subject company, and plan to use P/E ratios for comparable companies to determine what our P/E ratio should be, we need to define the P/E ratio the same way for the comparable companies as for our subject company. For example, if we use the latest five years average earnings as the earnings base for the subject company, we should use the latest five years average earnings as the base for each of the comparable companies. If we exclude extraordinary items from the earnings base of the subject company, we should exclude extraordinary items from the earnings of the comparable companies.

In other words, in defining prices and earnings to be used in the computation of comparative price/earnings ratios, as in defining any other variables to be used in the valuation, the measurement of the variables must be done on a consistent basis throughout the exercise. Furthermore, the definitions of what prices and what earnings were used should be stated clearly in the valuation report to leave no room for ambiguity in the mind of the reader. The foregoing discussion implies that the earnings base used for the subject company bears a relationship to earnings capacity somewhat similar to the relationship of the comparable companies' earnings bases to their respective earnings capacities. Adjustments should be made to the earnings base for any abnormal factors which would result in noncomparability. Some of the possible adjustments are discussed in Chapter 11.

Sources of price/earnings ratios. Usually the best guidance on what multiple a given stream of earnings is worth is found in what other people are willing to pay for comparable streams of earnings. The most important criterion of comparability is the degree of risk associated with the earnings stream. The various participants in a given industry are subject to at least a partially common set of risk factors, and generally have other relevant factors in common as well. Thus, the starting point to arrive at an appropriate price/earnings ratio for a particular company's shares is to find out the P/E ratios at which shares of other companies in the same industry or in similar industries are selling.

The most commonly used data for this exercise are the prices at which stocks of companies in the subject company's industry sell in the open market on a day-to-day basis. If possible, it also is desirable to obtain data on prices at which companies in the subject company's industry were acquired by other companies. An entire chapter in Part II is devoted to the mechanics of gathering and analyzing data on comparable companies.

Naturally, the more good comparables one is able to find, the more confidence one is likely to have in relying on this approach to the determination of an appropriate price/earnings multiple. Also, one intuitively tends to have more confidence in relying on such data, to the extent that the P/E ratios of the comparable companies are grouped in a reasonable range as opposed to being widely disparate. The degree of applicability of the P/E ratios so developed to the subject company will vary considerably from one case to another, depending on how many comparables one is able to find and how comparable they really are. In most cases, an appropriate P/E ratio for the subject company can be postulated somewhere within the range of the price/earnings ratios found for the comparable companies. The analyst must compare carefully the relevant strengths and weaknesses of the subject company with the comparable companies. Only in this way can he arrive at an informed and supportable judgment about where the subject company should fall within the range of price/earnings ratios of the comparable companies.

Relationships between price/earnings ratio and capitalization rate.   Unfortunately, the term _capitalization rate_ is a source of widespread confusion, because it is used profusely in the literature and practice of finance, and it is used with different meanings in different contexts. _To capitalize_ means _to compute or realize the present value of in money, as a periodical payment._ Thus, when we have applied an appropriate price/earnings multiple to a stream of earnings, we have capitalized that stream of earnings. In other words, we have applied one method of computing a present value of the stream of earnings. Thus, one properly might say, "We have chosen to capitalize the earnings at a multiple of seven."

The ambiguity is in the term _capitalization rate._ Some people use the term _capitalization rate_ interchangeably with the terms _price/earnings ratio_ and _price/earnings multiple._ It is more common, however, to find capitalization rate used interchangeably with the term _discount rate,_ that is, as used in the denominator of the present value formula presented in the preceding chapter on pricing the company by the discounted future earnings method. Used in this sense, the capitalization rate or discount rate can be defined as _the rate of expected return that the market requires for investments that are comparable in terms of risk and other characteristics._

Using this definition of capitalization rate, in the particular case where the earnings stream is considered to be flat, that is, a more or less constant level of earnings in perpetuity with no clearly discernable growth or decline projected, the capitalization rate and the price/earnings ratio are reciprocals of each other. If _A_ is a reciprocal of _B,_ this means that _A_ is 1 divided by _B._ If the price/earnings ratio is the reciprocal of the capitalization rate, the P/E ratio is 1 divided by the capitalization rate. For example, if the capitalization rate is 20 percent, then:

$$P/E \text{ ratio} = \frac{1}{\text{Capitalization rate}} = \frac{1}{.20} = 5.0$$

Remember, however, the notion that the capitalization rate and P/E ratios are reciprocals of each other is valid only to the extent of its implicit assumption, that no appreciable earnings growth or decline from the earnings base being used is reflected in the capitalization of earnings exercise.

If the expectation of future earnings growth is impounded in the price/earnings ratio, that ratio will be higher than the reciprocal of the capitalization rate. Take, for example, a stock selling at 20 times current earnings. The reciprocal of this P/E ratio would be (1 ÷ 20) = .05. Obviously, no one has any interest in investing for a 5 percent expected return on equity. The notion that the capitalization rate applicable to the company's equity, or the company's implied cost of equity capital would be 5 percent, is nonsense. The ratio of the market price of the company's shares to its current earnings in effect reflects two variables in one, that is, the capitalization rate and the market's expectations regarding the company's future earnings growth.

To illustrate this point with an example, we will refer to Exhibit 4–4 in the previous chapter, the present value of Ace Widget Company by the discounted future earnings method. As can be seen from even the pessimistic earnings forecast, Ace Widget Company is expected to achieve quite substantial earnings growth.

If we are willing to accept the most likely earnings forecast and discount that earnings stream at a 24 percent capitalization rate, the table shows the present value of the company works out to $338,785. The table does not provide data on the latest year's earnings, but the current year's earnings on this most likely estimate are projected at $40,000. On this basis, the appropriate price/earnings ratio for the company, using the current year's projected earnings as the earnings base, is:

$$\frac{\$338,785}{\$40,000} = 8.5x$$

The reciprocal of 8.5 is .118, but the company's capitalization rate as we have defined it is certainly not 11.8 percent. The price/earnings ratio of 8.5 times projected current earnings reflects a combination of the capitalization rate of 24 percent and acceptance of the most likely forecast of future earnings growth.

In the same example, if one is willing to accept the same set of earnings projections, but a capitalization rate of only 20 percent, then the appropriate P/E ratio for the company, using the current year's projected earnings as the earnings base, is:

$$\frac{\$433,840}{\$40,000} = 10.8x$$

Note that for a company with a projected earnings growth pattern such as this, a change in the capitalization rate has a more than proportional effect on the ratio of price to current earnings. As noted earlier, where the earnings are projected to be flat, a change in the capitalization rate has an exactly proportional inverse effect on the ratio of price to current earnings.

It thus can be seen that the price/earnings ratios at which publicly-traded stocks sell in the market impound two variables into a single figure, that is, the capitalization rate the market applies to the company's earnings, plus the market's expectations about the prospective future changes in the company's earnings. The analyst should explicitly recognize that these two factors are the components determining price/earnings ratios when he is using P/E ratios of public companies as a guide for determining an appropriate P/E ratio to apply to a closely-held company. To the extent that the subject company's earnings growth prospects are greater or less than the average for the public company comparables, the ratio of price to current or historical earnings should be greater or less than the average for its industry. To the extent that the subject company's risk factors, and, consequently, its appropriate capitalization rate, are less or greater than the average for the public company comparables, the ratio of price to current or historical earnings should be greater or less than the average for its industry.

The discounted future earnings approach is specific in identifying the relative impact of differences in the capitalization rate and differences in the assumptions regarding future earnings. While price/earnings ratios reflect these two factors, their relative impacts are not identified separately. The analyst must compare the subject company to the public companies and use his best judgment in arriving at an appropriate P/E multiple that reflects both an appropriate capitalization rate and the earnings prospects for the subject company.

Price/earnings ratios adjusted to a debt-free basis

In some cases the comparison of the market value to earning power among two or more companies that have significantly different degrees of financial leverage can be more meaningful if the prices and the earnings for the companies being compared are all adjusted to a debt-free basis. The objective is to compute a P/E ratio made up of the market value of the company's total capital as the numerator and the pro-forma earnings as if the company had no long-term debt as the denominator. This makes the ratios more comparative in the sense that distortions that might be introduced as the result of differences in financial leverage are alleviated.

For an example, let's say that our objective is to determine an appropriate price/earnings ratio for company A, a closely-held company, for the purpose of valuing its shares for an ESOP. The only guidance that we have been able to find is company B, whose shares are publicly traded. Our analysis indicates that company B is an excellent comparable, except for one major difference: Company A has no long-term debt outstanding. Company B's capital structure, however, is leveraged with long-term bonds, which also are publicly traded. Condensed balance sheets and operating statements for companies A and B are:

Condensed Balance Sheet

	A (Private)	B (Public)
Assets	$2,000,000	$2,000,000
Current liabilities	500,000	500,000
Long-term debt (12 percent)	0	500,000
Stockholders' equity	1,500,000	1,000,000
Shares outstanding	150,000	100,000
Book value per share	10.00	10.00

Condensed Operating Statement

	A (Private)	B (Public)
Sales	$5,000,000	$5,000,000
Operating expenses	4,200,000	4,200,000
Earnings before interest and taxes	$ 800,000	$ 800,000
Interest expense	0	60,000
Net income before taxes	$ 800,000	$ 740,000
Income taxes	320,000	296,000
Net income	$ 480,000	$ 444,000
Earnings per share	$3.20	$4.44
Market price per share		20.00
Price/earnings ratio		4.5

Looking at the above data, or, especially, just looking at the earnings without taking the difference in capital structure into account, one's initial reaction might be to use company B's P/E multiple of 4.5 to price company A's shares, which would result in (4.5 × $3.20) = $14.40 per share. But the earnings on company B's shares, being leveraged with long-term debt, are more risky than the earnings on company A's shares. As discussed in the previous section, this should call for a higher capitalization rate for company B, or a lower P/E ratio for company B's earnings than company A's to reflect company B's higher risk arising from the leverage. Of course, the effect on the P/E multiple of the higher risk for company B's earnings could be offset by a higher expected growth rate in earnings per share for company B. The adjustment of company B's data to a debt-free basis is an attempt to quantify the net effect of these factors in order to obtain a more appropriate P/E ratio to apply to the earnings of company A.

For the example, we will assume that company B's bonds are selling at a discount from par value and have an aggregate market value of $400,000. The aggregate market value of company B's common stock is (100,000 shares × $20) = $2,000,000. Therefore, the aggregate market value of company B's outstanding capital is ($400,000 + $2,000,000) = $2,400,000.

If company B did not have the debt outstanding, it would not have the interest expense. However, the higher pretax earnings would be subject to income tax, which we will assume to be at the rate of 40 percent. Adjusting for elimination of the interest expense, net of the tax effect, company B's earnings would be $480,000 on a debt-free basis. Dividing the aggregate market value of company B's capital by its debt-free earnings capacity gives a debt-free equivalent P/E ratio of ($2,400,000 ÷ $480,000) = 5.0. Applying this P/E ratio to company A's shares would result in (5.0 × $3.20) = $16.00 per share, compared with $14.40 per share using company B's P/E ratio on an unadjusted basis. Most practitioners would agree that the adjusted figures provide a better comparison between the two companies.

Use of this approach was called for by the case problem that was part of the 1980 version of the American Society of Appraisers examination for candidates in the field of business enterprise appraisal. The case problem from that exam and the solution using this approach are included in Appendix B.

Incidentally, it is not necessary that there be a public market for the debt securities of the comparable company or companies to make use of this approach. The computation of the market value of the debt is a simple exercise in present value arithmetic, using the formula presented in Chapter 4. The only thing the analyst needs to determine is the appropriate discount rate at which to capitalize the bonds. There is a very active market in private placements of corporate debt with insurance companies and other financial institutions. Someone active in this market, in investment banking or corporate finance, usually can provide a satisfactorily accurate discount rate on the basis of a brief study of the company's financial picture.

In some instances the analyst might go a step further and compare price/earnings ratios not only adjusted to a debt-free basis but also adjusted to a debt-free pretax basis. Generally, this would be applicable if the purpose of the valuation would result in the entity not remaining in its present independent form, such as in a comparative valuation of acquisition candidates, where the result would be that any acquired company would end up being subject to the acquirer's tax rate. If the potential acquiree had a significantly lower independent tax rate than the acquirer, the difference in the effect on value could be great enough to make it more attractive to remain independent than to sell for what the potential acquirer would be willing to pay!

CAPITALIZATION OF CASH FLOW

Cash flow is a term that is used with different meanings by different people in different contexts. Therefore, when discussing capitalization of cash flow for valuation purposes, it is necessary first to define what is meant by the term.

One popular definition of the term *cash flow* is *net earnings plus noncash expenses,* such as depreciation, amortization, and depletion. This concept also is sometimes called "cash earnings," or "income before depreciation." It can be a useful analytical tool for comparing companies that are accounting with markedly different useful lives or different depreciation methods for essentially similar plant and equipment.

One of the most common uses of capitalization of cash flow by this definition is in valuing real estate investment trusts (REITs) or real estate holding companies. For such companies, the depreciation charges typically leave little or no net earnings, and most analysts feel that a price to cash earnings ratio provides a better basis for comparison. It is easy to develop average ratios to use as benchmarks from the marketplace, since there are hundreds of REITs.

The term *cash flow* used in other contexts means a figure that reflects all cash inflows and outflows, including receipts and expenditures that affect the balance sheet but not the income statement. By this definition, cash outflows would include repayment of debt principal, investments in fixed assets, and additions to working capital. Cash inflows would include collection of debt principal, sales of assets, and reductions of net working capital. For mature companies or those with low rates of growth, such an analysis may yield valid comparative statistics. However, for younger, rapidly growing companies, cash flow measured in this manner is likely to be negative for several years.

In some cases, the capitalization of cash flow approach may be done on a debt-free basis, as discussed in the previous section on capitalization of earnings. There also may be cases where it may be useful to compare companies' debt-free cash flows adjusted to a pretax basis.

CAPITALIZATION OF DIVIDENDS

Capitalization of dividends plays a much less important role in valuation of business interests than capitalization of earnings. Revenue Ruling 59–60 states that dividends or dividend paying capacity should be one of the factors in the valuation of a business interest for federal estate or gift tax purposes. In court cases involving valuations of shares under dissenting stockholder appraisal rights, capitalization of dividends has been a factor specifically recognized in the courts' determinations of value in about half or less of the cases. Most potential acquirers are not specifically interested in the acquiree's dividend paying capacity, since the acquiree will not continue to operate as an independent entity.

If the valuation is of a controlling interest, then dividend paying capacity is more important than actual dividends paid, since the controlling stockholder has the discretion to pay or not to pay dividends as long as the company has the capacity to do so. In valuing a minority interest, however, the actual dividends the company pays usually are more important than the dividend paying capacity, since the minority stockholder generally cannot force the company to pay dividends—even if it has unquestionable capacity to do so.

Where the capitalization of dividends approach is used as an element in the valuation, it usually is by reference to dividend yields on comparable publicly-traded companies. For example, if comparable publicly-traded companies were found to have an average dividend yield (market price per share divided by annual dividends per share) of 5 percent, and the subject company paid dividends or was determined to have a dividend paying capacity of $1 per share, the capitalization of dividends approach is simply to divide the dividend paying capacity per share by the appropriate capitalization rate, in this case ($1.00 ÷ .05) = $20 per share implied value by the capitalization of dividends approach.

The typical closely-held company is not as well capitalized as its publicly-traded counterpart, and may have less dividend paying capacity per dollar of earning capacity than most of the publicly-traded companies with which it might be compared. Thus the use of capitalization of dividends as an element in the valuation may tend to have some dampening effect on the valuation conclusion, compared with the conclusion that might be reached using the capitalization of earnings approach alone.

There are situations in which capitalization of gross revenues is an appropriate approach to valuation. This can be one of several approaches considered in a particular valuation, and, in some instances, may even be the approach on which the greatest reliance is placed. The capitalization of gross revenues approach is applied most frequently to service businesses, such as advertising agencies, insurance agencies, mortuaries, professional practices, and some types of publishing operations. In a way, a capitalization of gross revenues approach can be considered a shortcut to a capitalization of earnings approach, since generally there is an implicit assumption that a certain level of revenues should be able to generate a certain level of earnings in a given type of business.

Asset value approaches are less useful for most service businesses than for merchandising or manufacturing businesses, because most service businesses are less dependent on major categories of assets, such as inventories and plant and equipment. Earnings may not be indicative of value, because it may be possible to make discretionary changes in the company's expenses that would substantially alter the company's earnings. The analyst may prefer to try to arrive at an appropriate multiple of gross revenues, as the valuation criterion, rather than attempt to make such adjustments to the company's earning power, or he may at least want to consider a multiple of gross revenues approach as a check against a valuation result based on an adjusted earnings approach.

The purpose of the valuation assumes even more than its normal degree of significance when deciding whether, or the extent to which, to rely on a capitalization of gross revenues approach to the valuation. Probably the most valid use of the multiple of gross revenues approach is when selling a service business, or when acquiring a service business. The acquirer can eliminate discretionary expenditures, may be able to improve earnings through tried and proven management techniques, and may create efficiencies by centralizing some of the functions in the acquirer's home office. Therefore, the acquirer may have reasonably reliable guidelines on what a given level of revenue production should be worth, regardless of the earnings that an independent entity may or may not be achieving with that level of revenue production.

Of course, if the acquirer is to rely on this approach, a very careful assessment must be made of the expected future continuity of the revenue production. It is not uncommon for an acquirer to pay top dollar to establish a branch by buying a strong independent company—only to experience a mass exodus of the sales force within a year or two (or sooner), because the personnel did not find working for the acquirer as attractive as working for the former independent entity.

On the other hand, if the service business is not going to sell out, but the stock is being valued for gift, ESOP, or other purposes, then the earnings may assume a greater weight in the valuation process, since changes that an acquirer might impose are not in prospect. Naturally, if the valuation is for estate tax purposes, it is necessary to assess the effect that the death of the owner might have on the future prospects of the business. In many service businesses, the death of a key person may reduce the value of the business to the net scrap value, if any, of the assets.

Guidance on arriving at an appropriate multiple of gross revenue for a particular business can be found both in public stock market data and in merger and acquisition data. There are quite a few publicly-traded companies in most service business categories, such as insurance agencies, advertising and public relations firms, and securities brokers. For most categories of service establishments there are trade associations or periodicals that publish data on prices of recent acquisitions.

ASSET VALUE APPROACHES

Asset value approaches to valuation of a business interest tend to carry relatively more weight, with respect to holding companies, than with operating companies, such as manufacturers, merchandisers, or service companies. Also, asset value approaches are more relevant to the extent that a significant portion of the assets are of a nature that could be liquidated readily if so desired, such as a portfolio of notes or contracts receivable for which there might be a ready market.

Nevertheless, the notion that a business interest is worth the value of its underlying assets is basically fallacious in most instances. Unless liquidation of the assets is a reasonable prospect, the value of the assets lies in their ability to generate earnings, rather than being an element of value that is distinct from the company's value based on its earning power. A strong asset base also contributes value, in that it enhances a company's ability to survive through periods of low or negligible earnings or losses.

Apart from the question about the degree of weight to attribute to an asset valuation approach versus other approaches, the asset value approach can be regarded as a two-step function. The first step is to arrive at the appropriate value of the net assets that relate to the business interest. The second step is to determine an appropriate ratio of the value of the business interest itself (i.e., the share of stock, the partnership interest, and so forth) to the underlying net asset value.

Determining the appropriate asset value

All serious practitioners of business valuations agree that book value is not necessarily an adequate proxy to represent the underlying net asset value of a business for valuation purposes, much less to represent the value of the business itself. However, book value is a figure that is available for almost all businesses. Furthermore, it is a value that different businesses have arrived at by some more or less common set of rules, usually some variation within the scope of generally accepted accounting principles (GAAP). Also, each asset or liability number that is a component of book value, as shown in the financial statements, represents a specific set of assets or obligations that can be identified in detail by referring to the company's records, assuming that the bookkeeping is complete and accurate. Therefore, book value usually provides the most convenient starting point for an asset value approach to the valuation of a business interest.

The nature and extent of adjustments that should be made to book value for the business valuation depend on many factors. One, of course, is the purpose of the valuation. Another, frequently a limiting factor, is the availability of reliable data on which to base the adjustments, both for the subject company and for other companies with which it might be compared in the course of the valuation process.

Revenue Ruling 59–60 is quite specific in stating that the asset values to be adjusted if the valuation is for gift or estate tax purposes are the nonoperating assets, or assets of the investment type. The ruling states:

Consideration also should be given to any assets not essential to the operation of the business, such as investments in securities, real estate, etc. In general, such nonoperating assets will command a lower rate of return than do the operating assets, although in exceptional cases the reverse may be true. In computing the book value per share of stock, assets of the investment type should be revalued on the basis of their market price and the book value adjusted accordingly.[1]

Revenue Ruling 59–60 also is applicable to valuations for ESOPs and for recapitalizations and other situations governed by the Internal Revenue Code.

Security values usually are easily obtainable from market quotations. Real estate appraisals may be expensive to obtain, and themselves may vary considerably depending on the purpose of the real estate appraisal. Tax assessment values may be a suitable basis for making adjustments to book values of real estate in some cases.

If it is considered appropriate to adjust operating plant and equipment values, the most common standard used in an asset value approach to a going-concern value of the business is the depreciated replacement cost value, which is the value that the SEC requires larger public companies to estimate in their annual 10–K forms. This means that an estimate needs to be made of the present cost to replace the facilities and the useful life. *Depreciated replacement cost* is defined as *the current replacement cost reduced by the percentage of the useful life that the existing facilities already have been in service.*

Part II of this book, especially Chapters 6 and 7 on company data, suggests information to collect that can be helpful in analyzing values. Chapter 11, Analyzing and Adjusting Financial Statements, discusses many adjustments to the balance sheet that might appropriately be made in an asset approach to valuation. The result of the exercise should be an adjusted book value or

---

[1]*Revenue Ruling 59–60 (1959–1 C.B. 237).*

adjusted net asset value that should be suitable as one of the inputs to further steps in the valuation process.

Ratio of stock value to asset value

When it has been determined that book value or some adjusted book value figure provides some useful representation of a company's underlying net asset values, the next step is to translate that figure into its implication for the value of the shares of stock or partnership interest being valued. This usually is done by reference to the relationship of the prices of comparable companies' stocks to their respective underlying net asset values. The data for the comparable companies may be based on prices of stocks traded on the open market or on prices paid in acquisitions, or both.

As in any aspect of valuation based on comparisons with other companies, the analyst must use all possible expertise to assure that the comparisons are as valid as possible within the limitations imposed by the availability of data. It may be possible to compute the ratio of market price to book value for a group of comparable companies that have stock trading in the public market, and apply a ratio somewhere within the range of such ratios to the book value of the subject company. If the book values of the subject company and the comparator companies were computed on comparable bases, this procedure should provide a reasonably realistic figure for the value of the business interest using the asset value approach.

If accounting methods were significantly different between the subject and comparator companies, then appropriate adjustments should be made before the market price to book value ratios are computed and applied to the valuation. There also can be significant other differences than accounting practices, such as differences in asset mix, that could raise questions about the validity of using the price to book value ratio of one company in valuing the stock of another.

Obviously, if one wants to use a ratio of market price to book values adjusted for depreciated replacement costs of the relevant assets, it is necessary to have the depreciated replacement cost data for the comparator companies as well as for the subject company. Such information is available for some of the larger public companies, and the nature and scope of the available information is discussed in Chapter 9, Data on Comparable Companies. To the extent that data are available, this can be a useful tool in making the asset value approach meaningful in valuing a business interest.

As with capitalization of earnings or other general categories of approaches to the business valuation, it may be fruitful to work out the results of two or more variations of asset value approaches. In most approaches, the work will result in a range of possible values. If the subject company's return on equity is high, compared to the comparables, the appropriate price to asset value ratio probably should be in the upper end of the relevant range, and vice versa.

If the analyst wishes to use stock price to net asset value ratios, where the different companies being compared have significantly different degrees of financial leverage, the technique of adjusting the data to a debt-free basis can be used. The essence of this technique is similar to that discussed earlier in the chapter for adjusting to a debt-free basis to obtain comparative price/earnings ratios for companies with different degrees of financial leverage. The technique is to compute a market price to book value ratio made up of the aggregate market value of the company's total capital as the numerator and the book value of the company's total capital as the denominator.

Going back to the example used earlier, company B (the public company) has a market price per share of $20 and a book value of $10, for a ratio of market price to book value of ($20 ÷ $10) = 2:1. If we apply this ratio to company A (the private company), which also happens to have a book value of $10 per share, the result would be (2 × $10) = $20 per share. But, note that company A also has half again as many shares outstanding as company B. Is it justified that the market value to book value per share ratio be the same for both companies in spite of such a considerable difference in their respective capital structures? Probably not.

We previously computed the aggregate market value of company B's capital to be $400,000 for its bonds and $2 million for its stock, or a total of $2,400,000. The book value of the bonds and the stocks taken together is $500,000 for the bonds and $1 million for the stock, or a total of $1.5 million. Therefore, the ratio of the aggregate market value of the company's total capital to the book value of its capital is ($2,400,000 ÷ $1,500,000) = 1.6. Applying this market value to book value ratio to company A's book value per share would result in (1.6 × $10) = $16 per share, compared with $20 per share using company B's market price to book value per share ratio on an unadjusted basis. Most practitioners would agree that the adjusted figures provide a better comparison between the two companies.

Incidentally, the fact that the adjusted market value to book value approach and the adjusted price/earnings approach each produce the identical value of $16 per share for company A stock occurs only because the figures for company B and company A were drawn in the example to be identical except for the leverage factor, just to help demonstrate the technique. It is interesting to note that, in this case, the distortion introduced by using company B's unadjusted ratios in valuing company A's shares was downwardly biased in valuing company A's shares on an earnings approach basis, and upwardly biased in valuing company A's shares on an asset value approach basis.

The technique of using the ratio of market value of total capital to book value of total capital also is demonstrated in the case problem in the American Society of Appraisers 1980 Business Enterprise Appraisal examination, included in this book as an appendix.

Sometimes different aspects of a single company are dissimilar enough that one part of the company should be valued in a different way than another

COMBINATION APPROACHES

part. This may be the case if the company has operations in two or more dissimilar industries, or if the company has a significant amount of nonoperating assets.

Where a company has two or more separate and different operations, if the financial information can be segregated adequately between them, the valuation of the total company might be approached virtually as if it were two or more separate and independent valuations, using the approach or approaches most applicable in each case.

Where a company has nonoperating assets, they may be valued separately from the operations. Perhaps the operations would be valued with primary reliance on a capitalization of earnings approach, and then some value attributable to the nonoperating assets could be added. Of course, if the valuation is to be divided in this way, any earnings generated by the nonoperating assets would have to be subtracted from the earnings base that would be capitalized in valuing the company's operations, or there would be a double counting of values.

The theory of valuing nonoperating assets separately from operating assets rests on the assumption that the nonoperating assets could be liquidated without impairing operations. Thus, if the market value of nonoperating assets is higher than book value, and the analyst is going to mark the nonoperating assets up to the market value to make the valuation, he also should consider offsetting factors. These might include the capital gains or ordinary income tax (as the case would be) that the company would have to pay if it liquidated the assets, any costs of liquidation, and whatever discounts would be appropriate to reflect the estimated time that would be required to liquidate and the risk that the actual amounts realized might be less than the market values as of the valuation date.

It also is common to find the reverse situation, that is, where it might be appropriate to value the company by a capitalization of earnings approach, but then subtract an amount for inadequacy of operating assets. This easily could be the case where net working capital is inadequate to support the level of business or where certain plant and equipment is in imminent need of replacement. The evaluation of such inadequacies may require more subjective judgment than the recognition of excess assets, but the potential problem of measurement does not render recognition of the concept of asset inadequacy any less important.

OTHER FACTORS TO CONSIDER

History of past transactions

Past transactions in the securities that are being valued should be considered for whatever past period might provide a reasonable guide to current value. The more the transactions, the larger the transactions, and the closer in time to the valuation date, the more weight past transactions should carry as an indicator of current value.

However, by far the most important criterion to consider in assessing the weight of past transactions is the extent to which they were on an arm's-length basis between fully informed and sophisticated parties. Transactions between family members or other closely-related parties may be accorded little or no weight in arriving at a fair current value.

The fact that there is no love lost among members of some families does not necessarily make any difference. In one fairly typical case that I recall, one family member had purchased some shares from another member a few months prior to an intrafamily gift of some shares. There was considerable animosity between the family member who had bought the shares and the one who had sold them, and the price bargaining had been every bit as intense as any arm's-length transaction. Nevertheless, the IRS agent handling the case was not willing to accord any weight at all to the price of the intrafamily sale in arriving at a value for the gift tax.

In some cases, bona fide offers to buy or sell that did not result in a transaction could carry some weight as an indicator of value. To be taken into serious consideration, such an offer normally would have to be documented in writing, be legally binding if accepted, and be made on an arm's-length basis.

Marketability

Ready marketability definitely adds value to a security, or, conversely, lack of marketability detracts from the value of the security vis-à-vis one that is otherwise comparable but readily marketable. Since interests in closely-held businesses do not, by definition, enjoy the ready market of a publicly-traded stock, this is a difference that must be considered when valuing an interest in a closely-held business by reference to prices of publicly-traded stocks.

There have been many court cases, especially those involving valuations for gift and estate tax purposes, that have taken a single lump discount to reflect marketability, minority interest, and other factors. However, it seems to me that the conceptual thinking in the valuation analysis can be more precise to the extent that it is possible to isolate and separately quantify the various valuation factors, especially the most important factors. The importance of the factor of marketability in the valuation has been gaining increasing recognition over the years. There is considerable evidence to suggest that the discount for the lack of marketability factor alone for a closely-held stock compared with a publicly-traded counterpart should average about 35 percent.

Most of Chapter 10 is devoted to analysis of data that can be used to help quantify appropriate discounts for lack of marketability.

Extent of "elements of control" versus minority position

If a minority interest in a closely-held business is valued by reference to day-to-day trading prices of publicly-held stocks, then minority interests are being compared with minority interests. The closely-held stock value should be discounted for marketability compared with the public stock, as discussed in the previous section, but not for minority interest.

If a minority interest in a closely-held business is being valued by capitalization of earnings, book value, adjusted book value, or whatever other approach, but without comparison to daily trading prices of public stocks, then discounts must be taken to reflect both the lack of marketability and the minority interest. It is not uncommon to find a minority interest discounted at 65 percent or more below the stock's underlying net asset value.

Conversely, if a controlling interest in a closely-held business is being valued with reference to day-to-day trading prices of public stocks, which are minority interests, it would be appropriate to add a premium for control to the price that otherwise would appear to be indicated. In valuing controlling interests in closely-held companies by reference to prices of publicly-traded stocks, it frequently works out that the discount for lack of marketability and the premium for control just about offset each other. This intuitively seems reasonable—at least by one way of looking at it. That is, public companies acquiring private companies tend to be reluctant to incur dilution by paying a higher price/earnings ratio than for what their own stock is selling. In effect, when a controlling stockholder sells to a public company, he is giving up control but gaining liquidity. Apart from other valuation factors, in many cases these two factors by themselves end up having the net effect of cancelling each other.

Voting rights. The matter of voting rights, of course, is inseparably related to the whole matter of control. There is very little empirical transaction data, and very little guidance from court decisions, that is helpful in quantifying the value of voting rights in various circumstances.

For small minority interests, what little market data are available suggests that voting rights are accorded little or no value. It intuitively seems reasonable that the value of voting rights should increase to the extent that those rights become meaningful. In one ESOP for which my company values the shares annually, for example, we have used a 5 to 7 percent difference in the value between voting and nonvoting shares. In that particular case, no single stockholder has voting control, so certain combinations of voting could result in certain minority interests constituting the swing votes.

Of course, if only a small percentage of a company's outstanding shares are of a voting class, and they can exercise wide discretionary powers over a substantial amount of resources, the voting rights could have significant value. Since little guidance is available, the quantification of such value will have to rely on a large dose of judgment.

Elements of control. Control positions versus minority positions are not necessarily cut-and-dried differences, but may be matters of degree. In most states a 51 percent interest in a corporation is not enough to control a company in all respects. Also, many other factors may limit the exercise of prerogatives normally associated with control. On the other hand, minority interests may not be totally bereft of control factors, as we just discussed, for example, in connection with potential swing votes.

The value of control is dependent on the ability to exercise any or all of a variety of rights typically associated with control. Consequently, if control is an issue in the valuation, the analyst should assess the extent to which the various elements of control do or do not exist in the particular situation, and assess the impact of each element on the value of control. The following is a checklist of some of the more common prerogatives of control:

1. Elect directors and appoint management.
2. Determine management compensation and perquisites.
3. Declare and pay dividends.
4. Sell or acquire treasury shares.
5. Acquire or liquidate assets.
6. Set policy and change the course of business.
7. Make acquisitions.
8. Select people with whom to do business and award contracts.
9. Change the articles of incorporation or by-laws.
10. Liquidate, dissolve, sell out, or recapitalize the company.

In the case of election of directors, if the company has noncumulative voting, then the whole pie belongs to the majority. If the company has cumulative voting, then some of the value that is attributable to the ability to elect directors will shift from the majority holder with less than enough to elect the whole board to the minority stockholders.

Many of the rights associated with control simply are rendered economically empty or of little value because of the company's financial condition. These could include the rights to decide on management compensation, dividends, stock or asset purchases, or acquisition of other companies.

Many typical control rights may be denied to a company through contractual restrictions. For example, indenture provisions in conjunction with debt obligations frequently prevent dividend payments, increased management compensation, liquidation of assets, acquisitions, or changes in the direction of business.

Government regulation of operations may preempt the usual prerogatives of control. For example, it is a lengthy and sometimes an even impossible process to liquidate companies in such regulated industries as insurance or utilities. Government regulation may prevent certain acquisitions, and, similarly, may prevent a company from selling out to certain other companies.

Most states require more than a simple majority vote to effect major changes in the corporate structure, such as changes in the articles of incorporation (which usually includes the authorized amount of stock available for sale), or liquidating, dissolving, selling out, or recapitalizing the company.

When any of the elements of control are lacking in a particular case, any value attributable to control must be diminished accordingly.

In certain cases, especially in merger and acquisition situations where vertical integration is an objective, the element of selecting people with whom to do business and awarding contracts can have a considerable value. For example, a wholesaler or retailer that is only marginally profitable might become an attractive acquisition candidate for a manufacturer seeking to lock up assured channels of distribution.

In summary, control or lack of it is not all black and white. Its impact on valuation must be analyzed on the basis of all the relevant circumstances of the particular case.

Other contractual rights or obligations

There can be such a variety of contractual rights or obligations affecting value that it is hard to generalize, except to say the analyst should attempt to identify and evaluate any existing rights or obligations that could affect the value.

The most common right or obligation connected with an interest in a closely-held company would arise from a buy-sell agreement. This book has an entire chapter, 21, on the subject. Certain rights or obligations also could be written into the company's by-laws. If, for example, a stockholder is required to offer his shares back to the company at book value before he can sell them to anyone else, it makes it pretty hard to value the shares much above book value, even though they might be worth much more in the absence of such a provision.

In valuing the general partner's interest in a limited partnership, potential costs that the general partner could be forced to incur as a result of his unlimited liability could have a severe negative impact on the value of the general partnership interest.

ANALYZING AND BALANCING THE VALUATION FACTORS

When all the relevant factors have been analyzed and assessed individually, they must be brought together to arrive at a final number that represents the valuation conclusion. Sometimes it will be obvious that a single approach should be relied on, such as a capitalization of earnings approach, where the asset base is negligible compared with the earnings, or an asset value approach, if the earnings are negligible or nonexistent. In other cases, two or more valuation approaches may yield results so close together that it matters little how much weight is awarded one approach.

However, the real world of business valuations is fraught with apparent inconsistencies, with different approaches to the valuation leading to markedly different results, which must be reconciled into a single number to be used for the valuation at hand.

An intuitively appealing method of dealing with this dilemma is to use the analyst's subjective but informed judgment and decide on a percentage weight that should be given the results of each relevant valuation approach used, and to base the final valuation on a weighted average of the results of the various factors. Suppose, for example, that the analyst is valuing a minority interest in a closely-held manufacturing company by comparing the publicly-traded stocks in the same industry. Since it is an operating company, but has a substantial asset base, he feels the appropriate capitalization of earnings approach should be 60 percent of the total weight, the capitalization of dividends approach 10 percent, and the asset value approach 30 percent. We will assume in this case that the company has not been able to generate a good rate of return on its asset base, so the result might come out in this way:

	Value per share	Weight	Total
Capitalization of earnings:			
$2.00 per share × 5.0 =	$10.00	.6	$ 6.00
Capitalization of dividends:			
$.60 per share ÷ .05 =	12.00	.1	$ 1.20
Asset value approach:			
$20.00 book value × .8 =	16.00	.3	4.80
			$12.00
Less: Discount for lack of marketability:			
.35 × 12.00		=	4.20
Value per share			$ 7.80

In the above case, while companies in the same industry generally are selling below book value, subject company is valued at a larger discount from book value than the average in its industry because of poorer earnings. However, the asset base is accorded some weight, and the company is not valued at as large a discount from book value as it would be if it were valued strictly on a capitalization of earnings basis. As it turns out, in the above case, the effect of the capitalization of dividends factor is neutral.

The main weakness of the above method is that no acceptable mathematical model is available to use in deriving the weights to be assigned to the results of each of the different valuation approaches. The relative weights to be assigned to each approach are dependent on the judgment of the analyst; however, it forces the analyst to present his thinking in clearly quantified terms. The method also has the appeal of being clear and simple to understand. If someone evaluating the results disagrees with some aspect of the analyst's judgment, the point of departure is readily identifiable, and it is easy to apply an alternate set of numbers and quickly recompute the result.

Court cases where values of stocks have to be determined under dissenting stockholders' appraisal rights have tended to rely on this method.

However, the wording of Revenue Ruling 59–60 does not embrace the method. The ruling states:

Because valuations cannot be made on the basis of a prescribed formula, there is no means whereby the various applicable factors in a particular case can be assigned mathematical weights in deriving the fair market value. For this reason, no useful purpose is served by taking an average of several factors (for example, book value, capitalized earnings and capitalized dividends) and basing the valuation on the result. Such a process excludes active consideration of other pertinent factors, and the end result cannot be supported by a realistic application of the significant facts in the case except by mere chance.[2]

In spite of the above wording, the method has been used successfully in many gift and estate tax cases, both at the level of dealing with the Service and

---

[2]*Revenue Ruling 59–60 (1959–1 C.B. 237) Sec. 7.*

also in cases decided in court. The wording of 59–60 indicates concern that the averaging or weighted average method leaves room for omission of consideration of pertinent factors. However, it is possible to use the basic weighted average of factors method and still, at one stage or another, incorporate consideration of all the pertinent factors that are mentioned in Revenue Ruling 59–60. As director of research for my own firm, for several years I directed my staff to avoid using this method of resolving differences in results of various approaches in tax cases because of the wording of 59–60. However, the method has obvious appeal for the reasons discussed. We have started using it for some tax cases, and, at least so far, have not had it rejected. Of course, we have been careful to demonstrate in each case that all other pertinent factors have been given active consideration and are reflected in the result to the extent applicable.

II
GATHERING DATA

6

COMPANY DATA—WRITTEN INFORMATION

FINANCIAL STATEMENTS
    Annual statements
    Federal income tax returns
    Interim statements

OTHER FINANCIAL SCHEDULES
    Aged receivables list
    Aged payables list
    Stockholder list
    Schedule of dividends paid
    Real estate and equipment lists and depreciation schedules
    Inventory list
    Officers and directors compensation schedule
    List of loans to and from officers, directors, and stockholders

MISCELLANEOUS FINANCIAL INFORMATION
    Schedule of key man life insurance
    List of past transactions in the stock or offers to buy
    Budgets or projections
    Capital requirements
    Order backlog
    Customer base
    Supplier list

EVIDENCE OF REAL AND PERSONAL PROPERTY VALUES
    Real and personal property tax assessments
    Insurance appraisals
    Independent appraisal reports

CONTRACTUAL OBLIGATIONS

OFF BALANCE SHEET ASSETS OR LIABILITIES

CORPORATE RECORDS

COMPANY HISTORY

BROCHURES, CATALOGS, AND PRICE LISTS

KEY PERSONNEL LIST

PATENTS, COPYRIGHTS, AND TRADEMARKS

TRADE ASSOCIATIONS AND INDUSTRY SOURCES

CONCLUSION

The appraiser should begin by getting a broad view of the industry involved, how the company fits into it, the competition, and company markets and products. This perspective will help to get the ball rolling in preparing lists of information needed.

There is some overlap between this chapter and the next chapter, since some information will be obtained as written materials, while in other cases similar information may be obtained through interviews or facility visits.

Exhibit 6–1 presents a checklist of documents and information commonly used in an appraisal. Every item on the list will not necessarily be required in every appraisal situation. There will be many instances where special circumstances necessitate reviewing certain documents beyond those indicated on the general checklist.

It would be an unusual and fortuitous circumstance to find every item on the checklist readily available. Therefore, it usually will be necessary to develop some of the needed information through interviews. The appraiser usually can get enough information in a preliminary meeting or through a few telephone calls to develop a reasonably good list of documents and information required for the appraisal assignment.

The appraiser can work from the list in Exhibit 6–1 and from the discussion in this chapter to develop a list applicable to the business in question, and to request that the business supply documents and written information to the extent reasonably available.

The appraiser can review the written material and supplement it, when necessary, by requests for additional written information and by interviews and facilities visits, or by reference to written information outside the company itself.

FINANCIAL STATEMENTS

Analysis of financial statements is nearly always the most important tool used in determining a company's value. If the valuation date is a year or more earlier than the time the appraisal is actually being conducted, statements for years subsequent to the valuation date normally are not considered. If litigation is involved, the general rule is that the valuation must be based on facts available on the valuation date. Occasionally a court might allow introduction of statements for periods following the valuation date to support the reasonableness of the projections made from facts available on the valuation date.

Annual statements

It is desirable, of course, that the annual statements be audited. In that case the statements will have been prepared in accordance with generally accepted accounting principles (GAAP) and will include footnotes explaining various items, such as inventory valuation methods and any unusual transactions.

However, the large majority of closely-held businesses do not go to the expense of having statements audited. Statements sometimes are prepared by outside CPAs without audit, and sometimes are prepared internally. They may

Exhibit 6–1
Company documents and information checklist

Financial statements
Annual statements for relevant period immediately prior to valuation date, typically five years or more
Federal income tax returns for same years
Interim statements (may be needed if valuation date removed from company's year-ends, or because needed to develop certain data)

Other financial schedules
Aged receivables list
Aged payables list
List of loans to and from officers, directors and stockholders
Depreciation schedule(s), including real estate and equipment lists, date of acquisition, cost, depreciation method and life, and net depreciated value
Inventory list
Officers and directors compensation schedule, including all employee benefits and expense allowances.
Stockholders list
Schedule of dividends paid

Miscellaneous financial information
Schedule of key-man life insurance
List of past transactions in the stock or offers to buy
Any available budgets or projections
Capital requirements
Order backlog
Customer base (list of largest customers with amount of sales to each in recent periods)
Supplier list (list of largest suppliers with amount of purchases from each in recent periods)

Evidence of real and personal property values
Copies of real and personal property tax assessments
Copies of insurance appraisals
Copies of any independent appraisal reports

Copies of contractual obligations
These would include, but not be limited to, such items as leases, loan agreements, franchise or distributorship agreements, contracts with customers and/or suppliers, buy/sell agreements, ESOP document, employment or non-competition agreements, etc.

Information regarding any off balance sheet assets or liabilities

Corporate records
Articles of incorporation and by-laws (or articles of partnership, as applicable)
Minute book

Company history

Product or service brochures, catalogs, price lists, etc.

List of key personnel, with company position, tenure with company and biographical data

List of patents and copyrights

List of trade association memberships and industry information sources

or may not include a set of footnotes that explain the accounting principles employed. To the extent that footnote details are omitted, the information that normally would appear in such footnotes, such as inventory valuation methods, must be furnished. To the extent that the financial statements are prepared on some basis differing from GAAP, such differences need to be explained, and usually adjusted to conform to GAAP presentation.

The most important annual statements are, of course, the income statement and the balance sheet. Two other statements frequently are useful in assessing the value of a business: the statement of changes in stockholders' equity (or an analysis of changes in the partners' capital accounts in the case of a partnership) and the statement of changes in financial position. (The latter sometimes is referred to as the "funds statement."[1])

One critical question is, "How many years of annual statements will be needed?" To the extent that there is any rule-of-thumb answer, the most commonly used period is five years. However, the answer conceptually must be that the statements cover a *relevant period*. What constitutes a relevant period means some period over which the statements are representative of the company's general operations leading up to and including the valuation date.

If the company made significant changes in its operations a few years ago, maybe only the last three or four years of statements prior to the valuation date have any relevance in determining the value of the business. But if the business has a long history and some or all of the recent years were somehow abnormal (such as might be the case in a cyclical peak or trough for an industry) seven, ten, or more years might be required to constitute a relevant period for evaluating the business.

Federal income tax returns

There can be many fully justifiable differences in reporting between federal income tax returns and financial statements prepared under GAAP. Discrepancies between tax returns and financial statements usually result from timing differences. Common examples include different methods of revenue recognition, straight-line versus accelerated depreciation, the accrual versus the flow-through method for investment tax credits, and capitalizing costs for book purposes while expensing them on the tax return.

If such differences exist, the analyst must use his professional judgment to determine which figures will provide the most appropriate basis for appraisal purposes. In general, the statements that most closely conform to industry practices would most fairly represent the company's financial position and earning power. The tax returns normally would *not* be relied upon when comparing the subject company to the price/earnings or price/book ratios derived from publicly-traded comparables.

Interim statements

The most common need for interim statements arises when the valuation date is sufficiently removed from the company's fiscal year-end that the year-end statements are not adequate for the valuation purpose.

Interim statements usually do not contain certain adjustments that typically are made when closing the books at the end of the year, such as those for physical inventory count, prepaid expenses, and a variety of accrual items. Therefore, to interpret interim statements and to use them in comparison with year-end statements, it may be necessary to obtain additional information to approximate such adjustments.

When interim statements are used to get data closer to the valuation date,

---

[1]The analysis to be done on the statements is covered in some detail in Part III of this book.

86

then interim statements for the comparable period of the previous fiscal year also should be obtained. In this way the two periods can be compared on a consistent accounting basis.

The other situation that sometimes gives rise to using interim statements in addition to annual statements is when it is desired to analyze certain variables, such as cash flow or inventory turnover, in detail. This analysis might be especially appropriate to gain a better understanding of businesses with pronounced seasonal variability in operations, where the analyst may wish to examine certain trends or patterns on a monthly or quarterly basis.

OTHER FINANCIAL SCHEDULES

Aged receivables list

The aged receivables list has important implications for the profitability and even the viability of the company. However, some smaller companies may not have prepared such a list. The purpose of examining this list is to recognize special situations affecting valuation. Accounts receivable usually will be listed alphabetically, sometimes categorized by customer group, with amounts spread into several columns (total, over 30 days, over 60 days, over 90 days, and over 120 days). Special circumstances regarding any individual account may be noted to the right of the line item or shown as a footnote. The date used usually is the same as the latest annual or interim statement, so that the total will reconcile with the amount shown on the statement.

If there are notes or other receivables besides normal trade receivables, these should be listed separately, with enough detail for the analyst to understand their nature and to evaluate them.

Aged payables list

The payables list usually is prepared in the same format as the receivables list. Again, the purpose is to alert the analyst to special situations that should affect the valuation.

Stockholder list

This list will be examined by the IRS and the courts if they are involved. The stockholder list should include the name of each stockholder and the number of shares of stock held by each. If there is more than one class of stock, the holdings of each class should be shown. If there are family or other relationships among the stockholders, these should be identified.

Schedule of dividends paid

The dividend schedule normally should cover the same time as the financial statements used. The schedule should show the date of each payment and the amount per share for each class of stock.

Real estate and equipment lists and depreciation schedules

Lists of property owned should include the acquisition date, a description adequate to identify each piece or group, the original cost, the depreciation method and life used, and the net depreciated value. The totals of such schedules should reconcile to line items in the financial statement.

For real estate, the size (acres of land and dimensions and square feet of floor space of buildings) should be shown, with a brief description of the construction and any special features. Date and costs of additions and remodeling also should be indicated.

The analyst should not rely on insurance appraisals, since replacement cost is not equivalent to depreciated values shown in the statements, nor the market value of used equipment.

The amount of detail desired in the inventory list will vary greatly from one appraisal to another. In any case, the total should be reconcilable to the inventory as shown on the financial statement, using whatever adjustments conform to the company's policy.

Inventory list

The company's write-down policy should be examined, and occasionally a market value adjustment needs to be made.

A compensation schedule usually should be prepared for the same number of years as the financial statements. It may provide a basis for adjustments to the income statements, offering evidence as to the company's earnings capacity.

Officers and directors compensation schedule

The compensation schedule should show, for each applicable year, all payments made to or for the benefit of each person in upper-level management. These would include such items as base salary, bonuses or commissions, amount paid into a pension, profit-sharing or other employee benefit funds, and other employee benefits. It also should include compensation other than cash, such as stock or options, company cars or other property used, and any significant expenses paid or reimbursed for business activities engaged in by the employee. The appraiser should be mindful at all times that the IRS sometimes attempts to depict compensation to owners of closely-held businesses as being excessive and tries to get dividend tax treatment for a portion of it. Avoiding involvement in such a disagreement can require careful phrasing of any comment adjusting owners compensation.

Since loans to or from company insiders or those connected with the company usually cannot be regarded strictly as arm's-length transactions, they should be listed and described separately from other receivables and payables.

List of loans to and from officers, directors, and stockholders

In many closely-held companies the loss of a single key man can have a significant impact on the company's operations. It is always desirable to know how much this risk is covered by life insurance. This insurance may have to be considered as part of the company's value.

MISCELLANEOUS FINANCIAL INFORMATION Schedule of key man life insurance

List of past transactions in the stock or offers to buy

To the extent that past transactions in the stock were of an arm's-length nature, they provide objective evidence of value. Thus, it is important not only to list all the stock transactions but also to indicate whatever relationships existed between the parties to make some judgment about the arm's-length nature of each transaction.

The transaction record usually should go back as far as the number of years of financial statements used. On this basis, past transaction prices can be compared with then-current book values, earnings, or other relevant variables.

If any bona fide offers have been received for the company's stock, especially in writing, these offers also can be considered evidence of value, even if the offers were not accepted. Again, such evidence of value carries greater weight to the extent that any offers or negotiations were on an arm's-length basis.

Budgets or projections

How closely-held companies prepare budgets varies greatly from one company to another. It ranges from virtually none to fairly detailed and accurate budgeting procedures. Since the value of a business interest ultimately depends on what the business will accomplish in the future, reasonable estimates of future expectations should be helpful in arriving at a value.

How far budgets or projections can be relied upon by the appraiser in arriving at the present value varies greatly. It depends both on the quality of the budgeting effort and on the purpose for which the valuation is being done. In cases where litigation or potential litigation is involved, the appraiser may or may not wish to take budgets or projections into consideration. But one should not rely on them heavily, because a court may totally reject the use of a budget or projection as a basis for determining value on the ground that it is too speculative.

On the other hand, in the merger situation, budgets or projections are widely used in determining value. We believe that in most cases a company that does excellent forward budgeting will command a better price on selling out than it would without a convincing set of forward budgets. To help in assessing the reliability of the company's budgeting, the appraiser may wish to obtain copies of past budgets and compare them with actual results.

Capital requirements

Since dividend paying capacity is one criterion of value of a business interest, the need for the company to retain cash versus its ability to pay out earnings is a factor the appraiser must consider. Capital requirements can arise from many sources, such as catching up on deferred maintenance (a common requirement with many small and medium-size businesses), increasing working capital, or making capital expenditures.

In making an acquisition, the acquirer certainly will want to consider needs for cash injections beyond the purchase price as part of his ultimate total cost.

For types of companies where order backlog is significant, the backlog on the valuation date should be compared with the backlog at one or more dates in the past. Comparison, especially with the backlog a year prior to the valuation date, is one indication of the company's prospects for the future that is solidly based on its past record.

Order backlog

The fewer customers the company relies on for its market, the more important an analysis of the customer base becomes. A convenient way to compile the customer base information is in simple tabular form. The analyst should list, in order of size of billings, the 10 to 20 largest customers in the latest year or fiscal period, with the dollar amounts of billings and the percentage of total billings accounted for by each. This information should be shown not only for the latest period but for several periods in the past. The columns for the past years should also show any customer that accounted for a significant proportion of the billings, even though not a current customer. If a budgeted figure for each customer is available for the current or forthcoming year, it is desirable to show that as well.

Customer base

Exhibit 6–2 presents a sample format for showing the customer base, using the top ten customers based on their budgets for the current year, and showing any others that have accounted for over 10 percent of revenues in any of the past four years. The analyst, of course, will use this information, along with information developed in interviews, in assessing the potential for customer turnover.

Like the customer base, the supplier list becomes more important if the suppliers are few in number. Also, it becomes more important in cases where availability of certain supplies in the future may be an important risk factor affecting the company. If this is a critical factor, then it is desirable to append a list of alternate sources to those being used currently. The supplier list could be shown in the same format as the customer base.

Supplier list

Tax assessments may not provide the best yardstick of asset values, but they are one category of objective information that is almost always readily available, and at least should be considered. Most tax-assessed values lean on the low side, compared with replacement costs or even depreciated replacement costs, although they may be well above liquidating value, especially for personal property.

EVIDENCE OF REAL AND PERSONAL PROPERTY VALUES

Real and personal property tax assessments

The analyst usually can obtain some local information on the broad relationship between tax-assessed values and market values for a particular jurisdiction. There are many jurisdictions where the tax-assessed value does not purport to represent market value, but rather some fixed percentage of market value, such as 30 percent. Of course, in those instances the analyst must adjust the figures upward to the market value directly implied by the

Exhibit 6-2

ANALYSIS OF CUSTOMER BASE
WESTERN ADVERTISING AGENCY
(Figures in 000's)

Customer	1980 (Budget)		1979		1978		1977		1976	
Agency Total	$9,863	100.0%	$8,160	100.0%	$6,943	100.0%	$5,961	100.0%	$4,820	100.0%
Runwell Sports Shoes	3,350	34.0	2,520	30.9	1,900	27.4	1,025	17.2	570	13.8
Pacific Cruises	2,500	25.3	1,750	21.4	750	10.8	...	...	...	...
Rainier Airline	1,100	11.2	639	7.8	...	...	...	...	...	...
Thunderegg Motels	800	8.1	...	...	...	...	...	...	...	...
Top-Flite Personnel	600	6.1	480	5.9	321	4.6	268	4.5	122	2.5
Henry's Hemlock Homes	400	4.1	768	9.4	1,123	16.2	822	13.8	630	13.1
Growling Pizza	325	3.3	278	3.4	257	3.7	210	3.5	115	2.4
Grand Pine Furniture	250	2.5	280	3.4	350	5.0	267	4.5	180	3.7
Coast Resorts Assn.	100	1.0	50	0.6	...	...	...	...	...	...
Siskiyou Ski School	50	0.5	35	0.4	...	...	...	...	...	...
Schludwiller Beer	...	...	112	1.4	381	5.5	732	12.3	1,223	25.4
Big Joe's Supermarkets	...	...	...	...	1,340	19.3	1,112	18.7	980	20.3
Leaping Leopard Air Frt.	...	...	...	...	...	...	1,130	19.0	750	15.6

Overall, total customer base has increased from 12 clients in 1976 to 19 clients in 1980.

tax-assessed value before making further adjustments, if any, for whatever systematic biases may be perceived to prevail in the particular jurisdiction.

As opposed to tax appraisals, insurance appraisals have some tendency to run on the high side, primarily to be sure that the insurance will be adequate to cover any potential loss. If it is demonstrated, following a casualty, that a company's insurance was far less than the value of the property insured, then the company may recover only a pro-rata portion of the loss, even though the loss involved only a portion of the total property insured. Insurance appraisals tend to be on the replacement basis, not on used values.

Insurance appraisals

Independent appraisals by qualified practitioners, if available, usually are considered more reliable as a guide to asset values than either tax or insurance appraisals. Such appraisals generally specify the approach taken, the assumptions made, and some guidance about appropriate interpretation and use for the appraisal. A replacement cost or depreciated replacement cost appraisal, for example, normally would be quite different than a liquidation value appraisal, and neither may be an appropriate appraisal for assets which are being used in some specific ongoing business situation.

Independent appraisal reports

The appraiser must evaluate all significant contractual obligations for potential positive or negative effect on a company's value. Contracts that may be significant to the value of a business or a business interest can cover a wide variety of subjects. Leases may be favorable or unfavorable. A long-term lease costing the company less than the current market usually would be a favorable factor. However, companies sometimes are saddled with long-term lease obligations on quarters no longer useful but for which the company is unable to find an alternate tenant. A lease about to expire may be an important problem to a company if it is not renewable or if renewal is available only at significantly increased cost. Some companies, such as retailing chains, have many leased locations. In those cases it may be appropriate to present a list of the leases with a summary of the provisions.

CONTRACTUAL OBLIGATIONS

Most loan agreements contain various requirements and restrictive covenants. One reason to read the loan agreements is to check whether there is danger the company might default from failure to meet any requirement of a loan agreement. Another consideration is the effect of any loan agreement restrictions on the company's dividend-paying capacity.

One of the key things to look for in franchise or distributorship agreements is the rights owned by the business under the agreement. It is common to find that such agreements are cancellable on relatively short notice, such as 30 days. Sometimes the rights under such agreements rest with an individual rather than with the corporation being valued. It also is common to find that whatever rights there might be under such agreements are nontransferable. The analyst should determine future mutual obligations and costs.

Customer contracts are significant items for some companies, such as for a manufacturer leasing its equipment to customers. Contracts to obtain key raw materials may be significant to some companies. An analysis of the terms and strengths of such contracts can be a necessary consideration in valuing the business.

Buy-sell or repurchase agreements with major stockholders may contain provisions that can have an impact on the company's shares to which they apply, and in many cases on all the outstanding stock as well. Provisions in such agreements may address the question of value directly, or may impose restrictions on transferability, which may have a bearing on the value of the shares affected. If the company has an employee stock ownership plan (ESOP), the terms of the buy-back provisions have a major bearing on the marketability of the shares involved, and thus must be considered when valuing ESOP shares.

Employment agreements with key personnel may have an effect on the company's value, as could important noncompetition agreements.

OFF BALANCE SHEET ASSETS OR LIABILITIES

One of the most common "off balance sheet" assets or liabilities is a prospective award or payment arising from a lawsuit. Inquiry should be made on any pending or potential suits, and details noted.

Another off balance sheet liability for some companies is unfunded pension requirements.

An important category of off balance sheet liabilities for many companies these days is the potential cost of compliance with environmental, OSHA, or other government requirements.

CORPORATE RECORDS

The articles of incorporation, along with any amendments, and with rights attaching to each class of stock outstanding, is information that is particularly important where more than one class of stock exists. There may be other information in the articles or by-laws of relevance to value. Certain items in the minute book may be important, especially if there are transactions with parties related to the company.

In a partnership, the rights and obligations of the partners should be contained in the articles of partnership.

COMPANY HISTORY

The appraiser must set the stage for placing the company in the context of its industry, especially its competition, as well as in the general economy.

A relatively brief history will suffice in most cases. The history should indicate how long the company has been in business, and some chronology of major changes, such as form of organization, controlling ownership, location of operations, and lines of business. Sometimes recognition of predecessor companies is appropriate as part of the background. Some companies have a relatively complex history, including transactions that may require detailed explanation to understand properly the company as of the valuation date.

The company should furnish the analyst a set of sales materials used, such as brochures, catalogs, and price lists. This will enable the analyst to familiarize himself with the company's products, services, and pricing, and also to evaluate the written sales materials. As with many of the written items furnished, these will help the analyst get an overview of the company and prepare relevant questions for visiting the company's facilities and personnel.

BROCHURES, CATALOGS, AND PRICE LISTS

Key personnel would include directors and officers, heads of departments or divisions, and anyone else whom the analyst believes plays an important role in the company's operation. The list should include, at minimum, the person's age, position, tenure with the company, and educational and professional credentials. It is desirable to include a description of present and past duties with the company and background prior to joining the company.

KEY PERSONNEL LIST

A list of patents, copyrights, and trademarks should include the dates and the items covered. It should have at least a brief description and preferably enough information to understand the items. The importance of these items, and the degree of detail necessary, varies greatly from one situation to another.

PATENTS, COPYRIGHTS, AND TRADEMARKS

It is helpful to have the company furnish a list of trade associations to which it belongs, or is eligible to belong, along with the addresses and the name of the executive director of the associations. The analyst then can contact the trade association for industry information.

In many industries there are other trade sources, such as trade journals or sources of composite data. The company usually can furnish a list of such sources.

TRADE ASSOCIATIONS AND INDUSTRY SOURCES

Gathering and analyzing the foregoing information will provide the analyst a framework from which to interview the company in person and to fill in relevant details significant to the valuation. The material needed will vary with the particular valuation and is a matter of judgment for the analyst.

CONCLUSION

7

COMPANY DATA—FIELD TRIPS AND INTERVIEWS

SCHEDULING THE SEQUENCE OF STEPS

HISTORY

OVERVIEW OF COMPANY POSITION AND OBJECTIVES

MARKETS AND MARKETING

MANAGEMENT

OPERATIONS
　Supplies
　Energy
　Labor
　Regulatory climate
　Plant and equipment
　Interview

FINANCIAL ANALYSIS
　Financial postion
　Analysis of profitability
　Identification of changes or aberrations
　Insurance
　Management emoluments
　Dividend policy
　Prior transactions or offers

CATCH-ALL QUESTION

INTERVIEWING PROFESSIONALS RELATED TO COMPANY
　Attorney
　Independent accountant
　Banker

OTHER OUTSIDE INTERVIEWS
　Customers
　Suppliers
　Competitors
　Former employees

CONCLUSION

The need for the valuation analyst to visit company facilities and to have personal contact with company personnel and other related people will vary greatly from one valuation situation to another. The extent of the field work necessary depends on many things, including the purpose of the valuation, the nature of the operation, and the size and complexity of the case. Also affecting field work is the degree to which the written material discussed in the previous chapter did or did not comprehensively cover many subjects.

The objectives of the field work range from gaining a broad, general perspective on the company and its operations to filling in necessary minutiae. My experience has been that a visit to the company's headquarters and operations adds substantial insight beyond what is gleaned solely from financial statements and other written material. Seeing operations first-hand and participating in face-to-face interviews make a company come alive to an analyst. Also, many details can be filled in more easily and more productively through conversation than with written material.

The analyst can get the most out of the field trip and interview process if he thinks and plans in terms of accomplishing three objectives. One is to gain a better overall understanding of the company. Another is to better understand and interpret the financial statements and other written information about implications for the company's valuation. The third objective is to identify change or potential change that might cause the company's future to be different from that indicated by a mere extrapolation of historical data.

In trying to establish the value of a business interest at some specified time, the analyst recognizes the necessity of going beyond the financial statements. Financial statements are based on historical costs, depreciation, and a set of variously applied accounting conventions that may or may not bear any significant relationship to current economic realities and values. The field trip and interviews should focus on establishing the relationship between the financial statements or other information gathered and the current economic values.

Furthermore, in only a small minority of cases is pure extrapolation of the past trend a valid indicator of the future results for any business enterprise. Therefore, the third focus of the field trip and interviews is to identify and evaluate the internal and external forces that will generate a set of future results differing from the past pattern.

Since the analyst usually is trying to assess the company on a going-concern basis, one area of inquiry is to identify patterns or aberrations from patterns that will help clarify what is and is not representative of ongoing expectations regarding the company.

SCHEDULING THE SEQUENCE OF STEPS

Scheduling the sequence of reading and analyzing various aspects of the written material, seeing the company's operations, and conducting interviews is a matter that needs to be worked out uniquely for each case. Scheduling the various steps should receive attention at the beginning, along with defining the valuation assignment, and should continue to receive attention throughout the valuation process.

It is usually best to have the field work interspersed with the analysis of the written material. By studying the financial statements and other basic information, the analyst can gain an overview of the company and prepare a list of specific questions that will make the field work more meaningful and productive. And after seeing the operation and talking with management, the analyst will be able to complete his reading and analysis of the written material with greater insight.

The field work also helps identify other steps to be taken. Among the myriad of written company materials discussed in the previous chapter, the field trip can resolve whether, or the extent to which, certain documentation is needed. Some items may be dismissed as irrelevant. Some documents may be consulted at the company offices, without making copies for the analyst's files. In other cases the field work may turn up circumstances suggesting the need for additional documentation. The field trip to the company also is helpful in identifying other sources of information to be consulted, such as trade associations, periodicals, government agencies, customers, suppliers, and competitors. Many questions can be asked that will be helpful in analyzing the financial statements, as discussed in Part III.

The initial screening process to identify comparable companies is a step that can start immediately at the beginning of the valuation process. However, seeing the subject company's facilities and talking with its management generally is helpful in making the final decision about what companies can be considered comparable. The field work also may bring to mind certain companies or categories of companies considered similar but overlooked in the comparable search process conducted at the analyst's office.

For these reasons, it usually is best to visit company facilities and interview management fairly early in the valuation process—after getting enough preliminary information to have a general overview of the company. Follow-up interviews then can be conducted, if needed, either in person or by telephone.

The following sections present a generalized discussion of interview topics. Naturally, the actual topics and the sequence in which they are covered will vary considerably from one situation to another.

HISTORY

The history of the company, although rarely the most exciting or most important part of the interview process, might be an appropriate beginning. This will give the analyst a perspective on how the business got where it is.

The history will cover when the business, or any of its predecessors, was founded, any acquisitions or divestitures along the way, any changes in the basic form of organization, any major changes in lines of business, and any major changes in the geographical areas served. The history also should cover major changes in ownership and how they came about, whether from owners buying into the business or from one generation succeeding another.

Although the total history of the business should be sketched briefly, the parts most relevant to the valuation analysis will usually be the most recent past. A chronology of major events will help the analyst decide how many years of the company's financial data are relevant to the current valuation, and identify any major changes in the business or special circumstance for which allowance should be made in analyzing the financial statements.

The analyst might well begin the discussion of the company's present position by asking the chief executive officer to describe his perception of the company's economic contribution. In other words, what does the company do, why does it need to be done, and what makes this company particularly well qualified to do it? What is the company's perception of the economic niche into which it fits, and how does it go about trying to do the best job of fitting there?

OVERVIEW OF COMPANY POSITION AND OBJECTIVES

These questions should lead to a general discussion of the industry in which the company operates, the company's particular role within that industry, and the company's lines of products or services.

The analyst should try to gain an understanding of how the company perceives the industry and the particular aspect of the industry within which it operates. What is the nature and rate of technological change and how does this help or hinder the company? What developments or trends are expected in the industry in the foreseeable future, and how do these circumstances impinge on the company? What special industry factors have a bearing on this particular company?

Some other points to include are how the company perceives its own major strengths and weaknesses, and the key factors that enable this company to operate profitably (such as a unique product or product line, brand name acceptance, marketing strength, and reputation for service). Also, to what extent is the company the master of its own destiny, and to what extent are its fortunes subject to outside forces over which it has no control?

If the company has relatively new operations, this might be a good place in the interview to inquire how management views their fit in the total picture and how the operations are working out. This should include the progress and prognosis for new products or services, locations, channels of distribution, and other aspects of the operation that may be in a developmental or transitional stage.

The analyst should explore with top management the company's program for capital expenditures, acquisitions, divestitures, and research and development. These inquiries should cover how much is being spent, for what, and how it is being financed. The analyst will want to know what kind of a program the company has for corporate development, including further development of existing products or markets, new products, or new markets.

The entire Pandora's box of inquiry named here obviously has such broad potential implications for the valuation, and will vary so much from one company to another, that only the most general discussion of these topics is possible within the scope of this chapter.

The analyst will want to evaluate the advantages of various prospective expenditures and the effect of their cost on the value of the company. The cost in the case of debt can be both the direct expense and the cost of the additional risk incurred by increasing the company's financial leverage. If expansion or acquisitions are to be financed by issuing additional stock, the analyst must assess the effect of the potential dilution.

The intent of present management on major aspects of future company policy is much more critical if a minority interest is being valued than in the case of a controlling interest. Nevertheless, even in the case of a controlling interest, most prospective buyers would want to know how management sees the major opportunities and problems facing the company, and how it would plan to deal with them.

The analyst should be trying to gain a context within which to assess the strength of the company's intangible assets, whether or not intangible assets may be carried on the company's books. Does the company have proprietary products or services? If so, what characteristics do they contribute to their market to give them comparative value over the competition? To what extent does the company benefit from brand names, trademarks, copyrights, or patents? How well protected are they and when do any important ones expire? Does the company enjoy goodwill arising from location, personnel, or other factors?

To use an analogy, the analyst at this state of the interviewing is trying to gain an understanding of what moves this machine, at least as those in the driver's seat see it, and what could accelerate it, slow it down, or bring it to a halt.

When the analyst is satisfied that he has obtained a sufficiently broad overview, the logical next step is a more detailed study of the company's markets and marketing.

MARKETS AND MARKETING

The interview on marketing should result in being able to identify and describe the company's markets and its program and degree of success in reaching those markets.

A major part of the marketing aspect of the interview should focus on competition. The analyst should make a list of those the company considers to be its competitors for each product or service and in each market segment it serves. An attempt should be made to quantify the market share for each segment held by the company and by each major competitor, and try to estimate the trends in these market shares.

A common tendency in such interviews is for the marketing manager to understate the company's competition, usually by defining too narrowly the groups of companies or products competing, or by not giving adequate credit to the product acceptability of one or more competitors or their ability to market. Many companies, especially smaller ones, tend to be blind-sided by potential competition that has not yet surfaced. The analyst should conduct the interview to probe for hints of these situations, and in many cases will augment the analysis with interviews of customers, suppliers, and competitors.

One of the most important aspects of the marketing interview is determining how the company competes. Is it through product differentiation, either by uniqueness or quality? Is it heavily based on providing superior service? Is it a matter of providing the customer wider selections or other conveniences? What is the company's pricing policy, and how is it forced to meet price competition?

It is important to identify not only the present competition but potential competition. Might another company usurp a portion of the market by opening a competitive location, or by innovating with a technologically comparable or superior product?

Who now uses and might use the company's products and services and why? The market should be defined both geographically and by category of customer. What is the economic outlook for the markets the company serves? What are the forces that determine the demand and the changes in demand for the company's products or services? Does the market have identifiable seasonal, cyclical, or secular characteristics? Are there technological changes in progress or in prospect that will alter the shape of the market? What does the company do to anticipate and cope with market change, and how effective are its efforts?

How does the company reach its market, both in promotional programs and channels of distribution? To what extent does this conform to or differ from industry norms?

As discussed in the previous chapter on written material, the analyst should try to assess the breadth and stability of the company's market. To what extent can the company rely on repeat business and customer continuity?

The interview also should discuss the marketing personnel. What is the degree of turnover? Where do the marketing people come from, and where do the ones leaving go? What is the structure and level of compensation for marketing people, and how does this compare with the competition?

The marketing interview is a logical time for the analyst to inquire about the order backlog on the valuation date, and how it compares with the level of a year earlier.

The analyst should ask about any changes in the marketing program that are in progress or anticipated. If the company apparently is not doing as well as it should in certain respects, what is it doing about that? If the company sees further opportunities, how does it plan to capitalize on them? If competitive forces or other problems are building up, what is the company doing to protect itself?

By the conclusion of the marketing discussion, the analyst should have a good grasp of the company's markets and competition and the company's marketing program *as the company sees them*.

MANAGEMENT

Analyzing the ability of management is one of the most subjective aspects of a company valuation. Yet, in many companies, it is a critical or even the most critical factor. Therefore, assessment of management should be a constant and conscious objective of the analyst throughout the field trip and interview process, regardless of what subject is being discussed.

The analyst should make a list or organization chart of the key management. He will be interested in the competence, breadth, and depth of present management. An important item to evaluate in most closely-held companies is the adequacy of provision for management succession, which usually runs from somewhat lacking to nonexistent.

As mentioned in Chapter 6, for each key person the analyst should inquire about age, health, and qualifications. Qualifications will include education and professional credentials, experience, background before joining the company, and history with the company.

Each person's compensation package and level of compensation should be noted. This will include participation in all employee benefit plans, fringe benefits, expense allowances, and other perquisites. Part of the reason for this inquiry is to help the analyst make judgments on whether key people are being compensated well enough to keep them from being lured to greener pastures. Another reason is to judge whether there may be excess compensation that could be reduced, if the company were to fall on hard times, either by direct reductions or by replacement of certain personnel with others who could do a comparable job at a lower cost.

The analyst should also inquire about the time and effort devoted by each of the key people, and what the true contribution is to the company's well-being. Many companies carry people, usually family members, at full salary even though they have only a figurehead role and work only occasionally. On the other hand, some senior people in a company may make a significant contribution because of experience and acumen, though devoting only limited hours per month.

OPERATIONS

Obviously, the line of questioning about operations is dependent on the type of company, whether manufacturing, merchandising, services, or whatever. The purpose, in any case, is to learn what operations the company carries out, how efficiently and effectively, and what the prospects are either for improvement or for deterioration.

Supplies

Supplies are vital to the operations of any business enterprise. The following questions should be answered in the interview process of the valuation case.

To what extent does the company fabricate versus assemble, and how much flexibility does it have in this respect? What are the key supplies and sources of those supplies? How much is the make-or-buy decision within the company's control as conditions change?

Continuity of availability and pricing are the two key factors that the analyst should pursue in the questioning about the company's supply situation. The extreme, which is not as rare as one might think, is the existence of a single source for a critical supply that could shut down the company's operations if it were cut off. Most distributorships, for example, can be terminated on 30 days' notice. For many manufacturing companies, one or more raw materials with limited sources of supply are essential to the operation.

The analyst should list key suppliers and alternates, including names of individuals with whom the company deals. He also should inquire about supplier contracts or agreements and terms. He may wish to contact suppliers, either to get additional information about the present or potential supply situation, or for references about the credit, reputation, or other attributes of the company.

Energy

While energy is itself a form of supplies, it is important enough in some company situations, especially manufacturing, to be discussed as a separate topic. Like other supplies, the critical factors are availability and price. What types of energy does the company use, how much (both in units and cost) does it use, and where do the energy supplies come from? What conservation efforts are being made? Is the company subject to temporary interruption of operations because of energy curtailment? If so, how severe could they be? Is there any possibility that lack of energy could cause permanent shutdown? What impact will future changes in energy costs have on the company's overall cost structure?

Labor

The analyst needs to be concerned with the continuity of labor availability and cost, as well as with the efficiency and effectiveness of the labor force. In taking the facilities tour, in addition to seeing the physical plant and operation, the analyst should be alert to obtain a feeling for labor morale and efficiency.

To what extent is the company unionized? If not, have there been attempts to unionize it? How does this compare with others in the industry? What is the history of strikes? What present contracts are there, when do they expire, and what are the prospects for satisfactory renewal, both in terms of acceptable costs and conditions and in terms of risks of work stoppage? How do company compensation levels compare with the industry? Is there an adequate pool of skilled labor in the area? What is the company's experience with personnel turnover, and how does this compare with industry norms?

Regulatory climate

The analyst should inquire about government regulations which may impinge on the company's operations. To what extent does the company face costs associated with environmental protection or with OSHA? The analyst may wish to examine government inspection sheets and question the costs of compliance.

Restrictions affecting the company's value might also be imposed by the industry. These restrictions would be in the form of quality standards or pricing pressures.

How much is the company subject to industry regulations? Are there prescribed quality standards in effect? If so, to what extent does the company have a problem meeting them? Are there restrictions on pricing, promotional activities, geographical or other expansion, on product innovation or other phases of the company's operations? What is the impact of these regulations on the company's earning capacity, flexibility, and other aspects affecting the company's value?

Plant and equipment

Usually a company representative will take the analyst on a tour of company facilities. How extensive and detailed this needs to be varies. One objective of the tour is to give the analyst a better idea of the company's operations from a physical viewpoint. Another is to make some evaluation of the physical plant's adequacy. The business enterprise appraiser will be making such an evaluation in a general sense only. If real estate or equipment appraisals are necessary, these usually will be made by appraisers who are specialists in those areas.

If the analyst will need to communicate some description of the operations or facilities, or both, to someone not having the opportunity to visit the facilities, such as a judge in a court case, then it may be desirable to take a set of pictures while on tour.

The analyst usually will want to include at least a brief description of the facilities in his report. For this purpose, it may be helpful to inquire about sizes, such as acres or square feet, of various sites or buildings. Some notes should be made of the type of construction, also.

The analyst will want to make some observations on the apparent efficiency of the location and layout and the condition of the facilities. Are they cramped? What is the schedule of use? How much unused capacity is available? What are the opportunities to expand capacity? Is the equipment modern? Is it well-maintained? In general, will the plant be adaptable to future cost savings, or will it be a source of increasing operating costs? These points should also be discussed with management.

Inventory

While touring the facilities the analyst will have the opportunity to observe inventories on hand. This can be any combination of raw materials, work in progress, or goods available for sale or shipment. The analyst is interested in how much inventory is obsolete, damaged, excessive, or inadequate. The analyst should ask for assistance in interpreting the status of inventory. The facilities tour offers a good time to inquire about inventory turnover and quality.

As discussed elsewhere in this book, there may be a significant amount of near-worthless inventory carried on the books, or there may be significant amounts of valuable inventory in stock that has been written off. Since this variable can have a large effect on reported earnings and net worth in some types of companies, it is a subject worth considerable attention.

Interviews that will aid in financial analysis may be conducted with the chief financial officer, controller, other company personnel, or the firm's outside accountant or attorney. For the most comprehensive results in conducting this stage of the interview process, the reader is referred to Part III, Financial Statement Analysis, especially Chapter 11, which suggests many possible adjustments to the financial statements. Many of the questions suggested by that chapter are not referred to separately in this section.

Interviews can contribute a great deal toward genuine understanding of a company's financial position, beyond simply what is shown on the financial statements, and the depth of inquiry will be beneficial.

Current assets. The reliability of the accounts receivable depends on the collectibility of the individual accounts. Go over the aging of accounts receivable with a financial officer, covering specific overdue accounts. One indicator of the receivables worth is the amount of bad debt write-offs during the previous couple of years. What is the policy for bad debt write-offs? Are there doubtful or disputed accounts beyond those reflected in the Allowance (or Reserve) for Doubtful Accounts? Are there accounts written off that probably will be collected? What is the average collection period? In other words, to what extent does the net Accounts Receivable figure represent an amount that is genuinely collectible, and how long will it take to collect it? What is the prognosis for collection of any notes or other receivables? Cash management techniques should be explored.

How is inventory accounted for? How does physical flow relate to the accounting flow? To what extent is the inventory figure representative of the value of the inventory in a going-concern context? What is the write-off policy?

Fixed assets. One objective of inquiry about fixed assets is to get some feeling for the extent to which the company's carrying values of fixed assets are comparable to other companies in the industry owning similar assets. This can be especially relevant if an asset value or comparative price-to-book value approach is to be a factor in the valuation.

How do the depreciation lives and methods compare with industry norms? What is happening to replacement costs of the kind of assets used in the business?

There should be a discussion of the probable time and cost to liquidate all or any part of the assets, as well as the potential net realizable value if possible liquidation is another factor to consider in the valuation.

Other assets. Intangible assets, such as goodwill or patents and trademarks or copyrights should be discussed, to get management's perception and to determine accounting practices and a legal context.

Current liabilities. Usually the most important purpose of inquiry regarding current liabilities is to get an understanding of the company's banking relationship. Does it have a line of credit? What are the costs and terms? Does the company have unused credit, or is it under pressure to pay down on a bank line?

Another important current liability is accounts payable. Practices in aging accounts payable should be determined. What are relationships with creditors? What are the terms of suppliers? Does the company have slack, or is it under pressure on how it uses its accounts payable? What are the terms, conditions, and expectations regarding other current liability items?

Capital structure. Questions that might be asked about the capital structure will vary greatly. If there is long-term debt maturing in the foreseeable future, what are the company's options and intentions about rolling it over? How much more term debt is available to the company, if such is needed or wanted, and from what sources and on what terms? Are personal guarantees necessary on company loans? If so, by whom and to what extent? Are they compensated adequately for these guarantees?

In order to investigate potential dilution, ascertain the prognosis as far as exercise of any convertible notes, puts, calls, warrants, or options. What changes in the capital structure might be anticipated? Will there be equity financing or debt financing?

In virtually every case the analyst will want to discuss who owns the shares currently outstanding and what their relationships are, one to another.

Off balance sheet items. Is there potential legal liability, such as liability for compliance with environmental protection, OSHA, or other government regulations? Is there product liability? Liability for service under warranties? Unfunded pension liability? Is the company a co-signer or guarantor on any debt? Is there any potential tax liability or refund? Are any tax losses carried forward? Are there leases on real or personal property, and what are the terms? Is litigation pending, and what is its substance?

Analysis of profitability

Budgeting is an important area of inquiry. To what extent does the company do profitability or cash flow budgeting, or both? How far into the future, in how much detail, and how often is it reviewed? How accurate have been the company's past budgets? A review of past and current budgets can be a good starting point in an attempt to gain greater insight into a company's profit history and potential. Does the company use budgeted versus actual comparisons?

In analyzing the company's sales, an attempt should be made to distinguish between changes in unit sales and price changes. Making this distinction should help the analyst in evaluating the company's outlook.

If the company is involved in multiple products or product lines, it is desirable to try to identify which are most profitable and why. What is the outlook for maintaining profitability of the good ones and improving profitability of the poor ones?

A useful area of discussion is the company's fixed and variable costs and their elements—that is, the degree of operating leverage. To what extent can increased or decreased volume be expected to affect the company's operating margins?

What elements have determined the company's effective tax rate in the past, and to what extent might the effective tax rate be different in the future?

What can be done to make the company more profitable? What will it cost? What are the risks?

Identification of changes or aberrations

To what extent are changes of a more or less predictable nature, such as seasonal, cyclical, or secular patterns? If accounts receivable, accounts payable, inventory, or other variables are abnormally high or low, why is this so and what are the implications?

Should any special circumstance be taken into account on the valuation date, such as unusual present or imminent competitive pressure, supply problems, or labor problems?

In analyzing past operations, what is reflected in the statements for various periods that would not be representative of the company's current and prospective operations? Such items could include results of discontinued operations or results that occurred under unusual conditions not likely to be repeated.

Were there any changes in accounting policy during the time under review?

Insurance

Whether insurance is carried can be significant to the company's viability. An uninsured catastrophe could wipe out the business. How adequate is the company's insurance coverage, if there is any? The questions about insurance should investigate the adequacy of key man life insurance, product and other liability insurances, and all forms of casualty insurance, including fire, theft, and business interruption. If no insurance is carried, adequacy of reserves should be determined.

Management emoluments

Many expenses that are of a management emolument nature may not be thought of as employee benefits or compensation to the closely-held company that has incurred such expenses as a matter of routine for a generation or more. The analyst, therefore, may have to do some probing to identify all such items and their magnitude.

The analyst should find out about the company's fleets of vehicles, including cars, boats, and airplanes. To what extent are they dispensable? What is the company supporting in terms of condominiums or recreational locations or activities? How big is the travel and entertainment budget, and how much could be trimmed? What salaries, bonuses, profit-sharing arrangements, or other benefits could be reduced or eliminated if necessary?

Dividend policy

Inquiry should be made to insure that the analyst has a complete record of past dividend payments. Beyond that, the analyst should assess both the company's dividend-paying capacity and intentions with regard to dividends, if dividend-paying capacity does exist. What is the policy?

Prior transactions or offers

The previous chapter suggested that the written material include a list of prior transactions in the stock. It might be a good idea in the interview to verify whether the record so furnished is complete. Somehow, it seems easy to overlook one or more past transactions. What price was paid for stock, or was it bonus stock at no cost to the recipient?

CATCH-ALL QUESTION

If the person doing the field work for a business valuation reviews this chapter and makes a list of questions applicable to the particular company, the result should be a reasonably comprehensive facility visit and set of interviews. This will be more true if the person is an experienced interviewer, because the ramifications of many interview subjects and techniques are not conducive to explanation in a book, much less in one easy chapter.

Nevertheless, even the most experienced interviewer may not ask just the right specific questions to elicit responses on every aspect bearing on the valuation. Therefore, somewhere near the end of the interview process, perhaps back with the chief executive officer or top management group (after having interviewed department heads), the analyst might ask a catch-all question. This can be something like: "Is there any information that you know of that hasn't been covered and which could have a bearing on the valuation of the company?"

This should help protect the analyst against material omissions in his questioning process, and place the burden on company management if they are deliberately withholding material information.

INTERVIEWING PROFESSIONALS RELATED TO COMPANY

It may not be necessary to interview outside professionals related to the company, but it usually is a good idea to get their names during the company interview in the event it might be desirable. It may be necessary to have management contact those individuals to grant them permission to release pertinent information or discuss company issues. Sometimes, interviews with the company's outside professionals are helpful not only for specific technical information but for independent viewpoints on certain aspects of the company.

Attorney

The most common reason to interview the company's attorney arises from the need for a legal interpretation about a company document or contract, or for an assessment of a pending lawsuit or potential litigation.

There are times when the analyst may work very closely with the company's attorney. If, for example, the company is structuring a recapitalization, buy-sell agreement, or an ESOP, the wording of the legal documents may have a considerable bearing on the valuation. In such cases, the attorney may want the valuation analyst's opinion about the impact of certain prospective provisions on the valuation for the wording of the documents.

Independent accountant

It may be necessary for the analyst to interview the company's outside independent accountant, usually for an explanation or interpretation of something in the financial statements, to consult working papers, or to obtain other detail to augment the statements. This is most likely to be necessary if the statements are not audited and do not contain all the footnote information that audited statements normally contain. If there is a qualification to the statement, the analyst may seek further amplification of details.

Banker

If the company's banking relationship is important, it is a good idea to hear first-hand how the banker perceives it. The banker also may be a good source of general information about the company and the industry.

OTHER OUTSIDE INTERVIEWS

Considerable discretion is called for in conducting certain outside interviews.

Customers

The company's customers can be a good source of information. They can tell why they use the company's products, and can discuss the outlook for their own businesses to help the analyst evaluate the continuing demand for the products or services.

The customers may be a much better source of information about the competition than the company itself. They can explain their own perceptions of differences in product design, quality, service, and pricing, and explain their own purchase decision criteria.

It's also desirable, if possible, to contact former customers to find out why they are no longer patronizing the company.

Suppliers

Suppliers can be good sources about the company, and may also be helpful in identifying and evaluating competition. Particularly if the company is dealing in a technological area, the suppliers may be able to explain technology changes in the industry and, in some cases, may be able to make some evaluation of the company's expertise.

Competitors

Many times it is possible to interview competitors. In the majority of cases this would have to be done without disclosing the purpose of the interview, to avoid violating any relationship of confidentiality. If the competitors are publicly-held companies, they are accustomed to being interviewed by analysts and the interview should be no problem. If the company is private, it is usually necessary to explain the purpose of the interview in a general sense, being careful not to divulge any confidences. It would be up to the private company, of course, whether it would be willing to cooperate.

The analyst may ask the competitor many of the same questions he would ask the subject company. For instance, demand, supply, and pricing factors, technological change in the industry, and relative merits of the products and services of the various companies in the industry might be discussed, including, of course, the company that is the subject of the analysis.

Former employees

Sometimes former employees can be useful as information sources—on why they left and about other aspects of the company as seen in hindsight and without continued involvement.

CONCLUSION

The preceding queries should provide the analyst a perspective on the company being valued and yield a multitude of details relevant to the valuation case assignment. What the analyst gets from the process will depend partly on the thoroughness of preparation and partly on the degree of cooperation provided by the company and those being interviewed.

8

INDUSTRY AND ECONOMIC DATA

COMPOSITE COMPANY STATISTICS
Source Book: Statistics of Income
Dun & Bradstreet *Key Business Ratios*
RMA Annual Statement Studies
Standard & Poor's Analysts Handbook
Trade associations

GENERAL INDUSTRY INFORMATION
Books and periodicals
Indexes to other sources

ECONOMIC DATA
U.S. government publications
Handbook of Basic Economic Statistics
State and local sources
Banks, utilities and private companies
Predicasts services
Sources of data on management compensation
Indexes to economic data

BIBLIOGRAPHY: INDUSTRY AND ECONOMIC DATA SOURCES

This chapter presents a listing and discussion of some sources of industry and economic information that can be useful in the business valuation. The sources are broken down into three categories:

1. Sources of composite balance sheet and income statement statistics for industry groups to be used for comparisons with the business being valued.
2. General industry information.
3. Economic information.

In some respects the breakdown between sources of industry information and sources of economic information is arbitrary, since there are considerable overlaps between these two categories. Many of the sources discussed in the next chapter on source of comparable company data also are sources of industry and economic data, even though many of them are not referred to separately in this chapter.

COMPOSITE COMPANY STATISTICS

Source Book: Statistics of Income

By far the most comprehensive set of composite company statistics is prepared by the Statistics Division of the Internal Revenue Service and published annually under the title *Source Book: Statistics of Income*. Its biggest weakness is that it runs about four years out of date.

The book is based on statistical sampling from over two million U.S. corporate tax returns. It is broken down basically by Standard Industrial Classification (SIC) groups. Each industry group is classified into 12 categories based on size of total assets. Exhibit 8–1 is a typical page from the *Source Book: Statistics of Income,* based on corporation income tax returns for accounting periods ended July 1975 through June 1976. The book that covered the returns for that period was published in January 1979.

Dun & Bradstreet *Key Business Ratios*

Dun & Bradstreet annually publishes a book titled *Key Business Ratios,* which shows 14 ratios for each of 800 SIC groups. The companies in each SIC group are broken down into three size categories, based on total sales. For each size category within each SIC group, the median and upper and lower quartile values are shown for each of the 14 ratios. Exhibit 8–2 is a sample of data from Dun & Bradstreet's *Key Business Ratios.* The book is published in October, covering data through the previous calendar year.

RMA Annual Statement Studies

The Robert Morris Associates *Annual Statement Studies* offer common size balance sheets and income statements, plus 16 ratios, for each of 310 SIC groups, with each SIC group broken down into four size categories, based on total assets. It is especially useful for comparisons with smaller companies. Except for the contractor industries, the largest of the four size categories in each industry is for companies with assets from $10 million to $50 million.

Exhibit 8–1
Sample page from *Source Book: Statistics of Income*

1975 CORPORATION

Wholesale and retail trade: Retail trade: Food stores

SOURCE BOOK OF STATISTICS OF INCOME
INCOME TAX RETURNS OF ACTIVE CORPORATIONS WITH ACCOUNTING PERIODS ENDED JULY 1975 THROUGH JUNE 1976--BALANCE SHEET, INCOME STATEMENT, AND INVESTMENT CREDIT ITEMS, BY MINOR INDUSTRY, BY SIZE OF TOTAL ASSETS
(ALL FIGURES ARE ESTIMATES BASED ON SAMPLES--MONEY AMOUNTS AND SIZE OF TOTAL ASSETS ARE IN THOUSANDS OF DOLLARS)

MINOR INDUSTRY 5400

SIZE OF TOTAL ASSETS

RETURNS WITH AND WITHOUT NET INCOME

	TOTAL	ZERO ASSETS	1 UNDER 100	100 UNDER 250	250 UNDER 500	500 UNDER 1,000	1,000 UNDER 5,000	5,000 UNDER 10,000	10,000 UNDER 25,000	25,000 UNDER 50,000	50,000 UNDER 100,000	100,000 UNDER 250,000	250,000 OR MORE
1 NUMBER OF RETURNS	29997	1160	17208	6059	3051	1414	865	93	61	37	21	16	12
2 TOTAL ASSETS	20059227	-	666540	959488	1082902	967401	1779443	632653	956071	1324351	1420245	2493718	7776415
3 CASH	1618137	-	85671	119738	172368	133436	1975[illegible]	66149	88455	114174	111094	188920	340474
4 NOTES AND ACCTS RECEIVABLE	1444044	-	52976	79207	61757	67173	124195	49913	52351	78108	97529	174202	606633
5 LESS: BAD DEBT ALLOWANCE	22852	-	360*	134*	216*	403*	3499	1416*	996	2805	2493	4580	5948
6 INVENTORIES	6961566	-	201078	279297	328403	277602	559556	181003	305876	494242	479274	870135	2965100
INVESTMENTS IN GOVT. OBLIG													
7 UNITED STATES	137268	-	-	-	-	1287*	4392*	2937*	2249	4194	-	50413	71796
8 STATE AND LOCAL	62968	-	-	-	250*	-	976*	118*	120	6960	-	19452	35092
9 OTHER CURRENT ASSETS	618553	-	15722	28064	39514	32288	60862	31384	35554	39730	29096	65033	241286
10 LOANS TO STOCKHOLDERS	79888	-	16826	9800	6602	7121	16372	1238*	2596	12052	6108	-	873
11 MORT AND REAL ESTATE LOANS	70774	-	6139*	13443*	4215*	1313*	3954	15355*	2898	13528	5552	2440	1937
12 OTHER INVESTMENTS	1335576	-	6653	63744	59792	77453	104792	20440	51299	69245	81978	155216	644964
13 DEPRECIABLE ASSETS	12160735	-	475609	556664	620823	576281	1062189	382139	627445	747072	947575	1583332	4581606
14 LESS: ACCUMULATED DEPR	5659216	-	248999	256075	295770	286040	507424	172440	272362	326325	424317	764029	2105435
15 DEPLETABLE ASSETS	7177*	-	1536*	-	432*	-	5208*	-	-	-	-	1	-
16 LESS: ACUMULATED DEPLETION	2708*	-	896*	-	144*	-	1668*	-	-	-	-	-	-
17 LAND	618289	-	12489	32476	29383	33374	75163	24398	43295	37277	56223	63395	210816
18 INTANGIBLE ASSETS (AMORT)	55189	-	11334	6357	4089	3459	10600	3053	1957	643	6735	4714	2248
19 LESS: ACCUMULATED AMORT	21082	-	6506	2218	595	443	3701	836	813	161	3446	1565	798
20 OTHER ASSETS	594921	-	37268	29125	51981	43500	69858	29178	15847	36417	29337	86639	165771
21 TOTAL LIABILITIES	20059227	-	666540	959488	1082902	967401	1779443	632653	956071	1324351	1420245	2493718	7776415
22 ACCOUNTS PAYABLE	4672096	-	148171	174226	249548	267565	495199	156640	239933	332945	317546	631871	1658252
23 MORT,NOTES,BONDS UNDER 1 YR	989122	-	50763	60230	62864	67427	129752	60230	65620	64840	53135	61390	312871
24 OTHER CURRTNT LIABILITIES	2034978	-	45499	69047	92452	76304	164433	50656	91342	118644	153970	214739	958192
25 LOANS FROM STOCKHOLDERS	360352	-	91017	85590	71235	40290	33096	1850*	8600	8531	17185	14	2944
26 MORT NOTES BONDS OVER 1 YR.	3260382	-	118497	208138	238147	194945	354066	96248	135893	191533	240660	437685	1044570
27 OTHER LIABILITIES	681904	-	20484	15546	15763	15446	19463	33679	20237	68352	38798	117366	316770
28 CAPITAL STOCK	1568784	-	151348	139436	119714	97447	153339	42649	72804	99906	115630	198634	377877
29 PAID-IN OR CAPITAL SURPLUS	1706550	-	34338	20371	23327	31876	42219	28333	39772	56237	92143	272187	1065747
30 RETAINED EARNINGS, APPROP	45934	-	1764*	7327*	1925*	4134*	3579*	3041*	1046	2594	-	5	20519
31 RETAINED EARNINGS, UNAPPROP	4943012	-	14476	190096	232730	183372	429661	163955	291219	395347	398203	611001	2032952
32 LESS: COST OF TREASURY STK	203887	-	9817*	10519*	24603	11405	45364	4828	10095	14578	7025	51174	14279
33 TOTAL RECEIPTS	113209989	364172	4871001	5156279	8309757	6441383	12014215	3704256	5951503	7826375	8387782	13329372	36853794
34 BUSINESS RECEIPTS	112074696	346843	4844282	5099429	8253664	6398197	11891878	3669495	5876633	7758158	8303756	13177250	36455111
INT U.S. GOVT OBLIGATIONS													
35 UNITED STATES	7069	-	-0*	-	300*	184*	139	35*	153	334	73	2706	3145
36 STATE AND LOCAL	2559	220	-	65*	-0*	-	219*	65*	72	374	475	945	124
37 OTHER INTEREST	100765	1198*	890	2801	4914	5476	8182	5077	4123	4367	8689	12428	42620
38 RENTS	280858	854*	1581*	17466	6928	5225	23021	8229	16345	7434	22186	28905	142684
39 ROYALTIES	7577	-	-0*	-	-	108*	692*	-	114	28	3	973	5659
40 NET S-T GAIN LESS L-T LOSS.	466	-	-	162*	-0*	-	-0*	75*	17	-	141	-	71
41 NET L-T GAIN LESS S-T LOSS.	28332	52*	968*	4939*	4349	2028	1575	929	1363	772	1585	1409	8363
42 NET GAIN, NONCAPITAL ASSETS	33902	2780*	1935*	2369	2414	322	4616	1390	771	820	1156	10730	4599
43 DIVIDENDS, DOMESTIC CORPS	6327	1*	-0*	958	201*	499	370	483	576	668	957	1341	273
44 DIVIDENDS, FOREIGN CORPS	8407	-	-	-	-	-	-	-	-	2	295	1	8109
45 OTHER RECEIPTS	659031	12224	21345	28090	36987	29344	83523	18478	51436	53418	48466	92684	183036
46 TOTAL DEDUCTIONS	111890749	363036	4885224	5089939	8231566	6371082	11872508	3657577	5856827	7707818	8292560	13168717	36393895
47 COST OF SALES AND OPERATION	88510350	287480	3696314	3991107	6766645	5096789	9544544	2901716	4721709	6156955	6602825	10179953	28564313
48 COMPENSATION OF OFFICERS	690257	3538	186771	126652	119065	79356	80917	13811	17616	16491	11574	17261	17205
49 REPAIRS	492074	1720	23027	21581	28154	26238	53381	16732	24599	34961	34731	81321	145629
50 BAD DEBTS	57392	1134*	2006	2157	3114	5898	6420	2428	1544	5798	2596	5091	19206
51 RENT PAID ON BUSINESS PROP.	1646861	10633	104780	72633	108419	81238	158666	56338	77899	121023	116434	208341	530457
52 TAXES PAID	1375957	4814	77218	72905	79570	67651	137292	43521	67479	91899	97053	177755	458800
53 INTEREST PAID	368954	1782	13034	23079	25705	28112	38650	13643	16655	16955	26512	47222	117605
54 CONTRIBUTIONS OR GIFTS	17481	16*	69	154	921	1058	1910	636	1123	1894	2544	2343	4813
55 AMORTIZATION	2906	10*	51	514	487	80*	428	83*	58	344	438	18	395
56 DEPRECIATION	1112931	3146	47702	47971	51937	47880	95214	32284	52654	66715	86726	134556	446146
57 DEPLETION	3776*	-	-0*	3082*	681*	-	-	-	1	10	2	-	-
58 ADVERTISING	1036673	2576	33840	52369	77271	81949	115137	32998	53432	70979	73168	120360	322594
59 PENSION,PROF SH, ANUTY PLAN	381758	282*	6503	7920	16760	12987	27749	9263	16411	22136	20074	44677	196996
60 EMPLOYEE BENEFIT PROGRAMS	392401	662*	5829	5922	13082	12589	30042	11863	16358	24475	40235	74901	156443
61 NET LOSS,NONCAPITAL ASSETS	14749	337*	900*	4349*	1620	1281	1728	621	677	1675	1022	408	131
62 OTHER DEDUCTIONS	15786229	44906	687180	657544	938135	827976	1580430	521640	788612	1075508	1176626	2074510	5413162
63 TOTAL RECEIPT LESS TOTAL DEDS	1319240	1136	-14223	66340	78191	70301	141707	46679	94776	118557	95222	160655	459899
64 CONST TAX INC FRM REL FG CORP	1951	-	-	-	-	-	-	-	-	-	-	333	1618
65 NET INCOME(LESS DEFICIT)	1318632	916	-14223	66275	78191	70301	141488	46614	94704	118183	94747	160043	461393
66 NET INCOME, TOTAL	1700875	6984	49436	94745	107285	91516	174571	56682	100927	130893	113716	187025	587095
67 DEFICIT, TOTAL	382243	6068	63659	28470	29094	21215	33083	10068*	6223	12710	18969	26982	125702
68 NET INC, LESS DEF, F 1120S.	64898	-2109*	-5965	5088	18114	26082	20249	3439	-	-	-	-	-
69 NET INC LESS DEF F1120-DISC	885*	-	-	-	-	885*	-	-	-	-	-	-	-
70 STAT SPEC DEDS 1120, F, L, M.	46539	537*	5605	5603	7144	4831	6485	2749	1504	788	2334	766	8193
71 NET OPERATING LOSS DEDUCT.	41576	536*	5605	4847	6974	4440*	6180	2342*	1019	211	1409	-	8013
72 W.H.T. CORP DEDUCTION	-	-	-	-	-	-	-	-	-	-	-	-	-
73 OTHER	4963	1*	-0*	756*	170*	391	305	407	485	577	925	766	180
74 INC SUBJ NORM, SUR, ALT TAX	1550149	6447	31384	74076	75833	57881	147703	50563	99430	130142	111389	186275	579026
75 NT LG-TM GAIN TAXED ALT RTE	11870	52*	127*	-	2348*	723*	692	263*	946	717	1540	279	4183
76 INCOME TAX (BEF CR), TOTAL	686110	1932	6441	18154	20659	20107	64267	23476	47024	62151	53125	89731	279043
77 NORM TAX,SURTAX AND ALT TAX	682543	1908	6441	17968	20536	20008	64160	23390	46894	61959	53005	89215	277059
78 TAX FR RECOMP PR YR INVCR	3567	24*	-0*	186*	123	99	107	86	130	192	120	516	1984
79 TAX FR RECOMP PR YR WINCR	-	-	-	-	-	-	-	-	-	-	-	-	-
80 ADDITIONAL TAX FOR TAX PREF	-0*	-	-	-	-0*	-	-	-	-	-	-	-	-
81 FOREIGN TAX CREDIT	5609	-	-	53*	-	-	-	-	-	-0	-0	123	5433
82 INVESTMENT CREDIT	85489	222*	936	1961	2888	1989	7584	2312	4980	6963	7529	10829	37296
83 WORK INCENTIVE CREDIT	53	-	-	-	-	-	3*	10*	12	10	-	13	5
DISTRIBUTION TO STOCKHOLDERS													
84 CASH AND PROP EXC OWN STK	251858	689*	8783*	1893*	11207	15501	17276	3784	11134	9692	916[illegible]	34045	128691
85 CORPORATIONS OWN STOCK	52235	-	-	-	50*	2080*	3440*	1342*	2176	679	15915	-	26553
INVESTMENT CREDIT ITEMS													
86 TOTAL COST INVES CR PROP	1260846	1767*	48543	57153	87017	48093	113945	33935	65509	77332	92614	149946	484992
87 TOTAL QUALIFIED INVESTMENT.	1122705	1646*	29115	44195	64898	33350	97066	28917	63019	72598	86646	143860	457395
88 TENTATIVE INVESTMENT CR	107836	146*	2165	3731	5731	2955	9419	2819	6123	7071	8483	14020	45173
89 INVESTMENT CR CARRYOVER	36744	629*	1108	1001	1635	3240	3459	1389	999	2247	2059	10644	8334
90 FORM 1120-DISC QUAL BUS RECPT	975*	-	-	-	-	975*	-	-	-	-	-	-	-

FOOTNOTES AT BEGINNING AND END OF FILM U.S. TREASURY DEPARTMENT INTERNAL REVENUE SERVICE

Source: U.S. Internal Revenue Service, *Source Book: Statistics of Income, 1975* (Washington, D.C.: U.S. Government Printing Office), p. 199.

Exhibit 8–2
Sample data from Dun & Bradstreet's
Key Business Ratios

ECONOMIC SECTOR: RETAIL

SIC: 5411 GROCERY STORES

	TO 50M	50-2MM	2MM+	TOTAL
CURRENT ASSETS	(1531)	(1901)	(765)	(4197)
TO	6.58	7.57	3.92	6.36
CURRENT DEBT	2.44	3.23	2.05	2.70
(TIMES)	1.16	1.71	1.38	1.43
NET PROFITS				
ON	5.71	4.90	2.30	4.27
NET SALES	1.99	2.19	1.31	1.79
(PERCENT)	.51	1.00	.70	.74
PROFITS				
ON	73.97	36.31	21.84	39.68
NET WORTH	32.87	20.75	13.84	20.17
(PERCENT)	8.89	10.36	7.98	9.32
PROFITS				
ON	83.67	67.51	51.95	68.37
WORKING CAPITAL	35.39	35.90	27.82	33.21
(PERCENT)	6.14	13.69	12.86	11.89
SALES				
TO	23.28	15.01	15.94	17.39
NET WORTH	10.29	8.37	9.61	9.18
(TIMES)	4.77	4.19	4.97	4.52
SALES				
TO	23.25	22.15	31.39	24.88
WORKING CAPITAL	11.67	13.00	16.94	13.07
(TIMES)	5.00	6.88	7.59	6.37
COLLECTION PERIOD				
(DAYS)				
SALES				
TO	20.1	21.3	25.9	22.0
INVENTORY	14.1	15.3	18.3	15.4
(TIMES)	9.7	10.1	13.0	10.4
FIXED ASSETS				
TO	126.1	76.6	92.9	92.2
NET WORTH	52.5	39.6	49.8	45.6
(PERCENT)	21.4	19.8	23.2	20.8
CURRENT DEBT				
TO	139.6	77.2	89.4	92.0
NET WORTH	39.2	30.0	43.1	35.9
(PERCENT)	8.0	10.5	18.4	11.5
TOTAL DEBT				
TO	294.3	125.6	139.6	166.3
NET WORTH	87.9	57.4	64.1	64.5
(PERCENT)	13.4	19.6	28.9	19.6
INVENTORY				
TO	127.2	121.9	158.4	129.0
WORKING CAPITAL	90.9	87.9	91.7	89.4
(PERCENT)	60.8	61.8	51.3	59.5
CURRENT DEBT				
TO	111.3	89.5	128.9	104.6
INVENTORY	52.0	46.3	85.1	55.3
(PERCENT)	19.6	20.0	45.4	22.2
FUNDED DEBTS				
TO	246.7	172.7	166.1	197.2
WORKING CAPITAL	117.6	78.4	67.8	87.4
(PERCENT)	40.8	29.3	16.9	28.0

Source: *Key Business Ratios, 1979* (New York: Dun & Bradstreet, 1979), p. 155.

The ratios are presented as a median and upper and lower quartile value for each size category within each industry group, and also as a composite of the four size categories for each industry group. Comparative historical data of three years prior to the latest year are shown for the common size statement figures and the 16 ratios for each SIC group, but are not broken down by size category within the group.

Data for contractor industries are shown in a separate section in a different format. There is a finance industry supplement, which shows a variety of ratios for several different types of finance companies. Also, a bibliography lists additional sources of composite financial data, especially sources that may specialize in data for a particular industry.

Exhibit 8–3 is a typical page from *RMA Annual Statement Studies*. This book is published in the latter part of each year, covering statements for fiscal years ending through March of the year of publication.

Standard & Poor's Analysts Handbook

Standard & Poor's publishes an *Analysts Handbook* annually, with monthly supplements available, listing per share income account and balance-sheet items and related ratios by industry group. The breakdowns are into about 100 industry groups, with data going back to 1947. The data include only the larger public companies followed by Standard & Poor's.

Exhibit 8–4 is a sample page from the *Analysts Handbook*. The annual edition comes out about midyear for statistics through the previous year.

Trade associations

Many industry trade associations collect financial statements from their members and compile composite industry financial data. Officers of the company being analyzed usually will know whether such data are available. Otherwise, the availability of this data usually can be determined by a call to the relevant trade association or associations.

GENERAL INDUSTRY INFORMATION

To organize this discussion, we classified general industry sources into two groups: books and periodicals (which are end sources of information in themselves), and indexes to other sources.

Books and periodicals

Trade associations and periodicals. A majority of all companies belong to one or more trade associations, most of which publish industry information that can be helpful in understanding better the industry in which the company is operating. In addition to data put out by trade associations themselves, many industries have one or several trade journals devoted to news and analysis of the industry. Trade association and other trade periodicals typically are one of the most useful sources of practical industry information for the valuation analyst.

The analyst can ask the subject company what trade associations are relevant to its industry and find out from either the company or the association what information they provide that might be useful in the analysis. He also might ask what trade journals might be helpful. As an adjunct or alternate to such inquiry, the analyst can consult any of various directories of trade associations and journals, some of which are referenced specifically in the next section and in the bibliography.

Standard & Poor's Industry Surveys and Statistical Service. The *S&P Industry Surveys* is a useful service, organized into 36 broad industry groups and indexed for references into about 500 subgroups. Each broad

Exhibit 8–3
Sample page from RMA Annual Statement Studies

RETAILERS · GROCERIES & MEATS
SIC# 5411

167(6/30-9/30/78)		191(10/1/78-3/31/79)			ASSET SIZE NUMBER OF STATEMENTS	6/30/76-3/31/77	6/30/77-3/31/78	6/30/78-3/31/79
0-250M 73	250M-1MM 113	1-10MM 134	10-50MM 38	ALL 358		ALL 307	ALL 351	ALL 358
%	%	%	%	%	**ASSETS** % %	%	%	%
12.0	10.5	11.8	10.0	11.2	Cash & Equivalents	10.6	10.9	11.2
4.4	6.2	5.3	3.0	5.2	Accts. & Notes Rec. - Trade(net)	5.6	5.4	5.2
36.5	33.7	32.7	35.4	34.1	Inventory	34.0	34.1	34.1
1.0	1.5	1.4	1.7	1.4	All Other Current	2.1	1.9	1.4
53.8	51.9	51.2	50.2	51.8	Total Current	52.3	52.3	51.8
34.5	35.9	36.9	38.7	36.3	Fixed Assets (net)	37.0	36.8	36.3
3.3	1.4	.6	2.4	1.6	Intangibles (net)	1.4	1.0	1.6
8.3	10.8	11.2	8.6	10.2	All Other Non-Current	9.2	10.0	10.2
100.0	100.0	100.0	100.0	100.0	Total	100.0	100.0	100.0
					LIABILITIES			
9.8	4.8	3.9	2.4	5.2	Notes Payable-Short Term	5.7	4.7	5.2
4.2	4.9	3.7	2.3	4.0	Cur. Mat.-L/T/D	4.7	4.2	4.0
17.2	20.1	23.5	24.7	21.3	Accts. & Notes Payable - Trade	20.4	20.8	21.3
4.7	6.0	6.1	8.3	5.8	Accrued Expenses	5.9	6.0	5.8
4.2	5.7	3.4	1.7	4.1	All Other Current	4.0	3.9	4.1
40.1	41.5	40.6	37.3	40.4	Total Current	40.7	39.5	40.4
27.1	21.7	19.3	22.3	21.9	Long Term Debt	21.3	21.9	21.9
.9	1.8	2.0	3.2	1.8	All Other Non-Current	1.8	2.0	1.8
31.9	35.0	38.1	37.3	35.8	Net Worth	36.2	36.7	35.8
100.0	100.0	100.0	100.0	100.0	Total Liabilities & Net Worth	100.0	100.0	100.0
					INCOME DATA			
100.0	100.0	100.0	100.0	100.0	Net Sales	100.0	100.0	100.0
77.1	76.7	78.7	80.7	77.9	Cost Of Sales	77.6	78.9	77.9
22.9	23.3	21.3	19.3	22.1	Gross Profit	22.4	21.1	22.1
20.4	21.3	19.6	17.2	20.0	Operating Expenses	19.9	19.2	20.0
2.4	2.0	1.7	2.1	2.0	Operating Profit	2.6	2.0	2.0
.3	.3	-.3	.3	.1	All Other Expenses (net)	.3	.1	.1
2.1	1.7	2.0	1.8	1.9	Profit Before Taxes	2.3	1.9	1.9
					RATIOS			
2.2	1.9	1.6	1.5	1.8		1.7	1.8	1.8
1.6	1.4	1.2	1.3	1.3	Current	1.3	1.3	1.3
1.0	.8	1.0	1.1	1.0		1.0	1.0	1.0
.8	.6	.6	.4	.6		.6	.6	.6
(72) .4 (111)	.4	(37) .4 (354)	.3	.4	Quick	(305) .3 (347)	.4 (354)	.4
.2	.2	.2	.2	.2		.2	.2	.2
0 INF	0 999.8	1 572.7	1 458.6	0 999.8		0 999.8	0 963.0	0 999.8
1 685.0	1 409.0	1 266.7	1 247.5	1 325.1	Sales/Receivables	1 326.9	1 319.7	1 325.1
2 162.8	3 120.2	4 100.4	2 160.5	3 120.7		4 103.0	3 113.0	3 120.7
17 21.0	16 22.2	16 23.5	20 18.1	17 21.7		17 21.2	16 22.6	17 21.7
22 16.6	25 14.6	22 16.9	26 14.2	23 15.8	Cost of Sales/Inventory	24 15.1	23 15.7	23 15.8
34 10.6	36 10.2	35 10.5	38 9.7	35 10.5		36 10.2	34 10.6	35 10.5
21.4	23.6	28.4	31.8	26.1		26.1	24.0	26.1
44.1	51.7	79.9	44.8	57.1	Sales/Working Capital	62.1	56.5	57.1
-352.6	-100.3	-881.2	101.5	-502.2		-370.2	-724.0	-502.2
8.1	10.3	10.5	12.4	9.9		11.0	11.0	9.9
(62) 3.8 (98)	4.8 (112)	4.4 (34)	5.4 (306)	4.5	EBIT/Interest	(251) 5.2 (276)	5.2 (306)	4.5
1.0	2.0	1.8	3.1	1.9		2.1	2.0	1.9
1.9	3.6	5.0	17.0	5.2		5.8	5.6	5.2
(13) .7 (48)	1.8 (91)	2.5 (31)	4.3 (183)	2.5	Cash Flow/Cur. Mat. L/T/D	(145) 2.5 (187)	2.5 (183)	2.5
.3	1.0	1.5	2.5	1.2		1.1	1.1	1.2
.6	.6	.6	.7	.6		.6	.6	.6
1.1	1.0	1.0	1.3	1.0	Fixed/Worth	1.1	1.0	1.0
2.4	2.2	1.8	1.8	2.0		1.9	2.0	2.0
1.0	1.0	1.0	1.1	1.0		.9	.9	1.0
2.1	2.1	1.7	2.0	1.9	Debt/Worth	1.8	1.7	1.9
6.0	4.3	3.4	3.0	3.9		3.7	4.3	3.9
102.6	43.3	39.3	36.5	43.3	% Profit Before Taxes/Tangible	57.3	45.4	43.3
(65) 40.0 (104)	28.0 (132)	23.2 (37)	24.9 (338)	25.6	Net Worth	(289) 27.9 (325)	25.7 (338)	25.6
9.7	13.6	8.3	18.2	12.8		13.8	12.5	12.8
20.3	16.3	13.6	13.4	15.6	% Profit Before Taxes/Total	18.0	17.6	15.6
12.6	8.3	8.5	9.8	8.9	Assets	11.0	9.4	8.9
1.6	4.0	2.8	5.5	3.1		3.7	3.2	3.1
47.8	36.5	29.5	21.6	32.4		30.8	33.5	32.4
24.2	18.3	19.6	15.6	19.6	Sales/Net Fixed Assets	18.8	19.4	19.6
10.8	9.8	11.3	10.2	10.7		9.9	11.0	10.7
10.1	8.5	8.6	7.2	8.5		8.2	8.5	8.5
6.5	5.4	6.4	6.4	6.2	Sales/Total Assets	5.9	6.1	6.2
4.6	3.8	4.4	5.0	4.4		4.4	4.3	4.4
.5	.5	.6	.6	.6		.6	.6	.6
(69) .9 (109)	.8 (126)	.8 (36)	.8 (340)	.8	% Depr., Dep., Amort./Sales	(278) .8 (334)	.8 (340)	.8
1.2	1.3	1.1	1.1	1.2		1.2	1.2	1.2
.8	.5	.7	.5	.7		.8	.8	.7
(48) 1.5 (83)	1.2 (91)	1.2 (26)	1.1 (248)	1.2	% Lease & Rental Exp/Sales	(214) 1.4 (243)	1.2 (248)	1.2
2.2	1.9	1.7	1.6	2.0		2.0	1.8	2.0
1.5	1.0	.5		.9		.8	.7	.9
(42) 2.7 (57)	1.6 (46)	.9	(150)	1.6	% Officers' Comp/Sales	(140) 1.8 (146)	1.2 (150)	1.6
4.5	2.4	2.0		2.6		3.2	2.7	2.6
74321M	3890006M	3170484M	6356957M	9990768M	Net Sales ($)	8298887M	10875064M	9990768M
9331M	61228M	473555M	1026949M	1571063M	Total Assets ($)	1452774M	1814079M	1571063M

©Robert Morris Associates 1979   M = $thousand   MM = $million

Source: *RMA Annual Statement Studies, 1979* (Philadelphia: Robert Morris Associates, 1979), p. 252.

industry group is given a fairly comprehensive background analysis report about once a year, with updates in the form of a shorter current analysis from time to time.

The *Standard & Poor's Statistical Service* is published monthly, providing statistical tables and charts on a wide variety of industry and other economic

Interpretation of Statement Studies Figures

RMA recommends that Statement Studies data be regarded only as general guidelines and not as absolute industry norms. There are several reasons why the data may not be fully representative of a given industry:

(1) The financial statements used in the *Statement Studies* are not selected by any random or statistically reliable method. RMA member banks voluntarily submit the raw data they have available each year, with these being the only constraints: (a) The fiscal year-ends of the companies reported may not be from April 1 through June 29, and (b) their total assets must be less than $50 million.

(2) Many companies have varied product lines; however, the *Statement Studies* categorize them by their primary product Standard Industrial Classification (SIC) number only.

(3) Some of our industry samples are rather small in relation to the total number of firms in a given industry. A relatively small sample can increase the chances that some of our composites do not fully represent an industry.

(4) There is the chance that an extreme statement can be present in a sample, causing a disproportionate influence on the industry composite. This is particularly true in a relatively small sample.

(5) Companies within the same industry may differ in their method of operations which in turn can directly influence their financial statements. Since they are included in our sample, too, these statements can significantly affect our composite calculations.

(6) Other considerations that can result in variations among different companies engaged in the same general line of business are different labor markets; geographical location; different accounting methods; quality of products handled; sources and methods of financing; and terms of sale.

For these reasons, RMA does not recommend the Statement Studies *figures be considered as absolute norms for a given industry. Rather the figures should be used only as general guidelines and in addition to the other methods of financial analysis. RMA makes no claim as to the representativeness of the figures printed in this book.*

data. There is some overlap between the *Statistical Service* and the *Standard & Poor's Analysts Handbook* discussed in the section on composite company statistics.

Paine Webber Handbook. The *Paine Webber Handbook of Stock and Bond Analysis* provides 31 chapters on how to analyze stocks, each chapter

Exhibit 8–4
Sample page from *Standard & Poor's Analysts Handbook*

FOODS-COMPOSITE *

Per Share Data—Adjusted to stock price index level. Average of stock price indexes, 1941-1943 equals 10.

	Sales	Oper. Profit	Profit Margin %	Depr.	Income Taxes	Earnings Per Share	Earnings % of Sales	Dividends Per Share	Dividends % of Earn.	Price 1941-43=10 High	Price 1941-43=10 Low	Price/Earn. Ratio High	Price/Earn. Ratio Low	Div. Yields % High	Div. Yields % Low	Book Value Per Share	Book Value % Return	Working Capital	Capital Expenditures
1946	60.12	4.37	7.27	0.52	1.45	2.06	3.43	0.80	38.83	19.81	15.90	9.62	7.72	5.03	4.04	13.01	15.83	9.84	1.11
1947	85.26	4.61	5.41	0.60	1.40	2.25	2.64	0.89	39.56	17.31	14.66	7.69	6.52	6.07	5.14	14.16	15.89	10.36	1.78
1948	89.06	4.06	4.56	0.71	1.32	1.86	2.09	1.06	56.99	15.91	13.79	8.55	7.41	7.69	6.66	15.20	12.24	10.87	1.94
1949	86.21	4.28	4.96	0.85	1.29	1.79	2.08	0.98	54.75	17.17	14.03	9.59	7.84	6.99	5.71	16.38	10.93	11.67	2.15
1950	88.94	5.26	5.91	0.93	1.91	2.12	2.38	1.07	50.47	18.52	16.53	8.74	7.80	6.47	5.78	17.47	12.14	11.91	1.53
1951	101.57	4.97	4.89	1.01	2.01	1.64	1.61	1.10	67.07	19.00	17.29	11.59	10.54	6.36	5.79	17.97	9.13	12.31	1.80
1952	101.61	5.01	4.93	1.06	2.00	1.54	1.52	1.03	66.88	19.26	17.32	12.51	11.25	5.95	5.35	18.38	8.38	12.49	1.58
1953	100.75	5.75	5.71	1.12	2.41	1.84	1.83	1.04	56.52	20.60	18.96	11.20	10.30	5.49	5.05	18.85	9.76	12.57	1.84
1954	100.27	5.35	5.34	1.20	2.04	1.68	1.68	1.12	66.67	25.21	20.53	15.01	12.22	5.46	4.44	19.39	8.66	12.61	1.86
1955	96.96	5.76	5.94	1.25	2.18	2.05	2.11	1.11	54.15	26.32	24.44	12.84	11.92	4.54	4.22	19.37	10.58	12.59	1.88
1956	90.71	5.88	6.48	1.21	2.22	2.19	2.41	1.16	52.97	25.85	23.53	11.80	10.74	4.93	4.49	19.64	11.15	12.68	2.10
1957	91.80	5.82	6.34	1.28	2.16	2.12	2.31	1.21	57.08	24.48	22.57	11.55	10.65	5.36	4.94	20.26	10.46	12.52	2.11
1958	93.78	6.08	6.48	1.34	2.38	2.23	2.38	1.24	55.61	34.33	25.05	15.39	11.23	4.95	3.61	21.34	10.45	13.45	1.83
1959	93.65	6.59	7.04	1.37	2.65	2.49	2.66	1.30	52.21	38.99	34.37	15.66	13.80	3.78	3.33	22.13	11.25	13.95	1.95
1960	93.26	6.77	7.26	1.41	2.72	2.57	2.76	1.41	54.86	52.31	37.14	20.35	14.45	3.80	2.70	23.05	11.15	14.00	2.10
1961	92.75	6.95	7.49	1.45	2.83	2.60	2.80	1.48	56.92	72.28	50.26	27.80	19.33	2.94	2.05	23.40	11.11	14.30	2.23
1962	95.87	7.34	7.66	1.57	2.91	2.71	2.83	1.58	58.30	66.75	47.51	24.63	17.53	3.33	2.37	24.10	11.24	14.78	2.59
1963	98.47	7.70	7.82	1.63	3.09	2.92	2.97	1.69	57.88	65.81	56.03	22.54	19.19	3.02	2.57	25.40	11.50	15.43	2.63
1964	103.66	8.20	7.91	1.70	3.11	3.31	3.19	1.79	54.08	71.03	66.05	21.46	19.95	2.71	2.52	26.83	12.34	15.86	3.07
1965	108.79	8.25	7.58	1.82	2.94	3.44	3.16	1.94	56.40	73.41	67.40	21.34	19.59	2.88	2.64	28.16	12.22	16.60	3.25
1966	119.93	9.09	7.58	1.95	3.17	3.81	3.18	2.05	53.81	68.90	50.41	18.08	13.23	4.07	2.98	28.79	13.23	16.99	3.75
1967	120.78	9.80	8.11	2.16	3.33	3.95	3.27	2.18	55.19	67.28	57.24	17.03	14.49	3.81	3.24	30.44	12.98	18.68	3.93
1968	127.40	10.00	7.85	2.22	3.88	3.91	3.07	2.25	57.54	75.93	59.30	19.42	15.17	3.79	2.96	31.63	12.36	19.91	3.77
1969	133.71	10.83	8.10	2.36	4.00	3.80	2.84	2.29	60.26	72.85	62.79	19.17	16.52	3.65	3.14	30.74	12.36	19.22	4.37
1970	140.46	11.70	8.33	2.40	4.16	4.23	3.01	2.34	55.32	69.70	54.32	16.48	12.84	4.31	3.36	32.28	13.10	20.50	4.69
1971	141.69	12.11	8.55	2.52	4.21	4.54	3.20	2.31	50.88	73.44	64.60	16.18	14.23	3.58	3.15	33.00	13.76	21.71	4.75
1972	151.65	12.52	8.26	2.59	4.34	4.76	3.14	2.34	49.16	80.96	69.14	17.01	14.53	3.38	2.89	34.85	13.66	23.43	4.80
1973	163.29	13.26	8.12	2.57	4.61	5.20	3.18	2.26	43.46	80.44	58.27	15.47	11.21	3.88	2.81	35.97	14.46	24.81	5.04
1974	191.86	14.94	7.79	2.68	5.07	5.71	2.98	2.30	40.28	65.70	41.68	11.51	7.30	5.52	3.50	39.38	14.50	28.65	5.95
1975	R203.41	R16.89	8.30	2.88	R6.04	6.59	3.24	2.51	38.09	73.68	51.60	11.18	7.83	4.86	3.41	R43.41	15.18	R31.04	R6.36
1976	P216.40	P16.76	7.74	P2.86	P6.79	P7.41	3.42	2.90	39.14	80.82	70.75	10.91	9.55	4.10	3.59	N.A.	...	N.A.	N.A.

Stock Price Indexes for this group extend back to 1926. * A Composite of Canned Foods Companies, Dairy Products, Meat Packing, and Processed Foods Companies. The component companies of the groups are shown on their respective pages, immediately following.

Source: *Standard & Poor's Analysts' Handbook, 1977.* New York: Standard & Poor's Corp., Inc.

devoted to a particular industry. Each chapter is organized a little differently, but generally tries to identify the key to analyzing the industry, general points about the industry, and questions that should be asked in analyzing a company in the industry. Part II of the book is an analysis of fixed-income securities, and also deals with special characteristics of a more limited group of industries with respect to analysis of their bonds and preferred stocks.

Brokerage house and other investment research reports. An almost endless variety of industry information is published by investment advisory services and brokerage house. Several such sources are referred to at various points in this book in discussions of specific types of information, and the indexing services discussed in the next section will lead to some of these sources. The availability of brokerage house information may be erratic, since it is published primarily for distribution to clients and is not widely distributed to libraries.

U.S. Industrial Outlook. In January of each year the U.S. Department of Commerce publishes the *U.S. Industrial Outlook,* which provides one-year and five-year projections for each of 200 industries, classified by SIC codes.

Each industry is discussed in both text and tabular statistics in terms of growth in key variables over the past six years as well as the outlook.

Banks. Almost all major banks publish economic information of one kind or another, and generally compile and publish information on specific industries that are indigenous to their respective service areas.

Federal and state agencies. The number of federal and state agencies that compile data is astronomical. Most of the material compiled by federal agencies is indexed somewhere in one or more of the indexing services discussed in the text or listed in the bibliography.

Indexes to other sources

Predicasts Index of Corporations and Industries. This index covers company, product, and industry information from over 750 financial publications, business-oriented newspapers, trade magazines, and special reports. Section 1 of the *Predicasts Index of Corporations and Industries* is arranged by industries, using SIC codes. Section 2 is alphabetical by company.

Business Periodicals Index. The *BPI* is one of the most widely used general indexes, covering a broad range of subjects and periodicals indexed. It is published monthly and cumulated quarterly and annually.

National trade and professional associations. An annual publication, *National Trade and Professional Associations of the United States and Canada,* lists more than 6,000 organizations. The book includes a key word index, which can be helpful in identifying associations that are related to a particular industry.

RMA Annual Statement Studies. The *RMA Annual,* discussed in an earlier section on composite statistics, also has a very useful bibliography of industry information sources in the back of the book.

Directories of information sources. A variety of books are very useful in locating sources of industry and business information. Three of these are *Business Information Sources,* by Lorna M. Daniells; *Directory of Business and Financial Services,* by Mary M. Grant and Norma Cote; and *Encyclopedia of Business Information Sources,* by Paul Wasserman. All three of these are annotated in the bibliography at the end of this chapter.

ECONOMIC DATA

There is such a huge variety of economic data available that this section will mention only a few specific sources and conclude with reference to some books and indexing services that can lead to whatever specific types of economic data one may be seeking. Also, several of the sources referenced earlier for compiling company and industry data are useful for broader economic data.

Apart from specific sources referenced here it should be assumed that the analyst is reading a number of general sources of business and economic data on a regular basis. These sources would include such publications as *The Wall Street Journal, Barrons, Forbes, Fortune, Financial World, Standard & Poor's Outlook,* and many other national and regional periodicals.

The plethora of U.S. government publications that contain one kind of economic data or another boggles the most creative imagination. Four of the most widely used, all monthly, are the *Federal Reserve Bulletin, Survey of Current Business, Business Conditions Digest,* and *Economic Indicators.* One of the most widely used annuals is the *Statistical Abstract of the United States.* For references to other U.S. government data, one can consult the *American Statistics Index.*

Federal Reserve Bulletin. Each monthly issue of the *Federal Reserve Bulletin* contains articles on monetary policy and things that affect the monetary climate, plus many pages of tables of domestic financial and nonfinancial statistics and international statistics. Of relevance to business valuations, one of the most useful aspects of the *Federal Reserve Bulletin* is to provide insights into many financial components of the economy that have a direct bearing on companies' cost of capital, especially various categories of interest rates.

Series include interest rates on various maturities of U.S. government obligations, new issues of AAA utility bonds, various grades of seasoned corporate bond issues, mortgages, bank prime rate, other short-term rates, preferred and common stock yields, various stock price indexes, housing permits, starts, and completions, various consumer and price indexes, and other economic series, such as gross national product and personal income. Most of the statistics are quoted monthly, going back for several months, and annually, going back a few years; some statistics are quoted on a quarterly basis. Since we have noted that capital costs are an important factor in business valuations, Exhibit 8–5 has a page from the *Federal Reserve Bulletin* that shows a variety of current money and capital market rates.

Survey of Current Business. Considered by some to be the most important single source for current business statistics, it covers a broad scope of business indicators, price series, employment figures, and business activity figures. There also is a biennial supplement, *Business Statistics,* which presents definitions and sources for the many statistical series, plus an historical record of the statistics.

Business Conditions Digest. Most of the emphasis in *Business Conditions Digest* is on the so-called cyclical indicators. These are classified by leading, coincident, and lagging indicators, and also classified by the type of economic process which each represents, such as employment, production, consumption, capital investment, inventory changes, prices and profits, and money and credit.

Economic Indicators. The Council of Economic Advisors prepares *Economic Indicators.* The statistics are grouped into several categories, including output, income, and spending; employment, unemployment, and wages; production and business activity; prices, money, credit, and security markets; federal finance; and international statistics.

Statistical Abstract of the United States. The annual *Statistical Abstract of the United States* is published by the U.S. Department of Commerce's Bureau of the Census, which keeps track of all kinds of things

Exhibit 8–5
Interest rates: Money and capital markets

1.36 INTEREST RATES Money and Capital Markets

Averages, percent per annum

Instrument	1977	1978	1979	1979 Dec	1980 Jan	1980 Feb	1980 Mar	1980 week ending Mar 1	Mar 8	Mar 15	Mar 22	Mar 29
							Money market rates					
1 Federal funds[1]	5.54	7.94	11.20	13.78	13.82	14.13	17.19	14.62	16.17	16.45	16.24	17.78
Commercial paper[2,3]												
2 1-month	5.42	7.76	10.86	13.35	13.07	13.62	16.55	14.46	15.92	16.75	16.84	16.61
3 3-month	5.54	7.94	10.97	13.24	13.04	13.78	16.81	14.77	16.22	16.95	17.04	16.95
4 6-month	5.60	7.99	10.91	12.66	13.60	13.60	16.50	14.68	16.02	16.50	16.70	16.70
Finance paper, directly placed[2,3]												
5 1-month	5.38	7.73	10.78	13.27	13.01	13.58	16.30	14.45	15.71	16.53	16.48	16.34
6 3-month	5.49	7.80	10.47	11.74	11.96	13.05	15.36	13.93	14.96	15.52	15.50	15.43
7 6-month	5.50	7.76	10.25	11.68	11.79	12.39	14.70	13.27	14.31	14.72	14.69	14.98
8 Prime bankers acceptances, 90-day[3,4]	5.59	8.11	11.04	13.31	13.15	14.01	17.10	15.10	16.59	17.24	17.22	17.29
Certificates of deposit, secondary market[5]												
9 1-month	5.48	7.88	11.03	13.36	13.26	13.93	16.81	14.88	16.15	17.21	16.97	16.84
10 3-month	5.64	8.22	11.22	13.43	13.39	14.30	17.57	15.45	16.87	17.71	17.82	17.80
11 6-month	5.92	8.61	11.44	13.42	13.46	14.58	17.74	15.74	17.11	17.77	17.90	18.07
12 Eurodollar deposits, 3-month[6]	6.05	8.74	11.96	14.51	14.33	15.33	18.72	16.46	17.16	18.58	18.98	18.99
U.S. Treasury bills[3,7]												
Secondary market												
13 3-month	5.27	7.19	10.07	12.04	12.00	12.86	15.20	13.78	15.37	15.32	14.76	15.55
14 6-month	5.53	7.58	10.06	11.84	11.84	12.86	15.01	13.82	14.90	15.02	14.83	15.42
15 1-year	5.71	7.74	9.75	10.92	10.96	12.46	14.03	13.53	13.94	15.02	13.89	14.39
Auction average[8]												
16 3-month	5.265	7.221	10.041	12.071	12.036	12.814	15.526	13.700	15.136	15.381	15.053	16.532
17 6-month	5.510	7.572	10.017	11.847	11.851	12.721	15.100	13.629	14.792	14.956	14.950	15.700
							Capital market rates					
U.S. TREASURY NOTES AND BONDS												
Constant maturities[9]												
18 1-year	6.09	8.34	10.67	11.98	12.06	13.92	15.82	15.24	15.77	15.68	15.58	16.25
19 2-year	6.45	8.34	10.12	11.39	11.50	13.42	14.88	14.70	15.03	14.67	14.72	15.16
20 2½-year[10]				10.90	11.15	14.00	14.65					
21 3-year	6.69	8.29	9.71	10.71	10.88	12.84	14.05	14.07	14.27	13.83	13.86	14.31
22 4-year[10]												
23 5-year	6.99	8.32	9.52	10.42	10.74	12.60	13.47	13.76	13.65	13.22	13.21	13.83
24 7-year	7.23	8.36	9.48	10.42	10.77	12.53	13.00	13.50	13.23	12.76	12.76	13.28
25 10-year	7.42	8.41	9.44	10.39	10.80	12.41	12.75	13.20	12.94	12.54	12.54	13.00
26 20-year	7.67	8.48	9.33	10.18	10.65	12.21	12.49	12.59	12.61	12.36	12.29	12.71
27 30-year		8.49	9.29	10.12	10.60	12.13	12.34	12.57	12.44	12.23	12.13	12.55
Composite[11]												
28 3 to 5 years	6.85	8.30	9.58	10.45	10.76	12.52	13.41	13.57	13.65	13.21	13.16	13.68
29 Over 10 years (long-term)	7.06	7.89	8.74	9.59	10.03	11.55	11.87	12.10	12.01	11.73	11.67	12.06
STATE AND LOCAL NOTES AND BONDS												
Moody's series[12]												
30 Aaa	5.20	5.52	5.92	6.50	6.58	7.28	8.16	8.00	8.00	8.15	8.25	8.25
31 Baa	6.12	6.27	6.73	7.42	7.60	8.12	10.30	9.00	10.40	10.40	10.40	10.00
32 Bond Buyer series[13]	5.68	6.03	6.52	7.22	7.35	8.16	9.17	8.72	8.94	9.08	9.20	9.44
CORPORATE BONDS												
33 Seasoned issues, all industries[14]	8.43	9.07	10.12	11.35	11.74	12.92	13.73	13.54	13.64	13.72	13.68	13.87
By rating groups												
34 Aaa	8.02	8.73	9.63	10.74	11.09	12.38	12.96	12.88	13.00	13.00	12.83	13.00
35 Aa	8.24	8.92	9.94	11.15	11.56	12.73	13.51	13.45	13.41	13.51	13.43	13.65
36 A	8.49	9.12	10.20	11.46	11.86	12.99	13.97	13.66	13.89	14.03	14.01	14.17
37 Baa	8.97	9.45	10.69	12.06	12.42	13.57	14.45	14.16	14.27	14.35	14.45	14.67
Aaa utility bonds[15]												
38 New issue	8.19	8.96	10.03	11.25	11.73	13.57	14.00	14.11	13.98	13.95	13.85	14.22
39 Recently offered issues	8.19	8.97	10.02	11.33	11.77	13.35	13.90	13.83	13.94	13.72	13.80	14.12
MEMO: Dividend/price ratio[16]												
40 Preferred stocks	7.60	8.25	9.07	10.06	10.14	10.55	11.26	10.83	11.11	11.34	11.43	11.61
41 Common stocks	4.56	5.28	5.46	5.53	5.40	5.24	5.77	5.41	5.49	5.72	5.94	6.31

1. Weekly figures are 7-day averages of daily effective rates for the week ending Wednesday; the daily effective rate is an average of the rates on a given day weighted by the volume of transactions at these rates.
2. Beginning November 1977, unweighted average of offering rates quoted by at least five dealers (in the case of commercial paper), or finance companies (in the case of finance paper). Previously, most representative rate quoted by those dealers and finance companies. Before Nov. 1979, maturities for data shown are 30–59 days, 90–119 days, and 120–179 days for commercial paper; and 30–59 days, 90–119 days, and 150–179 days for finance paper.
3. Yields are quoted on a bank-discount basis.
4. Average of the midpoint of the range of daily dealer closing rates offered for domestic issues.
5. Five-day average of rates quoted by five dealers (3-month series was previously a 7-day average).
6. Averages of daily quotations for the week ending Wednesday.
7. Except for auction averages, yields are computed from daily closing bid prices.
8. Rates are recorded in the week in which bills are issued.
9. Yield on the more actively traded issues adjusted to constant maturities by the U.S. Treasury, based on daily closing bid prices.

10. Each figure is an average of only five business days near the end of the month. The rate for each month is used to determine the maximum interest rate payable in the following month on small saver certificates. (See table 1.16).
11. Unweighted averages for all outstanding notes and bonds in maturity ranges shown, based on daily closing bid prices. "Long-term" includes all bonds neither due nor callable in less than 10 years, including several very low yielding "flower" bonds.
12. General obligations only, based on figures for Thursday, from Moody's Investors Service.
13. Twenty issues of mixed quality.
14. Averages of daily figures from Moody's Investors Service.
15. Compilation of the Board of Governors of the Federal Reserve System. Issues included are long-term (20 years or more). New-issue yields are based on quotations on date of offering; those on recently offered issues (included only for first 4 weeks after termination of underwriter price restrictions). on Friday close-of-business quotations.
16. Standard and Poor's corporate series. Preferred stock ratio based on a sample of ten issues: four public utilities, four industrials, one financial, and one transportation. Common stock ratios on the 500 stocks in the price index

Source: Board of Governors of the Federal Reserve System. *Federal Reserve Bulletin* (April, 1980), p. A27.

besides population. The 33 chapters of this volume run to about 1,000 pages. Some of the subjects of potential interest include labor force, employment, and earnings; income, expenditures, and wealth; prices; banking, finance, and insurance; business enterprise; energy; transportation; agriculture, forests, and forest products; fisheries; mining and mineral products; construction and housing; and manufactures.

American Statistics Index. In hundreds of pages it provides subject and name indexes to data in all the U.S. government publications. The service, and its monthly supplements, also include an abstracts section.

One privately sponsored publication of economic data is the *Handbook of Basic Economic Statistics*. It is available in an annual version with monthly supplements, a quarterly with monthly supplements, or a fully cumulative handbook every month. There are over 200 pages of tables on many aspects of industry, commerce, agriculture, and labor.

Handbook of Basic Economic Statistics

Various state agencies, especially departments of commerce and of economic development, put out large amounts of economic data about their states. Most states publish some kind of a listing or catalog of what they have available.

A useful source of information that most people seem to overlook is county courthouses. They keep data on such things as building permits, value of construction, real estate sales, employment, and levels of compensation that can be useful for certain valuation cases of a particular local orientation.

State and local sources

Many companies that serve a broad cross-section of the population compile economic data for various purposes, and much of it is available in published form. Because of the almost universal nature of the populations they serve, the two industry groups that tend to publish the most of such data are banks and utilities. Most large stock brokerage firms also have one or more staff economists and generally have available published analyses of the economic outlook and various aspects of it.

One of the advantages of bank, utility, and other private company data, compared with many of the government sources, is that the private company data tends to be more up to date. Another very important advantage to the valuation analyst is that private company sources tend to be more forward-looking than government sources. This is especially important in recognition of the fact that any business valuation has future expectations at least implicit in it, so the more explicit the available data on future expectations the better the valuation should be.

Banks, utilities, and private companies

Predicasts has very broad-based economic data available, both in published form and in computer-accessible form. One service, called "Prompt," provides 4,000 concise digests each month, covering developments in almost all broad industry groups. The digests are taken from about 500 original sources. Predicasts also publishes half a dozen other digest-type services.

In addition to the *Predicasts Index of Corporate Change* discussed in the next chapter, and the *Predicasts Index of Corporations and Industries* discussed earlier, Predicasts publishes European, international, and federal indexes.

Predicasts also has three statistical services. One is "Predicasts," and it abstracts forecasts and market data from articles in over 2,000 trade journals, business publications, newspapers, government reports, and special studies; it

Predicasts services

also provides historical data and short and long-range forecasts for 500 statistical series. "Worldcasts" provides similar material, worldwide. The annual *Basebook* gives historical annual data for over 25,000 statistical series.

Predicasts also offers special studies on each of a variety of industries, and a variety of special market reports (priced at several hundred dollars each). The company offers an on-line terminal system for computer access and several related services.

Sources of data on management compensation

Since the appropriate level of management compensation frequently is an issue in the valuation of a closely-held business, it is helpful to know where to turn for guidance on this subject. The most comprehensive set of compensation statistics is the Executive Compensation Service provided by the American Management Association. See the annotated bibliography at the end of this chapter for a description. Also in the bibliography is an index of sources of management compensation information titled *Executive Compensation: Selected References* compiled at Harvard University by Karen B. Tracy.

Indexes to economic and industry data

Many of the indexes to economic data have already been mentioned, such as the Predicasts indexes and the Predicasts services, the *American Statistics Index,* the *Business Periodicals Index,* and the *Business Information Sources* book by Lorna M. Daniells.

Another very important index, leaning more to economic information than to specific business information, is the *Public Affairs Information Service (PAIS).*

Many periodicals publish their own indexes. For example, *The Wall Street Journal* is indexed monthly and cumulated annually. The *Northwest Investment Review* is indexed quarterly and cumulated semiannually and annually. *Mergers and Acquisitions* is indexed annually.

The three directories mentioned earlier, *Business Information Sources, Directory of Business and Financial Services,* and *Encyclopedia of Business Information Sources,* all contain references to sources for a wide variety of economic data as well as to sources for data on specific industries.

BIBLIOGRAPHY: INDUSTRY AND ECONOMIC DATA SOURCES
(See also the bibliography on sources of company data at end of Chapter 9)

American Management Association. *Executive Compensation Service.* New York. (annual)

Series of eight reports dealing with salaries for different levels of job categories. Includes top management, middle management, professional and scientific, first line supervision, technicians, office personnel, sales personnel. Offers job descriptions, further broken down into categories like durable goods industries, with some by industry segments. Offers median pay, base pay, bonuses, average range of salaries.

American Statistics Index. Washington, D.C.: Congressional Information Services. (monthly, with annual cumulations)

"A comprehensive guide and index to the statistical publications of the U.S. government." In addition, ASI *1974 Annual and Retrospective Edition* gives coverage of federal government statistical publications in print on 1/1/74, as well as significant publications issued since the early 1960s.

Board of Governors of the Federal Reserve System. *Federal Reserve Bulletin.* Washington, D.C. (monthly)

Current U.S. banking and monetary statistics, and includes such basic business statistics as employment, prices, national income and construction. Includes the *FRB* index of industrial production.

Business Periodicals Index. New York: H.W. Wilson Co. (monthly, with quarterly and annual cumulations)

Covers wide range of business topics, including industries, published in various journals, with indexing arranged alphabetically by subject and author.

Council of Economic Advisers. *Economic Indicators.* Washington, D.C.: U.S. Government Printing Office (monthly)

Statistical charts and tables for basic U.S. economic indicators. Statistics are reprinted for at least six years and monthly or quarterly for the past year. Covers total output, income and spending; GNP in 1972 dollars, personal consumption expenditures; corporate profits; production and business activity; money, credit, and security markets.

Daniells, Lorna M. *Business Information Sources.* Berkeley: University of California Press, 1976.

Annotates sources arranged by subject, such as industry statistics. Somewhat out of date, but still very useful in research on individual cases. Indexed by title, author, and subject.

Grant, Mary M., and Cote, Norma, eds. *Directory of Business and Financial Services.* 7th ed. New York: Special Libraries Association, 1976.

Annotated reference book dealing exclusively with information services that provide continuous coverage of some facet of business activity, such as investment advisory services and commodity services. Arranged alphabetically by title, with a subject index. Describes 1,051 publications and represents 421 publishers.

Handbook of Basic Economic Statistics. Economics Statistics Bureau of Washington, D.C. (annual, with monthly supplements) Box 10163, Washington, D.C. 20018

Current and historic statistics on commerce, industry, labor, and agriculture, with more than 1800 statistical series included.

Key Business Ratios. New York: Dun & Bradstreet, Inc. (annual)

Balance sheet and profit and loss ratios based on a computerized financial statements file. The 14 key ratios are broken into median figures, with upper and lower quartiles. Covers over 800 lines of business, broken into three size ranges by net worth for each SIC.

National Trade and Professional Associations of the United States and Canada and Labor Unions. Washington, D.C.: Columbia Books, Inc. (annual)

Excellent source book to contact trade and industry sources for industry information. Lists about 6,000 national trade associations, labor unions, scientific or technical societies and other national organizations composed of groups united for a common purpose.

Paine Webber Handbook of Stock and Bond Analysis. Kiril Sokohoff, ed. in chief. New York: McGraw-Hill Book Co., 1979.

Discusses industry groups and offers keys to analyzing each industry.

Predicasts. Cleveland, Ohio: Predicasts, Inc. (quarterly)

Economic and market forecast index arranged by products with sources cited for further research.

Predicasts Index of Corporations & Industries. Cleveland, Ohio: Predicasts Inc. (weekly, with monthly and annual cumulations) 1101 Cedar Ave., Cleveland, OH. 44106

Index for current information on companies, products, and industries. Covers periodicals and a few brokerage house reports. Contains information on corporate acquisitions and mergers, new products, technological developments, and sociopolitical factors. Includes sections arranged by SIC number and alphabetically by company name.

Public Affairs Information Service Bulletin. New York: Public Affairs Information Service. (biweekly, with quarterly and annual cumulations)

"A selected subject list of the latest books, pamphlets, government publications, reports of public and private agencies and periodical articles, relating to economic and social conditions, public administration and international relations, published in English throughout the world."

RMA Annual Statement Studies. Philadelphia: Robert Morris Associates. (annual).

"Including comparative historical data and other sources of composite financial data." Composite balance sheets and income data, with selected ratios for over 300 lines of business. Includes bibliography of sources. Issued annually in October, covering fiscal year-ends 6/30 through 3/31.

Standard & Poor's Analysts Handbook. New York: Standard & Poor's Corp., Inc. (annual)

"Composite corporate per share data—by industries," for over 90 industries. Statistics and percentages cover 13 components, including sales, operating profits, depreciation, earnings dividends, and the like.

Standard & Poor's Industry Surveys. New York: Standard & Poor's Corp., Inc. (quarterly and annual)

Basic data on 36 important industries, with financial comparisons of the leading companies in each industry. Includes a "Basic Analysis" for each, revised annually. A "Current Analysis" is published quarterly for each industry. A monthly "Trends and Projections" includes tables of economic and industry indicators.

Standard & Poor's Statistical Service. New York: Standard & Poor's Corp., Inc.

Contains basic statistics on broad industry groups, supplemented monthly by current statistics. Includes security price index record by industry group.

Tracy, Karen B. *Executive Compensation: Selected References.* Boston: Baker Library, Harvard University, 1976.

Includes a section giving data sources for general salary statistics, and a number of sources for salary statistics for executives in various fields and industries.

U.S. Bureau of Census. *Statistical Abstract of the United States.* Washington, D.C.: U.S. Government Printing Office. (annual)

Summary of statistics on the social, political and economic organization of the United States.

U.S. Bureau of Economic Analysis. *Business Conditions Digest.* Washington, D.C.: U.S. Government Printing Office. (monthly)

Includes charts and statistical tables for leading economic time series. Sections include cyclical indicators: composite indicators and their components; cyclical indicators by economic process; diffusion indexes and rates of change; national income and product; prices, wages, and productivity; labor force, employment, and unemployment; government activities; U.S. international transactions and international comparisons.

U.S. Department of Commerce. Industry and Trade Administration. *U.S. Industrial Outlook.* Washington, D.C.: U.S. Government Printing Office. (annual)

Information on recent trends and outlook for about five years in over 200 individual industries. Narrative with statistics contains discussions of changes in supply and demand, developments in domestic and overseas markets, price changes, employment trends, capital investment.

U.S. Department of Commerce. *Survey of Current Business.* Washington, D.C.: U.S. Government Printing Office. (monthly)

Some narrative with charts and statistical tables, as well as tables of statistics in general business indicators; commodity prices; construction and real estate; domestic trade; labor force, employment, and earnings; finance; foreign trade of United States: transportation and communications; chemicals and allied products; electric power and gas; food and kindred products; and so on. Special statistical reports appear, such as the "National Income Issue"; "Local Area Personal Income"; "Corporate Profits"; "Plant & Equipment Expenditures"; "State and Regional Income."

U.S. Internal Revenue Service. *Source Book: Statistics of Income: Corporation Income Tax Returns.* Washington, D.C. (annual)

"Balance sheet, income statement, tax and investment credit items by major and minor industries, broken down by size of total assets." Tables provide more detailed industry data than appear in annual *Statistics of Income: Corporation Income Tax Returns.* Comes out four to five years late.

U.S. Internal Revenue Service. *Statistics of Income: Corporation Income Tax Returns.* Washington, D.C.: U.S. Government Printing Office. (annual)

Balance sheet and income statement statistics from a sample of corporate returns. Includes tables by major industry, by asset size, and so on. Includes historical summaries.

U.S. President. *Economic Report of the President.* Transmitted to Congress February (each year); together with the Annual Report of the Council of Economic Advisers. Washington, D.C.: U.S. Government Printing Office. (annual)

The *Annual Report* is the major part, discussing economic policy and outlook, economic trends of the year, and includes statistical tables relating to income, employment and production.

Wasserman, Paul, et al. *Encyclopedia of Business Information Sources.* 3d ed. Detroit: Gale Research Co., 1976.

Listing of information sources on subjects and countries, with basic statistics sources, directories, almanacs, periodicals, associations, handbooks, bibliographies, dictionaries, general works for each. Approximately 1,300 subjects are covered. Under each subject, a citation is provided for each source mentioned, including the address of the publisher and the price, where available.

9

DATA ON COMPARABLE COMPANIES

Throughout this book there is discussion of using publicly-traded company data as one source for guidance in the valuation of closely-held businesses. This chapter presents, on a step-by-step basis, some direction on how to locate and compile such information. The final section discusses sources of data on prices and terms of mergers and acquisitions that might prove relevant as guidance for another company's valuation.

The point of gathering data on comparable publicly-traded companies is to derive some bench marks by which to value the subject privately-held company. For example, if the public companies in the industry sell at price/earnings ratios higher than the overall market average, it is an indication of optimism in the public market regarding the future of the industry, and this optimism also should be reflected in the P/E ratio accorded the privately-held company. Similarly, the public market can provide bench marks about how the prices of shares of stock relate to such variables as book values, adjusted underlying net asset values, dividends, and gross revenues. Any or all of these parameters could have relevance to a specific valuation situation, as discussed elsewhere in this book.

The process of compiling a comprehensive list of comparable publicly-traded companies is not a simple one. There is no single source on which the analyst can rely and feel secure that his list is complete. For some industries, it is much easier to find a good comparable list than for others. A complete search requires creativity, ingenuity, and some degree of experience. This chapter presents the most comprehensive general sources available. If the analyst is not satisfied with the list developed through the use of such sources, he can consult trade association membership lists, regional investment publications, the subject company itself, and those companies discovered through the conventional processes in the endeavor to find additional comparable companies.

COMPILING A LIST OF PUBLICLY-TRADED COMPARABLES

Of all the criteria by which different companies may be judged comparable, the criterion on which attention most often is focused is the industry in which the company operates. In fact, Revenue Ruling 59–60 states specifically that of the factors that "are fundamental and require careful analysis in each case" for gift and estate tax valuations one is "the market price of stocks of corporations engaged in the same or a similar line of business having their stocks actively traded on a free and open market, either on an exchange or over-the-counter."[1]

Therefore, the starting point in compiling a list of comparable companies is a list of the companies that operate in the subject company's industry group. The most widely accepted categorization of industry groups is the U.S. government's *Standard Industrial Classification Manual,* which publishes and defines Standard Industrial Classification (SIC) codes. The latest edition of the

---

[1]Revenue Ruling 59–60, (1959–1 C.B. 237) Section 4.

manual is 1972, and a 1977 supplement indicates that a review of the manual is scheduled for 1982.

The search for comparable public companies should be as exhaustive as the scope of the particular valuation case permits. Frequently, the most obvious public companies in an industry are the largest ones, and for that and related reasons may not be as comparable to most closely-held companies as would some of the smaller, more obscure public companies. If, for example, one is valuing a local retail grocery chain, the appraiser would be best advised not to rely on data for those companies included in the Standard & Poor's retail grocery index, including such national giants as Safeway, Kroger, and A&P. The list would be more comparable if it included some small, regional grocery chains, most of which would be traded over-the-counter, and probably be virtually unknown outside their own regions.

Another reason why the appraiser should be comprehensive in the search for comparable companies is to be able to demonstrate that all companies that might be considered reasonably comparable were taken into account, and that the most comparable companies available were selected for analysis. The analyst must establish and adhere to an objective set of selection criteria, so that the final list will have no tendency to upwardly or downwardly bias the valuation result.

Developing a list of "suspects"

Three sources that can be used to develop a list of "suspects" (companies in the subject company's SIC group that might be useful as comparables) are the *Directory of Companies Required to File Annual Reports With the Securities and Exchange Commission; Standard & Poor's Register of Corporations, Directors and Executives;* and *Standard & Poor's Corporation Records.*

***SEC* Directory.** The latest SEC *Directory* as of this writing lists 9,831 companies. The coverage is defined as:

The Directory contains listings of companies required to file annual reports under the Securities Exchange Act of 1934 as of March 31, 1980. The Directory includes companies with securities listed on national securities exchanges, companies with securities traded over the counter which are registered under Section 12(g) of the Securities Exchange Act, and certain companies required to file pursuant to Section 15(d) of the Securities Exchange Act as a result of having securities registered under the Securities Act of 1935.[2]

While this is a good list, there are thousands of smaller companies that trade over-the-counter that are not included. Only companies with $1 million or more in assets and with 500 or more stockholders are subject to SEC filing requirements under Section 12(g) of the Securities Exchange Act.

---

[2]Securities and Exchange Commission, *Directory of Companies Required to File Annual Reports with the Securities and Exchange Commission,* (Washington, D.C.: U.S. Government Printing Office, March 31, 1980), p. 1.

Also, the SEC *Directory* excludes investment companies registered under the Investment Company Act of 1940, an important group to use as comparables for family investment holding companies. Data for investment companies can be found in Wiesenberger Investment Companies Services' *Investment Companies,* an annual publication with monthly supplements.

Another limitation of the SEC *Directory* is that it is usually a year or more out of date. As this is being published in 1981, the latest issue is a listing as of March 31, 1980. Disclosure (a set of services which will be discussed later in the chapter) publishes a more up-to-date list titled *SEC Filing Companies,* but it is arranged alphabetically only. The SIC codes are shown, but it would be necessary to comb through the whole list to pick out the companies in any particular SIC group.

Standard & Poor's Register.   The *S&P Register* lists far more companies than the SEC *Directory,* but does not distinguish which are public companies and which are private companies. If the company is public and has been quoted in the National Daily Quotation Service (referred to among stock brokers as the "pink sheets") within the preceding six months, it will be listed in the *National Monthly Stock Summary.* Therefore, both the *S&P Register* and the *National Monthly Stock Summary* can be used to develop a list of publicly quoted companies in a particular SIC group.

The *National Monthly Stock Summary* provides the price quotations at the end of the month, in most cases. The anaylst compiling the list of companies usually would want to use the monthly issue of the *National Monthly Stock Summary* that coincided with the valuation date.

Standard & Poor's Corporation Records.   For cases where budget or time constraints do not allow for the most exhaustive search for comparable companies, a short-cut method is to use the Classified Index of Industrial Companies that is published annually as a part of the *Standard & Poor's Corporation Records* instead of using the S&P *Register.* The index, classified by SIC code, includes every public company that appears in the *S&P Corporation Records.* The limitation is that there are some smaller public companies included in the *S&P Register* that are not included in the *Corporation Records.*

Having used these sources, the analyst will have compiled a list of companies in a particular SIC code that have a public trading market, along with their month-end price at or near the valuation date. At Willamette Management Associates, we call this the "suspect list." The next step is to learn more about the companies so that those obviously not comparable can be eliminated at an early stage, narrowing the group of companies under consideration to what we call a "prospect list."

Before moving on to the next step, it should be pointed out that the suspect list is not necessarily comprehensive about all public stocks that possibly could be comparables. A stock price quotation is included in the *National Monthly Stock Summary* only if the stock is listed on an exchange or if a stock brokerage firm pays a fee to have it quoted in the publication. There are many public stocks traded, mostly of smaller companies, for which no broker purchases the quotation services of the National Quotation Service. There is, however, no more comprehensive single price quotation source. Also, the S&P *Register* does not necessarily pick up every relevant company within an SIC group. Other potentially comparable companies may be added to the list from the analyst's personal knowledge, regional publications (e.g., the *Northwest Stock Guide*), or information obtained from stock brokerage firms.

Developing a list of "prospects"

Another section of the S&P *Register* gives the address of each company and a very brief summary of the company's products or business. For some of the companies, it will become obvious just from this brief description that they can be eliminated from consideration as possible comparables.

Either of two fairly comprehensive services can be consulted to obtain more detailed company descriptions—*Standard & Poor's Corporation Records* or *Moody's Manuals.* Each of the two services consists of several volumes. *Moody's Manuals* are separated into *Bank & Finance, Industrials, OTC Industrials, Public Utilities,* and *Transportation.* Although these two services are fairly comprehensive, not every public company is included. The analyst can find some additional descriptions in such regional publications as *Northwest Investment Review* and *Walker's Manual of Western Corporations.*

From these more detailed descriptions, it usually will be possible to eliminate several more companies from consideration. At this point the analyst will have to start using judgment about the criteria by which the final comparables list will be drawn. The longer the list of potential comparables, the more stringent the criteria can be, with the aim of offering a reasonably sizeable list. Ideally, each comparable company will do 100 percent of its business in the same industry as the subject company. Rarely will it be possible to develop such a list, because companies' activities tend to become increasingly diversified over the years. It is best not to draw the criteria for comparability too tightly here, since any questionable company still can be eliminated from the list at a later stage.

At this point, on the basis of some preliminary screening using a few standard published sources, the analyst has narrowed down a suspect list to a prospect list, a group of companies which he has reason to believe might be comparable enough to the subject company to provide some guidance in the valuation. There still may be some companies remaining on the suspect list about which no information is available in the manuals consulted. The analyst will have to decide whether to carry these companies to the next step, depending on time, budget, and the extent to which it does or does not appear that a satisfactory group of comparables will result from the remaining prospect list.

Narrowing the list to comparable companies

The next step is to contact the companies themselves and obtain their financial reports. This can be done by mail or by telephone, whichever is more convenient.

Even though they are publicly traded, the companies are not obligated to mail their financial reports to nonstockholders. However, most of them will be glad to do so, whether just to help make their company better known, or perhaps to gain a new stockholder in the process. In fact, I have serendipitously come across many good investments among smaller public companies in the process of doing research for the valuation of a closely-held company.

A few companies, for whatever reasons, will refuse, or at least not bother, to send out the requested information. If they are not required to file annual reports with the SEC, this may be a dead end unless it is possible to locate a stockholder or broker who has the reports. However, if they are one of the 9,831 corporations (as of March 31, 1980) required to file annual reports with the SEC, then copies of the reports can be ordered from a company called Disclosure, Inc., discussed later in the chapter.

In deciding what information to ask for, keep in mind two purposes are to be served by the data received from the companies. The first is to learn enough about them to make a final decision on whether to use the company on the comparables list. For each company for which that decision is positive, then the second purpose is to obtain the data that the analyst desires to tabulate for the comparable companies.

If the analyst has decided to rely on five years' data for the subject company, then it would be desirable to get five years' data for each of the comparable companies. Most companies summarize five years' data in their annual reports. Also, for those companies required to meet SEC filing requirements, it is desirable to obtain the Form 10-K for the latest year. Companies are required to include a more detailed description of their business and properties in this report than they are required to include in their annual stockholder reports. Also, the larger companies are required to include replacement cost accounting data in the Form 10-K, which can be useful in cases where the analyst desires to use the ratio of price to adjusted book value approach, as discussed in Chapter 5. In some cases, proxy statements may have useful additional information, such as officer compensation and details of actual or proposed transactions.

A list of the various forms required to be filed with the SEC, and a synopsis of the content of each, is included as Exhibit 9–1, later in the chapter. Different forms may contain information of particular relevance to various valuation situations. All of the SEC filings may be ordered through Disclosure, Inc.

Once all the information has been received and reviewed by the analyst, decisions must be made about which companies to include on the list of comparables for the case at hand. The more from which to choose, the easier this part of the task usually is, and the more useful the final comparable list probably will be. If many potential comparables are available, the analyst might decide to use only those which derive 80 percent or more of their revenues from the subject company's industry. If the list of prospects is skimpy, the analyst may settle for companies that derive half or more of their revenues from the subject company's industry. If plenty of comparables are available, the analyst may impose a size criterion. For example, if the subject company had $20 million annual revenues, the analyst might decide not to consider the largest companies, perhaps those with over $100 million revenues.

The critical matter at this point is that the analyst should establish objective criteria and include all companies that meet the criteria. If a company is eliminated, there should be a good reason why it is considered less comparable than the companies that are included. The reason is that the analyst must be very careful to avoid any bias in the process of selecting comparables—bias that could lead to some unjustified positive or negative impact on the valuation.

Obviously, the more unique the subject company, the more difficult to find a good list of comparables. In some cases, the analyst may have a group of companies which he feels can help to shed some light on the valuation question, but he may consider one or a few of the group more directly comparable to the subject company than the rest. In such cases, he may tabulate data for the whole group, but elect to accord more weight to the data for those which he considers more comparable.

Once in a while a subject company will be so unique that even an exhaustive search will fail to produce any companies that can be used as comparables. Keep in mind, however, that there are a lot of little public companies out there, over 30,000, that have sold stock through a public offering at one time or another and which are still operating. Also, if the purpose of the valuation is for federal gift or estate taxes, Revenue Ruling 59–60 states that the companies may be in the same "or similar" industries. This leaves the analyst latitude to exercise reasonable judgment in selecting companies from related industries, if it is not possible to find comparable companies in the subject company's exact industry group.

THE COMPARABLE SEARCH—A SAMPLE EXERCISE

For purposes of illustration, I have chosen as our subject company a small supermarket chain with operations in Oregon and Washington. The company does no wholesaling and no manufacturing; its operations are limited strictly to the retail grocery business.

I must emphasize at the outset that the depth of the comparable search will depend greatly on the time and budget constraints placed on the appraiser. It also will depend on how "easy" the particular search is (i.e., for some companies a rather cursory search will turn up a good list of comparables). However, if good comparables are not found initially, the appraiser is forced to dig deeper.

The first step of the search is to determine the appropriate SIC number. Skimming through the *Directory of Companies Required to File Annual Reports with the Securities and Exchange Commission,* we find the broad heading Wholesale & Retail Trade. Underneath is the heading we are looking for: SEC 541 Retail Trade—Grocery & Miscellaneous Food Stores lists 89 companies. From this it is easy to track down the more specific SIC number, which is SIC 5411 Grocery Stores. Looking in the S&P *Register,* we find that there are approximately 235 such companies listed under this SIC number. A third source is the directory in the S&P *Corporation Records*. There are 91 such companies in this list, which includes only those public companies covered by Standard & Poor's.

Given these lists, the decision must be made as to how exhaustive the comparable search is to be. For example, to be most exhaustive, the 235 companies in the S&P *Register* could be cross-checked with the *National Monthly Stock Summary* to determine which are publicly-traded. This is a long and tedious process for 235 companies. There still may be some companies in the SEC list not appearing on the SIC list. To be most comprehensive, the *public* companies in the SIC classification should be combined with those in the SEC classification.

Depending on the budget and time constraints, however, the appraiser may want to go directly to the SIC number in the *Corporation Records*. In the case of grocery stores, the list is especially large, and we believe that for our purpose we can get a representative group of comparables from these 91. However, if the list was considerably smaller, say 25 or less, we would be compelled to undertake the more exhaustive search described above.

The time consideration also should be emphasized. If the appraiser is under time constraints, as we will assume here, he may not have enough lead time to write or call for annual or 10-K reports but may have to rely solely on data published by Standard & Poor's, Moody's, or other secondary sources. If this is so, it makes no sense to make an exhaustive search to find the smallest comparables available, only to find that the financial data cannot be received in the allotted time period. Thus, if either Standard & Poor's or Moody's is to be the source of financial data, it also should be the source for compiling the original list.

For our purposes, we will use as our suspect list the 91 companies in the *Corporation Records*. The next step is to look up companies in the *Corporation Records* to see: (1) what their principal lines of business are, and (2) an indication of size. Often, a company is listed in a given SIC group, even though only a very small percentage of its business pertains to that number. These companies can be eliminated quickly, as can ones which are extremely large. The results of this initial screening, plus description and size, should be included as an appendix to the written case. This is illustrated in an appendix to the sample case in Chapter 15.

Once this list is compiled and the appraiser has had time to examine briefly the suspects, he must make up some objective selection criteria. For our grocery store, we have chosen:

1. Sales not to exceed $400 million.
2. Principal area of business (say 90 percent) must result from operation of supermarkets.
3. Companies which operate principally "convenience" stores will be eliminated.
4. Companies whose operations are principally wholesale will be eliminated.

In most comparable searches, companies which are in the process of reorganization or liquidation or both, are eliminated, as are those subject to a merger offer. We may be interested in information on companies which actually have been bought out. The final section of this chapter discusses information sources for such transactions.

From this initial screening, our original suspect list of 91 companies was trimmed to a prospect list of 17. As noted earlier, the reasons why the others were rejected should appear in an appendix if a complete written case report is required. It is important to be able to track every comparable suspect from its initial selection to either its ultimate use in the comparable table or the reason for its rejection.

The next step is to call for the annual, interim, and 10–K reports of the remaining 17 companies. Once these are received, stricter selection criteria can be outlined. The appraiser must outline in detail why some companies were rejected and others kept.

Our comparable search finally resulted in ten companies. While I believe this was an especially good comparable search, it does not insure in any way that the data derived will be conclusive, which can be a source of frustration for the appraiser.

The sample case, Chapter 15, presents the details of the comparable search, including the appendix listing the suspects and prospects that were eliminated, and why. Of course, as discussed earlier, the objective of compiling the public company data is to derive some parameters that can be applied to the valuation of the subject company. Particularly important are the ratios of the public company's prices to whatever variables the analyst has decided are relevant in the subject company's case, such as earnings, revenues, book value, and dividends. The sample case in Chapter 15 contains a fold-out page showing the tabulation of the data for the comparable companies, with an accompanying discussion of how the data were used in the valuation of the subject company. Note that it is important to compile the prices for the comparable companies on the date of the valuation of the subject company, or as close to it as possible.

MERGER, ACQUISITION, AND OTHER TRANSACTION DATA

While the previous sections of this chapter dealt with data on day-to-day trading prices of stocks, it frequently is useful to have data on the prices at which entire companies or operating units of companies have been sold, or the prices at which significant interests in companies changed hands. Such data are harder to find than daily stock trading data, since there are far fewer such transactions, and also because there is no centrally organized mechanism for collecting and making available such price information.

A number of sources can be monitored to obtain data on mergers, acquisitions, and other significant transactions. Three of these are SEC filings, the *Predicasts Index of Corporate Change,* and *Mergers & Acquisitions.* There is considerable overlap among these sources, and none lead the investigator to all the data he might like to have. Of course, if there is not a public company or unit of a public company involved in either side of the transaction, there is no obligation to make public disclosure of the data, and information availability is subject to the willingness of the parties to disclose it. Even where there are SEC filings because public companies are involved, the filings do not always include all the information that the valuation analyst would like to have. It frequently is necessary to make direct contact with the companies to get the information relevant to the valuation criteria used in the transaction.

SEC Filings

If a public company is involved in a transaction, the chances are there will be a related SEC filing of one kind or another. This includes initial public offerings by companies that formerly had been private, offers to buy out public companies, and acquisitions of private companies by public companies. Exhibit 9–1 lists the various forms filed with the SEC and gives a brief summary of the content of each.

Copies of all filings made with the SEC can be ordered either in paper copy form or on microfiche from Disclosure, Inc. Disclosure also sells three indexing services to SEC filings:

1. A monthly loose-leaf service containing a listing of all reports received by Disclosure during the preceding month (available on paper only).
2. A monthly cumulative index which lists all reports received by Disclosure back to January 1 of the current year (available on microfiche only).
3. A cumulative index listing all reports received by Disclosure from January 1, 1966, through the end of last calendar year (available on microfiche only).

Predicasts Index of Corporate Change

The *Predicasts Index of Corporate Change* is published quarterly and cumulated annually. It lists acquisitions alphabetically and by SIC code. It also gives a one-line description of the transaction and a reference to a periodical or other publication where the transaction is discussed in more detail. Exhibit 9–2 is a sample excerpt from the *Predicasts Index of Corporate Change*.

Mergers & Acquisitions

Published quarterly, *Mergers & Acquisitions* is subtitled *The Journal of Corporate Venture*. Each issue contains articles about mergers and acquisitions and also a "Mergers & Acquisitions Roster." The amount of information shown for each merger varies quite a bit from one to another. Exhibit 9–3 is a sample page from the "Mergers & Acquisitions Roster."

Exhibit 9–1
A guide to SEC corporate filings

DISCLOSURE

A basic purpose of the Federal securities laws is to provide disclosure of material financial and other information on companies seeking to raise capital through the public offering of their securities, as well as companies whose securities are already publicly held. This aims at enabling investors to evaluate the securities of these companies on an informed and realistic basis.

The Securities Act of 1933 is a *disclosure* statute. It generally requires that, before securities may be offered to the public, a registration statement must be filed with the Commission disclosing prescribed categories of information. Before the sale of securities can begin, the registration statement must become "effective," and investors must be furnished a prospectus containing the most significant information in the registration statement.

The Securities Exchange Act of 1934 deals in large part with securities already outstanding and requires the registration of securities listed on a national securities exchange, as well as over-the-counter securities in which there is a substantial public interest. Issuers of registered securities must file annual and other periodic reports designed to provide a public file of current material information. The Exchange Act also requires disclosure of material information to holders of registered securities in solicitations of proxies for the election of directors or approval of corporate action at a stockholder's meeting, or in attempts to acquire control of a company through a tender offer or other planned stock acquisition. It provides that insiders of companies whose equity securities are registered must report their holdings and transactions in all equity securities of their companies.

10-K

This is the official annual business and financial report which must be filed by most companies. The financial section (Part I) must be filed within 90 days of a company's fiscal year end. Supporting data (Part II) of the 10-K contains the information normally required in a proxy statement. It must be filed within 120 days of fiscal year-end if a proxy is not filed separately in that period. Schedules to financial statements may be filed by amendment within the 120-day limit. No other source of corporate information provides more comprehensive or current information about a company than this report, with its schedules, exhibits and amendments.

ITEMS REPORTED in FORM 10-K

Part I

1—*Business.* Identifies principal products and services of the company, principal markets and methods of distribution and, if "material," competitive factors, backlog and expectation of fulfillment, availability of raw materials, importance of patents, licenses, and franchises, estimated cost of research, number of employees, and effects of compliance with ecological laws; if there is more than one line of business, for each of the last five fiscal years a statement of total sales and net income for each line which, during either of the last two fiscal years, accounted for 10 percent or more of total sales or pre-tax income

2—*Summary of Operations.* Summary of operations for each of the last five fiscal years and any additional years required to keep the summary from being misleading (per-share earnings and dividends are included). Includes explanatory material describing reasons for changes in revenues, earnings, etc.

3—*Properties.* Location and character of principal plants, mines, and other important properties and if held in fee or leased

4—*Parents and Subsidiaries.* List or diagram of all parents and subsidiaries and for each named, the percentage of voting securities owned, or other basis of control

5—*Legal Proceedings.* Brief description of material legal proceedings pending; when civil rights or ecological statutes are involved, proceedings must be disclosed

6—*Increases and Decreases in Outstanding Securities.* Information for each security including reacquired securities, new issues, securities issued in exchange for property, services or other securities, and new securities resulting from modification of outstanding securities.

7—*Changes in Securities and Changes in Security for Registered Securities.* Material changes in rights of the holders of any class of registered security, or withdrawal or substitution of assets securing any class of registered securities of the registrant.

Exhibit 9-1 (Continued)

8—*Defaults upon Senior Securities.* Material defaults in the payment of principal, interest, sinking fund or purchase fund installment, dividend, or other material default not cured within 30 days

9—*Approximate Number of Equity Security Holders.* Holders of record for each class of equity securities as of the end of the fiscal year

10—*Submission of Matters to a Vote of Security Holders.* Information relating to the convening of a meeting of shareholders, whether annual or special, and the matters voted upon, with particular emphasis on the election of directors

11—*Executive Officers of the Registrant.* List of all executive officers, nature of family relationship between them, positions and offices held

12—*Indemnification of Directors and Officers.* General effect under which any director or officer is insured or indemnified against any liability which he may incur in his capacity as such

13—*Financial Statements and Exhibits Filed.* Complete, audited annual financial information, and a list of exhibits filed

Part II

14—*Principal Security Holders and Security Holdings of Management.* Identification of owners of 10 percent or more of any class of securities and of securities held by directors and officers according to amount and percent of each class

15—*Directors of the Registrant.* Name, office, term of office, and specific background data on each

16—*Remuneration of Directors and Officers.* List of each director and 3 highest paid officers with aggregate annual remuneration exceeding $40,000—and total paid all officers and directors

17—*Options Granted to Management to Purchase Securities.* Options granted to or exercised by directors and officers since the beginning of the fiscal year

18—*Interest of Management and Others in Certain Transactions.* Material changes in significant transactions of such things as assets, pension, retirement, savings or other similar plans, or unusual loans

Schedules

I. Marketable securities. Other security investments

II. Amounts due from directors, officers, and principal holders of equity securities other than affiliates

III. Investments in securities of affiliates

IV. Indebtedness of affiliates (not current)

V. Property, plant, and equipment

VI. Idebtedness of affiliates (not current)

VII. Reserves for depreciation, depletion, and amortization of property, plant and equipment

VIII. Intangible assets

IX. Reserves for depreciation and amortization of intangible assets

X. Bonds, mortgages, and similar debt.

XI. Indebtedness to affiliates (not current)

XII. Guarantees of securities of other issuers

XIII. Reserves

XIV. Capital shares

XV. Warrants or rights

XVI. Other securities

XVII. Supplementary profit and loss information

XVIII. Income from dividends (equity in net profit and loss of affiliates)

10-Q

This is the quarterly financial report filed by most companies, which, although unaudited, provides a continuing view of a company's financial position during the year. It must be filed within 45 days of the close of a fiscal quarter.

ITEMS REPORTED in FORM 10-Q

Part I
Financial Statements

1—Income Statement

2—Balance Sheet

3—Statement of source and application of funds

4—A narrative analysis of material changes in the amount of revenue and expense items in relation to previous quarters, including the effect of any changes in accounting principals

Exhibit 9-1 (Continued)

Part II

1—Legal Proceedings. Brief description of material legal proceedings pending; when civil rights or ecological statutes are involved, proceedings must be disclosed

2—Changes in Securities. Material changes in the rights of holders of any class of registered security

3—Changes in Security for Registered Securities. Material withdrawal or substitution of assets securing any class of registered securities of the registrant

4—Defaults upon Senior Securities. Material defaults in the payment if principal, interest, sinking fund or purchase fund installment, dividend, or other material default not cured within 30 days

5—Increase in Amount Outstanding of Securities or Indebtedness. Amounts of new issues, continuing issues or reissues of any class of security or indebtedness with a reasonable statement of the purposes for which the proceeds will be used

6—Decreases in Amount Outstanding of Securities or Indebtedness. Amounts of decreases, through one or more transactions, in any class of outstanding securities or indebtedness

7—Submission of Matters to a Vote of Security Holders. Information relating to the convening of a meeting of shareholders, whether annual or special, and the matters voted upon, with particular emphasis on the election of directors

8—Other materially Important Events. Information on any other item of interest to shareholders not already provided for in this form

8-K

This is a report of unscheduled material events or corporate changes deemed of importance to the shareholders or to the SEC—changes in the control of the registrant; acquisition or disposition of assets; institution of bankruptcy or receivership; change in auditor. The report is filed within 15 days of the occurrence of a reportable event.

10-C

"Over-the-counter" companies use this form to report changes in name and amount of NASDAQ-listed securities. It is similar in purpose to the 8-K.

Form 8

Form 8 is used to amend or supplement filings previously submitted. 1933 Act registration statements are amended by filing an amended registration statement (pre-effective amendment) or by the prospectus itself, as previously noted.

Annual Report to Shareholders

The annual report to shareholders is the document that most major companies use to communicate directly with their shareholders. Since it is not an official SEC filing, companies have considerable leeway in determining what types of information this report will contain, and how it is to be presented. It often provides nonfinancial details of the business which are not reported elsewhere, including forecasts of future programs and plans.

Listing Application

Like the ARS, a listing application is not an official SEC filing. It is filed by the company with the NYSE, AMEX or other stock exchange to document proposed new listings. Usually a Form 8-A registration is filed with the SEC at about the same time.

N-1R

This report is the equivalent of the 10-K for registered management-investment firms. In addition to annual financial statements, this report shows diversification of assets, portfolio turnover activity, and capital gains experience.

N-1Q

This is the quarterly report of registered management-investment firms, which must be filed within one month after the quarter has ended. The N-1Q shows changes in portfolio securities, including the number of shares bought, sold and owned at the end of the quarter for each stock in the company's portfolio.

Exhibit 9-1 (Continued)

Registration Statements

Registration statements are of two principal types: (1) "offering registrations filed under the 1933 Securities Act, and (2) "trading" registrations filed under the 1934 Securities Exchange Act.

"Offering" registrations are used to register securities before they may be offered to investors. Part I of the registration, a preliminary prospectus or "red herring," is promotional in tone; it carries all the sales features that will be contained in the final prospectus. Part II of the registration contains detailed information about marketing agreements, expenses of issuance and distribution, relationship of the company with experts named in the registration, sales to special parties, recent sales of unregistered securities, subsidiaries of registrant, franchises and concessions, indemnification of directors and officers, treatment of proceeds from stock being registered, and financial statements and exhibits.

"Offering" registration statements vary in purpose and content according to the type of organization issuing stock:

S-1 A generalized form which may be used for registration by an issuer when no other form is authorized or prescribed

S-2 Used by "development stage" companies other than insurance, investment or mining companies

S-3 Used by operating or development stage companies which mine for minerals other than oil and natural gas

S-4 Used by closed-end investment companies registered under the Investment Company Act of 1940 on Form N-8B-1

S-5 Used by open-end investment companies (mutual funds) registered under the Invest-Act of 1940 on Form N-8B-1

S-6 Used by unit investment trusts registered under the Investment Act of 1940 on Form N-8B-2

S-7 A short form which may be used by companies which have a relatively healthy operating history and have filed under both the Secrities Act of 1933 and 1934 in a timely manner

S-8 Used to register securities to be offered to employees under stock option and various other benefit plans

S-9 Rescinded in SEC Release No. 33-5791, December 20, 1976. Previously used as a short form similar to the S-7 for the registration of debt securities. The requirements are now incorporated in Form S-7.

S-10 Used for the registration of landowners' royalty interests, overriding royalty interests, participating interests, working interests, oil or gas payments, oil or gas fee interests, oil or gas leasehold interests and other producing and non-producing oil or gas interests or rights

S-11 Used by real estate companies, primarily limited partnerships and investment trusts

S-12 Used to register American Depository Receipts issued against securities of foreign issuers deposited with an American depository

S-13 Used for the registration of certificates, agreements, etc. relating to voting and voting-trust agreements

S-14 Used to register securities for the reorganization, merger, consolidation, transfer of assets or similar plan of acquisition

S-15 No such form currently used

S-16 A short form which may be used for the registration of securities to be offered for sale by current or future security holders

"Trading" registrations are filed to permit trading among investors on a securities exchange or in the over-the-counter market. Registration statements which serve to register securities for trading fall into three categories:

(1) Form 10 is used by companies during the first two years they are subject to the 1934 Act filing requirements. It is a combination registration statement and annual report with information content similar to that of SEC-required annual reports.

(2) Form 8-A is used by 1934 Act registrants wishing to register *additional* securities for trading.

(3) Form 8-B is used by "successor issuers" (usually companies which have changed their name or state of incorporation) as notification that previously registered securities are to be traded under a new corporate identification.

Exhibit 9-1 (Concluded)

INFORMATION CONTENT of SEC FILING FORMS

Information Attributes	10-K	N-1R	7-Q	10-Q	N-1Q	8-K	10-C	Proxy Statement	Prospectus	F-10	'34 Act 8-A	'34 Act 8-B	'33 Act "S" Type	ARS	Listing Application
Auditor															
Name	A	A	S					S	A	A			A	A	S
Opinion	A	A	S							A			A		
Changes						A		S							
Compensation Plans															
Equity	S	S	S					F	F	A			F		S
Monetary	S		S						F	A			F		S
Company Information															
Nature of Business	A								A	A			A	S	S
History	F									A			A	S	S
Organization and Change	F							A	S	S	A		F	A	S
Debt Structure	A	A						S	A	A			A	A	
Depreciation and Other Schedules	A								A	A	A		A		
Dilution Factors	A					F			A	A			A	A	
Directors, Officers, Insiders															
Identification	F								A	A	A		A	F	
Background	S								F	A	S		A	S	
Holdings	S							S	A	A	A		A		
Compensation	S							S	A	A	A		A		
Earnings: Earnings Per Share	A	A	A								A		A		
Financial Information															
Annual Audited	A	A							F	A			F	A	
Interim Audited	S							S	S				S		
Interim Unaudited	F		A	S					S				S		
Foreign Operations	A							S	A	A			A	S	F
Labor Contracts				S				S		F			F		
Legal Agreements	F			S				S		F			F		
Legal Counsel				S					A				A		S
Loan Agreements	F	S	F	S				S		F			F		
Plants and Properties	A			S					F	A			F	S	
Portfolio Operations															
Content					A										
Management		A													
Product-Line Breakout	A								A				A	S	
Replacement Cost Data	S														
Securities Structure	A						S		A	A			A		
Subsidiaries	A							S	A	A			A	S	S
Underwriting				S					A	A			A		
Unregistered Securities	S			S				S	F				F		
Block Movements	S					F		S		A					S

LEGEND
A always included: included—if occurred or significant
F frequently included
S special circumstances only

Proxy Statement

A proxy statement provides official notification to designated classes of stockholders of matters to be brought to a vote at a shareholders' meeting. Proxy votes may be solicited for changing the company name, transferring large blocks of stock, electing new officers, or many other matters. Disclosures normally made via a proxy statement may in some cases be made using Form 10-K (Part II).

Prospectus

When the sale of securities as proposed in an "offering" registration statement is approved by the SEC, any changes required by the SEC are incorporated into the prospectus. This document must be made available to investors before the sale of the security is initiated. It also contains the actual offering price, which may have been changed after the registration statement was approved.

Disclosure, Inc.

Executive Offices:

5161 River Road
Washington, DC 20016
Telephone: (301) 951-1300

National Sales Office:

120 Broadway
Suite 1502
New York, NY 10005
Telephone: (212) 732-5964

European Office:

37-39 Oxford Street
London WIR 2LL
England
Telephone: 01-434 1788
Telex: 83-7704

Source: Disclosure, Inc. *A Guide To SEC Corporate Filings.*

Exhibit 9–2
Sample Pages from *Predicasts Index of Corporate Change*

ACQUISITIONS

Sample Pages

Alphabetical
Access
to Acquisitions
Arranged by
Industry

Source: *Predicasts Index of Corporate Change*, sample page on acquisitions from brochure.

Exhibit 9–3
Sample page from *Mergers & Acquisitions*

ACME-CLEVELAND CORP.
(Cleveland, OH)   (acq.)
Year end: 9-30-78
Sales: $289,509,000
Net Inc.: $13,158,000

Nobur Manufacturing Co.
(North Hollywood, CA)
Nobur Products Corp.
(North Hollywood, CA)

TERMS: *Acme-Cleveland acquired all the shares of Nobur Manufacturing and Nobur Products for $1,200,000.*
DISPOSITION: Acme-Cleveland makes capital equipment and related parts and expendable cutting tools. Nobur Manufacturing and Nobur Products manufacture specialized cutting tools.
EFFECTIVE DATE: 8-17-79

ACTON CORP.
(Acton, MA)   (acq.)
Year end: 12-31-78
Revs.: $97,966,000
Net Inc.: $4,883,000

DeCoster Egg Farms Inc.
(Turner, MA)
Year end: 12-31-78
Sales: $47,800,000
Pre-tax Inc.: $4,200,000

TERMS: *Acton acquired all the shares of DeCoster Egg Farms for $17,200,000.*
DISPOSITION: Acton produces snack foods and operates CATV systems. DeCoster Egg Farms produces 1,500,000 dozen eggs weekly.
EFFECTIVE DATE: 9-10-78

AIDLIN AUTOMATION CORP.
(Sarasota, FL)   (acq.)

Arvin Automation Inc.
(Sarasota, FL)

TERMS: *Aidlin Automation acquired all the assets of Arvin Automation from Arvin Industries for an undisclosed consideration.*
DISPOSITION: Aidlin Automation and Arvin Automation manufacture automated machinery.
EFFECTIVE DATE: 9-18-79

AKZONA INC.
(Asheville, NC)   (acq.)
Year end: 12-31-78
Sales: $868,711,000
Net Inc.: $20,832,000

General Circuits Inc.
(Rochester, NY)
Garry Manufacturing Co.
(New Brunswick, NJ)
Year end: 12-31-78
Comb. Sales: $45,000,000

TERMS: *Akzona acquired all the shares of General Circuits and Garry Manufacturing for $45,000,000.*
DISPOSITION: Akzona manufactures synthetic textile fibers, wire, cable, and electronic/electrical devices, salt products, pharmaceuticals, diagnostic products, industrial chemicals, and fashion leather. General Circuits makes printed circuit boards, while Garry Manufacturing makes interconnect devices.
EFFECTIVE DATE: 8-9-79

ALASKA AIRLINES INC.
(Seattle, WA)   (acq. int. in)
Year end: 12-31-78
Revs.: $84,246,000
Net Inc.: $7,231,000

Wien Air Alaska Inc.
(Anchorage, Alaska)
Year end: 12-31-78
Sales: $62,495,000
Net Inc.: $482,000

TERMS: *Alaska Airlines acquired a 21.3 percent interest in Wien Air Alaska for an undisclosed consideration.*
DISPOSITION: Alaska Airlines provides service between Seattle and major cities in Alaska. Wien Air Alaska provids air service within Alaska.
EFFECTIVE DATE: 8-15-79

ALEXANDER'S INC.
(New York, NY)   (acq.)
Year end: 7-31-78
Sales: $432,618,000
Net Inc.: $4,280,000

Margo's La Mode Inc.
(Dallas, TX)
Year end: 12-31-78
Sales: $38,036,000
Net Inc.: $791,000

TERMS: *Alexander's acquired all the shares of Margo's La Mode at $10.30 a share for a total consideration of $9,500,000.*
DISPOSITION: Alexander's operates 15 department stores. Margo's is an apparel chain with 72 stores in the South.
EFFECTIVE DATE: 7-26-79

ALGEMENE BANK NEDERLAND N.V.
(Amsterdam, Holland)   (acq.)

La Salle National Bank
(Chicago, IL)
Year end: 12-31-78
Total Assets: $947,000,000

TERMS: *Algemene Bank Nederland acquired the La Salle National Bank from GATX for $82,000,000.*
DISPOSITION: Algemene Bank Nederland is one of the largest Dutch banks. La Salle National Bank is one of the largest banks in Ilinois.
EFFECTIVE DATE: 8-15-79

ALLIANZ VERSICHERUNGS A.G.
(Munich, Germany)   (acq.)

Fidelity Union Life Insurance Co.
(Dallas, TX)
Year end: 12-31-78
Net Inc.: $20,556,000

TERMS: *Allianz Versicherungs acquired all the shares of Fidelity Union Life Insurance at $72.50 per share. Total value of the transaction was $370,000,000.*
DISPOSITION: Allianz Versicherungs is a major West German insurance company. Fidelity Union Life Insurance writes individual and group life insurance policies and annuities.
EFFECTIVE DATE: 9-12-79

ALLIED BANCSHARES INC.
(Houston, TX)   (acq.)
Year end: 12-31-78
Loan Int.: $103,901,000
Net Inc.: $22,891,000

Cypress Bank
(Houston, TX)
Year end: 12-31-78
Dep.: $25,437,183
Mercantile Bancshares
(Houston, TX)
Year end: 12-31-78
Dep.: 82,500,000

TERMS: *Allied Bancshares acquired all the shares of Mercantile Bancshares for $12,500,000, and all the shares of Cypress Bank for $4,000,000.*
DISPOSITION: Allied Bancshares owns all the shares of Allied Bank of Texas and 18 other Texas banks.
EFFECTIVE DATE: 7-26-79

ALLIED BANCSHARES INC.
   (acq.)

Jetero Bank
(Houston, TX)

TERMS: *Allied Bancshares acquired all the shares of the Jetero Bank for $5,600,000.*
EFFECTIVE DATE: 8-22-79

Disclosure, Inc.   Business Information Service. Washington D.C. 5161 River Rd., Washington, D.C. 20016

Provides microfiche or xerox copies of various reports filed with the SEC. Individual orders or subscription packages available.

Mergers & Acquisitions, The Journal of Corporate Venture.   McLean, Va.: Information for Industry, Inc. (quarterly) Box 36, McLean, Va. 22101

Includes comprehensive bibliography, 1972; Roster cross-index 1966–1970. Journal has merger and acquisition-related articles, roster of joint ventures, news.

Moody's Banks & Finance Manual.   New York: Moody's Investors Service. (semiweekly, with annual cumulation)

Covers insurance, finance, real estate, and investment companies. Includes five to seven-year presentation of income accounts, balance sheets, financial and operating ratios, a detailed description of the company's business, including a complete list of subsidiaries, and a capital structure section, with details on capital stock and long-term debt, with bond and preferred stock ratings.

Moody's Industrial Manual.   New York: Moody's Investors Service. (semiweekly, with annual accumulation)

Covers companies listed on the New York and American Stock Exchanges, as well as companies listed on regional American exchanges. Includes five to seven years of financial information on income accounts, balance sheets, financial and operating ratios, a detailed description of the company's business, including a complete list of subsidiaries and a capital structure section, with details on capital stock and long-term debt.

Moody's OTC Industrial Manual.   New York: Moody's Investors Service (weekly, with annual cumulation)

Over-the-counter industrial corporations are covered, with history, background, mergers and acquisitions, subsidiaries, business and products, principal plants and properties, names and titles of officers and directors. Includes financial statements, and a description of capitalization, with financial and operating ratios.

Moody's Public Utility Manual.   New York: Moody's Investors Service (semiweekly, with annual cumulation)

Includes electric and gas utilities, gas transmission companies, and telephone and water companies. Covers financial statements and operating and financial ratios, with history, background, mergers and acquisitions, subsidiaries, business, construction programs, principal plants and properties, as well as data relating to rates, franchises, and contracts.

Moody's Transportation Manual.   New York: Moody's Investors Service (semiweekly, with annual cumulation)

Covers railroads, airlines, shipping, bus, and truck lines. Also covers oil pipelines, bridge companies, and auto and truck leasing and rental companies. Includes maps of many of the larger railroad systems, plus route maps of some large airlines. Statistics showing financial and operating results are given, with historical data, location and mileage, management and security descriptions.

National Daily Quotation Service.   New York: National Quotation Bureau, Inc. (daily)

Daily stock price quotations (referred to by brokers as the "pink sheets"). The national Quotation Bureau provides the service of compiling, for a fee, any history that is needed of past price quotations which it has published.

National Monthly Stock Summary.   New York: National Quotation Bureau, Inc. (monthly, with semiannual cumulations)

Contains "a summarization of market quotations which have appeared in the National Daily Services, or have been supplied by dealers on special lists." Lists many over-the-counter and inactively traded listed stocks. Supposedly cumulates semiannually, but quotations from monthlies do not always reappear in semiannual publication.

Northwest Investment Review.   Portland, Ore.: Willamette Management Associates, Inc. (weekly), 400 Willamette Bldg., Portland, OR 97204.

Detailed investment information includes feature articles, earnings reports and estimates, scheduled meetings for publicly-held companies in the Pacific Northwest, Intermountain area, Hawaii, Alaska and western Canada.

Northwest Stock Guide.   Portland, Ore.: Willamette Management Associates, Inc. (quarterly), 400 Willamette Bldg., Portland, OR 97204.

Offers statistical data in tabular form on over 350 publicly-held companies in Alaska, Colorado, Hawaii, Idaho, Montana, Oregon, Utah, Washington, Wyoming, and western Canada.

Predicasts Index of Corporate Change.   Cleveland, Ohio: Predicasts, Inc. (quarterly, with annual cumulations) 11001 Cedar Ave., Cleveland, Ohio 41106

Guide to information in periodicals and newspapers on mergers, acquisitions, and other organizational changes that affect corporate identity. Sections list companies by SIC and alphabetically, and includes special tabulations of name changes, new companies, reorganizations, bankruptcies, liquidations, subsidiary changes, foreign operations, joint ventures. Material is available in other Predicasts indexes.

Securities and Exchange Commission.   *Directory of Companies Required to File Reports with the Securities and Exchange Commission.* Washington, D.C.: U.S. Government Printing Office. (annual)

Listing of companies required to file under the Securities Exchange Act of 1934. Arranged alphabetically and by industry group.

Standard & Poor's Corporation Records.   New York: Standard & Poor's Corp., Inc. (annual, with bi-monthly supplements)

Company descriptions and supplementary news items, plus an index. Comparable to Moody's manuals. Covers companies having both listed and unlisted securities. Company information includes history, list of subsidiaries, principal plants and properties, business and products, officers and directors, comparative income statements, balance sheet statistics, selected financial ratios, and description of outstanding securities. *Daily News Section* provides updates.

Standard & Poor's Register of Corporation, Directors and Executives. New York: Standard & Poor's Corp., Inc. (annual)

Vol. 1: Corporations; alphabetically lists over 37,000 companies, gives brief summary description with addresses, telephone numbers, corporate officers and directors. Vol. 2: Individual listings, directors and executives section; lists alphabetically the individuals serving as officers, directors, trustees, partners, and so on. Vol. 3: Indexes; gives SIC classification, geographic index, and new additions.

U.S. Office of Management and Budget. *Standard Industrial Classification Manual, 1972.* Washington, D.C.: U.S. Government Printing Office. (supplement, 1977)

Useful for defining SIC codes.

Walker's Manual of Western Corporations. Long Beach, Calif.: Walker's Manual, Inc. (annual, with monthly supplements)

Describes publicly-owned financial institutions and corporations headquartered in the 13 western states and western Canada.

Wiesenberger Investment Companies Service. *Investment Companies.* Boston: Warren, Gorham & Lamont, Inc. (annual with monthly supplements)

"An annual compendium of information about Mutual Funds and Investment Companies . . . a complete explanation of their functions and their various uses to the investor . . . data on the background, management policy and salient features of all leading companies . . . management results, income and dividend records, price ranges, and comparative operating details."

10

DATA ON DISCOUNTS FOR LACK OF MARKETABILITY

All other things being equal, an interest in a business is worth more if the interest is readily marketable, or, conversely, worth less if it is not. It is well known that investors prefer liquidity to lack of liquidity. Interests in closely-held businesses are relatively illiquid, compared with most other investments. This problem may be compounded further by restrictions on transfer of interests found in buy-sell agreements in many companies. The problem that the appraiser of closely-held businesses must solve, of course, is to quantify the effect of marketability, or lack of it, in terms of its impact on the value of the specific business interest being considered.

One body of empirical evidence specifically isolates the value of the factor of marketability from all other factors. This is the body of data on transactions in letter stocks. A letter stock is identical in all respects to the freely-traded stock of a public company except that it is restricted from trading on the open market for some period. The duration of the restrictions will vary from one situation to another. Since marketability is the only difference between the letter stock and its freely-tradeable counterpart, the appraiser should try to find differences in price at which letter stock transactions take place, compared with open market transactions in the same stock on the same date. This provides some evidence about the price spread the market placed between a readily marketable security and one that is otherwise identical but subject to certain restrictions on its marketability.

MARKETABILITY DISCOUNTS EVIDENCED BY PRICES OF RESTRICTED STOCKS

Publicly-traded corporations frequently issue letter stock in making acquisitions or raising capital because the time and cost of registering the new stock with the SEC would make registration impractical at the time of the transaction. Also, founders or other insiders may own portions of a publicly-traded company's stock that never has been registered for public trading. Even though such stock cannot be sold to the public on the open market, it may be sold under certain circumstances in private transactions. Such transactions usually must be reported to the SEC, and so become a matter of public record. Thus, there is a body of data available on the prices of private transactions in restricted securities or letter stocks that can be used for comparison with prices of the same (but unrestricted) securities eligible for trading on the open market.

Since the data represent hundreds of actual arm's-length transactions, anyone who might consider negotiating a deal involving these securities (such as receiving letter stock in connection with selling out to a public company) would be well advised to be familiar with the information. Furthermore, courts frequently reference the data on letter stock discounts in determining the amount of discount for lack of marketability appropriate in valuing interests in closely-held companies.

In a major study by the SEC of institutional investor actions, one of the topics was the amount of discount at which transactions in restricted stock

SEC INSTITUTIONAL INVESTOR STUDY

(letter stock) took place, compared to the prices of otherwise identical but unrestricted stock on the open market.[1] The most pertinent summary tables from that study are reproduced as Exhibits 10–1 and 10–2.

Exhibit 10–1 (Table XIV-45 of the SEC *Institutional Investor Study*) shows the amounts of discount from open market price on letter stock transactions broken down by the market in which the unrestricted stock trades. The four categories are New York Stock Exchange, American Stock Exchange, Over-the-Counter (reporting companies), and Over-the-Counter (nonreporting companies). A reporting company is a publicly-traded company that must file Forms 10-K, 10-Q, and other information with the SEC, and a nonreporting company is a company that has stock that is publicly-traded OTC but is not subject to the same reporting requirements. A company traded OTC can avoid becoming a reporting company either by maintaining its total assets under $1 million or by maintaining its number of stockholders under 500. As discussed in Chapter 9, Data on Comparable Companies, because of their smaller size and other characteristics, the analyst may find nonreporting publicly-traded companies more comparable to the closely-held company being valued than some of the reporting public companies.

The table shows that the discounts on the letter stocks, compared to their free-trading counterparts, were the least for NYSE listed stocks, and increased, in order, for ASE listed stocks, OTC reporting companies, and OTC nonreporting companies. For OTC nonreporting companies, the largest number of observations fell in the 30 to 40 percent discount range. Slightly over 56 percent of the OTC nonreporting companies experienced discounts greater than 30 percent on the sale of their restricted stock compared with the market price of their free-trading stock. A little over 30 percent of the OTC reporting companies experienced discounts over 30 percent, and over 52 percent experienced discounts over 20 percent.

Exhibit 10–2 (Table XIV-47 of the SEC *Institutional Investor Study*) shows the amounts of discount from open market price on letter stock transactions broken down into six groups by annual sales volume of the subject companies. There was a strong tendency for the companies with the largest sales volumes to experience the smallest discounts, and the companies with the smallest sales volumes to experience the largest discounts. Well over half the companies with sales under $5 million (the three smallest of the six size categories used) experienced discounts over 30 percent.

DATA ON INVESTMENT COMPANY PURCHASES OF RESTRICTED STOCK

One of the outgrowths of the SEC *Institutional Investor Study* was SEC *Accounting Series Releases, No. 113,* dated October 13, 1969, and *No. 118,* dated December 23, 1970, which require investment companies registered under the Investment Company Act of 1940 to disclose their policies about the

---

[1]"Discounts involved in Purchases of Common Stock" in U.S. 92d Congress, 1st Session, House. *Institutional Investor Study Report of the Securities and Exchange Commission.* Washington, D.C.: U.S. Government Printing Office (March 10, 1971), 5:2444–2456. (Document No. 92-64, Part 5).

Exhibit 10–1
Table XIV-45 of SEC *Institutional Investor Study*: Discount by trading market

	-15.0% to 0.0%		0.1% to 10.0%		10.1% to 20.0%		Discount 20.1% to 30.0%		30.1% to 40.0%		40.1% to 50.0%		50.1% to 80.0%		Total	
Trading Mkt.	No. of Trans-actions	Value of Purchases (Dollars)	No. of Trans-actions	Value of Purchases (Dollars)	No. of Trans-actions	Value of Purchases (Dollars)	No. of Trans-actions	Value of Purchases (Dollars)	No. of Trans-actions	Value of Purchases (Dollars)	No. of Trans-actions	Value of Purchases (Dollars)	No. of Trans-actions	Value of Purchases (Dollars)	No. of Trans-actions	Value of Purchases (Dollars)
Unknown	1	$ 1,500,000	2	$ 2,496,583	1	$ 205,000	...	...	2	$ 3,332,000	...	...	1	$ 1,259,995	7	$ 8,793,578
NY Stk. Exch.	7	3,760,663	13	15,111,798	13	24,503,988	10	$ 17,954,085	3	11,102,501	1	$ 1,400,000	4	5,005,068	51	78,838,103
Amer. Stk. Exch.	2	7,263,060	4	15,850,000	11	14,548,750	20	46,200,677	7	21,074,298	1	44,250	4	4,802,404	49	109,783,439
Over-the-Counter (Reporting Co.)	11	13,828,757	39	13,613,676	35	38,585,259	30	35,479,946	30	38,689,328	13	9,284,047	21	8,996,406	179	178,477,419
Over-the-Counter (Non-Reporting Co.)	5	8,329,369	9	5,265,925	18	25,122,024	17	11,229,155	25	29,423,584	20	11,377,431	18	13,505,545	112	104,253,033
Total	26	$34,681,849	67	$52,337,982	78	$102,965,021	77	$110,863,863	67	$123,621,711	35	$22,105,728	48	$33,569,418	398	$480,145,572

Exhibit 10–2
Table XIV-47 of SEC *Institutional Investor Study*: Discount by sales of issuer

	50.1% or More		40.1% to 50.0%		30.1% to 40.0%		Discount 20.1% to 30.0%		10.1% to 20.0%		0.1% to 10.0%		Total	
Sales of Issuer (000's)	No. of Trans-actions	Size of Trans-actions (Dollars)	No. of Trans-actions	Size of Trans-actions (Dollars)	No. of Trans-actions	Size of Trans-actions (Dollars)	No. of Trans-actions	Size of Trans-actions (Dollars)	No. of Trans-actions	Size of Trans-actions (Dollars)	No. of Trans-actions	Size of Trans-actions (Dollars)	No. of Trans-actions	Size of Trans-actions (Dollars)
Less than $100	11	$2,894,999	7	$ 2,554,000	17	$19,642,364	16	$12,197,394	6	$12,267,292	9	$12,566,000	66	$ 62,122,049
$100 - $999	7	474,040	2	1,221,000	...	...	1	500,000	1	1,018,500	2	3,877,500	13	7,091,040
$1,000 - $4,999	8	4,605,505	13	8,170,747	12	10,675,150	15	9,865,951	10	9,351,738	3	2,295,200	61	44,964,291
$5,000 - $19,999	6	1,620,015	4	1,147,305	13	25,986,008	25	27,238,210	24	21,441,347	47	12,750,481	119	90,183,366
$20,000 - $99,999	3	605,689	3	4,372,676	6	11,499,250	8	11,817,954	18	22,231,737	17	36,481,954	55	87,009,260
$100,000 or More	2	1,805,068	...	...	2	2,049,998	3	7,903,586	10	24,959,483	7	10,832,925	24	47,551,060
Total	37	$12,005,316	29	$17,465,728	50	$69,852,770	68	$69,523,095	69	$91,270,097	85	$78,804,060	338	$338,921,066

Source: "Discounts involved in Purchases of Common Stock" in U.S. 92d Congress, 1st Session. House: Institutional Investor Study Report of the Securities and Exchange Commission. Washington, D.C.: U.S. Government Print Off. (March 10, 1971), 5:2444-2456. (Document No. 92-64, Part 5).

cost and valuation of their restricted securities. The result is that now an ongoing body of data is available on the relationship between restricted stock prices and their freely tradeable counterparts, which can provide empirical bench marks for quantifying marketability discounts.

Moroney study

In an article published in the March 1973 issue of *Taxes,*[2] Robert E. Moroney presented the results of a study of the prices paid for restricted securities by ten registered investment companies. There were 146 purchases reflected. The results of that study are reproduced as Exhibit 10–3.

Moroney points out:

It goes without saying that each cash purchase of a block of restricted equity securities fully satisfied the requirement that the purchase price be one "at which the property would change hands between a willing buyer and a willing seller, neither being under any compulsion to buy or to sell and both having reasonable knowledge of relevant facts." Reg. Sec. 20.2031-1(b).[3]

Moroney contrasts the evidence of the actual cash deals with the lower average discounts for lack of marketability adjudicated in most prior court decisions on gift and estate tax cases. He points out, however, that the empirical evidence on the prices of restricted stocks was not available as a bench mark to quantify marketability discounts at the times of the prior cases, and suggests that higher discounts for lack of marketability should be allowed in the future now that the relevant data are available. As Moroney puts it:

Obviously the courts in the past have overvalued minority interests in closely-held companies for federal tax purposes. But most (probably all) of those decisions were handed down without benefit of the facts of life recently made available for all to see.

Some appraisers have for years had a strong gut feeling that they should use far greater discounts for nonmarketability than the courts had allowed. From now on those appraisers need not stop at 35 percent merely because it's perhaps the largest discount clearly approved in a court decision. Appraisers can now cite a number of known arm's-length transactions in which the discount ranged up to 90 percent.[4]

In another article four years later, Moroney makes the point that courts have started to recognize higher discounts for lack of marketability:

The thousands and thousands of minority holders in closely-held corporations throughout the United States have good reason to rejoice because the courts in recent years have upheld illiquidity discounts in the 50 percent area.*

*Edwin A. Gallun, CCH Dec. 32,830(M), 33 T.C.M. 1316 (1974) allowed 55 percent. *Est. of Maurice Gustave Heckscher,* CCH Dec. 33,023, 63 T.C. 485 (1975) allowed 48 percent. Although *Est. of Ernest E. Kirkpatrick,* CCH Dec. 33,524(M), 34 T.C.M. 1490 (1975) found per share values without mentioning discount, expert witnesses for both sides used 50 percent—the first time a government witness recommended 50 percent. A historic event, indeed!

---

[2]Robert E. Moroney, "Most Courts Overvalue Closely-Held Stocks," *Taxes* (March 1973), pp. 144–54.

[3]Ibid, p. 151.

[4]Ibid., p. 154.

Exhibit 10–3
Original purchase discounts for restricted stocks (discounts from the quoted market value of the same corporation's "free" stock of the same class)

Investment Company		Original Purchase Discount	Number of Blocks
Bayrock Growth Fund, Inc., New York City (formerly Fla. Growth Fund)	4	blocks bought at discounts of 12%, 23%, 26%, 66%, respectively	4
Diebold Venture Capital Corp., New York City	6	blocks bought at discounts of 16%, 20%, 20%, 23%, 23%, 50%, respectively	6
Enterprise Fund, Inc., Los Angeles	10	blocks bought at discounts of 31%, 36%, 38%, 40%, 49%, 51%, 55%, 63%, 74%, 87%, respectively	10
Harbor Fund, Inc., Los Angeles	1	block bought at a discount of 14%	1
Inventure Capital Corp., Boston		At acquisition dates all blocks were valued at cost	---
Mates Investment Fund, Inc., New York City	1	block bought at a discount of 62%	1
New America Fund, Inc., Los Angeles (formerly Fund of Letters, Inc.)	32	blocks bought at discounts of 3%, 3%, 14%, 14%, 16%, 21%, 25%, 26%, 27%, 33%, 33%, 33%, 35%, 36%, 36%, 37%, 37%, 39%, 40%, 40%, 43%, 44%, 46%, 47%, 49%, 51%, 53%, 53%, 56%, 57%, 57%, 58%, respectively	32
Price Capital Corp., New York City	7	blocks bought at discounts of 15%, 29%, 29%, 32%, 40%, 44%, 52%, respectively	7
SMC Investment Corp., Los Angeles	12	blocks bought at 30% premium, discounts 4%, 25%, 26%, 32%, 33%, 34%, 38%, 46%, 48%, 50%, 78%, respectively	12
Value Line Development Capital Corp., New York City	35	blocks bought at discounts of 10%, 15%, 15%, 15%, 15%, 15%, 20%, 23%, 28%, 28%, 28%, 30%, 30%, 30%, 30%, 30%, 32.5%, 35%, 40%, 40%, 40%, 40%, 40%, 40%, 45%, 50%, 50%, 50%, 50%, 53%, 55%, 55%, 65%, 70%, 90%, respectively	35
Value Line Special Situations Fund, Inc., New York City	38	blocks bought at discounts of 10%, 13%, 15%, 15%, 17%, 17%, 20%, 20%, 20%, 23%, 25%, 25%, 25%, 26.5%, 27%, 27%, 30%, 30%, 30%, 30%, 30%, 30%, 30%, 30%, 33%, 37.5%, 40%, 40%, 40%, 40%, 45%, 55%, 55%, 56%, 56%, 60%, 81%, respectively	38

Source: Robert E. Moroney, "Most Courts Overvalue Closely-Held Stock," *Taxes* (March 1973), pp. 144–54.

Nevertheless, perhaps we appraisers ought to think of 35 percent or thereabouts as the norm, subject to adjustment up or down according to the facts of each case. We shall certainly gain strong support from many minority stockholders who have tried to sell at that level without getting so much as a nibble.[5]

---

[5]Robert E. Moroney, "Why 25 percent Discount for Nonmarketability in One Valuation, 100 percent in Another?" *Taxes* (May 1977), p. 320.

Maher study

Another well-documented study on marketability discounts for closely-held business interests was done by J. Michael Maher and was published in the September 1976 issue of *Taxes*.[6] Maher's approach was similar to Moroney's, comparing prices paid for restricted stocks with the market prices of their unrestricted counterparts. He found that funds were not purchasing restricted securities during 1974 and 1975, which were very depressed years for the stock market. Therefore, the data actually used covered the five-year period 1969 through 1973. The study showed that "The mean discount for lack of marketability for the years 1969–73 amounted to 35.43 percent."[7] He also eliminated the top 10 percent and the bottom 10 percent of purchases made in an effort to remove an especially high and low risk situation. The result was almost identical with the "outliers" removed, with a mean discount of 34.73 percent.

Maher concludes:

The result I have reached is that most appraisers underestimate the proper discount for lack of marketability. The results seem to indicate that this discount should be about 35 percent. Perhaps this makes sense because by committing funds to restricted common stock, the willing buyer (a) would be denied the opportunity to take advantage of other investments, and (b) would continue to have his investment at the risk of the business until the shares could be offered to the public or another buyer is found.

The 35 percent discount would not contain elements of a discount for a minority interest because it is measured against the current fair market value of securities actively traded (other minority interests). Consequently, appraisers should also consider a discount for a minority interest in those closely-held corporations where a discount is applicable.[8]

Solberg study of court decisions

Solberg[9] conducted a study of 15 cases in which the courts valued restricted securities. He discussed Revenue Ruling 77-287 and federal securities law, especially Rules 144 and 237. Of the 15 cases, the range of discounts from market value was 10 to 90 percent, with a median of 38.9 and a mean of 37.4 percent. He concluded:

The valuation of restricted securities is not a numbers game, and each case must stand on its own facts as presented to the court. Legal precedent, in terms of discounts granted in cases previously decided, is not as important as the nature, quality and quantity of the evidence and the skill with which that evidence is marshalled and presented. The cases indicate that the courts, if provided with the factual basis to do

---

[6]J. Michael Maher, "Discounts for Lack of Marketability for Closely-Held Business Interests," *Taxes* (September 1976), pp. 562–71.

[7]Ibid. p. 571.

[8]Ibid. p. 571.

[9]Thomas A. Solberg, "Valuing Restricted Securities: What Factors Do the Courts and the Service Look For," *Journal of Taxation* (September 1979), pp. 150–54.

so, are willing to grant significant discounts for restricted securities to properly reflect the economic realities of the marketplace.[10]

The results of the Solberg study are shown as Exhibit 10–4.

In 1977 the Internal Revenue Service specifically recognized the relevance of the data discussed in the foregoing sections in Revenue Ruling 77-287. The purpose of the ruling is "to provide information and guidance to taxpayers, Internal Revenue Service personnel, and others concerned with the valuation,

REVENUE RULING 77-287

---

[10]Ibid. p. 153.

Exhibit 10–4
Cases in which the court valued restricted securities

	Case Name and Citation	Discounts Considered	Market Price	IRS Value	Taxpayer's Value	Court's Value	Discount From Market
1.	Goldwasser, 47 BTA 445 (1942) aff'd 142 F.2d 555 (CA-2, 1944) cert. den.	Restricted Securities	$ 82.25	$ 75.88	$ 54.87	$ 68.00	17.3%
2.	Conroy, TCM 1958-6	Restricted Securities	$ 5.00	NA	$1.00-$2.00	$ 3.50	30%
3.	Victorson, TCM 1962-231	Restricted Securities	$ .85	$ .85	NA¹	$ .50	40%
4.	Simmons, TCM 1964-237 (involved two securities)	Restricted Securities and Blockage	$ 3.50 / $ 1.00	$ 2.75 / $ 1.00	NA¹ / NA¹	$ 2.75 / $ .75	21.4% / 25%
5.	Specialty Paper and Board Co., Inc., TCM 1965-208	Restricted Securities and Blockage	$ 5.12	$ 4.50	NA¹	$ 2.85	44.4%
6.	LeVant, 45 TC 185 (1965) rev'd 376 F.2d 434 (CA-7, 1967)	Restricted Securities	$ 39.06	$ 39.06	$ 31.50	$ 31.50	19.4%
7.	Husted, 47 TC 644 (1967)	Restricted Securities and Blockage	$ 11.25	$ 11.25	$4.20-$5.25	$ 7.00	37.7%
8.	Jacobowitz, TCM 1968-261	Restricted Securities	$ 10.00²	$ 10.00	$ 1.00¹	$ 4.50	55%
9.	Alves, DC Mo., 4/11/69	Restricted Securities and Voting Trust Certificates	$103.00⁴	$103.00	$ 77.25	$ 77.25	25%
10.	Bolles, 69 TC 342 (1977) (involved three securities)	Restricted Securities and Blockage	$ 22.62 / $ 14.30 / $ 12.60	$ 15.00 / $ 6.50 / $ 12.00 / $ 12.00⁶	NA¹ / NA¹ / NA¹ / $ -0-	$ 12.44 / $ 1.43 / $ 9.83 / $ -0-	45% / 90% / 22%
11.	Roth, TCM 1977-426	Restricted Securities and Blockage	$ 2.68	$ 2.00	$ .75¹	$ 1.07	60%
12.	Strouse, TCM 1978-55 (involved two dates)	Restricted Securities	$ 36.00 / $ 34.00	$ 34.00 / $ 32.00	$ 6.00 / $ 6.00	$ 21.00 / $ 19.20	40% / 43.5%
13.	Estate of Doelle, DC Mich., 5/19/73	Restricted Securities and Voting Trust	NA⁸	$ 3.12	$ .083	$ .085⁹ / $ .09⁹	NA¹⁰
14.	Wheeler, TCM 1978-208	Restricted Securities, Blockage Denied	$ 5.87	NA	$ 2.15	$ 5.29	10%
15.	Kessler, TCM 1978-491	Restricted Securities	$ 7.09	$ 4.96	$ .50	$ 3.67	48.2%

¹ Taxpayer argued that the stock had no ascertainable value due to Securities Act restrictions.
² Public offering took place 2½ months after the valuation date. Offering price to public was $10.
³ Taxpayer reported value initially at $5.50, but later changed his value to $1.00. Taxpayer's expert testified stock was worth $1.10.
⁴ Market price for shares was $101 bid, $105 asked. Plaintiff made gift of voting trust certificates representing shares and valued them at 75% of mean share value.
⁵ Taxpayer sought greater discounts than court allowed on debentures.

The court probably adopted the taxpayer's value on the warrants and common stock, but this is not clear from opinion.
⁶ Taxpayer had a guaranty of questionable enforceability that the three securities would have a total value of $45.50. IRS valued the guaranty agreement at $12.00. The Court disregarded the guaranty.
⁷ Reduced from $1.00 claimed on original tax return.
⁸ No evidence introduced as to market price.
⁹ Stock in voting trust was valued at $.085 and stock not in voting trust at $.09.
¹⁰ Cannot be computed without a market value figure.

Source: Thomas A. Solberg, "Valuing Restricted Securities." *Journal of Taxation* (September 1979), pp. 150–54. © 1979 *The Journal Of Taxation*. Reprinted with permission of author and publisher.

for Federal tax purposes, of securities that cannot be immediately resold because they are restricted from resale pursuant to Federal security laws."[11]

The ruling specifically references the SEC *Institutional Investor Study* and the values of restricted securities purchased by investment companies as part of the "relevant facts and circumstances that bear upon the worth of restricted stock."

CONCLUSION

The four studies discussed are quite consistent in indicating an average discount for lack of marketability of approximately 35 percent for restricted stocks of publicly-traded companies. Most such securities eventually will be registered, and become freely tradeable.

Shares of closely-held companies, most of which will never be freely tradeable, suffer more from lack of marketability than do restricted shares of publicly-traded companies. Once the analyst has made his best estimate of the price at which the shares involved in the valuation would sell if they were freely marketable, the discounts at which restricted securities of publicly-traded companies sell can provide useful guidance to determine an appropriate marketability discount.

---

[11]*Revenue Ruling 77-287 (1977-2 C.B. 319), Section 1.*

III

FINANCIAL STATEMENT
ANALYSIS

11

ANALYZING AND ADJUSTING FINANCIAL STATEMENTS

ADEQUACY OF ALLOWANCE AND RESERVE ACCOUNTS
   Allowance for doubtful accounts
   Reserves for self-insurance
   Pension liabilities

INVENTORY ACCOUNTING METHODS
   Fifo, Lifo, and other methods
   Write-down and write-off policies

DEPRECIATION METHODS AND SCHEDULES

DEPLETION

TREATMENT OF INTANGIBLES

CAPITALIZATION VERSUS EXPENSING OF VARIOUS COSTS

TIMING OF RECOGNITION OF REVENUES AND EXPENSES
   Contract work
   Installment Sales
   Sales involving actual or contingent liabilities
   Prior-period adjustments

ACCOUNTING FOR LEASES

ACCOUNTING FOR CERTAIN TAX ASPECTS
   Investment tax credits
   Tax loss carryforwards

TREATMENT OF INTERESTS IN AFFILIATES

EXTRAORDINARY OR NONRECURRING ITEMS
   Ordinary versus extraordinary items
   Other nonrecurring items
   Discontinued operations

OPERATING VERSUS NONOPERATING ITEMS

MANAGEMENT COMPENSATION AND PERQUISITES

TRANSACTIONS INVOLVING COMPANY INSIDERS

CONTINGENT ASSETS AND LIABILITIES

ADJUSTMENTS TO ASSET VALUATIONS
   Marketable securities
   Other assets

COMPUTATION OF EARNINGS PER SHARE
   Weighted average basis
   Primary versus fully diluted earnings

COMPUTATION OF BOOK VALUE PER SHARE

AN EXAMPLE OF THE EFFECT OF ALTERNATIVE ACCOUNTING METHODS

ADJUSTING BALANCE SHEET TO CURRENT VALUES

. . . within the framework of generally accepted accounting principles (GAAP) there is some latitude permitted in the preparation of financial statements.[1]

The financial analyst not only knows that the above statement is true but that it may be considered the understatement of the century. Rarely do any two firms follow exactly the same set of accounting practices in keeping their books and preparing their financial statements, even within the broad confines of generally accepted accounting principles. Furthermore, the typical closely-held company does not go to the expense of having financial statements audited, and many deviations from GAAP are encountered. Therefore, the analyst must evaluate each item and make adjustments for differences in accounting practices if two or more companies are to be compared, or if a company is to be measured against some industry or other standard.

Furthermore, all discussion of financial statement analysis in this book is subject to the caveat that generally accepted accounting principles are constantly being reviewed and changed. Accounting principles were prescribed by the Accounting Principles Board (APB) until 1974, when that function was taken over by the Financial Accounting Standards Board (FASB). The FASB is broader than the APB in that it includes representation from financial analysts and from corporate issuers of financial statements as well as from the accounting profession. The first FASB statement was issued toward the end of 1974, and as of this writing there already have been 37 such statements, many with sweeping implications for the use and interpretation of financial statements. In addition to the accounting requirements prescribed by the FASB, companies that are publicly traded are also subject to additional disclosure requirements prescribed by the SEC. The material in Part III is intended primarily as a framework for the nonspecialist rather than a comprehensive treatise on financial statement analysis, which is the subject of other complete books, some of which are referenced in the bibliography. The practitioner of business valuations must make it his business to have sources of information on the current status of accounting principles as they affect any particular business he may be valuing.

Since earning power is the most important element in the majority of business valuations, the point of analyzing income statements usually is to better understand and interpret the earning power that the income statements represent. Adjustments to the earning power as shown in the income statements generally fall into any or all of three categories:

1. Adjustments to the way the company has elected to account for what it has done.
2. Adjustments to reflect the likelihood that certain things in the future may be different than in the past, since certain aspects of past operations may not be representative of future earning power.

[1]George D. McCarthy and Robert E. Healy, *Valuing a Company: Practices and Procedures,* (New York: John Wiley & Sons, 1971), p. 16.

3. Adjustments for certain discretionary items, such as generous management bonuses.

Asset values also play a role to a greater or lesser degree in different valuation situations, so it may be appropriate to make certain adjustments to balance-sheet accounts for analytical purposes. Since the income statement and balance sheet are interdependent, some variables adjusted for income statement analysis will imply adjustments to the balance sheet. In other cases there may be appropriate balance-sheet adjustments, especially to nonoperating assets, that would not affect the company's ongoing earning power.

This chapter discusses the most common categories of adjustments to the income statement and to the balance sheet that the business valuation analyst may wish to consider. References to more complete discussions of the various items, including complete books on financial statement analysis, are included in the bibliography.[2]

This chapter first discusses adjustments that tend to arise from the differing treatment of measurements of asset and liability items, then moves to a number of items that arise from the treatment of revenue and expense items, and finally addresses a number of miscellaneous items.

ADEQUACY OF ALLOWANCE AND RESERVE ACCOUNTS

There is no end to the possible variety of reserve or allowance accounts that will be encountered from time to time. Each should be questioned and analyzed on its own merits. Some so-called reserve accounts should not be considered reserve accounts at all, but merely portions of equity that management has chosen to earmark for some future expenditure or contingency.

It is not uncommon to find that a company is either underreserved or overreserved for certain items. If underreserved, the effect is an overstatement of earnings because of inadequate reserve charges to expenses, with an accompanying overstatement of net asset value. If overreserved, the opposite is the case.

Allowance for doubtful accounts

Most companies carry accounts receivable, with some allowance deducted for potentially uncollectible accounts. The typical policy is to charge some percentage of credit sales to bad debt expense at the time the sales are made. Often a charge at the end of each month, reflecting that month's credit sales, is made with a credit to Allowance for Doubtful Accounts, which shows up as a deduction from Accounts Receivable on the balance sheet. Then as individual accounts are written off, they are credited against Accounts Receivable and debited against Allowance for Doubtful Accounts, with no direct effect on either earnings or net asset value at the time of the actual write-off.

---

[2]See, for example, Leopold A. Bernstein, *Financial Statement Analysis: Theory Application and Interpretation*, rev. ed. (Homewood, Ill.: Richard D. Irwin, 1978). © 1978 by Richard D. Irwin, Inc.

Since the expense charge actually represents an estimate of future write-offs, the analyst must make some judgment as to the accuracy of that estimate, at least in cases where the effect might be material. One way is to compare the historical percentage of bad debt losses to the percentage of current credit sales being charged to bad debt expense to see if too little or too much is being charged currently. Another approach is to compare the Aged Accounts Receivable schedule with the current Allowance for Doubtful Accounts to make a judgment on whether the allowance is reasonable relative to the amount of overdue accounts. Some companies tend to carry receivables on their books forever, with little or no doubtful account allowance, resulting in overstatement of earnings and net asset value. Other companies follow a very aggressive write-off policy, removing from their books many accounts which eventually are collected, tending to understate earnings and net asset value.

While looking at accounts receivable, the analyst should also check to see whether there may be any notes or other receivables which may be questionable, and make appropriate adjustments if indicated.

Reserve for self-insurance

Some companies elect to self-insure instead of paying premiums to insure against such contingencies as property and casualty losses or product liability. In these cases, the company should expense reasonable amounts to a self-insurance expense account as it goes along, building a reserve to cover potential losses when and if they occur.

For example, in an industry in which product liability claims are common, a company that elects not to carry product liability insurance should build up a reserve against which to charge potential claims. Failure to do so can be interpreted as an overstatement of earnings and net asset value. A reasonable adjustment for the analyst to make in such a case could be based on the amount that typical insurance premiums would cost if insurance were purchased.

It also is entirely possible, of course, that a company may be overreserved, indicating an appropriate upward adjustment in earnings and net asset value.

Pension liabilities

Many companies, especially older, larger companies, do not have their pension liabilities fully funded. If the financial statements are audited, unfunded pension liabilities will be indicated in a footnote. In some cases the effect can be substantial. The effect of unfunded pension liability is an item that the analyst should take into consideration where appropriate.

INVENTORY ACCOUNTING METHODS

Fifo, or "first in, first out," means that the first unit of an inventory item purchased is the first unit considered sold for accounting purposes. Lifo, or

Fifo, Lifo, and other methods

"last in, first out," means that the last purchased unit of an inventory item is the first unit considered sold for accounting purposes.

The difference between Fifo and Lifo accounting shows up in the ending inventory on the balance sheet, at the same time impacting the Cost of Goods Sold and thus the earnings.

To the extent that prices go up, Lifo results in lower figures for earnings and inventory than does Fifo. Since Lifo accounting is acceptable for federal income tax purposes, there has been a widespread trend for companies to adopt Lifo rather than Fifo inventory accounting in response to inflation.

If two or more companies are being compared for valuation purposes, the earnings and asset values of one or more should be adjusted when they are not all on the same inventory accounting basis, if the differences are substantial enough to have a material impact on the valuation.

Take a simple example of a company that started its accounting period with 30 widgets, which it purchased for $10 each, and purchased 60 more widgets during the accounting period at $15 each, then ended the period with an inventory of 40 widgets. The comparative Cost of Goods Sold under Fifo versus Lifo would be computed as follows:

	Fifo		**Lifo**	
Beginning inventory .... 30 units @ $10 =	$300	30 units @ $10 =	$300
Purchases .... 60 units @ $15 =	$900	60 units @ $15 =	$900
Goods available for sale	$1,200		$1,200
Ending inventory .... 40 units @ $15 =	$600	30 units @ $10 =	$300
		10 units @ $15 =	150
			$450
Cost of goods sold	$600		$750

In other words, under Lifo, the accounting perpetrates the fiction that the original units in the inventory are the ones that are still there. In the above case, if the sales were $1,000, the gross margin would be $400 under Fifo accounting and $250 under Lifo accounting.

For most companies that report on Fifo, the information is not readily available to enable the analyst to adjust earnings and inventory to the Lifo basis. If a company reporting on Lifo has audited statements, the footnotes will provide the information necessary to adjust earnings and inventory values from Lifo to Fifo. If the statements of a company reporting on Lifo are not audited, then the company's accountant should be able to provide the analyst with the necessary information to adjust to a Fifo basis. Therefore, because of the availability of the necessary information, if one or more companies' inventory accounting needs to be adjusted for comparative purposes, the adjustments usually have to be on the Lifo reporting companies to a Fifo basis.

Keep in mind that if an upward adjustment to earning power is made on the basis of adjusting from Lifo to Fifo earnings, such adjustment should be net of the related additional income taxes that would be incurred.

A few companies also account for inventory on some type of an average cost basis, but they are unusual enough not to warrant a discussion of that type of inventory accounting in this book.[3]

Regardless of whether the Fifo, Lifo, or average cost inventory method is used, most companies adhere to the "lower of cost or market" principle, which says that the carrying value should be reduced if the market value is less than cost. Market value for this purpose is defined as "current replacement cost except that market shall not be higher than net realizable value nor should it be lower than net realizable value reduced by the normal profit margin."[4]

Write-down and write-off policies

Implementation of the lower of cost or market principle varies tremendously—one company may have stockrooms full of obsolete inventory, while another company may have an aggressive program of automatic write-downs and write-offs of inventory on the basis of the number of months it has been in stock. Where a company goes to one extreme or the other in making or failing to make adjustments to inventory values, in its implementation of the lower of cost or market principle, appropriate adjustments to earnings and asset values may be necessary.

The three most common methods of computing depreciation charges, all acceptable to the IRS for income tax purposes, are straight line, declining balance, and sum of the years' digits. Regardless of which method is used, the decision as to the number of years' useful life over which the asset will be depreciated is of crucial importance.

DEPRECIATION METHODS AND SCHEDULES

The straight-line method simply charges depreciation on the asset in even increments over the asset's useful life. The declining-balance and sum-of-the-years'-digits methods are called "accelerated methods" because they charge a higher proportion of the total depreciation in the early years of the asset's useful life compared with the straight-line method.

In the declining-balance method, some multiple, such as two times or one and half times the normal depreciation rate, is used. For example, if an asset had a useful life of ten years, straight-line depreciation would be at the rate of 10 percent per year. Double declining balance depreciation would be at twice that rate, or 20 percent, but with the percentage always applied to the remaining depreciated balance. In other words, in the first year a $100,000 piece of equipment with a ten-year life would be depreciated at 20 percent of $100,000, or $20,000, leaving a depreciated balance of $80,000. The second year the asset would be depreciated at 20 percent of $80,000, or $16,000, leaving a depreciated balance of $64,000.

In the sum-of-the-years' digits method, the depreciation charge is a fraction

---

[3]For a discussion of the average cost method, see Bernstein, *Financial Statement Analysis,* pp. 125–26, 137–38.

[4]Ibid., p. 130.

whose denominator is the sum of the year's digits of the asset's useful life, and the numerator is the number of years remaining of useful life. Thus, for a ten-year useful life, the denominator is $(1 + 2 + 3 + 4 + 5 + 6 + 7 + 8 + 9 + 10) = 55$. The numerator the first year is 10, so the first year the depreciation charge is $10/55$ths of the asset's value, in the second year $9/55$ths, and so on. Exhibit 11–1 gives an example of the depreciation computations under each of the three methods for an asset costing $100,000 and depreciated over a ten-year life.

In some cases, a residual or salvage value at the end of the depreciable life may be assumed. In this case, the difference between the cost and salvage value is the depreciable amount. Note, however, that salvage value normally would not be deducted from cost in the declining-balance method, because that method never results in the asset being depreciated to zero.

Another depreciation method sometimes used is units of utilization. If a

Exhibit 11–1
Examples of depreciation computations

STRAIGHT LINE METHOD

Year	Computation	Year's Depreciation Charge	Cumulative Depreciation Charge	Balance After Depreciation
1	10% x $100,000	$10,000	$ 10,000	$90,000
2	10% x 100,000	10,000	20,000	80,000
3	10% x 100,000	10,000	30,000	70,000
4	10% x 100,000	10,000	40,000	60,000
5	10% x 100,000	10,000	50,000	50,000
6	10% x 100,000	10,000	60,000	40,000
7	10% x 100,000	10,000	70,000	30,000
8	10% x 100,000	10,000	80,000	20,000
9	10% x 100,000	10,000	90,000	10,000
10	10% x 100,000	10,000	100,000	0

200% DECLINING BALANCE METHOD

Year	Computation	Year's Depreciation Charge	Cumulative Depreciation Charge	Balance After Depreciation
1	20% x $100,000	$20,000	$ 20,000	$80,000
2	20% x 80,000	16,000	36,000	64,000
3	20% x 64,000	12,800	48,800	51,200
4	20% x 51,200	10,240	59,040	40,960
5	20% x 40,960	8,192	67,232	32,768
6	20% x 32,768	6,554	73,786	26,214
7	20% x 26,214	5,243	79,029	20,971
8	20% x 20,971	4,194	83,223	16,777
9	20% x 16,777	3,355	86,578	13,422
10	20% x 13,422	2,684	89,262	10,738

SUM OF THE YEARS' DIGITS METHOD

Year	Computation	Year's Depreciation Charge	Cumulative Depreciation Charge	Balance After Depreciation
1	10/55 (.18182) x $100,000	$18,182	$ 18,182	$81,818
2	9/55 (.16364) x 100,000	16,364	34,546	65,454
3	8/55 (.14545) x 100,000	14,545	49,091	50,909
4	7/55 (.12727) x 100,000	12,727	61,818	38,182
5	6/55 (.10909) x 100,000	10,909	72,727	27,273
6	5/55 (.09091) x 100,000	9,091	81,818	18,182
7	4/55 (.07273) x 100,000	7,273	89,091	10,909
8	3/55 (.05455) x 100,000	5,455	94,546	5,454
9	2/55 (.03636) x 100,000	3,636	98,182	1,818
10	1/55 (.01818) x 100,000	1,818	100,000	0

$100,000 asset is expected to provide 10,000 hours of useful service, it might be depreciated on the basis of $10 for each hour that it is used.

The analyst should make some judgment on the appropriateness of the depreciation schedule in an absolute sense, and also in a relative sense if comparisons are to be made with other companies. Consider the situation where a company is using an eight-year useful life for equipment that it manufactures and leases to customers, while almost everybody else in the industry is using a six-year useful life because the conventional wisdom says that the high degree of technological innovation in the industry is causing a six-year obsolescence cycle. The situation suggests that the analyst should make a downward adjustment to the earnings base and a downward adjustment to the net depreciated value of the equipment to reflect the apparently inadequate depreciation charges. There can be fairly wide ranges within the parameters of industry norms. Considerable research could be necessary to reach an informed judgment on the reasonable depreciation life for some types of assets.

Let's say that we are valuing a closely-held company by a multiple of earnings approach, and that about seven times earnings seems appropriate based on current market multiples of earnings at which publicly-traded companies in the industry are selling. Let's say, however, that the publicly-held companies are reporting for financial statement purposes on the basis of straight-line depreciation, while our company is reporting on an accelerated depreciation basis. The analyst would want to adjust the closely-held company's earnings to a straight-line basis (remembering also to adjust the related income taxes) before applying the publicly-traded company multiple, so that the earnings to be capitalized would be stated on a comparative basis. Usually a reasonable approximation is satisfactory for this kind of an adjustment.

DEPLETION

Depletion is the process of charging the cost of a natural resource to expense over the time during which it is extracted. It applies to such natural resources as metals and hydrocarbons in the ground and to timber stands.

The basic concept of depletion accounting is simple: If a natural resource cost $1 million and 5 percent of it is removed in a year, the depletion expense charged is 5 percent $\times$ $1,000,000 = $50,000. A like amount is credited to the Allowance for Depletion account on the balance sheet, reducing the net carrying value of the natural resource asset. The problems in application are basically problems of measurement. How much of the natural resource is there? What is included in "cost" of a natural resource undergoing continuous development? Where depletion is involved, the analyst should inquire about how it is measured and the extent to which the company's depletion accounting practices may conform to or depart from industry norms. While depletion is a relatively easy concept to define, it is a very difficult item to measure. Reasonable estimates can be subject to wide variations.

TREATMENT OF INTANGIBLES

Accounting for intangibles is one of the areas where practices vary most widely among different companies. The following are some examples of intangible assets:

1. Patents.
2. Trademarks.
3. Copyrights.
4. Goodwill.
5. Customer lists.
6. Employment contracts.
7. Covenants not to compete.
8. "Intangible drilling costs" or similar natural resource development costs.
9. Natural resource exploration rights.
10. Franchises.
11. Licenses.

Accounting principles state that intangibles are to be carried on the books at cost and amortized over their useful economic lives. However:

The costs of developing, maintaining, or restoring intangibles which are unidentifiable, have indeterminate lives, or are inherent in a continuing enterprise should be expensed as incurred. By contrast, such intangible assets which are purchased must be carried at cost and amortized over their useful lives and cannot be written down or written off at date of acquisition.[5]

Thus a company may have spent a great amount of money internally developing valuable intangible assets, with none of it shown on the balance sheet, while another company may show comparable intangible assets on the balance sheet and be charging amortization expenses as deductions from earnings because it purchased the intangibles instead of developing them internally.

If the intangible assets have true economic value to a company, that value should be reflected in earnings. As a broad generalization, the greater the extent to which a company's value tends to be more dependent on intangible than tangible assets, the greater the extent to which the valuation exercise should rely on a capitalization of earnings approach rather than on asset-oriented approaches.

For the purpose of comparing two or more companies with divergent accounting treatments, the simplest way for an analyst to adjust financial statements containing intangible items is to eliminate the intangible items from the balance sheets and to adjust the income statements to eliminate the effect of amortization charges.

CAPITALIZATION VERSUS EXPENSING OF VARIOUS COSTS

There are many cost items that fall into a gray area, where the decision to expense or to capitalize the expenditure is subjective. One category, for example, would be the question on how to draw the line between maintenance expenditures, which are expenses, and capital improvements, which are capitalized. For example, many seasonal operations, such as resorts and

---

[5]Ibid., p. 155.

food processing plants, maintain skeleton crews year-round. Their compensation generally is expensed, even though they may do improvements that probably would be capitalized if outside contractors were hired for the same job.

Companies that want to show a good bottom line will capitalize where the decision is marginal, while companies that want to minimize income taxes will elect to expense rather than capitalize wherever possible. The analyst should be alert to spot the many opportunities for choices between capitalization and expensing, and inquire into the company's tendencies in this respect on making judgmental conclusions about the quality of the company's earnings and balance sheet.

TIMING OF RECOGNITION OF REVENUES AND EXPENSES

Another area where certain types of companies have considerable latitude in their choice of accounting practices is in the timing of recognition of some of their revenues and expenses.

Contract work

Contract work can be accounted for either on a completed contract or a percentage of completion basis. The latter is conceptually preferable, but its implementation can only be as good as the estimates of the percentages completed. If the company being valued is in the contracting business, the accounting practices deserve careful scrutiny. This can be one of the most difficult areas for the outside analyst to evaluate critically. If it is a major issue in the valuation, it may require considerable inquiry into the company's records, as well as inquiry about industry experience for comparable situations.

Installment sales

When is a sale a sale? For years many companies booked huge profits by selling land on high face-value contracts with 5 or 10 percent down and the balance over extended periods at low interest. The down payments were not high enough to deter many buyers from defaulting, and even the good contracts were worth nowhere near their face value because of the low interest rate. Now both the AICPA[6] and the SEC[7] have issued guidelines to prevent such abuses, but still there is some latitude for differences in treatment from one company to another. Where installment sales are a significant part of a company's business, the analyst should look into their accounting treatment.

Sales involving actual or contingent liabilities

Sales involving actual future liabilities generally are those where certain services are due the customers in conjunction with the sale. These would include sales, such as service contracts and subscriptions, or products with

---

[6]AICPA *Industry Accounting Guide on Recognition of Profit on Sales of Real Estate,* 1973.

[7]SEC *Accounting Series Release No. 95.*

future servicing warranted for some period. The unearned portion of the revenues usually would be carried on the balance sheet as a liability item, commonly labeled Deferred Income, and transferred to income as it is earned. Considerable judgment may be involved about when such income should be recognized as revenue, so the analyst should give some scrutiny to the accounting treatment in companies that make sales involving future liabilities.

Sales involving contingent liabilities most commonly are where the customer has certain rights to return the product for a refund. If such contingent liabilities exist, the analyst should make some judgment about the adequacy of accounting for them because they affect the reported earnings and assets.

Prior-period adjustments

For a variety of reasons a company may find that its revenues or expenses, or both, were under- or overstated in certain prior accounting periods. The most common reasons are errors in accounting and under- or overpayment of income taxes. The company usually records such an adjustment in the accounting year when it is discovered. In assessing the company's earnings history, the analyst should spread the effect of the adjustment back over the prior periods to which it applies. Sometimes the information is available to allocate the adjustment with accuracy to the appropriate prior periods. In other cases, the information for a precise prior period allocation is not available. Even where a rough estimate of the appropriate allocation over prior periods is the best that can be done, it usually is better for analytical purposes to spread the adjustment on the basis of such an estimate rather than to leave it in the period in which it was reported.

ACCOUNTING FOR LEASES

In accordance with the Statement of Financial Accounting Standards No. 13, issued in November 1976, leases that are of a financial nature (those that transfer essentially all of the benefits and risks incident to the ownership of the property) must be capitalized as assets on the lessee's balance sheet. All other leases are accounted for as operating leases, that is, the lease payments simply expensed as incurred. Since there is room for argument in some cases about which method of accounting is appropriate, and since unaudited closely-held companies are less prone than audited public companies to adhere strictly to GAAP, the analyst should examine leases to make a judgment on whether any adjustments should be made to the company's accounting treatment for analytical purposes.

ACCOUNTING FOR CERTAIN TAX ASPECTS

Investment tax credits

If a company receives a $10,000 credit against its income taxes for buying $100,000 worth of capital equipment that has a useful life of five years, the $10,000 benefit to the company's earnings can be spread at the rate of $2,000 per year over the five-year asset life, or "flowed through" immediately to earnings in the year the asset is purchased. Almost all companies today use the flow-through method of accounting for investment tax credits. Therefore, in assessing a company's earning power base, the analyst should determine how much of each year's earnings resulted from investment tax credits, and whether the purchases that generated those credits will continue in future years at a comparable level.

An item that frequently causes controversy in a business valuation is the value of a tax loss carryforward. The amounts are shown in footnotes to company balance sheets rather than in the body because their value is contingent on generating future profits against which they can be used. The ability to generate such profits usually is questionable, since, if the company had an unbroken profit history, there would be no loss carryforwards.

As far as the income statement is concerned, tax loss carryforwards properly are classed as extraordinary credits in the periods in which they are used. They should be adjusted out of the earning power base in those periods for analytical purposes. It could be considered reasonable analysis to spread back the tax loss carryforward credits that actually were used, as an offset against the losses in the periods in which the tax loss carryforwards were generated.

Tax loss carryforwards

If a company owns 50 to 100 percent of another company's stock, it may either prepare consolidated statements or account for the subsidiary by the equity method. If a company owns 20 to 50 percent of another company's stock, it may account for it either by the equity method or by the cost method. If a company owns less than 20 percent of another company's stock, it accounts for it by the cost method.

Consolidated statements treat the parent and subsidiaries as if they were all one company, with minority interests in subsidiaries, if any, shown as deductions on the financial statements. When accounting is done by the equity method, the parent's share of earnings or losses of the subsidiary (net of intercorporate eliminations, if any) are shown on the parent company's income statement, and the carrying value of the interest in the subsidiary is adjusted accordingly on the parent company's balance sheet. When accounting is done by the cost method, the parent shows only dividends received on its income statement, and continues to carry the investment on its balance sheet at cost, except that accounting principles state the investment should be written down if it has a permanent impairment in its value. An analyst frequently would consider an adjustment appropriate on the basis of his evaluation, even though the accountant would not necessarily recognize permanent impairment.

The greatest distortions in the reporting of a parent company's overall results, of course, arise under the cost method, where earnings or losses of the subsidiary interest are not reflected in the parent's financial statement. If this is a significant factor, the analyst may wish to make appropriate adjustments.

TREATMENT OF INTERESTS IN AFFILIATES

170

On the other hand, either presenting consolidated statements or accounting on the equity method imply that a dollar of earnings of the subsidiary is worth a dollar to the parent, which is not necessarily true. There may be restrictions on distributions of the subsidiary's earnings due to loan agreements, regulatory authorities, or other reasons. Also, the analyst should check to be sure that the parent has made allowance for any income taxes incident to potential transfer of funds from subsidiary to parent.

EXTRAORDINARY OR NONRECURRING ITEMS

In analyzing a company's historical earnings as a guide to estimating the company's earning power base, the analyst should make every reasonable effort to distinguish between those past earnings which are representative of ongoing earning power and those which are not. The analyst should make adjustments to the income statements to eliminate the effects of past items that would tend to distort a reasonable representation of the company's current and future earning power. Much judgment is required in the implementation of this exercise.

Ordinary versus extraordinary items

Accounting Principles Board Opinion No. 30, issued in 1973, is very restrictive as to what may be reported as an "extraordinary" gain or loss. *APB Opinion No. 30* states that an item must be *both* unusual in nature and infrequent in occurrence to be categorized as extraordinary, and defined those two requirements as:

Unusual nature—the underlying event or transaction should possess a high degree of abnormality and be of a type clearly unrelated to, or only incidentally related to, the ordinary and typical activities of the entity, taking into account the environment in which the entity operates.
Infrequency of occurrence—the underlying event or transaction should be of a type that would not reasonably be expected to recur in the foreseeable future, taking into account the environment in which the entity operates.[8]

If an item meets the above definitions, it almost certainly could not be considered representative of ongoing earning power. That does not necessarily mean it should be totally ignored, however, since an extraordinary item could indicate a risk which may still face the company again in the future.

Other nonrecurring items

Since the use of the extraordinary designation is as restricted as it is, obviously many items do not meet the strict definition for accounting purposes but nevertheless should be regarded as being of a nonrecurring nature for analytical purposes. Some examples of such items would be:

1. Gains or losses on the sale of assets, especially where it is clear that the company does not have a continuing supply of assets available for sale.

---

[8]*APB Opinion No. 30,* 1973.

2. Gains or losses on disposition of a segment of the business.
3. Effects of a strike or of an extended period of unavailability of critical raw materials.
4. Effects of abnormal price fluctuations, such as the astronomical but short-lived inflation in sugar prices that occurred in 1974.

It is possible, of course, for any of the above or other types of unusual events to recur, to some greater or lesser extent. The analyst must make judgments about the likelihood of recurrence of such risks or unusual benefits in his decision on what adjustments should be made to historical earnings to best reflect a continuing earning power base.

Discontinued operations

Apart from any one-time gain or loss incident to the disposal or discontinuance of a segment of operations, there is also the matter of how to treat the operating earnings or losses that the segment of the business had been generating prior to discontinuance. Since those earnings or losses will not continue, the analyst may wish to adjust operating earnings by removing the effect of the discontinued operations, if the amounts can be isolated from the results of the other ongoing operations. The effect on the company's overall resources also should be considered, since loss of earnings from one source may be replaced by redeployment of the resources in another direction.

OPERATING VERSUS NONOPERATING ITEMS

Depending on the method of valuation that the analyst is using, it may be useful to distinguish between operating and nonoperating earnings, even if the nonoperating earnings are of a recurring nature. The nonoperating item most commonly found on financial statements is income from investments. It is suggested elsewhere in this book that it may be appropriate to value certain portions of a company, such as investments, on a market value approach, while operating portions of a company may rely primarily on a capitalization of earnings approach to valuation. If such a distinction is to be made in the valuation approach, that is, valuing nonoperating assets separately, then the analyst must be sure to exclude any income generated by the nonoperating assets from the base which is used to determine the capitalized earnings value of the operating portion of the company.

MANAGEMENT COMPENSATION AND PERQUISITES

In closely-held companies, it is common to find that compensation and perquisites to owners and managers may be based on the personal desires of owners and on the company's ability to pay rather than on the value of services performed for the company. How much the earning power base should be adjusted to reflect discrepancies between compensation paid and value of services performed depends on the purpose of the valuation.

Owners of successful closely-held businesses tend to take out what normally would be considered profits in the form of compensation and discretionary

172

expenses. This may be an effort to avoid the double taxation that arises from paying a corporate income tax and then paying a personal income tax on what is left from that paid in the form of dividends. It is not uncommon to find an owner/manager of a successful company drawing $150,000 annual compensation, even though his services to the company could be replaced for $60,000 per year. The extreme cases go much, much further.

If the owner/manager described in the previous paragraph wants to sell his business and retire, the difference between his compensation and what it will cost to replace him will become available as a part of pretax profits, and the earning power base should be adjusted accordingly in establishing the selling price of the business. On the other hand, if the principal owner in such a business wants to establish an ESOP, but plans to continue working and to continue a similar compensation program for the next ten years, then no adjustment should be made to the earning power base for an ESOP valuation, since the level of compensation can be expected to continue.

It also is common to find that management is undercompensated because of the company's lack of ability to pay. The analyst usually should assume that this will be corrected when adequate resources are available, and make an appropriate upward adjustment to the management compensation expense in estimating the company's earning power base.

A number of sources can provide the analyst some guidelines in assessing reasonable levels of management compensation. For example, *RMA Annual Statement Studies*[9] shows officers' compensation as a percent of sales for each industry group. As with other ratios provided in that service, each industry group is divided into four classes by asset size, and for each group the median and the upper and lower quartile values are shown for each variable.

The *Source Book: Statistics of Income*[10] also shows compensation of officers by industry group, broken down by asset size. It covers many more companies than RMA covers, and has 13 asset size categories. Its big drawback is that its latest edition usually is about four years out of date.

TRANSACTIONS INVOLVING COMPANY INSIDERS

The analyst should carefully scrutinize and evaluate any transaction involving owners or management.

One of the most common situations is to have the business lease premises from a person associated with the company. In such cases the analyst usually will wish to evaluate the extent that the lease amounts are equivalent to what the company would pay on an arm's-length basis. If not, then the appropriate adjustment depends on the situation, especially the length of time over which the present arrangement can be expected to continue.

Another common occurrence in closely-held businesses is loans to or from stockholders or officers. Here the analyst should examine the ability and intent

---

[9]*RMA Annual Statement Studies* (Philadelphia: Robert Morris Associates). Published annually.

[10]U.S. Internal Revenue Service, *Source Book: Statistics of Income* (Washington, D.C.: U.S. Government Printing Office). Published annually.

to repay. If there is little or no likelihood of collecting a receivable from an insider, then for analytical purposes it should be removed from the balance sheet. If interest is being accrued and is not likely to be collected, it should be adjusted out of the earnings used to evaluate the earning power base. Also common is to find a demand note payable in the current liability section of the balance sheet, even though there is no intent to pay any time soon or maybe ever. Interest may or may not be paid on it. For analytical purposes it may be more appropriate to treat such an item as if it were long-term debt—or even subordinated capital of a nature more like equity than debt.

One of the most difficult categories of items to treat analytically for valuation purposes is contingencies. The very nature of the fact that an item is a contingency defies precise quantification. Nevertheless, the valuation analyst must try to discover contingent assets and liabilities, whether they are on the financial statements in some form or other, or not, and to deal with them within the scope of the available information.

CONTINGENT ASSETS AND LIABILITIES

The commonest categories of contingent assets and liabilities are those which arise from litigation or potential litigation. If their outcomes were known, there would be no need for litigation. These situations are so varied that it is virtually impossible to generalize on how the analyst should treat them for a valuation. At least the analyst should be alert to attempt to investigate and evaluate contingencies.

It is generally agreed that marketable securities should be adjusted to fair market value for most asset valuation purposes. However, there is not necessarily total agreement that such an adjustment should be accompanied by a partially offsetting adjustment for the related income tax effects implied by the unrealized gain or loss to which the adjustment gives rise. Making the offsetting tax adjustment seems logical. There is more on the issue later in this book, in the chapters on gift and estate tax cases, in which treatment of the matter by the courts has been inconsistent.

ADJUSTMENTS TO ASSET VALUATIONS

Marketable securities

The appropriateness of adjusting various other categories of balance-sheet assets for business valuation purposes is very controversial, and depends partly on the situation. For gift and estate tax purposes, Revenue Ruling 59-60 states that values of assets of an investment nature (opposed to operating assets) should be adjusted. The theory apparently is that such assets could be liquidated without impairing the company's operations. Sometimes, however, that would not be true—if the assets are required to be maintained as loan collateral, or if they are necessary to maintain certain financial ratios that may be required by lenders or regulatory agencies. Other portions of this book discuss the appropriateness of adjusting different categories of asset values under various circumstances.

Other assets

COMPUTATION OF EARNINGS PER SHARE

Weighted average basis

Earnings per share should be computed on a weighted average basis, that is, the number of shares weighted by the length of time they have been outstanding. Let's say that a company had 100,000 shares outstanding at the beginning of the year, and issued 30,000 more shares on May 1. The 100,000 would be outstanding all year, and the 30,000 outstanding for eight months or two thirds of the year. The weighted average number of shares outstanding for the year would be computed as follows:

$$
\begin{array}{rcrcr}
1/3 & \times & 100,000 & \times & 33,333 \\
2/3 & \times & 130,000 & = & \underline{86,667} \\
\end{array}
$$

Weighted average
shares outstanding   120,000

If the earnings were $300,000, the proper computation of earnings per share would be $300,000 ÷ 120,000 = $2.50 per share.

Primary versus fully diluted earnings

In general, primary earnings per share are computed by dividing the earnings available to common equity by the weighted average number of common shares outstanding, plus "dilutive common stock equivalents." The definition and computations can be very technical, and the reader who has a need for this detail is referred to a competent technical accounting-oriented manual, such as Bernstein's.[11]

For analytical purposes, it seems that the earnings per share are best stated on a fully diluted basis, that is, showing the maximum potential dilution that could have resulted if all possible conversions and exercises of options and warrants had been exercised. Naturally, the effect of any interest or dividends paid on the convertible issues would have to be added back to the earnings base. Any conversions that would be antidilutive in their effect should not be included.

COMPUTATION OF BOOK VALUE PER SHARE

Book value per share is based on the number of shares outstanding at the end of the accounting period, not the weighted average, as is the case for computing the earnings per share. Also, book value normally is computed without considering possible dilutive effects of conversions, although the analyst may wish to make such a computation for analytical purposes.

Thus, the computation of book value per share usually is a simple matter of dividing the total common equity by the number of shares outstanding. On most balance sheets the common equity consists of the common stock account, any paid-in capital in excess of par or stated value, and the accumulated retained earnings or deficit. Of course, if there were any contingent payments on senior securities not shown on the balance sheet, such as preferred dividends in arrears, such amounts would have to be deducted from common equity in computing book value per share.

---

[11]Bernstein, *Financial Statement Analysis*, pp. 334–52.

Note that treasury stock (stock once issued and subsequently reacquired) is *not* included as part of the number of shares outstanding.

Several of the investment services, including the *S&P Corporation Records* (referenced elsewhere in this book), exclude intangibles in the computed book value per share that they show.

Exhibit 11–2
Example of the effect of the variety of accounting principles on reported income

RIVAL MANUFACTURING COMPANY
Consolidated Statement of Income
For Year Ended 19xx

	Method A	Method B
Net sales	$365,800,000	$365,800,000
Cost of goods sold (1) (2) (3) (4) (5)	(276,976,200)	(274,350,000)
	$ 88,823,800	$ 91,450,000
Research and development costs (6)	(7,326,000)	(7,000,000)
Selling, general, and administrative expenses (5) (7)	(44,600,000)	(35,700,000)
	$ 36,897,800	$ 48,750,000
Other income (expenses):		
Interest expenses	(3,085,000)	(3,095,000)
Net income—subsidiaries	1,538,000	1,460,000
Amortization of goodwill (8)	(390,000)	(170,000)
Miscellaneous expenses	(269,000)	(229,000)
Income before taxes	$ 34,691,800	$ 46,715,800
Taxes:		
Income taxes—deferred	(756,000)	(850,000)
Income taxes—current (9)	(16,716,900)	(22,397,900)
Reductions from investment tax credits (10)	10,400	758,400
Net income	$ 17,229,300	$ 24,226,300
Earnings per share	$5.74	$8.08

Explanations:

  (1) **Inventories:**
       A uses last-in, first-out
       B uses first-in, first-out
          Difference—$1,780,000
  (2) **Administrative costs:**
       A includes some administrative costs as period costs
       B includes some administrative costs as inventory costs
          Difference—$88,000
  (3) **Depreciation:**
       A uses sum-of-the-years'-digits method
       B uses straight-line method
          Difference—$384,200
  (4) **Useful lives of assets:**
       A uses conservative assumption—8 years (average)
       B uses liberal assumption—14 years (average)
          Difference—$346,000
  (5) **Pension costs:**
       A uses "maximum provision" under APB *Opinion No. 8*
       B uses "minimum provision" under APB *Opinion No. 8*
          Difference—$78,000
  (6) **Research expenses:**
       A charges as incurred
       B amortizes over 5 years
          Difference—$326,000
  (7) **Executive compensations:**
       A compensates executives with cash bonuses
       B compensates executives with stock options
          Difference—$840,000
  (8) **Goodwill from acquisition:**
       A amortizes over 10 years
       B amortizes over 40 years
          Difference—$220,000
  (9) **Taxes on subsidiary profits:**
       A makes provision as income earned
       B makes no provision until dividends received
          Difference—$67,000
 (10) **Investment tax credits:**
       A amortizes over useful lives of equipment
       B credits against current taxes
          Difference—$748,000

Source: Leopold A. Bernstein, *Understanding Corporate Reports: A Guide to Financial Statement Analysis.* (Homewood, Ill.: Dow Jones-Irwin 1974), p. 241. © 1974 by Dow Jones-Irwin, Inc.

AN EXAMPLE OF THE EFFECT OF ALTERNATIVE ACCOUNTING METHODS

Exhibit 11–2 illustrates the possible impact on reported earnings that can arise from different methods of accounting for a particular set of operations.

ADJUSTING BALANCE SHEET TO CURRENT VALUES

If it is appropriate to rely heavily on an asset approach in the valuation, the analyst may prepare a pro-forma balance sheet with some or all of the line items adjusted to current values. Depending on the valuation criteria to be used, the adjustments may affect only nonoperating assets or may affect all assets.

An example of such a balance-sheet adjustment exercise is shown as an exhibit in the sample case in Chapter 15.

12

OTHER ASPECTS OF FINANCIAL STATEMENTS

Besides the income statements and balance sheets, two others deserve attention for the additional information and the insight they can provide. These are the statement of changes in financial position and the statement of stockholders' equity. In a partnership, the counterpart to the latter is the statement of partners' capital accounts.

It also is desirable to understand what is and is not implied by various types of accountants' opinions regarding financial statements. To this end, this chapter discusses the accountants' opinions on audited statements, both "clean" opinions and "qualified" opinions, and also discusses two relatively new and lesser levels of accountants' opinions on financial statements, called "compiled" statement opinions and "reviewed" statement opinions.

STATEMENT OF CHANGES IN FINANCIAL POSITION

The statement of changes in financial position offers insight into the components of changes that take place during the accounting period in various line items on the balance sheet. It breaks down major items that caused balance-sheet variables to change, rather than just showing the net effect, which is all that can be gleaned from the balance sheet alone. It is helpful in analyzing the company's cash flow. It is especially useful to help the analyst understand the company's liquidity characteristics, and to help assess the company's potential capital needs.

The statement of changes in financial position as it is typically presented today is a product of *Accounting Principles Board* (APB) *Opinion No. 19*. It is essentially the statement known for years as the "statement of sources and applications of funds," commonly referred to as the "funds statement," but with some broadening.

In practice, the terms *funds* and *working capital* are used interchangeably. The basic purpose of the statement is to delineate the components of the change in net working capital (current assets minus current liabilities) from one balance sheet to the next.

APB 19 also requires that the statement of changes in financial position include any major financing or investment transactions, even though they may not affect any of the short-term asset or short-term liability accounts (the components of working capital). Such transactions could include the issuance of long-term debt or stock to acquire fixed assets, or the conversion of a convertible bond or preferred stock into common stock.

Exhibit 12–1 is an example of a statement of changes in financial position. Many people who address the question of a company's value fail to accord the statement of changes in financial position the attention that it deserves. I suggest that this statement be given careful scrutiny as one step in the valuation process.

STATEMENT OF STOCKHOLDERS' EQUITY

The statement of stockholders' equity shows inflows and outflows to the equity section of the balance sheet during the year, including earnings, dividends, and changes in shares outstanding. It reconciles the net equity

Exhibit 12–1
Statement of changes in financial position

Oregon Portland Cement Company

Statements of Changes in Financial Position

	Years ended December 31, 1979 and 1978	
	1979	1978
Sources of working capital:		
Net earnings	**$ 8,053,465**	6,844,603
Items which do not use (provide) working capital:		
Depreciation and depletion	**2,407,061**	2,633,962
Deferred income taxes	**694,100**	(21,100)
Other	**24,663**	150,148
Working capital provided by operations	**11,179,289**	9,607,613
Proceeds from exercise of employee stock options	**50,991**	51,385
Proceeds from issuance of treasury stock to employee benefit plans	**231,875**	124,009
Proceeds from long-term borrowings	**9,575,000**	17,000,000
Other sources	**—**	20,919
Decrease in working capital	**—**	2,534,628
	$21,037,155	29,338,554
Uses of working capital:		
Dividends	**935,346**	898,805
Current installments of long-term debt	**1,666,667**	450,000
Additions to fixed assets	**13,324,287**	27,915,614
Purchase of treasury stock	**30,214**	3,012
Other uses	**433,094**	71,123
Increase in working capital	**4,647,547**	—
	$21,037,155	29,338,554
Changes in components of working capital:		
Increase (decrease) in current assets:		
Cash	**(52,676)**	(767,911)
Short-term interest bearing deposits	**(775,413)**	3,611,796
Receivables	**1,275,821**	(744,908)
Inventories	**2,568,717**	(1,134,192)
Prepaid expenses	**(34,720)**	(35,712)
	2,981,729	929,073
Increase (decrease) in current liabilities:		
Current installments of long-term debt	**1,216,667**	50,000
Accounts payable	**(2,825,224)**	2,880,543
Accrued payroll and other expenses	**297,974**	857,579
Income taxes	**(355,235)**	(324,421)
	(1,665,818)	3,463,701
Increase (decrease) in working capital	**$ 4,647,547**	(2,534,628)

Source: Oregon Portland Cement Co., *1979 Annual Report.*

figure shown from one balance sheet to the next. It is a convenient source to help the analyst be sure that he takes proper account of the equity changes from one period to another, especially when computing per share figures, such as book value per share or earnings per share when there have been changes in the number of shares outstanding.

Exhibit 12–2 is a sample statement of stockholders' equity. Many closely-held companies do not bother to prepare a separate statement of stockholders' equity as part of their financial statements. If there are any complications about the equity accounts, the analyst preparing the materials for the company's valuation should make up such a statement so that all changes in the equity accounts are clearly presented.

STATEMENT OF PARTNERS' CAPITAL ACCOUNTS

The partnership counterpart of a statement of stockholders' equity is the statement of partners' capital accounts. In a corporation, each holder of a class of stock is treated identically in the equity section of the balance sheet, so

Exhibit 12–2
Statement of stockholders' equity

Oregon Portland Cement Company

Statements of Stockholders' Equity

Years ended December 31, 1979 and 1978

	Common Stock	Additional Paid-in Capital	Retained Earnings	Treasury Stock	Total Stockholders' Equity (Notes 4, 6, 7 and 8)
Balance at December 31, 1977	$956,376	5,410,159	16,949,857	585,777	22,730,615
Shares issued in connection with:					
Employee stock option plan, 3,915 shares	—	17,677	—	(33,708)	51,385
Employee savings and thrift plan, 1,828 shares	—	20,618	—	(37,952)	58,570
Employee tax reduction act stock ownership plan, 1,327 shares	—	42,648	—	(22,791)	65,439
Acquisition of 81 common shares	—	—	—	3,012	(3,012)
Net earnings	—	—	6,844,603	—	6,844,603
Dividends declared — $.97 per common share	—	—	(898,805)	—	(898,805)
Balance at December 31, 1978	$956,376	5,491,102	22,895,655	494,338	28,848,795
Shares issued in connection with:					
Employee stock option plan, 3,675 shares	—	(15,014)	—	(66,005)	50,991
Employee savings and thrift plan, 935 shares	—	29,349	—	(16,699)	46,048
Employee tax reduction act stock ownership plan, 3,766 shares	—	118,508	—	(67,319)	185,827
Acquisition of 544 common shares	—	—	—	30,214	(30,214)
Net earnings	—	—	8,053,465	—	8,053,465
Dividends declared — $1.00 per common share	—	—	(935,346)	—	(935,346)
Balance at December 31, 1979	$956,376	5,623,945	30,013,774	374,529	36,219,566

Source: Oregon Portland Cement Co., *1979 Annual Report.*

changes in equity do not need to be broken down by owner—only by class of stock. In a partnership, however, changes in each partner's capital account must be identified separately because, for various reasons, different partners may be treated differently. In effect, it is as if each partnership interest must be treated as a separate class of stock.

In a corporation, if a stockholder deposits or withdraws assets other than for stock, the transaction is recorded somewhere apart from the equity section on the company's books, just as if the transaction were with some other outside party than a stockholder. If the cash is paid to stockholders as dividends, all holders of a class of stock participate in proportion to their stock ownership. In a partnership, however, transactions involving deposit or withdrawal of partnership assets may be posted directly to one partner's capital account, thus changing that partner's relative ownership status vis à vis the other partners.

Also, it is common to find that each partner does not necessarily share in the earnings in the same proportion that he shares in the assets on liquidation. Therefore, the relative percentage of ownership of the overall partnership may shift among the various partners from period to period as different partners' capital accounts are credited with shares of the earnings or losses—shares that are out of proportion to their relative percentage interests, as shown by the partners' capital accounts at the beginning of the period.

The analyst valuing a partnership interest subject to any such complications probably will need to read the partnership agreement to be sure that he has a complete understanding of the rights of each partner. If one partner owns a 20

Exhibit 12–3
Statement of partners' capital accounts
For Year Ended December 31, 19XX

	Able	Baker	Total
Balance, January 1, 19XX	$300,000	$120,000	$420,000
Add: Capital Investments	---	30,000	30,000
	$300,000	$150,000	$450,000
Add: Net Income	60,000	36,000	96,000
	360,000	186,000	556,000
Less: Personal Drawings	50,000	30,000	80,000
Balance, December 31, 19XX	$310,000	$156,000	$476,000

percent interest in the capital account of a very profitable partnership, but is entitled to 60 percent of the earnings, his interest is not necessarily equal in value to another 20 percent interest that is entitled to a lesser participation in the earnings. Exhibit 12–3 is a sample statement of partners' capital accounts.

THE AUDITOR'S OPINION

If a company has its statements audited, the auditor's opinion becomes a part of the completed set of financial statements.

"Clean" opinions

A "clean" opinion consists of two paragraphs. The first paragraph states the scope of the audit, what basic financial statements were audited, and for what dates or periods. The second paragraph states that the figures are presented fairly in accordance with generally accepted accounting principles (GAAP). An

Exhibit 12–4
Auditor's "clean" opinion

To the Stockholders and Board of Directors of Georgia-Pacific Corporation:

We have examined the consolidated balance sheets of Georgia-Pacific Corporation (a Georgia corporation) and subsidiaries as of December 31, 1977 and 1976, and the related statements of consolidated income, surplus and changes in financial position for the years then ended. Our examination was made in accordance with generally accepted auditing standards, and accordingly included such tests of the accounting records and such other auditing procedures as we considered necessary in the circumstances.

In our opinion, the accompanying financial statements present fairly the financial position of Georgia-Pacific Corporation and subsidiaries as of December 31, 1977 and 1976, and the results of their operations and the changes in their financial position for the years then ended, in conformity with generally accepted accounting principles consistently applied during the periods.

ARTHUR ANDERSEN & CO.

Portland, Oregon,
February 10, 1978.

Source: Georgia-Pacific Corporation *1977 Annual Report.*

example of a clean opinion, Arthur Andersen's opinion on the statements of Georgia-Pacific Corporation for 1977, is shown in Exhibit 12–4.

There are three main categories of reasons why an auditor's opinion may be qualified: **"Qualified" opinions**

1. The scope of the examination somehow was limited, either by client's choice or by availability of data.
2. The figures do not fairly present the financial position of the company, either because of inadequate disclosure or because the accounting used was not in accordance with GAAP.
3. There are uncertainties about future events that the auditors feel are material enough, in their opinion, to warrant a qualification.

If the auditor's opinion is qualified, one or more paragraphs are added between the beginning and concluding paragraph, explaining the nature of the qualification or qualifications.

If the opinion is qualified because of limited scope, the analyst is basically in the same position as if the statements available to work with were not audited, at least on that portion of the statements not covered by audit. This should be only a minor disappointment to the analyst who is accustomed to valuing closely-held companies, since most closely-held companies do not have the luxury of audited statements anyway.

If the figures do not fairly present the company's position, the analyst must inquire about details of the inadequacy, and make whatever adjustments or allowances are necessary to get what he needs for analysis. The most commonly encountered departure from GAAP is the presentation of one or more items (or the whole set of statements) on a cash rather than an accrual basis.

The real befuddlement to the valuation analyst is a qualification "because of future uncertainties." Since the value of a company is dependent on the outlook for its economic future, any uncertainty about that future significant enough to warrant a qualification in the auditor's opinion must cause a problem in the company's valuation. The most common future uncertainties that give rise to a qualification in the auditor's opinion are litigation or potential litigation, and financial instability, in that the auditor questions the company's viability as a going concern. In cases where litigation or possible litigation is involved, the appraiser must apprise himself of the situation as thoroughly as possible and finally make a subjective judgment. If $1 million is at stake and the appraiser concludes there is a 30 percent probability that the company will lose, he probably will deduct more than $300,000 (.3 × $1,000,000) from his value because of the risk. The appraiser also will be very cautious about his value if there is doubt about the company's viability as a going concern. In any case, if such extreme uncertainties exist, the appraiser should include a qualification to that effect in his own appraisal report.

To give an example, in November 1978 a jury rendered a verdict against Georgia-Pacific, Weyerhaeuser, and Willamette Industries which was considered significant enough to require qualification to the audit reports on their respective financial statements. The qualification by Arthur Andersen & Co. was included in the 1978 and 1979 Georgia-Pacific statements, and was finally removed as a result of a related Court of Appeals action in May 1980. Arthur Andersen's qualified opinion on G-P's 1979 statements and also their report of May 15, 1980, removing the qualification are shown as Exhibit 12–5.

"COMPILED" AND "REVIEWED" FINANCIAL STATEMENTS

Effective July 1, 1979, the Accounting and Review Services Committee of the American Institute of Certified Public Accountants (AICPA) issued *SSARS 1* (*Statement on Standards for Accounting and Review Services 1*), titled "Compilation and Review of Financial Statements." This major breakthrough in accounting practice now provides standards for two levels of CPA reports short of a complete audit of a company's financial statements.

Such compilation and review services apply only to a nonpublic entity, defined as "Any entity other than one (a) whose securities trade in a public market either on a stock exchange (domestic or foreign) or in the over-the-counter market, including securities quoted only locally or regionally, or (b)

Exhibit 12–5
Auditor's qualified opinion and subsequent removal of qualification

To Georgia-Pacific Corporation:

We have examined the consolidated balance sheets of Georgia-Pacific Corporation (a Georgia corporation) and subsidiaries as of December 31, 1978 and 1979, the related statements of consolidated income (included in Item 2), surplus and changes in financial position for each of the five years in the period ended December 31, 1979, and the supporting Schedules V, VI, XII and XIII. Our examinations were made in accordance with generally accepted auditing standards and, accordingly, included such tests of the accounting records and such other auditing procedures as we considered necessary in the circumstances.

As more fully explained in "Legal Proceedings" on page 13, in November 1978, a jury rendered a verdict against the Corporation in the plywood antitrust litigation. The Corporation intends to continue defending this action. Management and counsel are not in a position to predict the extent of Corporation's liability, if any, in this matter.

In our opinion, subject to the effect of any adjustments that might have been required had the outcome of the litigation referred to in the preceeding paragraph been known, the financial statements referred to above present fairly the financial position of Georgia-Pacific Corporation and subsidiaries as of December 31, 1978 and 1979, and the results of their operations and the changes in their financial position for each of the five years in the period ended December 31, 1979, and supporting Schedules V, VI, XII and XIII present fairly the information required to be set forth therein, all in conformity with generally accepted accounting principles applied on a consistent basis.

ARTHUR ANDERSEN & CO.

Portland, Oregon
February 8, 1980
Source: Georgia-Pacific Corporation. *1979 Annual Report.*

Exhibit 12–5 (continued)

To Georgia-Pacific Corporation:

We have examined the consolidated balance sheets of Georgia-Pacific Corporation (a Georgia corporation) and subsidiaries as of December 31, 1978 and 1979, the related statements of consolidated income (included in Item 2), surplus and changes in financial position for each of the five years in the period ended December 31, 1979, and the supporting Schedules V, VI, XII, and XIII. Our examinations were made in accordance with generally accepted auditing standards and, accordingly, included such tests of the accounting records and such other auditing procedures as we considered necessary in the circumstances.

In our report dated February 8, 1980, our opinion was qualified as being subject to the effect of any adjustments that might have been required had the outcome of plywood antitrust litigation, described more fully in "Legal Proceedings" on page 13, been known. On May 9, 1980, the United States Court of Appeals for the Ninth Circuit denied enforcement of a February 1978 order of the Federal Trade Commission which found a violation of Section 5 of the Federal Trade Commission Act. After reviewing the opinion of the United States Court of Appeals, management has concluded that the Corporation's ultimate maximum liability, if any, on the plywood antitrust litigation would not have a material adverse effect on the financial position of the Corporation. Counsel in this proceeding has agreed with management's determination of the maximum ultimate liability. Accordingly, our present opinion on the financial statements, as presented herein, is different from that expressed in our previous report.

In our opinion, the financial statements referred to above present fairly the financial position of Georgia-Pacific Corporation and subsidiaries as of December 31, 1978 and 1979, and the results of their operations and the changes in their financial position for each of the five years in the period ended December 31, 1979, and supporting Schedules V, VI, XII and XIII present fairly the information required to be set forth therein, all in conformity with generally accepted accounting principles applied on a consistent basis.

ARTHUR ANDERSEN & CO.

Portland, Oregon
May 15, 1980

Source: Georgia-Pacific Corporation. Form 8 Amendment No. 1 to Form 10-K for fiscal year ended December 31, 1979.

---

that makes a filing with a regulatory agency in preparation for the sale of any class of its securities in a public market."[1]

The report defines "Compilation of financial statements" as:

Presenting in the form of financial statements information that is the representation of management (owners) without undertaking to express any assurance on the statements.[2]

The report defines "Review of financial statements" as:

Performing inquiry and procedures that provide the accountant with a reasonable basis for expressing limited assurance that there are no material modifications that should be made to the statements in order for them to be in conformity with generally

---

[1]*Statement on Standards for Accounting and Review Services,* issued by the Accounting and Review Services Committee, American Institute of Certified Public Accountants, Inc. (New York, December 1978), p. 2.

[2]Ibid., p. 3

Exhibit 12–6
Illustrative wording of accountants reports for compiled and reviewed statements

Report for Compiled Statement

The accompanying balance sheet of XYZ Company as of December 31, 19XX, and the related statements of income, retained earnings, and changes in financial position for the year then ended have been compiled by us.

A compilation is limited to presenting in the form of financial statements information that is the representation of management. We have not audited or reviewed the accompanying financial statements, and, accordingly, do not express an opinion or any other form of assurance on them.

Report for Reviewed Statement

We have reviewed the accompanying balance sheet of XYZ Company as of December 31, 19XX, and the related statements of income, retained earnings, and changes in financial position for the year then ended, in accordance with standards established by the American Institute of Certified Public Accountants. All information included in these financial statements is the representation of the management of XYZ Company.

A review consists principally of inquiries of company personnel and analytical procedures applied to financial data. It is substantially less in scope than an examination in accordance with generally accepted auditing standards, the objective of which is the expression of an opinion regarding the financial statements as a whole. Accordingly, we do not express such an opinion.

Based on our review, we are not aware of any material modifications that should be made to the accompanying financial statements in order for them to be in conformity with generally accepted accounting principles.

Source: *Statement on Standards for Accounting and Review Services No. 1,* "Compilation and Review of Financial Statements," issued by the Accounting and Review Services Committee, American Institute of Certified Public Accountants, Inc., New York, December 1978, pp. 7, 13. Copyright © 1979 by the American Institute of Certified Public Accountants, Inc.

accepted accounting principles or, if applicable, with another comprehensive basis of accounting.[3]

Exhibit 12–6 shows illustrative wording for accountants' reports for compiled and reviewed statements.

SSARS 2, effective November 30, 1979, is titled "Reporting on Comparative Financial Statements." It provides guidelines for practice and wording of accountants' reports when the statements are compiled or reviewed, or both, by the accountant for two comparative periods or for one of the comparative periods but not the other.

Exhibit 12–7 shows illustrative inquiries that may be made by the accountant in conjunction with the review of financial statements. If the analyst performing a company valuation has to work with statements that are neither audited nor reviewed, the suggested list of inquiries for accounting review should provide useful suggestions for questions that the analyst may wish to ask.

---

[3]Ibid., p. 3.

Exhibit 12–7
Illustrative inquiries to be made in review of financial statements

The inquiries to be made in a review of financial statements are a matter of the accountant's judgment. In determining his inquiries, an accountant may consider (a) the nature and materiality of the items, (b) the likelihood of misstatement, (c) knowledge obtained during current and previous engagements, (d) the stated qualifications of the entity's accounting personnel, (e) the extent to which a particular item is affected by management's judgment, and (f) inadequacies in the entity's underlying financial data. The following list of inquiries is for illustrative purposes only. The inquiries do not necessarily apply to every engagement, nor are they meant to be all-inclusive. This list is not intended to serve as a program or checklist in the conduct of a review; rather it describes the general areas in which inquiries might be made. For example, the accountant may feel it is necessary to make several inquiries to answer one of the questions listed below, such as item 3(a).

(1) **General**
    (a) What are the procedures for recording, classifying, and summarizing transactions (relates to each section discussed below)?
    (b) Do the general ledger control accounts agree with subsidiary records (for example, receivables, inventories, investments, property and equipment, accounts payable, accrued expenses, non-current liabilities)?
    (c) Have accounting principles been applied on a consistent basis?

(2) **Cash**
    (a) Have bank balances been reconciled with book balances?
    (b) Have old or unusual reconciling items between bank balances and book balances been reviewed and adjustments made where necessary?
    (c) Has a proper cutoff of cash transactions been made?
    (d) Are there any restrictions on the availability of cash balances?
    (e) Have cash funds been counted and reconciled with control accounts?

(3) **Receivables**
    (a) Has an adequate allowance been made for doubtful accounts?
    (b) Have receivables considered uncollectible been written off?
    (c) If appropriate, has interest been reflected?
    (d) Has a proper cutoff of sales transactions been made?
    (e) Are there any receivables from employees and related parties?
    (f) Are any receivables pledged, discounted, or factored?
    (g) Have receivables been properly classified between current and noncurrent?

(4) **Inventories**
    (a) Have inventories been physically counted? If not, how have inventories been determined?
    (b) Have general ledger control accounts been adjusted to agree with physical inventories?
    (c) If physical inventories are taken at a date other than the balance sheet date, what procedures were used to record changes in inventory between the date of the physical inventory and the balance sheet date?
    (d) Were consignments in or out considered in taking physical inventories?
    (e) What is the basis of valuation?
    (f) Does inventory cost include material, labor, and overhead where applicable?
    (g) Have write-downs for obsolescence or cost in excess of net realizable value been made?
    (h) Have proper cutoffs of purchases, goods in transit, and returned goods been made?
    (i) Are there any inventory encumbrances?

Exhibit 12-7 (continued)

(5) Prepaid Expenses

(a) What is the nature of the amounts included in prepaid expenses?

(b) How are these amounts amortized?

(6) Investments, Including Loans, Mortgages, and Intercorporate Investments

(a) Have gains and losses on disposal been reflected?

(b) Has investment income been reflected?

(c) Has appropriate consideration been given to the classification of investments between current and noncurrent, and the difference between the cost and market value of investments?

(d) Have consolidation or equity accounting requirements been considered?

(e) What is the basis of valuation of marketable equity securities?

(f) Are investments unencumbered?

(7) Property and Equipment

(a) Have gains or losses on disposal of property or equipment been reflected?

(b) What are the criteria for capitalization of property and equipment? Have such criteria been applied during the fiscal period?

(c) Does the repairs and maintenance account only include items of an expense nature?

(d) Are property and equipment stated at cost?

(e) What are the depreciation methods and rates? Are they appropriate and consistent?

(f) Are there any unrecorded additions, retirements, abandonments, sales, or trade-ins?

(g) Does the entity have material lease agreements? Have they been properly reflected?

(h) Is any property or equipment mortgaged or otherwise encumbered?

(8) Other Assets

(a) What is the nature of the amounts included in other assets?

(b) Do these assets represent costs that will benefit future periods? What is the amortization policy? Is it appropriate?

(c) Have other assets been properly classified between current and noncurrent?

(d) Are any of these assets mortgaged or otherwise encumbered?

(9) Accounts and Notes Payable and Accrued Liabilities

(a) Have all significant payables been reflected?

(b) Are all bank and other short-term liabilities properly classified?

(c) Have all significant accruals, such as payroll, interest, and provisions for pension and profit-sharing plans been reflected?

(d) Are there any collateralized liabilities?

(e) Are there any payables to employees and related parties?

(10) Long-Term Liabilities

(a) What are the terms and other provisions of long-term liability agreements?

(b) Have liabilities been properly classified between current and noncurrent?

(c) Has interest expense been reflected?

(d) Has there been compliance with restrictive covenants of loan agreements?

(e) Are any long-term liabilities collateralized or subordinated?

(11) Income and Other Taxes

(a) Has provision been made for current and prior-year federal income taxes payable?

(b) Have any assessments or reassessments been received? Are there tax examinations in process?

(c) Are there timing differences? If so, have deferred taxes been reflected?

(d) Has provision been made for state and local income, franchise, sales, and other taxes payable?

Exhibit 12–7 (continued)

(12) **Other Liabilities, Contingencies, and Commitments**

    (a) What is the nature of the amounts included in other liabilities?

    (b) Have other liabilities been properly classified between current and noncurrent?

    (c) Are there any contingent liabilities, such as discounted notes, drafts, endorsements, warranties, litigation, and unsettled asserted claims? Are there any unasserted potential claims?

    (d) Are there any material contractual obligations for construction or purchase of real property and equipment and any commitments or options to purchase or sell company securities?

(13) **Equity**

    (a) What is the nature of any changes in equity accounts?

    (b) What classes of capital stock have been authorized?

    (c) What is the par or stated value of the various classes of stock?

    (d) Do amounts of outstanding shares of capital stock agree with subsidiary records?

    (e) Have capital stock preferences, if any been disclosed?

    (f) Have stock options been granted?

    (g) Has the entity made any acquisitions of its own capital stock?

    (h) Are there any restrictions on retained earnings or other capital?

(14) **Revenue and Expenses**

    (a) Are revenues from the sale of major products and services recognized in the appropriate period?

    (b) Are purchases and expenses recognized in the appropriate period and properly classified?

    (c) Do the financial statements include discontinued operations or items that might be considered extraordinary?

(15) **Other**

    (a) Are there any events that occurred after the end of the fiscal period that have a significant effect on the financial statements?

    (b) Have actions taken at stockholder, board of directors, or comparable meetings that affect the financial statements been reflected?

    (c) Have there been any material transactions between related parties?

    (d) Are there any material uncertainties? Is there any change in the status of material uncertainties previously disclosed?

Source: *Statement on Standards for Accounting and Review Services No. 1*, "Compilation and Review of Financial Statements," issued by the Accounting and Review Services Committee, American Institute of Certified Public Accountants, Inc., New York, December 1978, pp. 24–25. Copyright © 1979 by the American Institute of Certified Public Accountants, Inc.

13

COMPARATIVE RATIO ANALYSIS

USE AND INTERPRETATION OF RATIO ANALYSIS

"COMMON-SIZE" STATEMENTS

SHORT-TERM LIQUIDITY MEASURES
Current ratio
Quick ratio (acid test ratio)
Accounts receivable turnover
Inventory turnover
Sales to net working capital

BALANCE SHEET LEVERAGE RATIOS
Total debt to total asset ratio
Equity to total asset ratio
Long-term debt to total capital ratio
Equity to total capital ratio
Debt to equity ratios

INCOME STATEMENT COVERAGE RATIOS
Times interest earned
Coverage of fixed charges
Coverage of preferred dividends

OPERATING PERFORMANCE RATIOS

RETURN ON INVESTMENT RATIOS
Return on equity
Return on total assets

ASSET UTILIZATION RATIOS

SAMPLE SUMMARY OF RATIO ANAYLSES

Properly used, analysis of financial statement ratios can be a helpful tool in a business valuation. Ratio analysis of the financial statements can be useful in identifying and quantifying some of a company's strengths and weaknesses, on an absolute basis and also relative to other companies or industry norms.

The implications gleaned from financial statement analysis may be taken into consideration in arriving at the value of the business or business interest in several ways. The most common method of incorporating the results of ratio analysis of financial statements into the final valuation is to make appropriate adjustments to the capitalization rate used when valuing earnings. To the extent that the ratios indicate sustainable growth, the business should be worth a higher multiple of current earnings than would be the case if such growth were not indicated. To the extent that ratios reveal high degrees of risk factors, the business should be worth less than if the risk factors were lower.

One use of ratio analysis is to compare a company's own figures over time. This can identify aspects of the business that demonstrate any improving or deteriorating trends. It can also give indications of levels of the different variables that have been normal within the experience of the period studied, as well as ranges that reveal the high and low parameters that the company has experienced for each variable over the time.

Another way to use ratio analysis is to compare the subject company with other companies, either specific companies or industry averages. Patterns of strength in the subject company compared to the similar companies would tend to help support a price-to-earnings or price-to-asset value in the high end of the range found in the industry. Conversely, poor ratios, compared to the similar companies, would suggest a lower value for the subject company on its earnings and asset values.

In comparing ratios from one period to another, or from one company to another, reasonable inquiry should be made on the extent that comparative ratios are based on comparable accounting policies. It was noted in a previous chapter that different choices among generally accepted accounting principles can result in wide variations in figures reported. If one is making a comparative analysis of a company's financial statements over time, appropriate allowance should be made if there were any changes in accounting policies during the period under analysis. When comparing a company with others in its industry, appropriate allowance should be made for any differences in accounting policies between the subject company and industry norms.

The relative significance of the various ratios will be different in each unique valuation situation. Certain ratios have greater significance for value in certain industries. In some situations a ratio may take on particular significance because it departs markedly from industry norms. The analyst must apply judgment to each individual case to select and evaluate figures significant to that situation.

If the analyst does the ratio computations prior to making the field trip to interview company personnel, the ratio analysis usually will generate some questions on reasons for any departures from industry norms. Of course, if the ratio work is done after the field trip, such questions can be covered in later telephone interviews.

Liquidity ratios can be helpful in resolving one of the common controversies in business valuations—, whether the company may have any excess assets above those required for its operating needs, or, conversely, whether it may have a shortfall in assets relative to its needs.

This chapter will discuss ratios that help to evaluate the company's financial position, looking first at those that measure short-term liquidity and then at the commonly used longer-term balance-sheet leverage ratios. The chapter then will discuss a variety of operating ratios. Each ratio will be illustrated by an example from our hypothetical manufacturer, Ace Widget Company, and a summary of Ace Widget Company ratios will be found at the end of the chapter.

"COMMON-SIZE" STATEMENTS

The first step in ratio analysis of financial statements usually is to prepare what sometimes are called "common-size" statements. These simply are statements with each line item expressed as a percentage of the total shown on the statement. On the balance sheet, each line item is shown as a percent of total assets. On the income statement, each item is shown as a percent of sales.

Exhibit 13–1 shows five years of balance sheets for Ace Widget Company, presented on a common-size basis. Exhibit 13–2 shows five years of income statements for Ace Widget Company presented on a common-size basis. A set of common-size statements also is presented in Chapter 15 as part of the Pagano Supermarkets, Inc., sample case.

SHORT-TERM LIQUIDITY MEASURES

Current ratio

The most commonly used short-term liquidity ratio is the current ratio. This is defined as *current assets divided by current liabilities*. Its most important significance is as an indicator of the firm's ability to pay its short-term liabilities on time. The old rule of thumb, that a satisfactory current ratio is 2.0:1, is not widely followed, because of vastly different conditions typical in different industries, such as typical accounts receivable collection periods and inventory turnover periods. Like most ratios, the adequacy of the current ratio for a given company can be gauged better by comparison with industry norms than by comparison with any absolute standard.

Using figures from Exhibit 13–1, the current ratio for Ace Widget Company for 1979 is:

$$\frac{\text{Current assets}}{\text{Current liabilities}} = \frac{\$950,000}{650,000} = \underline{\underline{1.46:1}}$$

Quick ratio (acid test ratio)

The next most commonly used ratio is the quick ratio, which some analysts refer to as the "acid test" ratio. It is defined as *the sum of cash and cash equivalents plus receivables* (usually all current assets listed above inventory),

Exhibit 13–1

ACE WIDGET COMPANY
Balance sheets—1975–1979

As of December 31

	1979		1978		1977		1976		1975	
ASSETS										
Current Assets:										
Cash	$ 100,000	5.7%	$ 100,000	6.3%	$ 100,000	6.7%	$ 80,000	5.7%	$ 75,000	5.6%
Marketable Securities	50,000	2.9	25,000	1.6	25,000	1.7	20,000	1.4	25,000	1.9
Receivables	400,000	22.9	400,000	25.0	375,000	25.0	350,000	25.0	350,000	25.9
Inventory	375,000	21.4	350,000	21.9	350,000	23.3	325,000	23.2	325,000	24.1
Prepaid Expenses	25,000	1.4	25,000	1.6	25,000	1.7	25,000	1.8	25,000	1.9
Total Current Assets	950,000	54.3	900,000	56.3	875,000	58.3	800,000	57.1	800,000	59.3
Fixed Assets:										
Land	200,000	11.4	200,000	12.5	200,000	13.3	150,000	10.7	150,000	11.1
Plant & Equipment - At Cost	1,000,000	--	850,000	--	725,000	--	725,000	--	650,000	--
Less: Accumulated Depreciation	400,000	--	350,000	--	300,000	--	275,000	--	250,000	--
Plant & Equipment - Net	600,000	34.3	500,000	31.2	425,000	28.4	450,000	32.2	400,000	29.6
Total Fixed Assets	800,000	45.7	700,000	43.7	625,000	41.7	600,000	42.9	550,000	40.7
Total Assets	$1,750,000	100.0%	$1,600,000	100.0%	$1,500,000	100.0%	$1,400,000	100.0%	$1,350,000	100.0%
LIABILITIES										
Current Liabilities:										
Notes Payable	$ 50,000	2.9%	$ 50,000	3.1%	$ 50,000	3.3%	$ 50,000	3.6%	$ 50,000	3.7%
Current Portion LTD	75,000	4.3	50,000	3.1	50,000	3.3	50,000	3.6	50,000	3.7
Accounts Payable	175,000	10.0	150,000	9.4	150,000	10.0	150,000	10.6	150,000	11.1
Accrued Expenses	150,000	8.6	100,000	6.3	100,000	6.7	100,000	7.1	100,000	7.4
Contingent Liab.-Oper. Lease	180,000	10.3	150,000	9.4	125,000	8.3	105,000	7.5	80,000	5.9
Interest Payable	20,000	1.1	25,000	1.6	25,000	1.7	20,000	1.4	20,000	1.5
Total Current Liabilities	650,000	37.1	525,000	32.8	500,000	33.3	475,000	33.9	450,000	33.3
Long-Term Debt	350,000	20.0	425,000	26.6	400,000	26.7	375,000	26.8	400,000	29.6
Total Liabilities	1,000,000	57.1	950,000	59.4	900,000	60.0	850,000	60.7	850,000	63.0
SHAREHOLDERS' EQUITY										
Common Stock	100,000	5.7	100,000	6.3	100,000	6.7	100,000	7.1	100,000	7.4
10% Preferred Stk. ($1 Par Val.)	100,000	5.7	100,000	6.3	100,000	6.7	100,000	7.1	100,000	7.4
Retained Earnings	550,000	31.4	450,000	28.0	400,000	26.6	350,000	25.0	300,000	22.2
Total Shareholders' Equity	750,000	42.9	650,000	40.6	600,000	40.0	550,000	39.3	500,000	37.0
Total Liabilities & Shareholders' Equity	$1,750,000	100.0%	$1,600,000	100.0%	$1,500,000	100.0%	$1,400,000	100.0%	$1,350,000	100.0%

All figures rounded to nearest .1%.
LTD = Long-Term Debt.

Exhibit 13–2

ACE WIDGET COMPANY
Income statements—1975–1979

For Years Ended December 31

	1979		1978		1977		1976		1975	
Sales	$3,500,000	100.0%	$3,100,000	100.0%	$3,000,000	100.0%	$2,750,000	100.0%	$2,500,000	100.0%
Cost of Goods Sold	2,500,000	71.4	2,250,000	72.6	2,200,000	73.3	2,050,000	74.5	1,875,000	75.0
Gross Profit	1,000,000	28.6	850,000	27.4	800,000	26.7	700,000	25.5	625,000	25.0
Operating Expenses	700,000	20.0	625,000	20.2	600,000	20.0	550,000	20.0	500,000	20.0
Operating Income	300,000	8.6	225,000	7.2	200,000	6.7	150,000	5.5	125,000	5.0
Interest Expense	20,000	0.6	25,000	0.8	25,000	0.8	20,000	0.7	20,000	0.8
Pre-Tax Income	280,000	8.0	200,000	6.4	175,000	5.9	130,000	4.7	105,000	4.2
Income Taxes	115,000	3.3	80,000	2.6	70,000	2.3	48,000	1.7	35,000	1.4
Net Income	165,000	4.7	120,000	3.8	105,000	3.5	82,000	3.0	70,000	2.8
Preferred Dividends	10,000	0.3	10,000	0.3	10,000	0.3	10,000	0.4	10,000	0.4
Earnings Available for Common Stock	$ 155,000	4.4%	$ 110,000	3.5%	$ 95,000	3.2%	$ 72,000	2.6%	$ 60,000	2.4%
Dividends Paid Per Share	$ 0.55		$ 0.60		$ 0.45		$ 0.22		$ 0.10	
Retained Earns. Per Share	1.00		0.50		0.50		0.50		0.50	
Earnings Per Share (Based on 100,000 shares in all periods.)	$ 1.55		$ 1.10		$ 0.95		$ 0.72		$ 0.60	
Effective Tax Rate	41.1%		40.0%		40.0%		36.9%		33.3%	

divided by current liabilities. For most companies the only other current asset of any significance is inventory, usually the slowest of the current assets to be converted to cash, from the short-term liquidity consideration. The old rule of thumb was that a satisfactory quick ratio is 1.0:1; but, like the current ratio, comparison with industry norms is more meaningful in most cases than comparison with an absolute standard.

Using figures from Exhibit 13–1, the quick or acid test ratio for 1979 is:

$$\frac{\text{Cash} + \text{Marketable securities} + \text{Receivables}}{\text{Current liabilities}} = \frac{\$100,000 + \$50,000 + \$400,000}{\$650,000} = \underline{\underline{.85:1}}$$

Accounts receivable turnover

The accounts receivable turnover can be expressed either as the number of times per year that the accounts turn over on the average, or as the average number of days required to collect accounts. A slow accounts receivable turnover (long average collection period) not only puts a strain on a company's short-term liquidity but could be indicative of the possibility of excessive bad debt losses.

Typically, the accounts receivable turnover ratio is computed by dividing net credit sales by average accounts receivable. If cash sales (as opposed to credit sales) are not significant, or if the figures available do not distinguish between cash and credit sales, then sometimes total sales may be used in the computation. Because of limitations on available data, average accounts receivable may have to be computed by averaging the receivables at the beginning and the end of the period. Averaging receivables figures at the end of each quarter or each month gives a more accurate picture, especially if the business is subject to seasonal variations. In any case, if the ratio is for comparative purposes, the level of least data availability among the comparators may limit the extent of fine tuning that is feasible to compute for this ratio.

Using data from Exhibits 13–1 and 13–2, the accounts receivable turnover for Ace Widget Company for 1979 as:

$$\frac{1979 \text{ Sales}}{(\text{Accounts receivable end } 1979 + \text{Accounts receivable end } 1978) \div 2} = \begin{array}{l}\text{Accounts} \\ \text{receivable} \\ \text{turnover}\end{array}$$

Or:

$$\frac{\$3,500,000}{(\$400,000 + \$400,000) \div 2} = \underline{\underline{8.75 \text{ times}}}$$

The number of times turnover is divided into 365 days expresses this variable in terms of average collection period. For Ace Widget Company this is 365 days divided by 8.75 times turnover, equalling 41.7 days average collection period. Incidentally, some analysts use 360 days instead of 365 days—a minor irritant among the many examples of inconsistencies in valuation practice.

The sales to receivables ratio reported in *RMA Annual Statement Studies*[1] is net sales for the year divided by accounts and trade notes receivable as of the end of the year. Therefore, if a comparison is to be made with RMA statistics, the ratio for the subject company should be computed in the same manner as the RMA ratio. For Ace Widget Company, this simplifies the computation to:

$$\frac{1979 \text{ sales}}{\text{Accounts receivable end 1979}} = \frac{\$3,500,000}{\$400,000} = \underline{8.75 \text{ times}}$$

Note that this ratio would differ from the above-mentioned ratio if the average accounts receivable were not equal to those of the year-end, which was the case with Ace Widget in 1979. This is equivalent to (365 ÷ 8.75) = 41.7 average days collection period.

Inventory turnover

The inventory turnover ratio typically is computed by dividing the cost of goods sold by the average inventory. As with accounts receivable turnover, a slow inventory turnover (long average holding period) not only puts a strain on the company's liquidity but could indicate obsolete or otherwise undesirable inventory.

Also, as with accounts receivable turnover, the ratio is more meaningful if it can be computed using quarterly or monthly inventory data, especially for companies with seasonal aspects in their operation; but data limitations make this impractical in more cases than not.

Using data from Exhibits 13–1 and 13–2, the inventory turnover for the Ace Widget Company for 1979 is:

$$\frac{1979 \text{ Cost of goods sold}}{(\text{Inventory end 1979} + \text{Inventory end 1978}) \div 2} = \text{Inventory turnover ratio}$$

Or:

$$\frac{\$2,500,000}{(\$375,000 + \$350,000) \div 2} = \underline{6.9 \text{ times}}$$

As with accounts receivable turnover, inventory turnover also can be expressed in terms of average number of days. For Ace Widget Company this is 365 days divided by 6.9 times inventory turnover, equaling 52.9 average days to sell inventory.

RMA Annual Statement Studies[2] reports inventory turnover in the same manner as accounts receivable turnover—dividing cost of sales only by ending inventory. If comparisons with RMA data are to be made, this computation should be made. For Ace Widget this simplifies the computation to:

[1]*RMA Annual Statement Studies, 1979* (Philadelphia: Robert Morris Associates, Inc.). Published annually. SEE Exhibit 8–3 for Interpretation of Statement Studies Figures.

[2]Ibid. SEE Exhibit 8–3 for Interpretation of Statement Studies Figures.

$$\frac{\text{1979 Cost of goods sold}}{\text{Inventory end 1979}} = \frac{\$2,500,000}{375,000} = \underline{\underline{6.7 \text{ times}}}$$

This is equivalent to (365 ÷ 6.7) = 54.5 average number of days of inventory holding period.

Net working capital is defined as *current assets minus current liabilities*. Net working capital is considered so important that its analysis is the subject of an entire separate financial statement, the statement of changes in financial position, discussed in Chapter 12. As a company's sales go up, if its current ratio, its accounts receivable collection period, and its inventory turnover remain constant, the working capital must go up, because the company will have to carry more receivables and inventory to support the increased level of sales.

A simplistic way to compute the sales to net working capital ratio is to divide sales for the fiscal year just ended by net working capital on the fiscal year-end. This can be useful when compared with the company's own past history and with other companies in the industry.

Using the figures from Exhibits 13–1 and 13–2, the sales to net working capital ratio is:

$$\frac{\text{Sales}}{\text{Current assets} - \text{Current liabilities}} = \frac{\$3,500,000}{\$950,000 - \$650,000} = \underline{\underline{11.7{:}1}}$$

A more sophisticated way to compute the ratio would be to use average net working capital, rather than to use ending net working capital as the denominator.

A high ratio of sales to net working capital results from a favorable turnover of accounts receivable and inventory, and indicates an efficient use of assets. However, a high sales to net working capital ratio also can indicate risk arising from possibly inadequate short-term liquidity. The economy and most industries are subject to some degree of cyclicality, in economic activity and in liquidity, which do not necessarily run exactly in tandem. The analyst should consider the highest reasonable level of sales that might be anticipated, couple it with the largest accounts receivable and the longest inventory turnover periods that might occur, and assess the adequacy of the working capital under that scenario.

Sales to net working capital

The general purpose of capital structure or balance-sheet leverage ratios is to aid in making some quantifiable statements about the long-term solvency of the business, and the ability of the business to deal with financial problems and opportunities as they may arise. As with most ratios, such analysis generally is most meaningful when compared with other companies in the same industry. Useful comparisons also can be made within the same company over time.

BALANCE-SHEET LEVERAGE RATIOS

Total debt to total asset ratio

Of the various balance-sheet ratios designed to measure the long-term adequacy of the company's capital structure, the total debt to total asset ratio probably is the one most popularly used. It is defined as *total debt divided by total assets*. This measures the total amount of the company's funding provided by creditors of all categories as a percentage of the company's total assets. Using figures from Exhibit 13–1, the total debt to total asset ratio for Ace Widget Company at the end of 1979 is:

$$\frac{\text{Total liabilities}}{\text{Total assets}} = \frac{\$1,000,000}{\$1,750,000} = \underline{\underline{0.57}}$$

Equity to total asset ratio

The equity to total asset ratio is sometimes just called the "equity ratio," and is computed by dividing the total equity by the total assets. It is equal to 1 minus the total debt to total asset ratio. Since these two ratios are merely two ways of stating the same thing, most analysts would include one or the other but not both in the presentation. Using figures from Exhibit 13–1, the equity to total asset ratio for Ace Widget at the end of 1979 is:

$$\frac{\text{Total equity}}{\text{Total assets}} = \frac{\$750,000}{\$1,750,000} = \underline{\underline{0.43}}$$

Long-term debt to total capital ratio

Unfortunately, there is considerable ambiguity in the terminology of financial statement analysis, especially in definitions of ratios. When some analysts say "debt ratio," they mean "debt divided by total assets," the ratio previously discussed. Other analysts say "debt ratio" to mean "long-term debt divided by total capital." Therefore, to avoid misinterpretation, it seems best to avoid the term *debt ratio* and use a title for the ratio that specifically defines the ratio intended.

There is a reasonably strong consensus that *total capital* should be defined as *total assets minus current liabilities*. Using figures from Exhibit 13–1, the long-term debt to total capital ratio for Ace Widget Company is:

$$\frac{\text{Long-term debt}}{\text{Total assets} - \text{Current liabilities}} = \frac{\$350,000}{\$1,750,000 - \$650,000} = \underline{\underline{0.32}}$$

The analyst should check to make sure that any ratios used for comparisons actually are computed by the same definitions—or the comparisons may be misleading. For example, some analysts include deferred taxes in the denominator as part of long-term capital, and others do not.

Equity to total capital ratio

This is simply 1 minus the long-term debt to total capital ratio, so there is usually no need to compute both. Using figures from Exhibit 13–1, the equity to total capital ratio for Ace Widget at the end of 1979 is:

$$\frac{\text{Total equity}}{\text{Total assets} - \text{Current liabilities}} = \frac{\$750,000}{\$1,750,000 - \$650,000} = \underline{\underline{0.68}}$$

Sometimes the debt is expressed as a ratio to equity, rather than to total assets. Again, some analysts prefer to focus on total debt and others just on long-term debt.

The RMA Annual Statement Studies[3] use total debt and use only tangible equity. In other words, the RMA debt to equity ratio is computed as:

Debt to equity ratios

$$\frac{\text{Total liabilities}}{\text{Total equity} - \text{Intangible assets}}$$

These ratios also sometimes are expressed in reverse; that is, equity to total debt or equity to long-term debt. There are numerous variations of balance-sheet leverage ratios, but the foregoing are the ones most frequently used.

INCOME STATEMENT COVERAGE RATIOS

In general, income statement coverage ratios are designed to measure the margin by which certain obligations of the company appear to be being met.

Times interest earned

The most popularly used of the income statement coverage ratios is times interest earned. It is designed to measure the firm's ability to meet interest payments. The times interest earned ratio is defined as *earnings before interest and taxes* (EBIT) *divided by interest*. Using figures from Exhibit 13–1, the times interest earned for Ace Widget Company for 1979 is:

$$\frac{\text{Earnings before interest and taxes}}{\text{Interest}} = \frac{\$300,000}{\$20,000} = \underline{\underline{15.0 \text{ times}}}$$

Note that the statements of Ace Widget Company are presented in the conventional manner, with interest shown as a separate deduction after operating income. Some closely-held companies do not present the statements in this way, so the EBIT figure may have to be computed, rather than taken directly from a line item on the income statement.

Coverage of fixed charges

The coverage of fixed charges is a more inclusive ratio, in that it includes coverage not only of interest but of other items. It is defined as *the sum of earnings before interest and taxes, plus fixed charges divided by fixed charges*. This definition leaves an almost unlimited spectrum of possibilities for determining what items of fixed charges to include. The most common items are lease payments and required installments of principal payments toward debt retirement.

In the Ace Widget Company example, the information shown in Exhibits

---

[3]Ibid. SEE Exhibit 8–3 for Interpretation of Statement Studies Figures.

13–1 and 13–2 is not totally adequate to compute this ratio. It is typical that the analyst may have to see some schedules or ask some questions beyond the normal statement presentations to acquire the information necessary to compute this ratio. Let's assume that the current portion of long-term debt shown in the current liability section of the balance sheet in Exhibit 13–1 is an annual required reduction of debt principal, and that the operating expenses as shown in Exhibit 13–1 include $180,000 per year lease payments on the premises occupied by the company. The coverage of fixed charges for Ace Widget then could be computed as:

$$\frac{\text{Earnings before interest and taxes} + \text{Lease payments}}{\text{Interest} + \text{Current portion of long-term debt} + \text{Lease payments}}$$

Or:

$$\frac{\$300,000 + \$180,000}{\$20,000 + \$75,000 + \$180,000} = \underline{\underline{1.7 \text{ times}}}$$

Coverage of preferred dividends

If a company has a preferred stock issue outstanding, it sometimes is useful to compute how adequate the earnings are to cover the preferred dividends. The simple way to do this is to divide the net income after taxes by the preferred dividend requirement; this can be a useful ratio. However, most analysts concur that a more meaningful coverage ratio is one which includes coverage of the interest payments on debt obligations as well as the preferred dividends. Since preferred stock dividends must be paid with after-tax dollars, the computation also must consider the tax requirements.

The balance sheet in Exhibit 13–1 shows 100,000 shares of 10 percent preferred stock are outstanding, with a par value of $1. This indicates a preferred dividend requirement of $.10 per share. The choice of a tax rate to use in the computation is a little bit arbitrary, because the rate will go up as the earnings (and thus the coverage) go up. In the example, the taxes are $115,000 on $280,000 of pretax income, or a 41.1 percent average rate. Using that rate and the EBIT from Exhibit 13–2, the preferred dividend coverage can be computed as:

$$\frac{\text{Earnings before interest and taxes}}{\text{Interest} + \text{Preferred dividends} \left(\dfrac{1}{1 - \text{Tax rate}} \right)}$$

Or:

$$\frac{\$300,000}{\$20,000 + \$10,000 \left(\dfrac{1}{1 - .41} \right)} = \underline{\underline{8.1 \text{ times}}}$$

Depending on the purpose of the analysis, some fixed charges in addition to interest (such as lease payments, and so on) also may be reflected in the calculations. If a company is considering issuing a preferred stock, a computation of the preferred dividend coverage would be a useful exercise to determine whether the anticipated dividend payments can, realistically, be met.

The four most commonly used measures of operating performance are gross margin, operating profit to sales, pretax income to sales, and net profit to sales. Since all are percentages of sales, they may be read directly from the common-size income statements, as shown in Exhibit 13–2.

Analysts will argue until doomsday whether return on equity or return on assets is a more meaningful measure of investment return. Proponents of return on equity say that the return on stockholder investment is what counts, and the majority adhere to this argument. However, proponents of return on assets say that management should be measured by the return on total assets utilized, without regard to the company's capital structure, which can have a considerable bearing on return on equity if return on assets is held constant. Each measure is useful for its own purpose.

Return on equity usually means return on common equity capital. If a company has preferred stock outstanding, then the analyst might consider computing return on total equity and return on common equity, since both can be useful measures. If making comparison with one or more ratios of return on equity for other companies that have preferred stock outstanding, the analyst should be sure that the ratios are being computed on the same basis for the subject company and for the comparator company.

Unless otherwise specified, return on equity means *after* taxes. Once in a while you will find someone, perhaps a broker trying to sell a business, quoting return on equity that has been computed on a pretax basis. This is very misleading, since income taxes are a very real cost, and the investor's return is what he has left after corporate taxes. In fact, if the computation is being made for a Subchapter S corporation, a partnership, or a sole proprietorship, then I recommend having the taxes that would be paid if it were a regular corporation be deducted from the net income before the computation is made. Sometimes there are legitimate reasons to compare companies' returns on equity on a pretax basis, but when doing so it should be specified clearly—and recognized by the parties using the data—that it is a departure from the conventional meaning and computation of return on equity.

One other issue to be resolved in the return on equity analysis is whether the selected equity base is the one at the beginning of the period, the end of the period, or the average for the period. There is consensus among analysts that the average equity provides the basis for the most meaningful analysis. The most commonly used method is to divide the earnings for the year by the average of the beginning and ending equity. If adequate information is available, this can be further fine tuned by averaging quarterly or monthly equity figures.

Since the return on equity is a percentage, the result should be the same whether the computations are made on a total company basis or on a per share basis, at least if there is no dilution. If a weighted average number of shares has been used in the per share earnings computation, this will work out if the average equity base is weighted in the same manner.

Using the data from Exhibits 13–1 and 13–2, the return on equity for Ace Widget Company for 1979 is:

$$\frac{\text{Net income} - \text{Preferred dividends}}{\text{Average common stockholders' equity}} = \frac{\$165,000 - \$10,000}{(\$650,000 + \$550,000) \div 2} = \underline{25.8\%}$$

On a per share basis, with 100,000 shares outstanding for Ace Widget, the computation is:

$$\frac{\text{Earnings per share}}{\text{Average book value per share}} = \frac{\$1.55}{(\$6.50 + \$5.50) \div 2} = \underline{25.8\%}$$

Return on total assets

The computations for return on total assets are similar to those for return on equity. One key difference is that interest, net of its related tax deduction, should be added back to the net income. A realistic analysis of return on total assets should not be influenced by how the company chooses to utilize debt in its capital structure.

Again, using figures from Exhibits 13–1 and 13–2, the computation of return on assets for Ace Widget Company for 1979 is:

$$\frac{\text{Net income} + \text{Interest} (1 - \text{Tax rate})}{(\text{Beginning total assets} + \text{Ending total assets}) \div 2}$$

Or:

$$\frac{\$165,000 + \$20,000 (1 - .41)}{(\$1,750,000 + \$1,600,000) \div 2} = \underline{10.6\%}$$

ASSET UTILIZATION RATIOS

Asset utilization ratios indicate how efficiently the firm is employing its assets in its operations. This series of ratios relates sales to each of several assets or asset groups. Ratios that are sometimes computed include sales to cash, to accounts receivable, to inventories, to working capital (discussed under liquidity ratios), to fixed assets, to other assets, and to total assets.

SAMPLE SUMMARY OF RATIO ANALYSES

Exhibits 13–3 and 13–4 provide samples of summaries of the ratio analyses discussed in the foregoing sections as applied to Ace Widget Company.

Exhibit 13–3 shows a number of statistics for Ace Widget, in comparison with industry averages compiled by *RMA Annual Statement Studies*. Exhibit 13–4 shows ratios for Ace Widget over a five-year period. Minor discrepancies between the figures shown in Exhibits 13–3 and 13–4 compared with figures in the text of the chapter are accounted for by the figures in the exhibits being computed on ending statement figures only rather than on averages of beginning and ending statement figures.

Exhibit 13–3
Ace Widget Company and Robert Morris Associates *Annual Statement Studies*—SIC No. 3544-Widget Maker (balance sheet and income data)

	RMA	ACE
Asset Size	$1-10MM	
Number of Statements	124	1979
ASSETS		
Cash & Equivalents	7.8%	8.6%
Accounts & Notes Receivable-Trade (Net)	24.9	22.9
Inventory	24.1	21.4
All Other Current	1.8	1.4
Total Current Assets	58.6	54.3
Fixed Assets (Net)	32.9	45.7
Intangibles (Net)	0.7	---
All Other Non-Current	7.8	---
Total Assets	100.0%	100.0%
LIABILITIES & NET WORTH		
Notes Payable — Short-Term	8.0%	2.9%
Current Maturing Long-Term Debt	3.6	4.3
Accounts & Notes Payable-Trade	13.2	10.0
Accrued Expenses	9.9	8.6
All Other Current	4.1	11.4
Total Current Liabilities	38.8	37.2
Long-Term Debt	12.1	20.0
All Other Non-Current	1.3	---
Net Worth	47.7	42.8
Total Liabilities & Net Worth	100.0%	100.0%
INCOME DATA		
Net Sales	100.0%	100.0%
Cost of Sales	75.2	71.4
Gross Profit	24.8	28.6
Operating Expenses	17.3	20.0
Operating Profit	7.5	8.6
All Other Expenses (Net)	1.0	0.6
Profit Before Taxes	6.5%	8.0%

Source: Robert Morris Associates' (RMA) *Annual Statement Studies*, 1978, copyright 1978, Philadelphia, PA. SEE Exhibit 8–3 for Interpretation of Statement Studies Figures.

Exhibit 13–3 (continued)
Ace Widget Company and Robert Morris Associates' *Annual*
Statement Studies—SIC No. 3544-Widget Maker (ratio analysis)

Asset Size Number of Statements	RMA $1-10MM 124	ACE
		1979
Current	2.1 1.6 1.1	1.5
Quick	1.3 0.8 0.6	0.9
Sales/Receivables	9.8 7.1 5.6	8.8
Cost of Sales/Inventory	10.7 5.8 4.0	6.7
Sales/Working Capital	5.4 9.2 31.4	11.7
EBIT/Interest	16.6 6.7 2.9	15.0
Cash Flow/Current Maturing Long-Term Debt	8.9 3.2 1.4	3.3
Fixed Assets/Net Worth	0.4 0.7 1.1	1.1
Debt/Net Worth	0.6 1.1 2.0	1.3
% Profit Before Taxes/Tangible Net Worth	35.9 21.9 12.8	37.3
% Profit Before Taxes/Total Assets	18.0 10.2 4.7	16.0
Sales/Net Fixed Assets	8.6 5.9 3.5	4.4
Sales/Total Assets	2.1 1.8 1.4	2.0
% Depreciation, Depletion, Amortization/Sales	1.9 2.8 4.0	1.4
% Lease & Rental Expense/Sales	0.5 1.3 1.9	5.1

Source: Robert Morris Associates' (RMA) *Annual Statement Studies*, 1978, copyright 1978, Philadelphia,
PA. SEE Figure 8–3 for Interpretation of Statement Studies Figures.

Exhibit 13–4
Ace Widget Company (selected ratios—1975–1979)

	For Years Ended December 31				
	1979	1978	1977	1976	1975
Short-Term Liquidity Measures:					
Current Ratio	1.5	1.7	1.8	1.7	1.8
Quick Ratio (Acid Test Ratio)	0.8	1.0	1.0	1.0	1.1
Accounts Rec. Turnover (Days)	41.7	47.1	45.6	46.5	51.1
Inventory Turnover (Days)	54.8	56.8	58.1	57.9	63.3
Sales to Net Work. Cap.	11.7	8.3	8.0	8.5	7.1
Balance Sheet Leverage Ratios:					
Total Debt to Total Asset	0.57	0.59	0.60	0.61	0.63
Equity to Total Assets	0.43	0.41	0.40	0.39	0.37
LTD to Total Capital	0.32	0.40	0.40	0.41	0.44
Equity to Total Capital	0.68	0.60	0.60	0.59	0.56
Total Liabilities to Total Tangible Equity	1.3	1.5	1.5	1.5	1.7
Income Statement Coverage Ratios:					
Times Interest Earned	15.0	9.0	8.0	7.5	6.3
Coverage of Fixed Charges	1.7	1.7	1.6	1.5	1.4
Coverage of Preferred Dividends	8.1	5.4	4.8	4.2	3.6
Return on Investment Ratios:					
Return on Equity	22.1%	17.6%	16.5%	14.4%	NA
Return on Common Equity	25.8%	21.0%	20.0%	18.0%	NA
Return on Assets	10.6%	8.7%	8.3%	6.9%	NA
Asset Utilization Ratios:					
Sales to Receivables	8.8	7.8	8.0	7.9	7.1
Sales to Net Work. Cap.		(See above)			
Sales to Net Fixed Assets	4.4	4.4	4.8	4.6	4.5
Sales to Total Assets	2.0	1.9	2.0	2.0	1.9

LTD = Long-Term Debt.

All figures rounded to nearest .1.

IV
PRESENTING THE REPORT

14

WRITTEN PRESENTATIONS

The form, scope, and content of written business appraisal reports can vary tremendously, depending on the nature and size of the business being appraised and, especially, on the use or uses to which the appraisal report may be put. In Chapter 2, Defining the Appraisal Assignment, the point was made that the assignment should include at least a general statement about the nature of the written output that is expected.

The scope and content of the written report are governed primarily by the legal requirements and the person or groups of people to be satisfied. Legal requirements can arise from federal and state tax laws, ERISA, the SEC, state statutes on contested property settlements or appraisal rights of dissenting stockholders, and various legally mandated fiduciary responsibilities of parties involved in a transaction. People who are to be satisfied include present and prospective parties at interest and their beneficiaries, representatives of whatever regulatory authorities may be involved, a judge and possibly a jury if litigation or potential litigation is involved, and all the related parties that may be involved, such as attorneys, CPAs, and trustees.

In the early planning of the valuation case, the analyst should think through the various legal requirements and parties that must be satisfied and plan the general form of the written report and the steps leading to it. If changes are made in the assignment during the course of the project, any implications for changes in the written report should be noted by a memo to the file, with a copy to the client if appropriate.

If litigation or potential litigation is involved, the analyst should work closely with the attorney in structuring the report. The analyst must respect the attorney's knowledge and interpretations of the laws involved, and also the attorney's methods of approaching and handling negotiations. In some cases, the attorney may wish a complete written report that puts all the cards on the table at the outset to assist in reaching a negotiated conclusion. In other cases, there may be very good reasons for the attorney to wish to hold some hole cards, so the written report, at least initially, may be very abbreviated. Budget often enters in. The attorney may feel there is a good chance of reaching a negotiated conclusion on the basis of a preliminary written report, and may wish to avoid incurring the cost of a completely documented report unless the early negotiations fail to result in an agreement. Where litigation is involved, it is usually safest to presume that the attorney has the best grasp of the laws and the postures of the parties involved, and that the attorney must orchestrate the development and implementation of the case.

In preparing a written report, it is a good idea to follow the American Society of Appraisers (ASA) Principles of Appraisal Practice, which set forth a list of items that the society feels should be included in any complete, formal appraisal report, whether the property being appraised is real estate, antiques, a business enterprise, or anything else. The relevant section of the ASA Principles of Appraisal Practice is presented in Exhibit 14–1.

It usually works best to place the definition of the appraisal assignment at the beginning of the written appraisal report. The brevity or detail that is

Exhibit 14–1

Report requirements section of ASA Principles of Appraisal Practice

8 APPRAISAL REPORTS

In preceding sections it was stated that good appraisal practice, as defined by the Society, requires the inclusion of certain specific explanations, descriptions, and statements in an appraisal report. These are summarized herewith. (These requirements do not apply to reports prepared by a staff appraiser for the exclusive and non-public use of his employer; but do apply to reports prepared by a public appraiser, i.e., one who offers his services for a fee to the general public.)

8.1 Description of the Property Which Is the Subject of an Appraisal Report

It is required that the property with which an appraisal report is concerned, whether tangible, intangible, real, or personal, be fully described therein, the elements of such description being: (a) identification, (b) legal rights and restrictions encompassed in the ownership, where these are not obvious, (c) value characteristics, and (d) physical condition, where applicable. (See Sec. 6.8)

8.2 Statement of the Objectives of the Appraisal Work

It is required that an appraisal report include a statement of the objectives for which the work was performed: to determine a value, to estimate a cost, to forecast an earning power, to ascertain certain facts, to reach conclusions and make recommendations for action in specified matters, etc. (See Sec. 2.1)

It is required that the meaning attached by the appraiser to any specific kind of value or estimated cost which is the objective of the appraisal undertaking be described and explained in the appraisal report. (See Sec. 6.1)

8.3 Statement of the Contingent and Limiting Conditions to Which the Appraisal Findings Are Subject

It is required that statements, information, and/or data, which were obtained by the appraiser from members of other professions, or official or other presumably reliable sources, and the validity of which affects the appraisal findings, be summarized or stated in full in the appraisal report and the sources given, so that verification desired by any user of the report may be accomplished. (See Sec. 6.4)

If an appraisal is a hypothetical one, it is required that it be labeled as hypothetical, that the reason a hypothetical appraisal was made be stated, and that the assumed hypothetical conditions be set forth. (See Sec. 6.5)

If an appraisal is a fractional appraisal, it is required that it be labeled as fractional and that the limitations on the use of the reported figure be stated. (See Sec. 6.3)

If a preliminary appraisal report is issued, namely, one in which the figures are subject to refinement or change, it is required that the report be labeled as preliminary and that the limitations on its use be stated. (See Sec. 7.6)

8.4 Description and Explanation in the Appraisal Report of the Appraisal Method Used

It is required that the method selected by the appraiser as applicable to the subject appraisal undertaking be described and explained in the appraisal report. (See Sec. 6.2)

8.5 Statement of the Appraiser's Disinterestedness

It is required that the appraiser include a statement in his appraisal report that he has no present or contemplated future interest in the subject property or any other interest which might tend to prevent his making a fair and unbiased appraisal or, if he does have such an interest, to set forth fully the nature and extent of that interest. (See Sec. 7.3)

8.6 Signatures to Appraisal Reports and the Inclusion of Dissenting Opinions

It is required that the party who makes the appraisal or who has the appraisal made under his supervision sign the appraisal report. (See Sec. 7.4)

It is required that all collaborating appraisers, issuing a joint appraisal report, who agree with the findings, sign the report; and that any collaborating appraiser who disagrees with any or all of the findings of the others, prepare, sign, and include in the appraisal report his dissenting opinion. (See Sec. 7.4)

Source: ASA Principles of Appraisal Practice and Code of Ethics, 1979.

appropriate will be a matter of judgment in each case. From that point on, the length and organization of the report leading to the conclusion will vary with the assignment. Suggestions for various situations are discussed in the following sections. If the report is more than a few pages in length, it usually is a convenience to the users of the report to have a brief summary of the conclusion included in the introductory section.

GENERAL PRINCIPLES OF A GOOD WRITTEN REPORT

The basic principles for writing a good business valuation report are similar to those for writing a good term paper or thesis. The reader must be able to understand the purpose and scope of the assignment, what was done to carry it out, what conclusion was reached, and what the logical flow of data and rationale was that led to and supported the conclusion. The report should be well organized, as comprehensive as the purpose calls for, well documented, and presented in a correct, consistent, and easily readable style. The entire content should be relevant to the purpose of the report, avoiding extraneous material.

The writer of the report should be conscious of the audience for the report and write it in such a manner that the intended audience will understand it and find it convincing. If terminology or references are used that would not be familiar to the intended audience, such items should be explained adequately so their relevance to the report and to the points being made will be understood. Each aspect of the conclusion(s) should be so clearly supported that no link in the chain of data and rationale leading to the conclusion is obscured and left to the reader's imagination.

One of the commonest shortcomings of all too many business valuation reports is inadequate documentation. Research people use the term *replicability* as one of the hallmarks of an acceptable research report. This means that the documentation should describe all the steps taken so adequately that the reader could duplicate the exercise. Whenever information or opinion is attributable to anyone besides the author of the report, the source should be cited adequately, so the reader can find and consult the source himself. In occasional instances where it is necessary to omit source citations because of confidentiality, the justification should be made obvious. Such documentation becomes particularly important if the work ever should have to be defended in court.

TAX-RELATED CASES

This section presents the written report format that the Willamette Management Associates staff has used fairly consistently for tax-related valuation reports. Although it is presented here as a format for tax-related reports, it is a good, generalized format that can be adapted with appropriate modifications to many other uses. Also, of course, most of the criteria and steps required in valuations for tax purposes have applicability in valuations for other purposes as well.

In general, tax-related cases are governed by Revenue Ruling 59–60. This applies to federal gift and estate tax cases, income tax cases, recapitalizations, and employee stock ownership plans. Most state revenue statutes follow the federal statutes quite closely, and the same format is equally applicable for state inheritance tax or income tax cases.

General organization of report

Following a brief introductory section that defines the assignment, summarizes the conclusion, and sets the stage for the detailed report, an organizational pattern which moves from the general to the specific seems to serve many purposes quite well. It provides a logical flow of data and analysis within which all the necessary considerations required in Revenue Ruling 59–60 can be incorporated.

Most situations seem to lend themselves well to be organized into five major sections, in the following order:

1. Introduction.
2. Economic data.
3. Industry data.
4. Company data.
5. The valuation exercise and conclusion.

Introduction

The introduction can be brief, conveying three key categories of information: (1) The assignment, (2) sources of information utilized, and (3) the valuation approach or approaches used and the conclusion.

The assignment. Defining the appraisal assignment was the subject of Chapter 2. It is logical to start the text of the report with the elements of the appraisal assignment which were discussed in that chapter.

The standard of value to be used is one aspect of the appraisal assignment. The most commonly used standard is fair market value. The standard of value not only should be stated but also be defined. This may be a paragraph within the appraisal assignment section of the introduction, or it may be treated separately as a brief section immediately following the appraisal assignment section.

Sources of information. After the description of the assignment is a convenient place to present a generalized list of the sources of information used. The degree of detail that is appropriate depends on the case. In essence this section of the report is a summary of the sources used as discussed in Part II (Chapters 6 through 10) of this book.

The financial statements and supporting schedules that were examined should be listed, including the years that were examined for each statement or category. Other company financial information used should be listed. If one or a few asset appraisal reports were examined, they might be listed separately; if many such reports were examined, they might be described in summary as a group. The same thing applies to leases or contracts. Other company data consulted should be listed if it is significant.

Facilities visited should be listed. If a few interviews were conducted, the names and positions of those interviewed might be listed; but if many interviews were conducted, the categories and scope of the interviews might be summarized.

Major sources of economic data, such as periodicals relied on, may be specified and other sources referred to generally. The same comment applies to industry data. The extent and nature of both economic and industry data that are relevant varies greatly from one case to another. The point is to summarize what sources were called upon for the case at hand.

Sources used to compile comparable company data should be listed. If specific sources were utilized in determining such factors as marketability or minority interest discounts, or both, it could be appropriate to reference them in the information sources section.

In most cases it is not necessary to include exact citations in this section, since such citations will appear in later sections when necessary. The purpose of the information source section is to summarize for the reader the sources that were consulted in the course of preparing the report. Hopefully, at this early stage of the written report, the reader will feel the background information that was collected and taken into consideration was adequate for the analysis and conclusion.

Valuation approach or approaches and conclusion. This section should indicate briefly the broad criterion or criteria used in reaching the valuation conclusion, such as capitalization of earnings, net asset value or adjusted asset values, or whatever. This should be followed by a brief statement of the conclusion reached.

Optional summary description of company. Sometimes it may be convenient for the reader to have a brief summary description of the company included in the introduction. If this is desired, it may be placed between the description of assignment and the sources of information section.

The brief description may include such information as how long the company has been in business, where it is located, and what it does. (Presumably, the form of organization, such as corporation, partnership, and so on, was covered under the definition of the entity being appraised in the assignment section, as discussed in Chapter 2.)

Economic section

The key word in choosing what should be included in the economic section is relevancy. What the reader wants to know about are those aspects of economic conditions that may have a bearing on the prospects for the subject company. If a company's business is tied to the economy of a particular region, then it would be appropriate to divide the economic section into two parts, the national economy and the economy of the region that is directly relevant.

Remember, if the report is a retrospective valuation (a valuation as of an earlier date), the economic section must follow the same rules as other sections, that is, the writer must be standing in time on the valuation date, using only economic data and forecasts available then, even though subsequent events may have produced different results. A discussion of what economic data might be included and where to find it is the subject of Chapter 8.

Industry section

The industry section should give the reader a primer on the nature of the industry involved and current conditions in the industry. This section should discuss the markets and end uses for the industry's products or services, and the factors that affect the potential growth and volatility in demand. If there are special supply factors, these should be pointed out.

The structure of the industry should be discussed. That is, how big is the industry, how many competitors are there, and how do they compete? Is the industry characterized by commoditylike price competition or by product differentiation?

Even though this section is on the industry rather than on the specific subject company, it is a good idea in many cases to make brief mention here of how the company fits into the industry, perhaps noting such things as its size relative to competitors and any specialized segments of the market it serves.

This can give the reader some grasp of the role or niche of the subject company within the context of its industry group.

Some companies clearly are engaged in two or more different industries. In such cases it usually is necessary to include a separate industry section in the report for each industry in which the company has significant involvement. Gathering industry data is the subject of Chapter 8.

Company section

The company section should be descriptive and analytical. That is, it should present the facts that the reader needs to know to understand the company, and it should analyze those facts and make qualitative judgments on the positive and negative aspects of the company that will have a bearing on its value.

In most written business valuation reports, the description and analysis of the company turns out to be the longest section. It could be organized into any number of subsections. In most cases the material that needs to be covered can be subsumed under the following five headings: (1) background, (2) operations, (3) management, (4) financial condition, and (5) ownership.

Background. The reader gains some perspective on the company by being apprised of when it started and of a brief chronology of major changes or events in its history. Such changes that might appropriately be included in this section would be name changes, changes in form of organization (e.g., from partnership to corporation), changes in location, changes in major line or lines of business, mergers with or acquisitions of other companies, startups of new operations, and changes in ownership control. Any significant or unusual events during or affecting the period under analysis should be mentioned, such as a major fire or strike that may have disrupted operations.

The section should conclude with a summary statement about the company's present position. For some companies this can be done in a single sentence, such as, "The company presently operates as a corporation manufacturing pine boxes in a single plant in Waukesha, Wisconsin." For other companies it may require an elaborate organization chart. There may be one or more subsidiaries. Various subsidiaries may be wholly or partially owned. The subsidiaries may be incorporated or they may be other forms of organization, such as general or limited partnerships. The subsidiaries may not all have the same fiscal year as the parent company. The parent company may reflect different affiliates by consolidated statements or by the equity or cost methods of accounting. The reader should be given a clear and complete picture of the company's structure.

Exhibit 14–2 is a sample of an organization chart designed to help the reader understand a company with several affiliates. Note that for each affiliate the information in the chart indicates the form of organization, the ownership percentage, the fiscal year, and the accounting method by which the affiliate is reflected on the parent company financial statements.

Operations. The operations section should list the company's operating locations and describe its products and services, markets, facilities, employee

Exhibit 14–2
Northern Hospitality Company and affiliates

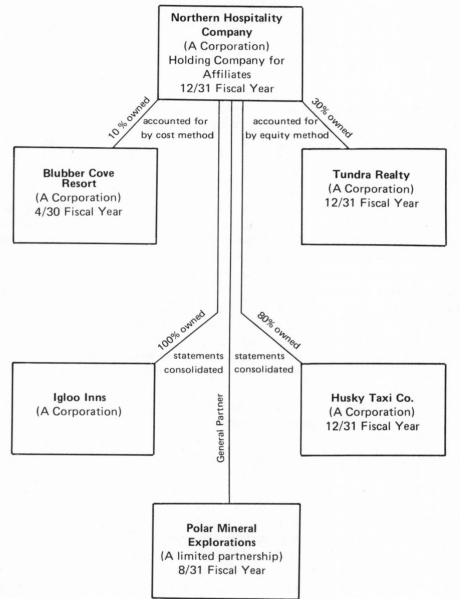

structure, and key information regarding supplies and suppliers, if applicable. It is completely arbitrary, of course, whether all this is included in a single section or separated into several sections, such as marketing, facilities and production, personnel, and supply situation.

If the company has proprietary products, the section should explain how the products serve the perceived market and how they differ from competition. In a sense, one might say that this section explains the economic justification for the company's existence, at least conceptually. This could be a good place in the report to include some qualitative judgments about just how strongly the company's existence really is justified. A discussion of the company's competition would be an appropriate part of this section.

The report should indicate which facilities are leased and which are owned. It should note the expiration dates of current leases and the extent to which they appear to be above, below, or near current market rates. It is desirable to include some qualitative judgment on the apparent condition and efficiency of the facilities. If there are any major problems on the horizon, such as a forced move or sharply increased costs because of a lease expiration or some major cash outlays needed to replace or update equipment, such problems should be pointed out.

The report should indicate approximately how many employees there are, and how many are seasonal and part-time versus full-time if such a segmentation is applicable to the company. It is desirable to indicate whether the employees are unionized, and, if so, what unions and when the current contracts expire. It also may be useful to include some qualitative comments about employee turnover or longevity and labor relations.

For some kinds of companies, continuity of sources of supply is a critical consideration. If so, the adequacy of supply sources should be addressed. If applicable, a list of key suppliers may be included at this point.

A review of Chapters 6 and 7 on gathering company data will bring to mind many other factors that might be included in the operations section for any given company.

Management. The management section can be handled by a brief description of the position and background of each of the key people, along with some qualitative evaluation of the adequacy of present management and provision for management succession. Most closely-held companies suffer from weakness in this area to some degree, and the report should address this issue.

Financial condition. The analysis of the financial condition is, at least quantitatively, the most critical part of the company description. This is the section of the report that will contain the data developed as discussed in Part III of this book (Chapters 11 through 13), Financial Statement Analysis.

This section will contain the income statement and balance-sheet spread sheets for the number of years used in the analysis, preferably common-sized, as shown in Exhibits 13–1 and 13–2. It also is desirable to show the key percentages for the common-size statements in comparison with industry norms. An example of such a comparison is shown in the second part of Exhibit 13–3. Also, this section will present whatever ratio analysis the analyst considers relevant, preferably in comparison with industry norms. An example of such a comparison is shown in the second part of Exhibit 13–3. If trend analysis has been done on sales, earnings, or other variables the results should be presented in this section. Charts are useful in presenting trend analyses.

The Statement of Changes in Financial Position or the Statement of

Stockholders' Equity, or both, may be included in this section if the analyst feels they will be helpful in discussing the financial condition of the company. Otherwise, they can be included as part of the current financial statements, which normally will constitute one of the appendixes.

If adjustments have been made to the financial statements, the adjustments also should be presented in this section. Alternatively, if there are not too many adjustments and they are not complicated, the writer may merely discuss them in the text.

In any case, the section on financial condition should make some judgments about the quality of earnings and the adequacy of the company's assets and capital position.

Distribution of ownership. It usually is desirable to indicate who owns how many shares or what percentage of the entity. This helps to identify the control group. It may be appropriate in this section to identify the various owners' relationships to the company and to each other. If there is more than one class of stock, the provisions and ownership distribution of each class should be presented.

Approaches used in valuation. The valuation section, of course, is the essence of the report. It usually opens with a discussion of the valuation approach or approaches that were used. If one or more approaches would seem on the surface to be applicable to the company but were rejected, there should be an explanation of why the seemingly appropriate ones were considered inapplicable to the situation. The various approaches that might be used are discussed in Part I, Principles of Business Valuation, especially Chapters 4 and 5, on the discounted future earnings approach and a variety of conventional approaches.

Valuation section

Comparable company data. After discussing the valuation approaches used, the next logical step is to introduce data on comparable companies that can provide some valuation bench marks. Such data can include prices at which public companies in the same industry trade in the open market relative to earnings, book value, and other criteria, and data on prices at which mergers or sales of comparable private companies took place, if available. Chapter 9 discussed the collection of such data and its uses. The sample case in Chapter 15 gives an example of a format for its tabular presentation.

Analysis and results of each valuation approach used. I suggest that a separate subsection be devoted to the rationale and computations for each valuation approach used, such as capitalization of current earning power, capitalization of dividends, ratio of fair market value per share to book value per share, or an adjusted asset value approach. Each such section usually will draw on the comparable company section for guidance as to appropriate price/earnings ratios, dividend capitalization rates, price to book value ratios, and the like, to apply to the earnings, assets, and other figures derived for the subject company.

Each section should explain the rationale about why the midpoint or upper or lower end of the range of comparable companies' price/earnings ratios and other statistics should be applicable to the subject company. Each section also should make clear the rationale for picking certain statistics for the subject company, especially the earning power capacity, which for many reasons may differ from the demonstrated current earnings level.

Analyzing and weighting the valuation approach results. If two or more valuation approaches are used, there will be two or more implied results, which may be close together or far apart. At this point the writer must explain the relative weight given to each approach, and how the particular weighting results in the conclusion reached. Problems and techniques to be used in accomplishing this were discussed in Chapter 5.

Discounts and premiums. As discussed earlier in the book, the most common discounts are for lack of marketability or minority interest or for both. If the data used in the comparable company section to derive price/earnings ratios and other valuation bench marks were market prices of publicly-traded stocks, these were, in fact, minority interests, so no further minority interest would be applicable. However, there usually should be some discount for lack of marketability for a closely-held stock compared with a publicly-traded counterpart.

Data on marketability discounts were presented in Chapter 10. To the extent that such adjustments are applicable to the case at hand, such adjustments should be presented, along with the appropriate rationale, at this stage of the report.

Conclusion. The final step is to summarize the key elements of the valuation and the conclusion reached. This usually can be done in a page or two. It usually is most helpful to the reader to have the summary and conclusion presented in tabular form.

Appendixes

The choices generally are quite arbitrary about how much supporting detail should be included in the written valuation report, and, of that included, which should be presented as tables or exhibits in the body of the report and which as appendixes. As with most aspects of the report, the writer should think about how much detail the audience for the report will want or need, and be guided accordingly.

Three items conventionally are included as appendixes in most reports. The first is a statement of the qualifications of the person or persons preparing the report. The second is a statement of the appraiser's independence of the company being appraised, or, if not independent, a statement of the appraiser's relationship to the company. The third appendix usually included is a statement of contingent and limiting conditions. The latter usually is a relatively simple statement of limitations of rights to use the report, and a statement to the general effect that the data used was from sources considered reliable but not guaranteed. Where the appraiser has reason to doubt the reliability or completeness of the data, a statement to that effect should be included.

The details of the comparable search may be included as an appendix, including the list of companies considered and the reasons for rejection of those considered but not used.

A complete sample report prepared generally in the format discussed in the previous sections is included as Chapter 15. Although somewhat abbreviated, due to space limitations in this book, it illustrates the key elements that would be included in most typical written reports.

REPORTS FOR BUY-SELL AGREEMENTS

It is desirable to have a written valuation report on a buy-sell agreement; this is discussed in Chapter 21. The report can range from a single-page memorandum to a full formal report, as discussed in the previous section.

Frequently, valuation reports prepared for buy-sell agreements also serve other purposes, such as to establish values for gift and estate taxes. If such be the case, the more detail included in the report, the better. A sample of a relatively short report suitable for a buy-sell agreement is included in an exhibit in Chapter 21.

BUYING OR SELLING SHARES IN COMPANY

If the company is selling or repurchasing some of its shares, a written valuation report generally is desirable. The extent of the report should depend on the size of the transaction and on whom the parties to the transaction are. The purpose of the written valuation report is partly to be sure that the parties to the transaction consider and understand all the factors involved in the valuation at the time, and that all parties are satisfied the transaction value is fair. It also is to prevent any later misunderstandings that sometimes result from not remembering exactly, or misinterpreting, what might have been said or intended.

There have been countless thousands of lawsuits many years after the fact because the price paid for a business interest somehow was unfair to the buyer or the seller. Such suits sometimes are brought by parties to the transaction, and sometimes by beneficiaries of parties to the transaction who had no direct involvement. Thorough documentation supporting the fairness of the value can be important protection to all parties in case questions about the transaction arise at a later time.

The well-documented written report is of particular importance where any of the parties to the transaction could be considered unsophisticated in determining the appropriate value, or where any party to the transaction is a trustee or has a fiduciary responsibility to other parties. It also is especially important if anyone involved in the transaction has any conflict of interest, such as being a member of the board of the buying or selling company and also being related to the buying or selling stockholder.

ACQUISITIONS

A written report making a recommendation about an acquisition may go well beyond the question of value to include the appropriateness of the acquisition in terms of its fit with the acquiring company. It also may include recommendations on actions to be taken when the acquisition is completed, such as which facilities to retain and which to dispose of.

It may be that the matters of corporate fit and policy already have been addressed by the acquirer's management, and the purpose of the valuation report is merely to determine a range within which the potential acquirer should be willing to negotiate price. If so, the person or persons responsible for the valuation report should know what changes the acquirer contemplates and what their effect will be on earnings and other variables. If, for example, the acquirer can get rid of a distribution center owned by the acquiree because it duplicates the acquirer's facilities, which have adequate excess capacity, not only will operating costs be reduced but the acquirer will recover a portion of the purchase price through the sale of the excess facility. The result may be that the acquiree is worth far more to the acquirer than it would be worth as a free-standing company.

Such synergistic benefits are a dimension not found in the report on a company considered by itself. The extent to which the synergistic benefits may be reflected in the valuation vary with the circumstances. If there is only one potential buyer who would enjoy such benefits, a seller may have considerable difficulty trying to insist on reflecting the benefits in the selling price. However, if there are several such potential buyers, the competition may lead to some reflection of the value of such benefits in the price. Most state statutes on appraisal rights of dissenting stockholders specify that such potential values are to be disregarded.

Of course, the acquisition report will rely much more on forward projections versus past history than the report for tax or litigation purposes. Also, it usually will be far less formal, since its purpose is primarily for internal use only in management decision making.

DUE DILIGENCE REPORT FOR PUBLIC OFFERING

When a company contemplates an offering of stock to the public, the SEC requires that certain due diligence work be undertaken to insure that the underwriters and all parties marketing the stock understand the selling company, including its financial condition and its limitations. This work may be done by the underwriter or by an independent third party.

The report is made available to representatives of the underwriting firm and the selling group. The written report usually is quite comprehensive, and is supplemented by one or more meetings between the person or persons preparing the report and the representatives of the underwriter and selling group to discuss the proposed offering and answer questions.

The due diligence report will contain most or all of the elements of a report prepared for tax purposes, but will have much more emphasis on the company's future prospects. It usually will contain earnings and cash flow projections and analyses of the factors that will tend to support or prevent the attainment of the projections. Subjective evaluative judgments that have been obtained from persons outside the company, such as from customers, distributors, suppliers, competitors, and bankers, should be included. The written report may identify the comments attributable to such source by name, or, in some cases of confidentiality, by category of source.

Exhibit 14–3 is a table of contents for a due diligence report prepared by Willamette Management Associates, Inc., for a 1980 "Reg A" offering of $1.5 million worth of common stock and warrants in Tax Corporation of America, a company that specializes in preparing income tax returns. Note that the sections conveying written analysis of the company are considerably more lengthy than in the sample report in the following chapter, and include 15 pages of just summaries of interviews with parties outside the subject company. Some consider it an anomaly in the U.S. securities laws that the SEC requires these reports be made available only to the underwriters and

Exhibit 14–3
Table of contents for due diligence report on Tax Corporation of America

TABLE OF CONTENTS

Source: Due diligence report by Willamette Management Associates, Inc.

selling group, and not to the public who are buying the securities. The buying public is allowed access only to the prospectus.

SELLING OUT

Two different types of written reports might be used in conjunction with selling out the company. One is oriented toward finding a buyer and convincing the prospective buyer of the merits of the company. The other is oriented toward the selling stockholders and their representatives, and is prepared for determining and documenting that the selling stockholders are getting a fair price for their interests.

Seeking a buyer

A written report designed to attract a buyer may more resemble a sales brochure than an analytical valuation report. It certainly will focus on the company's strengths and opportunities. Contrary to the reports prepared for

Exhibit 14–3 (Continued)

TABLE OF CONTENTS (Cont.)

Exhibit 14–3 (Concluded)

TABLE OF CONTENTS (Cont.)

Page

TABLES (Cont.)

other purposes, the reader should not be entitled to presume that the report is unbiased. The report may or may not name an asking price for the business. Exhibit 14–4 is a table of contents of a report prepared by the McDermott Group, a merger and acquisition company, for presenting a company to prospective buyers.

Protecting selling stockholders and their representatives

Many of the same comments that applied in the earlier section on buying or selling a partial interest in a company apply with equal or greater force to selling out the entire company. Someone needs to take the responsibility as watchdog to insure that the selling stockholders are being treated fairly. A thorough written report will help to insure that all factors have been considered at the time of the transaction, and, hopefully, will forestall any future accusations or lawsuits alleging that some party to the transaction or his beneficiary did not receive fair treatment.

As discussed elsewhere, unless the sellers are paid in cash, the dimension of the adequacy of the terms must be considered. If selling to another company for stock in the acquirer company, the written report really is tantamount to two separate reports, one on the value of the selling company and one on the value of the shares of the acquiring company. Furthermore, if the stock to be

Exhibit 14-4
Table of contents for presenting company.

VULCAN STEEL FOUNDRY COMPANY

INDEX

-3-

The McDERMOTT GROUP

Source: McDermott Group

received is restricted, the effect of the restriction on the value of the consideration received also must be addressed in the written report.

If the consideration received includes a debt instrument of some kind, the effect of this also should be addressed in the report. Two aspects of the debt instrument should be considered, the issuer's financial ability to meet the interest and principal payment schedule, and the true present economic worth of the instrument relative to its face value. It seems to me that sellers and their representatives sometimes act like ostriches with their heads in the sand on this latter point. If totally liquid, top institutional quality debt instruments are selling to yield 13 percent, then a 10 percent ten-year note, issued by a less than A-rated company, and having no market liquidity, cannot have an economic worth equal to its face value. In such cases, it seems that the written report should address the issue of the value of the consideration received.

Tender offers and statutory mergers are considered together here because in both cases the written output requirement usually is an opinion letter rather

TENDER OFFERS AND STATUTORY MERGERS

Exhibit 14–5
Brief form opinion letter

WILLAMETTE MANAGEMENT ASSOCIATES, INC.

220 S.W. ALDER STREET SUITE 203
PORTLAND, OREGON 97204
(503) 224-6004

November 28, 1975

Board of Directors
Mouldings, Inc.
P. O. Box 858
Marion, Virginia 24354

Gentlemen:

We have been retained by Mouldings, Inc. to render an independent opinion as to a price that would be fair and equitable for the public stockholders of Mouldings, Inc. to receive for their shares of stock under current conditions for the Company, its industry, and the securities markets.

In analyzing the Company and related information to arrive at a fair value, we studied the current and recent past financial statements of Mouldings, Inc. furnished to us by the Company; made a tour of the Company's physical facility in Marion, Virginia; interviewed Company officers with respect to the Company's operations and prospects; gathered industry data and data on competitive companies from published sources and personal interviews; reviewed the records of Mouldings, Inc. stock's price and trading volume history from 1969 through September, 1975; and compiled statistics on other tender offers made in the United States during the past year.

Based on our analyses of these data and assuming the accuracy of information furnished to us, we are of the opinion that $1.10 per share is a fair cash price for the public stockholders of Mouldings, Inc. to receive for their stock.

Sincerely,

WILLAMETTE MANAGEMENT ASSOCIATES, INC.

By

Shannon P. Pratt, C.F.A.
President

SPP:mp

Exhibit 14–6
Longer form opinion letter

VALUATION OF THE COMMON STOCK OF MOULDINGS, INC.
September 8, 1978
INTRODUCTION

Description of Assignment

Willamette Management Associates, Inc., was retained by Mouldings, Inc., to appraise the fair value of its public common stock as of the current date. The purpose of this valuation was to establish a fair cash value for shares held by Mouldings' minority stockholders in connection with a proposed merger of MLG Corp. into Mouldings, Inc. As a result of the proposed merger, the majority shareholders of the company, Mr. and Mrs. James T. Rash, will become the sole owners.

Methodology

In our appraisal of the stock of Mouldings, Inc., we first reviewed a previous valuation study performed by our firm in 1975. We also analyzed the company's last five years of annual audited financial statements and the interim unaudited financial statement for the most recent quarter. We examined the state of the overall economy and household furniture industry. We also reviewed the history of the stock's market price and trading volume, concentrating on the last 15 months. In addition, we conducted a search for publicly traded companies having operations and products comparable to Mouldings.

We visited Mouldings' corporate headquarters and sole manufacturing facility in Marion, Virginia, where we interviewed the president, the vice president of production, the treasurer and the vice president of sales. Topics discussed included the company's history, the industry, Mouldings' competitive market position, the outlook for the company in general and its products specifically, raw materials procurement, labor markets, the production process, corporate policies and management approach.

We have relied on the accuracy and completeness of the information and documents furnished by Mouldings, Inc.

Conclusion

Based on our analysis, we believe valuation methods based on net asset value, capitalization of earning power and the history of the stock's trading price on the American Stock Exchange are reasonable and appropriate factors to consider in the valuation of the common stock of Mouldings, Inc. Based on these factors, we believe a fair and equitable value for the stock of Mouldings, Inc., is $2.75 per share.

Between the time we started our analysis and the time we completed it, the company announced operating earnings for its first fiscal quarter ended July 31, 1978, of $.10 per share compared to $.05 for the comparable period the previous year. The market reacted with a sharp upward movement in the stock's price on the American Stock Exchange from 2⅜ to as high as 3⅛. Based on standard fundamental analysis and relative to the prices of other stocks in the current market, we feel that the stock reached a point of being at least fully priced if not slightly overpriced.

BACKGROUND

Industry Outlook

The household furniture industry is directly influenced by several economic variables, primarily housing starts, real personal disposable income, population and consumer confidence and buying patterns.

42

Source: Mouldings, Inc.'s, Notice of Special Meeting of Shareholders, November 21, 1978.

than a complete written report. The actual investigation and analysis underlying the valuation opinion must be at least as scrupulous as that required for valuations for other purposes; but the written report typically consists only of a very brief summary and conclusion.

A very brief (and common) form of opinion letter is shown as Exhibit 14–5. A longer form of opinion letter (less commonly used) is shown as Exhibit 14–6. The balance of the tabular data and notes supporting the opinion are kept in the analyst's files, to be used if necessary in case of questions,

Exhibit 14–6 (continued)

Based on our examinations of these variables, we believe that the outlook for the furniture industry should parallel that of the national economy, perhaps lagging by 6-9 months. We expect the outlook can best be characterized by a slow decline over the next 18 months. Over the longer term, this industry should keep pace with real growth in GNP, about 3.5-5%.

Mouldings' Position in Industry

Mouldings' products belong in the category of occasional furniture, as opposed to bedroom or dining room lines. The company does not compete with the larger manufacturers of high-priced, styled products. Rather, the company competes in a very narrow segment of the industry, defined primarily by price.

The company's annual sales represent an insignificant portion of the occasional furniture industry. Competing manufacturers are typically small, privately held companies and divisions or subsidiaries of larger diversified firms. Manufacturers are estimated to have excess capacity, with many plants operating on a single-shift basis, similar to Mouldings.

APPRAISAL OF THE STOCK'S FAIR VALUE

Analysis of Assets and Liabilities

The book value of Mouldings, Inc.'s common stock as of July 31, 1978, was $5,238,670, or $2.63 per share based on 1,992,933 shares.

Current Assets. The company's current assets are dominated by short-term investments, primarily certificates of deposit. Based on our review of the aging of accounts receivable, we feel the stated value and the related allowance for doubtful accounts fairly reflect the probable collectible value of the receivables. Inventories are valued on the first-in/first-out basis. We believe the stated value of inventories approximates current market values.

Land and Buildings. There have been no recent appraisals on the land and buildings. The majority of the 40 acres of land owned by Mouldings is not commercially usable. Further, rising land prices in the area probably have been largely offset by having the land flooded for the first time ever in 1977.

A 350,000 square foot general purpose steel building houses the company's corporate offices and manufacturing facility. It was constructed in 1970. Inflation in building costs is probably offset by the fact that other general purpose buildings in the area are available for sale or lease. Considering these factors, we believe Mouldings' depreciated book value of its land and buildings may be a reasonable approximation of its underlying value.

Machinery and Equipment. There have been no recent appraisals of Mouldings' machinery and equipment. The company designs and constructs its own machinery and equipment, most of which is notably single purpose and would be difficult to sell. One aircraft, a Mitsubishi MU-2, is still owned by the company after selling three other aircraft over the last three years. The aircraft is used for sales and marketing activities. Management is attempting to sell the aircraft, unsuccessfully to date.

Liabilities. The company has no long-term debt. The current liabilities and deferred income tax accrual appear to be fairly stated.

Valuation. Based on our review of Mouldings' assets and liabilities, we believe that the net book value per share of $2.63 is reasonably representative of the company's true underlying net asset value.

Capitalization of Earnings

Income statements covering fiscal years 1977 and 1978 reflect the performance of Mouldings' current operations. Pre-1977 statements are not directly comparable due to a different product mix.

43

negotiations, or in the event of the necessity of an appraisal under dissenters' stockholder rights.

The opinion letter described in the foregoing section on tender offers and statutory mergers represents a final opinion based on the presumption that a thorough analysis and valuation has been completed. On the other hand, there are many situations where the client desires a preliminary opinion as a matter of guidance on how to proceed in various situations. In other words, the client needs a ballpark estimate—to decide what to do, or to guide him in

PRELIMINARY OPINION LETTERS

Exhibit 14–6 *(continued)*

Earnings. Earnings for the latest 12 months indicate that the current earning power of Mouldings is $769,000, or $.38 per share. Based on our examination of the company's history, current product mix and management, in conjunction with the outlook for the furniture industry and the general economy, we believe this level of earnings should be sustainable for some time. However, since Mouldings has no contractual relationship with its single major customer, there can be no assurance that these earnings can be sustained.

Appropriate Price/Earnings Multiple. As a guide in selecting a reasonable and appropriate capitalization rate, or price/earnings ratio, we reviewed several broad market indexes and the S&P furniture index.

PRICE/EARNINGS RATIOS OF
SELECTED BROAD INDUSTRY AND MARKET INDEXES
As of June 30, 1978

Standard & Poor's Furniture Industry	9.6
Standard & Poor's Composite Index	8.7
Standard & Poor's Industrial Index	9.1
Dow Jones Industrial Index	10.0

While these price/earnings multiples range from 8.7 to 10.0, we feel a lower capitalization rate is warranted for Mouldings. More substantial companies are contained in all the indices, characterized by greater financial strength, greater stock liquidity, greater management depth, and significantly greater diversification of both products and customers. The companies comprising the Standard & Poor's furniture group offer, in addition to many of the same elements mentioned above, superior brand name recognition and broader market distribution of higher priced products. Furthermore, most pay dividends. Mouldings' policy is not to pay dividends.

We also reviewed data on publicly traded companies whose businesses are comparable to the company's. The three companies which we believe are most comparable had price/earnings ratios of 6.1, 6.3 and 14.2. All were selling below their net asset values. The average market price was 17% below the average net book value. However, two of the three companies are part of the household furniture industry, but (a) compete in a higher price level of the industry than Mouldings and (b) offer styled products uncharacteristic of Mouldings' product line. Despite operating in a like competitive industry segment, the third company serves the construction industry and does not market its products under a private label. Although these three firms were the most comparable we could find, we discount direct comparison between these companies and Mouldings because of the uniquely competitive market it serves.

Based on the distinctions above, we believe a price/earnings multiple of 7.5 is reasonable and appropriate for Mouldings, Inc.

Valuation. Using the latest 12 months' reported earnings and our estimate of an appropriate and reasonable P/E ratio, we believe that $2.85 per share ($.38 x 7.5) represents the value of Mouldings' common stock based on capitalization of its earnings.

Valuation Summary

We have examined two fundamental valuation approaches in assessing the fair value of Mouldings, Inc. These approaches were an analysis of the company's net asset value and capitalization of earnings. The values indicated by these approaches were $2.63 and $2.85 per share, centered about $2.75 per share. Considering all these factors, and on the basis of the information available to us at this time, we view Mouldings, Inc., as being fully valued at $2.75 per share.

44

negotiating a particular situation. Any of a large variety of situations can raise the need for a preliminary opinion, such as estate planning, partnership dissolutions, divorces, potential dissenters to a statutory merger, desire to respond to a buyout feeler, consideration of establishing an ESOP, and many more.

The preliminary opinion letter must clearly state that the opinion is preliminary, with some language to the general effect that the investigation was superficial. The figures usually are presented as a range rather than a point estimate, and usually there should be a qualification to the effect that further investigation may lead even to a figure outside the preliminary range.

Exhibit 14–6 *(concluded)*

QUALIFICATION OF APPRAISERS

This appraisal report was prepared by Willamette Management Associates, Inc:, an investment adviser registered with the Securities and Exchange Commission. Willamette Management conducts valuation studies of both publicly held and privately held ongoing business enterprises for a variety of purposes, including public stock offerings, tender offers, mergers and acquisitions, federal gift and estate tax cases and other litigation.

In addition, Willamette Management publishes the quarterly NORTHWEST STOCK GUIDE and semi-monthly NORTHWEST INVESTMENT REVIEW, which include statistics and analyses of publicly held companies operating in the Northwest/Intermountain area of the United States.

Willamette's Director of Research is Shannon P. Pratt, a Chartered Financial Analyst and a Certified Financial Planner. He holds a doctorate in finance and has participated extensively in corporate valuation studies.

Pratt is the senior faculty member of the Chartered Financial Analyst National Review Workshop, which is the education forum for financial analysts wishing to attain the C.F.A. designation. In addition, he has published work on valuation of publicly owned and closely held corporations, relationship between risk and rate of return for common stocks, corporate insider trading and stock market returns, and cost of equity capital for public utilities.

Gregory A. Gilbert received his B.A. in Economics at Yale University and completed his formal education with an M.S. in Industrial Administration at the Massachusetts Institute of Technology in 1966. For 12 years he has been an investment analyst following a widely diversified list of companies. Gilbert is Associate Director of Research at Willamette Management Associates, Inc.

Jeff Morgan holds a Master of Business Administration degree with a concentration in finance and has been a security analyst with Willamette Management Associates, Inc., for one year.

A preliminary opinion, although not a binding conclusion, can be quite valuable for someone trying to make a major business decision, such as whether or not to pursue a merger, ESOP, recapitalization, or other course of action. It also can be valuable for someone deciding whether to pursue a valuation action in a divorce, dissent to the merger, or other potential legal action.

15

A SAMPLE CASE

APPRAISAL OF THE

FAIR MARKET VALUE OF

PAGANO'S SUPERMARKETS INC.

Prepared by

Shannon P. Pratt C.F.A.
Director of Research

and

Greg Gilbert
Associate Director of Research

and

Mark P. Pagano
Research Analyst

of

WILLAMETTE MANAGEMENT ASSOCIATES, INC.

June 1980

Pagano's Supermarkets, Inc. is a case contrived to illustrate the application of many of the principles and procedures presented in the first 14 chapters of this book. It also incorporates a few of the points made in Chapter 20 on ESOPs.

The hypothetical company is not intended to be patterned after any real-world company. The reader should not be concerned whether or not any of the assumptions bear resemblance to the reader's perception of reality in the retail grocery industry. The point of the case simply is to demonstrate one possible way of organizing a written valuation report, and to illustrate by example the application of a variety of procedures commonly used in valuation reports.

The reader also should keep in mind that the valuation date used, March 31, 1980, represented a point of extremely high capital costs and extremely low values in the U.S. capital markets by any historical standards.

This report has been prepared for the confidential use of Pagano's Supermarkets by Willamette Management Associates, Inc. It was made by and/or under the direct supervision of the undersigned using standard valuation techniques and practices.

Shannon P. Pratt, C.F.A.
President & Director of Research

TABLE OF CONTENTS

TABLES

APPENDICES

INTRODUCTION

Description of the Assignment

Willamette Management Associates, Inc., was retained by Pagano's Supermarkets Inc., an Oregon corporation, to appraise the fair market value of that company's stock as of March 31, 1980. The purpose of the valuation will be for a prospective Employee Stock Ownership Plan (ESOP), which Pagano's is now contemplating. The ESOP stock will represent a minority interest relative to the company's total outstanding stock.

Definition of Fair Market Value

Fair market value is considered to represent a value at which a willing seller and willing buyer, both being informed of the relevant facts about the business, could reasonably conduct a transaction, neither party acting under any compulsion to do so.

Among other factors, this appraisal takes into consideration all elements of appraisal listed in Internal Revenue Service Ruling 59-60, which provides guidelines for the valuation of closely-held stocks. Revenue Ruling 59-60 states that all relevant factors should be taken into consideration, including the following:

(1)   The nature of the business and the history of the enterprise from its inception.
(2)   The economic outlook in general and the condition and outlook of the specific industry in particular.
(3)   The book value of the stock and the financial condition of the business.
(4)   The earning capacity of the company.
(5)   The dividend-paying capacity.
(6)   Whether or not the enterprise has goodwill or other intangible value.
(7)   Sales of the stock and the size of the block of stock to be valued.
(8)   The market price of stocks of corporations engaged in the same or a similar line of business having their stocks actively traded in a free and open market, either on an exchange or over-the-counter.

Sources of Information Utilized

Several sources of information were used to complete this appraisal. Audited financial statements for the years ending December 31, 1975-1979 were examined. A list of marketable securities was reviewed as was an aging of accounts receivable. Tax assessments of the company's land were utilized. A prospective employee stock ownership plan was examined.

We toured the company's corporate headquarters adjacent to a supermarket in Portland, Oregon. President A. B. Pagano was interviewed to gain a better understanding of the company and its markets. Mr. Pagano was most cooperative in supplying all information that was desired. The firm's accountant, S. B. Brink, of the firm of J. C. Curti and Associates, was also cooperative in answering questions regarding the financial statements.

Information on comparable companies was provided primarily by **Standard & Poor's Corporate Records**. Information on the industry was provided by the U.S. **Industrial Outlook** and the **Standard & Poor's Industry Survey**. Information on the Regional economy was provided by the Washington State Department of Commerce and Economic Development, the Washington State Office of Financial Management, and the Economics Department of the U.S. National Bank of Oregon. Data on the National Economy was provided by a variety of sources.

Valuation Approach and Conclusion

Three basic valuation approaches were utilized in the valuation of Pagano's Supermarkets Inc.: capitalization of earnings, a price/book value approach, and an adjusted net asset value approach. The first two methods rely heavily on data derived from comparable publicly-traded companies. In the final analysis, the weighting allocated to the respective approaches was 65% to capitalization of earnings, 20% to the ratio of price-to-book value, and 15% to adjusted net asset values.

Based on these approaches and these weightings, it is our opinion that the value of Pagano's Supermarkets Inc., on a publicly-traded equivalent basis, is $3,050 per share.

A 10% discount for lack of marketability was deemed appropriate for the prospective ESOP shares in question, yielding a fair market value for the shares of $2,745 per share.

APPRAISAL OF ECONOMIC CONDITIONS

The National Economy

The Commerce Department's latest report on economic activity indicates the economy is slowing. Real GNP grew at a 2.1% seasonally adjusted annual rate in the fourth quarter following a 3.1% rise in the third. 1979's annual growth rate of 2.3% follows increases of 4.4% in 1978 and 5.3% in 1977. Government economists, discouraged by rapid increases in consumer prices, voiced concern that the continued growth in the economy could help lead to higher prices by fueling an inflation psychology.

The failure of the economy to run out of steam has led to a dramatic increase in the rate of inflation. 1979's 13.3% increase in the consumer price index was higher than the 12.2% in 1974, and the steepest since the end of wartime price controls, which sent prices surging 18.2% in 1946. While personal income rose 12.0% during the year, consumers suffered a decline in real purchasing power.

In an effort to ease inflation, the Federal Reserve, has sent interest rates sky-rocketing. In October 1979, the Fed increased the discount rate, the rate on loans to member commercial banks by the New York Federal Reserve Bank, to 12% from 11%. In February 1980, the rate was increased again, to 13%. These moves have forced short-term and long-term interest rates to record levels. The prime rate is currently 18½% from 12% at the beginning of 1978.. 13-week Treasury Bills are currently yielding approximately 15.05%, up 5.7 percentage points since the end of 1978.

The unemployment rate in January increased to a seasonally adjusted 6.2% of the labor force, from 5.9% in December. That brought the jobless rate to its highest level since July 1978, and marked the first time in 17 months that the rate has broken out of a narrow range between 5.7% and 5.9%. The Bureau of Labor Statistics indicated there is a clear deterioration in the labor market. However, there is not enough evidence yet to indicate that the unemployment rate is in for a serious downturn.

The increase in interest rates is beginning to affect the housing market. February housing starts were 1.334 million units on a seasonally adjusted annual basis, the lowest level since December 1975. February's rate was 6.3% below January's, and 9.2% below the year-earlier rate. Housing starts for 1979 were 1,742,500 units, down 14% from 1978. The seasonally adjusted rate of building permits in February declined also. The Commerce Department reported that

2

February building permits were 7.0% below the January rate and 1.4% below the rate of a year earlier. For the year, most economists expect housing starts to be in the 1.3 to 1.5 million unit range.

In summary, although the economic indicators are not yet delivering a clear signal as to the direction of the economy, the Carter administration is expecting a brief and mild recession. The number one problem facing the administration is inflation. Neither Carter nor his advisors hold out much hope for rapid progress. The administration is expecting improvement in the overall inflation rate, predicting consumer prices will rise 10.4% in 1980, down from 13.3% in 1979.

Inflation should continue to dampen consumers' purchasing power in 1980, and the personal savings rate is likely to rise from its currently low level. Real consumer purchases of goods and services are forecast to decline ¼% to 1% in 1980, the first decline since 1974. As consumer spending slows, businesses are likely to trim expenditures, and inventory accumulation will probably decline further. Housing starts may also decline a bit more.

The administration does not expect declines in real GNP to extend much past mid-1980, and believes economic growth will resume later in the year. Measured from fourth quarter of 1979 to fourth quarter of 1980, real GNP is expected to decline between ¾% and 1¼%, after growing 0.8% in the similar period ending in 1979.

The Regional Economy

Washington State Economy. According to a December 1979 report issued by the Washington State Department of Commerce and Economic Development, growth of the state's economy slowed in 1979 from the record pace achieved in the prior two years. However, growth remains well above the national averages, reinforcing the strength of the regional economy vis-a-vis the nation. Although Washington will not be spared the effects of a national recession, the impact should be less severe than in other parts of the country.

Total employment in the state increased by 111,000 workers, or 6.2% for the year ending September 1979, down from the gains present in the prior two years, but still representing a very healthy increase. During the year, the unemployment rate dropped six-tenths of a percentage point to 6.7%, although this still remains above the national average of 5.8%. Despite brisk economic activity, the state has traditionally recorded an unemployment rate above the national average stemming primarily from seasonal considerations and an above-average rate of net in-migration.

Gains in manufacturing employment continued to be dominated by the state's aerospace industry, especially The Boeing Company. Aerospace employment rose approximately 20% during the year ending in September. The "other durable goods" sector, which includes instruments and related products, exhibited the second largest year-to-year increase, rising 14.8%. Strong demand and the corporate growth of such companies as Hewlett-Packard, Tektronix and National Semiconductor have aided the growth of the state's electronics industry.

Not all manufacturing industries registered employment gains. Sensitive to the downturn in housing starts, the state's lumber and wood products industry fell slightly for the year ending in September. Moreover, recent actions by the Federal Reserve indicate the housing industry may be adversely impacted over an extended period.

The state's non-manufacturing industries enjoyed the largest absolute employment gains. The trade and service industries have benefited most from the state's

3

economic expansion. Increased levels of personal income, population growth, and household formation translate directly into benefits for the state's service industries.

Consistent with the state's employment advances has been the growth of personal income. Despite forecasted growth of over 15% for the year, continued double-digit inflation will hold down real personal income gains to less than 5%.

Following are some of the economic forecasts of the Washington State Office of Financial Management:

(1) Employment growth will continue to slow through the first half of 1980, caused by a weakened national economy. The wood products industry should see the largest declines. Growth of the manufacturing sector, especially the electronics industry, should spur above-average employment gains in following years.

(2) Inflation should peak in the first quarter of 1980, although only modest improvement is expected over the remainder of the year. High inflation should cause a decline in real wages in 1980.

(3) Personal income growth should remain in the 14 to 15% range in 1980 and 1981. Growth in real income could be minor in 1980 and recover a bit in 1981.

Oregon State Economy. With the national recession picking up steam and the resulting adverse effect on the housing industry, Oregon's real growth rate will at best be flat in 1980. Construction and the forest products industry should be especially hard hit, while the electronics, instruments, and aerospace industries should provide some year-to-year stability.

Specifically, the Economics Department of the U.S. National Bank of Oregon projects:

(1) Non-agricultural wage and salary employment flat or down modestly.
(2) Large job losses in the lumber, forest products, and construction industries.
(3) Unemployment hitting double-digit rates as job growth stops and population growth continues.
(4) Inflation matching gains in personal income resulting in no real growth.

Oregon's employment situation has been erratic through the first part of 1980. The unemployment rate fell from 6.7% in January to 6.3% in February and climbed back to 6.8% in March. The majority of employment declines have occurred in the lumber and wood products industry. The apparel and textile industries have also experienced some minor layoffs. Sectors recording employment gains included the electrical equipment, instruments, and food processing industries. However, these industries will find it increasingly difficult to offset lumber and wood products losses.

Oregon's agricultural industry could face a serious price-cost squeeze during 1980. The supply of most farm and food products is plentiful and farm prices have been low. While farm prices could be up only 3 to 5%, farm costs are likely to jump 15% or more. Thus, while total farm receipts should approximate last year's level, income could be down by as much as 20 to 25%. One bright spot in the agricultural sector in 1980 will be the continued high demand from the export market.

4

APPRAISAL OF THE GROCERY INDUSTRY

Overview

Prospects for the grocery industry look good for 1980. The outlook calls for a moderating of food price inflation, which has been of concern to the Carter administration. Although recent developments suggest intensified competition, the current tranquil competitive environment should preserve or improve margins. The installation of electronic scanners and sales of higher-margined general merchandise items are other positive factors.

Although much more recession-resistant than most industries, the grocery business will not be spared the effects of a prolonged recession. A downturn in sales of discretionary non-food items is expected, while slowing sales growth and high financing costs discourage capital expansion. Convenience stores, the fastest growing segment of the business, may be impacted even harder, as the lower prices of the larger stores may now outweigh the time saved by shopping at the smaller marts.

Inflation Boosts Earnings

Supported by a projected 11% rise in food prices, sales and earnings of most grocery chains were expected to be significantly improved in 1979. Retail food price increases are expected to moderate in 1980.

Margins in 1980 could come under pressure from two sources. In an effort to explain rising retail food prices and declining farm prices, President Carter summoned industry leaders to Washington, D.C. in August 1979. The charge of excessive profiteering, whether true or not, may have a restraining effect on prospective price increases. Second, the possibility of price wars would lead to greater emphasis on discount pricing, and Safeway has recently been very aggressive in this regard.

However, growing sales of higher-margined non-food items, more efficient utilization of physical facilities, and greater use of electronic scanning equipment should provide some protection for margins.

New Marketing Concepts

The U.S. grocery industry has long operated on very thin profit margins, due mainly to intense competition. Because there is little to differentiate one supermarket from the next, pricing is crucial.

However, pricing is not the only way to compete. In an effort to improve margins, some grocers have begun experimenting with two new store formats: (1) the "superstore," which provides one-stop shopping for all the customer's needs (food and non-food alike) and (2) the "warehouse" or "limited assortment" store, which concentrates on cost-cutting by providing a reduced line of groceries with a minimum of service. Both concepts have been growing in popularity.

Another new concept in the industry is the sale of generic items. Some large chains have been increasing promotion of their own private labels as an alternative to the generics. The longer-range prospects for generics are largely dependent on the level of food price inflation and consumers' perception of their quality.

Scanning Systems Grow in Popularity

The most significant cost-control development for the grocery industry in recent years has been electronic scanner check-out system. The Ford Marketing

5

Institute estimates that as of the end of July 1979, there were 1,025 scanner-equipped stores in operation, representing a large increase from the 562 at 1978's year end. Further growth may be restricted by suppliers' capacity for the production of the required hardware.

The effect on profits of using scanners can be immense. Some estimate that scanners can increase pre-tax profits by as much as 2% of sales, which would more than double profits for many stores.

In addition to increasing cashier speed and accuracy, scanning has also eliminated the need for price marking. However, the elimination of price marking has met with strong opposition from union leaders for fear of losing jobs. From the industry's viewpoint, labor is by far the largest operating expense, and any means of lowering labor costs should receive avid interest.

Convenience Stores Continue Growth

The fastest growing segment of the food store business is the convenience store, with 1978 sales rising 18% over year-earlier levels. Since 1970, the number of such stores has grown by an average of nearly 12% per year. Growth in 1978 was 8%.

The primary competitive advantage of convenience stores is their time-saving attribute. Most are located in heavy traffic locations with a large customer base located nearby. Experience has shown that shoppers are reluctant to face supermarket crowds for just a few items.

The latest trend in convenience store operations is the introduction of hot take-out food and soda fountains in an effort to compete with the fast-food industry.

Margins Key to Profits

Whatever economic scenario develops in1980, supermarkets can be comforted by the relative inelasticity of food demand. However, stable sales volume does not necessarily result in stable profits. The high rate of food price inflation in the last two years has actually been an aid to margins. Margins may decline in 1980 if food-price inflation moderates as expected.

Rising energy costs, increased government surveillance, higher costs of borrowing, and indications of growing price competition will be of concern to the industry. Of greater importance is a new development on the labor scene, as two industry labor groups have merged to create one of the largest unions in the country. What effect this will have on margins remains to be seen.

Overall, 1980 could be a favorable year for the supermarket industry. In the absence of widespread price wars and intense pressure from government or other public groups for lower prices, margins should remain at acceptable levels.

FUNDAMENTAL POSITION OF THE COMPANY

Background

Pagano's Supermarkets Inc. was founded in 1958 by current President and principal shareholder, A. B. Pagano. Starting with one store in Portland, Oregon, the company has expanded to its present size, operating 12 stores across Oregon and Washington, with current revenues totaling nearly $40 million. The last acquisition was that of SP Markets, a small chain of three supermarkets in the Spokane area, in 1977. The company ran into considerable operational problems at the time of this acquisition, which have since been resolved.

6

Operations

The locations of the company's 12 stores are as follows: Portland, (4); Seattle (3); Lynnwood; Vancouver, Washington; and Spokane, (3). The Spokane stores are easily the smallest, averaging 7,500 square feet versus approximately 20,000 square feet for the remaining nine. The company owns the property and buildings of the two Portland stores. The remainder are leased. Management forecasts no problems with renewing any of the leases at competitive rates. All buildings are of fairly modern construction and design.

Although the company prides itself on quality service at competitive prices, there is very little to distinguish Pagano's firm from the typical supermarket. The product mix is fairly typical of the industry. In fiscal 1979, the mix was as follows: groceries — 65%, meat — 15%, produce — 10%, and non-food — 10%.

Competition exists from many regional and national chains such as Safeway, Fred Meyer and Albertson's. In addition, there are numerous independent stores with which the company must compete. Competition in the industry is intense. Management believes market share has been increasing slightly in recent years. The company believes its stores are located in areas exhibiting above-average population growth.

Approximately 60% of the company's non-salaried employees are unionized. Labor relations have generally been satisfactory, although the company experienced a week-long work stoppage in 1977 during contract negotiations. This was the first in the company's history. All current contracts expire June 30, 1980. Management does not expect any contract difficulties this time around.

Management

Mr. A. B. Pagano, 57, is President and Chairman of the Board. Prior to founding the company, he spent 15 years in the grocery business. His last position was as vice president of a major chain in Portland.

Mr. C. D. Pagano, 51, is Vice President of Operations. He is the brother of A. B., and a co-founder of the chain. Prior to joining the company, Mr. Pagano also had extensive experience in the grocery business.

Mr. A. C. Labadie, 48, is the Secretary. He has held this position since 1969. Prior to that time, Mr. Labadie was employed by Albertson's.

Mr. D. A. Schue, 36, is the Controller, having held this position since 1974. Prior to that time he was employed by Arthur Andersen and Company. Mr. Schue is a certified public accountant.

Mr. M. P. Pagano, 29, is the Treasurer, having been employed in this position since 1977. He holds an MBA in finance from Stanford Business School and is a Chartered Financial Analyst. He is the son of Mr. A. B. Pagano.

It is generally assumed that the junior Mr. Pagano is being groomed for the position of president when his father retires. However, retirement appears five to ten years away and the senior Mr. Pagano will still stay on in an advisory role.

The Board of Directors consists of the five executive officers, plus Dr. E. F. Pagano, a shareholder and brother of the two founders. He contributed a portion of the initial capital, but is inactive in the business. Mr. Pagano is a practicing physician. If the board does approve an ESOP, it will be Dr. Pagano's shares which will be purchased for the employees.

Current ownership of the stock is as follows:

7

	Shares	Percent
A. B. Pagano	500	62.5%
C. D. Pagano	200	25.0
E. F. Pagano	100	12.5
Total Shares	800	100.0%

There have never been any transactions in the company's stock.

Trend Analysis

Income Statement. Table I presents a five-year income statement summary for Pagano's Supermarkets. Sales have shown a very steady increase, rising from $24.0 million in 1975 to $40.0 million in 1979, a compound annual growth rate of 13.6%. Sales growth began to slow slightly in 1979, rising 11.1%.

The gross margin has also been fairly steady, although we note that recent margins are down from the levels achieved in 1975 and 1976. The lower level achieved in 1977 is attributable to price cutting associated with the new store openings. The steady gross margins are indicative of the industry.

As a percentage of sales, operating expenses declined considerably in 1976 and 1977, but have shown gradual increases in 1978 and 1979. Although the increases are not large, with the typically low margins characteristic of the industry, even small increases can materially impact the bottom line.

Interest expense rose considerably in 1977 as a result of the increased indebtedness associated with the SP Markets acquisition. In 1978 and 1979, the lower borrowings were partially offset by higher rates.

With the exception of 1977, pre-tax margins have been fairly steady, ranging from 2.1% in 1979 to 2.5% in 1975. However, we note that the trend has generally been downward. Net income has followed the trend of pre-tax profits, with the effective tax rate remaining in a fairly narrow range of 41% to 44%.

In summary, Pagano's Supermarkets Inc. has been consistently profitable, with sales exhibiting steady increases on the order of 13%. However, sales growth has been slowing and the trend of profit margins has been downward, the net effect being that income has been increasing, but at a decreasing rate.

Balance Sheet. Table II is a similar five-year balance sheet array. Inventory is easily the largest current asset, typically accounting for nearly 70% of all current assets. Small cash balances are maintained, although the company does have a portfolio of marketable securities. The latter was reduced markedly in 1977 as the company sold a portion to help finance the SP Markets acquisition.

Receivables do not constitute a major portion of current assets, since goods are sold for cash. Current assets have generally been increasing as a percentage of total assets, with the exception of 1977, when a significant amount of fixed assets were acquired.

The company owns the land and buildings of its original two stores. The remainder are leased. The land is carried at its purchase price of $400,000. Significant additions to buildings and equipment are again evident in 1977, due to the SP acquisition. At December 31, 1979, Pagano's plant and equipment were approximately 32% depreciated.

"Other" assets are comprised of the goodwill associated with the 1977 acquisition and the *net* cash value of insurance policies on the principals of the company. For book purposes, the goodwill is being amortized over a 40-year period, although the amortization is not a tax deductible expense. Total assets of the company have risen from $4.0 million in 1975 to $6.6 million in 1979, a compound annual growth rate of 13.3%.

8

TABLE I

PAGANO'S SUPERMARKETS INC.

INCOME STATEMENTS – 1975-1979
(All figures in 000's, except per share)

Years Ended December 31

	1979		1978		1977		1976		1975	
Sales	$40,000	100.0%	$36,000	100.0%	$32,000	100.0%	$27,000	100.0%	$24,000	100.0%
Cost of Goods Sold	31,600	79.0	28,440	79.0	25,600	80.0	20,800	77.0	18,000	75.0
Gross Margin	8,400	21.0	7,560	21.0	6,400	20.0	6,200	23.0	6,000	25.0
Operating Expenses	7,425	18.6	6,630	18.4	5,810	18.2	5,500	20.4	5,320	22.2
Operating Income	975	2.4	930	2.6	590	1.8	700	2.6	680	2.8
Interest Expense	125	0.3	130	0.4	140	0.4	80	0.3	80	0.3
Pre-Tax Income	850	2.1	800	2.2	450	1.4	620	2.3	600	2.5
Income Taxes	350	0.9	350	1.0	200	0.6	270	1.0	250	1.0
Net Income	$ 500	1.2%	$ 450	1.3%	$ 250	0.8%	$ 350	1.3%	$ 350	1.5%
EPS (based on 800 shares in all periods)	$625.00		$562.50		$312.50		$537.50		$537.50	
Effective Tax Rate	41.2%		43.8%		44.4%		43.5%		41.7%	

9

TABLE II

PAGANO'S SUPERMARKETS INC.
BALANCE SHEETS – 1975-1979
(All figures in 000's)

As of December 31

	1979		1978		1977		1976		1975	
ASSETS										
Current Assets:										
Cash	$ 300	4.5%	$ 300	4.8%	$ 100	1.7%	$ 200	4.4%	$ 100	2.5%
Marketable Securities	200	3.0	200	3.2	200	3.5	350	7.8	350	8.8
Receivables	400	6.0	400	6.4	350	6.1	250	5.6	200	5.0
Inventory	2,500	37.7	2,200	35.0	2,000	34.8	1,750	38.9	1,600	40.0
Prepaid Expenses	150	2.3	150	2.4	100	1.7	100	2.2	50	11.2
Total Current Assets	3,550	53.5	3,250	51.8	2,750	47.8	2,650	58.9	2,300	57.5
Fixed Assets:										
Land	400	6.0	400	6.4	400	6.9	400	8.9	400	10.0
Plant & Equip.-At Cost	3,100		2,900		2,800		1,800		1,600	
Less: Accum. Deprec.	(1,000)		(800)		(650)		(500)		(400)	
Plant & Equip.-Net	2,100	31.7	2,100	33.4	2,150	37.4	1,300	28.9	1,200	30.0
Net Fixed Assets	2,500	37.7	2,500	39.8	2,550	44.3	1,700	37.8	1,600	40.0
Other Assets:										
Excess of Purchase Price Over Net Assets of Acquired Company	380	5.8	390	6.2	400	6.9	--	--	...	...
Cash Value of Life Insurance, Net of Policy Loans	200	3.0	140	2.2	50	1.0	150	3.3	100	2.5
Total Other Assets	580	8.8	530	8.4	450	7.9	150	3.3	100	2.5
Total Assets	$6,630	100.0%	$6,280	100.0%	$5,750	100.0%	$4,500	100.0%	$4,000	100.0%

10

TABLE II (Cont.)

PAGANO'S SUPERMARKETS INC.

BALANCE SHEETS – 1975-1979

(All figures in 000's)

As of December 31

	1975		1976		1977		1978		1979	
LIABILITIES										
Current Liabilities:										
Notes Payable	$ 250	6.2%	$ 250	5.6%	$ 300	5.2%	$ 250	4.0%	$ 300	4.5%
Cur. Maturing LTD	150	3.8	150	3.3	200	3.5	200	3.2	200	3.0
Accounts Payable	1,000	25.0	1,100	24.4	1,400	24.3	1,500	23.9	1,600	24.1
Accrued Expenses	300	7.5	300	6.7	400	7.0	400	6.3	450	6.8
Other Current Liabilities	100	2.5	100	2.2	100	1.7	150	2.4	150	2.3
Total Current Liabilities	1,800	45.0	1,900	42.2	2,400	41.7	2,500	39.8	2,700	40.7
Long-Term Debt	600	15.0	650	14.4	1,150	20.0	1,130	18.0	780	11.8
Total Liabilities	2,400	60.0	2,550	56.6	3,550	61.7	3,630	57.8	3,480	52.5
STOCKHOLDERS' EQUITY										
Common Stock	800	20.0	800	17.8	800	13.9	800	12.7	800	12.1
Retained Earnings	800	20.0	1,150	25.6	1,400	24.4	1,850	29.5	2,350	35.4
Total Stockholders' Equity	1,600	40.0	1,950	43.4	2,200	38.3	2,650	42.2	3,150	47.5
Total Liabilities & Stockholders' Equity	$4,000	100.0%	$4,500	100.0%	$5,750	100.0%	$6,280	100.0%	$6,630	100.0%

LTD = Long-Term Debt.

11

The liability half of the balance sheet has been relatively stable. Current liabilities typically account for nearly 40% of total assets. Accounts payable easily constitutes the largest single current liability.

The acquisition in 1977 is amply evidenced by a 77% increase in long-term debt. The debt has been pared down considerably since that time, standing at $780,000 at December 31, 1979, or only 11.8% of total assets. This is the lowest percentage level of the last five years.

Due to continual increases to retained earnings, stockholders' equity has risen at a compound rate of 18.5%. At December 31, equity stood at nearly $3.2 million, or 47.5% of total assets, the highest level of the past five years. However, if only *tangible* equity is included, the compound growth rate would drop to 14.7% and equity as a percent of tangible assets would drop to 44.3%, still high by historical standards.

In summary, the composition of the company's assets tends to be progressing in a step-wise fashion. Current assets have been rising faster than fixed assets, while the latter tend to rise in spurts concurrent with a major expansion of facilities. Similarly, the earnings of the company are high enough to reduce past indebtedness, which may also increase in spurts to finance major capital expenditures.

Sources and Uses Statement. Examination of the "Statement of Changes in Financial Position," shown in Table III, will further clarify the sources and uses of the company's funds. With the exception of 1977, virtually all of the company's financing was provided internally. In 1977, long-term debt and increases in life insurance loans provided other sources of funds.

The major use of funds was the acquisition in 1977, although minor additions to fixed assets were made in other years. In 1978 and 1979, debt reduction has been a primary use of funds. Working capital has been on the increase.

Ratio Analysis. When assessing a firm's performance over time, ratio analysis is perhaps even more revealing than a review of income statement or balance sheet.

As evident from Table IV, Pagano's current ratio has been fairly steady at 1.3. The quick ratio has exhibited similar performance, averaging nearly 0.35. No clear trend is evident in either.

Leverage ratios confirm what was alluded to earlier, i.e., except in years of significant capital expansion, funds provided from operations are sufficient to maintain the facilities and redeem existing debt. Interest coverage has not been a problem.

The activity ratios have also been extremely stable. Total asset turnover has ranged between 6.0 and 6.4. Fixed asset turnover has been slightly more diverse, ranging from 14.3 to 16.4. Inventory turnover has also been steady, especially during the past three years. Again, no clear improving or deteriorating trend is evident.

With the exception of 1977, the operating profitability ratios have been quite steady. None differ markedly from the norm.

Comparative Industry Analysis

While trend analysis is most helpful in identifying any improving or deteriorating trends, or identifying any deviations from the norm, it gives no indication of how the subject company's balance sheet and operating performance compares to similar-size firms in the industry. This is accomplished with the use of **Robert Morris Associates' (RMA)** Annual Statement Studies, the industry data for which is included in Table V.

12

TABLE III

PAGANO'S SUPERMARKETS INC.

STATEMENT OF CHANGES IN FINANCIAL POSITION — 1976-1979

(All figures in 000's)

	Years Ended December 31			
	1979	1978	1977	1976
SOURCES OF FUNDS				
From Operations:				
Net Income	$ 500	$ 450	$ 250	$ 350
Depreciation & Amortization	210	160	150	100
Total from Operations	710	610	400	450
Increases to Long-Term Debt	---	--	500	50
Increase fr. Life Insurance Loans	---	--	100	---
Total Sources of Funds	710	610	1,000	500
USES OF FUNDS				
Increases to Plant & Equip.	200	100	1,000	200
Excess of Purchase Price				
Over Net Assets Acquired	---	---	400	--
Redemption of LTD	350	20	---	---
Decrease in Life Ins. Loans	60	90	---	50
Total Uses of Funds	610	210	1,400	250
Increase (Decrease) in Working Capital	$ 100	$ 400	$(400)	$ 250

TABLE IV

PAGANO'S SUPERMARKETS INC.

RATIO ANALYSIS — 1975-1979

	Period Ending December 31				
	1979	1978	1977	1976	1975
LIQUIDITY					
Current Ratio	1.31	1.30	1.15	1.39	1.28
Quick Ratio	0.33	0.36	0.27	0.42	0.36
LEVERAGE					
Total Debt/Total Assets	52.5%	57.8%	61.7%	56.6%	60.0%
LTD/Total Capitalization	19.8%	29.9%	34.3%	25.0%	27.3%
EBIT/Interest	7.8	7.2	4.2	8.8	8.5
ACTIVITY					
Sales/Avg. Total Assets	6.2	6.0	6.2	6.4	6.3
Sales/Avg. Fixed Assets	16.0	14.3	15.1	16.4	15.7
Cost of Goods Sold/ Avg. Inventory	13.4	13.5	13.7	12.4	12.0
PROFITABILITY					
% Pre-Tax Inc./Sales	2.1	2.2	1.4	2.3	2.5
% Pre-Tax Inc./Avg. Assets	13.2	13.3	8.8	14.6	15.8
% Pre-Tax Inc./Avg. Equity	29.3	33.0	21.7	34.9	40.7

LTD = Long-Term Debt.

13

TABLE V

PAGANO'S SUPERMARKETS INC. &
ROBERT MORRIS ASSOCIATES' (RMA) ANNUAL STATEMENT STUDIES —
SIC NO. 5411-RETAILERS-GROCERIES & MEATS

BALANCE SHEET & INCOME DATA

	RMA	PAGANO'S	
Asset Size	$1-10MM		
No. Statements	134		
		1979	1978
ASSETS			
Cash & Equivalents	11.8%	7.5%	8.0%
Accounts & Notes Receivable	5.3	6.0	6.4
Inventory	32.7	37.7	35.0
Other Current	1.4	2.3	2.4
Total Current Assets	51.2	53.5	51.8
Fixed Assets - Net	36.9	37.7	39.8
Intangibles-Net	0.6	5.8	6.2
Other Non-Current Assets	11.2	3.0	2.2
Total Assets	100.0%	100.0%	100.0%
LIABILITIES & NET WORTH			
Notes Payable	3.9%	4.5%	4.0%
Current Maturing Long-Term Debt	3.7	3.0	3.2
Accounts & Notes Payable	23.5	24.1	23.9
Accrued Expenses	6.1	6.8	6.4
Other Current Liabilities	3.4	2.3	2.4
Total Current Liabilities	40.6	40.7	39.8
Long-Term Debt	19.3	11.8	18.0
Other Non-Current Liabilities	2.0	---	---
Net Worth	38.1	47.5	42.2
Total Liabilities & Net Worth	100.0%	100.0%	100.0%
INCOME DATA			
Net Sales	100.0%	100.0%	100.0%
Cost of Sales	78.7	79.0	79.0
Gross Profit	21.3	21.0	21.0
Operating Expenses	19.6	18.6	18.4
Operating Profit	1.7	2.4	2.6
All Other Expenses (Credits)	(0.3)	0.3	0.4
Profit Before Taxes	2.0%	2.1%	2.2%

14

Source: Robert Morris Associates' *Annual Statement Studies, 1979*. Copyright 1979. Philadelphia, Pa. SEE Exhibit 8–3 for Interpretation of Statement Studies Figures.

Note that certain ratios for the company differ from those used in the trend analysis. RMA uses slightly different methods for computing certain of these ratios, which we must conform to for comparative purposes. The time lag should also be noted. The most current RMA data available covers fiscal years ending June 1978 through March 1979. The most current data for the subject company is December 1979.

Although Pagano's total current assets are nearly identical to the industry norm, their composition is weighted more toward inventory and less toward cash and equivalents. The assets are slightly less liquid than the industry norm. Fixed assets also compare reasonably well.

However, the biggest discrepancy stems from intangibles and other non-current assets. Pagano's intangibles account for nearly 6% of total assets versus only 0.6% for the industry. Offsetting this is the company's lack of various "other" non-current assets, which account for only 2-3% of assets compared to nearly 11% for RMA.

Pagano's total current liabilities are very much in line with the industry norm, with no significant deviations apparent in any of the components.

The capitalization of the company is substantially different, however, Pagano being significantly less leveraged than the industry. At December 31, 1979, Pagano's long-term debt accounted for 11.8% of total assets and equity was 47.5% versus 19.3% and 38.1%, respectively, for the industry.

On the income statement, Pagano's gross margin in recent years has been nearly identical to the industry. Operating expenses have been slightly less, however, resulting in an average operating margin over the last two years of 2.5% versus 1.7% for the industry.

Surprisingly, the industry's net non-operating income (expense) figure is positive, apparently indicating income derived from investments, equipment dispositions or other sources. Interest is usually the largest non-operating expense, and because of Pagano's less leveraged financial position, we would have expected these expenses to be less than for the industry. However, it is still important to note that Pagano's operating performance relative to the industry is better than the pre-tax figures would indicate.

The RMA ratios, shown in Table VI, provide added insight into the company's performance. The RMA data divides the 134 surveyed companies into quartiles, the middle ratio representing the median, with 25% of all companies surveyed lying above and below the top and bottom quartile values, respectively.

The company's current ratio is very much in line with the norm, although the quick ratio is slightly below, again indicating the higher than normal investment in inventory.

The debt/net worth ratio is improved over 1978 and lies above the industry norm. Similarly, interest charge coverage is much higher than "normal."

Activity ratios are the only areas where the company fails to meet or exceed industry standards. Both total asset and fixed asset turnover are below par, but still lie far above the bottom industry quartile. Inventory turnover shows slightly more divergence from the industry norm.

The profitability ratios, i.e., pre-tax return on assets and tangible equity, lie well above the industry norm. The industry is characterized by high turnover and low profit margins. In Pagano's case, higher than normal margins more than offset lower than normal turnover.

In summary, while we have pointed out any deviations Pagano may have from the industry norm, we should emphasize that all these deviations were relatively

15

TABLE VI

PAGANO'S SUPERMARKETS INC. &
ROBERT MORRIS ASSOCIATES' (RMA) ANNUAL STATEMENT STUDIES —
SIC NO. 5411-RETAILERS-GROCERIES & MEATS

RATIO ANALYSIS

Asset Size No. Statements	RMA $1-10MM 134	PAGANO'S	
		1979	1978
Current	1.6 1.2 1.0	1.3	1.3
Quick	0.6 0.4 0.2	0.3	0.4
Debt/Net Tangible Worth	1.0 1.7 3.4	1.3	1.6
EBIT/Interest	10.5 4.4 1.8	7.8	7.2
Sales/Total Assets	8.6 6.4 4.4	6.0	5.7
Sales/Fixed Assets	29.5 19.6 11.3	16.0	14.4
Cost of Sales/Inventory	23.5 16.9 10.5	12.6	12.9
% Profit Before Taxes/Total Assets	13.6 8.5 2.8	12.8	12.7
% Profit Before Taxes/Tangible Net Worth	39.3 23.2 8.3	30.7	35.4

16

Source: Robert Morris Associates' *Annual Statement Studies, 1979.* Copyright 1979. Philadelphia, Pa. SEE Exhibit 8–3 for Interpretation of Statement Studies Figures.

minor. Note that not one ratio lies above or below the top and bottom industry quartiles, quite an unusual occurrence in a private company valuation. In this sense, Pagano's Supermarkets can be regarded as a "typical" grocery chain.

Current Financial Condition

As indicated by the previous sections, Pagano's current financial position compares favorably to both historical and industry standards. The company's liquid assets were shown to be slightly less than "normal." However, the marketable securities which are carried on the books at $200,000 have a current market value of $250,000.

Receivables are usually not significant to a grocery store. An analysis of the aging of receivables as of December 31, 1979 indicated that past-due accounts (over 90 days) had been reserved for adequately.

Inventory is computed on the LIFO basis. Had FIFO been used, reported inventory would have been $500,000 higher at year-end. Pagano's policy of writing off excess inventory was found to be in conformity with industry norms.

The company's land is carried at its purchase price of $400,000. Current tax assessments put the value at $550,000. The depreciation methods and estimates of useful lives on the remainder of fixed assets were found to be in conformity with industry standards.

The goodwill associated with the 1977 purchase of SP Markets is being amortized over 40 years. Intangible assets totaled $380,000 at year-end.

The $300,000 of notes payable outstanding are part of a $500,000 line of credit with interest at prime plus 1%. The majority of long-term debt carries interest at 8 to 12%. The loan agreements require minimum levels of working capital to be maintained and prohibit the payment of dividends. The company has complied with all restrictive provisions.

Stockholders' equity totaled $3.15 million at year-end. Tangible equity stood at $2.77 million. The common stock ownership has already been discussed.

APPRAISAL OF FAIR MARKET VALUE

Valuation Approaches Utilized

A capitalization of earnings approach will be the valuation method relied upon most heavily in the appraisal of Pagano's Supermarkets Inc. As in most valuations of ongoing concerns, earnings are given primary emphasis in the appraisal. In the case of Pagano's Supermarkets, a stable operating history provides a good estimation of the firm's current earning power and excellent comparable companies provide a capitalization rate for which we have an above-average degree of confidence.

We also took asset values into consideration, using two asset value approaches. One utilized the ratios of price-to-book value for the publicly-traded comparable companies. The other examined the assets of Pagano's Supermarkets and computed an adjusted net asset value.

The Comparable Search

To develop the "suspect" list of companies for our comparable search, we started with a list of all companies in SIC No. 5411 — Grocery Stores, which are listed in **Standard & Poor's Corporate Records**. There are 91 such companies.

17

These 91 companies are listed in Appendix A, while Appendix B describes their principal lines of business and gives an indication of size in terms of sales. Reviewing these data, we set objective selection criteria. For Pagano's the criterion selected were:

(1) Sales not to exceed $400 million.
(2) At least 90% of business must result from the operation of supermarkets.
(3) Companies which operate principally "convenience" stores to be eliminated.
(4) Companies whose operations are principally wholesale to be eliminated.

During this selection, 74 companies were eliminated for reasons detailed in Appendix C. Annual, interim and 10-K reports were then requested for the 17 remaining companies and stricter selection criteria were outlined. Seven more companies were eliminated for the reasons outlined in Appendix D.

Data on the remaining ten companies surviving the search is included in Table VII.

Capitalization of Earnings

Two basic pieces of information are needed to value a company by the capitalization of earning power approach — an appropriate figure for earning power and an appropriate capitalization rate.

In the case of Pagano's Supermarkets, we have stressed the stability of income. There have been no quantifiable non-recurring items which have distorted income one way or the other. Sales have steadily increased and margins have been stable. One adjustment that could be made is to eliminate the amortization of goodwill, but this is not material. In summary, reported net income is a good estimation of current earning power.

On the other hand, to this point we have based the valuation entirely on one year's earnings. What if earnings should dramatically turn up or down in 1980? Should we still capitalize current earnings? In order to provide some degree of stability to the valuation, we also computed five-year average and weighted average earnings as follows:

Year	Earnings Per Share	Average Earnings				Weighted Average Earnings
1979	$ 625.00		x 5	=	$3,125.00	
1978	562.50		x 4	=	2,250.00	
1977	312.50		x 3	=	937.50	
1976	537.50		x 2	=	1,075.00	
1975	537.50		x 1	=	537.50	
	$2,575.00 /5 =	$515.00			$7,925.00 /15 = $528.33	

Similar computations were also made for the comparable companies in Table VII. Note that both average and weighted average earnings for Pagano's are significantly below the latest 12 months' figures.

The comparable table will prove valuable in determining the appropriate price/earnings ratio to be utilized. For the latest 12 months earnings, the P/E ranges from 3.3 to 10.0, with a mean and median of 5.6 and 5.7, respectively. However, note that for the two highest P/E's (10.0 and 9.1), latest 12 months earnings are less than half of the prior fiscal year, indicating the ratios are

18

skewed upward. If these are eliminated, the mean and median drops to 4.4 and 3.8, respectively. We estimate that 4.5 is the most representative P/E for the group. We also note that at March 31, 1980, the stock market in general appeared to be at a cyclical low caused in large part by record interest rates.

Aside from determining a "normal" P/E for the comparable companies, we must determine the direction and extent the company in question should deviate from the norm. In the case of Pagano's Supermarkets, we think there should be a net upward adjustment for the following reasons:

(1) The company's historical performance has been very steady with a strong underlying growth trend evident.
(2) The balance sheet is stronger than the industry, thus entailing less fixed charges and decreasing risk.
(3) 40% of the comparable companies use FIFO accounting, which tends to overstate earnings and understate P/E's.
(4) Prospects for economic activity in Pagano's marketing area appear brighter than nationally.

On the negative side, we note that Pagano's is much smaller than the comparables and is restricted from paying a dividend.

Not only do we think that Pagano's deserves a higher than "average" ratio, we believe the normal P/E in the market may be temporarily depressed due to what appears to be a pronounced cyclical market downturn. For the purposes of an ESOP especially, we would hope to minimize any wide variations in market swings.

In summary, we think the company's latest 12 months earnings should be capitalized at a rate of 5.5, yielding a publicly-traded equivalent value of $3,438 per share.

The same analysis is used for average and weighted average earnings. The mean and median P/E for five-year average earnings are 5.7 and 5.3, respectively. However, the 11.0 of Shopwell skews the mean upward. We feel the 5.3 median is representative for the group. For the reasons already outlined, we believe Pagano's deserves a higher than average P/E and have chosen 6.5 in this regard. Capitalizing average earnings of $515 per share by a P/E ratio of 6.5 yields a publicly-traded equivalent value of $3,348 per share.

Weighted average earnings are probably superior to a straight average because the most recent years' data are given primary emphasis. The mean P/E on the comparables is again skewed upward by two figures that lie outside the relevant range. Excluding these, the mean drops to 5.3, which compares well to the median of 5.1. In this case, we again feel Pagano's deserves a P/E of 6.5, yielding a value of $3,434 per share.

Price/Tangible Book Approach

A second valuation approach will determine the relationship between price and tangible book value of the comparables. These ratios are also shown in Table VII. With a mean of .49 and a median of .47, we believe .50 appears representative for the group. As with the P/E, we again believe Pagano's deserves a price/book ratio, which is higher than "normal" for two primary reasons:

(1) Pagano's return on equity is much higher than the average of the comparables. Note that the three companies that had returns near Pagano's had ratios of .58, .59 and .60.
(2) Since 40% of the comparables are on FIFO, their equity figures are necessarily higher and price/book ratios necessarily lower than the LIFO companies.

20

(3) As with the P/E's, we think the normal ratio may be temporarily depressed.

Because of these factors, it is our opinion that Pagano's deserves a price/book ratio of .65, or approximately 30% above the current industry norm. This yields a publicly-traded equivalent value of $2,251 per share.

However, since the FIFO discrepancy can be quantified, we can take one alternative approach. By utilizing the footnotes to the financial statements of the publicly-traded companies, we can convert all companies to a FIFO basis. This is done in Table VIII, which computes new equity figures and price/book ratios based on FIFO figures. A representative industry price/book ratio is now approximately .40, while Pagano's adjusted book value has risen to $4,087.50 per share. Applying an approximate 30% premium for the high return on equity and current market conditions, we estimate a ratio appropriate for Pagano's of .55, yielding a publicly-traded equivalent value of $2,248 per share.

Adjusted Net Asset Approach

A third valuation approach is simply to adjust the firm's assets from a cost basis to an approximation of market. These will be four primary adjustments:

(1) Eliminate intangible assets.
(2) Convert securities to market value from cost.
(3) Convert inventory from LIFO to FIFO.
(4) Mark up fixed assets to an approximation of market. The only adjustment will be to land.

The latter three adjustments must be net of any income taxes. The adjustments are summarized in Table IX, and the adjusted balance sheet is shown as Table X.

The new adjusted net asset figure is $3,175,000, or $3,969 per share. Strictly by coincidence, this happens to approximate the equity shown on the financial statements.

This figure is not directly comparable to the publicly-traded equivalent figures previously derived. The latter figures were all computed using ratios derived from per share prices of the publicly-traded comparables. These shares represent small minority interests in the respective companies, therefore need no adjustment when valuing the prospective ESOP shares of Pagano's, which are also small minority interests.

However, in an adjusted net asset value approach, per share data from public companies is not utilized. Since we have no implicit minority interest discount which is automatically built-in to the valuation, an explicit discount must be taken. It should be emphasized to the reader that a 10% interest in $1 million worth of net assets is not equal to 10% ownership in the stock of a company that owns $1 million of net assets. The minority shareholder has little or no control over the use or disposition of those assets.

On the basis of empirical data we have available to us, we believe a 35% minority interest discount is appropriate to put the shares on a publicly-traded equivalent basis. This would yield a value of .65 x $3,969, or $2,580 per share.

Valuation Summary

In valuing the prospective ESOP shares of Pagano's Supermarkets, we have utilized three basic valuation techniques to derive six prospective values. These are summarized in Table XI.

21

TABLE VIII
PAGANO'S SUPERMARKETS & COMPARABLE COMPANIES
ADJUSTED TO A FIFO INVENTORY BASIS

	Shares Outs. Yr.-End (000)	Tang. Book Val. Sh.	Inv. Method	LIFO Reserve (000)	Tang. FIFO Book Value	Price 3/31/80	Price/ Tang. FIFO Book
A.T. Bayless Mkts.	1,181	$21.44	LIFO	$2,133	$23.25	10-5/8B	0.46
King Kullen Groc.	688	33.18	LIFO	1,272	35.03	13-1/4B	0.38
Mayfair Super.	1,212	2.14	LIFO	NA	NA	2B	---
Motts Super.	1,427	13.32	FIFO	---	13.32	7-3/4	0.58
Seaway Food	1,648	15.71	LIFO	7,728	20.40	9-1/4B	0.45
Shopwell	1,115	12.92	FIFO	---	12.92	3-3/4	0.29
Star Super.	862	20.14	LIFO	3,463	24.16	12-1/8	0.50
Thorofare Mkts.	1,245	11.09	FIFO	---	11.09	3-1/2	0.32
Victory Mkts.	1,520	8.17	FIFO	---	8.17	2-1/4B	0.28
Village Super.	587	13.67	LIFO	726	14.91	6B	0.40
					Mean		0.41
					Median		0.40
PAGANO'S	0.800	3,462.50	LIFO	500	4,087.50		

22

TABLE IX

PAGANO'S SUPERMARKETS INC.

SUMMARY OF ADJUSTMENTS TO BALANCE SHEET

MARKETABLE SECURITIES:	
At Market	$ 250,000
At Cost	— 200,000
Pre-Tax Gain — Short-Term	50,000
(1 — Tax Rate)	x (1 — .46)
Post-Tax Gain	$ 27,000

INVENTORY:	
FIFO Basis	$3,000,000
LIFO Basis	— 2,500,000
Pre-Tax Gain	$ 500,000
(1 — Tax Rate)	x (1 — .46)
Post-Tax Gain	$ 270,000

LAND:	
Assessed Value	$ 550,000
At Cost	— 400,000
Pre-Tax Gain	150,000
(1 — Tax Rate)	(1 — .28)
Post-Tax Gain	$ 108,000
Stockholders' Equity (As Reported)	$3,140,000
Intangible Assets	— 380,000
Tangible Stockholders' Equity	$2,770,000

ADDITIONS TO ASSETS, NET OF		
RELATED TAX LIABILITIES:		
Marketable Securities	$ 27,000	
Inventory	270,000	
Land	108,000	
Total Net Additions to Assets		405,000
Adjusted Stockholders' Equity		$3,175,000

23

TABLE X

PAGANO'S SUPERMARKETS INC.

ADJUSTED BALANCE SHEET — AS OF DECEMBER 31, 1979
(All figures in 000's)

	At Cost	Adjustment	As Adjusted
ASSETS			
Current Assets:			
Cash	$ 300	---	$ 300
Marketable Securities	200	$ 50	250
Receivables	400	---	400
Inventory	2,500	500	3,000
Prepaid Expenses	150	---	150
Total Current Assets	3,550	550	4,100
Fixed Assets:			
Land	400	150	550
Net Plant & Equipment	2,100	---	2,100
Total Fixed Assets	2,500	150	2,650
Goodwill	380	(380)	---
Cash Value of Life Insurance	200	---	200
Total Assets	$6,630	$ 320	$6,950
LIABILITIES & STOCKHOLDERS' EQUITY			
Current Liabilities	$2,700	---	$2,700
Prospective Taxes	---	$ 253	253
Total Current Liabilities	2,700	253	2,953
Non-Current Liabilites:			
Long-Term Debt	680	---	680
Other Non-Current Liabilities	100	---	100
Prospective Taxes	---	42	42
Stockholders' Equity	3,150	25	3,175
Total Liabilities & Stockholders' Equity	$6,630	$ 320	$6,950

TABLE XI
PAGANO'S SUPERMARKETS INC.
VALUATION SUMMARY
(On a Publicly-Traded Equivalent Basis)

	Value Per Share
Capitalization of Earnings:	
Current Earnings	$3,438
Average Earnings	$3,348
Weighted Average Earnings	$3,434
Price/Book Approach:	
Tangible Book Approach	$2,251
FIFO Adjusted Tangible Book Approach	$2,248
Adjusted Net Asset Value	$2,580

24

If we had to choose one figure which would characterize the capitalization of earnings approach, $3,400 per share would appear appropriate. Similarly, $2,250 per share reasonably reflects the figures indicated by the price/book approach, while $2,580 is derived for the adjusted net asset approach.

The question now arises as to how much weight should be afforded the different approaches. Because we are valuing an ongoing concern, earnings must be given primary emphasis. We have accorded capitalization of earnings 65%, or approximately two-thirds of the total weight. However, assets must also be taken into account. Of the 35% of the weight allocated to the asset value approaches, we have accorded 20% to the price-to-book value approach and 15% to the adjusted net asset value approach. In summary, we feel a 65-20-15 weighting is justified, yielding a value of $3,047 per share.

Valuation Method	Value Per Share		Weighting		Weighted Value Per Share
Capitalization of Earnings	$3,400	x	65%	=	$2,210
Price/Book Approach	$2,250	x	20%	=	$ 450
Adjusted Net Asset Approach	$2,580	x	15%	=	$ 387
Per Share Value					$3,047

Rounding slightly, it is our opinion that the value of Pagano's Supermarkets Inc., on a publicly-traded equivalent basis, is $3,050 per share.

Marketability Discount

That $3,050 per share is a publicly-traded equivalent value, does not necessarily mean that this is the fair market value of the shares in question. This is because there is one key difference between the shares in a public company versus a private company — that being the lack of marketability of shares in the latter.

If one wishes to dispose of shares of a publicly-traded company, all one has to do is call a local stockbroker. However, it's no easy task to dispose of shares in a private company.

The marketability (liquidity) afforded by the public marketplace has value. Empirical studies have shown that "letter stocks," defined as similar in every way to normal stock except possessing stringent marketability restrictions, typically sell at a 30% to 35% discount from their non-letter counterparts. This discount is for their lack of marketability.

However, in the case of an ESOP, a willing buyer of the shares is usually referenced in the ESOP agreement. Depending on the terms of the plan and the track record of actually redeeming stock, we normally use a marketability discount ranging from 5% to 20%. In the case of Pagano's the plan is worded so as to insure the employee-shareholder can have the shares redeemed at his option — except when the company is in an unusually illiquid position — a fairly liberal plan. Appropriate sections of the ESOP are included in Appendix E. However, the company has not yet established a record of redeeming shares immediately for each, so some discount is necessary.

In summary, we feel a 10% discount for lack of marketability is appropriate.

25

Conclusion

Applying a 10% marketability discount to the publicly-traded equivalent value of $3,050 per share yields a fair market value of the prospective ESOP shares of $2,745 per share.

The results of the entire valuation are summarized in Table XII.

TABLE XII

PAGANO'S SUPERMARKETS INC.

SUMMARY OF VALUATION PROCEDURES

(All figures are per share, unless otherwise noted)

Valuation Approaches					Point Est.
CAPITALIZATION OF EARNINGS:					
Current Earnings	$625	x 5.5	=	$3,438	$3,400
Average Earnings	$515	x 6.5	=	$3,348	
Weighted Average Earnings	$528.33	x 6.5	=	$3,434	
PRICE/BOOK APPROACH:					
Tangible Book	$3,462.50	x .65	=	$2,251	
FIFO Adjusted Tangible Bk.	$4,087.50	x .55	=	$2,248	$2,250
ADJUSTED NET ASSET VALUE:					
(Not Per Share)					
Stockholders' Equity				$3,150,000	
Adjustments (net of tax effect):					
Intangible Assets				(380,000)	
Marketable Securities				27,000	
Inventory				270,000	
Land				108,000	
Adjusted Stockholders' Equity				$3,175,000	
Per Share				3,969	
(1 — Minority Interest Discount)		x		(1 — .35)	
Publicly-Traded Equivalent Value					$2,580

WEIGHTING OF APPROACHES:

	Value	Weighting		Weighted Val.
Capitalization of Earnings	$3,400	x 65%	=	$2,210
Price/Bk. Approach	$2,250	x 20%	=	$ 450
Adj. Net Asset Val.	$2,580	x 15%	=	$ 387
				$3,047
WMA Estimate of Value Per Share on a Publicly-Traded Equivalent Basis				$3,050
(1 — Marketability Discount)			x	(1-.10)
Fair Market Value Per ESOP Share				$2,745

26

5411 Grocery Stores

ALBERTSON'S INC.
ALLIED SUPERMARKETS, INC.
ALTERMAN FOODS, INC.
AMERICAN STORES CO
AMFAC, INC.
APPLEBAUMS' FOOD MARKETS, INC.
ARDEN-MAYFAIR, INC.
ASSOCIATED BRITISH FOODS LIMITED
A. J. BAYLESS MARKETS, INC.
BIG V SUPERMARKETS, INC.
BORMAN'S INC.
BRUNO'S, INC.
CANADA SAFEWAY LIMITED
CAVENHAM (USA) INC.
CIRCLE K CORP.
CLABIR CORP
CONSOLIDATED FOODS CORP.
CONVENIENT INDUSTRIES OF AMERICA, INC.
COOK UNITED, INC.
CULLUM COMPANIES, INC.
DMI FURNITURE INC.
DAYLIGHT INDUSTRIES INC.
DILLON COMPANIES, INC.
FAIRMONT FOODS CO.
FIRST NATIONAL SUPERMARKETS INC.
FISHER FOODS, INC.
164 SOUTHERN BOULEVARD CORP.
FOOD FAIR INC.
FOOD TOWN STORES, INC.
FOODARAMA SUPERMARKETS, INC.
GAMBLE-SKOGMO, INC.
GIANT FOOD INC.
GLOSSER BROS., INC.
GODFREY CO.
GRAND UNION CO.
THE GREAT ATLANTIC & PACIFIC TEA COMPANY, INC.
HANNAFORD BROS. CO.
HOP-IN FOOD STORES, INC.
HORNE & PITFIELD FOODS, LIMITED
INTERNATIONAL BASIC ECONOMY CORP.
JEWEL COMPANIES, INC.
JIFFY FOODS CORP.
JURGENSEN'S INC.
KELLY, DOUGLAS & CO., LTD.
KING KULLEN GROCERY CO., INC.
THE KROGER CO.
LANECO, INC.
LIL' CHAMP FOOD STORES, INC.
LOBLAWS LIMITED
LUCKY STORES INC.
MALONE & HYDE, INC.
MARSH SUPERMARKETS, INC.
MAYFAIR SUPER MARKETS INC.
FRED MEYER, INC.
MINI MART CORP.
MOTT'S SUPER MARKETS, INC.
MUNFORD, INC.
NASH-FINCH COMPANY
NATIONAL CONVENIENCE STORES INC.
NATIONAL TEA CO.
NIAGARA FRONTIER SERVICES, INC.
THE OSHAWA GROUP LTD.
PENN TRAFFIC CO.
PNEUMO CORP.
PROVIGO INC.
PUEBLO INTERNATIONAL INC.
RED FOOD STORES, INC.
RUDDICK CORPORATION
SAFEWAY STORES, INC.
SAGE INTERNATIONAL INC.
SCHULTZ SAV-O STORES, INC.
SEAWAY FOOD TOWN, INC.
SHOP & GO, INC.

SHOP RITE FOODS,INC.
SHOPWELL, INC.
SOBEYS STORES, LTD.
SOUTHLAND CORP.
STAR SUPERMARKETS, INC.
STEINBERG INC.
STOP & SHOP COMPANIES INC.
SUNSHINE-JR. STORES, INC.
SUPERMARKETS GENERAL CORP.
THOROFARE MARKETS, INC.
THRIFTIMART, INC.
TWIN FAIR INC.
VICTORY MARKETS, INC.
VILLAGE SUPER MARKET INC.
WALDBAUM, INC.
J. WEINGARTEN, INC.
WEIS MARKETS, INC.
WINN-DIXIE STORES, INC.

5422 Freezer and Locker Meat Provisioners

DOUGHTIE'S FOODS, INC.
THOROFARE MARKETS, INC.

5431 Fruit Stores and Vegetable Markets

BEATRICE FOODS CO.
NASH-FINCH COMPANY

5441 Candy, Nut, and Confectionery Stores

BARTON'S CANDY CORP.
CHOCK FULL O'NUTS CORP.
FANNY FARMER CANDY SHOPS, INC.
HICKORY FARMS OF OHIO, INC.
SOUTHLAND CORP.
WOMETCO ENTERPRISES, INC.

5451 Dairy Products Stores

CARVEL CORP.
CROWLEY FOODS, INC.
DELLWOOD FOODS, INC.
FUQUA INDUSTRIES, INC.
INTERNATIONAL DAIRY QUEEN, INC.
ROYAL OAK DAIRY LTD.
SOUTHLAND CORP.

5462 Retail Bakeries—Baking and Selling

COLE NATIONAL CORPORATION
THE HORN & HARDART CO.
INGREDIENT TECHNOLOGY CORP.

5463 Retail Bakeries—Selling Only

NIAGARA FRONTIER SERVICES, INC.

5499 Miscellaneous Food Stores

FAIRMONT FOODS CO.
GIANT FOOD INC.
HICKORY FARMS OF OHIO, INC.
JEWEL COMPANIES, INC.

27

APPENDIX B

COMPANIES LISTED IN SIC NO. 5411 — GROCERY STORES, WHICH ARE INCLUDED IN STANDARD & POOR'S CORPORATE RECORDS — 91 COMPANIES

	Sales $MM	Description — S&P
Albertson's	$2,269	Operates 317 supermarkets in Western states. Also 47 super drug/grocery stores in Southwest.
Allied Supermarkets		Company is in process of Chapter XI bankruptcy proceedings.
Alterman Foods	436	Operates 93 supermarkets in Metropolitan Atlanta area.
American Stores	4,183	Through subsidiaries, operates food, drug, general merchandise stores & restaurants.
Amfac		Diversified.
Applebaum's Foods Mkts.		Acquired by National Tea Co. 7/27/79 for $15.25 per share.
Arden-Mayfair Inc.	449	Operates 108 supermarkets in California, Oregon, Washington, Arizona & Nevada. Name changed to Arden Group.
A.J. Bayless Markets	260	Operates 57 supermarkets in Arizona.
Assoc. British Foods Ltd.		Limited information available.
Big V Supermarkets	295	Operates supermarkets & drug stores in New York.
Borman's Inc.	784	Operates 80 supermarkets, 50 drug stores and 10 convenience stores in Michigan.
Bruno's Inc.	386	Operates 50 supermarkets & 54 drug stores in Alabama, Tennessee and Georgia.
Canada Safeway Ltd.	1,985	Operates 300 grocery stores, primarily in Canada.
Cavenham (USA) Inc.	2,399	Holding company, owning all common shares of Grand Union.
Circle K Corp.	439	Operates 1,158 retail drive-in grocery stores, 695 of which also sell gasoline.
Clabir Corp.	83	Food & retail activities account for less than half of revenues.
Consolidated Foods Corp.		Diversified.
Convenient Ind. of America		Operates & franchises 316 convenience food stores and 218 gasoline stations. Name changed to Conna Corp.
Cook United	416	Specialty retail outlets, discount department stores & wholesale distribution.
Cullum Companies, Inc.	783	Operates supermarkets & drug stores primarily in Dallas area. Mfg. accounts for 8.2% revenue.
DMI Furniture		Limited information available.
Daylight Industries		Limited information available.
Dillon Companies, Inc.	1,792	Operates supermarkets, convenience stores and junior department stores.
Fairmont Foods Co.	562	Mfr. dairy products, operates convenience stores.
First Nat'l. Supermarkets	1,112	Operates 256 supermarkets & 18 retail food warehouses.
Fisher Foods, Inc.	1,452	Operates 158 supermarkets & 11 no-frills warehouse stores.
564 Southern Blvd. Corp.	1,496	Assets sold to MM Supermarkets of NY Inc. & Tropical Brands Packing Corp.
Food Fair, Inc.		In process of Chapter XI proceedings.
Food Town Stores, Inc.	416	Operates 85 supermarkets, primarily in North Carolina.

28

Foodarama Supermarkets	413	Operates 44 supermarkets, primarily in New York/New Jersey area.
Gamble-Skogmo	1,955	General merchandiser of variety of products.
Giant Food, Inc.	1,081	Operates 117 self-service supermarkets in Washington, D.C., Maryland & Virginia.
Glosser Bros. Inc.	146	Operates discount department stores.
Godfrey Co.	318	Company distributes food & other products to Sentry Supermarkets.
Grand Union Co.	2,399	Operates 840 supermarkets, primarily in Eastern U.S.
Great Atlantic & Pacific Tea Co.	7,470	Operates 1,771 retail food stores in U.S. & Canada.
Hannaford Bros. Co.	378	Wholesale & retail distribution through 107 supermarkets & 17 retail drug stores.
Hop-In Food Stores, Inc.	43	Company operates 132 convenience stores, most of which offer gasoline.
Horne & Pitfield Foods Ltd.		Amalgamated 11/78 with a subsidiary of M. Loeb.
Inter'l. Basic Economy Corp.	67	Company is very diversified.
Jewel Companies, Inc.	3,516	Operates 364 food stores which account for 76.3% of business.
Jiffy Foods Corp.		Fast food restaurants, importing & trading.
Jurgensen's, Inc.		Information not available.
Kelly, Douglas & Co. Ltd.		Wholesale distribution of packaged, fresh & frozen foods.
King Kullen Grocery Co.	318	Operates 53 self-service supermarkets in New York.
The Kroger Co.	9,029	Operates 1,234 supermarkets & 504 drug stores.
Laneco, Inc.	139	Operates food (78%) & department stores in eastern Pennsylvania & western New Jersey.
Lil' Champ Food Stores	25	Operates 128 retail drive-in groceries.
Loblaws Ltd.	3,073	Largest retailer of food products in Canada (grocery stores); owns 81% of Nat'l. Tea Co.
Lucky Stores, Inc.	4,658	Company operates food (61%) & department stores (27%).
Malone & Hyde, Inc.	1,616	Wholesale grocery distribution (79%), retail food & drug stores (19.5%).
Marsh Supermarkets	392	Operates supermarkets, convenience stores & drug stores in Indiana & Ohio.
Mayfair Super Markets Inc.	266	Operates chain of supermarkets in New Jersey.
Fred Meyer, Inc.	927	Operates 61 retail stores in the West; also wholesale food distribution services.
Mini Mart Corp.		Information not available.
Mott's Super Markets, Inc.	211	Operates 23 supermarkets in Connecticut & Massachusetts.
Munford, Inc.	260	Operates drive-in convenience food stores.
Nash-Finch Company	760	Distributes food products.
Nat'l. Convenience Stores	320	Operates retail convenience food stores.
National Tea Co.	919	Operates chain of 214 supermarkets in 10 states.
Niagara Frontier Services	464	Diversified food retailer, wholesaler & franchiser.
The Oshawa Group Ltd.	1,337	Wholesale food distributor (44.9%), retail food (28.1%) & general merchandise (20.2%).
Penn Traffic Co.	330	Operates 64 supermarkets & 6 department stores.
Pneumo Corp.	627	Operates chain of supermarkets & wholesale food distribution (77%); aerospace (18%).

29

Provigo Inc.	2,037Cdn.	Food & drug distributor.
Pueblo Int'l., Inc.	296	Operates 36 supermarkets in Puerto Rico.
Red Food Stores, Inc.	206	Operates 34 supermarkets primarily in Tennessee. Shareholders are to vote on liquidation.
Ruddick Corp.	389	Yarn & thread operations (23%), supermarkets (73%).
Safeway Stores	12,551	Largest food retailer in U.S.
Sage Int'l. Inc.	25	Operates discount department stores.
Schultz Sav-O Stores	219	Conducts wholesale food business & operates Piggly Wiggly stores under franchise agreement.
Seaway Food Town, Inc.	285	Operates supermarkets in Ohio & Michigan.
Shop & Go, Inc.	94	Operates 379 self-service convenience stores.
Shop Rite Foods, Inc.	181	Operates Piggly Wiggly supermarkets & convenience food stores in Texas.
Shopwell, Inc.	272	Operates chain of retail food stores in New York state.
Sobeys Stores, Ltd.	308Cdn.	Limited information available.
Southland Corp.	3,077	Country's largest operator & franchiser of convenience food stores.
Star Supermarkets, Inc.	228	Operates 50 supermarkets in New York state.
Steinberg Inc.	1,918	Large Canadian food retailer.
Stop & Shop Cos.	1,762	Supermarkets account for 67% of revenue. Department, drug, tobacco and specialty items account for the remainder.
Sunshine-Jr. Stores	94	Operates 316 convenience food stores in Southeast U.S.
Supermarkets General	2,062	Supermarkets (86%), home centers & department stores.
Thorofare Markets	218	Operates 64 supermarkets.
Thriftimart, Inc.	368	Operates retail/wholesale outlets in Los Angeles & Las Vegas.
Twin Fair Inc.		Operates discount department stores.
Victory Markets, Inc.	229	Operates 84 supermarkets, primarily in New York.
Village Super Market Inc.	232	Operates 20 supermarkets in New Jersey.
Waldbaum, Inc.	941	Operates 129 self-service supermarkets in New York, Connecticut & Massachusetts.
J. Weingarten, Inc.	566	Operates 100 supermarkets, primarily in Texas.
Weis Markets, Inc.	518	Operates 101 supermarkets, primarily in Pennsylvania.
Winn-Dixie Stores, Inc.	4,931	Operates 1,174 food stores in the South & Southeastern U.S.

APPENDIX C

REASONS FOR REJECTION IN INITIAL SCREENING — 74 COMPANIES

Albertson's Inc.	Too large.
Allied Supermarkets	In process of Chapter XI proceedings.
Alterman Foods	Too large.
American Stores	Too large.
Amfac Inc.	Too diversified.
Applebaums Food Markets	Acquired.

30

Arden Group	Too large.
Associated British Foods Inc.	Limited information available.
Borman's Inc.	Too large.
Bruno's Inc.	Over half of stores are drug stores.
Canada Safeway Ltd.	Too large.
Cavenham (USA) Inc.	Too large.
Circle K Corp.	Primarily convenience stores.
Clabir Corp.	Supermarkets are not primary business.
Consolidated Foods	Too diversified.
Convenient Ind. of America	Convenience stores. Name changed to Conna Corp.
Cook United	Too diversified.
Cullum Companies	Too large.
DMI Furniture	Limited information available.
Daylight Industries	Limited information available.
Dillon Companies	Too large.
Fairmont Foods	Too large.
First National Supermarkets	Too large.
Fisher Foods	Too large.
564 Southern Boulevard	Assets sold.
Food Fair	In process of liquidation.
Food Town Stores	Too large.
Foodarama Supermarkets	Too large.
Gamble-Skogmo	Too large.
Giant Foods	Too large.
Glosser Bros.	Operates department stores.
Godfrey Co.	Food distributor.
Grand Union	Too large.
Great Atlantic & Pacific Tea Co.	Too large.
Hop-In Food Stores	Convenience stores.
Horne & Pitfield Foods Ltd.	Merged.
International Basic Economy	Diversified.
Jewel Companies	Too large.
Jiffy Foods Corp.	Restaurants.
Jurgensens, Inc.	Limited information available.
Kelly, Douglas & Co., Ltd.	Wholesaler.
Kroger Co.	Too large.
Lil' Champ Food Stores	Convenience stores.
Loblaws, Ltd.	Too large.
Lucky Stores Inc.	Too large.
Malone & Hyde Inc.	Primarily a wholesaler.
Fred Meyer Inc.	Too large.
Mini Mart Corp.	Limited information available.
Munford Inc.	Convenience stores.
Nash-Finch	Too large.
National Convenience Stores	Convenience stores.
National Tea Co.	Too large.
Niagara Frontier Services	Too diversified.
The Oshawa Group Ltd.	Too large.
Pneumo Corp.	Too large.
Provigo Inc.	Too large.
Pueblo International, Inc.	Operates in Puerto Rico.
Red Food Stores	In process of liquidation.
Ruddick Corp.	Supermarkets not high enough percentage of business.

31

Safeway Stores Inc.	Too large.
Sage International	Department stores.
Schultz Sav-O Stores	Large portion in wholesale.
Shop & Go Inc.	Convenience stores.
Sobey's Stores	Limited information available.
Southland Corp.	Too large.
Steinberg	Too large.
Stop & Shop	Too large.
Sunshine Jr. Stores	Convenience stores.
Supermarkets General	Too large.
Twin Fair Inc.	Department stores.
Waldbaum Inc.	Too large.
J. Weingarten Inc.	Too large.
Weis Markets Inc.	Too large.
Winn-Dixie Stores Inc.	Too large.

APPENDIX D

REASONS FOR REJECTION IN SECONDARY SCREENING — 7 COMPANIES

Big V Supermarkets	Operates 26 supermarkets, 8 discount drug stores, owns 5 shopping centers. Too many non-supermarket operations.
Hannaford Bros.	Company is primarily a food distributor.
Laneco Inc.	Supermarkets provide only 78% of revenue.
Marsh Supermarkets	Operates 62 supermarkets, 108 convenience stores and drug stores.
Penn Traffic Co.	Department stores & dairy processing account for 15% of business.
Shop Rite Foods	Company has not been profitable since 1975.
Thriftimart	Large portion of operations are wholesale.

APPENDIX E

EXCERPTS FROM PAGANO'S SUPERMARKETS PROSPECTIVE ESOP AGREEMENT RELATING TO MARKETABILITY

5.4-2   Each participant, beneficiary or a donee of the company shares received by the participant shall have an option to sell company shares received from the plan, or any part of them, to the company. For a period of six months after company shares are distributed to a participant or beneficiary, the participant, beneficiary or participant's donee shall have the right to require the company to purchase the shares at fair market value determined in accordance with subparagraph 9.3. The option shall be exercised by the seller given written notice to the company. Payment for the purchase of company shares may, at the election of the company, be either in a lump-sum or in substantially equal annual, quarterly or monthly installments over a period not to exceed five years from the date the company purchases the shares. If an installment payment is elected, the first installment shall be due within 30 days of the date the option was exercised. At the election of the seller the installment payments may be extended

32

beyond five years, but not to exceed ten years. As security for an installment payment, the seller shall be given a promissory note which provides for the acceleration of the balance in the event of a default. If the term of an installment payment for company shares exceeds five years, the seller shall receive adequate security for the outstanding amount of the promissory note. The promissory note shall bear interest at a rate equal to the prevailing interest rate then being charged for first mortgage loans on residential real estate in Portland, Oregon.

5.4-3   After the close of the company's taxable year in which the option under subparagraph 5.4-2 lapses, the company will notify each person who failed to exercise an option of the fair market value of company shares. Each such person shall then have three months from the date the valuation information is mailed to require the company to purchase all or any part of the company shares on the terms provided in paragraph 5.4-2. Thereafter, the company shall have no obligation to purchase the shares under subparagraph 5.4-2 or this subparagraph.

INDEPENDENCE OF APPRAISERS

Neither Willamette Management Associates, Inc., nor the individuals involved with this appraisal have any present or contemplated future interest in the subject property or any other interest which might tend to prevent making a fair and unbiased appraisal.

APPENDIX F

QUALIFICATION OF APPRAISERS

This appraisal report was prepared by Willamette Management Associates, Inc., an investment adviser registered with the Securities and Exchange Commission. Willamette Management conducts valuation studies of both publicly-held and privately-held ongoing business enterprises for a variety of purposes including public stock offerings, tender offers, mergers and acquisitions, federal gift and estate tax cases, divorces, and other cases involving litigation and Employee Stock Ownership Trusts.

In addition, Willamette Management publishes the quarterly Northwest Stock Guide and semi-monthly Northwest Investment Review, which include statistics and analyses of publicly-held companies operating in the Northwest/Intermountain area of the United States. Willamette Management also maintains an extensive investment research library with files and reference manuals and services on publicly-held companies located throughout the nation.

Willamette's Director of Research is Shannon P. Pratt, a Chartered Financial Analyst. He holds a doctorate in finance and has participated extensively in corporate valuation studies, including expert testimony in court and in settlement hearings with the Internal Revenue Service on numerous occasions. Mr. Pratt received his Doctorate in Finance from Indiana University. He holds the designation of Certified Financial Planner, and is a Senior Member, Business Enterprise Valuation of the American Society of Appraisers. From 1964 to 1969 he was Associate Professor and Director of the Investment Analysis Center at Portland State University.

Gregory A. Gilbert received his B.A. in Economics at Yale University and completed his formal education with an M.S. in Industrial Administration at the

33

Massachusetts Institute of Technology in 1966. Since that time he has been an investment analyst following a widely diversified list of companies. The customers for his research represented the entire spectrum of major financial institutions, centered primarily in New York, Boston, Hartford, Milwaukee and Chicago. At Monness, Williams, and Sidel, one of the two firms he was associated with before Willamette Management Associates, he was Managing Partner in Charge of Administration in addition to his normal sales and research duties. Mr. Gilbert is Associate Director of Research at Willamette Management Associates, Inc.

Mark P. Pagano is a Research Analyst for Willamette Management Associates, Inc. Mr. Pagano has a Bachelor of Science degree from Lewis & Clark College with majors in both Business Administration and Economics.

APPENDIX G

CONTINGENT AND LIMITING CONDITIONS

This appraisal is subject to the following contingent and limiting conditions:

1. Information, estimates, and opinions contained in this report are obtained from sources considered reliable; however, no liability for such sources is assumed by the appraiser.

2. Client company and its representatives warranted to appraiser that the information supplied to appraiser was complete and accurate to the best of client's knowledge; and that any reports, analysis, or other documents prepared for it by appraiser will be used only in compliance with all applicable laws and regulations.

3. Possession of this report, or a copy thereof, does not carry with it the right of publication of all or part of it, nor may it be used for any purpose by any but the client without the previous written consent of the appraiser or the client, and in any event only with proper attribution.

4. Appraiser is not required to give testimony in court, or be in attendance during any hearings or depositions, with reference to the company being appraised, unless previous arrangements have been made.

5. The various estimates of value presented in this report apply to this appraisal only, and may not be used out of the context presented herein.

34

16

COURT TESTIMONY

Court testimony is challenging to an expert witness because it is part of an adversary proceeding. If the opposite side were willing to accept the witness's valuation, there probably would be a settlement instead of a trial. Indeed, the majority of cases reach settlement at some stage before reaching trial, especially if the witness has prepared his case thoroughly and the attorney has been able to draw on the expert's valuation research in negotiating with the opposite side. Thus, if the case goes to court, sharp disagreement is inevitable. Competent and thorough preparation must culminate in a clear and convincing presentation.

While generally it is important for a person doing a business valuation to be objective and unbiased, it is essential when legal testimony is involved. One school of thought says that the courts tend to make decisions spliting opposing positions down the middle, so the appraiser on one side of an issue must take an extreme position because the opposition will do so, and, thus, taking an extreme position is the only strategy that will lead to a fair result in the court. I do not adhere to this philosophy. I believe that the expert witness should arrive at a figure that he expects to present and to defend without compromise on cross-examination. In the majority of cases, I believe that a rigorously prepared and presented objective case will prevail over an extreme position, which a competent judge will tend to discredit.

All of the elements of defining the appraisal assignment, which were discussed in Chapter 2, should be included in the process of making and accepting the assignment where legal testimony may be involved, and certain aspects should be given special consideration. Also, the date of retention of the appraiser should be noted, since it is a point about which opposing counsel may inquire.

MAKING AND ACCEPTING THE ASSIGNMENT

The client seeking an expert witness on the valuation of a business or business interest will want someone who is competent and articulate, whose valuation concepts and conclusions will not be diametrically opposed to those of the client, and who has no conflict of interest. Usually the attorney will assume the role of middleman between the client and the prospective witness.

The qualifications of the witness can be established fairly readily from his credentials and reputation. Establishing whether there is a concurrence of valuation philosophy and whether there is any conflict of interest usually requires some delicate conversation between the attorney and the prospective witness.

In some cases, the client or the attorney, or both, may not be tentatively or irrevocably committed to preconceived notions about value, and may rely on the guidance of the independent business appraiser. This probably is the best of all situations, especially in that an open-minded attitude on the part of the client relying on an expert is the most likely condition to lead to a settlement

Concurrence of valuation philosophy

short of trial. However, in the real world there are few participants without preconceived ideas, and some are more receptive to change in the light of new evidence than others.

To establish whether there is a concurrence of valuation philosophy, the attorney may wish to approach the prospective witness with a hypothetical scenario. This way the attorney can get some idea of the approaches and parameters the witness would use in reaching the value conclusion, without revealing the name of the client or identifying the business interest to be valued. If the attorney decides that the witness would be unacceptable in the particular situation, he can back off, without incurring the risk that evidence would surface later in testimony about another appraiser having offered a preliminary opinion that was adverse to the specific case.

One of the nuances in this exercise is that the initiative to establish valuation parameters should be in the hands of the prospective witness, rather than in the hands of the attorney or client. In other words, the witness should establish valuation parameters independently, rather than being led by a priori thinking of the attorney or client. A witness generally has more credibility in court because it is established that he was hired to ascertain a value independently, not to testify to some value that was predetermined by the interested party.

This preliminary exploration is as valuable to the witness as to the client, since no reputable appraiser wants to be under pressure to testify to a value which he cannot support professionally. If it appears that this would be the situation, the witness should decline the assignment. Within a very few minutes of dialogue between an experienced attorney and an experienced appraiser, it usually is possible to determine whether the appraiser can be helpful as a witness.

Of course, if the attorney finds that the thinking of the proposed witness is far apart from that of the client, and the attorney believes in the expertise of the appraiser, the attorney may decide that the appraiser could be helpful in moving the client away from an untenable position, thus perhaps facilitating an otherwise impossible settlement. The attorney simply has to use his best judgment in advising his client on whether to get the prospective appraiser involved in such circumstances.

Conflicts of interest

At a very early point in the proceeding, the attorney must disclose the name of the client to the prospective witness to ascertain there is no conflict of interest. Normally, it is also necessary to identify the party or parties on the opposite side of the case. In general, the witness should be in a position of independence to the parties on both sides of the case.

The most common type of conflict of interest (apart from having been retained already by the party on the opposite side of the case) would be having some financial interest in the entity involved which would call the witness's independence into question. However, it is possible also that the prospective witness may have some personal or business relationship with some party on one side of the case or the other that would cause him to decline the assignment, even if the relationship would not cause the witness's independence or credibility to be called into question.

If the prospective witness is willing to accept the assignment but there is a question in his mind whether there could be any conflict of interest, the witness should disclose all the relevant facts to the attorney. The attorney then should make the judgment on whether the credibility of the witness might be impeachable on the grounds of conflict of interest.

Compensation

The critical point regarding compensation is that it must be agreed that the witness will be compensated either on a flat fee or on an hourly basis, or some combination thereof, regardless of the outcome of the case. Any compensation agreement that is based on how the case comes out absolutely destroys the witness's independence in testimony.

From the viewpoint of the witness, the danger in agreeing to do the entire project on a flat fee basis is that the hours required for some of the later elements, such as depositions, working with the attorney to prepare for court, and actual time spent in court, are out of the witness's control. Therefore, the project may be broken down into stages. The research and preparation of the basic information for the oral testimony and preparation of the supporting exhibits may be one stage, on a fixed fee basis. Then the time spent on negotiations, depositions, working with the attorney to prepare for court, and actual court time may be charged on an hourly basis.

The attorney may wish to break down the project into more phases. For example, he may want a less detailed report that can be used as a basis for negotiations as a first phase, with a more complete and well-documented report to follow if the negotiations fail to result in a settlement. The attorney and the witness must cooperate to structure the compensation so it is flexible enough to accomodate the many uncertainties that must be coped with where litigation is involved, but rigid enough that the witness cannot become a party at interest to the outcome of the case.

PREPARING THE PRESENTATION

Where legal controversy is involved, there is no substitute for thorough homework and preparation. You virtually have to prepare not only your own case but the other side's case as well. It is essential for the expert valuation witness to attempt to anticipate any potential weaknesses that the opposing attorney may seize upon in cross-examination and to be prepared to defend against them. Also, the expert witness should be prepared to critique the case presented by the opposing side.

Basic preparation and documentation

The basic research itself should follow the principles and procedures outlined in Parts I, II, and III. As discussed in Part I, where legal testimony is involved, reliance needs to be placed to the greatest extent possible on facts, not on conjecture.

Documentation is the keynote at every step. It makes no difference how well the witness himself is convinced of the validity of his facts and conclusions unless the witness is able to convince the court.

If the witness were presenting the company in question to a prospective buyer, it might be valid to presume some knowledge and sophistication on the part of the buyer about the business or industry involved. However, such knowledge can not be presumed on the part of the court. Every fact on which the witness intends to rely in reaching the conclusion must be presented with whatever supporting documentation is necessary to convince the court that the fact should, indeed, be relied upon.

Also, if the witness were presenting the company to a prospective buyer and the buyer was interested, but believed that the facts were inadequate to reach a decision, the buyer might issue an invitation to do additional homework and offer another audience in two weeks. The witness must assume that the court will make its decision based on the initial presentation, however inadequate it may be and however interested the court may be in reaching an equitable determination. The luxury of a second chance to present the case is rarely available to the expert witness, so the research had better be thorough the first time.

Hearsay

The witness can anticipate that the attorney on the opposite side probably will object to any testimony the witness offers that might be classified as hearsay. The term refers broadly to any information the witness may have obtained from third parties without personal verification. The witness should not, however, avoid collecting information and opinions from other people if these are relevant. The judge has a great deal of latitude in deciding what he will or will not listen to, and usually he wants to hear anything that might be helpful in reaching an equitable decision. Especially if there is no jury, most judges are reluctant to disallow any potentially relevant testimony on technical grounds. Once the witness has been qualified to testify as an expert before the court, judges tend to be amenable to learning from the witness any relevant information the witness had considered in forming his opinion, even if the testimony of the witness includes statements that would be disallowed as hearsay in some other legal proceedings. The judge then will make his own determination on what weight, if any, to accord any statements in the testimony.

Nevertheless, the witness runs the risk that anything that could be considered as hearsay may be disallowed or accorded little or no weight in the court's deliberations. Therefore, the witness should take all feasible steps to make any research that might possibly be considered as hearsay be both admissible and convincing. If the witness is surveying customers, suppliers, or competitors to obtain information on industry practices, then the larger the sample, the better. To the extent that the witness can use specific names and companies to identify who said what, the testimony might be more acceptable than if the sources had to be kept confidential.

Just to be on the safe side, the witness should so structure his research and conclusion that anything that could be considered as hearsay is not essential to the conclusion, even though it may lend considerable support to the conclusion if accepted.

If the witness does not have the cooperation of the management of the business being valued, it usually is difficult to obtain all the information necessary to do the valuation job thoroughly. It is the responsibility of the witness to apprise the attorney about what documents will be needed from the company, what facility visits will be desired, and what people need to be interviewed. This must be done very early, so that any foot-dragging by uncooperative parties on the opposite side will not succeed in frustrating the analyst's ability to complete a thorough valuation study.

Discovery

The witness also should keep the attorney informed on the timeliness and adequacy of information received. The attorney then can follow up to obtain any necessary additional data, and can report accurately to the court on the timeliness and adequacy of information supplied.

A part of the homework preparatory to testifying on an issue of valuation is to read the prior court cases that are relevant to the one at hand. I specifically recommend reading the full texts of the cases, rather than only the digests provided by various services. The digest services are very useful as regular day-to-day reading to keep up on the field generally, but are not an adequate substitute for the detail needed when addressing a specific case. It also can be helpful to read relevant articles analyzing particular cases or categories of cases.

Reading prior cases and articles

This book offers a fairly detailed analysis of a few tax cases; they were selected to be representative of some of the most frequently occurring valuation issues. Also, the bibliography lists the leading tax reporting services which index court cases.

The expert witness and the attorney need to spend some time working together to prepare the presentation. The witness should know what areas of questions he is expected to answer, so he can prepare answers that are direct and complete. The attorney needs to know what evidence the expert witness has prepared, so he can be sure to get all of it presented. Some attorneys like to put the expert witness on the stand and ask one broad question, such as, "Will you please describe your investigation and findings as to the value of XYZ Company?" Most attorneys (and most judges) prefer that the attorney ask a series of questions which will develop the case logically and point by

Outlining the presentation

point in a question and short answer format between the attorney and the witness.

In some instances, the judge may issue a pretrial order requiring each side of the case to prepare and exchange formal, written reports, and then to find areas of agreement and disagreement among themselves, and limit the verbal testimony to the unresolved issues. I think it is harder to convey to the court the full context of a case in this way. Unless a written report is required by the court, I prefer to prepare only the tables and exhibits in written form, and to present the text of the case verbally in the attorney/witness question and answer format.

The attorney may prepare a list of 20 to 50 questions, usually leading the witness through the testimony in more or less the following sequence:

1. Identification and qualifications of witness.
2. Description of assignment.
3. Conclusion.
4. Steps taken in carrying out the assignment.
5. Findings.
6. Repeat the conclusion.

Qualifying the witness.   The qualifying of the witness as an expert is an essential first step to establish the witness's credibility in the eyes of the court. This step usually will establish not only the witness's expertise on the subject of business valuation but also his position and affiliations, making it clear that he is independent of the company being valued and of the parties to the suit.

Description of assignment.   The description of the assignment usually will include when the witness was retained and by whom, and what the assignment was, including the standard of value to be used. This information will be similar to that included in the Description of Assignment section of a written report, as discussed in Chapter 2.

The matter of compensation to the witness may or may not be raised, either by the attorney on direct examination or by the opposing attorney on cross-examination. Whether the witness's compensation is on a flat fee or an hourly basis, it is a good idea for the witness to come to court prepared to answer the question on how many hours have been spent in preparation. If the witness has carried out all the steps in the valuation process suggested in this book, a good many hours will have been spent, and testimony to that effect lends further support to the thoroughness of the preparation.

Summary of conclusion.   Once the witness has been qualified and the assignment defined, most attorneys like to ask the witness to state the conclusion that was reached, before starting into the description of the research undertaken. This is very much like stating a summary of the conclusion at the end of the introduction in the written report. Some attorneys prefer to wait until the entire research project has been described before presenting the conclusion. In this, as in all other procedural matters in testimony, the attorney's judgment should prevail.

Description of steps taken. The description of the steps taken in reaching the valuation conclusion should include a combination of the Sources of Information Used portion of the written report format, plus brief statements on what was obtained from the various sources. For example, in listing persons interviewed, the witness might tell at this point in the testimony what subjects were discussed. In listing written information sources, the witness also might tell what pieces of information were obtained from each source.

Findings. The oral testimony about the findings of the research should cover all the rest of the information discussed in the chapter on the written report. This includes pertinent aspects of the economic outlook, the industry in which the company operates and its position in that industry, a description of the company, and the analysis leading to the valuation conclusion.

Final conclusions. In stating the conclusion—even though it usually is obvious, from differing results of the various approaches used, that there is some reasonable range of possible values—the attorney typically will ask the witness for one single figure that represents the witness's best judgment of value. The attorney probably will ask the witness to restate the standard of value used at the time the conclusion is presented. The attorney usually will ask whether all the procedures followed in the valuation have been in accordance with generally accepted business valuation techniques and procedures.

An important part of the preparation for court testimony, of course, is the exhibits which will be presented. These usually include the qualifications of the witness that would be included as an appendix to a written report, all the tabular statistical data for the written report, and whatever charts, pictures, or other supporting material that may be of assistance to the court in understanding the business and how it should be valued. **Exhibits**

Courtroom testimony is an event in which I believe the old adage, "One picture is worth a thousand words." The witness probably has visited the company's operating locations and toured them. The judge very likely has not. Since it is unlikely the court will go to the facilities, the next best thing is to bring the facilities to the court. In effect, if through pictures the witness can give the court a "walking tour" of the business being valued before getting into the financial analysis, this should help give the court a better understanding of what it is all about, and hopefully make the financial analysis more meaningful.

Most business valuation cases are tried before a judge without a jury. Even if the parties have a right to a jury trial in the particular situation, attorneys on both sides usually opt to waive the right in business valuation cases. This is partly because of the extra time and cost involved in dealing with a jury. It also is because of the potential difficulty met in educating a lay jury sufficiently on the complexities of a business valuation to have any reasonable confidence that a fair decision will be reached by the jury, however conscientious and well-intentioned the jury members may be. Consequently, the pictures used in the courtroom usually can be in the form of prints that the judge can see and which can be entered as official exhibits. If the trial is before a jury, the attorney and witness may wish to present the pictures in slide form, so all parties in the courtroom can see the same thing while the witness is describing the company's operations.

For exhibits of a size and format that can be copied readily, such as 8½ x 11-inch or 11 x 17-inch pages and as would be included in a written report, it is convenient to prepare an extra set for the judge to look at, in addition to the set to be labeled by the clerk and entered as the official exhibit in the court record. This will make it convenient for the judge to look at the tables and other exhibits while the witness is discussing them in direct testimony, as well as during cross-examination. It also is a courtesy to provide a set of copies for the attorney on the opposing side.

The exhibits the witness proposes to use should be reviewed with the attorney who will conduct the examination, to be sure that they all are legally admissable. A sample list of exhibits appropriate for a simple, basic case is shown as Exhibit 16–1.

DEPOSITIONS

The term *depose* means *to state under oath but not in open court*. It is common practice for the opposing attorney to take a witness's deposition some time before the trial. There are several reasons for this. One is for the opposing attorney to attempt an assessment of the relative strengths of the opposing sides for guidance on whether to consider offering or accepting a settlement, and, if so, on what basis. Another reason is to try to learn enough about the witness and his testimony in advance to prepare a cross-examination that will be damaging to it. Another reason sometimes is that an

Exhibit 16–1
Typical list of exhibits to be submitted with court testimony on business valuation

Qualifications of Witness

Pictures of Business Facilities

Latest Five Years Financial Statements for Subject Company

Five-Year Summary of Subject Company's Balance Sheets

Five-Year Summary of Subject Company's Income Statements

Subject Company Financial Ratios Compared with Industry Norms

Market Price Data for Comparable Publicly-Traded Companies

Summary Statistics of Valuation Approaches Used and Conclusion

(The above list applies to a simple, basic case, and should be expanded to include whatever additional material may be relevant in each specific case.)

attorney may hope to embarrass or discredit a witness by bringing out inconsistencies between what is in the deposition and what he testifies to at trial.

Unless there is some unusual pretrial order, the other side cannot force the witness to complete the entire research and preparation of the testimony ahead of the trial date. Obviously, a witness cannot disclose the results of research that he has not yet done. Also, the witness has the right to check and recheck data as thoroughly as he wishes. If he finds an error at any time between the deposition date and the court date, he should correct it. If the opposing attorney tries to embarrass him in court over the inconsistency, the witness should state frankly that the material at the time of the deposition was preliminary, and that the process of checking the material disclosed an error which subsequently was corrected.

The opposing attorney may harangue the witness in the deposition proceeding for not being as prepared as the opposing attorney would like. This is not the witness's problem. The schedule of preparation for the trial, and for any deposition, negotiation, or other proceeding related to it, is a matter between the witness and the attorney who is representing the client.

The witness has the right to receive, read, and make any corrections to the transcript of his own deposition, or he may waive that right. I recommend exercising that right. For one thing, although court reporters do an incredibly fast and accurate job in general, they do make mistakes, and occasionally mistakes are made that can change the sense of a point. Also, reading over the transcript of his own deposition is a constructive exercise for the witness, in that it helps to call attention to any weakness or disorganization, which then can be corrected prior to the trial.

ON THE STAND

Perhaps the most critical thing for the witness to keep in mind on the stand is that he must be objective and unbiased, not an advocate. An advocate is defined as "one who pleads the cause of another," or "one who supports something as a cause." Pleading and supporting the client's cause is the role of the attorney. The role of the witness is to present the facts as they are and to use his professional expertise to interpret those facts to reach an objective conclusion.

Direct examination

The witness must be careful not to omit any material facts, even (or especially) if their implications are not supportive of the client's case. Always assume that the attorney and the expert witness for the opposite side will be properly prepared (whether you really believe that or not), and that they will not allow any adverse facts to be overlooked. If the witness omits consideration of material facts, his credibility with the court will be in question, whether the omission is because of incompetence or because of advocacy.

It also is essential that the witness not distort any of the facts or their interpretations. Straightforward is a good key word to go by.

278

Another key element on the stand is that the witness must be responsive to the questions that are asked. This means that the witness first must pay attention to the question and be sure that he understands it. He should pause long enough before answering to be *sure* that the answer will be responsive to the question. If the witness is not sure whether he understands the question, he should ask for a clarification.

Answers should be concise but complete. How far to go is a matter of judgment. The thing to avoid is the introduction of material or ideas that are not relevant to the question. There is a fine line of judgment, however. Occasionally a question will be worded in such a manner that a direct answer without clarification could leave a misleading impression. In such cases, the witness should volunteer the necessary clarification. (Of course, such questions are more likely to come from the attorney on the other side on cross-examination, either because he doesn't understand the material or because he deliberately wishes to lead the witness into leaving a false impression.)

The witness should speak distinctly and slowly enough for the judge and attorneys to understand what is being said and for the court reporter to type it into the record. If it is necessary to use proper names or esoteric terminology, it is desirable to spell them so the court reporter can enter them correctly into the record.

The timing of entering the exhibits with the testimony is a matter of preference. Sometimes it is convenient to enter the entire set of exhibits at the beginning of the testimony. However, many attorneys feel, and I generally concur, that entering the exhibits one at a time with the relevant part of the testimony helps to keep the attention of the court focused on the subject immediately at hand. After the verbal qualification of the witness, the witness's credentials in writing may be entered as an exhibit. From that point forward, each exhibit can be introduced immediately before the witness discusses it, so the judge can look at it as the witness describes and interprets it.

The witness should not be surprised if the opposing attorney raises frequent objections. He may object to the form or substance of a question, to an answer given by a witness, or to the introduction of an exhibit. When an objection is raised, the witness must pause while the attorneys fight it out, then proceed when so instructed by the judge or by the attorney conducting the examination.

Cross-examination

It is the job of the opposing attorney to expose to the court any weaknesses in the witness's testimony. The witness should not take this personally.

The attorney may attempt to discredit the witness in various ways. He may ask questions designed to attack the witness's competence to present expert testimony on the valuation issue at hand. He may ask questions designed to bring out possible conflicts of interest that would call the independence of the witness into question. If the witness has testified in previous cases, the witness should assume that the opposing attorney has read the transcripts of such cases and will ask questions that will bring out any inconsistencies between previous testimony and the present testimony.

As discussed in the previous section, in preparing the direct testimony the witness also must prepare for cross-examination. If the witness did not use some particular approach, one that may seem reasonable on the surface, he should be prepared to explain why. If he did not use a company as a comparable, he should be prepared to explain why the company was disqualified as a comparable. (This particular problem will be taken care of almost automatically if the procedures outlined in Chapter 9, Data on Comparable companies, are followed and documented.)

If the witness has done his homework thoroughly, the cross-examination actually can be quite helpful to the case. In one case, the attorney conducting the cross-examination asked a series of questions on why I had not used certain valuation approaches and why I had not used certain comparable companies. In response to each question, I replied that I had considered using the approach or the comparable company, and explained why it was inappropriate to use for the case at hand. Finally, I overheard a colleague of the examining attorney sitting next to him whisper, not too discreetly, "Let's get this guy off the stand. He's hurting us." As it turned out, the attorney was destroying his own case. The approaches and prospective comparables in question were ones that the opposition's expert witness had researched and planned to use. With each answer explaining why the particular approach or company was rejected, I was rebutting his expert witness's testimony, which hadn't even been presented yet!

As mentioned earlier, some attorneys use a cross-examination technique of asking questions in a manner designed to leave the court with an impression that the attorney might like to convey, but which may be misleading. A favorite ploy is to frame a complicated question, which was carefully designed to leave a certain impression, and then demand a yes or no answer. The witness should realize that he cannot be compelled to limit his answer to yes or no if it is not a completely appropriate answer. The witness has the right to clarify the answer, and he should demand to be allowed to do so if he feels that failure to clarify would leave a misimpression. The witness should try to remain courteous, but must be firm and not allow himself to be bullied by an overbearing attorney on cross-examination.

Since the cross-examination can refer to any point in the witness's previous testimony at any time, it is helpful if the witness can keep his notes and copies of exhibits reasonably well-organized on the stand, so he can find the appropriate material fairly quickly when responding to questions on different aspects of the testimony. Exhibits will be numbered by the court as they are entered, and there probably will have been other exhibits entered in earlier aspects of the case. Therefore, witness's Table II may be the court's Exhibit 15. As the exhibits are entered, the witness should write the court's exhibit number at the top of his own copy, since that usually is how the exhibit will be identified when the witness is called to discuss it in cross-examination.

The witness should be aware that the opposing attorney has the right to examine and make copies of any notes or papers that the witness takes to the stand for reference. The witness should check his papers to make sure that nothing is there that might be embarrassing.

One thing that a witness absolutely must avoid is attempting to bluff if he does not know an answer. If the court suspects the witness is bluffing on any answer, it could cast doubt on the credibility of the witness's entire testimony. If the witness does not know the answer, he must say so. Also, if the witness has made some error in his data, he should admit and correct it, making whatever adjustment to his conclusion the correction would indicate.

Redirect examination

Even when the cross-examination has been completed, it is not yet time for the witness to breathe a sigh of relief. The attorney who conducted the original examination usually will want to put the witness back on the stand for redirect examination. The general purpose of this is to expand any points brought out in the cross-examination that the attorney feels should be elaborated. This is the attorney's opportunity to counter possible misimpressions that might have been left with the court on the cross-examination, and to reinforce any positions about which the cross-examination may have raised doubts.

If there is a recess between cross- and redirect examinations, and the witness feels the need to further clarify any points, he should make his feelings known to the attorney, so the attorney can ask the appropriate questions. If the witness feels strongly that something should be brought out on redirect examination and there is no scheduled recess, he can request a conference with the attorney.

In fact, the witness can request a conference with the attorney at any time during the proceedings if he wishes to communicate in private or needs guidance in some respect.

The redirect and recross examinations can go back and forth for some time, limited only by the restraint of the attorneys and the patience of the judge.

The judge may break in at any time during the direct examination, cross-examination, or any part of the proceedings, to ask questions. Some judges are more prone to do so than others—it usually is a good sign. At least the judge is paying attention, and judges often ask penetrating and perceptive questions. Also, the witness should prefer that the judge ask for clarification of something the witness has left unclear or omitted, rather than just leaving the issue alone.

ASSISTING IN EXAMINATION OF OPPOSITION WITNESSES

The expert witness also can assist the attorney during the examination of the expert or experts for the other side of the case, both at the deposition stage and in the courtroom. At the deposition, the witness can suggest to the attorney areas of examination or specific questions, or both, that would help reveal the substance and validity of the opposition's position. Following the deposition stage, the attorney may wish to consult with his own witness on the merits or lack thereof of the opposition's case about the issue of valuation, to help decide whether to pursue settlement negotiations, and to determine a range of values within which it might be reasonable to reach a compromise settlement.

If the case is not settled and goes to court, the witness can hear the direct testimony of the opposing expert, can provide the attorney with a critique of it, can suggest subjects and questions for the cross-examination, and can make suggestions for rebuttal testimony. Sometimes the attorney for the opposition will try to blunt the effectiveness of such assistance from a good expert witness by moving to have the witnesses in the case barred from the courtroom during the other witnesses's testimony. If the court grants such a motion, then the attorney must take good notes on the opposing witness's testimony, or have someone else take notes, and then review them and the opposing witness's exhibits with the attorney's own witness prior to cross-examination.

V
USING THE BUSINESS VALUATION

17

ESTATE PLANNING AND TAX VALUATIONS

The present estate and gift tax base . . . could be entirely washed away if taxpayers put a strong effort into doing so. The fact that any substantial amount of tax is now being collected can be attributed only to taxpayer indifference to avoidance opportunities or the lack of aggressiveness on the part of estate planners. . . . For those who do not want to contribute their estates to the government (or to charity), there is an impressive array of strategies for moving wealth from one generation to another outside the purview of estate and gift taxation.[1]

The two most important objectives of estate planning for the owner of the closely-held business are:

1. Provision for liquidity for himself or his heirs, or both.
2. Minimization of gift, estate, and inheritance taxes.

Liquidity during the owner's lifetime can be provided by going public, selling out the company, selling shares to an ESOP, or selling shares by other means. Liquidity at the owner's death can be provided by any of the same means or by a buy-sell agreement funded by life insurance. Chapter 20 discusses ESOPs, Chapter 21 discusses buy-sell agreements, and Chapter 22 discusses other types of transactions, such as mergers, acquisitions, and purchases and sales of minority interests.

Minimization of transfer taxes can be accomplished through both the structuring and the timing of the interests transferred. The next two sections of this chapter discuss general techniques of estate planning as they apply to the stock of a closely-held company, and the specific technique of recapitalization. Regardless of structure and timing of transfers, the valuation aspect is critical in any case. The final section of this chapter discusses the guidelines for valuation for tax purposes, and includes as exhibits the complete texts of the most relevant IRS rulings. Chapters 18 and 19 analyze a number of particularly instructive cases where disputed tax valuations have been resolved in court.

The material in this book generally is limited to discussion of issues regarding valuation. Anyone involved in a tax case also should consult a competent attorney and a CPA for guidance on legal and tax implications of any particular situation.

In general, estate planning techniques to minimize transfer taxes revolve around timing transfers, when the value of the stock is relatively low, and so structuring the transfers that they have the least possible value.

The more rapidly a company is growing in value, the more important it is to effect stock transfers to heirs early, rather than later after the value has increased. However, if the business is of a cyclical nature, it may be possible to time transfers at a cyclical trough in the company's value.

MINIMIZING TAXES BY A SERIES OF TIMELY MINORITY INTEREST TRANSFERS

---

[1]George Cooper, "A Voluntary Tax? New Perspectives on Sophisticated Estate Tax Avoidance," *Columbia Law Review* (March 1977), p. 164.

For structure, the best technique usually is to plan transfers as a series of small minority interests. To begin, a married couple can give up to $20,000 in value to each of as many heirs as they wish, each year, without federal gift tax. More important for transfers of substantial size, however, is that, at least under the law and court rulings at this writing, minority interests are entitled to substantial discounts in value per share compared with the per-share value of a controlling interest. As a broad generality, the less significant the fractional interest as it relates to control or potential control of the company, the greater the discount that is applicable.

Discounts for lack of marketability are discussed in Chapter 10. Minority shares in closely-held companies can be valued for tax purposes by estimating their potential market value as publicly-traded stock and then discounting them for lack of marketability. In general, the smaller the minority interest, the greater the extent to which this approach can be applied to its fullest extent. Since most public stocks at this writing in 1980 sell substantially below their underlying net asset values, as was demonstrated in the comparable table in Chapter 15, the net result can be that transfers of shares of closely-held companies can be made at quite large discounts below net asset values. Illustrations of such discounts are included in the analysis of certain tax valuation cases in the next two chapters.

INCORPORATING FAMILY ASSETS BEFORE TRANSFERRING

Because of the discounts discussed in the previous section, it may be worthwhile to consider incorporating various family assets into a family-controlled holding company before transferring them to heirs. The assets could be almost anything, such as marketable securities, real estate, art, coins, or collectibles of any kind. Since publicly-traded securities of companies holding such assets (such as closed-end investment companies and REITs) sell at a discount from underlying net asset value, so should shares of family-controlled corporations. Interests in such closely-held companies also are entitled to be valued at a further discount for lack of marketability.

Of course, in making the decision to incorporate a family holding company to execute a portion of the family estate plan in this manner, it must be realized that the justification for the discounted values is real and not contrived. That is, the heir who receives a gift of minority shares of a family holding company representing an undivided interest in a portfolio of assets will not have control over those assets. Owning 15 percent of the assets and owning 15 percent of the stock of the company that owns the assets are two different things. The power to liquidate, transfer assets, declare dividends, and exercise all the other various elements of control will not go to the donee. There also may be income tax considerations, so such a move should not be undertaken without the aid of competent tax counsel. If the donor understands and is satisfied with the various implications, the creation of a family-owned holding company could be a tax-saving feature as a part of the total estate plan.

A recapitalization can be an effective tool in estate planning to freeze the value of the older generation's estate and have the future appreciation in the value of the business accrue to the younger generation. The recapitalization also can accomplish several other desirable objectives, such as allowing active members of management to maintain continuity of voting control and providing income to selected owners who have a need for it. While it is most common to use the recapitalization technique for a corporation, it also is possible to use essentially the same technique to create a multi-class partnership.[2]

A corporate recapitalization involves dividing the equity of the company into two or more classes of stock, the provisions of each class being designed to serve the objective of a particular owner or group of owners. In its simplest form, the recapitalized company would have the value of its common stock divided into one class of common and one class of preferred, but the possible variations to serve different circumstances and objectives are limitless.

Let's say that we have a growing company operated by a father and son, that the father owns all the stock, and that we have estimated the fair market value at $1 million. Assume also that the father desires that all the future growth in the value of the company inure to the benefit of the son, rather than further building the value of the father's estate. The total value of the $1 million can be reallocated to a common stock and a fixed-dividend preferred, say on the basis of $100,000 worth of common and $900,000 worth of preferred. If the father has not used his lifetime unified gift and estate tax exemption, he can give the $100,000 worth of common stock to his son with no gift tax payment. If in five years the value of the total business grows to $2.5 million, but the value of the preferred stays constant, the value of the business interest in the older generation's estate has been frozen at $900,000, while the value of the younger generation's interest has grown to $1.6 million.

The technique obviously can be a tremendously powerful tool to reduce potential estate tax consequences in a growing family company. The recapitalization technique used for this purpose is perfectly acceptable to the IRS as long as two criteria are met.[3] First, the total value assigned to the company at the time of the recapitalization must be acceptable under the guidelines of Revenue Ruling 59–60. This requires an analysis and report similar to that which would be done to establish a gift or estate tax or ESOP value. Second, the allocation of total value must be made properly among whatever classes of stock are used. The essence of the problem here usually is to avoid the possible pitfall of allocating too little to the common and too much

---

[2]Byrle M. Abbin, "Using the Multi-class Partnership to Freeze Asset Values for Estate Planning Purposes," *The Journal of Taxation* (February 1980), pp. 66–69.

[3]Of course, a business purpose must be met. However, courts have found that estate planning for shareholders in a closely-held company does constitute a valid business purpose. If one is in doubt about being able to satisfy the business purpose requirement, it may be advisable to seek a private letter ruling. For a good discussion of basic requirements of a recapitalization, and tax treatment, as well as other aspects of recapitalizations, see Robert L. Littenberg, "The Use of Recapitalizations in Estate Plans under the 1976 Tax Reform Act," *Tax Institute, University of Southern California* 30 (1978): 719–73.

to the preferred, since the common typically will be transferred, and the taxpayer does not want to be in the position of incurring a substantial gift tax if the IRS subsequently determines that the value of the transfer was considerably above the amount allocated in the recapitalization.

As Littenberg states:

Accurate valuation of a corporation and the stocks and/or securities to be exchanged and issued in connection with a recapitalization is absolutely essential. Failure to achieve accurate valuation can result in either unexpected gift tax or income tax liabilities. . . .

In most instances the most prudent course to pursue is to engage the services of a qualified expert to make the valuation and prepare a supporting written report which can be provided to the Service on audit.[4]

The income, voting, redemption, and liquidation rights can be assigned to the various classes of stock in almost any desired manner. Typically, those who desire income, such as a retiring key owner or family member, will receive dividend-paying preferred stock, while those desiring growth of value will receive common. Stock with voting rights may be used for those active in the affairs of the company, and nonvoting stock used for inactive owners. Sometimes voting rights on a class of stock will be conditioned on some event, such as failure to pay dividends for a two-year period. A class of stock can even have voting rights that terminate with the death of a specified individual, so that control of the corporation will not remain in the estate of the deceased.

Dividends on preferred stocks can be cumulative, noncumulative, or partially cumulative on almost any basis the company wants to set. The dividend payment can be fixed, adjustable on some sort of formula, or participating. A preferred stock can be convertible or nonconvertible.

Typically, each class of stock will be subject to its own buy-sell agreement provisions. The corporation may or may not retain an option to redeem one or more classes of preferred stock. Also, a preferred stock may have a put feature, that is, an option on the part of the holder to sell it back to the corporation on some specified basis.

All of the foregoing factors have a bearing on the relative values of the different classes of stock. They present unique challenges to the appraiser, because there is little empirical data available to use as guidelines to assess the value impact of each feature. Furthermore, there is a notable lack of court cases that have set any precedents on the relationship between various special features of preferred stocks and their values.

The starting place in evaluating a preferred stock usually is an analysis of the yields available on preferred stocks in the public marketplace. A tabulation of such yields in early 1980 is shown as Exhibit 4–3.

The prices of publicly-traded preferred stocks relative to their yields are only a starting point, however, because the characteristics of a closely-held preferred stock can be significantly different, with some factors adding to or

---

[4]Littenberg, "The Use of Recapitalizations," pp. 732–33.

detracting from relative value. The quality of the dividend-paying capability may be lower for the closely-held company, although not necessarily so. I call attention to the definition of the B classes of S&P preferred stock quality ratings, stated in Exhibit 4–3, which do not suggest that the stocks necessarily are pillars of dividend-paying strength.

Another difference is in marketability, where the public stock, by definition, is publicly salable, while the private stock is not. However, the markets for many public preferred stocks are quite thin, and there may be substantial spreads between bid and asked prices, not only for those traded in the OTC market but for those listed on exchanges as well. The private company may more than compensate for the lack of a public market for its preferred through its buy-sell agreement mechanism, or, especially, by the use of a put option in the preferred.

The put feature can be especially useful in helping to establish value for a preferred stock in cases where the desired value might be questionable on the basis of the stock's dividend features alone. The put feature not only guarantees marketability, but usually even guarantees it at a specified minimum price, a feature notably absent in the public marketplace.

One of the features that can have a wide range of value implications under different circumstances is voting rights. For the few public companies which have both nonvoting and voting stocks trading simultaneously, the price differential usually is very small. However, if a question of significant or total degree of control is involved, the value of voting rights can make a considerable difference. For example, if a preferred stock were noncumulative, its value should be substantially enhanced if that class of stock has voting control, since it can control dividend as well as other important policies. Alternatively, the noncumulative preferred stock's value could be enhanced by the right to assume voting control in the case of nonpayment of dividends for some specified time.

The appraiser simply has to make a reasoned judgment of the factors affecting the relative value of the securities of each class in a recapitalization situation in light of all the facts unique to this situation. Because of the considerable impact on value that can result from the various features, it is becoming increasingly common for the appraiser to work intimately with the attorney, CPA, and client, starting from the very outset of a proposed recapitalization program.

GUIDELINES FOR FEDERAL GIFT AND ESTATE TAX VALUATIONS

The basic guidelines for the valuation of closely-held stocks are contained in Revenue Ruling 59–60, which is included in its entirety as Exhibit 17–1. Revenue Ruling 59–60 is modified slightly by Revenue Ruling 65–193, included as Exhibit 17–2. Revenue Ruling 68–609, included as Exhibit 17–3, discusses a "formula method" (sometimes referred to by practitioners as the "treasury method") for arriving at value for intangibles, but states that, "The 'formula' approach should not be used if there is a better evidence available from which the value of intangibles can be determined." Finally, Revenue

Exhibit 17–1
Revenue ruling 59–60

In valuing the stock of closely-held corporations, or the stock of corporations where market quotations are not available, all other available financial data, as well as all relevant factors affecting the fair market value must be considered for estate tax and gift tax purposes. No general formula may be given that is applicable to the many different valuation situations arising in the valuation of such stock. However, the general approach, methods and factors which must be considered in valuing such securities are outlined.

SECTION 1. PURPOSE.

The purpose of this Revenue Ruling is to outline and review in general the approach, methods and factors to be considered in valuing shares of the capital stock of closely-held corporations for estate tax and gift tax purposes. The methods discussed herein will apply likewise to the valuation of corporate stocks on which market quotations are either unavailable or are of such scarcity that they do not reflect the fair market value.

SECTION 2. BACKGROUND AND DEFINITIONS.

.01 All valuations must be made in accordance with the applicable provisions of the Internal Revenue Code of 1954 and the Federal Estate Tax and Gift Tax Regulations. Sections 2031(a), 2032 and 2512(a) of the 1954 Code (sections 811 and 1005 of the 1939 Code) require that the property to be included in the gross estate, or made the subject of a gift, shall be taxed on the basis of the value of the property at the time of death of the decedent, the alternate date if so elected, or the date of gift.

.02 Section 20.2031-1(b) of the Estate Tax Regulations (section 81.10 of the Estate Tax Regulations 105) and section 25.2512-1 of the Gift Tax Regulations (section 86.19 of Gift Tax Regulations 108) define fair market value, in effect, as the price at which the property would change hands between a willing buyer and a willing seller when the former is not under any compulsion to buy and the latter is not under any compulsion to sell, both parties having reasonable knowledge of relevant facts. Court decisions frequently state in addition that the hypothetical buyer and seller are assumed to be able, as well as willing, to trade and to be well informed about the property and concerning the market for such property.

.03 Closely-held corporations are those corporations the shares of which are owned by a relatively limited number of stockholders. Often the entire stock issue is held by one family. The result of this situation is that little, if any, trading in the shares takes place. There is, therefore, no established market for the stock and such sales as occur at irregular intervals seldom reflect all of the elements of a representative transaction as defined by the term "fair market value."

SECTION 3. APPROACH TO VALUATION.

.01 A determination of fair market value, being a question of fact, will depend upon the circumstances in each case. No formula can be devised that will be generally applicable to the multitude of different valuation issues arising in estate and gift tax cases. Often, an appraiser will find wide differences of opinion as to the fair market value of a particular stock. In resolving such differences, he should maintain a reasonable attitude in recognition of the fact that valuation is not an exact science. A sound valuation will be based upon all the relevant facts, but the elements of common sense, informed judgment and reasonableness must enter into the process of weighing those facts and determining their aggregate significance.

.02 The fair market value of specific shares of stock will vary as general economic conditions change from "normal" to "boom" or "depression," that is, according to the degree

Source: 1959–1 C.B. 237.

Ruling 77–287, included as Exhibit 17–4, amplifies Revenue Ruling 59–60 by giving specific recognition to criteria to determine an appropriate discount for lack of marketability.

If the analyst follows the valuation procedures presented in this book with a reasonable degree of thoroughness, the requirements of these revenue rulings basically should be met. Consequently, beyond including the relevant rulings as exhibits, the text of this section will be limited to calling attention to a few

Exhibit 17-1 (*continued*)

of optimism or pessimism with which the investing public regards the future at the required date of appraisal. Uncertainty as to the stability or continuity of the future income from a property decreases its value by increasing the risk of loss of earnings and value in the future. The value of shares of stock of a company with very uncertain future prospects is highly speculative. The appraiser must exercise his judgment as to the degree of risk attaching to the business of the corporation which issued the stock, but that judgment must be related to all of the other factors affecting value.

.03 Valuation of securities is, in essence, a prophesy as to the future and must be based on facts available at the required date of appraisal. As a generalization, the prices of stocks which are traded in volume in a free and active market by informed persons best reflect the consensus of the investing public as to what the future holds for the corporations and industries represented. When a stock is closely held, is traded infrequently, or is traded in an erratic market, some other measure of value must be used. In many instances, the next best measure may be found in the prices at which the stocks of companies engaged in the same or similar line of business are selling in a free and open market.

SECTION 4. FACTORS TO CONSIDER.

.01 It is advisable to emphasize that in the valuation of the stock of closely-held corporations or the stock of corporations where market quotations are either lacking or too scarce to be recognized, all available financial data, as well as all relevant factors affecting the fair market value, should be considered. The following factors, although not all-inclusive are fundamental and require careful analysis in each case:

(a) The nature of the business and the history of the enterprise from its inception.
(b) The economic outlook in general and the condition and outlook of the specific industry in particular.
(c) The book value of the stock and the financial condition of the business.
(d) The earning capacity of the company.
(e) The dividend-paying capacity.
(f) Whether or not the enterprise has goodwill or other intangible value.
(g) Sales of the stock and the size of the block of stock to be valued.
(h) The market price of stocks of corporations engaged in the same or a similar line of business having their stocks actively traded in a free and open market, either on an exchange or over-the-counter.

.02 The following is a brief discussion of each of the foregoing factors:

(a) The history of a corporate enterprise will show its past stability or instability, its growth or lack of growth, the diversity or lack of diversity of its operations, and other facts needed to form an opinion of the degree of risk involved in the business. For an enterprise which changed its form of organization but carried on the same or closely similar operations of its predecessor, the history of the former enterprise should be considered. The detail to be considered should increase with approach to the required date of appraisal, since recent events are of greatest help in predicting the future; but a study of gross and net income, and of dividends covering a long prior period, is highly desirable. The history to be studied should include, but need not be limited to, the nature of the business, its products or services, its operating and investment assets, capital structure, plant facilities, sales records and management, all of which should be considered as of the date of the appraisal, with due regard for recent significant changes. Events of the past that are unlikely to recur in the future should be discounted, since value has a close relation to future expectancy.

(b) A sound appraisal of a closely-held stock must consider current and prospective economic conditions as of the date of appraisal, both in the national economy and in the industry or industries with which the corporation is allied. It is important to know that the company is more or less successful than its competitors in the same industry, or that it is

points in Revenue Ruling 59–60. The following two chapters provide discussion of a variety of key factors in the context of various positions taken and decisions reached in court cases.

Revenue Ruling 59–60, Section 3, "Approach to Valuation," makes the general point that the public marketplace best reflects the consensus of the

Approach to valuation

Exhibit 17–1 (continued)

maintaining a stable position with respect to competitors. Equal or even greater significance may attach to the ability of the industry with which the company is allied to compete with other industries. Prospective competition which has not been a factor in prior years should be given careful attention. For example, high profits due to the novelty of its product and the lack of competition often lead to increasing competition. The public's appraisal of the future prospects of competitive industries or of competitors within an industry may be indicated by price trends in the markets for commodities and for securities. The loss of the manager of a so-called "one-man" business may have a depressing effect upon the value of the stock of such business, particularly if there is a lack of trained personnel capable of succeeding to the management of the enterprise. In valuing the stock of this type of business, therefore, the effect of the loss of the manager on the future expectancy of the business, and the absence of management-succession potentialities are pertinent factors to be taken into consideration. On the other hand, there may be factors which offset, in whole or in part, the loss of the manager's services. For instance, the nature of the business and of its assets may be such that they will not be impaired by the loss of the manager. Furthermore, the loss may be adequately covered by life insurance, or competent management might be employed on the basis of the consideration paid for the former manager's services. These, or other offsetting factors, if found to exist, should be carefully weighed against the loss of the manager's services in valuing the stock of the enterprise.

(c) Balance sheets should be obtained, preferably in the form of comparative annual statments for two or more years immediately preceding the date of appraisal, together with a balance sheet at the end of the month preceding that date, if corporate accounting will permit. Any balance sheet descriptions that are not self-explanatory, and balance sheet items comprehending diverse assets or liabilities, should be clarified in essential detail by supporting supplemental schedules. These statements usually will disclose to the appraiser (1) liquid position (ratio of current assets to current liabilities); (2) gross and net book value of principal classes of fixed assets; (3) working capital; (4) long-term indebtedness; (5) capital structure; and (6) net worth. Consideration also should be given to any assets not essential to the operation of the business, such as investments in securities, real estate, etc. In general, such nonoperating assets will command a lower rate of return than do the operating assets, although in exceptional cases the reverse may be true. In computing the book value per share of stock, assets of the investment type should be revalued on the basis of their market price and the book value adjusted accordingly. Comparison of the company's balance sheets over several years may reveal, among other facts, such developments as the acquisition of additional production facilities or subsidiary companies, improvement in financial position, and details as to recapitalizations and other changes in the capital structure of the corporation. If the corporation has more than one class of stock outstanding, the charter or certificate of incorporation should be examined to ascertain the explicit rights and privileges of the various stock issues including: (1) voting powers, (2) preference as to dividends, and (3) preference as to assets in the event of liquidation.

(d) Detailed profit-and-loss statements should be obtained and considered for a representative period immediately prior to the required date of appraisal, preferably five or more years. Such statements should show (1) gross income by principal items; (2) principal deductions from gross income including major prior items of operating expenses, interest and other expense on each item of long-term debt, depreciation and depletion if such deductions are made, officers' salaries, in total if they appear to be reasonable or in detail if they seem to be excessive, contributions (whether or not deductible for tax purposes) that the nature of its business and its community position require the corporation to make, and taxes by principal items, including income and excess profits taxes; (3) net income available for dividends; (4) rates and amounts of dividends paid on each class of stock; (5) remaining amount carried to surplus; and (6) adjustments to, and reconciliation with, surplus as stated on the balance sheet. With profit and loss statements of this character available, the appraiser should be able to separate recurrent from nonrecurrent items of income

investing public, and concludes by suggesting as a measure of value "the prices at which the stocks of companies engaged in the same or a similar line of business are selling in a free and open market." The section also recognizes that the value can change as a result of internal factors affecting the company and external economic factors. The section emphasizes the complexity of the factors affecting valuation and the degree of uncertainty involved.

Exhibit 17–1 (*continued*)

and expense, to distinguish between operating income and investment income, and to ascertain whether or not any line of business in which the company is engaged is operated consistently at a loss and might be abandoned with benefit to the company. The percentage of earnings retained for business expansion should be noted when dividend-paying capacity is considered. Potential future income is a major factor in many valuations of closely-held stocks, and all information concerning past income which will be helpful in predicting the future should be secured. Prior earnings records usually are the most reliable guide as to the future expectancy, but resort to arbitrary five-or-ten-year averages without regard to current trends or future prospects will not produce a realistic valuation. If, for instance, a record of progressively increasing or decreasing net income is found, then greater weight may be accorded the most recent years' profits in estimating earning power. It will be helpful, in judging risk and the extent to which a business is a marginal operator, to consider deductions from income and net income in terms of percentage of sales. Major categories of cost and expense to be so analyzed include the consumption of raw materials and supplies in the case of manufacturers, processors and fabricators; the cost of purchased merchandise in the case of merchants; utility services; insurance; taxes; depletion or depreciation; and interest.

(e) Primary consideration should be given to the dividend-paying capacity of the company rather than to dividends actually paid in the past. Recognition must be given to the necessity of retaining a reasonable portion of profits in a company to meet competition. Dividend-paying capacity is a factor that must be considered in an appraisal, but dividends actually paid in the past may not have any relation to dividend-paying capacity. Specifically, the dividends paid by a closely-held family company may be measured by the income needs of the stockholders or by their desire to avoid taxes on dividend receipts, instead of by the ability of the company to pay dividends. Where an actual or effective controlling interest in a corporation is to be valued, the dividend factor is not a material element, since the payment of such dividends is discretionary with the controlling stockholders. The individual or group in control can substitute salaries and bonuses for dividends, thus reducing net income and understating the dividend-paying capacity of the company. It follows, therefore, that dividends are less reliable criteria of fair market value than other applicable factors.

(f) In the final analysis, goodwill is based upon earning capacity. The presence of goodwill and its value, therefore, rests upon the excess of net earnings over and above a fair return on the net tangible assets. While the element of goodwill may be based primarily on earnings, such factors as the prestige and renown of the business, the ownership of a trade or brand name, and a record of successful operation over a prolonged period in a particular locality, also may furnish support for the inclusion of intangible value. In some instances it may not be possible to make a separate appraisal of the tangible and intangible assets of the business. The enterprise has a value as an entity. Whatever intangible value there is, which is supportable by the facts, may be measured by the amount by which the appraised value of the tangible assets exceeds the net book value of such assets.

(g) Sales of stock of a closely-held corporation should be carefully investigated to determine whether they represent transactions at arm's length. Forced or distress sales do not ordinarily reflect fair market value nor do isolated sales in small amounts necessarily control as the measure of value. This is especially true in the valuation of a controlling interest in a corporation. Since, in the case of closely-held stocks, no prevailing market prices are available, there is no basis for making an adjustment for blockage. It follows, therefore, that such stocks should be valued upon a consideration of all the evidence affecting the fair market value. The size of the block of stock itself is a relevant factor to be considered. Although it is true that a minority interest in an unlisted corporation's stock is more difficult to sell than a similar block of listed stock, it is equally true that control of a corporation, either actual or in effect, representing as it does an added element of value, may justify a higher value for a specific block of stock.

Factors to consider

Section 4, "Factors to Consider," lists the eight key factors and elaborates on each. In any written valuation case involving taxes, the appraiser should review Section 4 to be sure that each of the eight points has been addressed and considered at some point in the total valuation process.

Section 4.02(c) notes that, "In computing the book value per share of stock, assets *of the investment type* should be revalued on the basis of their

Exhibit 17–1 (*continued*)

(h)   Section 2031(b) of the Code states, in effect, that in valuing unlisted securities the value of stock or securities of corporations engaged in the same or a similar line of business which are listed on an exchange should be taken into consideration along with all other factors. An important consideration is that the corporations to be used for comparisons have capital stocks which are actively traded by the public. In accordance with section 2031(b) of the Code, stocks listed on an exchange are to be considered first. However, if sufficient comparable companies whose stocks are listed on an exchange cannot be found, other comparable companies which have stocks actively traded on the over-the-counter market also may be used. The essential factor is that whether the stocks are sold on an exchange or over-the-counter there is evidence of an active, free public market for the stock as of the valuation date. In selecting corporations for comparative purposes, care should be taken to use only comparable companies. Although the only restrictive requirement as to comparable corporations specified in the statute is that their lines of business be the same or similar, yet it is obvious that consideration must be given to other relevant factors in order that the most valid comparison possible will be obtained. For illustration, a corporation having one or more issues of preferred stock, bonds or debentures in addition to its common stock should not be considered to be directly comparable to one having only common stock outstanding. In like manner, a company with a declining business and decreasing markets is not comparable to one with a record of current progress and market expansion.

SECTION 5. WEIGHT TO BE ACCORDED VARIOUS FACTORS.

The valuation of closely-held corporate stock entails the consideration of all relevant factors as stated in section 4. Depending upon the circumstances in each case, certain factors may carry more weight than others because of the nature of the company's business. To illustrate:

(a)   Earnings may be the most important criterion of value in some cases whereas asset value will receive primary consideration in others. In general, the appraiser will accord primary consideration to earnings when valuing stocks of companies which sell products or services to the public; conversely, in the investment or holding type of company, the appraiser may accord the greatest weight to the assets underlying the security to be valued.

(b)   The value of the stock of a closely-held investment or real estate holding company, whether or not family owned, is closely related to the value of the assets underlying the stock. For companies of this type the appraiser should determine the fair market values of the assets of the company. Operating expenses of such a company and the cost of liquidating it, if any, merit consideration when appraising the relative values of the stock and the underlying assets. The market values of the underlying assets give due weight to potential earnings and dividends of the particular items of property underlying the stock, capitalized at rates deemed proper by the investing public at the date of appraisal. A current appraisal by the investing public should be superior to the retrospective opinion of an individual. For these reasons, adjusted net worth should be accorded greater weight in valuing the stock of a closely-held investment or real estate holding company, whether or not family owned, than any of the other customary yardsticks of appraisal, such as earnings and dividend-paying capacity.

SECTION 6. CAPITALIZATION RATES.

In the application of certain fundamental valuation factors, such as earnings and dividends, it is necessary to capitalize the average or current results at some appropriate rate. A determination of the proper capitalization rate presents one of the most difficult problems in valuation. That there is no ready or simple solution will become apparent by a cursory check of the rates of return and dividend yields in terms of the selling prices of the corporate shares listed on the major exchanges of the country. Wide variations will be found even for companies in the same industry. Moreover, the ratio will fluctuate from year to year depending upon economic conditions. Thus, no standard tables of capitalization rates applicable to closely-held corporations can be formulated. Among the more important factors to be taken into consideration in deciding upon a capitalization rate in a particular case are: (1) the nature of the business; (2) the risk involved; and (3) the stability or irregularity of earnings.

market price and the book value adjusted accordingly." (Emphasis supplied.) It is important to recognize that this requirement to adjust asset values is specific in saying that it applies to assets "of the investment type," not operating assets.

Exhibit 17–1 (*continued*)

SECTION 7. AVERAGE OF FACTORS.

Because valuations cannot be made on the basis of a prescribed formula, there is no means whereby the various applicable factors in a particular case can be assigned mathematical weights in deriving the fair market value. For this reason, no useful purpose is served by taking an average of several factors (for example, book value, capitalized earnings and capitalized dividends) and basing the valuation on the result. Such a process excludes active consideration of other pertinent factors, and the end result cannot be supported by a realistic application of the significant facts in the case except by mere chance.

SECTION 8. RESTRICTIVE AGREEMENTS.

Frequently, in the valuation of closely-held stock for estate and gift tax purposes, it will be found that the stock is subject to an agreement restricting its sale or transfer. Where shares of stock were acquired by a decedent subject to an option reserved by the issuing corporation to repurchase at a certain price, the option price is usually accepted as the fair market value for estate tax purposes. See Rev. Rul. 54-76, C.B. 1954-1, 194. However, in such case the option price is not determinative of fair market value for gift tax purposes. Where the option, or buy and sell agreement, is the result of voluntary action by the stockholders and is binding during the life as well as at the death of the stockholders, such agreement may or may not, depending upon the circumstances of each case, fix the value for estate tax purposes. However, such agreement is a factor to be considered, with other relevant factors, in determining fair market value. Where the stockholder is free to dispose of his shares during life and the option is to become effective only upon his death, the fair market value is not limited to the option price. It is always necessary to consider the relationship of the parties, the relative number of shares held by the decedent, and other material facts, to determine whether the agreement represents a bonafide business arrangement or is a device to pass the decedent's shares to the natural objects of his bounty for less than an adequate and full consideration in money or money's worth. In this connection see Rev. Rul. 157 C.B. 1953-2,255, and Rev. Rul. 189, C.B. 1953-2,294.

SECTION 9. EFFECT ON OTHER DOCUMENTS.

Revenue Ruling 54-77, C.B. 1954-1,187, is hereby superseded.

Source: 1959–1, C.B. 237.

As discussed previously in this book, Section 4.02(d) notes that the profit and loss statements to be considered should be for a "representative period." The section states that the appraiser should separate recurrent from nonrecurrent items and operating income from investment income. It suggests putting more weight on recent years if there appears to be a trend in the earnings pattern.

Section 4.02(h) again emphasizes the prices of stocks of publicly-traded companies in the same or similar lines of business should be considered, and

Exhibit 17–2
Revenue ruling 65–193

Revenue Ruling 59-60, C.B. 1959-1, 237, is hereby modified to delete the statements, contained therein at section 4.02(f), that "In some instances it may not be possible to make a separate appraisal of the tangible and intangible assets of the business. The enterprise has a value as an entity. Whatever intangible value there is, which is supportable by the facts, may be measured by the amount by which the appraised value of the tangible assets exceeds the net book value of such assets."

The instances where it is not possible to make a separate appraisal of the tangible and intangible assets of a business are rare and each case varies from the other. No rule can be devised which will be generally applicable to such cases.

Other than this modification, Revenue Ruling 59-60 continues in full force and effect.

Source: 1965–2, C.B. 370.

that as much care should be taken as possible in analyzing the companies to select the ones that are most comparable.

Weight to be accorded various factors

Section 5, "Weight to be Accorded Various Factors," essentially makes the point that earnings should be accorded the most weight in valuing operating companies and that asset values should be accorded the most weight in valuing holding companies.

The section also notes that assets should be adjusted to market values for closely-held investment or real estate holding companies, in the same sense that investment-type assets should be adjusted to market values if they are a factor in an operating company. For family-held investment companies, comparisons of per share value to underlying asset value then can be made on the basis of the ratios of market value to net asset value for closed-end investment companies, since such companies report the values of their assets at market on a regular basis. For closely-held real estate holding companies, the derivation of a per share value by reference to publicly-traded real estate holding companies is not quite as easy, since most real estate companies do not report the market values of their assets. It is helpful, however, that in the last two or three years quite a few REITs have started reporting market values. There now are enough reporting such market values that a table of REITs with the ratios of market prices to adjusted asset values can be constructed to provide guidance on the valuation of closely-held real estate holding company shares.

Incidentally, the search for public real estate holding companies to use as comparables for closely-held real estate holding companies is a situation where the use of the typical SIC Code approach does not work very well. Most of the public companies in the SIC Code category for real estate holding companies are more real estate development companies than holding companies. Therefore, REITs generally must be used as comparables for closely-held real estate holding companies. Certain adjustments must be made in the comparison, of course, such as a discount on the comparative value of the closely-held family shares for the fact that they do not enjoy the same income tax advantages as REITs.

Capitalization rates

Section 6, "Capitalization Rates," makes further references to publicly-traded shares, and notes that appropriate capitalization rates vary considerably both among companies and over time due to economic conditions.

Average of factors

Section 7, "Average of Factors," is the section referred to in Chapter 5 that discourages use of a mathematical weighting of various factors. The reason is, "Such a process excludes active consideration of other pertinent factors. . . ." However, as noted in Chapter 5, with examples presented in

Exhibit 17-3
Revenue ruling 68-609 (formula method)

The "formula" approach may be used in determining the fair market value of intangible assets of a business only if there is no better basis available for making the determination; A.R.M. 34, A.R.M. 68, O.D. 937, and Revenue Ruling 65-192 superseded. (1968-2, C.B., 327).

REVENUE RULING 68-609[1]

The purpose of this Revenue Ruling is to update and restate, under the current statute and regulations, the currently outstanding portions of A.R.M. 34, C.B. 2, 31 (1920), A.R.M. 68, C.B. 3,43 (1920), and O.D. 937, C.B. 4, 43 (1921).

The question presented is whether the "formula" approach, the capitalization of earnings in excess of a fair rate of return on net tangible assets, may be used to determine the fair market value of the intangible assets of a business.

The "formula" approach may be stated as follows:

A percentage return on the average annual value of the tangible assets used in a business is determined, using a period of years (preferably not less than five) immediately prior to the valuation date. The amount of the percentage return on tangible assets, thus determined, is deducted from the average earnings of the business for such period and the remainder, if any, is considered to be the amount of the average annual earnings from the intangible assets of the business for the period. This amount (considered as the average annual earnings from intangibles), capitalized at a percentage of, say 15 to 20 percent, is the value of the intangible assets of the business determined under the "formula" approach.

The percentage of return on the average annual value of the tangible assets used should be the percentage prevailing in the industry involved at the date of valuation, or (when the industry percentage is not available) a percentage of 8 to 10 percent may be used.

The 8 percent rate of return and the 15 percent rate of capitalization are applied to tangibles and intangibles, respectively, of businesses with a small risk factor and stable and regular earnings; the 10 percent rate of return and 20 percent rate of capitalization are applied to businesses in which the hazards of business are relatively high.

The above rates are used as examples and are not appropriate in all cases. In applying the "formula" approach, the average earnings period and the capitalization rates are dependent upon the facts pertinent thereto in each case.

The past earnings to which the formula is applied should fairly reflect the probable future earnings. Ordinarily, the period should not be less than five years, and abnormal years, whether above or below the average, should be eliminated. If the business is a sole proprietorship or partnership, there should be deducted from the earnings of the business a reasonable amount for services performed by the owner or partners engaged in the business. See **Lloyd B. Sanderson Estate v. Commissioner**, 42 F. 2d 160 (1930). Further, only the tangible assets entering into net worth, including accounts and bills receivable in excess of accounts and bills payable, are used for determining earnings on the tangible assets. Factors that influence the capitalization rate include (1) the nature of the business, (2) the risk involved, and (3) the stability or irregularity of earnings.

The "formula" approach should not be used if there is better evidence available from which the value of intangibles can be determined. If the assets of a going business are sold upon the basis of a rate of capitalization that can be substantiated as being realistic, though it is not within the range of figures indicated here as the ones ordinarily to be adopted, the same rate of capitalization should be used in determining the value of intangibles.

Accordingly, the "formula" approach may be used for determining the fair market value of intangible assets of a business only if there is no better basis therefor available.

Chapter 18, a mathematical weighting approach frequently is used in practice, even by government representatives, and relied on in court decisions, in spite of the wording of this section. My firm now uses the mathematical weighting process frequently, for the reasons discussed in Chapter 5, but making sure

Exhibit 17–3 (concluded)

See also Revenue Ruling 59-60, C.B. 1959-1, 237, as modified by Revenue Ruling 65-193, C.B. 1965-2, 370, which sets forth the proper approach to use in the valuation of closely-held corporate stocks for estate and gift tax purposes. The general approach, methods, and factors, outlined in Revenue Ruling 59-60, as modified, are equally applicable to valuations of corporate stocks for income and other tax purposes as well as for estate and gift tax purposes. They apply also to problems involving the determination of the fair market value of business interests of any type, including partnerships and proprietorships, and of intangible assets for all tax purposes.

A.R.M. 34, A.R.M. 68, and O.D. 937 are superseded, since the positions set forth therein are restated to the extent applicable under current law in this Revenue Ruling. Revenue Ruling 65-192, C.B. 1965-2, 259, which contained restatements of A.R.M. 34 and A.R.M. 68, is also superseded.

Source: 1968–2, C.B. 327.

that this process does not exclude active consideration of any other pertinent factors.

Restrictive agreements

Section 8, "Restrictive Agreements," makes the point that, to be binding for estate tax valuation purposes, a price fixed under a buy and sell agreement must be binding during the life as well as at the death of the stockholders, and not "a device to pass the decedent's shares to the natural objects of his bounty for less than an adequate and full consideration in money or money's worth."

Summary

Although Revenue Ruling 59–60 was written over 20 years ago, it shows considerable insight into the basic criteria and processes for valuing closely-held stocks. With minor modifications and amplification, it has stood the test of time.

Nevertheless, the nature of the process necessarily leaves much room for subjectivity and disagreements. Interpretations by IRS agents and by courts have been somewhat less than totally consistent. It is not a subject that is susceptible to such sharp definition of criteria that gray areas can be eliminated. The next two chapters will demonstrate the issues, opposing positions, and outcomes for a group of cases selected to be representative of most of the major issues commonly involved in disagreements in federal tax valuation cases.

Exhibit 17–4
Revenue ruling 77–287

Valuation of securities restricted from immediate resale. Guidelines are set forth for the valuation, for Federal tax purposes, of securities that cannot be immediately resold because they are restricted from resale pursuant to Federal securities laws; Rev. Rul. 59-60 amplified. (1977-2, C.B. 319).

REVENUE RULING 77-287

SECTION 1. PURPOSE.

The purpose of this Revenue Ruling is to amplify Rev. Rul. 59-60, 1959-1 C.B. 237, as modified by Rev. Rul. 65-193, 1965-2 C.B. 370, and to provide information and guidance to taxpayers, Internal Revenue Service personnel, and others concerned with the valuation, for Federal tax purposes, of securities that cannot be immediately resold because they are restricted from resale pursuant to Federal securities laws. This guidance is applicable only in cases where it is not inconsistent with valuation requirements of the Internal Revenue Code of 1954 or the regulations thereunder. Further, this ruling does not establish the time at which property shall be valued.

SECTION 2. NATURE OF THE PROBLEM.

It frequently becomes necessary to establish the fair market value of stock that has not been registered for public trading when the issuing company has stock of the same class that is actively traded in one or more securities markets. The problem is to determine the difference in fair market value between the registered shares that are actively traded and the unregistered shares. This problem is often encountered in estate and gift tax cases. However, it is sometimes encountered when unregistered shares are issued in exchange for assets or the stock of an acquired company.

SECTION 3. BACKGROUND AND DEFINITIONS.

.01 The Service outlined and reviewed in general the approach, methods, and factors to be considered in valuing shares of closely-held corporate stock for estate and gift tax purposes in Rev. Rul. 59-60, as modified by Rev. Rul. 65-193. The provisions of Rev. Rul. 59-60, as modified, were extended to the valuation of corporate securities for income and other tax purposes by Rev. Rul. 68-609, 1968-2 C.B. 327.

.02 There are several terms currently in use in the securities industry that denote restrictions imposed on the resale and transfer of certain securities. The term frequently used to describe these securities is "restricted securities," but they are sometimes referred to as "unregistered securities," "investment letter stock," "control stock," or "private placement stock." Frequently these terms are used interchangeably. They all indicate that these particular securities cannot lawfully be distributed to the general public until a registration statement relating to the corporation underlying the securities has been filed, and has also become effective under the rules promulgated and enforced by the United States Securities & Exchange Commission (SEC) pursuant to the Federal securities laws. The following represents a more refined definition of each of the following terms along with two other terms — "exempted securities" and "exempted transactions."

(a) The term "restricted securities" is defined in Rule 144 adopted by the SEC as "securities acquired directly or indirectly from the issuer thereof, or from an affiliate of such issuer, in a transaction or chain of transactions not involving any public offering."

(b) The term "unregistered securities" refers to those securities with respect to which a registration statement, providing full disclosure by the issuing corporation, has not been filed with the SEC pursuant to the Securities Act of 1933. The registration statement is a condition precedent to a public distribution of securities in interstate commerce and is aimed at providing the prospective investor with a factual basis for sound judgment in making investment decisions.

Exhibit 17–4 (*continued*)

(c)   The terms "investment letter stock" and "letter stock" denote shares of stock that have been issued by a corporation without the benefit of filing a registration statement with the SEC. Such stock is subject to resale and transfer restrictions set forth in a letter agreement requested by the issuer and signed by the buyer of the stock when the stock is delivered. Such stock may be found in the hands of either individual investors or institutional investors.

(d)   The term "control stock" indicates that the shares of stock have been held or are being held by an officer, director, or other person close to the management of the corporation. These persons are subject to certain requirements pursuant to SEC rules upon resale of shares they own in such corporations.

(e)   The term "private placement stock" indicates that the stock has been placed with an institution or other investor who will presumably hold it for a long period and ultimately arrange to have the stock registered if it is to be offered to the general public. Such stock may or may not be subject to a letter agreement. Private placements of stock are exempted from the registration and prospectus provisions of the Securities Act of 1933.

(f)   The term "exempted securities" refers to those classes of securities that are expressly excluded from the registration provisions of the Securities Act of 1933 and the distribution provisions of the Securities Exchange Act of 1934.

(g)   The term "exempted transactions" refers to certain sales or distributions of securities that do not involve a public offering and are excluded from the registration and prospectus provisions of the Securities Act of 1933 and distribution provisions of the Securities Exchange Act of 1934. The exempted status makes it unnecessary for issuers of securities to go through the registration process.

SECTION 4. SECURITIES INDUSTRY PRACTICE IN VALUING RESTRICTED SECURITIES.

.01   **Investment Company Valuation Practices.** The Investment Company Act of 1940 requires open-end investment companies to publish the valuation of their portfolio securities daily. Some of these companies have portfolios containing restricted securities, but also have unrestricted securities of the same class traded on a securities exchange. In recent years the number of restricted securities in such portfolios has increased. The following methods have been used by investment companies in the valuation of such restricted securities:

(a)   Current market price of the unrestricted stock less a constant percentage discount based on purchase discount;

(b)   Current market price of unrestricted stock less a constant percentage discount different from purchase discount;

(c)   Current market price of the unrestricted stock less a discount amortized over a fixed period;

(d)   Current market price of the unrestricted stock; and

(e)   Cost of the restricted stock until it is registered.

The SEC ruled in its Investment Company Act Release No. 5847, dated October 21, 1969, that there can be no automatic formula by which an investment company can value the restricted securities in its portfolios. Rather, the SEC has determined that it is the responsibility of the board of directors of the particular investment company to determine the "fair value" of each issue of restricted securities in good faith.

.02   **Institutional Investors Study.** Pursuant to Congressional direction, the SEC undertook an analysis of the purchases, sales, and holding of securities by financial institutions, in order to determine the effect of institutional activity upon the securities market. The study report was published in eight volumes in March 1971. The fifth volume provides an analysis of restricted securities and deals with such items as the characteristics of the restricted securities purchasers and issuers, the size of transactions (dollars and shares), the marketability discounts on different trading markets, and the resale provisions. This research project provides some guidance for measuring the discount in that it contains information, based on the actual experience of the marketplace, showing that, during the period

Exhibit 17–4 (continued)

surveyed (January 1, 1966, through June 30, 1969), the amount of discount allowed for restricted securities from the trading price of the unrestricted securities was generally related to the following four factors:

(a) **Earnings.** Earnings and sales consistently have a significant influence on the size of restricted securities discounts according to the study. Earnings played the major part in establishing the ultimate discounts at which these stocks were sold from the current market price. Apparently earnings patterns, rather than sales patterns, determine the degree of risk of an investment.

(b) **Sales.** The dollar amount of sales of issuers' securities also has a major influence on the amount of discount at which restricted securities sell from the current market price. The results of the study generally indicate that the companies with the lowest dollar amount of sales during the test period accounted for most of the transactions involving the highest discount rates, while they accounted for only a small portion of all transactions involving the lowest discount rates.

(c) **Trading Market.** The market in which publicly-held securities are traded also reflects variances in the amount of discount that is applied to restricted securities purchases. According to the study, discount rates were greatest on restricted stocks with unrestricted counterparts traded over-the-counter, followed by those with unrestricted counterparts listed on the American Stock Exchange, while the discount rates for those stocks with unrestricted counterparts listed on the New York Stock Exchange were the smallest.

(d) **Resale Agreement Provisions.** Resale agreement provisions often affect the size of the discount. The discount from the market price provides the main incentive for a potential buyer to acquire restricted securities. In judging the opportunity cost of freezing funds, the purchase is analyzing two separate factors. The first factor is the risk that underlying value of the stock will change in a way that, absent the restrictive provisions, would have prompted a decision to sell. The second factor is the risk that the contemplated means of legally disposing of the stock may not materialize. From the seller's point of view, a discount is justified where the seller is relieved of the expenses of registration and public distribution, as well as of the risk that the market will adversely change before the offering is completed. The ultimate agreement between buyer and seller is a reflection of these and other considerations. Relative bargaining strengths of the parties to the agreement are major considerations that influence the resale terms and consequently the size of discounts in restricted securities transactions. Certain provisions are often found in agreements between buyers and sellers that affect the size of discounts at which restricted stocks are sold. Several such provisions follow, all of which, other than number (3), would tend to reduce the size of the discount:

(1) A provision giving the buyer an option to "piggyback," that is, to register restricted stock with the next registration statement, if any, filed by the issuer with the SEC;

(2) A provision giving the buyer an option to require registration at the seller's expense;

(3) A provision giving the buyer an option to require registration, but only at the buyer's own expense;

(4) A provision giving the buyer a right to receive continuous disclosure of information about the issuer from the seller;

(5) A provision giving the buyer a right to select one or more directors of the issuer;

(6) A provision giving the buyer an option to purchase additional shares of the issuer's stock; and

(7) A provision giving the buyer the right to have a greater voice in operations of the issuer, if the issuer does not meet previously agreed upon operating standards.

Institutional buyers can and often do obtain many of these rights and options from the sellers of restricted securities, and naturally, the more rights the buyer can acquire, the lower the buyer's risk is going to be, thereby reducing the buyer's discount as well. Smaller buyers may not be able to negotiate the large discounts or the rights and options that volume buyers are able to negotiate.

Exhibit 17–4 (*continued*)

.03 **Summary.** A variety of methods have been used by the securities industry to value restricted securities. The SEC rejects all automatic or mechanical solutions to the valuation of restricted securities, and prefers, in the case of the valuation of investment company portfolio stocks, to rely upon good faith valuations by the board of directors of each company. The study made by the SEC found that restricted securities **generally** are issued at a discount from the market value of freely tradable securities.

SECTION 5. FACTS AND CIRCUMSTANCES MATERIAL TO VALUATION OF RESTRICTED SECURITIES.

.01 Frequently, a company has a class of stock that cannot be traded publicly. The reason such stock cannot be traded may arise from the securities statutes, as in the case of an "investment letter" restriction; it may arise from a corporate charter restriction, or perhaps from a trust agreement restriction. In such cases, certain documents and facts should be obtained for analysis.

.02 The following documents and facts, when used in conjunction with those discussed in Section 4 of Rev. Rul. 59-60, will be useful in the valuation of restricted securities:

(a) A copy of any declaration of trust, trust agreement, and any other agreements relating to the shares of restricted stock;

(b) A copy of any document showing any offers to buy or sell or indications of interest in buying or selling the restricted shares;

(c) The latest prospectus of the company;

(d) Annual reports of the company for 3 to 5 years preceding the valuation date;

(e) The trading prices and trading volume of the related class of traded securities 1 month preceding the valuation date, if they are traded on a stock exchange (if traded over-the-counter, prices may be obtained from the National Quotations Bureau, the National Association of Securities Dealers Automated Quotations (NASDAQ), or sometimes from broker-dealers making markets in the shares);

(f) The relationship of the parties to the agreements concerning the restricted stock, such as whether they are members of the immediate family or perhaps whether they are officers or directors of the company; and

(g) Whether the interest being valued represents a majority or minority ownership.

SECTION 6. WEIGHING FACTS AND CIRCUMSTANCES MATERIAL TO RESTRICTED STOCK VALUATION.

All relevant facts and circumstances that bear upon the worth of restricted stock, including those set forth above in the preceding Sections 4 and 5, and those set forth in Section 4 of Rev. Rul. 59-60, must be taken into account in arriving at the fair market value of such securities. Depending on the circumstances of each case, certain factors may carry more weight than others. To illustrate:

.01 Earnings, net assets, and net sales must be given primary consideration in arriving at an appropriate discount for restricted securities from the freely traded shares. These are the elements of value that are always used by investors in making investment decisions. In some cases, one element may be more important than in other cases. In the case of manufacturing, producing, or distributing companies, primary weight must be accorded earnings and net sales; but in the case of investment or holding companies, primary weight must be given to the net assets of the company underlying the stock. In the former type of companies, value is more closely linked to past, present, and future earnings while in the latter type of companies, value is more closely linked to the existing net assets of the company. See the discussion in Section 5 of Rev. Rul. 59-60.

.02 Resale provisions found in the restriction agreements must be scrutinized and weighed to determine the amount of discount to apply to the preliminary fair market value of the company. The two elements of time and expense bear upon this discount; the longer the buyer of the shares must wait to liquidate the shares, the greater the discount. Moreover, if the provisions make it necessary for the buyer to bear the expense of registration, the greater the discount. However, if the provisions of the restricted stock agreement make it possible for the buyer to "piggyback" shares at the next offering, the discount would be smaller.

Exhibit 17–4 (concluded)

.03 The relative negotiation strengths of the buyer and seller of restricted stock may have a profound effect on the amount of discount. For example, a tight money situation may cause the buyer to have the greater balance of negotiation strength in a transaction. However, in some cases the relative strengths may tend to cancel each other out.

.04 The market experience of freely tradable securities of the same class as the restricted securities is also significant in determining the amount of discount. Whether the shares are privately held or publicly traded affects the worth of the shares to the holders. Securities traded on a public market generally are worth more to investors than those that are not traded on a public market. Moreover, the type of public market in which the unrestricted securities are traded is to be given consideration.

SECTION 7. EFFECT ON OTHER DOCUMENTS.

(Rev. Rul. 59-60, as modified by Rev. Rul. 65-193, is amplified.)

Source: 1977–2, C.B. 319

BIBLIOGRAPHY: GIFT, ESTATE, INHERITANCE AND INCOME TAXES AND RECAPITALIZATIONS

Articles: Gift, estate, inheritance and income taxes

Allen, John T., Jr. "Washington Saves the Farm? The Peculiar Remedy of IRC Section 2032A." *Taxes* 56 (April 1978):205–12.

Banks, Warren E. "Legal Issues in Securities Valuation." *Tax Executive* 25 (1973):89–100.

_____. "Present Value and the Close Corporation." *Taxes* 49 (January 1971):33–44.

Barnett, Bernard. "Resolving Close Corporation Stock Values in IRS Proceedings." *Tax Adviser* 7 (January 1976):19–24.

Barton, Robert M. "Methods of Terminating Stockholder Interests in Closely-Held Corporations." *Institute on Federal Taxation, New York University* 32 (1974):811–31.

Bell, E. Folsom, and Earls, Lawrence W. "How to Reduce the Potential Estate Tax Bite on Stock of a Closely-Held Corporation." *Taxation for Accountants* (November 1973) p. 273.

Bills, Charles W. "Reduction in Value of Closely-Held Stocks due to Income Tax Liabilities." *Taxes* 44 (July 1966):487–90.

Blackstone, Franklin, Jr., et al. "How to Put a Price on a Close Corporation: Attorney, CPA, Banker, and Appraiser Give Views." *Taxation for Accountants* 7 (August 1971):104–10.

Bock, C. Allen, and McCord, John H. "Estate Tax Valuation of Farmland under Section 2032A of the Internal Revenue Code: An Analysis of the Recently Proposed Treasury Regulations." *Southern Illinois University Law Journal* (August 1978), pp. 145–77.

Boles, Richard J. "Special Use Valuation for Land Can Be Effective Tax Saver Despite Its Complexity." *Taxation for Lawyers* 7 (September/October 1978):74–80.

Bomeli, Edwin C. "Valuation of Closely-Held Securities for Estate and Gift Tax Purposes." *Tax Counselors Quarterly* 6 (1962):145–63.

Bosland, Chelcie C. "Tax Valuation by Compromise." *Tax Law Review* 19 (1963):78–89.

Braitman, Howard L. "The Eye of the Beholder: A Fresh Look at Fair Market Value." *Taxes* 52 (May 1974):269–76.

Bratt, David A. "Material Participation and the Valuation of Farm Land for Estate Tax Purposes under the Tax Reform Act of 1976." *Kentucky Law Journal* 66 (1977–1978):848–88.

Bravenec, Lorence L., and Olsen, Alfred J. "How to Reap Estate Tax Benefits through Use of the Alternative Valuation of Farmland." *Journal of Taxation* 48 (March 1978):140–47.

Brody, Marvin D., and Berger, Jordan. "Formulas May Be Used to Value Closely-Held Businesses in Light of IRS Opposition." *Estate Planning* 4 (November 1977):394–400.

_____. "A Guide to Valuation of Closely-Held Corporations for Federal Estate and Gift Tax Purposes." *Barrister* 4 (Summer 1977):49–55.

Bromley, Robert G. "A Closer Statistical Look at Tax Court Compromise." *Taxes* (May 1979) pp. 325–30.

Butala, John H., Jr. "Valuation of Closely-Held Corporations." *Institute on Estate Planning, University of Miami* 7 (1973):1400–34.

_____. "Valuation of Securities of Closely-Held Corporations." *Western Reserve Law Review* 14 (1963):193–206.

Byars, R.B. "Sections 6166 and 6166A Elections—Estate Planning Opportunities." *Taxes* 57 (April 1979):265–69.

Carter, T. Heyward, Jr. "Application of Section 2032A to the Valuation of Timberland for Federal Estate Tax Purposes." *South Carolina Law Review* 29 (1978):577–625.

Castleman, Don R. "The Use of Restrictive Agreements in Estate Tax Valuation of Farmlands and Other Properties." *Kentucky Law Journal* 64 (1975–1976):785–99.

Cohan, John R. "Valuation of Interests in Closely-Held Businesses." *Taxes* 44 (July 1966):504–9.

_____. "Valuation of Interests in Closely-Held Businesses." *Trusts & Estates* 105 (July 1966):334–37.

Conway, John J. "Valuation of Stock in a Close Corporation for Estate Tax and Gift Tax Purposes." *Western Reserve Law Review* 14 (1963):188–93.

Coolidge, H. Calvin. "Valuation of Closely-Held Businesses: Emphasis on Full Disclosure of Facts." *Illinois Bar Journal* 65 (November 1976):160–62.

Cooper, George. "A Voluntary Tax? New Perspectives of Sophisticated Estate Tax Avoidance." *Columbia Law Review* 77 (March 1977):161–247.

Eber, Victor I. "How to Establish Value for Close Corporations that Will Withstand an IRS Audit." *Estate Planning* 4 (Autumn 1976):28–33.

Elin, Howard F. "How the Service's Own Guidelines Are Used to Value the Stock of a Closely-Held Corporation." *Taxation for Accountants* 1 (January/February 1967):370–73.

Englebrecht, Ted D., and Davison, Dale L. "A Statistical Look at Tax Court Compromise in Estate and Gift Tax Valuation of Closely-Held Stock." *Taxes* 55 (June 1977):395–400.

Englebrecht, Ted D. "Valuation of Closely-Held Oil and Gas Corporations for Estate and Gift Tax Purposes." *Oil and Gas Tax Quarterly* 25 (December 1977):273–88.

————. "A Reply, Analysis, and Extension of a Closer Statistical Look at Tax Court Compromise." *Taxes* (September 1979) pp. 607–14.

————. "Valuation of Closely-Held Stock for Estate and Gift Tax Purposes." *Journal of Small Business Management* 16 (July 1978):24–28.

"The Estate and Gift Tax Valuation of Closely-Held Holding Company Stock." *Virginia Law Review* 50 (March 1964):337–52.

"Estate Planning Treatment of Closely-Held Companies." *Institute in Estate Planning, University of Miami* (1975), pp. 1–44.

"The Family Farm and Use Valuation—Section 2032A of the Internal Revenue Code, Comment." *Brigham Young University Law Review* (1977), pp. 353–428.

"Federal Estate and Gift Tax Taxation: Amended Regulations Change Valuation for Estate and Gift Taxes." *Duke Law Journal* (Winter 1966), pp. 248–60.

"Federal Estate Tax—Valuation of a Deceased Spouse's Interest in Community Owned Stock," *Washington Law Review* 55 (December 1979):271–82.

"Federal Taxation—Valuation of In-Kind Dividends by Personal Holding Companies—Treasury Regulation Section 1.562–1(a)," *New York Law School Review* 25 (1980):741–58.

Fellows, Mary Louise, and Painter, William H. "Valuing Close Corporations for Federal Wealth Transfer Taxes: A Statutory Solution to the Disappearing Wealth Syndrome." *Stanford Law Review* 30 (May 1978):895–933.

Field, William R. "Market Value of Stock and Debt as Evidence of Value." *National Tax Journal* 25 (1972):243–58.

Fiore, Owen G. "Ownership Shifting to Realize Family Goals, including Tax Savings." *Institute on Federal Taxation, New York University* 37 (1979):38.1–38.52.

Fisher, Donald M. "Capitalization Rates." *National Tax Journal* 25 (1972):263–91.

Flynn, Kevin. "*United States* v. *Cartwright*—A New Estate Tax Valuation Criterion for Mutual Fund Shares." *Southwestern Law Journal* 27 (December 1973):890–96.

Gelman, Milton. "An Economist-Financial Analysts' Approach to Valuing Stock of a Closely-Held Company." *Journal of Taxation* (June 1972) pp. 353–54.

Golden, William C. "Tax Consequences of Selected Milestones in the Life of a Closely-Held Corporation." *Taxes* 55 (December 1977):837–51.

Gordon, Emanuel L. "What Is Fair Market Value?" *Tax Law Review* 8 (1952):35–62.

Graham, John R. "Valuation of Stock in Closely-Held Corporations: An Estate Planner's Dilemma." *CLU Journal* 30 (July 1976):36–41.

Grant, Irving M. "Selected Estate Planning Problems in the Use of Subchapter S Corporations." *Tax Institute, University of Southern California* 31 (1979):99–1008.

Greene, Scott. "Valuation and Inclusion of Community Property in the Gross Estate: A New Approach." *Houston Law Review* 15 (October 1977):93–109.

Greenwald, William I. "Pricing the Stock of a Closely-Held Corporation for Federal Estate Taxation—Part I." *New York State Bar Journal* 46 (October 1974):421–26.

————. "Pricing the Stock of a Closely-Held Corporation for Federal Estate Taxation—Part II." *New York State Bar Journal* 46 (November 1974):535–42.

Hammond, Pierce A., Jr., and Victor, Raymond M. "How to Sustain a Lower Valuation for Stock of a Closely-Held Investment Company." *Journal of Taxation* 25 (July 1966):40–42.

Hanna, Francis M. "Excedrin Headache Number 2032A: Special Use Valuation of Farm Real Estate." *Journal of the Missouri Bar* 34 (October/November 1978):476–81.

Hardy, Donald J. "Valuation: A Financial Planning Tool for Closely-Held Corporations." *Trusts & Estates* 113 (September 1974):584–87, 623–27.

Harley, Colin E. "Dealings between Closely-Held Corporations and Their Stockholders." *Tax Law Review* 25 (March 1970):403–27.

Harnack, Don S. "Techniques in Preparing a Valuation Case." *Institute on Federal Taxation, New York University* 30 (1972):163–84.

Hartwig, Joseph D. "Valuation Problems before the Internal Revenue Service and the Tax Court." *Institute of Federal Taxation, New York University* 13 (1955):1143–59.

Hill, J. Jeptha. "Estate Planning for the Closely-Held Corporation and Its Owner." *Alabama Lawyer* 40 (January 1979):122–48.

Hjorth, Roland L. "Special Estate Tax Valuation of Farmland and the Emergence of a Landholding Elite Class." *Washington Law Review* 53 (1978):609–62.

Hoffman, William H., Jr. "How Conclusive Is an Estate Tax Valuation in Determining Income Tax Basis?" *Journal of Taxation* 23 (July 1965):34–37.

Holloway, Ronald E. "Closely-Held Corporations—Pre-Termination Planning." *Institute on Federal Taxation, New York University* 32 (1974):785–809.

Holzman, Robert S. "When Actual Sales May Not Establish Fair Market Value for Securities." *Journal of Taxation* 29 (September 1968):134–35.

Hood, Edwin T., and Logan, Catherine Poindexter. "Close Corporations in Estate Planning after the Tax Reform Act of 1976." *Journal of Corporation Law* 2 (Winter 1977):207–303.

Hood, Edwin T., et al. "Tax Consequences for Corporate Divisions of the Family Farm Corporation." *Journal of Corporation Law* 4 (Fall 1978):1–61.

_____. "Special Elections: The Use of Sections 6166, 6166A and 303 of the Internal Revenue Code." *UMKC Law Review* 47 (Summer 1979):485–565.

Horvitz, Selwyn A. "Retention of Control: The Implication of the Byrum Case." *Institute on Federal Taxation, New York University* 32 (1974):235–67.

Huff, William S. "Tax Reform Act Workshop—Special Valuation of Farm and Closely-Held Business Property. Special Lien: Recapture Status." *Institute on Estate Planning, University of Miami* 11 (1977):3–3.23.

Jefferies, John J. and Walker, George B. "Special Estate Planning Considerations for the Owners of Closely-Held Corporations." *Estate Planning* 7 (March 1980):90–98.

Jensen, Herbert L. "Stock Valuation Formulas for Estate and Gift Taxes." *Trusts and Estates* 117 (April 1978):238–42, 248–49.

Johnson, Lyle R.; Shapiro, Eli; and O'Meara, Joseph, Jr. "Valuation of Closely-Held Stock for Federal Tax Purposes: Approach to an Objective Method." *University of Pennsylvania Law Review* (1951) pp. 166–95.

Jones, Robert L. "Valuation of Interests in Real Estate Partnerships." *The Estates, Gifts and Trusts Journal* 1 (January/February 1979):23–28.

Kaminski, Gerald F. "Estate and Gift Taxes. . . ." *University of Cincinnati Law Review* 28 (1969):579–82.

Kanter, Burton W. "Using Revaluation Clauses to Avoid Gifts under Holding Company Plans." *Trusts & Estates* 116 (June 1977):388–90, 432–34.

Kascle, Esther. "Valuation of Closely-Held Corporations." *Taxes* 43 (July 1965):454–62.

Keir, Loyal E. and Argue, Douglas W. "Choosing a Forum for Tax Litigation." *Practising Lawyer* 22 (October 1976):63–68.

Kelley, Donald H. "The Utility of the Close Corporation in Estate Planning and Administration." *Notre Dame Lawyer* 49 (December 1973):334–65.

_____. "Estate Planning for Farmers and Ranchers." *Practical Lawyer* 20 (February 1974):13–28.

_____. "The Farm Corporation as an Estate Planning Device." *Nebraska Law Review* 54(2) (1975):217–61.

_____. "Farmland Values for Estate Tax Purposes." *Practical Lawyer* 22 (January 1976):71–80.

Kirby, Jack Arthur. "How to Plan for New Special Rules of Valuing Farm and Close Corporation Real Estate." *Estate Planning* 4 (January 1977):94–100.

Koehn, Travis J. "Internal Revenue Code Section 2032A." *South Texas Law Journal* 19 (1978):315–19.

Korner, Jules G. "Issues and Problems in Valuing Closely-Held Business Interests for Estate Tax Purposes, Especially Partnership Interests." *Institute on Federal Taxation, New York University,* 30 (1972):185–207.

Lamson, Jeffrey E. "Factors that Will Substantiate the Valuation of a Closely-Held Corporation." *Journal of Taxation* 34 (April 1971):226–29.

Lauritzen, Christian M., II. "The Valuation Problem—Some Practical Solutions." *Tax Counselor's Quarterly* 6 (1962):251–93.

Lawinger, Ernest J. "Appraising Closely-Held Stock—Valuation Methods and Concepts." *Trusts & Estates* 110 (October 1971):816–19, 872–74.

Leffingwell, Douglas C. "Covenants Not to Compete: What Factors the Courts Consider in Valuing Them Today." *Journal of Taxation* 34 (January 1971):20–22.

Leimberg, Stephen R. "What to Look Out for in Setting Value on Assets for Estate Tax Purposes." *Taxation for Accountants* 9 (August 1972):108–20.

Lemann, Thomas B. "Government Use of Jury Trials in Tax Cases." *Taxes* 55 (October 1977):680–85.

Lindeberg, Frederic H. "Estate Planning Benefits for Small Farmer Increased By Provisions of Tax Reform Act." *Taxation for Accountants* 18 (April 1977):238–43.

Llewellyn, Don W., et al. "Selling a Close Corporation: Should Stock or Assets Be Sold for Maximum Tax Benefits?" *Taxation for Accountants* 17 (1976):98–103.

Macris, R. N. "Open Valuation and the Completed Transfer: A Problem Area in Federal Gift Taxation." *Tax Law Review* 34 (Winter 1979):273–317.

Maher, John Michael. "Impact of Keyperson Insurance on the Valuation of Closely Held Business Interests." *Trusts & Estates* 118 (August 1979):39–40.

Marks, Seymour. "Little Publicized Valuation Regs. Mean Higher Estate and Gift Taxes." *Journal of Taxation* 22 (May 1965):286–89.

Martin, Gerald R., and Sanford, E. Halsey. "Applying Fair Market Value Appraisal Techniques to Closely-Held Preferred Stock." *Taxes* 56 (February 1978):108–15.

Martin, Spencer J. "Factors the IRS and the Courts Are Using Today in Valuing Closely-Held Shares." *Journal of Taxation* 36 (February 1972):118–20.

Marvel, C. C. "Valuation for Tax Purposes as Admissible to Show Value for Other Purposes." *39 A.L.R. 2d 209* (1955, supp. 1977, 1979).

Matthews, Stephen F., and Stock, Randall. "Section 2032A: Use Valuation of Farmland for Estate Tax Purposes." *Idaho Law Review* 14 (1977–1978):341–62.

Megna, Michael S. "Appraising Closely-Held Share Capital." *Trusts & Estates* 177 (September 1978):56–65.

Minasian, T. L. and Welz, E. K. "Guidelines for Determining When

Discount on Preferred Stock Will Create Taxable Income," *Journal of Taxation* 53 (July 1980):2–4.

Mona, Joseph. "Amortization and Valuation of Intangibles: The Tax Effect Upon Sports Franchises." *Loyola of Los Angeles Law Review* 12 (December 1978):159–78.

Morris, Edward W. "TRA's Effect on Closely Held Business." *Trusts and Estates* 116 (April 1977):227–30.

Moyer, Reed. "Analyzing the Factors that Control the Value of Shares of a Closely-Held Corporation." *Taxation for Accountants* 21 (July 1978):48–52.

Myers, Marshall N. "The Tax Factors to Consider in Selling a Closely-Held Corporation." *Practical Accountant* 8 (January/February 1975):45–50.

Neuwahl, Malcolm H. "Incorporation of a Portfolio Consisting of Marketable Securities—A Useful Tax-Planning Technique." *University of Miami Law Review* 28 (Winter 1974):395–438.

Normand, Tom. "Special Use Valuation of Farmland for Estate Tax Purposes: Arrangements for Material Participation." *Baylor Law Review* 30 (Spring 1978):245–75.

Norris, John R. "Valuation of Stock of Closely-Held Corporations for Estate Tax Purposes." *Taxes* 46 (March 1968):183–90.

O'Brien, Kevin O'Shaunnessy. "Estate Planning for Farmers and Ranchers under Section 2032A." *Denver Law Journal* 55 (1978):347–64.

Pinney, Charles A., Jr. "The Busy New Executors under TRA-1976; Selected Problems under I.R.C. Section 6166." *Tax Institute, University of Southern California* 31 (1979):971–90.

"Planning for the Disposition of a Closely-Held Business." *Federal Tax Coordinator 2d. Special Study* (July 5, 1979).

Prey, Merle. "Capitalized Earnings as an Evidence of Value—Amount to be Capitalized." *National Tax Journal* 25 (1972):259–62.

"Problems in Valuing Stock of a Close Corporation." *Institute on Federal Taxation, New York University* 23 (1965):1261–92.

Rhodes, Harry H., III. "How to Reduce the Value of Farms and Other Closely-Held Businesses while Keeping Assets." *Estate Planning* 7 (January 1980):38–41.

Rice, Ralph S. "The Valuation of Closely Held Stocks: A Lottery in Federal Taxation." *University of Pennsylvania Law Review* 98 (1949–1950):367–99.

Ring, A. A. "Valuation Principles." *National Tax Journal* 25 (1972):233–36.

———. "Determining the Rate of Capitalization for Conversion of Utility Company's Earnings Into Value." *National Tax Journal* 25 (1972):293–309.

Schwingle, C. J. "Valuation of a Family Business." Tulane Tax Institute 12 (1969):231–54.

Scott, Edwin W. "Taxation—Valuation of Securities in a Close Corporation for Federal Estate Tax Purpose." *Villanova Law Review* 8 (Fall 1962):92–104.

Smith, Gordon V. "Valuing Closely-Held Stock of Regulated Companies." *Trusts & Estates* 117 (August 1978):491–96.

Starkey, Lawrence V., Jr. "Valuation of Closely-Held Corporation Stock: Book Value versus Capitalization of Earnings." *Estate Planning* 2 (Autumn 1974):37–41.

Tierney, Joseph E., Jr. "A New Approach to the Valuation of Common Stock of Closely-Held Companies." *Journal of Taxation* 17 (July 1962):14–18.

Tilzer, Ira L. "Should an Appraisal of Fair Market Value Be the Subject of a Criminal Prosecution?" *Journal of Taxation* 50 (March 1979):180–82.

"Valuation of a Close Corporation for Estate Tax Purposes." *New York Law Forum* 11 (1965):315–21.

"Valuation of Closely-Held Stock for Federal Estate Tax Purposes under Sect. 2031(b) of Internal Revenue Code of 1954 (26 USCS 2031 (b), and Implementing Regulations." *22 A.L.R. Fed. 31* (1975, supp. 1979).

Valuation of Gift Property for Purposes of Gift Tax." *60 A.L.R. 2d 1304* (1958, supp. 1976).

Vass, David T. "Factors that Are Presently Being Emphasized in Valuing a Closely-Held Corporation." *Journal of Taxation* (June 1973) pp. 356–58.

Vondran, John J. "Updating the McCandless Doctrine: Taxing of Reasonable Compensation Paid by Closely-Held Corporations." *John Marshall Journal of Practice and Procedure* 12 (Fall 1978):113–33.

Ward, L. D. "Planning for Farmers after the 1976 Tax Reform Act and the 1978 Revenue Act: Special Use Valuation under Section 2032A." *Institute on Estate Planning, University of Miami* 13 (1979):12.1–12.31.

Watts, David E. "The Fair Market Value of Actively Traded Securities." *Tax Lawyer* 30 (Fall 1976):51–84.

Weed, John B. "Techniques in Valuation of Close Corporations." *Institute on Federal Taxation, New York University* 20 (1962):597–607.

"What is Your Corporation Worth?" *Federal Tax Coordinator 2d. Special Study* (September 1, 1977).

"What Matters Are Protected by Attorney—Client Privilege or Are Proper Subject of Inquiry by Internal Revenue Service where Attorney Is Summoned in Connection with Taxpayer—Client under Federal Tax Examination." *15 A.L.R. Fed 771.*

Wheeler, Jon D. "New Valuation Provisions for Farms and Other Property Can Reduce Estate as Much as $500,000." *Taxation for Accountants* 19 (July 1977):42–47.

Whittenburg, G. E. "Recent IRS Rulings on Section 306 Stock." *Trusts & Estates* 117 (December 1978):766–67.

Wiegratz, Wyon F. "Special Valuation of Real Estate: Opportunities and Pitfalls." *Trusts & Estates* 118 (November 1979):38–45.

Wilkins, Robert P. "The Supreme Court's Cartwright Decision: Does It Signal New Valuation Disputes?" *Journal of Taxation* (July 1973) pp. 2–5.

Williams, Wayne. "Valuation of Closely-Held Corporations." *Trusts and Estates* 110 (March 1971):184–88.

Wormser, Rene A. "Siphoning-off Growth: Ways to 'Freeze' Assets at Present Value for Estate Tax Savings." *Trusts & Estates* 112 (February 1973):94–96.

"Your Guide to Successful Tax Settlements." *Federal Tax Coordinator 2d. Special Study* (March 15, 1979).

Zaritsky, H. "Amortization of Intangibles: How the 1976 TRA and Laird (556 F. 2d 1224) Affect Sports Franchises." *Journal of Taxation* 48 (May 1978):292–96.

Zaritsky, Howard M. "How the 1978 Act Affects Estate Planning for Farms and Closely-Held Businesses." *Journal of Taxation* 50 (May 1979):275–81.

Books: Gift, estate, inheritance and income taxes

Bishop, John A., and Rosenbloom, Arthur H. *Federal Tax Valuation Digest, Business Enterprises, and Business Interests, 1979.* Boston: Warren, Gorham & Lamont, 1979.

Englebrecht, Ted Dewin. *"An Empirical Investigation into the Valuation of Closely-Held Corporations by the Tax Court for Estate and Gift Tax Purposes."* Unpublished doctoral diss., University of South Carolina, 1976.

Grunewald, Adolph E. *Stock Valuation in Federal Taxation.* East Lansing: Michigan State University, Bureau of Business and Economic Research, 1961.

Huggins, Kenneth M. *'The Valuation of Closely-Held Corporations for Estate and Gift Tax Purposes."* Unpublished doctoral diss., Texas Tech University, 1973.

Lehrman, Albert M. *Tax Desk Book for the Closely-Held Corporation.* Englewood Cliffs, N.J.: Institute for Business Planning, Inc., 1978.

Mertens, Jacob, Jr. *Law of Federal Income Taxation.* Revised by James J. Doheny. Chicago: Callaghan & Co., 1976. (Cumulative supplement, 1979.) (Chap. 59: Problems of Valuation.)

Articles: Recapitalizations

Abbin, Byrle M. "Gift, Estate, and Income Tax Exposure from Recapitalizing Closely-Held Companies." *Institute on Estate Planning, University of Miami* 10 (1976):1200–08.5.

————. "Using the Multi-Class Partnership to Freeze Asset Values for Estate Planning Purposes." *Journal of Taxation* 52 (February 1980):66–71.

Berall, Frank S. "Recapitalizing Close Corporation May Be Planning Solution for Major Stockholders." *Estate Planning* 3 (Winter 1976):96–104.

Collins, William E. "Outline on Estate Planning Alternatives to Recapitalizations and Holding Companies for Closely Held Family Corporations," *Real Property, Probate and Trust Journal* 15 (Spring 1980):88–98.

Dan, Merwyn E. "Updated Analysis of Tax Planning for Closely-Held Corporations and Their Shareholders." *Taxes* 56 (December 1978):897–903.

Faber, Peter L. "Avoid Tax Problems in Planning Recapitalizations." *Trusts & Estates* 119 (January 1980):67–73.

Freasier, B. Roland, Jr. "An Analysis of the Use of Estate Planning Recapitalizations under Current Law." *Journal of Taxation* 51 (July 1979):40–43.

Henderson, Gordon D. "Use of Different Classes of Stock in Maintaining Control in the Close Corporation." *Institute on Federal Taxation, New York University* 24 (1966):531–54.

Howard, Alex W. "Estate Planning via Recapitalization of Closely-Held Corporations." *Mergers & Acquisitions* 11 (Fall 1976):4–9.

Jensen, Herbert L., and Crumbley, D. Larry. "Structuring a Tax-Free 'A' Reorganization," *Mergers & Acquisitions* 14 (Summer 1979):39–44.

Leung, T. S. Tony. "Valuing Preferred Stock in a Recapitalization: What Weight to Give Its Special Provisions," *Estate Planning* 7 (September 1980):270–74.

Littenberg, Robert L. "The Use of Recapitalizations in Estate Plans under the 1976 Tax Reform Act." *Tax Institute, University of Southern California* 30 (1978):719–73.

Meyers, R. M. "Outline on Valuation Problems in Estate Freezing Techniques," *Real Property Probate & Trust Journal* 15 (Spring 1980):112–17.

Milefsky, Norman R. "How Closely-Held Corporations Can Be Used to Achieve Estate Planning Aims." *Journal of Taxation* 52 (January 1980):18–23.

"Recapitalizations in Estate Planning." *CPA Journal* 47 (March 1977):53–57.

Reed, Charles H. "The Advantages of a Preferred Stock Recapitalization in Closely-Held Corporation Situations." *Taxes* 45 (September 1967):596–603.

Rosenkranz, Stanley. "Recapitalizing the Closely-Held Corporation." *Institute on Estate Planning, University of Miami* 9 (1975):10-1 – 10-17.

Simon, Stanley C. "Iconoclastic Thoughts on the Capitalization of Family Corporations." *Tax Counselors Quarterly* 8 (March 1964):9–14.

Weinberg, Michael D. "Using Preferred Stock to Solve Close Corporation Continuity Problems." *Journal of Taxation* 31 (July 1969):46–50.

Williams, Richard A. "Using a Recapitalization to Reallocate Equity Interests and Perpetuate Closely-Held Status." *Institute on Federal Taxation, New York University* 32 (1974):715–30.

Wolfberg, Stephen. "Uses of Preferred Stock in Tax Planning for Closely-Held Corporations." *Taxes* 44 (January 1966):52–64.

18

ANALYSIS OF THE CENTRAL TRUST COMPANY CASE—A LESSON IN FEDERAL GIFT TAX VALUATION

In spite of the court's final opinion, almost exactly splitting the difference between the values posited by the opposing parties, I think that the most informative court case for the student of business valuations to study is the *Central Trust* case.[1] This is primarily because of the judge's very thorough written opinion. The opinion outlines the testimony of five different witnesses on the value of the stock in question, critiques many aspects of the testimony, and gives a detailed explanation of the rationale for the court's final decision.

BACKGROUND

Heekin Can Company, a well-established manufacturer of cans for the food industry, had 254,125 shares outstanding in 1954, of which 180,510 were owned by 79 persons who were related to James Heekin, the founder.

On August 3, 1954, Albert E. Heekin gifted 30,000 shares, the gifts composed of 5,000 shares to each of six trusts created for the benefit of his three sons, each son being the beneficiary under two trusts. Following his death on March 10, 1955, the executors of his estate filed a gift tax return in which the value of the stock was fixed at $10 a share. On October 28, 1957, however, they filed an amended gift tax return and a claim for refund, contending that the correct value of the Heekin Can Company stock on August 3, 1954, was $7.50 per share.

On October 25, 1954, James J. Heekin and his wife, Alma Heekin, gifted 40,002 shares, the gifts composed of 13,334 shares to each of three trusts created for the benefit of his three children and their families. Gift tax returns were filed in which the value of the stock was similarly declared to be $10 per share. However, on January 21, 1958, James filed an amended gift tax return and a claim for refund, also contending that the correct value of the stock on October 25, 1954, was $7.50 a share, and on the same day, the executor of Alma's estate (she having died on November 9, 1955) filed a similar amended return and claim for refund.

The commissioner of the Internal Revenue subsequently determined that the stock was worth $24 per share on the gift dates, and gift taxes were paid on the deficiency on that basis. The Central Trust Company, as executor for the estates of the donors, filed for a refund, claiming a value of $7.50 per share on the gift dates.

In 1951 and 1952 there had been 44 transactions in the stock totaling 13,359 shares, all at $7.50 per share. These transactions resulted from the desire of descendants of a partner of James Heekin, the founder, to liquidate their interests, and all the sales were made to Heekin family members, employees, or friends. In 1953 the only transaction in Heekin stock was a 100-share sale from one Heekin employee to another. In 1954 the only transaction in Heekin stock was a 200-share sale also from one Heekin employee to another.

---

[1] *Central Trust Co.* v. *United States*, 305 F. 2d 393 (1962).

Book value was $33.15 per share on June 30, 1954, and $33.55 on September 30, 1954. The company paid a cash dividend at the annual rate of $.50 per share, which had been paid each year from 1946 through 1954, except when the company had an extraordinary loss in 1950, when the dividend was omitted, and 1951, when only $.25 was paid. The company was in a sound financial position, with a current ratio of better than 3 to 1, and current assets exceeding total liabilities by a ratio of almost 2 to 1.

The trial took place in the U.S. Court of Claims in 1962. At the trial, the taxpayers produced three independent expert witnesses, and the government one. A spokesman for the government also testified on the government's valuation. The court stated that:

> Where, as in the present cases, the problem is the difficult one of ascertaining the fair market value of the stock of an unlisted closely held corporation, it is not surprising that, in assisting the court to arrive at an "informed judgment," the parties offer the testimony of experts. In such a situation, the opinions of experts are peculiarly appropriate.[2]

The court's opinion provides a thorough explanation of the positions of the different expert witnesses on various aspects of the valuation, and the court's assessment of those positions.

OPPOSING POSITIONS

Taxpayer's first expert witness

Taxpayer's first expert used $1.77 per share as an earning power base. This was arrived at using an unadjusted and unweighted average of the full years' 1952, 1953, and 1954 earnings, which he capitalized at a P/E ratio of 6 to 1. He capitalized the dividend at 7 percent. He discounted book value by 50 percent because of the age and "multi-storied inefficiency" of the company's two main plants. He assigned weights of 40 percent to capitalization of earnings, 20 percent to capitalization of dividends, 20 percent to the book value approach, and 20 percent to past sales of the stock. He then took a 25 percent discount for lack of marketability. The first expert did not utilize comparable publicly-traded companies in his deliberations, on the basis that he felt none could properly be compared with Heekin. This analysis produced the result as follows:

Earning Power								
$ 1.77	×	6	=	$10.62	×	.4	=	$ 4.25
Dividends								
$ .50	÷	.07	=	7.14	×	.2	=	1.43
Book value								
$33.20	×	50%	=	16.60	×	.2	=	3.32
Prior sales								
$ 7.50					×	.2	=	1.50
								$10.50
Less 25 percent discount for lack of marketability							=	2.62
Value per share							=	$ 7.88

[2]Ibid., p. 399.

Taxpayer's second expert used $1.68 as an earning power base. This figure represented an unadjusted and unweighted average of the full years' 1950 through 1954 earnings. He tabulated that 11 publicly-traded companies in the container industry sold at an average price/earnings ratio of 10 over the five-year period, and capitalized Heekin's earnings at 8 times, which he considered appropriate for a "marginal" company. From the result of this calculation, he took a 14.1 percent discount to move the price back to the August gift date, "derived by calculating the general rise in a relatively large group of certain other industry stocks between August 3 and December 31."[3]

Taxpayer's second expert used $.35 per share as the dividend base, the average for the 1950–54 period. He capitalized it at 6 percent, noting a 5.1% average dividend yield for his 11 publicly-traded companies and higher yields available on other general groups of industrial stocks.

He assigned weights of 40 percent to capitalization of earnings, 40 percent to capitalization of dividends, 10 percent to book value, and 10 percent to prior sales. He used a 15 percent discount for lack of marketability.

This analysis produced the following result:

Earning Power							
$ 1.68	×	8	=	$13.44			
$13.44	−	14.1%	=	11.55	× .4	=	$ 4.62
Dividends							
$ .35	÷	.06	=	5.83	× .4	=	2.33
Book value							
$33.23					× .1	=	3.32
Prior sales							
$ 7.50					× .1	=	.75
							$11.02
Less 15% discount for lack of marketability						=	1.65
Value per share						=	$ 9.37

This witness then rounded the figure to $9.50. Using the same method, he valued the October gift at $9.65, based on a lesser downward adjustment in the earning power component of the valuation.

Taxpayer's third expert used the years 1949–53 to compute an earnings base, and adjusted the income statements to eliminate abnormal and nonrecurring items. He used eight companies in the container industry to derive a P/E ratio of 11.82. He also derived a value that he called the "earnings paid out" basis, which reflected both dividends and interest on long-term debt ("earnings paid out on capital invested"). He adjusted the book value to a "value based on invested capital."

He assigned weights of 33⅓ percent to the capitalized earnings value, 33⅓ percent to the "earnings paid out on capital invested" value, 16⅔ percent to

[3]Ibid., p. 400.

the value based on invested capital, and 16⅔ percent to the prior stock sales. He used a 20 percent discount for lack of marketability.

This analysis produced the result:

Earning power				
$13.78	×		.3333	=	$ 4.59
"Earnings paid out on capital invested"				
$ 9.59	×		.3333	=	3.20
Book value (or "value based on invested capital")				
$31.34	×		.1667	=	5.22
Prior sales				
$ 7.50	×		.1667	=	1.25
				$14.26
Less 20 percent discount for lack of marketability			=	2.85
Value per share			=	$11.41

The witness also noted that he would discount only 17.5 percent for lack of marketability if the transaction were viewed as one 30,000 share block and not three 10,000 share blocks, which would result in a price of $11.76 per share.

The same witness, using the same method, derived a value of $9.40 per share for the October gifts, the sharp difference being attributable to drops in the market prices of the public companies used as comparables between the August and October valuation dates. He noted that he would use a price of $9.47 if the transaction were regarded as one block of 40,000 shares rather than three blocks of 13,334 shares each. No explanation was given in the case about why this differential should be smaller than that used in the August gifts.

Government's independent expert witness

The government's expert used earnings for 1950 through September 1954, with certain adjustments. He also computed earnings for the 12 month periods ended June 30 and September 30, 1954, the ends of the quarters immediately prior to the two valuation dates. He considered eight publicly-traded container companies as possible comparables, and ended up relying on two as the only ones he considered comparable to Heekin. Based on these two comparables, he applied a P/E ratio of 7.24 to the adjusted earnings of $2.21 per share for the 12 months ended June 30, and a ratio of 8.29 times the $1.84 adjusted net profit per share for the 12 months ended September 30.

He evaluated the stock on a dividend yield basis by capitalizing dividends at 3.13 percent on the August valuation date, and 3.28 percent on the October valuation date, which dividend yields he derived from the comparable companies. For a dividend figure, he used the average for the 4.5 years preceeding the valuation dates, thus including the atypical period when no dividends were paid. The details of the weighting and computations are not given in the case opinion, but the witness finally took a discount of "almost 20 percent" for lack of marketability, resulting in a figure of $16.00 for the August date and $15.25 for the October date. He then noted that this final value also approximated the company's current assets less all of its liabilities, without giving any value at all to its plants, equipment, or other noncurrent assets.

Government's staff witness

The government staff witness computed "representative earnings" for Heekin at $1.89 per share, based on 1953 and 1954 adjusted earnings. He found an average P/E ratio of 13 on current earnings of 11 container companies. This would produce a capitalized earnings value of $24.57 per share, which the government witness arbitrarily valued at $22.50.

The government staff witness noted that the average market price to book value ratio was 1.4, and on this basis concluded that Heekin stock would not sell for less than its book value of about $33 per share.

Based on seven of the eleven comparables used in the earnings capitalization, the government staff witness capitalized Heekin's $.50 dividend at 3.75 percent. He ignored prior sales and denied the applicability of any discount for lack of marketability. He then assigned weights of 50 percent for capitalized earnings, 30 percent for capitalization of dividends, and 20 percent for book value.

This analysis produced the result as follows:

Earning power		
$ 1.89 × 13	= $24.57	
Arbitrarily reduced to	22.50 × .5 =	$11.25
Dividends		
$ .50 ÷ .0375	= 13.33 × .3 =	4.00
Book value		
$33	× .2 =	6.60
Value per share	=	$21.85

COURT'S POSITIONS

Comparative appraisal method

The court stated:

. . . the comparative appraisal method is a sound and well-accepted technique. In employing it, however, every effort should be made to select as broad a base of comparative companies as is reasonably possible, as well as to give full consideration to every possible factor in order to make the comparison more meaningful.[4]

In discussing the study offered by the government's expert witness, the court observed, in part, that:

. . . it has certain weaknesses . . . , the principal one being the limitation of the comparative companies to two, one of which, Crown Cork & Seal, leaves much to be desired as a comparative because its principal business is the manufacture of bottle caps and bottling machinery, an entirely different business.[5]

In commenting on the government's own witness's use of comparables, the court stated:

---

[4]Ibid., p. 407.

[5]Ibid., p. 406.

. . . the selection of such companies as American Can and Continental Can as comparatives—companies held in esteem in the investment world—will obviously give an unduly high result. It simply is not fair to compare Heekin with such companies and to adopt their market ratios for application to Heekin's stock. Furthermore, defendants's use of the comparatives is confusing. The employment of different comparatives for different purposes is unorthodox. When the comparative appraisal method is employed the comparatives should be clearly identified and consistently used for all purposes.[6]

Capitalization of earnings

The court recognized that capitalization of earnings should be the most important factor in the valuation of a manufacturing company. It also recognized that earnings should be adjusted to eliminate abnormalities and nonrecurring events. It also recognized that earnings (or any other factors) should be considered only to the extent of information available up to the time of the valuation date, and should be brought as current to the valuation date as reasonably possible. Finally, the court required that any trend in earnings be considered, which it did by using a weighted average rather than a simple average of past earnings in deriving an earning power base. All four of the foregoing principles are consistent with generally accepted business appraisal procedures.

Earnings most important factor.   On earnings being the most important factor, the court stated:

. . . it is generally conceded that, as stated in the Revenue Ruling, in evaluating stocks of manufacturing corporations such as Heekin, earnings are the most important factor to be considered.[7]

Adjustments to earnings.   On elimination of abnormalities, the court stated:

. . . it is accepted valuation practice, in ascertaining a company's past earnings, to attempt to detect abnormal or nonrecurring items and to make appropriate eliminations or adjustments.[8]

The court listed the adjustments it considered appropriate as:

In these cases, this normalizing process should require (a) the elimination from the years 1950 to 1952 of the abnormal, nonrecurring losses incident to its financing subsidiary, which had been completely liquidated by 1952; (b) the elimination of the abnormally large 1951 profits due to the Korean war; (c) the redistribution of the expenses attributable to the establishment subsequent to 1951, of a retirement plan, which expenses, although borne in later years, were also applicable to 1950 and 1951, thereby overstating 1950 and 1951 profits and similarly depressing 1953 and 1954 profits; (d) the shift from 1954 to 1951 of the renegotiation refund paid with respect to excessive 1951 profits; (e) the elimination from 1954 of the abnormally

---

[6]Ibid., p. 408.

[7]Ibid., p. 404.

[8]Ibid., p. 403.

large charge relating to the accrual in 1954 of certain expenses actually attributable to 1955, . . . which resulted in the doubling up of 2 years of such expenses in 1954, as permitted by a then recent change in the tax laws.[9]

Use only data available up to valuation date. The court criticized those witnesses who used data past the valuation date:

. . . in using the Company's full 1954 financial data, and then working back from December 31, 1954, to the respective dates, data were being used which would not have been available to a prospective purchaser on the gift dates. The valuation of the stock must be made as of the relevant dates without regard to events occurring subsequent to the crucial dates.[10]

The court also criticized failure to utilize data available as close in time as possible preceding the valuation date:

. . . the converse situation applies with respect to the data used by the third expert. His financial data only went to December 31, 1953, since the Company's last annual report prior to the gift dates was issued for the year 1953. But the Company also issued quarterly interim financial statements, and by the second gift date, the results of three-quarters of 1954 operations were available. In evaluating a stock, it is essential to obtain as recent data as is possible as section 4 of the Revenue Ruling makes plain. Naturally, an investor would be more interested in how a corporation is currently performing than what it did last year or in even more remote periods. Although the use of interim reports reflecting only a part of a year's performance may not be satisfactory in a seasonal operation such as canning, it is possible here to obtain a full year's operation ending on either June 30 or September 30, 1954, which would bring the financial data up closer to the valuation dates.[11]

The court's solution was to consider the four full years 1950 through 1953, plus the 12 months ended June 30 for the August valuation date and the 12 months ended September 30 for the October valuation date.

It should be noted that the foregoing does not totally close the door on the use of some projections or forecasts, if available. For example, had the company had a budget for its full year 1954 earnings, and if it would have been available to prospective stock purchasers on the valuation date, such budget properly could have been considered. Even so, as noted earlier in the book, courts usually put far less reliance on budgets or projections than on actual reported earnings and other data.

Recognition of earnings trend. The court criticized the expert witnesses for merely using average earnings in arriving at an earning power base, rather than considering any trend in earnings. The court noted that an investor would be expected to pay more for a share of a company with a rising earnings trend, rather than one with a declining earnings trend if the five-year

---

[9]Ibid., p. 409.

[10]Ibid., p. 403.

[11]Ibid., p. 403.

average were the same for both companies. "Greater weight should fairly be given to the most recent years and periods."[12]

The court handled this matter by a weighted average, assigning a weight of 1 to the 1950 earnings, 2 to 1951, 3 to 1952, 4 to 1953, and 5 to the latest 12 months preceding each valuation date.

Capitalization of dividends

Determination of appropriate dividend rate. The court rejected using the past five years' average dividend as a base, making the point that the five-year period was not representative of current dividend-paying capacity because it included an abnormal period when the dividend was temporarily suspended because of an extraordinary loss.

In accepting the current $.50 per share rate as the dividend paying capacity base, the court noted that the payment as a percentage of earnings was less than the industry average as demonstrated by the comparable public companies, but that this was justified because:

. . . no substantially larger payment, at least for some time to come, could reasonably have been anticipated. Heekin's equipment was, as shown, not modern and the Company was in need of relatively large sums for equipment and plant modernization if it hoped to continue to be a competitive factor in the industry. For such a program, the Company would have to depend almost entirely on retained earnings. A further limitation on the Company's dividend-paying capacity was its repayment obligations on its long-term debt. Annual installments on principal of $150,000 had to be made through 1965, plus 20 percent of the net income (less $150,000) for the preceding year.[13]

Determination of appropriate rate at which to capitalize dividend. The court basically took the position that the appropriate capitalization rate should be that shown by the marketplace for the publicly-traded comparables:

. . . in capitalizing the dividend at 6 and 7 percent, as did two of the experts, rates of return were used which well exceeded those being paid at the time by comparable container company stocks.[14]

Use of book value

The government's independent expert witness characterized the consideration of book value as a defensive factor in the valuation, describing the net asset factor as "one which keeps a stock price from declining to zero when earnings become zero or even when losses are suffered and when a price-to-earnings ratio would therefore become meaningless."[15] The court seemed to agree, in general, with this assessment.

---

[12]Ibid., p. 409.

[13]Ibid., p. 409.

[14]Ibid., p. 404.

[15]Ibid., p. 405.

The court downplayed the importance of the record of prior stock sales in this case, primarily because the bulk of the prior sales took place too far in the past from the valuation date, and when conditions were not comparable, because the company was just recovering from its loss position. Less important (in this particular case), the court also questioned the extent to which the transactions were actually made on an arm's-length basis.

The court stated that the taxpayer's expert witnesses "all give undue weight as a factor to the $7.50 price of the prior stock sales."[16] The court explained the rationale for its position in this way:

Almost all of these sales occurred in the relatively remote period of 1951 and early 1952. Only one small transaction occurred in each of the more recent years of 1953 and 1954. . . . Furthermore, the $7.50 price of the 1951 and 1952 sales evolved in early 1951 during a period when the Company was experiencing rather severe financial difficulties due to an unfortunate experience with a subsidiary which caused a loss of around $1 million, and when, consequently, the Company found itself in a depleted working capital position and was paying no dividends. Further, there is no indication that the $7.50 sales price evolved as a result of the usual factors taken into consideration by informed sellers and buyers dealing at arm's length. Fair market value presupposes not only hypothetical willing buyers and sellers, but buyers and sellers who are informed and have "adequate knowledge of the material facts affecting the value." *Robertson v. Routzahn*, 75 F.2d 537, 539 (C.C.A.6th); Paul, Studies in Federal Taxation (1937), pp. 193–4. The sales were all made at a prearranged price to Heekin employees and family friends. The artificiality of the price is indicated by its being the same in 1951, 1952, 1953, and 1954, despite the varying fortunes of the Company during these years and with the price failing to reflect, as would normally be expected, such differences in any way.[17]

It should be clear from the foregoing explanation that the court was not downplaying the importance of prior sales as a valuation criterion in general, if they were at arm's length and under circumstances where the economic factors determining the prices were comparable to those on the valuation date. The court simply felt the prior sales generally failed to meet such standards. Even so, the court did not disregard the prior sales completely, as will be seen in the following summary section.

The court recognized that a discount for lack of marketability must be used if valuing the stock with reference to publicly-traded comparables. Referring to the government's position on this issue, the court stated that ". . . the refusal to make any allowance for lack of marketability contributes further to the unrealistic nature . . ."[18] of the government's fair market value estimate.

---

[16]Ibid., p. 402.

[17]Ibid., p. 402.

[18]Ibid., p. 408.

However, all of the expert witnesses in this case approached the quantification of the appropriate marketability discount on the basis of the "cost of flotation," that is, how much it would cost to make a public offering of the shares involved. On this basis, the court found that the discounts for lack of marketability offered by the experts were too high, and accepted a discount of 12.17 percent based on a prior study of flotation costs, which the court cited.

I believe that this was a major conceptual error in the case, and the only major procedure which subsequent cases have not generally followed, as will be seen in the next chapter. The assumption implicit in using flotation cost as a basis for determining the discount for lack of marketability is that such a flotation is a viable possibility. That generally is not the case for minority stockholders. Depending on conditions, it might not even be a viable possibility for a controlling position.

Obviously, the adoption of the premise that flotation cost should be the basis for determining the marketability discount was not the court's fault, since the expert witnesses were the ones who suggested it, and the premise was not refuted in the testimony. Also, the data on discounts for lack of marketability discussed in Chapter 10 were not available at the time of this case. Subsequent cases have recognized that a public flotation normally is not a viable alternative, at least for minority stockholders, and, consequently, discounts for lack of marketability in most subsequent cases have been significantly higher.

Court's final summary

Earning power. The court used a weighted average of the latest five years' earnings for the earning power base. For both valuation dates the court gave a weight of 1 to the 1950 earnings, 2 to the 1951 earnings, 3 to the 1952 earnings, and 4 to the 1953 earnings, all adjusted as discussed earlier. For the August 3, 1954, valuation date the court applied a weight of 5 to the earnings for the 12 months ended June 30, 1954. For the October 25, 1954, valuation date the court applied a weight of 5 to the earnings for the 12 months ended September 30, 1954. This resulted in a weighted average earning power base of $1.93 for the August 3 valuation date and $1.79 for the October 25 valuation date.

Dividends. The court said that it could reasonably be anticipated that Heekin would continue its $.50 annual dividend. However, limitations on its dividend paying capacity made it unlikely that it would be increased, so that the current dividend rate appeared to approximate the firm's dividend-paying capacity.

Book value. The book value of Heekin stock was $33.15 at June 30, 1954, and $33.55 at September 30, 1954.

Comparable public companies. The court selected five of the public companies submitted by the witnesses as suitable to use for the valuation. The court discussed this procedure:

. . . it is . . . appropriate to select as closely comparable companies as is possible whose stocks are actively traded . . . ,and to ascertain what ratios their market prices bear to their earnings, dividends, and book values. The application of such ratios to Heekin would then give a reasonable approximation of what Heekin's stock would sell for if it too were actively traded. . . .

. . . five of them, . . . are, while by no means perfect comparables, certainly at least reasonable satisfactory for the purpose in question. . . . In addition, five companies give a sufficiently broad base. . . .

After similarly computing the earnings, as adjusted, of the comparatives for the same periods as Heekin . . . and similarly weighting them to give effect to the trend factor . . . the average ratio of their market prices to their adjusted earnings as of August 3 and October 25, 1954 (the "price-earnings" ratio) was 9.45 and 9.84 to 1, respectively. . . .

Similarly, the comparatives' dividend payments for the 12 months ending June 30 and September 30, 1954, . . . show an average yield of 3.50 and 3.56 respectively. . . .

As to book value, the average market prices of the comparatives were 83.96 and 86.39 percent, respectively, of the book values of their common stocks on said dates. . . .[19]

Weighting of factors. The court then accorded 50 percent weight to the capitalization of earnings, 30 percent weight to the capitalization of dividends, and 20 percent weight to the ratio of price to book value. This analysis produced these results:

								August 3, 1954	October 25, 1954
Earning power									
$ 1.93	×	9.45	=	$18.24	×	.5	=	$ 9.12	
$ 1.79	×	9.84	=	$17.61	×	.5	=		$ 8.81
Dividends									
$ .50	÷	.0350	=	$14.29	×	.3	=	4.29	
$ .50	÷	.0356	=	$14.05	×	.3	=		4.22
Book Value									
$33.15	×	.8396	=	$27.83	×	.2	=	$ 5.57	
$33.55	×	.8639	=	$28.98	×	.2	=		$ 5.80
								$18.98	$18.83
Less 12.17% discount for lack of marketability						=	2.31	2.29
Value per share							=	$16.67	$16.54

Past transactions, other factors, and conclusion. The court concluded:

. . . while the sales of Heekin stock at $7.50 warrant, as hereinabove pointed out, only minimal consideration, the figures derived from the above formula give them no cognizance whatsoever. "Giving important weight to the figure of $16.67 produced by the application of the comparative appraisal method as applied herein, but viewing it in light of all the facts and circumstances involved in these cases, it is concluded that

---

[19]Ibid., pp. 409–10.

the fair market value of the 30,000 shares given on August 3, 1954, was $15.50 per share.[20]

The court then went on to state that the company's prospects were no less bright as of October 25, 1954, and that the fair market value on that date also was $15.50 per share.

---

[20]Ibid., p. 411.

19

OTHER FEDERAL GIFT AND ESTATE TAX CASES

This chapter discusses three federal gift and estate tax cases involving transfers of interests in a total of five companies. They illustrate a variety of issues, such as primary reliance on capitalization of earnings versus asset values, and several aspects of discounts for minority interest, lack of marketability, and other factors.

KIRKPATRICK CASE

Background

On the date of his death, April 17, 1968, Ernest E. Kirkpatrick owned minority interests in two closely-held corporations.

The decedent owned 1,091 shares out of 2,512 shares outstanding, or 43.43 percent of French Tool & Supply Company (French Tool). Decedent's grandson owned 875.5 shares, or 34.85 percent, and decedent's daughter owned 545.5 shares, or 21.71 percent.

The decedent also owned 130 shares out of 2,000 shares outstanding, or 6.5 percent, of French Oil Company (French Oil). L. R. French, Jr., owned 1,805 shares, or 90.25 percent. Decedent's daughter owned 65 shares, or 3.25 percent.

French Tool operated an International Truck dealership (and a related rig-up shop), a Chrysler-Plymouth dealership, and was engaged in oil production and in ranching. The oil business consisted of some producing and some nonproducing properties. Ranching operations consisted of a 50 percent undivided ownership in two cattle and sheep ranches.

French Oil owned 22 producing oil leases. It also owned the other 50 percent undivided interest in the two cattle and sheep ranches referred to in the previous paragraph, plus a 100 percent interest in a 1,280-acre ranch used occasionally for grazing. French Oil also sold oilfield tubular goods.

Neither French Tool nor French Oil had ever paid any dividends. There had never been an outside sale of either stock. In 1960 French bought 870 shares of French Oil for $287 per share from his former wife as part of a property settlement connected with a divorce.

French Tool Company

On the original tax return the taxpayer had valued the French Tool stock at $353.63 per share. In the deficiency notice, government valued it at $600.34 per share, which was the book value on the latest interim statement prior to the valuation date. At the trial, the taxpayer claimed a value of $216 per share for the French Tool stock, while government claimed $500 per share.

Taxpayer's position. Taxpayer's expert witness relied primarily on the capitalization of earnings approach for the valuation of the French Tool stock. The testimony is summarized as:

He estimated that, based on numerous publicly-owned companies with financial prospects similar to French Tool's, decedent's stock, if it had been marketable, would have sold at eight times the company's earnings for the 12-month period ending March 31, 1968, or $432 per share. He then applied a 50-percent discount to this figure to reflect the nonmarketability of the stock, the lack of dividends, and the fact that a purchaser of decedent's interest would have no effective voice in the company's management. Thus, he concluded that, on April 17, 1978, decedent's 1,091 shares of French Tool stock had a fair market value of $216 per share.[1]

Government's position. Government's expert witness relied primarily on the value of the underlying assets for the valuation of the French Tool stock. He adjusted the book value upward to reflect an appraisal of the 50 percent owned ranch land in excess of the cost basis. He then discounted 50 percent from the resulting value to reflect the stock's lack of marketability and the decedent's minority interest.

Court's position. The court found the taxpayer's capitalization of earnings approach to the valuation of the shares more persuasive than the government's underlying asset value approach. The text of the court's opinion is:

On the date of the decedent's death, French Tool was actively engaged in three separate lines of business. Although it owned interests in large amounts of real estate, its land holdings constituted an integral part of its ongoing ranching business. Thus, since French Tool was clearly an operating company actively engaged in selling products and services to the general public, we think that primary consideration should be given to its earnings and prospects for future profits as opposed to the value of its underlying assets. See *Levenson's Estate* v. *Commissioner* (60–2 USTC 969), 282 F. 2d 581, 586 (3d Cir. 1960); Rev. Rul. 59–60, sec. 5(b), 1959–1 C. B. 237.

From this perspective, we think that a prospective purchaser of decedent's French Tool stock, in examining the company's financial position on April 17, 1968, would discover a number of factors that would have a depressing influence on the value of decedent's shares.

Such an examination would reveal that, for a number of years, French Tool's ratio of current assets to current liabilities had been about one-to-one. The company's net earnings had fluctuated widely for the past several years and, in fiscal year ending June 30, 1967, the company showed a net loss of approximately $3,000. It had a significant amount of long-term debt that approximately equaled stockholder's equity. The company had never paid any dividends and had not been in a financial position to do so. Finally, the stock was not marketable, and a purchaser of decedent's 43.43 percent interest in French Tool would probably have had little or no voice in the company's management due to the fact that the majority interest was held by decedent's daughter and grandson.

However, we think these negative factors would be offset somewhat by the fact that the company's fiscal year ending June 30, 1968, was quite profitable in relation to past years.* Also, although the company's net earnings had been quite low for the past several years, its cash flow position (net income plus depreciation) had been much more favorable. Finally, even though the chances on April 17, 1968, were minimal that French Tool would be liquidated in the foreseeable future, we think the rather high adjusted book value of the company's underlying assets would have been an attractive feature to a prospective purchaser of decedent's stock.

After taking all of these factors into consideration and after adjusting the value of the underlying assets to reflect the $94 per acre value of the Ranch,† we find

---

[1]*Estate of Ernest E. Kirkpatrick*, 1975–344 T.C.M. (CCH) p.1499.

decedent's 1,091 shares of French Tool stock to have been worth $300 per share on April 17, 1968.[2]

*"Although French Tool's June 30, 1968, financial data would not have been available to a prospective purchaser of decedent's stock on April 17, 1968, the company maintained monthly balance sheets and earnings statements. The financial data for the nine-month period ending March 31, 1968, would have been available and clearly forecasted the profitability of the 1967–68 fiscal year."

†"We cannot accept (taxpayer's witness's) contention that the value of decedent's French Tool stock would not be increased if we found the Ranch to be worth more than $80 per acre. While we think that little weight should be given to the value of the company's underlying assets, to adopt (taxpayer's witness') position is, in effect, to ignore their value altogether. This we cannot do. See *Estate of Lida R. Tompkins* (Dec. 15,182(M)), T.C. Memo. 1961–338."

The foregoing opinion is instructive, because it generally is consistent with the lines of reasoning found in similar cases, but perhaps articulated more clearly than in some cases.

French Oil Company

On the original tax return the taxpayer had valued the French Oil stock at $287.36 per share. In the deficiency notice, government valued it at $882.73 per share, which was the book value on the latest interim statement prior to the valuation date. At the trial, taxpayer claimed a value of $171 per share for the French Oil stock, while government claimed $650 per share.

Taxpayer's position. Taxpayer's expert witness felt he could not approach the French Oil valuation on a capitalization of earnings basis because most of the recent earnings resulted from collection of old receivables, which previously had been written off and from the sale of oil leases, neither of which were continuing earnings sources and without which the company would have lost money. He thus decided to estimate a liquidating value, and estimated that a minority shareholder might "gamble" about a quarter of liquidating value to accept the risks involved.

Government's position. Government's expert witness approached French Oil the same way as he did French Tool—adjusting the book value upward to reflect increased value in the ranchland, and then discounting 50 percent from the resulting adjusted asset value to reflect lack of marketability and minority interest.

Court's position. The text of the court's decision and rationale is:

In making our determination that decedent's 130 shares of French Oil stock were worth $250 per share on the date of his death, we did not feel comfortable with either expert's method of valuation. We found (taxpayer's witness') hypothetical amount that a purchaser would "gamble" in order to obtain a certain return on his investment to be too speculative to warrant our total reliance. With respect to the method utilized by (government's witness), we think the facts presented clearly show that French Oil, like French Tool, was an operating company on the date of decedent's death. Thus, we think (government's witness) gave excessive consideration to the value of the company's underlying assets in making his valuation.

We think that a prospective investor would view French Oil primarily from the standpoint of its history and prospects as a profit-making corporation.

---

[2]Ibid., p.1500.

An examination of its financial position as of April 17, 1968, reveals that the company was in rather poor shape. Its ratio of current assets to current liabilities had been about one-to-one for a number of years, and its long-term debt was quite high in relation to stockholder's equity. Its ranching business consistently operated at a loss and, although the company showed modest profits for its fiscal years ending August 31, 1965, 1966, and 1967, had it not been for the items of extraordinary income (collection of bad debts and sale of certain oil leases), the company would have lost money in each of these years.

Surely a prospective purchaser would have taken into account the fact that, as of April 17, 1968, all of French Oil's bad debts had been collected and would have realized that the company could not continue to sell its oil and gas leases indefinitely.

Moreover, French Oil had never paid any dividends in its 33 years of existence. Decedent's 130 shares were nonmarketable and represented a mere 6.5 percent of the company's issued and outstanding stock. A purchaser of decedent's interest would have had no voice in the company's management since the company was run by French who owned approximately 90 percent of its stock and served as president and chief executive officer.

As we found with French Tool, however, French Oil's cash flow position was more favorable than its net earnings position. Also, notwithstanding the minimal chances that the company would be liquidated, we think a prospective purchaser would place some importance on the rather high adjusted book value of the underlying assets.

After taking all of these factors into account, we find that $250 per share would have been a fair price for decedent's 130 shares of French Oil stock.[3]

GALLUN CASE

Background

On September 29, 1969, Edwin A. Gallun (taxpayer) made a gift of 400 shares of common stock of A. F. Gallun & Sons Corporation to members of his family. This was a little over 2.5 percent of the 15,722 shares of stock outstanding, of which Gallun owned 4,617.5 shares, or 28.7 percent.

The company owned a leather tanning operation, with related land, buildings, and equipment, plus an investment portfolio of stocks and bonds with a market value of $18,087,263 on September 30, 1969, the company's fiscal year-end.

Earnings per share were $30.89 in fiscal 1968 and $54.78 in 1969, much of which came from the investment portfolio. Dividends paid per share were $18 in fiscal 1968 and $23 in fiscal 1969. Book value at September 30, 1969, was $418.02 per share. Net asset value after adjusting the investment portfolio from cost to market value was $1,283.02 per share.

Taxpayer filed a gift tax return reporting the value of the 400 shares at $369.24 per share. Government filed a notice of deficiency, valuing the stock at $661.37 per share.

Points of agreement and issues involved

The two expert witnesses for the taxpayer and the one for government all agreed that the company was a combined operating company and investment

---

[3]Ibid., p.1501.

company, and, therefore, the tannery operations should be valued as an operating company, and the investment portfolio be regarded as an investment company.

There also was agreement that an adjustment to the value of the investment portfolio for blockage was necessary for two large blocks of stock. This reduced the value of the investment portfolio from $18,087,263 to $16,204,439, which reduced the adjusted net asset value from $1,283.02 per share to $1,163.26 per share.

The main issues in the case were the determination of proper discounts for various factors, such as lack of marketability, retention of income not present in a publicly-traded investment company, minority interest, and the potential capital gains tax if the stocks and bonds were to be liquidated by the corporation. At the time of the trial, government's expert witness was advocating only a 20 percent discount, while taxpayer's expert witnesses were advocating much greater discounts.

On the tannery operation, the court made these observations:

Court's position

The tannery operation is one of only a few remaining in the United States and represents an industry that is declining. . . . The performance of the tannery operation has been mediocre and it would be difficult to find an investor willing to invest in such an operation.[4]

The court valued the tannery operation at $900,000, or the equivalent of about $57 per share, a little less than half the portion of the company's book value attributable to the tannery.

The text of the conclusion of the court's opinion states:

In arriving at our determination we have rejected the argument of (taxpayer) that a discount should be allowed for a potential capital gains tax that would result if the investment portfolio were to be liquidated. The record does not establish that the management of the portfolio had any immediate plans to liquidate the investment portfolio. Furthermore, it is possible that the management at some time in the future may dispose of certain or all of the investment assets without incurring a capital gains tax. Under these circumstances, such a discount is not appropriate. See *Estate of Frank A. Cruikshank* (Dec. 15,941), 9 T. C. 162 (1947); *Estate of Alvin Thalheimer* (Dec. 32,714(M)), T.C. Memo. 1974–203.

On the other hand, we believe that the (government's) witness erred in refusing to discount the value of the stock to account for a corporate entity intervening between the investment assets and the owner of Gallun stock. (Government's) witness reasoned that the Corporation could be compared to eight publicly-traded, closed-end investment companies and that accordingly no discount was in order because the stock in the closed-end investment companies was not selling at a discount at the time of the gift. We do not agree that such a comparison is valid, since the shares of the

---

[4]*Edwin A. Gallun*, 1974–284 T.C.M. (CCH) p.1320

closed-end investment companies are readily marketable and the companies are entitled to certain tax benefits as regulated investment companies.

Taking into account not only the arguments we have discussed but also the additional factors brought to our attention by the parties, we have concluded that the net asset value of the investment portfolio should be discounted by 55 percent. Thus, we find that the fair market value of the investment portion of the Corporation's business was $7,292,000. Adding the value of the tannery operation to this figure, dividing by the number of shares outstanding and rounding, we find the fair market value of the Corporation's stock was $520 on the date in issue.

Based on the $23 dividend in 1969, the highest in a five-year period, the return on the Corporation's stock would be 4.4 percent at $520. Considering the declining state of the tannery industry and the nonmarketable nature of the Corporation's stock, we do not believe that an investor would be willing to accept a lower return. This factor was an additional consideration in convincing us that a substantial discount of underlying net asset value was necessary.[5]

Commentary on court's opinion

I think that three observations on the above court opinion are important.

First, I do not interpret the court's opinion as a rejection of the validity of the general approach of using publicly-traded, closed-end investment companies as useful comparables in valuing privately-held investment companies. Indeed, many other cases have relied on that approach. The court's opinion merely is there are at least two important differences between public and private investment companies, marketability and tax treatment, and it would not be valid to make the comparison without appropriate adjustments for those differences.

Second, the paragraph indicating that government erred in refusing to discount the value of the stock to account for a corporate entity intervening between the assets and the owner of the stock is extremely cogent. It is all too common for some people to jump to the conclusion that the value of a share of stock is its proportionate share of the value of the underlying assets, whereas the fact is that ownership of stock is not a legal claim on a proportionate share of the assets at all. This point was discussed in Chapter 3.

My third point is that the court's rejection of taxpayer's argument, that a discount should be allowed for a potential capital gains tax which would result if the investment portfolio were to be liquidated, is inconsistent with many other cases. The courts are so inconsistent and frequently ambiguous on their treatment of this point that the appraiser cannot predict reliably which way it will be resolved in any particular case.

My own opinion is that the trapped-in capital gains tax on unrealized appreciation is clearly a deferred liability that requires recognition. Strong support for this position is found in the American Institute of Certified Public Accountants official guidelines for the preparation of personal financial

---

[5]Ibid., p.1321.

statements, where assets with unrealized appreciation are adjusted to market value. They unequivocally take the position that any upward adjustment to market value must be accompanied by a deduction for the related capital gains tax. The text of the AICPA position is:

An accrual for income taxes on net unrealized appreciation (the difference between the tax basis of the net assets and estimated value) is required in the presentation of the estimated value column in personal financial statements. This accrual is necessary because the estimated values cannot generally be realized without incurring taxes.[6]

On January 8, 1969, William T. Piper, Sr., made gifts, to his son and to 11 trusts for the benefit of his grandchildren, of 100 percent of the outstanding stock of two investment companies, known as Piper Investment Company (Piper Investment) and Castanea Realty Company, Inc. (Castanea).

The two companies had somewhat similar asset portfolios, each consisting of unregistered shares of Piper Aircraft Corporation (PAC) common stock, whose shares were listed and traded on the New York Stock Exchange, plus some income-producing real estate. Piper Investment owned 37,500 shares of PAC, and Castanea owned 67,500, out of a total of 1,644,890 shares of PAC outstanding. The real estate had been purchased primarily to avoid the problem of having the two investment companies classified as personal holding companies.

No dividends were ever paid by either Piper Investment or Castanea, nor was any salary or other compensation ever paid to Piper, who, until the time of the gifts, was the only shareholder in both corporations.

Piper individually owned 73,920 shares of PAC separate from the two investment companies, and Piper family members collectively owned 28 percent of the outstanding PAC stock. Neither Piper nor any of his beneficiaries had any contractual rights to require the filing of a registration statement with the SEC covering the PAC shares, nor to annex shares to a registration statement otherwise being filed by PAC. No SEC filing by PAC was contemplated at the time. On the basis of the then-current NYSE quoted price for PAC stock and the then-current fair market values of the various real estate holdings, the adjusted net asset value of Piper Investment was about $178 per share, and the adjusted net asset value of Castanea was about $370 per share.

On the gift tax return, taxpayer valued Piper Investment at $76.68 per share, and government's notice of deficiency valued it at $101.89 per share. On the gift tax return, taxpayer valued Castanea at $158.59 per share, and government's notice of deficiency valued it at $226.15 per share.

One of the issues in the case was the value of the unregistered shares of Piper Aircraft Company stock owned by the two investment companies. Government claimed that the stock was not restricted, even though unregis-

PIPER CASE

Background

Discount for unregistered shares of listed stock

---

[6]AICPA, *Audits of Personal Financial Statements* (New York, 1968), p. 5.

tered, and that no discount from the NYSE quoted price was appropriate. Taxpayer claimed that the stock was restricted, and that there could be significant inhibitions standing in the way of registering it, so a full discount for lack of marketability was appropriate, such as would be applied to letter stock.[7]

The court held that the stock was restricted, in the sense that it could not be sold without registration. However, the court also noted that Piper was chairman of the board, and three sons were included among the other seven directors. On the basis of these facts, along with the significant family ownership position, the court decided that Piper and his associates could force registration if they so desired. Therefore the marketability discount to be applied directly to the value of the PAC stock should be only the costs of registration and sale. Noting that this would be less for unregistered shares of a company already trading on the NYSE than for a company with no public market, the court, on the basis of expert witness testimony submitted, determined the appropriate marketability discount for the PAC shares to be 12 percent.

With this marketability discount on the PAC shares, the adjusted net asset value of Piper Investment was $158.58 per share, and the adjusted net asset value of Castanea was $327.71 per share.

"Portfolio discount"

The parties agreed that the portfolios should be valued at some discount from their underlying net asset value, but disagreed on the appropriate amount of a "portfolio discount."

Both of the government's expert witnesses relied on prices of publicly-traded, closed-end investment companies in arriving at their opinion on an appropriate portfolio discount. One government witness proposed a discount of 7.7 percent from net asset value based on the market prices of 14 publicly-traded nondiversified investment companies. The other government witness used a group of 24 closed-end investment companies, which he found ranged from a discount of 16.7 percent to a premium of 82.4 percent, and concluded that, because of Piper Investment's and Castanea's relatively unattractive portfolios, the highest discount, approximately 17 percent, should be applied.

Taxpayer's witness did not present evidence of his own on this point. The text of the court's conclusion on the "portfolio discount" is this:

. . . we are hampered in our evaluation of the testimony of (taxpayer's) valuation expert because (taxpayer) has failed to supply us with any data with which to analyze (taxpayer's witness') statements. He stated that the only conclusion that could be drawn from the list of companies from which (government's witness) derived his discount was that an inverse correlation existed between the size of an investment

---

[7]The general concepts and typical discounts for lettered stock are discussed in Chapter 10, Data on Discounts for Lack of Marketability.

company's assets and the size of the discount from net asset value, and that, because of their small size, Piper Investment and Castanea were comparable only to the three smallest companies considered by (government's witness), for which the discounts averaged over 40 percent. Since taxpayer has presented no data to enable us to evaluate the validity of (taxpayer's witness') statements, we can accord them little weight.

Taxpayer has also failed to introduce specific data to support his assertion that Piper Investment and Castanea were substantially inferior to the worst of the companies considered by (government's witness). Taxpayer made no attempt to elicit evidence as to the portfolios of the companies considered by (government's witness), and taxpayer's expert witness only on (one government witness') and not on (other government's witness') report. We have only the fact that the companies considered by (government witness) were publicly-traded from which to infer that their portfolios were superior to those of Piper Investment and Castanea. We have taken account of the lack of a public market for the stock of Piper Investment and Castanea separately.

On the basis of the record before us, we conclude that the discount selected by (government's witness) was too low, but that there is insufficient evidence to support taxpayer's position that the discount should be higher than that proposed by (government's other witness). Therefore, we find that 17 percent is an appropriate discount from net asset value to reflect the relatively unattractive nature of the investment portfolios of Piper Investment and Castanea.[8]

At the time of this writing, 1980, the average discounts from net asset value are somewhat higher than at the time of this case, so utilization of the same procedure very likely could result in a larger discount. Also, the language of the court's opinion leads me to believe that the court could have been persuaded to accept a larger discount in this aspect of the case if the taxpayer's witness had presented more thorough evidence, such as comparative portfolio analysis, on why Piper Investment and Castanea should have been compared more closely with the investment companies selling at larger discounts.

Discount for lack of marketability

In addressing the discount for lack of marketability, one of the government's witnesses took the position that the discount should be based on the cost of a public flotation. The other government witness and the witness for the taxpayer took the position that Piper Investment and Castanea would not make attractive public offerings, and the marketability discount should be based on the difference between what stocks tend to sell for on the private placement market, compared with the publicly-traded market. The text of the court's opinion on this issue is:

We find this reasoning persuasive and reject the position of (government's witness) that a discount based on the costs of a secondary public offering should be employed since we find no support in the record for his premise that a public distribution would be an efficient method of disposing of the Piper Investment and Castanea stock. The situation in respect of the stock of these two companies stands in sharp contrast to the

---

[8]*Estate of William T. Piper, Sr.*, 72 T.C. (P-H) 88, p.594.

situation vis-à-vis the PAC stock where a previously registered and actively traded listed security was involved.

Government argues that any further discount for the costs of disposing of the Piper Investment and Castanea stock beyond the costs of a registration and public offering is rendered superfluous by the discounts for restrictions on the PAC stock and for the nondiversified nature of the investment companies' assets. However, because there was no established public market for the stock of Piper Investment and Castanea, and because the gifts were of minority interests in the investment companies, we believe that an investor would consider a purchase of the stock, which was the subject of the gifts, to involve risks and disadvantages which a direct investment in PAC stock would not entail and which are additional to the weaknesses in the investment companies' portfolios.[9]

Both the government witness who opted for the private placement market as a criterion for determining the discount and the taxpayer's witness agreed that the SEC *Institutional Investor Study*[10] provided an appropriate basis for quantifying the relevant discount.

Using various tables in the SEC *Institutional Investor Study* for discounts for private placement transactions, government's witness determined that a further 24 percent discount would be necessary, while taxpayer's witness claimed that the correct discount to be derived from the study should be 43.8 percent. The text of the court's position on this point and its final conclusion as to the value of the shares is:

We have examined the *Institutional Investor Study* in light of the objections raised by taxpayer. The study reveals an upward trend in the average discount throughout the period studied, January 1966 through June 1969, with a higher than average discount for the stock of companies with relatively low earnings. *Institutional Investor Study*, supra, at 2454, Table XIV-50. The study also shows a preference for purchases direct from the issuer in private placements of stocks of closely-held companies rather than secondary securities. *Institutional Investor Study*, supra, at 2416 n. 86, and 2419. Furthermore, a stock with a less active public market tended to sell in private placements at a higher discount. *Institutional Investor Study*, supra, at 2445. The Study also indicates that investment advisors were unlikely to be purchasers of stock like that of Piper Investment or Castanea, though it does not indicate, as (taxpayer) would have us believe, that only a venture capital company would purchase that stock since a considerable proportion of the private placements with banks and life insurance companies involved restricted common stocks of privately-held companies. *Institutional Investor Study*, supra, at 2419.

After carefully reviewing the *Institutional Investor Study* and considering all the arguments raised by taxpayer and government, we conclude that a further discount of 35 percent would have been required in a private placement of the Piper Investment and Castanea stock, in view of conditions in the private placement market on the valuation date, the possible purchasers of the stock in a private placement, and the earnings and other attributes of Piper Investment and Castanea.

---

[9]Ibid., pp.594–95.

[10]Use of this study and subsequent related studies to quantify appropriate discounts for lack of marketability is discussed in Chapter 10.

After applying the discount for the weaknesses in Piper Investment's and Castanea's portfolios and the 35 percent discount required to market their stock in private placements, we arrive at a per share value of $85.55 for Piper Investment and $176.80 for Castanea.[11]

Note that the above text makes reference to the fact that "the gifts were of minority interests." This is appropriate, because multiple gifts typically are each viewed as minority interests, even though the total amount given constituted a controlling interest. The valuation was on a minority interest basis, because it was made by comparison with sales of closed-end investment companies on the open market, which sales are, in fact, sales of minority interests.

The reader should be alerted to the fact that under the present Unified Gift and Estate Tax rules, any gift made three years before death is automatically construed as being in contemplation of death, and included in the donor's taxable estate (with credit for any gift taxes that may have been paid). In a case like this one, were the donor, under current law, to die within three years of the gifts, it is likely that the values for estate tax purposes would be adjusted upward to reflect a controlling interest instead of a group of minority interests.

Also, in December of 1979, the IRS issued a Technical Advice Memorandum on a case to the effect that a 100 percent interest, all given away at one time as three one-third interests, would be treated as one controlling interest instead of three minority interests for gift tax purposes. This IRS T.A.M has not yet been tested in court.

Taxpayer proposed a discount for potential capital gains tax at the corporate level because Piper Investment and Castanea had a basis of less than $1 per share in their PAC stock. As in the *Gallun* case, the court rejected this position.

In one sense, however, some relief was indirectly granted the taxpayer on that point in this case. That is, the portfolio discount was based on ratios of market prices to net asset values for closed-end investment companies. In the literature analyzing why such companies fairly persistently tend to sell at discounts from net asset value, the existence of trapped-in capital gains is consistently cited as one of the reasons. Thus, by granting a discount by reliance on closed-end investment company discounts, some relief from trapped-in capital gains tax liability is reflected. In this case, of course, it was rather nominal, since the average trapped-in capital gain for the public closed-end companies would have been only a small fraction of the value of the portfolio, compared with the large amount in the Piper case.

Treatment of trapped-in capital gain

---

[11]Ibid., p.595.

20

EMPLOYEE STOCK OWNERSHIP PLANS

The Employee Retirement Income Security Act of 1974 (ERISA) elevated employee stock ownership plans (ESOPs) to the status of statutorily defined employee pension benefit plans.[1] The ESOP is defined as *a qualified retirement plan designed to invest primarily in the employer's securities, thus providing a means for employees to have an ownership interest in the company for whom they work.*

The two primary benefits of an ESOP to a company and its stockholders are the income tax advantages and the means to provide liquidity to existing stockholders and their beneficiaries. This chapter presents a bare bones introduction to basic features of ESOPs. A fairly extensive special bibliography on ESOPs is included at the end of this chapter.

The regulations do not define "primarily." While most ESOPs are invested entirely in the employer's securities, various interpretations have suggested that the plan might need to be invested only to 50 percent or more in the employer's securities.

Employer securities can include common or preferred stock or debt. ERISA Title I does not provide for issuance of warrants or stock purchase options as part of an ESOP.

The ESOP can be used in either the publicly-traded or closely-held corporation, and can be used either separately or with other employee benefit plans. As in other employee benefit plans, there must be a nondiscriminatory definition of the group of employees who will be eligible to participate.

Usually the company can contribute up to 15 percent of the eligible payroll to the ESOP plan as a tax deductible expense, as in other employee benefit plans. In some circumstances the tax deductible contribution can be as high as 25 percent of eligible payroll.

The contribution can be made either in cash or in the employer company's securities; the contribution also can be some combination of the two. If the contribution is made in cash, all or part of the cash may be used to purchase stock from existing shareholders. The cash contribution is a deductible expense to the company. If the contribution is made in securities, the value of the securities contributed is the amount considered to be a tax-deductible expense.

The securities must carry a "put option" feature, which enables the employee or his beneficiary to sell the securities back to the corporation or to the ESOP[2] on death or severance from the company. The ESOP itself cannot

INTRODUCTION TO ESOPs

Basic features of ESOPs

Put option

---

[1] As used in practice, there is no distinction between the term *ESOP* (Employee Stock Ownership Plan) and *ESOT* (Employee Stock Ownership Trust). An ESOP is, by definition, a trusteed plan, so a trust necessarily is involved. For the purpose of this book the term *ESOP* will be used.

[2] In certain limited instances, such as banks where put options to the company are prohibited by federal regulation, the purchaser could be a third party.

be compelled to purchase the shares, but the employer company can grant the ESOP the option to purchase shares that are put to the company. Thus, the nature of the ESOP is such that it provides its own market for the securities. This can be a useful means to provide liquidity for existing shareholders of a closely-held corporation.

Right of first refusal

ESOP shares can be subject to a right of first refusal in favor of the ESOP itself or of the issuing corporation, but not in favor of another shareholder or third party. The right of first refusal must lapse not later than 14 days after the security holder gives notice of a third-party offer to purchase.

Voting rights

In closely-held companies, the voting rights that accrue to ESOP shares normally are exercised by the ESOP trustees. Voting rights need be "passed through" to the ESOP beneficiaries only on matters which, either by law or corporate articles, require more than a majority vote of stockholders. In public companies, voting rights are passed through to plan participants.

Life insurance

Contributions to the ESOP, but not loan proceeds received by it, may be used to purchase key man life insurance. The general rules that apply to the purchase of key man life insurance by the ESOP are similar to those applicable to other qualified employee benefit plans.

The insurance proceeds normally may be used to purchase stock for the ESOP from the estate of a deceased shareholder. The shareholder's estate may be contractually bound to offer the securities to the ESOP. However, the ESOP may not be contractually bound to buy the securities.

Leveraged ESOPs

The ESOP also can be used with corporate borrowings. The ESOP borrows money from a bank, and uses the money to purchase employer securities. The ESOP pledges the securities as collateral for the loan, and the employer company also guarantees the loan.

The company then makes annual contributions to the ESOP, which the ESOP uses to pay off the loan, with proportionate amounts of securities released from the loan collateral with each payment. (Note that the flow of cash contributions to the ESOP should be planned to match or exceed the schedule by which the employees' stock interests are scheduled to vest.)

The effect is that the company repayments of principal as well as interest are tax-deductible expense to the corporation. Of course, there is stock dilution, since additional shares are issued. Exhibit 20–1 presents schematic diagrams of how two leveraged ESOP situations work.

TRAESOPs

The term *TRAESOP* (also sometimes *TRASOP*) is an acronym for an ESOP that takes advantage of additional investment tax credits made

ESOPs As A Cash-Raising Aid To Owners

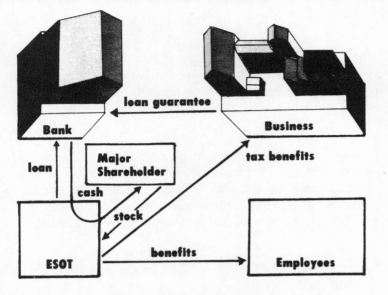

ESOPs As A Capital Formation Opportunity

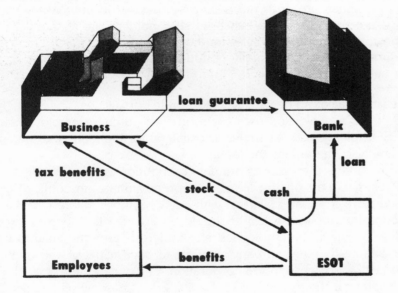

available under the Tax Reduction Act of 1975. By meeting certain additional requirements, a company with an ESOP can obtain 1 percent to 1.5 percent additional investment tax credit.

VALUATION OF ESOP SHARES

One recent and quite comprehensive book devoted entirely to ESOPs states, "The valuation . . . may be the most difficult and important task in administering an ESOP."[3] The book goes on to explain why this is so:

It is difficult because no formula can be devised that is generally applicable to all valuation issues and important because higher valuations in favor of officers, shareholders, or highly compensated employees may result in the disqualification of the ESOP due to discriminatory benefits. Further, improper valuations may cause an exempt loan to lose its exempt status, resulting in a prohibited transaction.[4]

In general, the valuation criteria for ESOP shares are the same as the criteria for valuing shares for gift and estate tax purposes.[5] Certain aspects peculiar to ESOPs are discussed in the following sections.

As of this writing, no court cases have been decided specifically on ESOP valuation issues. Furthermore, while there are reams of literature on ESOPs (as indicated in the special bibliography on ESOPs in this chapter), very little of the literature addresses itself to ESOP valuation issues, and none of it in any depth. Therefore, the opinions in the following sections about special ESOP valuation considerations have arisen largely from my own reasoning and from the experience of my associates and myself in valuing ESOP shares, and could be subject to refinement or change in the light of additional experiences, rulings, and court decisions.

Need for independent appraisal

Because of the fiduciary responsibility of the ESOP trustees, the desirability of having the value determination made by a qualified independent party is even stronger than in other cases where Revenue Ruling 59–60 criteria are applicable.

The regulations require that the valuation be made in good faith, and add a "safe harbor" provision that this requirement generally can be satisfied by having the initial and annual valuations done by a qualified independent appraiser. The Practising Law Institute book referred to earlier discusses this subject:

In most cases, an annual appraisal by a person who customarily makes such an appraisal, and who is independent of any party involved in transactions with the ESOP, will be deemed to be the appropriate determination of value. Such an appraisal would nevertheless be subject to challenge in regard to a transaction between an ESOP and a disqualified person.

Although an annual independent appraisal is encouraged, the size of many ESOPs may not justify the cost. For these ESOPs, it is possible for the plan fiduciaries to determine the value of securities on the appropriate valuation date by apply-

---

[3]Joseph P. Bachelder, III, ed., *Employee Stock Ownership Plans* (New York: Practising Law Institute, 1979), p. 310.
[4]Ibid., p. 310.
[5]*Rev. Ruling 59–60*, modified by *Rev. Ruling 65–193*, amplified by *Rev. Ruling 77–287*.

ing the relevant factors, methods and approaches set forth in the published Revenue Rulings.

A fiduciary determination of value may, however, create an inherent conflict of interest, or its appearance, since recognized methods and approaches may result in quite different value determinations. As a fiduciary must discharge his duties solely in the interest of participants and beneficiaries, and may not act on behalf of a party whose interests are adverse to the interests of participants or beneficiaries, the selection of one recognized valuation method over another that results in a lower value for the securities may subject the fiduciary to charges that he is acting on behalf of the employer. Additionally, the Department of Labor will not at present issue rulings regarding the adequacy of consideration under a specific formula. Therefore, the fiduciary and the ESOP are in a precarious position with respect to fiduciary determinations of value.[6]

One of the controversial issues in ESOP share valuation is the treatment of the ESOP contribution itself as it affects the measurement of the company's earning power base when a capitalization of earning power approach is used as a part of the valuation procedure.

Effect of ESOP on earning power base

Cash contribution. If a cash contribution is made and the cash is used to buy stock from an existing stockholder, the cash goes out of the company and into another stockholder's pocket, so it would seem that no part of that deduction should be added back in determining the earning power base. On the other hand, the argument can be made that if the company were to sell out, the buyer might eliminate the ESOP expense, and, therefore, in valuing the stock for acquisition, consider the earning power base to be what the fully taxed earnings would be without the ESOP. To really evaluate this latter argument, one needs to inquire about the extent to which the ESOP is regarded as a "frosting" benefit by the employees, versus the extent to which other employee benefit expenses would need to be incurred to satisfy and hold the employees if the ESOP were eliminated.

For some small companies that are managed in such a way that most of the pretax earnings are paid into the ESOP, the choice of how to treat the ESOP contribution can make a huge difference in the earning power base. There is not a clear-cut answer about how to deal with this problem, and, as noted earlier, there have been no judicial decisions involving this point. One way is to put relatively more reliance on asset-oriented or other approaches. The appraiser will have to rely on his expert judgment in light of the facts in each case.

Stock contribution. If the contribution is made in stock, then the value of the contribution really remains within the company. The cash that would have been paid out stays in the cash account or is spent on other assets, and the capital account is increased by the value of the stock. Thus, it would seem logical that the "expense" deducted as a result of this transaction be added

[6]Bachelder, *Employee Stock Ownership Plans*, p. 311.

340

back into net earnings in computing the earning power base. (Of course, the effect of this will be offset at least partially by the effect of dilution, discussed in the next section.)

The argument to this reasoning is the converse of the argument in favor of adding back the contribution when it is made in cash. That is, without the ESOP, the pre-ESOP earnings would be fully taxable, and a buyer would consider only a fully taxed earnings base without the ESOP in deliberations on what to pay in an acquisition. This argument, then, would lead one to add back to the earning power base the amount of the ESOP contribution, less the taxes that otherwise would have to be paid if there were no ESOP contribution. It would seem that this would be the minimum adjustment that should be made to net earnings in this case.

Taking account of dilution

When the contribution to the ESOP is made in stock, more shares of stock will be outstanding. This must be taken into consideration in computing the value per share. The following calculation will yield the appropriate value per share:

$$\frac{\text{Total value of stock} - \text{ESOP contribution}}{\text{Number of shares outstanding before contribution}}$$

Then one merely needs to divide the price per share thus derived into the dollar amount of the contribution to determine the number of shares to be contributed.

Marketability discount

Another controversy in ESOP share valuation is whether, or the extent to which, there should be some discount applied for lack of marketability.

In a previous chapter we saw that it frequently was reasonable to discount a minority interest in a closely-held company with no market for its stock 35 percent or more, compared to an otherwise comparable but freely tradeable minority interest in a publicly-held company. Some would take the position that an ESOP share should not be subject to a marketability discount because the ESOP creates its own market. I think that the question has to be analyzed individually for each ESOP situation, and that the answer lies in how good the ESOP market is. Most of the answer will be found by analyzing the wording of the "put" feature of the ESOP agreement. The more favorable it is to the stockholder, the less the appropriate marketability discount, compared to the price that would be appropriate if the stock were publicly-traded. Other factors to consider are the company's financial strength and its past performance in ESOP stock redemptions.

The regulations allow the company to take up to five years (ten in some circumstances), at a reasonable rate of interest, to complete the payments for stock tendered under an ESOP put provision. What constitutes a "reasonable" interest rate under capital market conditions of the 1980s is a matter open to considerable judgmental differences among reasonable people. (See

Chapter 21, Buy-Sell Agreements, for suggestions on setting a reasonable interest rate.) The shorter the payout period and the higher the interest rate, the lower the appropriate marketability discount. In most of the ESOP valuations with which I have been associated, a marketability discount of between 5 percent and 20 percent has been applied to reflect these factors.

Keep in mind that a discount is meaningless unless the base from which the discount is taken is clearly defined and understood. In the foregoing discussion, the assumption is that the shares are being priced by reference to prices of publicly-traded shares which can be considered comparable. Such shares are, themselves, minority interests. Therefore, the above range of discounts of 5 percent to 20 percent strictly reflects the factor of marketability.

Some companies have a policy of redeeming ESOP shares for cash when tendered, and have established a track record of doing so, even though the ESOP document allows an extended redemption period at the director's discretion. In such cases, where management indicates an intention to continue such a policy, and where the company's financial position appears capable of supporting it, it would seem that a zero marketability discount would be justifiable.

Treatment of excess management compensation

In the chapter on adjusting the income statement to derive an appropriate earning power base to capitalize, it was suggested that an upward adjustment to earnings might be appropriate if management were drawing more compensation than would be necessary to replace them. It seems, however, that such an upward adjustment would not be appropriate for the valuation of ESOP shares, because one normally would presume that the compensation policy would continue. The extent to which the compensation policy might be subject to change would be an appropriate area of inquiry in the field interviews with the control persons in the company.

The foregoing sections have pointed to several areas where the per share valuation for ESOP purposes may be less than the valuation per share if the company were to sell out. If the shares were valued conservatively for ESOP purposes, and the company were to sell out subsequently at a higher price, the ESOP shareholders suddenly would have a windfall profit on their shares, in some cases very substantial. This possibility does not pose any inconsistency in valuation techniques. In fact, it happens to shareholders in public companies every day when tender offers are made at substantial premiums over existing market prices.

CRITERIA FOR EXTABLISHING AN ESOP

As noted at the beginning of this chapter, the two primary benefits of an ESOP to a company and its stockholders are the income tax advantages and the means to provide liquidity to existing stockholders and their beneficiaries.

I believe that these advantages are not compelling enough reasons to establish an ESOP unless the company's existing stockholders have a genuine desire to have reasonably broad ownership of the company's securities by employees, since the "eligibility to participate" criteria must be nondiscriminatory.

If there is a genuine desire to have employee ownership, then the decision criteria turn toward weighing the costs versus the benefits. The primary costs are legal, accounting, and valuation. Most of the legal cost is in establishing the plan, and typically will run a few thousand dollars.

The accounting costs involve determination of what employees are eligible to participate and to what extent, as well as computation of vested and forfeited interests and schedules of payments to those who have tendered stock to the company. These costs are similar to other employee benefit plans, probably in the low four figures per year for typical $1 million to $10 million net worth companies with 10 to 100 participants.

In 1980, the initial cost of valuation for a typical, straightforward company is running in the mid to upper four-figure range, although it could be higher or lower. If there are no significant changes in company operations, the cost of annual updates may run about half the cost of the initial valuation.

The key to cost effectiveness, then, is whether the company has enough eligible payroll and enough profitability to make these costs worthwhile. There is no clear-cut answer about how much eligible payroll and profitability are necessary to make the ESOP expenditures worthwhile, since the determination will vary with the motivations of different people and the circumstances of different situations.

BIBLIOGRAPHY: ESOPs

Articles

American Institute of Certified Public Accountants. "Recommendations on Accounting for Employee Stock Ownership Plans." (Statement of Position 76–3).

Binns, W. Gordon, Jr. "ESOPs: A Joint Piece of the Action." *Financial Executive* (September 1975), pp.48–54.

Burck, Charles G. "There's More to ESOP than Meets the Eye." *Fortune* (March 1976), pp.128–33.

Clausen, Paul T. "ESOP Stock Valuation: A Case for Liquidity." *Trusts & Estates* 115 (June 1976):419–21.

Crichton, John H. "ERISA to ESOP to Capital." *Pension World* 14 (June 1978): 58–60, 62–65.

Curtis, John E., Jr. "ESOP, TRASOP Rules Clarified and Changed By the Technical Corrections Act of 1979," *Journal of Taxation* 52 (May 1980):304–306.

Daniel, John I., III. "Employee Stock Ownership Plan (ESOP) Used to Sell a Small, Closely-Held Corporation." *Louisiana Certified Public Accountant* 35 (Summer 1976):41–46.

"ERISA 1974 Act." *Pension & Welfare News* (November 1974).

"ESOP: Employee Ownership." *Wall Street Week No. 520* (December 12, 1975). Owings Mills, Md.: Maryland Center for Public Broadcasting.

"An ESOP Fable—Plan Must be for Participants' Benefit." *I.A.F.P. Financial Planning Update* (October 1979), pp.1–3.

"ESOPs—An Explanation for Employees." (March 1978) Prepared by the staff of the Senate Committee on Finance. Reproduced at CCH Pension Plan Guide Sect. 42,023.

"Employee Stock Ownership Trusts: Tax Advantages for Estate Planning in Close Corporations." *Yale Law Journal* 84 (June 1975): 1519–39.

Epstein, Michael F. "Foundation for a Successful TRASOP Plan." *Pension World* 14 (December 1978):8–10,11.

Faley, R. Scott, and Sussman, Richard L. "The Tax Aspects of Employee Stock Ownership Plans." *American University Law Review* 26 (Spring 1977): 593–631.

Fishman, Jacob. "Use of an Employee Stock Ownership Plan in the Closed Corporation." *Taxes* 55 (July 1977):443–56.

Forbes, Wallace F., and Partland, Donald P. "Valuing Securities for Employee Stock Ownership Plans." *Business Horizons* (August 1976), pp.74–83.

Gates, Jeffrey R., et al. "TRASOPs—More Attractive after the Revenue Act of 1978." *Financial Executive* 47 (January 1979):44–50.

Harris, Arthur F. M. "ESOPs . . . and the Pre-ESOP Shareholder." *Pension World* (November 1975), pp.57–60.

Humphreys, W. R. "From TRASOP to CESOP." *Taxes* 57 (May 1979): 319–23.

Kaplan, Jared. "ESOP's Fable." *Taxes* (December 1975), pp.898–912.

Larson, M. E., Jr., and Wolf, D. A. "Employee Stock Ownership Plans and The ESOP Credit after the Revenue Act of 1978." *Public Utilities Fortnightly* 103 (March 15, 1979):38–41.

Lawinger, Ernest J. "Current Techniques for Reliably Valuing Close Corporation Stock for Estate and ESOT Purposes." *Estate Planning* 3 (Autumn 1975):32–37.

_____ "Financial Impact of an ESOP on a Closely-Held Corporation." *Pension & Profit Sharing Tax Journal* 2 (1976):141–60.

_____ "Valuations of Closely-Held Common Stock for Employee Stock Ownership Plans." Prentice-Hall Inc, *Pension Service* (April 22, 1977), pp.1177–87.

Lee, M. Mark. "Valuing Closely-Held Stock for ESOP Purposes Is No Simple Matter." *Pension & Profit Sharing Tax Journal* 1 (1975):310–19.

_____ "Valuing Closely-Held Stock for ESOP Purposes Is No Simple Matter, Part II." *Pension & Profit Sharing Tax Journal* 2 (1975):29–45.

Lieberman, Paul. "Employee Stock Ownership Trusts: 1978 Developments." *Tax Advisor* (March 1979).

Ludwig, Ronald L., and Curtis, J.E., Jr. "Benefits of Employee Stock Ownership Plans Affected Markedly by the 1978 Revenue Act." *Journal of Taxation* 50 (January 1979):15–18.

Ludwig, Ronald L. "Conversion of Existing Plans to Employee Stock Ownership Plans." *American University Law Review* 26 (Spring 1977):632–56.

Lund, Harry A.; Casey, Walter J.' and Chamberlain, Philip K. "A Financial Analysis of the ESOT." *Financial Analysts Journal* 32 (January/February 1976):55–61.

Menke, John D. "ESOP's New Look under the Final Regulations." *Journal of Pension Planning and Compliance* (May 1979), pp. 213–38.

_____ "The ESOP as Defined by Final IRS Regulations." *CLU Journal* 33 (October 1979):61–79.

Moffitt, Donald. "How Stock-Ownership Plans for Employees Can Solve Tough Problems in Small Firms." *The Wall Street Journal* (August 7, 1978).

Nichols, Cathy A. "ESOTs: A Tool for Divestiture." *Mergers & Acquisitions* (Winter 1977) pp.4–9.

Parrs, Eugene. "Unscrambling the ESOP Omelet," *Taxes* 58 (March 1980):171–74.

Reade, K. Deane, Jr. "ESOT—Spells a New Employee Benefit." *Pension & Welfare News* (April 1976), pp.49–57.

Reum, Robert, and Reum, Sherry Milliken. "Employee Stock Ownership Plans: Pluses and Minuses." *Harvard Business Review* 7 (August 1976):133–43.

Rock, David F., and Brooks, Raymond D. "ESOP May Facilitate Tax-Free Transfer of Interest in Closely-Held Corporations." *Taxes* 56 (January 1978):43–47.

Rumack, F. W., and Von Wodtke, H. "Effect of the Tax Reform Act of 1976 on Employee Benefit Plans." *Financial Executive* 46 (Summer 1978):52–58.

Schaumburg, Donald B. "An Objective Look at ESOPs Opportunities, Problems and Alternatives." *Taxes* (February 1976), pp. 68–81.

Sherman, Gerald H., and Lewis, Stewart M. "The ESOP Fallacy." *Journal of Pension Planning and Compliance* 3 (May 1977):226–47.

Susman, Gerald S., and Borgman, Charles L. "ESOPs Can Be a Useful Tool for Both Financial and Estate Planning." *Estate Planning* 5 (July 1978):224–28.

Teague, Burton W. "In Review of the ESOP Fable: The Pros and Cons of Employee Stock Ownership Plans." *The Conference Board Record* (February 1976), pp.10–13.

Weisman, David E. "Employee Stock Ownership Plans: IRS Proposed Regulations and the Tax Reform Act of 1976—A Policy Analysis." *Wayne Law Review* 23 (September 1977): 1373–94.

Wolff, R. L., and Timber, C. J. "Leveraged Employee Stock Ownership Plans and the Closely-Held Corporation." *Tulsa Law Journal* 14 (1979):477–90.

Books

Bachelder, Joseph E., III, ed. *Employee Stock Ownership Plans*. New York: Practising Law Institute, 1979.

Frisch, Robert A. *The Magic of ESOT*. Rockville Centre, N.Y.: Farnsworth Pub. Co., 1975.

_____ *The Triumph of ESOP*. Rockville Centre, N.Y.: Farnsworth Pub. Co., 1977.

Hewitt Associates. *ESOPS: An Analytical Report*. Deerfield, Ill., no date. A 60-page pamphlet prepared for the Profit Sharing Council of America.

Lynch, William B. *Employee Stock Ownership Trusts*. Los Angeles: Lynch & Nelson, p.c., 1976. A 51-page pamphlet prepared for the Northwestern Mutual Life Insurance Co. Handy for those considering ESOT. Gives eight case examples of applications. Only three pages in entire pamphlet on valuation of stock: pp. 13–15.

Menke, John D. *How to Analyze, Design, and Install an Employee Stock Ownership Plan*. Greenvale, N.Y.: Panel Publishers, 1976.

Scharf, Charles A. *Guide to Employee Stock Ownership Plans: A Revolutionary Method for Increasing Corporate Profits*. Englewood Cliffs, N.J.: Prentice-Hall, Inc., 1976.

21

BUY-SELL AGREEMENTS

Buy-sell agreements are commonly used in closely-held corporations or partnerships to provide for liquidation of the interest of a withdrawing or deceased shareholder or partner. These agreements fall into three categories:

1. *Repurchase agreements* (also called *entity purchase agreements* or *redemptions*), where the issuing corporation or partnership buys the interest from the withdrawing party or from the estate of the deceased party.
2. *Cross-purchase agreements,* where one or more other individuals or entities buys the interest from the withdrawing party or from the estate of the deceased party.
3. *Hybrid agreements,* where the issuer will buy a portion of the interest and other stockholders or partners will buy a portion.

Either type of agreement may be either mandatory, that is, binding on both parties, or optional on the part of one of the parties, usually the purchaser. Sometimes agreements are written to be optional during an owner's lifetime, and mandatory for a decedent's estate.

It is not necessary that the same agreement apply to all the owners of a particular entity. One or a few owners may be subject to an agreement while others are not, or different owners may be subject to different agreements. For example, it is common to find minority owners of an enterprise subject to a buy-sell agreement while the controlling owner is not. In limited partnerships, provisions applicable to limited partners normally would be different than those applicable to general partners.

The provisions of any buy-sell agreement should, of course, be designed to carry out best the objectives of all the parties to the agreement. From the viewpoint of one who would be a seller under the agreement, the purpose usually is to provide liquidity in the case of withdrawal from the business or death. From the viewpoint of one who would be a purchaser, the purpose usually is to provide continuity of ownership and management without possible interference from outside parties. From the viewpoints of both seller and purchaser, the purpose also is to establish the circumstances under which the agreement will become effective and a means by which the price and terms of the transaction will be determined.

As Hartwig aptly put it:

The particular method selected by the parties for the determination of the price to be paid for the interest will, of course, depend on their attitudes toward each other and their objectives with respect to survivors, their beneficiaries and the business entity.[1]

One consideration in the choice between the cross-purchase versus redemption form of buy-sell agreement is the number of shareholders or partners involved. The more there are, the more complicated the cross-

---

[1]J. D. Hartwig, "Valuing an Interest in a Closely-Held Business for the Purpose of Buy/Sell Agreements, and for Death Tax Purposes," *Tax Institute, University of Southern California Institute on Federal Taxation* (1974), p. 237.

purchase plan becomes relative to the redemption. In the cross-purchase arrangement, the number of party-to-party relationships, life insurance policies required if so funded, and so on, rises geometrically with the number of parties involved. Also, the transfer of life insurance policies on other parties held in the estate of a decedent could give rise to a taxable incident. One solution to these problems is to create an insurance trust agreement, but this requires the drafting of another complicated agreement. In the redemption type of agreement, life insurance policies are owned by the corporation, so there is no administrative or tax problem arising from the necessity to transfer policies at the death of one party.

As far as the parties to the agreement are concerned, once all the intents and implications of the proposed agreement have been explored, fully understood, and agreed upon by all parties, then the task is to translate the conceptual agreement to a definitive written agreement. Attitudes and relationships change, and it cannot be assumed that any ambiguity in the buy-sell agreement will be resolved amicably when the time comes for a transaction to take place under the agreement. My own experience has demonstrated time and time again that most disputes relating to buy-sell agreements arise because one or several of the details of the agreement were not adequately defined.

For example, I testified as an expert witness in an arbitration case over the value of a business interest under a buy-sell agreement where the document was so ambiguous about the applicable valuation date that the attorney required me to analyze and testify to the valuation of the interest for four different dates that the arbitration panel conceivably could select as being applicable in the circumstances. The value differences on the different dates were considerable, because the business was undergoing a series of significant and not totally predictable changes during the relevant time period. The ambiguity as to the applicable valuation date substantially increased the time and cost involved for the analysis as well as the uncertainty of the outcome of the arbitration.

Hartwig makes the point of the typical lack of adequate definition even when the valuation criterion for the buy-sell agreement is simply book value:

Rarely do the agreements define book value; identify whether the books kept for tax purposes or for business purposes are intended; or whether such book value shall be computed as of the date of death, as of the end of the month preceding death, as of the end of the last regular accounting period of the entity, as of the end of the fiscal year of the entity nearest the date of death, or as of some other date.[2]

There are, of course, many aspects of the buy-sell agreement that must be defined adequately besides the valuation question. These, as well as in-depth discussions of specific valuation issues, are addressed in the references contained in the special bibliography on buy-sell agreements appended at the end of this chapter. Consistent with the scope of this book, the balance of this

---

[2]Ibid., pp. 238–39.

chapter will confine itself primarily to the matter of valuation questions relating to the buy-sell agreement.

ESTABLISHING THE BUY-SELL AGREEMENT PRICE

Almost by definition the setting of a value for a business to be covered by a buy-sell agreement is an essential feature of that agreement. Too often it is also the most neglected feature of the agreement, set in an arbitrary, unprofessional manner almost as an afterthought.[3]

One unique aspect of the price-fixing mechanism in a buy-sell agreement, as opposed to other valuation problems, is the extreme uncertainty about when a future event will occur to trigger a transaction under the agreement. This is one of the key reasons why there is no single approach to the problem of establishing the price for a buy-sell agreement that can be recommended as completely satisfactory to serve all situations.

Most of the price-fixing mechanisms in buy-sell agreements fall broadly into one or a combination of three categories:

1. Negotiation among the parties.
2. Some type of formula based on the financial statements, such as book value, some type of adjusted book value, capitalization of earnings, or some combination of such variables.
3. Independent outside appraisal.

Certain other approaches occasionally found in buy-sell agreements are in general disfavor with attorneys and other professionals who frequently are involved with buy-sell agreements. Some agreements call for the value established for estate tax purposes to be determinative for the transaction price. This is exactly the opposite of the more typical logic, which would seek to establish a desired transaction price that would also be determinative for estate and inheritance tax purposes. Besides, having the estate tax value determine the price has the obvious disadvantage of encouraging an upward bias in the negotiations between the executor and the IRS in setting the price, so that both the estate and the government will collect more money.

Another approach that is sometimes used, but generally disparaged in the literature written by practitioners, is to have one party make an offer if he wants to buy out the other, with the provision that if the other party rejects it, he must buy out the offering party on the same terms. This does not seem to work well in practice and may be quite unfair, because both parties probably will not have equal financial capability to buy out each other.

Negotiation among the parties

Many practitioners believe that negotiation among the parties, usually annually, is the best approach to setting the buy-sell agreement price. The

---

[3]Orville B. Lefko, "Buy-Sell Agreements and Appraisals," *Michigan State Bar Journal* (February 1976), p. 116.

parties themselves usually have the most intimate knowledge of their own estate objectives, and also of their attitudes toward each other. They also may have a better idea than anyone else about how much the business is worth; but in most cases, owners would benefit from professional outside guidance on that point.

The problems with this approach arise when the annual valuation is neglected (the incidence of that neglect is amazingly common), or when the parties cannot agree. The buy-sell agreement must make provision for dealing with both these possible eventualities.

The most common method of handling potential neglect of the annual valuation is to provide that if the price is not set annually on a timely basis, after some period (typically 18 to 24 months following the last price agreement) the price-fixing mechanism automatically reverts to either a formula approach or an independent appraisal. In the latter case, it is necessary either to name the appraisal firm or to specify the method by which the appraiser will be selected. If a firm or person is named, provision must be made for an alternate selection procedure if the named appraiser is unable to serve.

Some buy-sell agreements provide for two or three appraisers to submit reports to an arbitration panel, which will make the final determination in case of a dispute, but this can get quite expensive.

One suggestion for avoiding the problem of neglecting the annual valuation is to ask one of the company's professional advisors, such as the attorney, accountant, insurance agent, or appraiser, to put a memo in his tickler file to remind the company to make its annual valuation.

Reversion to formula or outside appraisal approaches is also the most common type of provision to deal with the circumstances where the parties cannot agree on a value through negotiation.

Formula approaches

I am generally opposed to formula approaches for setting the price in a buy-sell agreement, because the result usually turns out to be unfair to one party or the other when the transaction eventually occurs. As this book indicates, the valuation process should reflect a complex set of factors, usually too complex to be embodied adequately in a formula. A formula that might produce an appropriate value in one year might not do so in another year when circumstances in the company and the economy are different. Having made this point, we will consider some of the formulas most commonly found for fixing the price in a buy-sell agreement.

The commonest basis for a formula approach is to use book value or some type of adjusted book value. In earlier chapters the point has been made that book value only occasionally coincides with the going-concern value or fair market value of a business or business interest. Book value tends to come closest to going-concern value in a business that has a high proportion of its total assets in current assets, such as receivables and inventories which can be liquidated at near face value.

One of the attractions of using book value, of course, is its simplicity. Even so, it needs to be well defined. Some buy-sell agreements call for book value with certain adjustments, such as adding back the Lifo inventory reserve or adjusting certain assets to current market value. Unless extremely carefully defined, such adjustments can be subjects of dispute among the parties. Some agreements specify an independent appraiser or accountant to make the adjustments and avoid disputes among the parties.

Of course, if a business is on a cash basis it is almost always necessary to make some adjustments to book value to reach a price that more nearly approximates an accrual basis book value, at least going so far as to recognize the receivables and payables.

If a net asset value approach is used in a repurchase agreement funded by life insurance, keep in mind that the company's net asset value will be increased by the proceeds of the policy on the stockholder's death, a fact which should be reflected in the value.

If a capitalization of earnings formula is used, it seems almost essential to base it on an average or weighted average of several years' earnings to avoid aberrations in the result that could occur from one or two exceptionally good or poor years. Of course, as discussed elsewhere in this book, earnings should be adjusted to eliminate extraordinary items, although, again, such adjustments could be a source of disputes. The capitalization rate or multiplier is a critical variable, and a multiplier that is appropriate one year might not be appropriate another year because of changing economic conditions. One possible way to reflect changes in the appropriate multiple of earnings would be to tie it to some market or industry multiple, such as, for example, using 80 percent of the current earnings multiple on the relevant Standard & Poor's industry group.

Of course, a formula can use any type of combination of net asset value and capitalization of earnings approaches, weighted appropriately for the type of business involved.

One common criticism of formula approaches based on the balance sheet or the income statement, or both, is that closely-held companies have considerable latitude in reporting figures within the boundaries of generally accepted accounting principles, as well as control over such important variables as paying compensation to owner/employees versus retaining earnings. For this reason, controlling stockholders have the power to make decisions that could be detrimental to the minority stockholder whose value will be determined by a formula approach. This is one reason why some formula approaches are based on a percentage of gross revenues rather than net earnings or book value, especially in service-type businesses, on the theory that a certain amount of gross revenues should be able to produce a certain amount of net profit if the controlling owners so desire.

In any approach based on a multiple or percentage of earnings or revenues, recognition should be given to whatever loss of earnings or revenues will occur from the death of the owner.

Independent outside appraisal

Lefko presents a nine-point case for the advantage of having a formal, independent outside appraisal, kept current with periodic updates:

1. The Courts give great emphasis to formal appraisals and opinions of expert witnesses as to the valuation of interests in closely-held businesses.
2. A professionally done, formal appraisal allows and promotes proper estate planning.
3. A buy-sell agreement containing a professionally prepared formula appraisal may avoid costly litigation in the case of a dispute between owners of the stock or, for example, in a divorce action.
4. A formal, professionally prepared appraisal is more likely to assure fair treatment to all concerned.
5. Just as preventive medicine and preventive maintenance on machinery is usually less costly than emergency treatment or repairs, and is more effective (less down-time), so is an appraisal prepared for a buy-sell agreement likely to be better prepared and less costly than one done in an emergency atmosphere of a death, a divorce, etc.
6. As periodic updates are made, the appraiser becomes increasingly knowledgeable as to the economics of the individual business and the industry of which it is a part.
7. A professional appraisal provides not only an opinion as to the value of a closely-held business, but also an analysis of that business from a management consultant's point of view.
8. Knowing the value of a closely-held business allows proper planning of mergers, acquisitions, reorganizations, a sale of the business, a stock option plan, etc.
9. The underwriters generally have the last word as to the price at which a previously closely-held stock will be offered to the public. In planning a public offering, however, it cannot fail to be helpful to the owners of a corporation to know the worth of their stock.[4]

The obvious disadvantage of the formal appraisal with regular updates is the cost. However, the appraisal does not necessarily have to result in quite as lengthy and detailed a report as an ESOP valuation, since there usually are fewer beneficiaries to be satisfied, and the appraiser and the directors do not have to be concerned with meeting ERISA requirements.

Whether or not a complete, formal written appraisal report is done when pricing the buy-sell agreement, some degree of guidance from an independent professional business appraiser usually is helpful to arrive at a satisfactory value that will be equitable to all parties and that will forestall subsequent disputes arising from a buy-sell agreement.

Philosophy: Should the price be high, low, or in the middle?

Since we know that business valuations rarely can be made with undisputable precision, there usually will be some relevant range of reasonable prices that will be acceptable to the IRS, and, possibly, to all the parties. In other

---

[4]Ibid., pp. 120–24.

words, as Matsen gently puts it, "in light of several available methods of valuing closely-held shares and the notable subjectivity involved in such valuations, some flexibility in setting the price is possible."[5]

Appraisers of real estate, equipment, or other physical property frequently include a statement that their appraisal is accurate to within plus or minus 10 percent. Few business interests can be appraised within such tolerances. Just look at how widely the prices of many publicly-traded stocks fluctuate over relatively short periods. For many closely-held businesses it is not unreasonable for the high end of a value range to be 50 percent above the low end of the range. For highly dynamic or speculative businesses, the reasonable range may be much wider.

Considering this flexibility, if the buy-sell agreement price is to be determined by an independent outside appraiser, the appraiser should be given some guidance on the philosophy among the parties to the agreement about whether they want to lean toward one end or the other of the relevant range. Alternatively, the appraiser can present the parties with a relevant price range, and they can make a decision based on their wishes. Of course, it is not uncommon for the different parties to the agreement to have different circumstances and objectives which motivate them toward opposite pricing philosophies. In general, in arm's-length bargaining, one would expect parties who would expect to withdraw earlier to opt for a higher value, while parties who expect to survive in the business longest would opt for a lower value. If the decision is left to the outside appraiser, it is, of course, incumbent on the appraiser to balance these conflicting self-interests in the fairest possible manner.

The consensus among the many articles that address this subject leans from the middle of the range to a somewhat conservative valuation. There are several valid arguments for leaning toward a conservative value. One, of course, is lower tax consequences. Another is to lessen the burden of funding, however it is accomplished. Another is that, recognizing that the valuation is an imprecise matter, the parties have a tendency to feel that they enhance their favorable working relationship with each other by leaning over backwards (a little) to be fair to each other. Also, there is some feeling that if some benefit is to be gained in the pricing by one party or another, it most properly should accrue to those who will remain with the business, since they may need it and deserve it the most.

In a very close family situation, it is common to find the desire to minimize the price so that the tax consequences will be minimized. In these instances, it is especially important to have thoroughly documented justification of the price or basis selected, since the combination of a low price and a nonarm's-length family situation certainly will invite the scrutiny of the IRS and the state taxing authorities.

---

[5]Jeffrey R. Matsen, "A New Look at Business Buy-Out Agreements," *Practical Lawyer* (July 1979), p. 57.

Finally, of course, there are a few mavericks who philosophize that the buy-sell agreement price should be maximized. This is the position taken by Stern:

In essence I have abandoned the quest for the "true value" of the stock. Frankly, the disparities are so great in the valuation of stock of a closely held corporation made by the adversary parties' experts in contested cases, and the "willing buyer, willing seller" standard is so hypothetical that there need be no embarrassment in advising people to look for other approaches.

I now urge clients to consider fixing the highest price they can afford to have their corporation fund through insurance, after taking into account pension and profit-sharing plan death benefits and other life insurance which the business pays for. If the grand total (susceptible of being readily financed by the corporation) is so great that it shocks the parties' sensibilities, it can always be reduced.[6]

Stern admits, however, "It is properly arguable that my approach is more of a plan of mutual insurance than a determination of stock value." Of course, the comments also should be considered in light of their source. Although Stern is an attorney, he also has been a faculty member at a number of CLU institutes, and the article appeared in the *CLU Journal*, the official journal of the life insurance industry.

TERMS AND FUNDING

Two decisions that necessarily are integrally related in creating the buy-sell agreement are the provisions for payment terms and for funding.

Terms can run anywhere from immediate cash to payments spread out over several years, usually with interest. Funding can come from life insurance, from retained earnings in the case of a redemption, or from personal assets in the case of a cross-purchase. In some cases borrowings may be used to fund either a redemption or a cross-purchase. In order for a buy-sell agreement to work it is essential that funding adequate to carry out its terms be available one way or another, so provision for funding is an essential ingredient for a viable buy-sell agreement.

Term payment provisions

From the purchaser's viewpoint, the typical reason to prefer a term payment program to cash is to ease the funding burden. From the seller's viewpoint, the attraction of an installment payment program is to spread out the capital gains tax over several of the seller's tax years.

If a term payment plan is used, careful consideration must be given to establishing the interest rate, because this is really an integral part of the pricing decision. Careful consideration also should be given to the matter of collateral or other protection to insure that the seller will receive the contractual payments fully and on a timely basis.

---

[6]Milton H. Stern, "A Different Approach to Price-Fixing in Stockholders' Stock Purchase Arrangements," *CLU Journal* 28 (July 1974): 22–23.

As discussed elsewhere in this book, if the rate of interest on a term contract is below the market rate of interest for similar instruments, at the time of the transaction, the true value received by the seller is less than the face value of the contract. Similarly, if the interest rate is above the relevant market rate, then the true value is greater than the face value. The arithmetic for computing the present value of a contract bearing interest above or below a comparable market rate is shown in Chapter 4.

However, in setting the interest rate in the buy-sell agreement, we face the problem that market rates of interest fluctuate considerably over time, and we have no way of knowing at what time in the future the buy-sell transaction will be triggered, nor what the market level of interest rates will be then. There are several possible approaches to dealing with this dilemma.

One approach is simply to agree on an interest rate in spite of these uncertainties, and to hope that it does not prove to be grossly off the mark in the future. If the price under the buy-sell agreement is set by annual negotiation or appraisal, then the interest rate could be reviewed and adjusted annually at the same time. Another alternative is to set the interest rate by tying it to some index of interest rates at the time of the transaction. The interest rate index used should represent intermediate-to long-term rates, since such rates fluctuate less than short-term rates and because they would be more appropriate for a term payment contract. The yield on *Barron's* intermediate grade bonds or *Moody's* BBB bonds could provide appropriate guidelines to set the interest rate. The agreement could specify that the index rate or some specified amount above or below the index rate be used, depending on the credit of the company involved, the degree of security provided, and the desires of the parties to the agreement.

It might be appropriate to use an interest rate index that represents securities whose maturities coincide with the payout terms of the buy-sell agreement. For example, an index representing five-year maturities could be used if the payout term is five years. The *Federal Reserve Bulletin* gives indexes of interest rates on U.S. Treasury bonds maturing in 1, 2, 3, 5, 7, 10, 20 and 30 years.

Income tax considerations could imply the desirability of some tradeoff between the price and the interest rate. The portion of the contract payments designated as interest will be a deductible expense to the buyer and ordinary income to the seller. The portion of the contract payments designated as principal will not be deductible to the buyer (unless there is an ESOP involved), and will be taxed as capital gains to the seller to the extent that they exceed the seller's basis. Thus, if the seller is in a low tax bracket and the buyer a high tax bracket, it may be advantageous to structure the program to increase the interest rate and lower the price. Conversely, if the seller is in a high tax bracket and the buyer a low tax bracket, it may be advantageous to lower the interest rate and increase the price.

The buy-sell agreement should also make provision for adequate collateral or security for the seller in a term payment agreement. If adequate funds are available, the money could be placed in a series of certificates of deposit with maturities matched to the payment schedule, with a lien on the CDs in favor of the seller. Other security could be in the form of a mortgage or lien on physical assets, such as real estate or equipment. It is also common to require that certain financial criteria be met, such as some minimum level of working capital, some specified minimum current ratio, and some specified maximum debt-to-equity ratio. A typical sanction to enforce such protective standards would be to provide that the entire amount becomes due and payable immediately if any of the standards are violated. These are the types of protections that a bank would require in making a bank loan, and many people feel that a seller of a business interest should be no less well protected.

Funding the buy-sell agreement with life insurance

Life insurance can serve as an important source of funding for stock purchase agreements pertaining to deceased shareholders. The advantages of using life insurance for this purpose are several. First, deceased shareholders' estates get paid in cash, eliminating their need to rely on the continued prosperity of the corporation. Second, the corporation's investment in the cash value of an ordinary life policy is a business asset. Third, any excess insurance carried by the corporation over and above the value of the stock purchase agreement can be retained as earned surplus.

Two types of life insurance are available, ordinary and term. Premiums on ordinary life insurance are level during the life of the policy or over a specified period of years. Part of each premium is set aside as cash value, against which the insured can borrow. Over a period of time, ordinary life policies can build up substantial cash values. Annual renewable term insurance, on the other hand, charges for the pure cost of insurance over a specified period, and builds no cash reserves. Premiums are lower at the front end of the policy than ordinary life rates, but are raised each year. After age 65 new term policy coverage is not generally available, although preexisting annual renewable policies can often be carried to age 100.

Ordinary life, if affordable, is generally preferable to term coverage for permanent insurance needs, because of the expense of term insurance in late years. Further, the cash value of ordinary life policies can be used as a valuable borrowing tool.

Rather than merely purchasing insurance outright, it is possible to borrow against the cash value of ordinary life policies to pay the premiums, and deduct the interest cost on the loan from the policy owners' gross income for federal tax purposes. The desirability of financing life insurance purchases through borrowing depends on the policy owner's tax bracket. It is usually possible to structure borrowings so that a level death benefit, net of the borrowings, can be maintained, and this generally is a desirable objective.

Under Section 264 of the Internal Revenue Code, interest on loans obtained to finance life insurance purchases is tax-deductible only in the following four instances:

1. Where in the first seven years of the policy no more than three annual premiums are borrowed.
2. When the interest on the policy loan for the taxable year does not exceed $100.
3. When the interest was paid on a policy loan because of an unforeseen substantial increase in the taxpayers' financial obligations.
4. When the policy loan was incurred in connection with the taxpayers' trade or business.

Differences between legal decisions and Reg. Sec. 1.264-4(d)(4) of the Treasury over interpretation of exception 4 makes it desirable in practice to fund life insurance purchases under exception 1, to avoid costly litigation and problems with the IRS.

One final point is that, when establishing the price under a buy-sell agreement that is funded by life insurance, the price normally takes cash values under the policies into consideration, but does not take into consideration the death benefit under the policies over and above cash values.

INCOME TAX CONSIDERATIONS

There are at least three categories of income tax considerations to take into account in drafting, pricing, and funding a buy-sell agreement. The relative importance of consideration will vary with the circumstances from one business to another. The three income tax related questions to consider are these:

1. Could a corporate redemption of shares be construed as a distribution subject to ordinary income tax as a dividend?
2. In the case of a buy-sell agreement fully or partially funded by life insurance, who will pay the premiums?
3. In the case of a buy-sell agreement fully or partially funded by retained earnings, is there danger of being taxed on excessive accumulated earnings?

There also are special income tax considerations pertinent to Subchapter S corporations.

It is beyond the scope of this book and the author's expertise to present an exhaustive analysis of the income tax considerations to be taken into account with a buy-sell agreement. Besides, the regulations change faster than this book can be revised. I consider it essential that the corporation or partnership employ professional assistance that is competent to provide expert advice on the income tax, as well as on gift and estate tax implications of various provisions of any proposed buy-sell agreement.

For those who want to do some homework on this subject, many of the references in the special bibliography at the end of this chapter contain discussions of income tax aspects of buy-sell agreements. The purpose of this section is merely to make the reader aware of the major income tax implications that should be considered in deciding on the type of agreement to use, and on the provisions, pricing, terms, and funding.

Redemption construed as distribution

In general, when a corporation makes a payment to a shareholder, it is considered a dividend and taxed to the recipient at ordinary income tax rates. Such tax treatment can be avoided in corporate redemptions under buy-sell agreements only if certain conditions are met. The conditions, which are complex, are set out in Sections 302 and 303 of the Internal Revenue Code. The conditions deal with such items as the proportion of a decedent's gross and taxable estate constituted by the value of the close-held stock redeemed, and how much of the stock is redeemed relative to the total holdings of the stockholder or to the estate tax liability and other estate expenses. Under some circumstances, because of family "attribution" rules, it may even be impossible to avoid the taxation as a distribution in a redemption situation.

This problem is avoided completely in the cross-purchase agreement, as opposed to the corporate repurchase agreement, since the cross-purchase involves no payout from the corporation. Also, the prospect of taxability as a distribution may augur for a hybrid (combined cross-purchase and repurchase) agreement in a case where the corporation could buy only enough stock to pay estate taxes and expenses without the transaction being taxed as a distribution, and the rest of the stock could be purchased by other shareholders.

In some cases it might be appropriate for the question of taxation as a distribution to be considered in establishing the stock redemption price. Since valuation is not an exact science, there almost always is some range of acceptable values. Under some marginal circumstances, for example, the requirements on the percentage of a decedent's estate that was represented by the value of the closely held stock might be met by electing to use a price in the upper end of the range of acceptable values.

Payment of life insurance premiums

Life insurance premiums to fund a buy-sell agreement are not tax deductible. Therefore, an analysis should be made about the comparative net tax impact of having the premiums paid by the corporation versus having them paid by the shareholders.

Incidentally, premiums for insurance used to fund purchases under an ESOP have been made tax deductible as of this writing, which is one comparative advantage of repurchase through an ESOP versus a non-ESOP buy-sell agreement.

Accumulated earnings tax

If a corporation generates and holds retained earnings "beyond the reasonable needs of the business," a special accumulated earnings tax may be imposed. As in many, if not most, federal income tax concepts, there are no clearly defined and measurable rules on the circumstances that trigger such a tax. In general, to avoid it in conjunction with retained earnings held for stock redemption, it should be shown that some business advantage is served, beyond just serving primarily the personal purposes of shareholders.[7]

There are two special considerations to take into account in creating a buy-sell agreement for a Subchapter S corporation. One is that the agreement should be drafted in such a way as would prevent the occurrence of any events that can cause termination of the Subchapter S status. The other problem arises from the fact that all profits from the corporation's tax year are taxable to the shareholders on the last day of the corporation's tax year, regardless of when during that year any other shareholder's shares may have been sold, either to the company or to other shareholders. The pricing and share sale or redemption mechanism should take this factor into account.[8]

Special Subchapter S corporation tax considerations

Generally speaking, the price as determined by a buy-sell agreement will be binding on the Internal Revenue Service for estate tax purposes if the value falls within the range of what would be determined under Revenue Ruling 59–60 at the time of death. Of course, that value would be binding anyway even in the absence of a buy-sell agreement, but usually is easier to substantiate, or at least it usually is more readily acceptable to the IRS in the presence of a buy-sell agreement, especially to the extent that the agreement value was established by arm's-length negotiation.

However, a price established by a buy-sell agreement may be binding on the IRS for estate tax purposes even if it is lower than what would be established under Revenue Ruling 59–60 at the time of death under some circumstances. A review of the law, the literature, and the court cases indicates that the most important criterion is the extent to which the price was established on an arm's-length basis. The following is the complete text of Section 8 of Revenue Ruling 59–60, which addresses the effect of stockholder agreements on gift and estate tax values:

Frequently, in the valuation of closely held stock for estate and gift tax purposes, it will be found that the stock is subject to an agreement restricting its sale or transfer. Where shares of stock were acquired by a decedent subject to an option reserved by the issuing corporation to repurchase at a certain price, the option price is usually accepted as the fair market value for estate tax purposes. See Rev. Rul. 54–76, C. B. 1954–1, 194. However, in such case the option price is not determinative of fair market value for gift tax purposes. Where the option, or buy and sell agreement is the result of voluntary action by the stockholders and is binding during the life as well as at

RELEVANCE OF BUY-SELL AGREEMENT VALUES TO ESTABLISH GIFT AND ESTATE TAX VALUES

---

[7]For an excellent discussion of this point, *see* Martin D. Ginsburg et al., *Corporate Buy-Sell Agreements* (September 1979), pp. 25–40.

[8]For a discussion of this point, *see* Bruce E. Turner and Charles Dillingham, "Most Buy-Sell Agreements Will Require Revision as a Result of the Tax Reform Act of 1976," *Taxation for Accountants* 18 (March 1977): 138–46.

the death of the stockholders, such agreement may or may not, depending upon the circumstances of each case, fix the value for estate tax purposes. However, such agreement is a factor to be considered, with other relevant factors, in determining fair market value. Where the stockholder is free to dispose of his shares during life and the option is to become effective only upon his death, the fair market value is not limited to the option price. It is always necessary to consider the relationship of the parties, the relative number of shares held by the decedent, and other material facts, to determine whether the agreement represents a bona fide business arrangement or is a device to pass the decedent's shares to the natural objects of his bounty for less than an adequate and full consideration in money or money's worth. In this connection see Rev. Rul. 157 C.B. 1953–2, 255, and Rev. Rul. 189, C.B. 1953–2, 294.[9]

As can be seen, the buy-sell agreement price may be binding for estate tax purposes but not binding for gift tax purposes, on the basis that the transaction price is binding on the estate but during lifetime could be changed by negotiation among the parties. One criterion considered is whether the price determined by the buy-sell agreement was reasonable when the agreement was executed, even if subsequent events resulted in the price being abnormally low at time of death. In a recent article, Jeffrey R. Matsen, principal in a law firm and professor of law, summed up the recent trend in court rulings regarding acceptability of buy-sell agreement prices for estate tax values as follows:

. . . owners can no longer rely on an arbitrary valuation placed in an otherwise valid, enforceable, arm's-length buy/sell agreement, made for justifiable business purposes. It is becoming increasingly important that the valuation be one which can stand on its own merit as the actual worth of the shares represented, at least at the time of the agreement is entered into.[10]

Matsen cites as an example the *Slocum* case,[11] in which the court upheld the buy-sell agreement price for estate tax purposes by holding that the facts existing at the time the agreement was entered into were controlling as to whether it had a valid business purpose rather than a tax avoidance purpose.

It should also be pointed out that a value fixed by a buy-sell agreement may be legally binding on the estate for transaction purposes even if it is not binding on the IRS for estate tax purposes. This could result in a situation where the estate ends up paying taxes on a substantially higher value than the price the estate actually receives.

Matsen concludes his discussion of the potential acceptability or lack of it of the buy-sell agreement price for estate tax purposes with:

A valuation made in consideration of all the factors set forth earlier in this article [covered in previous chapters of this book] is the first step in persuading the Service. . . .

---

[9]*Revenue Ruling 59–60, 1959–1 C.B. 237, Section 8.*

[10]Jeffrey R. Matsen, "Establishing the Price for Closely-Held Business Buy-Sell Agreements," *Journal of Corporate Taxation* (Summer 1978), p. 150.

[11]*Slocum* v. *United States,* 256 F. Supp. 763 (S.D.N.Y. 1966).

The second, and perhaps equally important step in persuading the Service to accept the agreed valuation is to make a record of the valuation process at the time when the valuation actually takes place. Although not expressly mentioned in any case, regulation, or ruling, it is inherently understandable that substantiation and justification documented at the time the transaction occurs, and long before the Service becomes an interested party, will have significant probative and persuasive value.

For maximum effectiveness, the record should contain at least a memorandum of the valuation procedure used, perhaps as an exhibit to the corporate minutes or to the agreement itself; or if the size and financial position of the corporation so warrant, an independent appraisal should be considered.

In addition to bolstering and substantiating the value/price structure set up in the buy-sell agreement, a memorandum valuation or an independent appraisal will have several incidental benefits to the owner, and to the company itself. It will help the principals of the business to focus on the positive and negative aspects of their enterprise and perhaps assist them with short-term and long-range financial planning for the company. Moreover, it will assist the business owners in planning their estates and making personal financial decisions about the status of their business interests.[12]

---

[12]Matsen, "Establishing the Price," pp. 150–51.

APPENDIX: SAMPLE SUMMARY VALUATION MEMORANDUM

TO: File
RE: Valuation of the Common Stock of ABC Furniture, Co., Inc.

The purpose of this memorandum is to make a review of the operation of ABC Furniture Co., Inc. and to establish a value for the shares of the company. We have been informed that this valuation will be used as a basis for the valuation of the stock pursuant to a buy-sell agreement to be entered into by the shareholders of the company.

I VALUATION PROCESS

(Herein, a summary of the valuation factors discussed in the article can be included.)

II THE COMPANY

A **History.** ABC Furniture Co. was started in 1963 as a sole proprietorship by James P. Client. Mr. Client had been in the furniture business as a salesman and retail store manager prior to the establishment of his own furniture business. In his capacity as furniture salesman and manager of a furniture store, Mr. Client had noted the lack of quality in specialized furniture on the market for retail purchase to the average customer. He felt that he should be able to design and construct custom-made furniture at a reasonable price which would be of much higher quality than those generally available for retail purchase to middle-income customers and that there would be a viable market for such high-quality furniture if the consumer was educated as to the difference in quality of furniture on the retail market.

During the early years of the business, Mr. Client labored diligently in establishing a manufacturing process for his high-quality furniture. It was a long and arduous haul, but he felt he could develop a system of merchandising based upon owning his own retail outlets for marketing his furniture once he was able to set up and establish an efficacious manufacturing process. By 1969, Mr. Client had three retail outlets in addition to his factory, and the business was definitely a solid, viable entity.

He incorporated the business in 1969 as ABC Furniture Co., Inc., and over the years all of the profits and earnings of the company were poured back into it in order to set up and establish more retail outlets. By 1975, the company had fourteen retail outlets and gross sales approximating $3 million. During 1974 and 1975, the corporation experienced some difficulties due to the national recession and energy crisis; however, the company bounced back to have extremely profitable years in 1976 and 1977. The corporation now has twelve retail outlets and plans on opening two more stores this year. All of the retail outlets are in Los Angeles and Orange Counties; however, management of the company feels that there is a great potential for further expansion into the rest of the Southern California area, i.e., San Diego, Riverside, San Bernardino, and Fresno, as well as possibly north in the Bay Area. The company's present factory operation could be increased with relative ease so as to supply enough furniture for up to twenty-five retail outlets.

B **Nature of the Business.** ABC Furniture Co., Inc. is an independent manufacturer and retailer of high-quality custom-made furniture. Approximately 85 percent of the company's sales are made from the company's twelve retail outlets. The remaining 15 percent of sales are made on a wholesale basis principally to the Los Angeles-based Custom Interior Design, Inc. and less significantly to Wallace Manufacturing Company also based in Los Angeles County. The company is very particular and selective about its retail outlets and relies on good locations and community advertising. Management feels that the company's biggest asset is that nobody makes as fine quality furniture as the company makes selling for the price it charges through its retail divisions and that, accordingly, in the absolute sense, the company really has no competition.

Its principal competitor is Truly Fine Furniture, Inc. which has fifty stores in the Southern California area. However, Truly Fine is presently in a Chapter 11 bankruptcy proceeding, is heavily undercapitalized, and operates on the premise of selling a much lower quality (in the opinion of company management) line of furniture.

III SALES AND PROFITS

A **Sales.** The company has experienced the following sales history since January 1973:

    1973 — $2,800,000
    1974 — $3,200,000
    1975 — $2,800,000
    1976 — $2,800,000
    1977 — $3,000,000

B **Profits.** The company's profits before taxes for the years beginning with 1973 are as follows:

    1973 — $25,000
    1974 — ($50,000) — loss
    1975 — ($35,000) — loss
    1976 — $175,000
    1977 — $225,000

The company intends to open two new retail outlets before the end of 1978, and these operations should substantially increase total volume in sales as well as the projected profits. The marked increase in profits in 1976 and 1977 is atttributable not only to increased sales in 1977, but also to substantially lower selling expenses as a result of better fiscal control and more efficacious marketing policies.

IV PLANT

The company has a long-term lease for its factory in Santa Fe, California. The factory facility includes the manufacturing operational area as well as storage space for raw materials and finished goods. The production capacity of the factory is estimated by management to be almost double what production is at the present time. It is significant to note that the cost of production is not anticipated to increase in the same proportion as production, which will result in higher operating profits and lower costs of goods sold.

V ASSETS

The most recent balance sheet of the company (unaudited) is dated March 31, 1978. As is indicated, the company is in a very healthy cash flow position as a result of an excess of $95,000 on hand as cash in banks. Moreover, over 50 percent of the company's assets is made up of inventory which can be readily turned into cash. The fixed asset valuation is somewhat conservative because the figures used are probably closer to historical book values in comparison to true reproduction values.

VI MANAGEMENT

The President and Chairman of the Board of ABC Furniture Co., Inc. is James P. Client. Mr. Client is the majority shareholder of the company, and the other two principal members of management and minority shareholders are his son, Pierpont J. Client, General Manager and Chief Executive Officer of the corporation, and D. I. Figure, the corporation's Comptroller. Mr. Client, as has been previously stated, formed the company as a sole proprietorship in 1963 and has been continuously active thereafter in building up and operating the company. His son, Pierpont, has been with the company for more than ten years and has been involved as the General Manager of the company for a substantial period of time. Mr. Figure had over fifteen years of experience in the banking industry and is currently serving as Comptroller and Chief Financial Officer of the corporation. He has demonstrated extreme competence with respect to the financial and accounting operation of the business. It is obvious that Mr. Client, his son, Pierpont, and Mr. Figure have the energy, the ability, and the experience to take the company from the very strong foundation on which it now rests to greater heights and higher profits.

VII   FINANCIAL CONDITIONS

A **Balance Sheet Analysis.** The balance sheet of March 31, 1978 will be used for purposes of our analysis. Current asset ratio is 89 percent, which is extremely strong. This is represented principally by the sum of $95,000 as cash in banks and the sum of $272,000 as inventory.

The net book value of the company pursuant to the March 31, 1978 balance sheet is $138,807. It is anticipated that by December 31, 1978 the net worth of the company will be increased by over $125,000 because of profits during the remainder of the calendar year. On the whole, a balance sheet analysis of the company is not particularly revealing nor helpful in establishing any definitive fair market value of the company.

B **Sales and Income Analysis.** In presenting this analysis of sales and income, the financial statements for the company as of December 31, 1977 and December 31, 1976, and the financial statements of the company for the three-month period ending March 31, 1978 were examined. As was already pointed out, net profit for the year 1977 increased drastically over prior years. Of course, one reason for this is the fact that the corporation had expanded rapidly during previous years, thereby incurring expenses and costs that used up much of its profits. Moreover, the recession and energy crunch in 1974 and 1975 drastically hurt the company and the industry in general. From the examination we have undertaken, it is our opinion that the company appears to be on a much more sound and substantial fiscal foundation now than in the years 1973, 1974, and 1975. Accordingly, much weight should be given to the profits generated during the years 1976 and 1977.

VIII   COMPARISON WITH ANOTHER CLOSELY-HELD MANUFACTURING COMPANY

In order to assist in compiling a valid appraisal, we have made a comparison of ABC Furniture Co., Inc. with another closely-held manufacturing company in a similar industry which our firm was recently involved with as a result of a majority shareholder selling out to a minority shareholder. Although the net book value of the other company is substantially higher than that of the ABC Furniture Co., Inc., gross sales are considerably less and profit before federal income tax was only $125,000. That particular company was valued at $1 million, using earnings of $125,000 and a multiplier of 8. That corporation had a history of profits in the $50,000 to $100,000 range but was in a much more tenuous cash flow position and had a much greater debt-service expense. It should be noted, however, that the sale contemplated a buy-out over a five- to seven-year period at a relatively low (8 percent) interest rate, which may have had something to do with the buyer's consenting to the million dollar valuation. Moreover, the buyer was looking upon the company not only as an investment but as a means of livelihood and was definitely considering the salary and employee benefits that he could withdraw from that company in agreeing to pay the purchase price he did.

IX   COMPARISON OF PUBLIC COMPANIES

Comparison of values of publicly-held companies are important because they evidence values placed on similar companies as determined by the investment community at large. It is recognized that comparison, even of companies in the same industry, is difficult, however, at best, because product lines differ, the size of the companies differ, and the public view of management capabilities, goodwill, and future profits vary over a tremendously wide range. Furthermore, smaller public companies are generally traded over the counter where a market float in the stock may be rather thin and, hence, market prices may reflect conditions in the market more than operations of the company. And, as mentioned previously, a discount factor for closely-held stock representative of having no public market in some cases may justify the use of a lower multiplier than a publicly-traded stock with well-established markets.

With these reservations in mind, an examination of comparable public companies similar to ABC Furniture Co., Inc. was undertaken. We have selected two companies with characteristics somewhat similar to ABC Furniture Co., Inc. The first is the Barrymore Furniture Co., a New York Stock Exchange company that is a large international conglomerate that not only manufactures furniture for wholesale distribution but is also involved in the national contract business, health-care products, home furnishings, casket operations, financing operations, and various international operations. Price-earnings ratios were down substantially in both companies in the year 1974; however, they were on the upbeat in 1975 and increased in1976 and 1977. The second company selected is the Best Furniture Manufacturing Co. which is engaged primarily in the production and sale at wholesale of a diversified line of furniture under the Best trademark. Its price-earnings ratios were as follows: 1976 — 7.19; 1975 — 6.69; 1974 — 11.92.

The Barrymore Company price-earnings ratios for the same periods were as follows: 1976 — 11.92; 1975 — 10.81; 1974 — 9.23. We consider these price-earnings ratios a good indication of the multiplier that should be used in valuing closely-held businesses of a similar nature.

X   DETERMINATION OF VALUE

The following major factors are considered both implicitly and explicitly in determining the value for ABC Furniture Co., Inc.:

(1)   History of financial data as may be appropriate to estimate continuation of future expected profitability.

(2)   Management. (An experienced and capable management team, but somewhat limited in depth in that it seems to rest primarily upon the shoulders of three individuals.)

(3)   Comparison of the values of publicly-held companies which operate businesses of a nature somewhat similar to ABC Furniture Co., Inc.

(4)   Consultation with management as to the nature and operation of the business and future prospects of the business.

(5)   Study of the financial history of operations of the company.

Without consideration of management factors and the short history of profitability, a multiplier of 10 or above could possibly be supported with respect to the fair market valuation of the stock of the company if, in fact, the earnings figure was computed on a conservative basis. For purposes of our determination, we have adopted the earnings figure of $175,000, which represents the earnings the company generated in 1977. Although the company expects to earn at least $225,000 in 1978, we feel the $175,000 figure is realistic in view of the prior history of profits of the company. We feel, based upon our experience in valuing privately-held companies and upon a review of all of the factors listed above as well as our comparison of a company in a similar industry and of an operation of a somewhat similar nature to ABC Furniture Co., Inc., that a price-earnings multiplier of 8 would accurately reflect the market price for purposes of this valuation for the stock of ABC Furniture Co., Inc. In this regard, we have taken into account the lack of a public market, the regional nature of the company's operations, the lack of a permanent in-depth management team, and the rather high amount of current liabilities (accounts payable) as reflected on the March 31, 1978 balance sheet. On the other hand, positive factors with respect to this particular valuation include the marked increase in profits in 1976 and 1977, the projected earnings and capacity for increased sales and profits, the increased sales volume in 1978, and the relative ease with which the present factory operations of the company could be increased so as to generate more sales and profits.

Accordingly, applying the multiplier of 8 to the true earnings figure of $175,000, we arrive at a value of the corporation of $1,400,000. However, we feel it is realistic to apply a discount to this figure for lack of marketability of any one shareholder's interest in the amount of $200,000 (approximately 15 percent). Therefore, based on our understanding that there are 100 shares of par value $100 common stock issued and outstanding in the corporation, each share would be worth $12,000.

NOTE: Financial statements should be attached to the memorandum as exhibits along with any other pertinent data or documentation such as a prospectus or company report if available, some appropriate company advertising material, and perhaps a detailed list of equipment and inventory if available and appropriate.

Source: Jeffrey R. Matsen, "Establishing the Price for Closely-Held Business Buy-Sell Agreements," *Journal of Corporate Taxation* 5 (Summer 1978): 134–156. Reprinted by permission from *The Journal of Corporate Taxation*, volume 5, Number 2, Summer 1978, Copyright © 1978, Warren, Gorham and Lamont Inc., 210 South Street, Boston, Mass. All rights reserved.

BIBLIOGRAPHY: BUY-SELL AGREEMENTS

Articles

Abrams, Allan E. "Tax Planning for Agreements Disposing of a Shareholder's Closely-Held Stock at Death." *Journal of the Missouri Bar* 27 (September 1971): 445–66.

Basi, Burt A. "Want Your Business to Go on? Try Using Buy-Sell Agreements." *Industrial Distribution* 68 (May 1978): 75–77.

Black, Louis E. "Partnership Buy-Sell Agreements." *Institute on Federal Taxation, New York University* 36 (1978): 51–74.

Borgsdorf, Charles W. "How Stock Redemptions Can Be Used as an Effective Business and Tax Planning Tool." *Taxation for Lawyers* 8 (January/February 1980):230–34.

Brown, Leon B. "How to Plan and Draft a Stock Purchase Agreement Relating to the Death of a Shareholder in a Closely-Held Corporation." *Tax Institute, University of Southern California* (1956), pp. 519–48.

Buechner, Robert W. "Dynamic Use of Profit Sharing Plan-Funding a Buy-Out with Before-Tax Dollars." *CLU Journal* 33 (January 1979):61–66.

Chan, Lionel. "Planning a Sec. 303 Redemption." *Tax Adviser* 7 (January 1976):4–9.

Corneel, Frederic G. "Valuation Techniques in Buy-Sell Agreements: Effect on Gift and Estate Taxes." *Institute on Federal Taxation, New York University* 24 (1966):631–69.

_____. "Effect of the 1976 Tax Reform Act on Stock Buy-Out Agreements and Other Close Corporation Plans." *Boston College Law Review* 19 (1977–1978):509–29.

Curtis, Sally Morrow, and Moore, Michael L. "Tax Free Redemption of Stock Should Be Considered in Estate Plan of Owner of Close Corporation." *Estate Planning* 2 (Autumn 1974):32–36.

Dan, Merwyn E. "An Updated Analysis of Tax Planning for Closely-Held Corporations and Their Shareholders." *Taxes* 56 (December 1978):897–903.

Denenberg, Howard M. "Stock Purchase Agreement: Redemption Usually, but not Always, Preferable to Cross Purchase." *Taxation for Accountants* 21 (August 1978):76–83.

Englebrecht, Ted D., and DeCelles, Michael. "Family Discord and Section 302 Stock Redemptions: A Review and Analysis." *Taxes* 58 (January 1980):43–50.

Fitzgerald, Michael O. "Estate Tax Implications of Close Corporate Stock Redemptions." *Trusts & Estates* 117 (April 1978):245–47.

Forster, Richard H. "Valuing a Business Interest for the Purposes of a Purchase and Sale Agreement." *Stanford Law Review* 4 (1951–1952):325–48.

Garrity, Vincent F. "Buy-Sell Agreements." *Pennsylvania Bar Association Quarterly* 46 (March 1975):190–99.

Ginsburg, Martin D., et al. *Corporate Buy-Sell Agreements.* Xerox Copy (1979).

Glickman, David G. "Stock Purchase Agreement." *ALI-ABA Course Materials Journal* 3 (October 1978):65–85.

Gorman, Joseph G. "The Buy-Sell Agreement as a Dispositionary Device: Tax and Valuation Problems in Transferring Corporate, Partnership and Real Estate Interests at Death." *Institute on Federal Taxation, New York Univeristy* 34 (1976): 1591–1620.

Hartwig, Joseph D. "Valuing an Interest in a Closely-Held Business for the Purpose of Buy-Sell Agreements and for Death Tax Purposes." *Tax Institute, University of Southern California* 26 (1974):215–75.

Hyatt, Jack N. "Approaches in Drafting Buy-Sell Agreements to Secure Planning Benefits under New Rules." *Estate Planning* 4 (September 1977):344–48.

Kahn, Douglas A. "Mandatory Buy-Out Agreements for Stock of Closely-Held Corporations." *Michigan Law Review* 68 (November 1969):1–64.

Kimbrough, A. R. "Buy-Sell Agreements." *Trusts & Estates* 97 (October 1958):925–28.

Kinkead, Sidney Clay, Jr. "Drafting an Effective Buy-Sell Agreement with Emphasis on Estate Tax Valuation of Close Corporate Stock." *Kentucky Law Journal* 53 (1964–1965):373–78.

Kuntz, Joel D. "Stock Redemptions Following Stock Transfers—An Expanding 'Safe Harbor' under Section 302(c)(2)(B)." *Taxes* 58 (January 1980):29–42.

Lefko, Orville B. "Buy-Sell Agreements and Appraisals." *Michigan State Bar Journal* 55 (February 1976):116–27.

Linowes, Harry M. "The Why and How of Corporate Buy-Out Agreements." *Tax Adviser* 6 (November 1975):654–58.

Linstroth, Paul J. "Stock Redemptions under Sections 302 and 306 of the 1954 Code and Tax Planning for Shareholders Terminating Their Interest in Closely-Held Corporations: Revenue Ruling 77–455." *Creighton Law Review* 11(2) (1978):1259–75.

Litman, Neal S. "Buy-Sell Agreements for a Closely-Held Corporation." *Florida Bar Journal* 50 (Novermber 1976):555–58.

Lundgren, Donald. "Estate Planning with the Corporation Buy-Out Agreements." *New York State Bar Journal* 48 (February 1976):115–18, 135–39.

Lynch, W. B. "New Look at Buy-Sell Agreements." *Tax Institute, University of Southern California* 30 (1978):775–99.

MacDougall, Francis. "Closely-Held Corporations: Insurance Planning for Redemptions and Buy-Sell Agreements." *Estate Planning* 5 (January 1978): 52–56.

Matsen, Jeffrey R. "Establishing the Price for Closely-Held Business Buy-Sell Agreements." *Journal of Corporate Taxation* 5 (Summer 1978):134–56.

_____. "A New Look at Business Buy-Out Agreements." *Practical Lawyer* 25 (July 1979):43–64.

Milston, Martin, and Cohn, Theodore. "Personal and Business Aspects of Stockholder Agreements." *Journal of Accountancy* (October 1967), pp. 41–45.

Page, David Keith. "Setting the Price in a Close Corporation Buy-Sell Agreement." *Michigan Law Review* 57 (1958–1959):655–84.

Painter, William Steene. "Stock-Purchase Transactions upon the Death of a Shareholder of a Closely-Held Corporation." *Mississippi Law Journal* 45 (November 1974):1191–1233.

Polasky, Alan N. "Planning for the Disposition of a Substantial Interest in a Closely-Held Business." *Tax Counselors' Quarterly* 6 (June 1962):195–216.

_____. "Planning for the Disposition of a Substantial Interest in a Closely-held Business, Part II." *Tax Counselors Quarterly* 6 (September 1962):319–42.

Pratt, James W., and Whittenburg, Gerald E. "How to Avoid Dividend Treatment when Planning the Redemption of Closely-Held Stock." *Taxation for Accountants* 16 (March 1976):146–50.

Rachlin, Robert. "An Analysis of the Impact of the Carryover Basis Rules on Close Corporation Buy-Out Arrangements." *CLU Journal* 33 (July 1979):54–60.

Ross, Sander B. "Buy-Out Agreement for Transfer of Stock in Family Corporation: Tax Planning." *Estate Planning* 1 (Winter 1974):103–09.

Simmons, Sherwin P. "Planning for Closely-Held Businesses." *Real Property, Probate, and Trust Journal* 12 (Winter 1977):644–52.

Stechel, Ira. "Restrictive Buy-Sell Agreements Can Limit Estate Tax Value of Business Interest." *Journal of Taxation* 44 (June 1976):360–66.

Stern, Milton H. "Buy-Sell Agreements." *Institute on Federal Taxation, New York University* 19 (1961):653–72.

_____. "A Different Approach to Price-Fixing in Stockholder's Stock Purchase Arrangements." *CLU Journal* 28 (July 1974):21–23.

Sturm, Maurice. "Fresh Start Basis and Stock Buy-Sell Agreements." *Practical Lawyer* 24 (March 1978):89–94.

Swanson, Robert D. "Cross-Purchase, Stock Redemption or Hybrid: Which Type of Buy-Sell Agreement Is Best?" *Taxation for Accountants* 24 (January 1980):34–38.

Thomas, Richard L. "How to Use a Buy-Sell Agreement to Protect a Client's Business and to Save Estate Taxes." *Estate Planning* (September 1979), pp. 258–64.

Tinio, Ferdinand S. "Valuation of Corporate Stock under Buy-Out or 'First Option' Agreement Giving Option to or Requiring Corporation or Other Stockholders to Purchase Stock of Deceased or Withdrawing Stockholders." *54 A.L.R. 3d 790* (1973, supplement 1979).

Turner, Bruce E., and Dillingham, Charles. "Most Buy-Sell Agreements Will Require Revision as a Result of the Tax Reform Act of 1976." *Taxation for Accountants* 18 (March 1977):138–46.

"The Use of Life Insurance to Fund Agreements Providing for Disposition of a Business Interest at Death." *Harvard Law Review* 71 (1958):687–712.

Wark, Jerry W. "Section 303 Stock Redemptions: A Post-1976 Tax Reform Act Appraisal." *Notre Dame Lawyer* 53 (June 1978):913–33.

Weinstock, Harold. "Buy-Sell Agreements." *Trust & Estates* 105 (April 1966):338–41.

Books

Guild, Alden. *Stock-Purchase Agreements and The Close Corporation.* 2d ed. Montpelier,: National Life Insurance Co., 1973.

Hull, Addis E. *Stock Purchase Agreements in Estate Planning— With Forms.* 2d ed. Englewood Cliffs, N.J.: Prentice-Hall, Inc., 1979.

22

SELLING OUT, GOING PUBLIC, AND OTHER TRANSACTIONS

SELLING OUT OR DIVESTING
Valuation of a forward-looking exercise
Finding a buyer and negotiating
Cash versus terms
Earn-outs (contingency payments)
Selling out for stock

VALUING PROSPECTIVE ACQUISITIONS

DISSENTING STOCKHOLDER APPRAISAL RIGHTS

GOING PUBLIC
Legal forms of registration
Selling stock to the public
Pricing and terms of the offering
Once the company is public

This last chapter gives brief discussions of a variety of types of transactions for which a value of all or part of a business must be determined. The general bibliography at the end of the book provides the reader a rather substantial body of source material, directed to the various situations discussed in this chapter.

The section on appraisal rights of dissenting stockholders is especially pertinent, since it discusses a set of circumstances in which valuations are subject to legal challenge and resolution by the courts. If every evaluation were done initially with conscious consideration to the possibility that it might be challenged in court, the result probably would be better valuations and fewer challenges.

In selling a business, as in selling almost anything, one should do homework thoroughly and put one's best values forward.

SELLING OUT OR DIVESTING

The sale of all or a part of a business is a forward-looking transaction. That is, the primary interest of the buyer will be in how much he will be able to earn on his investment. Therefore, the best approach in valuing the business for a sale usually is the discounted future earnings (DFE) approach presented in Chapter 4.

Valuation a forward-looking exercise

Use of the DFE approach requires several years' earnings projections with enough credibility to be convincing to a potential buyer. If such budgeting has been done for several years, and it can be demonstrated that actual results have approximated budgeted projections, the current projections generally will be far more convincing to a potential buyer than if such budgeting has not been done previously. For this and many other reasons, it is desirable to anticipate the possibility of the sale of the business and to plan accordingly, even though the prospective sale may be only a possibility and not a likelihood.

A valuation by the DFE approach also should be backed up by valuation by the other methods discussed in Chapter 5. This provides a cross-check on the DFE valuation and adds support to the credibility of the asking price as indicated by the DFE valuation. In general, the greater the amount by which the DFE valuation exceeds the valuation based on historical data, the more difficult it will be to convince the buyer of the realism of the value. If the projected profits are so far in excess of historical profits that any buyer would be skeptical that they could be achieved, but the owner of the business is convinced of their reality, then the best decision usually would be to keep running the business a while longer to demonstrate how the early portions of the projections can be achieved.

Besides doing a detailed and convincing job on forward budgeting, companies considering selling also should take steps to clean up their financial statements. They should attempt to remove self-dealing items, such as loans to or from officers, and any odd or unusual items, so the statements can be analyzed comparatively with other companies in the industry.

As discussed earlier in the book, certain industries have unique characteristics that lend themselves to certain specialized techniques or approaches in their valuation. In such cases, the approaches conventionally used in the particular industry should be considered. They may be used instead of some of the more general approaches discussed in this book, or, and usually preferably, in addition to the more general approaches as a further cross-check on the reasonableness of a particular value. As discussed earlier, approaches focusing on gross revenues frequently are employed in selling service-type businesses, such as advertising, public relations, insurance, and various types of brokerage agencies, professional practices, and mortuaries. The bibliography contains references to specialized aspects of analyzing businesses in a variety of specific industries.

Finding a buyer and negotiating

As discussed in Chapter 9, the exercise of going through the comparables search will have the ancillary benefit of developing a partial list of potential buyers. Other likely buyers would include customers or suppliers who might be interested in vertical integration, or companies in related fields that might be interested in diversification.

Even if a company has a fairly good prospect list, it usually works out best to employ professional assistance to locate a buyer and negotiate a deal. A professional intermediary usually can keep the identity of the seller confidential up to the point where a seriously interested buyer has been located. The experience of a good professional intermediary can be very helpful in locating a buyer and in structuring and negotiating the terms of a deal. Negotiations and reasonable compromise frequently tend to progress much more smoothly—and with less risk of a deal falling apart—when a professional third-party intermediary is involved.

There are no hard and fast guidelines on how to find the right intermediary who can sell any particular business. However, business intermediaries tend to fall into two broad categories, "business brokers" and "mergers and acquisition specialists."

The former, the business brokers, tend to work in a limited geographical area and handle small localized businesses, such as stores, restaurants, cocktail lounges, taverns, and similar enterprises. Real estate brokers frequently become involved in the sale of local businesses, and some have a specialist or a special department to handle such transactions.

Merger and acquisition specialists tend to operate either regionally or nationally. They may be independent merger and acquisition firms, or they may be departments of other types of institutions, such as commercial banks or stock brokerage firms with investment banking capabilities.

If the initial business valuation has been done by an independent valuation firm not engaged in the merger and acquisition business, then the valuation firm should be able to make unbiased referrals to specific firms or to a type of firm that would be appropriate for selling a particular business. Of course, the independent business appraisal firm also should be able to offer unbiased guidance on the relative advantages of different methods for a seller to gain liquidity, such as selling out, going public, or forming an ESOP.

When selling out, one of the critical decisions is whether the stock of the business or the assets will be sold. The compelling consideration in making this choice usually is the tax consequences, because they affect the buyer and the seller. It is essential to employ competent tax counsel in reaching this decision.

Cash versus terms

A commonly heard expression is, "I'll pay you any price you want, if you let me name the terms." This deserves more consideration than most people accord it. Terms other than cash can be effective to ease the tax burden to the seller and to ease the buyer's front-end cash requirements. However, the practical effect of most sets of terms is to reduce the true present value of the deal to something less than the face value.

For example, consider a case where a business is sold for $1 million, with nothing down, on a contract at 8 percent interest, paid off in equal payments at the end of each year for 20 years. What is the present cash value of this sale?

The value is computed by using the present value formula, shown in Chapter 4. As noted, it can be implemented easily by using a hand business calculator that has discounting and compounding functions or by using the tables in Appendix A.

The first step is to determine the appropriate capitalization rate to apply to the contract. As discussed in Part I, the appropriate rate is the return available on other contracts or instruments of similar maturity, risk, and investment characteristics. The main factors to consider in assessing the risk are the degree of protection provided, through collateral and protective covenants in the sale contract, and the coverage of principal and interest payments, available from whatever is the source of payment of the contract. To be conservative, we will assume that the market rate of return on comparable contracts is 15 percent, although during 1980 the rate of return on most contracts was higher than that. Using a hand calculator that computes annuities, the annual payment on the contract just described is $101,852. The present value of that contract would be computed as:

$$PV = \sum \frac{FV_i}{(1 + r)^n}$$
$$= \sum \frac{\$101,852}{(1 + .15)} + \frac{\$101,852}{(1 + .15)^2} + \cdots + \frac{\$101,852}{(1 + .15)^{20}}$$
$$= \underline{\$637,525}$$

In other words, in the above case, the present value of the contract is less than 65 percent of the face value of the contract.

The previous paragraph noted that collateral and covenants are important factors to consider in assessing the risk of the contract when selling on terms instead of cash. Covenants usually cover such things as requiring some minimum amount of net working capital to be maintained, some maximum debt to equity ratio, and some other protections so that cash to be used in payments on the contract will not be drawn off for other uses. The longer the term of the contract, the less the down payment, and the lower the ratio of the funds available to the amount of the payments, the stronger the collateral and the covenants should be.

Earn-outs (contingency payments)

If the seller's projections of future profits are higher than the buyer is willing to accept and pay for, the solution sometimes used is called an "earn-out." Here, the buyer agrees to a mimumum price—but also agrees to additional payments when profits will exceed some agreed-upon level. This can be a satisfactory way for the seller to prove the earnings potential that he projects, and thus be paid for it. However, I would recommend the use of an earn-out sale only where the seller remains in the operating managment control of the business during the period of the earn-out. Otherwise, the seller's projections may fail to be met, because the operating policies the seller assumed in making the projections may not be carried out as anticipated.

Selling out for stock

When selling stockholders receive stock of the acquiring corporation instead of cash, the transaction usually is treated as a tax-free exchange, thus avoiding payment of capital gains tax at the time of the transaction. The stock received may be either registered or unregistered.

If the stock is registered, this means that the selling shareholders receiving the stock may sell it on the open public market at any time. In this case it is desirable to make an analytical report on the acquiring company available to the selling shareholders, so each shareholder can make his own decision about retaining or selling the stock received.

Unregistered stock may be stock of another closely-held corporation or it may be unregistered shares of a publicly-traded corporation. In such cases the valuation task is effectively doubled, since both the acquiring and the selling companies must be valued to determine an appropriate exchange ratio.

If selling out a public company for stock, the transaction and the subsequent rights of the selling stockholders to dispose of the stock are governed by SEC Rules 144 and 146. Typically, the selling stockholders are restricted from selling the public company's stock that they received for a period of two years. After that, the amount that can be sold at any given time is a percentage of the public company stock's average trading volume. During the two-year restricted period the stock may be sold in an exempt private transaction, under certain circumstances.

In past years there have been many instances of private companies selling out to public companies whose stocks happened to be selling at inflated prices at the time, only to watch the public company's stock price plummet 50 percent or more before the recipient was legally eligible to put it on the market. SEC rules now provide for a private company contemplating selling out to a public company to retain a qualified offeree representative to analyze the valuation and analyze other nonlegal aspects of the proposed transaction for the selling stockholders. The offeree representative is strictly responsible to the selling stockholders, even though the prospective acquirer may pay for the offeree representative's services.

SEC regulations regarding stock transactions are complex and subject to frequent change. Anyone contemplating a stock transaction should retain the services of expert legal counsel familiar with such transactions, as well as qualified appraisal consultation.

VALUING PROSPECTIVE ACQUISITIONS

Valuation of a prospective acquisition should be guided by the same criteria as if you were selling out your own company. The valuation is primarily a prospective, rather than a retrospective exercise, applied to the entity under consideration.

Most companies considering making an acquisition have a fairly good idea whether the prospect will make a good fit from an operational standpoint. On the other hand, few potential acquirers seem to be able to take an objective approach on how much should be paid. Many acquirers become so excited about an acquisition being a good fit that they succumb to paying an economically unjustifiable price; the result is that it may be many years, if ever, before the benefits of the acquisition can be translated into a reasonable rate of return on the investment made. At the other extreme, many good acquisitions are thwarted by the inability of the acquirer to place an adequate value on the acquiree, and thus, to offer a reasonable price. This book, I hope, will provide guidance away from those uneconomic extremes and toward a reasonable middle ground in which mutually beneficial negotiations can take place. Independent outside valuation counsel frequently can be helpful in this respect.

One important question in some cases is, How much added value from the synergy of a merger should be reflected in the price offered the prospective acquiree? Ideally, one might expect this prospective benefit to be divided between the acquirer and acquiree, so that the acquiree receives a premium above its value as a free-standing company, while the acquirer still buys it on the basis that its rate of return on investment will be higher than what is available on alternative investments.

As a practical matter, the realities of the merger market tend to be a dominant factor influencing the outcome in such situations. If there is only one potential acquirer for whom the synergy would have significant economic benefit, the price offered to the seller is not likely to reflect a very large proportion of that synergistic benefit. If, on the other hand, there are many acquirers competing to obtain the benefits available from a limited number of potential sellers, a large proportion of the economic value of the synergy may go to the seller.

DISSENTING STOCKHOLDER APPRAISAL RIGHTS

Most states give minority stockholders the right to dissent if a company sells out, merges, consolidates, sells substantially all of its assets, or undergoes some other fundamental change. In most cases, the dissenters' remedy is to have the value of their shares appraised—and be paid that value in cash.

If a minority stockholder wishes to dissent, most states require that the decision to dissent be registered in writing at or within a few days following the stockholder meeting when the corporate action in question was approved by the majority of stockholders. Most statutes specify that the valuation date to be used in the appraisal will be the day prior to the stockholder action. The implication is that the potential effect of the action itself on the value of the shares, such as some synergistic benefit between acquirer and acquiree, will not be taken into consideration. A typical example of this point is the phrasing of an Ohio court opinion, which stated, "There shall be excluded from such value any appreciation or depreciation resulting from the proposal acted upon at said meeting."[1]

The most ambiguous aspect of most state statutes on dissenting stockholder appraisal rights is lack of a clear definition of value. An excellent article in the *Harvard Law Review* on valuation of dissenter's stock stated the problem concisely: "The statutes do not define value, and different techniques of valuation can produce wide variations."[2] A California court opinion included the following note regarding this state of confusion:

Many writers prefer some . . . definition, such as . . . "fair cash value," or as "intrinsic value" or "real value" or "fair value," etc. We do not know what those terms or others like them mean, and we suspect that the writers who advocate them do not know either.[3]

There is a leaning on the part of the courts toward acceptance of fair market value as a standard of value in dissenting stockholder cases, but this is by no means unanimous. Most statutes still contain the more ambiguous language, such as *fair value* or *fair cash value* as a standard of value. These terms seem to suggest that there may be some underlying or intrinsic value that is different from fair market value.

The *Harvard Law Review* article also addresses the issue of why the value for a dissenting stockholder action might be different than the value for tax purposes:

---

[1]*Vought v. Republic-Franklin Ins. Co.,* 117 Ohio App. 389, 392, 192 N.E. 2d 332, 333 (1962).

[2]"Valuation of Dissenters' Stock under Appraisal Statutes," 30 *Harvard Law Review,* (May, 1966): 1453.

[3]*Gallois v. West End Chemical Co.,* 185 Cal.App.2d 767,774, 8 Cal.Rptr. 596 (1960); quoted in Edwin M. Rams, "Judicial Valuation of Dissenting Shareholder Interests," *Lincoln Law Reviews* (1973):76.

Some appraisers and courts tend to assume that accounting valuations of corporations and of stock, for other purposes, can serve as models for appraisal valuation. Although this may sometimes be true, more often the method should depend on the reason for the valuation. For example, it might be supposed that the techniques applied in valuing corporate shares for federal estate or gift tax purposes would be equally applicable to the appraisal remedy. But in a tax appraisal the stockholder or his beneficiary does not part with his interest in the earnings and growth of the company. Valuation merely establishes a figure on which to base the tax. In the appraisal situation, however, anticipated earnings are especially important because the dissenter is surrendering his opportunity to share in the future of the company. Moreover, in an estate tax valuation the corporation is not directly affected by the outcome, whereas in valuing the dissenter's stock a balance must be struck between the interests of the minority stockholder and those of the corporation.[4]

Whether the standard of value used is "fair market value," "fair value," or some other standard, there had been a strong tendency for appraisers and courts to utilize the weighted average method of balancing out the various factors affecting the value, such as earning capacity, asset values, dividends, and prior transactions in the company's shares or other evidence of market value. As a broad generality, the proportionate weights applied to these various factors in dissenting stockholder cases have been consistent with the appropriate weightings discussed for other purposes elsewhere in this book.

As might be expected, the outcomes of cases brought by dissenting stockholders have varied widely. In one case in which I testified, the company had sold out for $3.75 per share, and the stockholders who dissented were awarded $9 per share.[5] At the other end of the spectrum, there have been many cases where dissenters have incurred thousands of dollars of legal fees and years of delay in getting their money, only to be awarded the amount originally offered.[6] Once a stockholder has dissented, he cannot be assured of receiving the amount of the original offer.

From the viewpoint of the directors or controlling stockholders desiring to effect a sell-out or merger, the best procedure to avoid the likelihood of a dissenter stockholder suit is to retain an independent outside appraisal to provide an opinion on the fairness of the terms on behalf of the stockholders as an integral part of the selling or merging process. Ideally, the report and the appraisers themselves would be made available to answer questions of any stockholders who might have any doubts about the fairness of the terms or how the price was arrived at and justified.

From the viewpoint of the minority stockholder, if he has doubts about the fairness of the value after receiving all the available information from the company, the first step would be to retain an independent appraiser to obtain a preliminary opinion on the value. If there appears to be a significant

---

[4]"Valuation of Dissenters' Stock," pp. 1454–55.

[5]Charles Humble, "Court Upholds 'Little Guy' . . ." *Oregon Journal* (June 29, 1976) (3)–9.

[6]For example, see *Matter of Dimmock v. Reichold Chemicals Inc.,* 41 N.Y.2d 273, 360 N.E.2d 1079, 392 N.Y.S.2d 396 (1977); *Application of Dorsey,* 31 Misc.2d 747, 221 N.Y.S.2d 927 (Sup.Ct.N.Y. Co. 1961); *Lewis v. Bogin,* 337 F.Supp. 331, 334 (S.D.N.Y. 1972.

discrepancy in value, then the stockholder can pursue his dissenter's appraisal rights.

GOING PUBLIC

The primary reasons for a closely-held company to go public are to raise capital and to gain liquidity for existing stockholders. Some managements also feel there is benefit from the degree of exposure and prestige associated with being a public company.

The primary disadvantage of going public is cost—both the cost of the initial offering and the ongoing cost of complying with public company reporting requirements. Some managements also consider the information disclosure requirements imposed on a public company to be a serious disadvantage, for competitive, personal, or other reasons.

Furthermore, the price of a public company's stock can be subject to volatile (and not necessarily rational) price swings. If the price is exhorbitantly high, it can render new stock options nearly useless as a form of management compensation. If the price is unduly depressed, which can be the case for extended periods, it can impose a hardship on those who need or desire to sell. One advantage of the closely-held company ESOP over the public market is that the annual independent professional valuation may produce a more orderly market at a more rationally determined price level than might be the case when the stock is subject to the whim of the public market, especially for a small company.

For the company that may want to consider a public offering, this section offers a brief primer on what options are available as legal forms of registration and also as avenues for selling the stock. There also are discussions of pricing and terms in connection with the initial offering, and legal reporting requirements and desirable investor communications procedures to follow once the company is public.

The material in this section is offered only as a broad guide, and not as a technical treatise on legal requirements. Securities regulation is one of the most specialized and complex areas of U.S. law. Anyone contemplating a public securities offering should consult with competent counsel who is experienced in working with securities law.

Legal forms of registration

There are three primary forms of federal registration. Going from the most to the least complex, these are known as the S–1, the S–18, and the Regulation A. There is also an abbreviated form, a Rule 242 filing. Private placements may be exempt from federal regulation if they meet certain requirements. In some states a registration with the SEC automatically qualifies the securities for sale in the particular state. However, the majority of states require registration if securities are to be offered in the state, even though they also are registered with the SEC.

Some states impose criteria that are in some respects more stringent than the federal criteria. The point of SEC registration is to require full disclosure of material information. Oregon, for example, not only requires full disclosure but also requires that the offering be "fair, just, and equitable." It is up to the state Corporation Commission to determine whether each proposed offering meets this latter standard. Many offerings that have been approved by the SEC and by other states have been rejected in Oregon for not meeting the "fair, just, and equitable" standard.

Federal registration can be avoided if the securities are offered only in a single state. However, there are several disadvantages to such an offering.

S–1 registration. The most comprehensive securities registration form is the S–1. There is no limit to the amount of capital that can be raised under an S–1 registration form. The securities may all be offered by the issuer, all by one or more existing stockholders, or any combination thereof. Once an S–1 registration has been approved by the SEC it can be offered in any or all states in which it also has been approved or which automatically allow federally registered offerings.

The S–1 is the most lengthy and detailed of the securities registration forms. Thus it normally entails the greatest legal, accounting, and printing costs. The S–1 must be filed with the SEC headquarters office in Washington, D.C. Besides being the most costly, the S–1 filing also tends to require the most lead time to complete and gain SEC approval. It is not uncommon to take six months or more to prepare and amend the document to the satisfaction of the SEC.

S–18 registration. On April 23, 1979, the SEC adopted the Form S–18 Registration Statement. It may be used for offerings up to $5 million, of which not more than $1.5 million may be for the account of selling shareholders. It may be used by most types of companies, but not by natural resource companies, investment companies, or certain other types of companies.

The form omits some of the information required in the full S–1 registration. Perhaps more important is that it may be filed at any of the regional offices of the SEC, rather than at the headquarters in Washington, D.C., if the issuer so desires. The regional offices usually are less backlogged and provide speedier approval than the Washington, D.C., headquarters.

During 1979 there were 41 Form S–18s filed with the SEC, 27 of which completed the registration process and became effective during the year. A survey by the SEC indicated that the registration costs were less on the average than for comparable S–1 registrations. The SEC survey also indicated that average processing time was shorter for the S–18s than for comparable Form S–1s, and that issuers who took advantage of the Form S–18 regional office filing option experienced shorter processing times than those issuers who elected to file at the commission's headquarters office. Our office has done the due diligence work for several of the early S–18 offerings. Our contact with the issuing companies, their attorneys and bankers, and their underwriters indicate that this modified registration procedure will be quite helpful in making it more feasible for smaller companies to complete successful public offerings.

Regulation A registration. Congress has authorized the SEC to allow the more abbreviated "Reg A" registration to be used for offerings up to $2 million. At the time of this writing, the SEC has implemented this authority to the extent of allowing Reg A filings for offerings up to $1.5 million. The securities may be offered by the issuing corporation, by existing stockholders, or any combination thereof. The Reg A may be filed at the regional SEC offices, and is less costly and time-consuming than the S–1 or S–18.

Rule 242 sales and private placements. Effective February 25, 1980, the SEC adopted Rule 242 to facilitate small offerings to a limited number of purchasers. The maximum offering under the rule is $2 million. The securities may be sold to any number of accredited persons, defined to include institutional type purchasers, purchasers of at least $100,000 of securities, and the issuer's officers and directors. It also allows the securities to be sold to up to 35 other nonaccredited purchasers. No general advertising or solicitation is permitted for sales under this rule, and securities sold under it cannot be resold without registration as an exemption therefrom. To the extent that sales are made to nonaccredited persons under the rule, a portion of the information required in the Form S–18 must be furnished to the purchasers.

Securities usually are exempt from registration if they are sold on a private placement basis. A seller contemplating a private placement of securities should consult legal counsel to be sure that the offering will qualify as being exempt from registration.

Intrastate offering. If all of the securities in a public offering are offered and sold only to the residents of a particular state, the offering needs to be registered only with that state and not with the SEC. There is no limit on the number of dollars that can be raised nor on the number of people to whom the securities may be offered. The costs and time required run substantially less than for an S–1 registration, more in line with a Reg A offering.

Many companies have successfully used intrastate offerings to raise millions of dollars. However, intrastate offerings have some serious disadvantages.

For one thing, the seller may inadvertently violate the securities laws by selling to someone who is not a bona fide resident of the state in which the offering is registered. Second, the purchaser may not resell to other buyers outside the state for a considerable time. This severely limits the aftermarket liquidity of the offering, thus reducing its attractiveness. Broker-dealers in the stock market do not like to deal in securities that are subject to intrastate restrictions, because they are afraid of inadvertently violating the securities laws by selling to a non-bona fide resident of the state of the offering. An intrastate offering thus tends to suffer considerably from lack of marketability, compared with an offering registered with the SEC under the S–1, S–18, or Reg A registration provisions.

Selling stock to the public

If a company decides to make a public offering, it must decide whether to use the services of an investment banker or attempt to sell the securities itself.

In most cases it works out much better to use the services of an investment banker.

Most companies tend to think that it will be much easier to sell the stock to the public than actually turns out to be the case. Amid rose-tinted enthusiasm for their own company, they tend to overestimate the zeal with which the investing public will gobble up their securities. Many of the outside people who look fondly on the company may not be security investors at all. Those who are may not happen to have any liquid resources available at the time of the offering. It is the business of an investment banker to keep in touch with a large number of active investors at all times. A good investment banker will have a pretty good idea of how much of a particular offering he can reasonably expect to sell to his clientele at any particular time. Working with a competent investment banker substantially reduces the risk of the offering failing or falling short of raising the desired amount of capital.

Another major disadvantage of a do-it-yourself offering is the lack of an aftermarket. An investment banker who handles the sale of an offering, frequently with the participation of a number of stock brokerage firms in the selling group, usually arranges to have the stock quoted on a regular basis OTC (over the counter) following the offering. It usually is difficult to interest brokers in doing this if they did not participate in the sale in the first place. Therefore, securities sold by the companies themselves usually suffer from lack of marketability for an indefinite time after the offering, many of them forever.

Selecting an investment banker. The investment banking firm selected to handle the offering should be large enough to be able to get the entire offering sold, and, preferably, should be well represented in the areas where the issuing company is best known.

If the offering is relatively small, a regional investment banking firm usually is the best choice. In fact, all of the S–18 offerings sold by brokers in 1979 were through regional investment bankers, not national houses. Inquiry should be made on what investment bankers have established a successful track record in selling offerings of the size and type contemplated. An outside independent valuation consultant or corporate finance consultant usually can be quite helpful to the company in this respect. Such a consultant also can be helpful in guiding the issuing company to a reasonable level of underwriting fees for a given size and type of issue.

The best market for the company's securities usually is where the company is located or where it is most visible. For this reason, it is desirable to choose an investment banker who is well represented in the issuing company's area.

Firm underwriting versus best efforts offering. The term *firm underwriting* means *the underwriting firm guarantees the issuer of the securities that the issuer will receive the agreed-upon proceeds of the offering.* In other words, the underwriter is obligated to pay the issuer the net proceeds that have been contracted whether or not the underwriter is successful in selling the entire issue at the public offering price. Firm underwritings generally are undertaken on behalf of the larger and better established issuers of securities.

Smaller companies, especially those going to the public market for the first time, and those of a somewhat speculative nature, frequently have to settle for a best efforts offering. This means that the underwriting firm will use its best efforts to sell the entire offering, but does not guarantee it.

A best efforts offering can prescribe that a certain amount must be sold, and if not sold, have the money returned to the purchasers; or it may prescribe that whatever amount has been sold by a pre-determined date then be turned over to the issuer, with the offering closed at that point. Exactly what arrangement will be appropriate will depend to some extent on the purpose of the offering. If the purpose is to build a new plant, which will require some minimum amount of capital, there usually will be a minimum amount of proceeds that will be acceptable. If the offering is for another purpose, such as repayment of debt or building up working capital, it might not be necessary to set any minimum amount.

Most best efforts issues are sold out in full, but certainly not all. When it is necessary to do an offering on a best efforts basis, it is especially important to make a good assessment of the capability of the investment banking firm to sell the full amount of the offering.

Pricing and terms of the offering

The pricing of public offerings relies very heavily on the analysis of prices at which other comparable publicly traded securities are selling in the market-place. When a company makes its first public offering, usually most or all of the proceeds will go to the company rather than to the selling shareholders. Most practitioners agree that it is a good idea to price the initial offering a little on the conservative side in the hope that the market will establish and maintain a rising price trend. This generally is considered preferable to setting the price as high as possible, which increases the risk that investors could suffer losses either if the company has a bit of misfortune or if bad market conditions are encountered, thus jeopardizing the viability of future offerings.

Sometimes an initial offering can be made more attractive to the investing public by structuring it some other way than straight common stock. For example, a convertible bond offers the investor some interest income, plus a security that is senior to the common stock. Another popular structure is to issue units, which can consist of either debt or equity-type securities with warrants attached. There is almost no limit to the possible ramifications in creative structuring of an offering. This is a matter that the investment banker will want to address. The experience of the investment banker should be very helpful in this respect.

Once the company is public

Following a public securities offering, a company is subject to ongoing legal requirements to report financial and other information to the SEC and to stockholders. It also is desirable to have an ongoing program of communications with existing and prospective stockholders and brokers beyond the minimum reporting and information distribution required by law.

Legal reporting requirements. A public company must report regularly to stockholders and also must comply with the additional requirements of the annual 10–K, quarterly 10–Q, and special events 8–K which must be filed with the SEC. The various required forms and their contents are summarized in Exhibit 9–1. If a company goes public using an S–18 registration, its annual reporting requirements on Form 10–K are ameliorated for two years to the extent that the company need only update the disclosures required in Form S–18.

Investor communications and relations. There are many good reasons to maintain an active investor relations program beyond the minimum required by law. For one thing, a consistent investor relations program can help to maintain an active trading market in the stock at a reasonable price. Also, the company very likely will want to go to the public market with an additional offering at some future time. The better appreciated the company is in the financial markets, the easier an additional offering at a reasonable price will be.

As conditions stand in the early 1980s, there are tens of thousands of public securities competing for a limited amount of public interest in owning those securities. A company contemplating a public offering should plan to commit a budget for an ongoing program of investor relations to maintain public interest in the stock once the initial offering has been accomplished.

APPENDIX A
PRESENT VALUE TABLES

Finding the present value (discounted future earnings method)

PRESENT VALUE OF ONE DOLLAR DUE AT THE END OF N YEARS

HOW TO USE:

Suppose that you want to determine the present value of $1,331 that is to be paid three years from now, and you require a 10% discount rate. Substituting in the formula $PV = \dfrac{A_i}{(1+r)^n}$, we have $\dfrac{\$1,331}{(1+.10)^3}$. Instead of working out this somewhat complicated operation, we can use Appendix Table A-1 to find the answer. Going to the "10%" column and then down to row "3" (n = 3 years), we find the value .75131. To find the present value of $1,331 paid three years from now using a 10% discount rate, we **multiply** $1,331 by the value found in the table, .75131. This results in a present value of approximately $1,000 ($1,331 x .75131 = $999.99).

To find the present value of any amount, multiply that amount by the corresponding value found in the table for the discount rate being used and the number of years until payment.

More detailed compound value and present value tables are available, including a booklet entitled **Compound Interest Tables** published by Union Carbide Corp. and available from its public relations department (270 Park Ave., N.Y.C.) at no cost.

PRESENT VALUE OF AN ANNUITY OF ONE DOLLAR FOR N YEARS

HOW TO USE:

Suppose that you want to determine the present value of an income stream of $1,000 to be paid in each of the next 3 years, and you require a discount rate of 10%. Substituting in the formula $PV = \Sigma \dfrac{A_i}{(1+r)^n}$, we have:

$$\frac{\$1,000}{(1+.10)^1} + \frac{\$1,000}{(1+.10)^2} + \frac{\$1,000}{(1+.10)^3}$$

Instead of working out this somewhat complicated operation, we can use Appendix Table A-2 to find the answer. Going across to the "10%" column and then down to row "3" (n = 3 years), we find the value 2.4868. To find the present value of an income stream of $1,000 paid in each of the next three years using a 10% discount rate, we **multiply** $1,000 by the value found in the table, 2.4868. The result is a present value of $2,486.80 ($1,000 x 2.4868 = $2,486.80).

To find the present value of any income stream, **multiply** the annual payment amount by the corresponding value found in the table for the discount rate being used and the number of years payments are to be received.

Source: Shannon P. Pratt and Craig S. Hugo, "Pricing a Company by the Discounted Future Earnings Method," *Mergers & Acquisitions* (Spring 1972), p. 26. Reprinted with permission from *Mergers & Acquisitions* (Spring 1972), © 1972 Information for Industry, Inc. 229 S. 18th Street, Philadelphia, Pennsylvania 19103. All rights reserved.

APPENDIX TABLE A-1
Present Value of One Dollar Due at the End of n Years

n	1%	2%	3%	4%	5%	6%	7%	8%	9%	10%	n
1	.99010	.98039	.97007	.96154	.95238	.94340	.93458	.92593	.91743	.90909	1
2	.98030	.96117	.94260	.92456	.90703	.89000	.87344	.85734	.84168	.82645	2
3	.97059	.94232	.91514	.88900	.86384	.83962	.81630	.79383	.77218	.75131	3
4	.96098	.92385	.88849	.85480	.82270	.79209	.76290	.73503	.70843	.68301	4
5	.95147	.90573	.86261	.82193	.78353	.74726	.71299	.68058	.64993	.62092	5
6	.94204	.88797	.83748	.79031	.74622	.70496	.66634	.63017	.59627	.56447	6
7	.93272	.87056	.81309	.75992	.71068	.66506	.62275	.58349	.54703	.51316	7
8	.92348	.85349	.78941	.73069	.67684	.62741	.58201	.54027	.50187	.46651	8
9	.91434	.83675	.76642	.70259	.64461	.59190	.54393	.50025	.46043	.42410	9
10	.90529	.82035	.74409	.67556	.61391	.55839	.50835	.46319	.42241	.38554	10
11	.89632	.80426	.72242	.64958	.58468	.52679	.47509	.42888	.38753	.35049	11
12	.88745	.78849	.70138	.62460	.55684	.49697	.44401	.39711	.35553	.31863	12
13	.87866	.77303	.68095	.60057	.53032	.46884	.41496	.36770	.32618	.28966	13
14	.86996	.75787	.66112	.57747	.50507	.44230	.38782	.34046	.29925	.26333	14
15	.86135	.74301	.64186	.55526	.48102	.41726	.36245	.31524	.27454	.23939	15
16	.85282	.72845	.62317	.53391	.45811	.39365	.33873	.29189	.25187	.21763	16
17	.84438	.71416	.60502	.51337	.43630	.37136	.31657	.27027	.23107	.19784	17
18	.83602	.70016	.58739	.49363	.41552	.35034	.29586	.25025	.21199	.17986	18
19	.82774	.68643	.57029	.47464	.39573	.33051	.27651	.23171	.19449	.16351	19
20	.81954	.67297	.55367	.45639	.37689	.31180	.25842	.21455	.17843	.14864	20
21	.81143	.65978	.53755	.43883	.35894	.29415	.24151	.19866	.16370	.13513	21
22	.80340	.64684	.52189	.42195	.34185	.27750	.22571	.18394	.15018	.12285	22
23	.79544	.63414	.50669	.40573	.32557	.26180	.21095	.17031	.13778	.11168	23
24	.78757	.62172	.49193	.39012	.31007	.24698	.19715	.15770	.12640	.10153	24
25	.77977	.60953	.47760	.37512	.29530	.23300	.18425	.14602	.11597	.09230	25

Present Value of One Dollar Due at the End of n Years

n	11%	12%	13%	14%	15%	16%	17%	18%	19%	20%	n
1	.90090	.89286	.88496	.87719	.86957	.86207	.85470	.84746	.84034	.83333	1
2	.81162	.79719	.78315	.76947	.75614	.74316	.73051	.71818	.70616	.69444	2
3	.73119	.71178	.69305	.67497	.65752	.64066	.62437	.60863	.59342	.57870	3
4	.65873	.63552	.61332	.59208	.57175	.55229	.53365	.51579	.49867	.48225	4
5	.59345	.56743	.54276	.51937	.49718	.47611	.45611	.43711	.41905	.40188	5
6	.53464	.50663	.48032	.45559	.43233	.41044	.38984	.37043	.35214	.33490	6
7	.48166	.45235	.42506	.39964	.37594	.35383	.33320	.31392	.29592	.27908	7
8	.43393	.40388	.37616	.35056	.32690	.30503	.28478	.26604	.24867	.23257	8
9	.39092	.36061	.33288	.30751	.28426	.26295	.24340	.22546	.20897	.19381	9
10	.35218	.32197	.29459	.26974	.24718	.22668	.20804	.19106	.17560	.16151	10
11	.31728	.28748	.26070	.23662	.21494	.19542	.17781	.16192	.14756	.13459	11
12	.28584	.25667	.23071	.20756	.18691	.16846	.15197	.13722	.12400	.11216	12
13	.25751	.22917	.20416	.18207	.16253	.14523	.12989	.11629	.10420	.09346	13
14	.23199	.20462	.18068	.15971	.14133	.12520	.11102	.09855	.08757	.07789	14
15	.20900	.18270	.15989	.14010	.12289	.10793	.09489	.08352	.07359	.06491	15
16	.18829	.16312	.14150	.12289	.10686	.09304	.08110	.07078	.06184	.05409	16
17	.16963	.14564	.12522	.10780	.09293	.08021	.06932	.05998	.05196	.04507	17
18	.15282	.13004	.11081	.09456	.08080	.06914	.05925	.05083	.04367	.03756	18
19	.13768	.11611	.09806	.08295	.07026	.05961	.05064	.04308	.03669	.03130	19
20	.12403	.10367	.08678	.07276	.06110	.05139	.04328	.03651	.03084	.02608	20
21	.11174	.09256	.07680	.06383	.05313	.04430	.03699	.03094	.02591	.02174	21
22	.10067	.08264	.06796	.05599	.04620	.03819	.03162	.02622	.02178	.01811	22
23	.09069	.07379	.06014	.04911	.04017	.03292	.02702	.02222	.01830	.01509	23
24	.08170	.06588	.05322	.04308	.03493	.02838	.02310	.01883	.01538	.01258	24
25	.07361	.05882	.04710	.03779	.03038	.02447	.01974	.01596	.01292	.01048	25

APPENDIX TABLE A-1 (Cont.)
Present Value of One Dollar Due at the End of *n* Years

n	21%	22%	23%	24%	25%	26%	27%	28%	29%	30%	n
1	.82645	.81967	.81301	.80645	.80000	.79365	.78740	.78125	.77519	.76923	1
2	.68301	.67186	.66098	.65036	.64000	.62988	.62000	.61035	.60093	.59172	2
3	.56447	.55071	.53738	.52449	.51200	.49991	.48819	.47684	.46583	.45517	3
4	.46651	.45140	.43690	.42297	.40960	.39675	.38440	.37253	.36111	.35013	4
5	.38554	.37000	.35520	.34111	.32768	.31488	.30268	.29104	.27993	.26933	5
6	.31863	.30328	.28878	.27509	.26214	.24991	.23833	.22737	.21700	.20718	6
7	.26333	.24859	.23478	.22184	.20972	.19834	.18766	.17764	.16822	.15937	7
8	.21763	.20376	.19088	.17891	.16777	.15741	.14776	.13878	.13040	.12259	8
9	.17986	.16702	.15519	.14428	.13422	.12493	.11635	.10842	.10109	.09430	9
10	.14864	.13690	.12617	.11635	.10737	.09915	.09161	.08470	.07836	.07254	10
11	.12285	.11221	.10258	.09383	.08590	.07869	.07214	.06617	.06075	.05580	11
12	.10153	.09198	.08339	.07567	.06872	.06245	.05680	.05170	.04709	.04292	12
13	.08391	.07539	.06780	.06103	.05498	.04957	.04472	.04039	.03650	.03302	13
14	.06934	.06180	.05512	.04921	.04398	.03934	.03522	.03155	.02830	.02540	14
15	.05731	.05065	.04481	.03969	.03518	.03122	.02773	.02465	.02194	.01954	15
16	.04736	.04152	.03643	.03201	.02815	.02478	.02183	.01926	.01700	.01503	16
17	.03914	.03403	.02962	.02581	.02252	.01967	.01719	.01505	.01318	.01156	17
18	.03235	.02789	.02408	.02082	.01801	.01561	.01354	.01175	.01022	.00889	18
19	.02673	.02286	.01958	.01679	.01441	.01239	.01066	.00918	.00792	.00684	19
20	.02209	.01874	.01592	.01354	.01153	.00983	.00839	.00717	.00614	.00526	20
21	.01826	.01536	.01294	.01092	.00922	.00780	.00661	.00561	.00476	.00405	21
22	.01509	.01259	.01052	.00880	.00738	.00619	.00520	.00438	.00369	.00311	22
23	.01247	.01032	.00855	.00710	.00590	.00491	.00410	.00342	.00286	.00239	23
24	.01031	.00846	.00695	.00573	.00472	.00390	.00323	.00267	.00222	.00184	24
25	.00852	.00693	.00565	.00462	.00378	.00310	.00254	.00209	.00172	.00142	25

APPENDIX TABLE A-2
Present Value of an Annuity of One Dollar for n Year

n	1%	2%	3%	4%	5%	6%	7%	8%	9%	10%	n
1	.9901	.9804	.9709	.9615	.9524	.9434	.9346	.9259	.9174	.9091	1
2	1.9704	1.9416	1.9135	1.8861	1.8594	1.8334	1.8080	1.7833	1.7591	1.7355	2
3	2.9410	2.8839	2.8286	2.7751	2.7232	2.6730	2.6243	2.5771	2.5313	2.4868	3
4	3.9020	3.8077	3.7171	3.6299	3.5459	3.4651	3.3872	3.3121	3.2397	3.1699	4
5	4.8535	4.7134	4.5797	4.4518	4.3295	4.2123	4.1002	3.9927	3.8896	3.7908	5
6	5.7955	5.6014	5.4172	5.2421	5.0757	4.9173	4.7665	4.6229	4.4859	4.3553	6
7	6.7282	6.4720	6.2302	6.0020	5.7863	5.5824	5.3893	5.2064	5.0329	4.8684	7
8	7.6517	7.3254	7.0196	6.7327	6.4632	6.2098	5.9713	5.7466	5.5348	5.3349	8
9	8.5661	8.1622	7.7861	7.4353	7.1078	6.8017	6.5152	6.2469	5.9852	5.7590	9
10	9.4714	8.9825	8.5302	8.1109	7.7217	7.3601	7.0236	6.7101	6.4176	6.1446	10
11	10.3677	9.7868	9.2526	8.7604	8.3064	7.8868	7.4987	7.1389	6.8052	6.4951	11
12	11.2552	10.5753	9.9539	9.3850	8.8632	8.3838	7.9427	7.5361	7.1607	6.8137	12
13	12.1338	11.3483	10.6349	9.9856	9.3935	8.8527	8.3576	7.9038	7.4869	7.1034	13
14	13.0038	12.1062	11.2960	10.5631	9.8986	9.2950	8.7454	8.2442	7.7861	7.3667	14
15	13.8651	12.8492	11.9379	11.1183	10.3796	9.7122	9.1079	8.5595	8.0607	7.6061	15
16	14.7180	13.5777	12.5610	11.6522	10.8377	10.1059	9.4466	8.8514	8.3125	7.8237	16
17	15.5624	14.2918	13.1660	12.1656	11.2740	10.4772	9.7632	9.1216	8.5436	8.0215	17
18	16.3984	14.9920	13.7534	12.6592	11.6895	10.8276	10.0591	9.3719	8.7556	8.2014	18
19	17.2261	15.6784	14.3237	13.1339	12.0853	11.1581	10.3356	9.6036	8.9501	8.3649	19
20	18.0457	16.3514	14.8774	13.5903	12.4622	11.4699	10.5940	9.8181	9.1285	8.5136	20
21	18.8571	17.0111	15.4149	14.0291	12.8211	11.7640	10.8355	10.0168	9.2922	8.6487	21
22	19.6605	17.6580	15.9368	14.4511	13.1630	12.0416	11.0612	10.2007	9.4424	8.7715	22
23	20.4559	18.2921	16.4435	14.8568	13.4885	12.3033	11.2722	10.3710	9.5802	8.8832	23
24	21.2435	18.9139	16.9355	15.2469	13.7986	12.5503	11.4693	10.5287	9.7066	8.9847	24
25	22.0233	19.5234	17.4131	15.6220	14.0939	12.7833	11.6536	10.6748	9.8226	9.0770	25

Present Value of an Annuity of One Dollar for *n* Years

n	11%	12%	13%	14%	15%	16%	17%	18%	19%	20%	n
1	.9009	.8929	.8850	.3772	.8696	.8621	.8547	.8475	.8403	.8333	1
2	1.7125	1.6901	1.6681	1.6467	1.6257	1.6052	1.5852	1.5656	1.5465	1.5278	2
3	2.4437	2.4018	2.3612	2.3216	2.2832	2.2459	2.2096	2.1743	2.1399	2.1065	3
4	3.1024	3.0373	2.9745	2.9137	2.8550	2.7982	2.7432	2.6901	2.6386	2.5887	4
5	3.6959	3.6048	3.5172	3.4331	3.3522	3.2743	3.1993	3.1272	3.0576	2.9906	5
6	4.2305	4.1114	3.9976	3.8887	3.7845	3.6847	3.5892	3.4976	3.4098	3.3255	6
7	4.7122	3.5638	4.4226	4.2883	4.1604	4.0386	3.9224	3.8115	3.7057	3.6046	7
8	5.1461	4.9676	4.7988	4.6389	4.4873	4.3436	4.2072	4.0776	3.9544	3.8372	8
9	5.5370	5.3282	5.1317	4.9464	4.7716	4.6065	4.4506	4.3030	4.1633	4.0310	9
10	5.8892	5.6502	5.4262	5.2161	5.0188	4.8332	4.6586	4.4941	4.3389	4.1925	10
11	6.2065	5.9377	5.6869	5.4527	5.2337	5.0286	4.8364	4.6560	4.4865	4.3271	11
12	6.4924	6.1944	5.9176	5.6603	5.4206	5.1971	4.9884	4.7932	4.6105	4.4392	12
13	6.7499	6.4235	6.1218	5.8424	5.5831	5.3423	5.1183	4.9095	4.7147	4.5327	13
14	6.9819	6.6282	6.3025	6.0021	5.7245	5.4675	5.2293	5.0081	4.8023	4.6106	14
15	7.1909	6.8109	6.4624	6.1422	5.8474	5.5755	5.3242	5.0916	4.8759	4.6755	15
16	7.3792	6.9740	6.6039	6.2651	5.9542	5.6685	5.4053	5.1624	4.9377	4.7296	16
17	7.5488	7.1196	6.7291	6.3729	6.0472	5.7487	5.4746	5.2223	4.9897	4.7746	17
18	7.7016	7.2497	6.8399	6.4674	6.1280	5.8178	5.5339	5.2732	5.0333	4.8122	18
19	7.8393	7.3658	6.9380	6.5504	6.1982	5.8775	5.5845	5.3162	5.0700	4.8435	19
20	7.9633	7.4694	7.0248	6.6231	6.2593	5.9288	5.6278	5.3527	5.1009	4.8696	20
21	8.0751	7.5620	7.1016	6.6870	6.3125	5.9731	5.6648	5.3837	5.1268	4.8913	21
22	8.1757	7.6446	7.1695	6.7429	6.3587	6.0113	5.6964	5.4099	5.1486	4.9094	22
23	8.2664	7.7184	7.2297	6.7921	6.3988	6.0442	5.7234	5.4321	5.1668	4.9245	23
24	8.3481	7.7843	7.2829	6.8351	6.4338	6.0726	5.7465	5.4509	5.1822	4.9371	24
25	8.4217	7.8431	7.3300	6.8729	6.4641	6.0971	5.7662	5.4669	5.1951	4.9476	25

APPENDIX TABLE A-2 (Cont.)
Present Value of an Annuity of One Dollar for n Years

n	21%	22%	23%	24%	25%	26%	27%	28%	29%	30%	n
1	.8264	.8197	.8130	.8065	.8000	.7937	.7874	.7813	.7752	.7692	1
2	1.5095	1.4915	1.4740	1.4568	1.4400	1.4235	1.4074	1.3916	1.3761	1.3609	2
3	2.0739	2.0422	2.0114	1.9813	1.9520	1.9234	1.8956	1.8684	1.8420	1.8161	3
4	2.5404	2.4936	2.4483	2.4043	2.3616	2.3202	2.2800	2.2410	2.2031	2.1662	4
5	2.9260	2.8636	2.8035	2.7454	2.6893	2.6351	2.5827	2.5320	2.4830	2.4356	5
6	3.2446	3.1669	3.0923	3.0205	2.9514	2.8850	2.8210	2.7594	2.7000	2.6427	6
7	3.5079	3.4155	3.3270	3.2423	3.1611	3.0833	3.0087	2.9370	2.8682	2.8021	7
8	3.7256	3.6193	3.5179	3.4212	3.3289	3.2407	3.1564	3.0758	2.9986	2.9247	8
9	3.9054	3.7863	3.6731	3.5655	3.4631	3.3657	3.2728	3.1842	3.0997	3.0190	9
10	4.0541	3.9232	3.7993	3.6819	3.5705	3.4648	3.3644	3.2689	3.1781	3.0915	10
11	4.1769	4.0354	3.9018	3.7757	3.6564	3.5435	3.4365	3.3351	3.2388	3.1473	11
12	4.2785	4.1274	3.9852	3.8514	3.7251	3.6060	3.4933	3.3868	3.2859	3.1903	12
13	4.3624	4.2028	4.0530	3.9124	3.7801	3.6555	3.5381	3.4272	3.3224	3.2233	13
14	4.4317	4.2646	4.1082	3.9616	3.8241	3.6949	3.5733	3.4587	3.3507	3.2487	14
15	4.4890	4.3152	4.1530	4.0013	3.8593	3.7261	3.6010	3.4834	3.3726	3.2682	15
16	4.5364	4.3567	4.1894	4.0333	3.8874	3.7509	3.6228	3.5026	3.3896	3.2832	16
17	4.5755	4.3908	4.2190	4.0591	3.9099	3.7705	3.6400	3.5177	3.4028	3.2948	17
18	4.6079	4.4187	4.2431	4.0799	3.9279	3.7861	3.6536	3.5294	3.4130	3.3037	18
19	4.6346	4.4415	4.2627	4.0967	3.9424	3.7985	3.6642	3.5386	3.4210	3.3105	19
20	4.6567	4.4603	4.2786	4.1103	3.9539	3.8083	3.6726	3.5458	3.4271	3.3158	20
21	4.6750	4.4756	4.2916	4.1212	3.9631	3.8161	3.6792	3.5514	3.4319	3.3198	21
22	4.6900	4.4882	4.3021	4.1300	3.9705	3.8223	3.6844	3.5558	3.4356	3.3230	22
23	4.7025	4.4985	4.3106	4.1371	3.9764	3.8273	3.6885	3.5592	3.4384	3.3254	23
24	4.7128	4.5070	4.3176	4.1428	3.9811	3.8312	3.6918	3.5619	3.4406	3.3272	24
25	4.7213	4.5139	4.3232	4.1474	3.9849	3.8342	3.6943	3.5640	3.4423	3.3286	25

APPENDIX B
AMERICAN SOCIETY
OF APPRAISERS
EXAMINATION
SAMPLE CASE

Webb Manufacturing Corporation, a sample problem patterned after the 1980 American Society of Appraisers' examination.

THE CASE

You have been retained by Thomas Webb, chairman of the board of Webb Manufacturing Corporation (Webb) to evaluate an offer for the purchase of the company. You have been asked to express an opinion of the fair market value of this closely-held, family-operated business.

Your opinion is required to guide the directors in their deliberations on the adequacy of the proposed offer.

You have been further instructed that you are to give no consideration to any tax liabilities which may accrue as a result of the proposed transaction.

Webb's current financial statement follows for your study before answering the five questions.

WEBB MANUFACTURING CORPORATION
Balance Sheet
Assets

Cash		$600,000
Prepaid expenses		150,000
Accounts receivable	$1,125,000	
Less: Reserve for bad debts	(75,000)	1,050,000
Inventory		2,700,000
Equipment	3,300,000	
Less: Depreciation	(1,125,000)	2,175,000
Buildings	750,000	
Less: Depreciation	(150,000)	600,000
Land		225,000
Total assets		$7,500,000

Liabilities and Net Worth

Accounts payable	$1,125,000
Accrued expenses	225,000
Notes and mortgages payable	
Due within one year	150,000
Long term	-0-
Capital stock	2,250,000
Retained earnings	3,750,000
Total liabilities and net worth ...	$7,500,000

WEBB MANUFACTURING CORPORATION
Condensed operating statement

	Current year		5-year average	
	Amount	Percent of sales	Amount	Percent of sales
Net sales	$15,000,000	100.0	$13,950,000	100.0
Less cost of sales	(11,250,000)	(75.0)	(10,575,000)	(75.8)
Gross profit	3,750,000	25.0	3,375,000	24.2
Selling expense	1,125,000	7.5	1,012,500	7.3
General expense	750,000	5.0	637,500	4.6
Administrative expense	750,000	5.0	712,500	5.1
Operating expense ...	2,625,000	17.5	2,362,500	17.0
Pretax income	1,125,000	7.5	1,012,500	7.3
Less federal income taxes	(532,500)	(3.6)	(525,000)	(3.8)
Net income	$ 592,500	4.0	$ 487,500	3.5
Depreciation charged to operations	$ 262,500		$ 225,000	

Your inspection of the facilities and discussions with management indicates the following:

1. The company manufactures and sells a line of products under the Webb name which have a reputation in the industry for quality, accuracy, and dependability.
2. The company is known and respected within the industry for the technical competence and know-how of its management and personnel.
3. The company has a number of patents, trademarks, and trade names which are considered important.
4. While machinery and equipment are judged in good condition and adequate to sustain a substantial increse in business, the plant is very crowded and additional warehousing space is desperately needed. A 22,500-square-foot addition to the plant is in the early stages of construction, and its total cost is estimated to be $150,000.
5. In addition to their salaries, which are considered in line with those paid in the industry, the four top officers of the company, Mr. Webb and his three sons, have been receiving year-end bonuses for the past several years. These bonuses have aggregated $135,000 per year during the period under review.
6. As a further aid in the current negotiations, the company has just had its plant property and equipment appraised by an independent appraiser. This appraisal indicates a total fair market value of the facilities of:

```
Land ..................  $300,000
Buildings, including
  new warehouse
  addition ..............   750,000
Equipment .............  2,775,000
                        $3,825,000
```

Your inspection leads to the conclusion of an average remaining economic life of 33 years on the buildings and 10 years on the machinery and equipment. In your computations, assume that these values will form the new basis for depreciation of these assets under the new ownership.

Your analysis of other companies engaged in the same line of business discloses three publicly-owned corporations, suitable for comparables. Pertinent financial, operating, and marketing information on these companies discloses selected information, which appears in the following tabulation.

Companies comparable to Webb Manufacturing Corporation

	Company 1	Company 2	Company 3
Current assets	$11,250,000	$ 2,700,000	$ 9,000,000
Net plant, property, and equipment	6,750,000	2,250,000	4,500,000
Other assets	750,000	300,000	—
Total assets	$18,750,000	$ 5,250,000	$13,500,000
Current liabilities	$ 3,750,000	$ 825,000	$ 3,000,000
Long-term debt	6,000,000	—	3,750,000
Stockholders' equity	9,000,000	4,425,000	6,750,000
Total liabilities and capital	$18,750,000	$ 5,250,000	$13,500,000
Sales			
Current	$37,500,000	$11,250,000	$26,250,000
5-year average	33,750,000	10,500,000	22,500,000
Gross profit margin			
Current	25.0	30.0	20.0
5-year average	23.7	28.5	22.5
Net profit			
Current	1,500,000	487,500	900,000
5-year average	1,200,000	450,000	825,000
Net profit margin			
Current	4.0	4.3	3.4
5-year average	3.6	4.3	3.7
Depreciation charged			
Current	750,000	262,500	525,000
5-year average	690,000	225,000	487,500
Interest expense			
Current	420,000	—	210,000
5-year average	270,000		225,000
Number of shares outstanding	200,000	130,000	225,000
Current market price per share	$67.50	$45.00	$37.50

QUIZ ON WEBB MANUFACTURING CORPORATION AND COMPARABLE COMPANIES

Given the preceding information the appraiser must answer the following questions, showing all computations and work notes. Questions 1, 2a, 2b, 4, and 5 each carry 15 points, with question 3 carrying 50 points, for a total of 125.

Further assumptions or instructions:

a.   No premium for control or ownership of the entire business enterprise.
b.   Base your answers only on the information given in the problem.

c. Even if you do not consider that they will affect your answer, comment on any adjustments to earnings which are indicated.

d. Assume a 50 percent tax rate in your computations.

1. Determine the adequacy of Webb's working capital compared to other companies in the business. Is there an excess or deficiency indicated? Give reasons for your answer.
2. *a.* In valuing the Webb business enterprise, what adjustments to the operating statement are indicated?
   b. Are any adjustments to the earnings of the comparative companies indicated?
3. What is the indicated value of the Webb business enterprise as reflected in the capital stock of the company?
4. Assuming Current Assets and Liabilities at book value, what is the indicated value of the intangible assets?
5. From the buyer's standpoint, would it generally be more desirable to purchase the stock or the assets of the corporation? Give reasons for your answer.

The following is a representative set of satisfactory answers written under the time constraints of actual test conditions.

Determine the adequacy of Webb's working capital compared to the other companies in the business. Is there an excess or deficiency indicated? Give reasons for your answer.

Current ratio—Webb

Cash	$600,000	
Prepaid expenses	150,000	
Accounts receivable (net)	1,050,000	
Inventory	2,700,000	
Total current assets		$4,500,000
Accounts payable	$1,125,000	
Accrued expenses	225,000	
Notes and mortgages due within one year	150,000	
Total current liabilities		$1,500,000

$$\text{Current ratio} \quad \frac{\$4,500,000}{\$1,500,000} = 3:1$$

Total current assets	$4,500,000
Less total current liabilities	(1,500,000)
Net working capital	$3,000,000

Sales To net working capital—Webb (current year basis)

$$\frac{\text{Sales, current year} \quad \$15,000,000}{\text{Working capital} \quad 3,000,000} = 5.0 \text{ times}$$

Current ratio—comparable companies

$$\text{Company 1} \quad \frac{\$11,250,000}{3,750,000} = 3.0:1$$

Company 2	$\dfrac{\$ 2,700,000}{825,000}$ =	3.27:1
Company 3	$\dfrac{\$ 9,000,000}{3,000,000}$ =	3.0:1

Sales to net working capital—Comparable companies

Company 1 ..... $\dfrac{\$37,500,000}{7,500,000}$ = 5.0 times

Company 2 ..... $\dfrac{\$11,250,000}{1,875,000}$ = 6.0 times

Company 3 ..... $\dfrac{\$ 6,250,000}{6,000,000}$ = 4.375 times

Discussion. On the basis of current ratio, Webb is almost exactly in line with the three comparable companies, indicating no excess or deficiency by this measurement.

However, on an absolute (versus comparative) basis, 3:1 is generally considered a pretty high current ratio. Working capital may be considered high on this basis. Also, the company has no long-term debt, so there would appear to be plenty of room for borrowing if necessary.

Also by the sales/working capital comparison, Webb seems to be right on the industry average.

Question 2

a. In valuing the Webb business enterprise, what adjustments to the operating statement are indicated?

Answer

Add $135,000 per year to pretax earnings, or $62,500 aftertax earnings to reflect bonuses paid to management above industry average compensation.

Adjust pro-forma depreciation on stepped-up basis, as instructed. Using straight-line depreciation, this would mean:

Per year

Buildings (including new warehouse) ...... $750,000 ÷ 33 yrs. =	$ 22,727
Equipment ....2,775,000 ÷ 10 yrs. =	277,500
New depreciation	$300,000
Current year depreciation	(262,500)
Additional depreciation cost	$ 37,727
Less 50 percent federal income tax	(18,863)
Downward adjustment to pro-forma earnings	$ 18,864

Question 2 (continued)

b. Are any adjustments to the earnings of the comparable companies indicated?

Answer

Since Webb has no long-term debt, but two of the three comparable companies do have, I will adjust the earnings of the two companies with long-term debt to a debt-free basis for purposes of comparison.

Webb does not specify the amount of interest on its $150,000 short-term debt, and the comparable companies do not specify whether all of their interest is on the long-term debt. I will assume that it is, and do the arithmetic of the adjustments based on all of the debt.

Company 1. Current interest is $420,000. With a 50 percent tax rate, net profit would be adjusted upward $210,000, or to $1,710,000 on a debt-free basis. Average interest is $270,000, so average net profit would be adjusted upward 50 percent of that, or $135,000 to $1,335,000 average profit.

Company 3. Current interest is $210,000; 50 percent of that is a $105,000 upward adjustment, or to $1,005,000 current net profit on a debt-free basis. Average interest is $225,000, so 50 percent would be a $112,500 upward adjustment to the $825,000 average profit, or $937,500 average profit.

What is the indicated value of the Webb business enterprise as reflected in the capital stock of the company?

Question 3

Answer

Adjusted earning power—Webb (see answer to 2*a*)

	Current year	*5-year average*
Net Income	$592,500	$487,500
Compensation adjustment	67,500	67,500
Depreciation adjustment	(18,863)	-0- *
Current year indicated earning power:	641,137	
5-year indicated earning power		$555,000

*In the 5-year average no depreciation adjustment was used, nor necessary, since stepped-up basis applied only to new owners based on the case instructions.

Price/earnings ratios for comparable companies, adjusted to debt-free basis (see answer to 2*b*)

Company 1

Current net profit
    adjusted to debt-free basis . . . . $ 1,710,000
Market value of equity . . . .$67.50 × 200,000 shares
    or $13,500,000
Add: Long-term debt   6,000,000
Market value of capital $19,500,000
    $19,500,000 ÷ $1,710,000 profit = 11.4 × current profit
5-year average net profit
    adjusted to debt-free basis from 2*b*: . . . . $ 1,335,000
    $19,500,000 ÷ $1,335,000 profit = 14.6 × 5-year average profit

Company 2

Current net profit
    (no long-term debt) . . . .$487,500 ÷ 130,000 shares
    or $3.75/share
Market price of $45.00/share . . . . . .÷ $3.75/share = 12.0 P/E ratio on current earnings
Average net profit . . . .$445,000 ÷ 130,000 shares
    or $3.46/share
Market price of $45.00/share . . . . . .÷ $3.46/share = 13.0 P/E ratio on 5-year average profit

Company 3

Current net profit
    adjusted to debt-free basis (from 2*b*) . . . . $ 1,005,000
Market value of equity . . . .$37.50 × 225,000 shares
    or . . . . $ 8,437,500
Add: Long-term debt   3,750,000
Market value of capital $12,187,500

$12,187,500 ÷ $1,005,000 profit = 12.1 × current profit
5-year average net profit
  adjusted to debt-free basis .... $ 937,500
    $12,187,500 ÷ $937,500 profit = 13.0 × 5-year average profit

Therefore, the price/earnings ratio on debt-free basis is:

	Current earnings	*5-year average*
Company 1	11.4	14.6
Company 2	12.0	13.0
Company 3	12.1	13.0

The text makes Webb sound pretty good, so I will use a ratio of 12, the median and a little above the mean.

Adjusted current earnings $641,137
                ×   12 P/E
Indicated value, based on
  capitalization of adjusted
  current earnings .... $7,694,000.

and being more or less consistent, 14 is a little above mean for the 5-year average price/earnings ratio.

5-year average adjusted
  earnings $555,000
                ×   14 P/E
Indicated value, based on
  capitalization of 5-year
  average adjusted earnings: $7,770,000

Book value—Comparable companies
  Formula

$$(a) \quad \frac{\text{S/H equity}}{\text{Outstanding shares}} = \text{Book value per share}$$

$$(b) \quad \frac{\text{Market price}}{\text{Book value}} = \text{Price/book ratio}$$

Company 1

    (a) $9,000,000 ÷ 200,000 = $45.00/ share

    (b) $67.50/share ÷ $45.00/share = 1.5 price/book ratio

Company 2

    (a) $4,425,000 ÷ 130,000 = $34.04/share

    (b) $45.00/share ÷ $34.04/share = 1.32 price/book ratio

Company 3

    (a) $6,750,000 ÷ 225,000 = $30.00/share

    (b) $37.50/share ÷ $30.00/share = 1.25 price/book ratio

                    Median: 1.32
                    Mean: 1.36

Since Webb seems to be pretty good, let's try

$$1.4 \times \text{Book value of } \$6,000,000 = \$8,400,000$$

indicated value based on price to book ratios of comparables. I did not adjust Webb's book value upward to reflect asset appraisals because comparable companies are likely to be subject to similar adjustments.

The price to book value ratios also could be done on a basis adjusted to the debt-free status of Webb.

Company 1—Adjustments

Market value of equity	$13,500,000	
Plus: Long-term debt	6,000,000	
		$19,500,000
Book value of equity	$ 9,000,000	
Plus: Long-term debt	6,000,000	
		15,000,000
Market value/book value ratio . . .		1.3

Company 3—Adjustments

Market value of equity	$ 8,437,500	
Plus: Long-term debt	3,750,000	
		$12,187,500
Book value of equity	$ 6,750,000	
Plus: Long-term debt	3,750,000	
		$10,500,000
Market value/book value ratio . . .		1.16

Using adjusted market value of capital to book value ratios they are summarized as:

Company 1	1.3
Company 2	1.32
Company 3	1.16

Median: 1.3
Mean: 1.26

Consistent with previous analyses we will use:

$$1.3 \times \text{Book value of } \$6,000,000 = \$7,800,000$$

indicated value on this basis. (This is not adjusted for asset appraisals, as previously explained.)

Summary of value for Webb

Indicated value—based on capitalization of adjusted current earnings	$7,694,000
Indicated value—based on capitalization of adjusted 5-year average earnings	$7,770,000
Indicated value—based on price/book ratios, comparable companies adjusted to debt-free basis (preferable to unadjusted)	$7,800,000
For an operating company, the earnings approach tends to take precedence. In this case the results are so similar that I will round to	$7,800,000.

Assuming current assets and liabilities at book value, what is the indicated value of the intangible assets? **Question 4**

Answer

First, the case indicates an appraisal for real and personal property so Webb's book value will be adjusted starting with book value of $6 million.

	Appraisal	Book value	Adjustment
Land	$ 300,000	$ 225,000	+ $ 75,000
Equipment	2,775,000	2,175,000	+ 600,000
Building, includes new addition*	750,000	600,000	-0-
Total adjustments ...			$ 675,000

*Warehouse is "in early stages of construction," so we don't know how much of present book value reflects the warehouse. If, for simplicity, we assume none, then no adjustment to book value is necessary for this item.

Summary

Book value	$6,000,000	
Upward adjustments	675,000	
Adjusted book value		$6,675,000
Indicated value	$7,800,000	
Adjusted book value	(6,675,000)	
Indicated value of intangibles ...		$1,125,000

Question 5

From the buyer's standpoint would it generally be more desirable to purchase the stock or the assets of the corporation? Give reasons for your answer.

Answer

The buyer in this case is better off purchasing assets rather than stock because a stepped-up basis for depreciation is indicated. However, this could also be accomplished by a purchase followed by the liquidation and merger into another existing or newly created company.

Also, however, the buyer purchasing assets rather than stock generally avoids potential hidden contingent liabilities, such as product liability suits or something else out of the past. Such problems can be at least partially addressed in stock purchases by indemnification agreements.

APPENDIX C
BIBLIOGRAPHY

INDEXES, BIBLIOGRAPHICAL SOURCES, AND JOURNALS
GENERAL
  Articles
  Books
MARKETABILITY, MINORITY INTEREST, AND SO ON
  Articles
DISSENTERS' STOCK
  Articles
MERGERS AND ACQUISITIONS
  Articles
GOODWILL AND OTHER INTANGIBLES
  Articles

Separate subject bibliographies relevant to certain chapters have been appendixed to those chapters:
  Chap.   8. Industry and Economic Data
  Chap.   9. Data on Comparable Companies
  Chap. 17. Estate Planning and Tax Valuations
  Chap. 20. Employee Stock Ownership Plans
  Chap. 21. Buy-Sell Agreements

Indexes, bibliographical sources, and journals

Accountants' Index; Supplement. New York: American Institute of Certified Public Accountants. (annual)

Latest edition is two to three years old. Alphabetical arrangements by author and subject of accounting-related topics.

American Digest System. St. Paul, Minn.: West Publishing Co. (monthly and cumulative)

Includes *General Digest, Dicennial Digests.* Digests court cases reported in Reporter System, such as *Pacific Reporter 2d (P. 2d).* An index to judicial decisions, "Covering state and federal courts embraced in National Reporter System." Includes digests of cases arranged by subject and a table of cases. Monthly digest cumulates eventually into Dicennial Digest.

American Jurisprudence, and *American Jurisprudence 2d. (Am. Juris. 2d).* Rochester, N.Y.: Lawyers Cooperative Publishing House.

This encyclopedia of national coverage has over 400 alphabetically arranged topics or titles intended to cover the entire field of American law. It briefly summarizes rules of law and cites supporting authorities. *Am. Juris. 2d* is designed to supersede *Am. Juris.* and is still being published. Kept up-to-date by annual cumulative pocket supplements.

American Jurisprudence Proof of Facts (Am. Juris. P.O.F.). Rochester, N.Y.: Lawyers Cooperative Publishing House.

Planned for use with *Am. Juris.* Gives sample courtroom presentations.

American Law Reports (A.L.R.) Rochester, N.Y.: Lawyers Cooperative Publishing Company.

Includes *A.L.R., A.L.R. 2d, A.L.R. 3d,* and *A.L.R. Federal.* Compilations of annotations, each annotation being a complete and detailed treatise on a practical point of law, and based on all cases on the subject. Regularly updated with references to all later cases in point. Still being published.

Bishop, John A., and Rosenbloom, Arthur H. *Federal Tax Valuation Digest: Business Enterprises and Business Interests.* Boston, Mass.: Warren, Gorham & Lamont, 1979.

Digests selected federal tax cases from 1945 through mid-1978. Well-indexed and cross-referenced. Publisher plans an "updating service yearbook."

Business Periodicals Index (BPI). New York: H.W. Wilson Co. (monthly, with quarterly and annual cumulations)

Covers range of business topics published in various periodicals, with alphabetical arrangement by subject and author.

Canada Valuation Service. Toronto: Richard De Boo Ltd., 1980.

Looseleaf book, updated periodically. Written by Ian R. Campbell, this service has some application to the United States as well as Canada, and cites some U.S. cases and articles.

Corpus Juris Secundum (C.J.S.). Brooklyn, N.Y.: American Law Book Co.

This competitor to *Am. Juris. 2d.* is arranged similarly and provides the same type of coverage. Still being published.

Daniells, Lorna M. *Business Information Sources.* Berkeley: University of California Press, 1976.

Annotated bibliography arranges materials by broad subject category. It has index by title, author, and subject.

Federal Tax Articles. Chicago: Commerce Clearing House, Inc. (monthly)

This provides annotations of articles on federal income, estate, gift, and excise taxes that have appeared in legal, accounting, tax, and other professional journals, and in the proceedings of major tax institutes. The contents are arranged to correspond to the Internal Revenue Code section numbers. Included are author and subject indexes.

Federal Tax Coordinator 2d. New York: Research Institute of America, Inc. (annual loose-leaf service)

"A series of clearly stated professional briefs backed up by citations to the Code, Regulations, Rulings and Decisions which apply tax thinking . . . shows how the law applies, points up dangers, clarifies uncertainties, suggests what can be done most profitably." Arranged by broad subjects, with excellent index and finding tables.

Federal Tax Coordinator 2d. Special Studies. New York: Research Institute of America, Inc.

Supplement to *Federal Tax Coordinator 2d.*

Federal Tax Coordinator 2d. Weekly Alert. New York: Research Institute of America, Inc.

Supplement to *Federal Tax Coordinatory 2d.*

Federal Taxes. Englewood Cliffs, N.J.: Prentice-Hall Inc. (annual loose-leaf service, with periodic updates)

Arranged by IRC section number, this service annotates and discusses laws, rulings, regulations, and decisions relating to taxes. Competitor to C.C.H. *Standard Federal Tax Reporter.*

Financial Accounting Standards; Original Pronouncements as of July 1, 1979. Stamford, Conn.: Financial Accounting Standards Board, 1979.

Contains FASB Statements of Financial Accounting Standards, Statements of Financial Accounting Concepts, and Interpretations, and AICPA pronouncements.

Goldstein, Gersham. *Index to Federal Tax Articles.* Boston: Warren, Gorham & Lamont, 1975. (quarterly, cumulative supplements)

This subject arrangement of tax-related articles has convenient coverage of valuation topics.

Grant, Mary M., and Cote, Norma, eds. *Directory of Business and Financial Services.* 7th ed. New York: Special Libraries Association, 1976.

Annotated reference book dealing exclusively with information services which provide continuous coverage of some facet of business activity, such as investment advisory services and commodity services. Arranged alphabetically by title, with a subject index.

Index to Legal Periodicals. New York: H.W. Wilson Co. (monthly with cumulations).

Primarily an index of Anglo-American legal periodicals by author and subject, this is published monthly except September, with quarterly and semiannual cumulations and a bound annual cumulative issue. Includes a combined alphabetically arranged subject and author index, a table of cases, and a book review index.

IRS Letter Ruling Reporter. Chicago: Commerce Clearing House, Inc. (weekly) Official texts of Internal Revenue Service written determinations, i.e., technical advice memoranda and determination letters, which recite the relevant facts, explain the applicable provisions of law, and show the application of the law to the facts. Covers those issued by the IRS after October 31, 1976. Such letter rulings are not to be cited for precedent.

Journal of Taxation. Boston: Warren, Gorham & Lamont for Tax Research Group. (monthly)

"A national professional journal of current news and comment for tax practitioners." Contains some articles on valuation-related topics as well as notes on relevant rulings and decisions.

Mergers & Acquisitions, The Journal of Corporate Venture. McLean, Va.: Information for Industry, Inc. (quarterly)

Includes comprehensive bibliography, 1972; roster cross-index 1966–1970. Journal has merger and acquisition-related articles, roster of joint ventures, news.

Mertens, Jacob, Jr. *Law of Federal Income Taxation.* Chicago: Callaghan & Co., 1976. (cumulative supplement, 1979)

Chapter 59: Problems of Valuation. Multi-volume set discusses tax law and provides cumulative supplements covering legislation, regulations, rulings, and decisions.

National Reporter System. St. Paul, Minn.: West Publishing Co. (monthly and cumulative)

Includes *Pacific Reporter, Northwestern Reporter,* and other regional reporters. Includes all decisions of the highest courts in each state and of intermediate appellate courts; seven regional reporters, four federal court series, the *New York Supplement,* and *California Reporter* publish many, but not all of the written decisions by nearly every "judicial tribunal" now acting in the United States, including many decisions not appearing in any other report.

Shepard's Citators. Colorado Springs, Colo.: Shepard's Citations, Inc.

Multi-volume series gives citations for court decisions relating to particular cases. Arranged to coordinate with West Publishing Co.'s National Reporter System. Used for checking final disposition of particular cases and for finding related cases.

Shepard's Code of Federal Regulations Citations. Colorado Springs, Colo.: Shepard's Citations, Inc.

Cites cases relevant to particular C.F.R. sections by order of C.F.R. section number.

Standard Federal Tax Reporter. Chicago: Commerce Clearing House, Inc. (Annual loose-leaf service with periodic updates)

Arranged by code section number, this service annotates and discusses the Internal Revenue Code, tax regulations, rulings, and decisions. Competitor to Prentice-Hall's *Federal Taxes.*

Tax Management Portfolios. Washington, D.C.: Tax Management, Inc.

Each portfolio is devoted to a specific tax problem area and is designed for and written by tax practitioners. Each portfolio has three main sections: detailed analysis, working papers, bibliography and references, and is kept up to date by supplements when developments warrant.

No.52–2d. *Corporate Recapitalizations.* Washington, D.C.: 1974. (Tax Management Portfolios, No.52–2d)

No.354. *ESOPs and TRASOPs.* Washington, D.C.: 1979. (Tax Management Portfolios, No.354)

No.147–4th. *Practice Before the IRS.* Washington, D.C.: 1977. (Tax Management Portfolios, no.147–4th)

No. 202–3d. *Reasonable Compensation.* Washington, D.C.: 1974 (Tax Management Portfolios, No.202–3d)

No. 153–2d. *Tax Court—Trial of Case.* Washington, D.C.: 1974 (Tax Management Portfolios, No. 153–3d)

No.221. *Valuation of Shares of Closely Held Corporations.* Washington, D.C.: 1974. (Tax Management Estates, Gifts, and Trusts Portfolios, No.221)

Wasserman, Paul, et al. *Encyclopedia of Business Information Sources.* 3d ed. Detroit: Gale Research Co., 1976.

Listing of information sources on subjects and countries, with basic statistics sources, directories, almanacs, periodicals, associations, handbooks, bibliographies, dictionaries, and general works for each.

Articles: General

Banks, Warren E. "Measuring the Value of Corporate Stock." *California Western Law Review* 11 (Fall 1974):1–59.

_____. "The Accounting Balance Sheet as a Guide to Stock Value." Detroit College of Law Review 1978(1978):241–259.

Bateman, Ronald H. "Appraising the Going Concern." *Appraisal Journal* 39 (October 1971):526–34.

Bell, Lawrence M. "Valuation and the Probability of Bankruptcy in Chapter X." *American Bankruptcy Law Journal* 52 (Winter 1978):1–22.

Bishop, Maurice F. "Legal Aspects of the Income Approach to Market Value." *Alabama Lawyer* 31 (1970):79–85.

"Compilation and Review of Financial Statements," American Institute of Certified Public Accountants. Accounting and Review Services Committee. *Statement on Standards for Accounting and Review Services, No. 1* (December 1978).

Danzig, L.H. and Robison, R.A. "Going Concern Value Reexamined," *Tax Adviser* 11 (January 1980):32–36.

Drymalski, Raymond, Jr. "Valuation of Stock of a Subchapter S Corporation—A New Form of Business Organization." *Illinois Bar Journal* 56 (April 1968):672–89.

Everett, Robert F. "What Is the Business Worth?" *Real Estate Today* 11 (October 1978):46–50.

"Forensic Economics—Valuation of Businesses and Business Losses." *16 Am. Juris. P.O.F. 253* (1978, supplement 1979).

Gregory, W.A. "Stock Transfer Restrictions in Close Coporations," *Southern Illinois University Law Journal* 1978 (December 1978):477–99.

Hoopes, Townsend. "Appraising Managements." *C.F.A. Readings in Financial Analysis* pp. 177–85. Homewood, Ill.: Richard D. Irwin, Inc., 1977.

Houston, Jamie Giles, and Mounger, Dalton McBee. "Valuation of Shares in a Closely-held Corporation." *Mississippi Law Journal* 47 (September 1976):715–42.

Lang, Robert Todd, and Cooper, Stephen H. "Fairness I (and) II." *Review of Securities Regulation.* Vols. 12, 21 (II. December 5, 1979), pp. 831–36.

Lembke, Valdean C. "Determination of Reporting Basis for Long-Term Intercorporate Investment." *Mergers & Acquisitions* (Fall 1979), pp. 14–17.

Leslie, Eugene C. "Valuation of Close Corporation Stock." *CLU Journal* 21 (July 1967):12–22.

Martin, Spencer J. "Factors Used in Valuation of Closely-Held Stock." *National Public Accountant* 20(5) (May 1975):12–16.

McClellan, William A. "Valuation of Closely-Held Securities: Accounting Know-How Is the Key." *Journal of Accountancy* 121 (March 1966):47–55.

"Meaning of 'Book Value' of Corporate Stock." *51 A.L.R. 2d 606* (1957, supplement 1978–1979).

Neuhauser, Paul M. "The Two-Step Method of Valuation: One Step Backwards?" 51 *Iowa Law Review* (1966):321–64.

Newton, Grant W., and Ward, James J., Jr. "Valuation of a Business in Bankruptcy." *CPA Journal* 46 (August 1976):26–32.

Olson, Irving J. "Valuation of a Closely-Held Corporation." *Journal of Accountancy* 128 (August 1969):35–47.

Olson, Olof W. "Valuation of a Going Concern." *Valuation Magazine* (December 1973), pp. 118–25.

O'Neal, F. Hodge, and Janke, Ronald R. "Control Arrangements in Close Corporations." *Practical Lawyer* 20 (January 1974):27–42.

"Pennsylvania—Regulations for Valuing Capital Stock." *CPA Journal* 49 (April 1979):58–59.

Pratt, Shannon P. and Hugo, Craig S. "Pricing a Company by the Discounted Future Earnings Method." *Mergers & Acquisitions* 7 (Spring 1972):18–32.

Rappaport, Alfred. "Do You Know the Value of Your Company?" *Mergers & Acquisitions* (Spring 1979), pp. 12–21.

Redman, Arnold L., and Sirmans, C. F. "Regional/Local Economic Analysis: A Discussion of Data Sources." *Appraisal Journal* 45 (April 1977):261–72.

"Reporting on Comparative Financial Statements." American Institute of Certified Public Accountants. Accounting and Review Services Committee. *Statements on Standards for Accounting and Review Services, No. 2* (October, 1979).

Schilt, J.H. "Objection to the Excess Earnings Method of Business Appraisal," *Taxes* 58 (Fall 1980):123–26.

_____. "Pitfalls in the Valuation of Closely Held Companies," *Trusts & Estates* 119 (June 1980):44–47.

Schons, Larry H. "Valuation of Close Corporate Shares in Oregon." *Oregon Law Review* 57 (1978):309–21.

Schreier, W. T., and Joy. O. Maurice. "Judicial Valuation of 'Close' Corporation Stock: Alice In Wonderland Revisited." *Oklahoma Law Review* 31 (Fall 1978):853–85.

Sears, Gerald A., and Sucsy, Lawrence G. "The Expert's Role in Company Valuation." *Practical Lawyer* 17 (January 1971):11–34.

Shulkin, Martin B., and Goren, Richard A. "Purchase or Sale of a Closely-Held Corporation—an Overview." *Massachusetts Law Review* 63 (October 1978):211–19.

Silton, Lawrence C. "Valuation of Closely-Held Corporations." *Trusts & Estates* 116 (February 1977):82–85, 120–21.

Smith, S.K. "Court Decisions Now Recognize Valuation Discounts for Community Property Interests," *Journal of Taxation* 53 (July 1980):28–31.

Steinberg, Robert E. "New Approach to Rule 10b–5: Distinguishing the Close Corporation." *Washington University Law Quarterly* 1978 (Fall 1978):733–63.

Strobel, Caroline D. "Reorganization of Professional Corporations: an Analysis of Some Recent Private Letter Rulings," *Taxes* 58 (May 1980):347–53.

Treanor, R.B. and Johnson, Jack. "Valuation of Community Property Minority Interests Reflect Judicial Inconsistencies," *Journal of Taxation* 52 (June 1980):356–60.

"Use of Appraisals in SEC Documents." *University of Pennsylvania Law Review* 122 (November 1973):138–61.

"Valuation of Stock of Closely-Held Corporations." *2 Am. Juris. P.O.F. 2d 1* (1974, supplement 1979).

Walker, C.E.O., and MacBride, Dexter D. "Valuation of the Closely-Held Business: Viewpoint of the Appraiser." *Valuation* 23 (March/April 1976):2–12.

Books: General

Balachandran, M. *A Guide to Trade and Industry Statistics.* Ann Arbor, Mich.: Pierian Press, 1977.

Berman, Daniel S. *Going Public: A Practical Handbook of Procedures and Forms.* Englewood Cliffs, N.J.: Prentice-Hall, Inc. 1974.

Bernstein, Leopold A. *Financial Statement Analysis: Theory, Application and Interpretation.* Rev. ed. Homewood, Ill.: Richard D. Irwin, Inc., 1978.

Bierman, Harold and Smidt, Seymour. *The Capital Budgeting Decision.* 4th ed. New York: Macmillan Co., 1975.

Bosland, C. C. *Valuation Theories and Decisions of the S.E.C.* New York: Simmons-Boardman Pub. Co., 1964.

Desmond, Glenn M., and Kelley, Richard E. *Business Valuation Handbook.* Llano, Calif.: Valuation Press, 1977.

Desmond Glenn M. *How to Value Professional Practices.* Marina del Rey, Calif.: Valuation Press, 1980.

The 1980 Dow Jones-Irwin Business Almanac. Ed. by Sumner N. Levine. Homewood, Ill.: Dow Jones-Irwin, 1980.

Valuable reference source provides synopses of major legislation enacted in 1978 and 1979; regulatory agencies; finance and accounting, largest corporations, stock market discussion and data; commodities market; money and financial institutions; banks and other financial insititutions; advertising and the media; employment, wages and productivity; price data; economic indicators, gross national product and income; production, construction and business activity; federal, state, and local finance; international business; world population and GNP by country; economic indicators by country; a business information directory; etc.

Ellentuck, Albert B. *Practical Merger Techniques for Buying and Selling a Business: Successful Tax and Financial Strategies.* Chicago: Commerce Clearing House, Inc., 1974.

Fox, Byron E., and Fox, Eleanor M. *Corporate Acquisitions and Mergers.* (2 vols.) New York: Matthew Bender, 1971.

Furst, John S., and Moore, Cordell B. *Valuation of Closely-Held*

Corporate Stock. New York: Coopers & Lybrand, 1975. (pamphlet, 24 pages)

Graham, Benjamin, and McGolrick, Charles. *The Interpretation of Financial Statements*. 3d rev. ed. New York: Harper & Row, 1975.

Handy as a primer or elementary reference for a person who lacks a basic accounting foundation.

Graham, Benjamin; Dodd, David L.; and Cottle, Sidney. *Security Analysis Principles and Technique*. 4th ed. New York: McGraw-Hill Book Co., 1962.

Guardino, Joseph R. *Accounting, Legal and Tax Aspects of Corporate Acquisitions*. Englewood Cliffs, N.J.: Prentice-Hall, Inc., 1973.

Hawkins, David F. *Corporate Financial Reporting: Text and Cases*. Rev. ed. Homewood, Ill.: Richard D. Irwin, Inc., 1977.

Helfert, Erich A. *Valuation: Concepts and Practice*. Belmont, Calif.: Wadsworth Pub. Co., 1966.

Jurek, Walter. *How to Determine the Value of a Business*. Stow, Ohio: Quality Services, Inc., 1977.

_____. *A Reference Manual of Practical Information on Buying or Selling a Business*. Stow, Ohio: Quality Services, Inc., 1977.

Lasry, George. *Valuing Common Stock: The Power of Prudence*. New York: AMACOM, 1979.

Levine, Sumner N. *Financial Analyst's Handbook*. (2 vols.) Homewood, Ill.: Dow Jones-Irwin, 1975.

McCarthy, George D., and Healy, Robert E. *Valuing a Company: Practices and Procedures*. New York: Wiley-Interscience, 1971.

Ness, Theodore, and Vogel, Eugene L. *Taxation of the Closely-Held Corporation*. 3d ed. Boston: Warren, Gorham & Lamont, 1976.

O'Neal, F. Hodge. *Close Corporations: Law and Practice*. 2d ed. (2 vols.) Chicago: Callaghan & Co., 1971.

Plant, Peter G., and Dolin, Armin H. *Agency Mergers and Acquisitions*. Cincinnati: National Underwriter Co., 1969.

Practising Law Institute. *Valuation of Closely-Held Businesses*. 2d ed. *Estate Planning and Administration Course Handbook Ser. No. 38.* New York: Practising Law Institute, 1973.

_____. *Estate and Financial Planning for the Closely-Held Corporation*. (Tax Law & Estate Planning Series No. 107. New York: Practising Law Institute, 1980.

_____. *Tax Planning for the Closely-Held Corporation*. Tax Law & Estate Planning Course Handbook Ser. Vol. 123. New York: Practising Law Institute, 1978.

Robinson, Gerald J. *Going Public: Successful Securities Underwriting*. 2d ed. New York: Clark Boardman Co., 1972.

Sanzo, Richard. *Ratio Analysis for Small Business*. Small Business Management Series, no. 20. 4th ed. Washington, D.C.: Small Business Administration, 1977.

Scharf, Charles A. *Acquisitions, Mergers, Sales and Takeovers; a Handbook with Forms*. Englewood Cliffs, N.J.: Prentice-Hall, Inc., 1971.

Scharf, C. *Techniques for Buying, Selling and Merging Businesses*. Englewood Cliffs, N.J.: Prentice-Hall, Inc., 1964.

Schreiber, Irving, ed. *How to Take Money Out of a Closely-Held Corporation*. Rev. ed., (Loose-leaf.) Greenvale, N.Y.: Panel Publishers, 1971.

Stephens, Richard B.; Maxfield, Guy B.; and Lind, Stephen A. *Federal Estate and Gift Taxation*. 4th ed. Boston: Warren, Gorham & Lamont, Inc., 1978.

Winter, Elmer L. *Complete Guide to Making a Public Stock Offering*. 3d ed. Englewood Cliffs, N.J.: Prentice-Hall, Inc. 1972.

Woolery, Arlo. *The Art of Valuation*. Indianapolis: Heath, 1978.

Transcript of a two-day panel discussion on valuation of public utilities and railroads for ad valorem tax purposes.

Articles: Marketability, minority interest, and so on

Bowers, L. Thomas. "Share Premiums: They Aren't Your Profits." *Business Horizons* 21 (October 1978):61–64.

Coolidge, H. Calvin. "Fixing Value of Minority Interest in a Business; Actual Sales Suggest Discount as High as 70 Percent." *Estate Planning* (Spring 1975), pp. 138–40.

Dant, Thomas W., Jr. "Courts Increasing Amount of Discount for a Minority Interest in a Business." *Journal of Taxation* (August 1975), pp. 104–09.

"Discounts Involved in Purchases of Common Stock." *Institutional Investor Study Report of the Securities and Exchange Commission*. Document no. 92-64, part 5, 5 (March 10, 1971):2444–56. In U.S. 92d Congress, 1st Session. House. Washington, D.C.: U.S. Government Printing Office.

Feld, Alan L. "The Implications of Minority Interest and Stock Restrictions in Valuing Closely Held Shares." *University of Pennsylvania Law Review* 122 (April 1974):934–53.

_____. "Current Techniques for Valuing Minority Stock Interest or Stock with Restrictions." *Taxation for Lawyers* 3 (January/February 1975):244–49.

Finebaum, Murray L. "Disposal and Valuation of Restricted Securities." *Trusts & Estates* 110 (October 1971):840–43, 847.

Friedlob, George Thomas. "Effect IRS Gives to Restrictions in Determining Value of Stock Varies." *Taxation for Accountants* 22 (June 1979):350–53.

Granda, John A. "An examination of the Neglected Role of Sale-of-Control Law and Theory in the Valuation of a Control Block of Stock for Federal Estate-Tax Purposes." *Journal of Corporation Law* 2 (Fall 1976):91–114.

Greenside, Myron. "Discounts in the Valuation of Stock of Closely-Held Investment Corporations." *Massachusetts CPA Review* 50 (July/August 1976):33–34.

Lyons, William P., and Whitman, Martin J. "Valuing Closely-Held Corporations and Publicly-Traded Securities with Limited Marketability: Approaches to Allowable Discounts from Gross Values." *Business Lawyer* 33 (July 1978):2213–29.

Maher, J. Michael. "Discounts for Lack of Marketability for Closely-Held Business Interests." *Taxes* (September 1976), pp. 562–71.

_____. "Application of Key Man Discount in the Valuation of Closely-Held Businesses." *Taxes* 55 (June 1977):377–80.

_____. "An Objective Measure for a Discount for a Minority Interest and a Premium for a Controlling Interest." Taxes (July 1979), pp. 449–54.

Moroney, Robert E. "Most Courts Overvalue Closely-Held Stock." *Taxes* (March 1973), pp.144–54.

_____. "Why 25 Percent Discount for Nonmarketability in One Valuation, 100 Percent in Another?" *Taxes* (May 1977), pp.316–20.

Person, Stanley. "Valuation of Minority Interest Transferred in Contemplation of Death." *CPA Journal* 50 (February 1980):61–62.

Securities and Exchange Commission. *Accounting Series Releases:*

"Accounting Series Release, No. 113: Statement regarding Restricted Securities." *Commerce Clearing House, Inc. Federal Securities Law Reporter,* pp.62,283–62,288.

"Accounting Series Release, No. 118: Accounting for Investment Securities by Registered Investment Companies." *Commerce Clearing House, Inc. Federal Securities Law Reporter,* pp.62,293–62,298.

Smith, David O. "Closely-Held Stock: Corporate Control Gains Importance as Element of Stock Valuation," *Taxation for Lawyers* 4 (September/October 1975):78–81.

Solberg, Thomas A. "Valuing Restricted Securities: What Factors Do the Courts and the Service Look For?" *Journal of Taxation* (September 1979), pp.150–54.

Trout, Robert R. "Estimation of the Discount Associated with the Transfer of Restricted Securities." *Taxes* 55 (June 1977):381–85.

"Valuation of Corporate Stock for Purposes of Succession, Inheritance, or Estate Tax, as Affected by Quantity Involved." *23 A.L.R. 2d 775 (1952, supplement 1970, 1979).*

"What Is Your Corporation Worth? Part 2: Minority Interest." *Federal Tax Coordinator 2d. Special Study* (September 29, 1977).

Articles: Dissenters' stock

Banks, Warren E. "A Selective Inquiry into Judicial Stock Valuation." *Indiana Law Review* 6 (1972):19–44.

Birk, David R. "Shareholders' Appraisal Process: Need for Reform." *New York State Bar Journal* 51 (June 1979):274–77, 314–21.

"Corporations—Appraisal Statutes—Elements in Valuation of Corporate Stock." *Michigan Law Review* 55 (March 1957):689–96.

"Corporation Law—Dissenting Stockholder's Right of Appraisal-Determination of Value." *N.Y.U. Law Review* 28 (1953):1021–30.

"Duty and Liability of Closely Held Corporation, Its Directors, Officers, or Majority Stockholders, in Acquiring Stock of Minority Shareholder." *7 A.L.R. 3d 500* (1966).

Hotchkiss, David L. "Corporations—Fair Value for Dissenting Shareholders under the Pennsylvania Appraisal Statute." *Dickinson Law Review* 78 (Spring 1974):582–96.

Macrae, Howard T., Jr. "Dissenting Stockholders' Rights in Virginia: Exclusivity of the Cash-Out Remedy and Determination of 'Fair Value.' *University of Richmond Law Review* 12 (Spring 1978):505–33.

Manning, Bayless. "The Shareholder's Appraisal Remedy: An Essay for Frank Coker," *Yale Law Journal* 72 (Spring 1962):223–32.

"Note—Corporation Law—Dissenting Stockholder's Right of Appraisal—Determination of Value." *New York University Law Review* 28 (May 1953):1021–32.

Rams, Edwin M. "Judicial Valuation of Dissenting Shareholder Interests." Lincoln Law Review 8 (1973):74–89.

"Reconsideration of the Stock Market Exception to the Dissenting Shareholder's Right of Appraisal." *Michigan Law Review* 74 (April 1976): 1023–66.

Rogers, J. Steven. "Dissenting Shareholder's Appraisal Remedy." *Oklahoma Law Review* (Summer 1977):629–43.

"Valuation of Dissenter's Stock under Appraisal Statutes." *Harvard Law Review* 30 (May 1966), pp. 1453–74.

"Valuation of Stock of Dissenting Stockholders in Case of Consolidation or Merger of Corporation, Sale of its Assets, or the Like." *48 A.L.R. 3d 430* (1973, supplement 1979).

Articles: Mergers and acquisitions

Alberts, William W., and McTaggart, James M. "The Short-Term Earnings Per Share Standard for Evaluating Prospective Acquisitions." *Mergers & Acquisitions* 12 (Winter 1978):4–18.

Blaylock, Michael I. "The Buy-Sell Deal: Tax and Practical Considerations in Setting the Purchase Price of a Going Business." Xerox copy. *Hawaii Tax Institute, Seminar No. 2.* November 1, 1978.

Bradley, James W., and Korn, Donald H. "Bargains in Valuation Disparities: Corporate Acquirer versus Passive Investor." *Sloan Management Review* 20 (Winter 1979):51–64.

Brudney, Victor. "Efficient Markets and Fair Value in Parent Subsidiary Mergers." *Journal of Corporation Law* 4 (Fall 1978):63–86.

Byrd, William M. and Dean, James D. "Costs of Investigating Prospective Businesses: Federal Tax Consequences." *Mergers & Acquisitions* 12 (Fall 1977):28–33.

Chambers, John C., and Mullick, Satinder K. "Determining the Acquisition Value of a Company." *Management Accounting* (April 1970), pp.24–31,39.

Chirelstein, Marvin A., et al. "'Fairness' in Mergers between Parents and Partly-Owned Subsidiaries." New York: *Practising Law Institute. Institute on Securities Regulation* 8 (1977):273–308.

Corcoran, James M., Jr. "Checklists for Transferring a Business." *Practical Lawyer* 20 (March 1974):65–76.

Einhorn, Stephen. "Notes on the Decision to Keep or to Sell a Small Business." *Mergers & Acquisitions* 12 (Summer 1977):29–31.

Ely, Bert. "The Impact of the 1978 Tax Cut Bill on Mergers and Acquisitions." *Mergers & Acquisitions* (Summer 1979), pp. 4–13.

Gooch, Lawrence B., and Grabowski, Roger J. "Advanced Valuation Methods in Mergers and Acquisitions." *Mergers & Acquisitions* 11 (Summer 1976):15–29.

Heath, John, Jr. "Valuation Factors and Techniques in Mergers and Acquisitions." *Financial Executive* 40 (April 1972):34–43.

_____. "Appraisal Processes in Mergers and Acquisitions." Mergers & Acquisitions (Fall 1974), pp. 4–21.

Jensen, Herbert L. and Crumbley, D. Larry. "Simplifying the Type E Reorganization." Mergers & Acquisitions 13 (Fall 1978):4–7.

Kellogg, Douglas E. "How to Buy a Small Manufacturing Business." Harvard Business Review (September–October 1975), pp.92–102.

LaFleur, Gerald W. "The Financial Investigation of Acquisition Candidates—How it Affects the Purchase Price." In Acquisitions 1978, edited by Lewis B. Merrifield III, pp. 7–21. New York: Practising Law Institute, 1978.

Lorne, Simon M. "Reappraisal of Fair Shares in Controlled Mergers." University of Pennsylvania Law Review 126 (May 1978): 955–88.

Malernee, James K., and Kirby, Jack. "Measuring Return in Acquisition Analysis." Mergers & Acquisitions (Spring 1979), pp. 18–21.

"Merger Is Tax Free Despite Rescission, Redemption Features." Journal of Taxation 49 (August 1978):87–88.

Rappaport, Alfred. "Financial Analysis for Mergers and Acquisitions." Mergers & Acquisitions 10 (Winter 1976):18–36.

Reilly, Robert F. "Pricing an Acquisition: A 15-Step Methodology." Mergers & Acquisitions (Summer 1979), pp.14–31.

Rosenbloom, Arthur H., and Howard, Alex W. "Bootstrap Acquisitions and How to Value Them." Mergers & Acquisitions (Winter 1977), pp. 18–26.

Stoloff, Alfred H. "Corporate Combinations: Mergers, Consolidations, Asset and Stock Purchases." Oregon Law Review 45(3) (April 1966):161–83.

Taft, Robert S. "Acquiring the Closely-Held Corporation." St Johns Law Review 44–A (Spring 1970):1144–52.

"Tax-Free Merger of Closely-Held Corporation into Mutual Fund." Journal of Taxation 49 (December 1978):372–73.

Thomson, Marty. "Management Buyouts: An Overview." Mergers & Acquisitions 11 (Summer 1976):4–6.

_____. "Management Buyouts: The Inside Story," pp. 7–14.

Vaughn, Robert, Jr. "How to Acquire a Closely-Held Business." Practical Lawyer 22(1) (January 1976):11–19.

Wallner, Nicholas. "Leveraged Buyouts: A Review of the State of the Art, Part I." Mergers & Acquisitions 14 (Fall 1979):4–13.

_____. "Leveraged Buyouts: A Review of the State of the Art, Part II." Mergers & Acquisitions 14 (Winter, 1980):16–26.

Westin, Richard A. "Mutual Fund Mergers with Closely-Held Corporations." Mergers & Acquisitions 14 (Summer 1979):32–38.

Wines, William R., and Bentley, William R., Jr. "Are Tax Loss Carryovers Worth Anything Today?" Mergers & Acquisitions 13 (Spring 1978):17–19.

Articles: Goodwill and other intangibles

Adams, Fred M. "Professional Goodwill as Community Property: How Should Idaho Rule?" Idaho Law Review 14 (Spring 1978):473–91.

Alexander, Donald C. "Valuation of Intangibles." Institute on Federal Taxation, New York University 20 (1962):567–85.

Bergman, Gregory M. "Valuation of Goodwill." Los Angeles Bar Journal 53 (August 1977):87–98.

Blaine, Davis R. "Valuation of Goodwill and Going Concern Value." Mergers & Acquisitions (Spring 1979), pp.4–11.

Blum, Marc P. "Valuing Intangibles: What Are the Choices for Valuing Professional Sports Teams?" Journal of Taxation 45 (November 1976):286–88.

Davis, Michael E. "Valuation of Professional Goodwill upon Marital Dissolution." Southwestern University Law Review 7 (Spring 1975):186–205.

"Depreciability of Going Concern Value." University of Pennsylvania Law Review 122 (December 1973):484–97.

Dostart, Thomas J. "Professional Education as a Divisible Asset in Marriage Dissolutions." Iowa Law Review 64 (March 1979):705–21.

"Evaluation of Interest in Law Firm or Medical Partnership for Purposes of Division of Property in Divorce Proceedings." 74 A.L.R. 3d 621 (1976, supplement 1979).

Ganier, P.K. "Treatment of Goodwill: Allocating a Lump-Sum Purchase Price Among Mixed Assets of a Going Business," Journal of Corporate Taxation 7 (Summer 1980):111–36.

"Going Concern Value Can Exist Even Without Goodwill." Taxation for Lawyers 5 (January/February 1977):229–30.

"Goodwill." 5 Am. Juris. P.O.F. 505 (1960, supplement 1979).

"Goodwill." 38 Am. Juris. 2d (1968), and Section 8 (supplement 1979).

"Goodwill." 38 C.J.S. (1943) and Section 3 (supplement 1979).

Habeeb, Wade R. "Accountability for Good Will of Professional Practice in Actions Arising from Divorce or Separation." 52 A.L.R. 3d 1344 (1973).

Hauserman, Nancy R., and Fethke, Carol. "Valuation of a Homemaker's Services." Trial Lawyers' Guide 22 (Fall 1978):249–66.

Lurvey, Ira H. "Professional Goodwill on Martial Dissolution: Is it Property or Another Name for Alimony?" California State Bar Journal 52 (January/February 1977):27–30.

Lyons, James R. "Valuation of Good Will and Covenant not to Compete, How to Distinguish between Them." Journal of Taxation 16 (April 1962):228–30.

Maleck, Sidney. "Loss of Business Goodwill in Eminent Domain Proceedings." California State Bar Journal 53 (January/February, 1978):32–35.

Paulsen, Jon. "Goodwill and Going Concern Value Reconsidered." Mergers & Acquisitions 14 (Winter 1980):10–13.

Pinnell, Robert E. "Divorce after Professional School: Education and Future Earning Capacity May Be Marital Property." Missouri Law Review 44 (Spring 1979):329–40.

Projector, Murray. "Valuation of Retirement Benefits in Marriage Dissolutions." Los Angeles Bar Bulletin 50 (April 1975):229–38.

"Proof of Business Loss—Valuation of Goodwill of Professional Practice." *16 Am. Juris. P.O.F. 2d 375.*

"Retail Business Goodwill: Survey of Prices Paid." *Business Valuation, Monograph no. 3* (1980), p. 15.

Shipley, W. E. "Accountability for Good Will on Dissolution of Partnership." *65 A.L.R. 2d 521* (1959, supplements 1978, 1979).

Udinsky, Jerald H. "An Economists' View of Professional Goodwill in a Community Property Setting." *Community Property Journal* 5 (Spring 1978):91–96.

Walzer, Stuart B. "Marital Dissolution: Valuation of Good Will in Business and Professional Practices." *Tax Institute, University of Southern California Law Center* 27 (1975):377–414.

Wiener, Hilton M. "Going Concern Value: Goodwill by any Other Name?" *Tax Lawyer* 33 (Fall 1979):183–97.

Wise, Sherry Marcus. "Settlement of a Community Partnership Interest upon Separation or Divorce." *Tulane Law Review* 51 (April 1977):700–16.

406

INDEX

Intrastate offering, 377
Inventory
  accounting methods, 162–64
  turnover, 197–98
Investment banker, selection of, 376
Investment companies, purchases of restricted stock, 148–55
Investment tax credits, 169–70
Investor communications and relations, 379–80

J–K

Jurek, Walter, 40
Kingery v. Department of Revenue (inheritance tax case), 38
Kirkpatrick, Ernest E. (tax case), 151, 324–27

L

Lasry, George, 34
Last in, first Out (LIFO), 162–64
Leases, accounting for, 169
Lefko, Orville B., 348, 351
Letter stocks, 148–55, 330–34
Leverage, measures of, 198–200
Leveraged ESOP, 337
Levin v. Midland Ross Corp. (dissenting stockholder case), 30–31
Lewis v. Bogin (dissenting stockholder case), 374
Life insurance
  adequacy of, 6–7
  funding buy-sell agreement, 353–54, 357
  funding through ESOP, 337
Liquidity, measures of, 193–202
Litigation
  pending by or against company, 93, 107–08
  preparation for trial involving valuation issue, 272–77
Littenberg, Robert L., 288
Loss of business opportunity, 13

M

McCarthy, George D., 160
Maher, J. Michael, 153
Marketability, 35, 74, 147–55, 259–60, 311–21, 324, 34
  in ESOP, 341–42
Matsen, Jeffrey R., 352, 359
Matter of Dimmock v. Reichold Chemicals, Inc. (dissenting stockholder case), 374
Mergers and Acquisitions-The Journal of Corporate Venture, 136, 143
Messing, Morris M. (gift tax case), 20
Minority interest
  Central Trust Case, 309–321
  IRS Letter Ruling, 334
  other cases, 323–34
  series of transfers, 5, 334
Moody's Manuals, 131
Moroney, Robert E., 151–52

N

National Quotation Bureau
  National Daily Quotation Service, 130
  National Monthly Stock Summary, 130
National Trade and Professional Associations (annual directory), 119
Nonrecurring items, 171–72
Northwest Investment Review, 131

O

Offeree representative, 12
Opinion letter, 226–30
Outlining legal testimony, 274–76

P

Paine Webber Handbook of Stock and Bond Analysis, 117–18
Partners' Capital Accounts, Statement of, 181–83
Past transactions, history of as valuation factor, 36, 73–74, 310–21
Perquisites, 36, 172–73
Piper, William T. (tax case), 330–334
Predicasts, 122–23
  Index of Corporate Change, 136, 142
  Index of Corporations and Industries, 119
Preferred stock, dividend yield summary, 48
Present value
  arithmetic of, 41
  example, 42
  tables, 381–87
Price/earnings ratio
  debt-free basis, 64–66, 393–95
  definition of, 60–61
  relationship to capitalization rate, 62–64
  sources of, 61–62
Prior period adjustments, 169
Projected data, 29–31
Public Affairs Information Service, 123
Public offerings, 375–80
Purpose of appraisal, 21–23
Put option, 336–37

Q

Qualifications to auditor's opinion, 184–86
Qualifying the witness, 275
Quick ratio, 193–95

R

Rams, Edwin M., 373
Ratios, 191–206, 248–51, 392–93
  coverage of fixed charges, 200–01
  coverage of preferred dividends, 201–02
  current, 193
  debt to equity, 200
  equity to total assets, 199
  equity to total capital, 199–200
  long-term debt to total capital, 199
  price/earnings, 60–66
  price/earnings, debt free basis, 64–66
  quick (acid test), 193–95
  return on equity, 202–03
  return on total assets, 204
  sales to net working capital, 198
  sources of, 61–62
  stock value to asset value, 71–72
  times interest earned, 200
  total debt to total assets, 199
Recapitalization, 288–90
Redemption agreements; *see* Repurchase agreements
Regulation A registration, 375, 377
Reorganizations, 14
Repurchase agreements, 346

This book has been set Linotron 606, in 11 and 10 point Souvenir Light, leaded 2 points. Part numbers are Souvenir Light Roman; chapter numbers are Souvenir Light Arabic. Part titles are 36 point Souvenir Light; chapter titles are 30 point Souvenir Light. The size of the type page is 42 by 50 picas.